# Constructing Meaning

# Constructing Meaning

## Balancing Elementary Language Arts

SECOND EDITION

### Joyce Bainbridge

### Grace Malicky

UNIVERSITY OF ALBERTA

WITH A CHAPTER ON DRAMA

BY PAT PAYNE

**Harcourt Canada**

Harcourt Canada

Toronto  Montreal  Fort Worth  New York  Orlando
Philadelphia  San Diego  London  Sydney  Tokyo

Special thanks to all of the children who granted us permission to reprint the writing samples contained in this book.

Photo credits:  Cathie Archbould, 1, 22, 28, 43, 97, 104, 129, 157, 169, 182, 198, 207, 215, 227, 237, 265, 299, 307, 331, 339, 375, 396, 414
Paul Williams, 62
Birgitte Nielsen, 117, 142, 362
Brett Lamb, 278

**Canadian Cataloguing in Publication Data**
Bainbridge, Joyce, 1944–
— Constructing meaning : balancing elementary language arts

2nd ed.
Includes index.
ISBN 0-7747-3660-7

1.   Language arts (Elementary). 2. English language—Study and teaching (Elementary). 3. Language experience approach in education. I. Malicky, Grace, 1944– . II. Title.

LB1575.8.E38 2000        372.6'044        C99-932189-7

Acquisitions Editor: Heather McWhinney
Developmental Editor: Lise Dupont
Production Editor: Shana Hayes
Production Coordinator: Cheryl Tiongson

Copy Editor: Georgina Montgomery
Permissions Coordinator:  Patricia Buckley
Cover and Interior Design: Liz Harasymczuk
Typesetting and Assembly: Liz Harasymczuk
Printing and Binding: Tri-Graphic Printing

Harcourt Canada
55 Horner Avenue, Toronto, ON, Canada M8Z 4X6
Customer Service
Toll-Free Tel.: 1-800-387-7278
Toll-Free Fax: 1-800-665-7307

This book was printed in Canada.
 2 3 4 5    03 02 01

# Preface

Research has long shown that children develop their language abilities through interacting meaningfully with people in their daily lives — in storytime, at mealtimes, during chores, and while playing. When children enter school, they continue this process through using language in purposeful ways across the entire school curriculum. Learning is enhanced through interactions with teachers, parents, and others both within and outside the school context. In the school setting, teachers play a crucial role in maximizing children's language development. They serve as language models, providing a stimulus for thinking and for exploring ideas and talking about them, and in demonstrating literacy in action.

This textbook is an introduction to teaching elementary language arts from an integrated, balanced, and social constructive perspective. It is intended for both preservice and inservice elementary school teachers. As in the first edition, we provide a comprehensive theoretical framework accessible to beginning teachers and a range of ideas related to different areas of the language arts. New in this edition, however, is a more explicit focus on a social constructivist theory of learning and greater emphasis on balance in language arts classrooms.

Another major change in this edition is the addition of a chapter on technology in the language arts classroom. We made this addition in recognition of the increasing role of technology in language learning and of the importance of viewing and representing in language arts programs. Based on recommendations from colleagues and reviewers, we have also integrated suggestions for assessing children's language abilities into chapters on oral language, emergent literacy, reading, and writing. Readers who have seen the first edition will note changes in the ordering of chapters and in the packaging of chapters on reading and writing.

Consistent with social constructivist views, we begin each chapter with a graphic organizer that provides readers with an overview of topics and subtopics to be considered. To invite readers to construct their own meaning as they read, we present brief scenarios at the beginning of chapters, pose questions based on these scenarios, and use transitions between major sections of chapters to encourage reflection and prediction. Definitions of terms in boldface type are presented in a glossary at the end of the book. Included in many chapters are book lists, examples of teaching/learning activities, and samples of children's reading, writing, and oral language. We end each chapter with a summary, a short annotated list of selected professional resources for readers who wish to pursue an area further, and lists of both children's and professional materials referenced.

In Chapter One, we present our theoretical framework and encourage readers to reflect on their notions of how children learn. We also introduce the dimensions of language learning included in most language arts programs: speaking, listening, reading, writing, viewing, and representing. Because we hold a social constructivist view of learning, we devote considerable attention in this chapter to the social context of learning. We end the chapter with an indication of what we mean by balance in language arts classrooms.

Chapters Two through Nine provide specific suggestions for assessment and instruction in speaking, listening, reading, and writing. In Chapter Two, we describe the structure of language and present perspectives on language acquisition. This is followed by an exploration of how language functions in different social contexts and how language functions in learning in general. At the end of the chapter, we present suggestions for enhancing listening and speaking in classrooms and for assessing children's oral language abilities.

The focus of Chapter Three is emergent literacy. In this chapter, we begin by describing perspectives on early reading and writing development, as well as components of emergent literacy. We then provide suggestions for assessing young children's literacy development and for planning appropriate programs to meet their needs. We end the chapter by describing specific instructional techniques to foster early literacy development.

Reading is the focus of Chapters Four through Six. We begin in Chapter Four by describing various theoretical perspectives on reading and techniques for assessing children's reading abilities and needs. In Chapters Five and Six, we suggest specific instructional techniques to help children develop reading strategies, beginning with comprehension and critical literacy and then moving to word identification and fluency. We end Chapter Six by briefly considering reading intervention programs.

Chapters Seven, Eight, and Nine are devoted to writing. In Chapter Seven, we examine models and forms of writing, the process of composing, and guidelines for implementing a writing workshop. In Chapter Eight, we focus on the role of writing in learning across the curriculum, describing strategies for working with journal writing, learning logs, research reports, and study skills. The final chapter on writing deals with techniques for assessing children's writing as well as conventional aspects of writing.

We believe that children's literature has a critical role to play in children's language development. Therefore, in Chapters Ten and Eleven, we provide lists of children's books (with a heavy emphasis on Canadian content), as well as information on selecting children's literature and on responding to literature through a range of activities involving response groups, journals, drama, and visual arts.

Chapters Twelve and Thirteen focus on viewing and representing. In Chapter Twelve, Pat Payne introduces various forms of drama and shows how these can be used in the classroom to help children represent meaning. In Chapter Thirteen, we address issues related to the use of computers in classrooms, ways to help children learn *with* computers, criteria for selecting software, and ways to help children become effective and critical users of media.

The final chapter is designed to help teachers plan and implement language arts programs to meet the needs of all learners. We begin in Chapter Fourteen by acknowledging that no one organizational structure is best for all classrooms. We then go on to suggest ways that materials, time, space, and students can be organized to maximize learning in different contexts. The chapter concludes with a brief section on reporting to parents.

# Acknowledgements

We wish to thank all the children, teachers, undergraduate students, graduate students, and colleagues who have helped us understand the nature of the teaching and learning of language arts during our years as students and teachers. Particular appreciation is expressed to the teachers who took the time to write about their classroom experiences and to the children who provided samples of their reading, writing, and oral language.

We wish to acknowledge the significant contribution of Pat Payne, who drew on her knowledge of language arts to write the chapter on drama. One of the most complete descriptions of drama available in any language arts textbook, this chapter models integration in action.

As well, we are very grateful to John Proctor, whose careful reading of all chapters helped us achieve greater consistency in theoretical perspective and format throughout the text. In particular, we note his significant contribution to the writing of the first chapter and the chapter on technology in the language arts. Pat Campbell's contribution to the section on miscues in the chapter on assessment, Sylvia Pantaleo's contribution to the chapters on children's literature, and Shelley Peterson's contributions to the chapters on writing are also gratefully acknowledged.

We also appreciate the assistance of Tracey Derwing in providing feedback on the linguistics aspects of the chapter on oral language, and the assistance of Norma Nocente, Mike Carbonaro, Thalia Hartson, and Pam Steeves in developing the chapter on technology in the language arts. In addition, we received valuable comments and suggestions from instructors at our own and other universities, as well as from the following reviewers selected by Harcourt Canada: Marc Glassman, Memorial University of Newfoundland; Dale Hayes, Brandon University; Susan Lloyd, Queen's University; Adele Woolfe, The University of Western Ontario; and Meguido Zola, Simon Fraser University.

Finally, we wish to thank the editorial staff at Harcourt Canada for encouraging us to write a second edition of this book and for providing advice and support during its development.

Joyce Bainbridge
Grace Malicky
University of Alberta

## A Note from the Publisher

Thank you for selecting *Constructing Meaning: Balancing Elementary Language Arts*, Second Edition, by Joyce Bainbridge and Grace Malicky. The authors and publisher have devoted considerable time to the careful development of this book. We appreciate your recognition of this effort and accomplishment.

We want to hear what you think about the second edition of *Constructing Meaning*. Please take a few minutes to fill in the stamped reply card at the back of the book. Your comments, suggestions, and criticisms will be valuable to us as we prepare new editions and other books.

# Contents

# Chapter Twelve Drama in the Elementary Classroom 330
by Patricia A. Payne

# Chapter Thirteen Technology in the Language Arts Classroom 362

# Chapter Fourteen Planning and Organizing Language Arts Programs 396

# Introduction to Language Learning

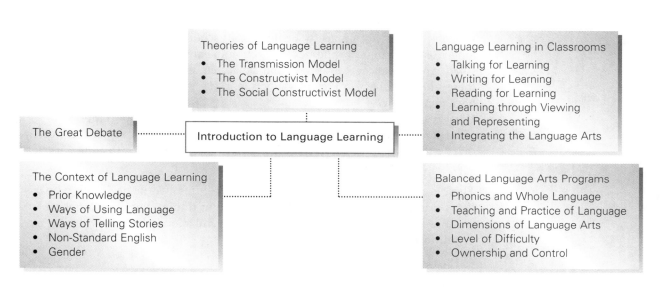

**Theories of Language Learning**
- The Transmission Model
- The Constructivist Model
- The Social Constructivist Model

**Language Learning in Classrooms**
- Talking for Learning
- Writing for Learning
- Reading for Learning
- Learning through Viewing and Representing
- Integrating the Language Arts

**The Great Debate**

**Introduction to Language Learning**

**The Context of Language Learning**
- Prior Knowledge
- Ways of Using Language
- Ways of Telling Stories
- Non-Standard English
- Gender

**Balanced Language Arts Programs**
- Phonics and Whole Language
- Teaching and Practice of Language
- Dimensions of Language Arts
- Level of Difficulty
- Ownership and Control

Chad Lee, a recent university graduate, is eagerly anticipating his first teaching assignment as a Grade 1 teacher. At the beginning of the summer, he meets with his principal, who tells him that the teachers in the school have moved away from transmission models of learning. Instead, she explains, programs focus on children using their language to actively construct meaning as they engage in learning experiences. She requests that, prior to the beginning of the school year, Chad develop a statement of his beliefs and intentions related to children's language and learning. She indicates that these will form the basis for planning and implementing a balanced language arts program in his classroom. ∎

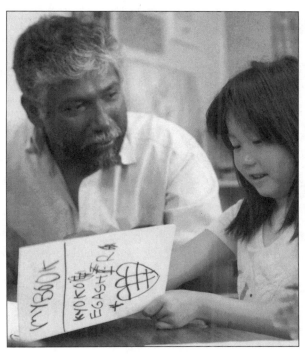

lthough Chad's situation may be particular to new teachers, it parallels the task faced by experienced teachers as they engage in a reflective process to adjust their planning each day, week, and year that they are in the classroom (Schön, 1987). Most of Chad's current ideas of language learning come from notions of how he personally learned to read and write. He knows this awareness needs to be developed and honed if he is to be effective in helping 25 to 30 eager 6- to 7-year-olds join the "**literacy** club" as competent and confident readers and writers (Smith, 1988). He begins by thinking about what he needs to learn.

- What does it mean to have students "construct meaning," and how does this differ from transmitting knowledge?
- Chad hears daily advertisements for **phonics** programs that imply these programs will meet needs not currently being met in schools. Is it true that schools no longer teach phonics? Is phonics instruction the answer to all reading problems?
- Chad remembers the workbooks and skillsheets from his past experiences. Are these still in vogue? Do they play any role in classrooms? If not, what have they been replaced by?
- What is a balanced language arts program? Why is balance important?
- Chad knows that classes at his new school are more ethnically and culturally diverse than when he was in school. In what ways will he need to adjust instruction to account for this diversity?

These are some of the questions that Chad asks himself as he begins his preparation for teaching language arts. Before you begin reading this chapter, take a few minutes to think about your past experiences and about what you will soon face in your own classroom. What are some of your questions?

## The Great Debate

In this section, we introduce two apparently conflicting views of how children learn to read and consider the role these theoretical orientations have played, and continue to play, in educational decisions.

For most of the twentieth century, language arts educators and theorists have been searching for the best way to teach reading (Crawford, 1995). In 1967, Jeanne Chall referred to the ongoing claims made by educators and researchers involved in this search as the "great debate." Essentially, the debate has centred on the relative efficacy of two approaches to the teaching of reading — "decoding individual sounds and words, or relating to the meaning of larger units of text from the outset" (Millard, 1997, p. 33).

One of the central themes of the debate hinges on the manner in which reading and writing are defined.

- Proponents of one view hold that reading and writing are made up of hierarchical sets of skills that children need to develop in a predetermined order, often through practice and drill.
- Proponents of the other view hold that reading and writing are skills that children learn and develop by engaging in the act of reading itself, in much the same way that they learn to listen and talk — without any apparent direct instruction.

Although these theoretical orientations may be described in a variety of ways, the former is generally called a basic skills approach, while the latter has become known as the **whole language** approach. The debate has been more sharply focussed in reading, although similar stances have been taken with regard to writing.

Participants and observers alike have decried the pendulum-like swings in practice that have resulted from the great debate. The past two decades have witnessed two particularly dramatic changes in language arts education:

1. a marked swing toward whole language in the 1980s, and

2. a move back to phonics-based instruction in the mid-1990s when the promise of whole language programs was not realized in increased scores on achievement tests.

The latter swing was accelerated by the publication of Marilyn Adams' book, *Beginning to Read*, in 1990. From her extensive review of research on beginning reading, she concluded that direct and systematic phonics instruction is the most effective way to teach reading.

One positive outcome of the phonics/whole language debate has been that it has kept reading and writing on the political agenda. This has resulted in additional government funding for early literacy programs in many jurisdictions. However, a negative outcome of the debate is the continuing search for the "best way" to teach reading and writing, the search for a one-size-fits-all solution. Entrepreneurs have been capitalizing on this search by publishing phonics programs aimed at parents frustrated with what they feel is happening in schools.

Today, most educators recognize that teaching children to read and write is not as simple as presented by those who propose "quick-fix" methods and solutions. There never was, and never will be, one best way to help children learn to read and write. Recognizing that this is the case, many educators are therefore now devoting their efforts to a search for "best practices," and combining these into what have become known as "balanced literacy programs" (Frepon and Dahl, 1998).

As we move into the twenty-first century, many programs are being driven by best practices rather than a coherent theoretical framework about how children learn. While the movement toward balanced programs is long overdue, only by framing balanced literacy within a coherent theory will teachers have an adequate basis for meeting the needs of individual learners in today's classrooms. Without a coherent theory of language learning, educators remain vulnerable to "the fads of literacy instruction" (Hiebert, 1991, p. 4).

That's what this book is about — helping teachers like you construct the theoretical and practical knowledge of language learning that you need in order to develop and implement an effective balanced language arts program. We begin by delving into what it means to know something and how knowledge is developed.

## Theories of Language Learning

In this section, we consider three ways of thinking about knowledge and learning — transmission, **constructivism,** and social constructivism. To a great extent, transmission and constructivist theories reflect the underlying premises of the two positions in the "great debate."

## The Transmission Model

In the past, learning was often equated with transmitting information. Knowledge was what students could recall. It was a quantitative notion, emphasizing facts and someone else's knowledge to be learned and reproduced on demand. Teachers had the knowledge, and it was their job to transmit this knowledge to their students. They appeared to assume that there was a direct conduit between their minds and those of their students and that knowledge could travel, unchanged, through this conduit.

The transmission model still dominates in some classrooms. In these classrooms

- tasks are defined and set by the teacher,
- the teacher is entirely responsible for monitoring students' progress and evaluating their learning,
- learning is thought of as linear and proceeding in incremental stages,
- skills, knowledge, and attitudes are viewed as separate, and the teacher assumes responsibility for building student competence in each area,
- teacher talk predominates, and
- students' learning is equated with their ability to correctly answer questions, complete workbooks and skillsheets adequately, and score well on objective tests.

In language arts classrooms where transmission is the underlying theory, teachers provide the type of instruction presented in Box 1.1.

**Box 1.1   Sample Activities in Transmission Language Arts Classrooms**

- Teachers assign the topics children write about and evaluate their writing.
- Teachers assign children stories to read from basal reading series and rely on teacher guides for activities and instructional ideas.
- Teachers set purposes for reading and determine the ways students respond to the reading.
- Teachers teach word recognition and comprehension as separate components or aspects of reading.
- Teachers ask questions about stories to test children's understanding of the author's ideas.
- Teachers present skills in a sequential order.
- Teachers rely on workbooks and skillsheets to provide practice in reading and writing skills.

## The Constructivist Model

Today, few educators believe that direct transmission of information between two people's minds is possible. Think about the last time you went to a movie with your friends and discussed the movie afterwards. Although there may have been many similarities in the meaning constructed by each of you, there were also likely some subtle and sometimes not-so-subtle differences. You might think that meant your friends were not paying attention or that they didn't understand the movie. In fact, however, it reflects the constructive nature of all meaning making and the impact of individual experiences on that process.

Today, many educators emphasize the individual or personal construction of meaning and understanding (Brooks and Brooks, 1993; Lauritzen and Jaeger, 1997). The focus is on students actively making meaning and solving problems. This view is particularly prominent in the areas of mathematics and science, where discovery learning has been promoted for decades.

The theoretical base for this thinking comes from the work of Piaget (1972), who focussed on the individual meaning-making process and on the development of higher levels of thinking. He conceptualized cognitive operations as being the same across cultures and social contexts. His ideas have been translated into hands-on activities designed to develop children's concepts and thinking processes (Richardson, 1997).

Box 1.2 presents some of the types of activities that predominate in language arts classrooms where constructivism is the underlying theory. As you can see, there are substantial and profound differences between transmission and constructivist classrooms.

**Box 1.2    Sample Activities in Contructivist Language Arts Classrooms**

- Children choose their own topics for writing.
- Children brainstorm ideas and jot these down to serve as a reference as they write.
- Children make decisions about form, format, and style and evaluate their own effectiveness as writers.
- Teachers use "high quality" children's literature, both fiction and non-fiction, in the classroom.
- Teachers provide opportunities for children to interact with what they are reading by making predictions, forming hypotheses, and asking questions before and during reading.
- Children respond personally to what they read.
- Teachers teach reading and writing skills and strategies based on children's needs as they engage in "real" reading and writing.

## The Social Constructivist Model

If constructivism is new to you, you likely have many questions at this point. For example:

- Are all interpretations or compositions equally valid and "good" if no one meaning of a text is *the* meaning?
- What role does the teacher play in helping children with reading comprehension or written composition if the construction of meaning is primarily an individual process?
- How are shared meanings developed?

Social constructivism deals with these kinds of questions.

Let's return to the example of you and your friends discussing a movie you attended together. Equally important as differences among your constructions of meaning are similarities. None of us constructs meaning in a vacuum. Instead, we make sense of our experiences within a particular social group, and this occurs within a broader societal and cultural context. The more similar the socio-cultural backgrounds of you and your friends, the more similar will be the meanings you construct. In other words, the social context of learning has a significant impact on the construction of meaning.

Social constructivism has its origins in the work of Vygotsky (1978), who theorized that the ways we think are learned primarily through social interactions and that the ways we learn language develop as a result of our use of language in social contexts. According to Vygotsky, children are active in their own development, but other people in their immediate social context also play an important role. He hypothesized a **zone of proximal development**. This is the "area of difficulty just beyond the point at which the child can solve problems independently; it is the area in which the child can solve problems in collaboration with others, especially with an adult or more competent peer" (Lindfors, 1987, p. 273). When they work collaboratively, people negotiate and develop shared meanings.

But not everyone has an equal voice in these negotiations. The view of one person or group is often privileged over that of others. To illustrate this, we return one last time to the movie discussion with your friends. Even within your small group, some people's meanings are given greater credibility than others'. Your gender, race, socioeconomic status, and language abilities all have an impact on how your ideas are viewed by other people. Social constructivists who take a critical stance recognize these inequalities and encourage each of us to become aware of our biases and of how we may knowingly or unknowingly value the ideas of one gender, race, or class over those of another.

To help teachers become aware of these inequalities, Edelsky (1994) asks the following questions:

- Who decides what is a "good" story?
- Who decides what children write about?
- Who decides whose turn it is to talk?
- Who decides whose meaning of a text is acceptable?
- Who decides what books are in the classroom?
- Whose view of the world is represented in these books?

---

**Box 1.3**    **Sample Activities in Social Constructivist Language Arts Classrooms**

- Children brainstorm ideas and share their ideas with others.
- Children share their writing with one another, discuss revisions in the group context, and engage in peer editing.
- Teachers provide opportunities for children to share ideas when making predictions, forming hypotheses, and discussing responses to their reading.
- Children work co-operatively on activities designed to help them develop reading and writing strategies.
- Children and teachers discuss how people of different genders, races, cultures, socio-economic groups, and age levels are portrayed in stories and books.
- Children and teachers examine and explore themes that focus on and celebrate diversity, acceptance, care, and mutual support.

---

When teachers base their teaching on social constructivism, they actively and consciously go beyond the activities that characterize constructivist classrooms to recognize the social nature of all learning. Teachers and children in these classrooms engage in the types of activities presented in Box 1.3.

A summary of the three major theories of learning discussed in this section is presented in Table 1.1. As authors of this text, we continue to construct and reconstruct theories of language learning with each new conversation, teaching experience, or article we read. At this point, however, the social constructivist view most adequately reflects what we believe about language learning. You may or may not hold a similar view, but you now have some understanding of what educators mean when they talk about constructing meaning.

## Language Learning in Classrooms

In this section, we briefly describe the various dimensions of language learning and the need to integrate these dimensions into the curriculum and children's lives.

Most learning is mediated through language. In classrooms, language is the most common vehicle for helping children construct concepts and principles and for enabling children to share those concepts, principles, and operations with others. Both oral and written language are used in this way, and they are used in every aspect of the curriculum.

Although in practice we often move seamlessly among talking, writing, reading, and other dimensions of language, provincial programs of study and curriculum guides generally separate these dimensions when outlining goals for language arts programs. The dimensions most commonly included in these materials are:

- speaking,
- listening,
- writing,
- reading,

**Table 1.1**   Three Orientations to Teaching and Learning

|  | Transmission | Constructivism | Social Constructivism |
|---|---|---|---|
| Underlying assumptions | Reality is objective and exists outside the individual | Reality is subjective and exists only as it relates to the individual | Reality is a social construct |
|  | Knowledge is transmitted — meanings are reproducible and constant | Knowledge is constructed — meanings vary with the individual | Knowledge is negotiated — meanings vary with the context or situation |
| Goal of education | Development of specialized knowledge and skills | Development of personally relevant knowledge and skills | Development of socially relevant knowledge and skills |
| Role of the teacher | Develop and manage teaching sequences and schemes | Create learning contexts that involve active learning | Create learning contexts that encourage ownership of learning |
|  | Present information, instruct, transfer knowledge | Scaffold or support individual learning | Support individual and collaborative learning |
| Role of the learner | Essentially passive — externally motivated | Active — internally motivated | Active — internally and socially motivated |

- viewing, and
- representing.

Here we combine the first two in a section on talking, and also present viewing and representing together.

## Talking for Learning

In the past, a quiet classroom was valued as a good classroom, and a teacher who managed a quiet class was respected and rewarded as an effective teacher. Today, we understand more fully the role of talking in learning and realize that effective classrooms often feature much focussed talk. The role of speaking and listening in learning includes speaking and listening both to others and to self. Sometimes the talk is an internal dialogue. It is usually more effective, however, if the talk is conducted with another person. As Piaget (1973) indicated, it is only then that we encounter cognitive conflict. He and Margaret Donaldson (1978) maintain that learning is a continuous process of making hypotheses, encountering conflicts, and resolving them by forming new hypotheses.

In effective classrooms, teachers organize children in many ways for different purposes. For instance:

- When children need to share a finished piece of writing, or talk with one another about a piece of writing in progress, space is provided in the classroom.
- When children are reading in pairs, they use various spaces around the room where they can read to each other.
- Science groups cluster around the tables where the activities are taking place, and discussion accompanies that activity.

- On some occasions, children need to be alone and working independently. Such occasions include time for composition, time for personal reading, and time for personal study.

Talk for learning includes questioning, focussing attention, problem solving, brainstorming, and making understanding more precise and more retrievable. These purposes apply to all areas of the curriculum and to all learning tasks. It is important that children have quiet time for their own work, and in our schools in the past, that was not a problem. Creating time and space for group work and the attendant speaking and listening was more problematic.

One of the greatest concerns expressed by beginning teachers is loss of control in the classroom. Often, when children are talking together it may appear that the teacher has lost control. However, if children and their ideas are respected, and if talk is valued, then indeed some control will be given up to the students. Of necessity, certain aspects of control become the shared responsibility of the teacher and the students.

In social constructivist classrooms, the idea that there is always one right answer to a question—and that the teacher has that answer—is rejected. In these classrooms, children discover answers for themselves and come to realize that there are many ways of answering the same question, depending on their context, point of view, and experience. They also begin to understand why some answers may be considered right and others wrong. When children are given the opportunity to express their thoughts and explain or justify their understandings, they develop confidence in their abilities as learners and thinkers. Talking freely and openly together is a major way in which human beings share understandings and develop new personal and shared perspectives on the way the world works.

## Writing for Learning

Fulwiler (1987) outlined five basic assumptions about language and learning, three of which relate specifically to writing for learning:

1. First, when people articulate connections between new information and what they already know, they learn and understand that new information better (Bruner, 1966).

2. Second, when people write about new information and ideas — in addition to reading, talking, and listening — they learn and understand them more fully (Britton, Burgess, Martin, McLeod, and Rosen, 1975).

3. Third, when people care about what they write and see connections between their writing and their own lives, they both learn and write more effectively (Moffett, 1968).

Barnes (1976, p. 76) maintains that writing is a way for people to take an active part in their own learning. He says, "As pupils write they can — under certain circumstances — reshape their view of the world, and extend their ability to think rationally about it." Writing for understanding gives learners the opportunity to examine ideas until they have clarified them. The advantage of writing about ideas as they are being processed is that the learner is forced to focus on them to a far greater degree than when simply talking about them. Talked-over ideas are easily lost; we may be distracted and lose the thread of our thoughts. Writing provides a record of where we have been in our thinking. We can go back and re-examine writing and get an overall picture of the development of our ideas and where we need to focus next. As D'Arcy (1989, p. 2) says, we can "retain, re-collect, re-construct, re-create, and re-present." We engage in what Moffett has termed "the revision of inner speech" (1979, p. 278).

## Reading for Learning

"Learning to read" rather than "reading to learn" has been at the centre of the great debate on reading (Crawford, 1995). Throughout this debate, educators have been more concerned *that* children learn how to read than with *why* or *how* they might use the reading skills and strategies developed. Some view reading development as proceeding in two distinct stages. Children first learn to read and then they read to learn. This dichotomy is reflected in a focus on basic reading skills with young children and on reading in the content areas with older students.

Most educators now realize that the two stages of learning to read and reading to learn are neither separate nor sequential. Learning to read is enhanced when children are engaged in purposeful and meaningful reading activities, and that process continues throughout their lives. As adults, we develop and extend our reading strategies every time we encounter a new task, such as reading a manual for a new computer program, using the computer catalogue in the library, or navigating the Internet. In effect, each time we read we become more adept and competent readers, the act of reading in and of itself engendering a "self-improving system" (Clay, 1993).

The recognition that learning to read and reading to learn occur simultaneously has led to a change in the type of reading material provided in language arts classrooms. Most current language arts series include a wide range of different **genres**, including poetry, stories, and informational material. Although informational materials are still viewed as being at the heart of reading for learning, Rosenblatt (1989) has helped us realize that it is our stance or purpose for reading that determines whether we take information away from texts (**efferent response**) or become part of the world created by texts (**aesthetic response**). She has also helped us realize that we can change our stance during the reading of any one text, and that the two stances are not mutually exclusive. We can all think of informational texts that both drew us into the world being portrayed and helped us construct ideas to take away. We can also think of novels that have changed the way we view ourselves or other people.

There has also been a change in how content area reading is taught in many classrooms. In the past, educators examined content area materials, developed a list of reading skills specific to each area, and designed tasks to develop each of the skills. As Gordon, Sheridan, and Paul (1998) point out, inundating students with page upon page of strategies has done little to increase their content area literacy. They recommend instead that reading, writing, talking, and viewing be an integral part of content learning and of the subject area curriculum.

## Learning through Viewing and Representing

Although language is often central, it is not the only way meaning is constructed. Every time we collect data through our senses, we interpret it and then add a modified or new construction to our awareness. Similarly, we may choose to represent meaning through media other than language. In schools, students usually do this through music, art, dance, and dramatic presentation. Most often in daily life, though, meaning is created through the interplay of many media. This is clearly evident in the example of the shared movie experience discussed earlier in this chapter. The meanings you and your friends created in response to the movie were probably as much related to the visual images and sound effects as they were to the dialogue in the movie. Thus, your personal construction of the "meanings" contained in the movie was related to the subtle interplay of language, sound, and visual images and their interaction with your background experiences, biases, and intentions. These non-linguistic ways of constructing meaning are commonly referred to in school settings as viewing and representing (Common Curriculum Framework for English Language Arts, 1996).

According to Brooks and Brooks (1993), one of the hallmarks of a constructivist classroom involves opportunities for students to explore "big ideas" in depth. When the questions students explore are related to social and cultural issues, media representations of reality often form part of the investigation. These include photography, recordings, radio, film, television, videotape, video games, computers, the performing arts, and virtual reality (Whipple, 1998). Students develop specific encoding and interpretive skills that allow them to view and examine the world represented by the media. These visual aspects of "language" are sometimes classed as a form of media literacy (Sinclair, 1996). According to Sinclair (1996, p. 27), media literacy is built upon four key concepts:

1. All media are a construction achieved by a process of selecting images, codes, and conventions.
2. Audiences develop their own meanings from media texts.
3. Creators of commercial media are subject to commercial implications and reflect many influences.
4. All media contain values and ideology.

In a program based on social constructivism, students are given opportunities to view media from a critical perspective, examining them for bias. Similarly, students explore the multiple ways by which they can represent meaning, either without or in combination with language, stretching the boundaries of meaning. Teachers are sensitive to the omnipresent multimedia environment in which their students are immersed, and they help students to develop the complex viewing and representing skills that allow them to negotiate successfully within this world.

## Integrating the Language Arts

There are at least three different levels of **integration** that can be considered in elementary classrooms. One involves the integration of the dimensions of language learning with one another. This capitalizes on reading–writing connections, speaking–writing connections, viewing–representing connections, and so on. For example, knowledge about how stories are organized helps children to construct meaning when both reading and writing. Knowledge about the relationship between letters and sounds helps children to both spell and identify words. Teaching the language arts in an integrated way helps children transfer strategies and knowledge developed in one language context to another.

A second level of integration involves language across the curriculum, a movement founded in the United Kingdom in the 1960s by James Britton and his colleagues at the London Institute for Education. More recently, the concepts of this movement have become known simply as language for learning. There are no aspects of the school curriculum where language does not play a major part. Music, health, mathematics, science, social studies, art, and physical education all have subject-specific language — a vocabulary and a way of speaking about that subject that must be learned.

But just as important is the language children bring to a subject and through which they process their thinking about that subject.

Studies on the role of language in learning have emphasized the need for learners to find meaning in the world through the use of language as a tool of exploration. Vygotsky (1962), Polanyi (1969), Britton (1970), and Halliday (1975) have all argued for the use of language in a **heuristic,** or exploratory, way so that students can make greater personal sense of their learning. The work of Britton (1970) and Moffett (1968) has promoted the understanding that language is a major medium through which learners "re-present" experience and the world to themselves. Language encodes experience, but it also takes us beyond the actual experience to reflect and interpret it. It frees us from the immediate context of our lives so that we can imagine and discuss things we have never actually experienced and things we want to know more about.

The third level of integration goes beyond the curriculum when children bring their own knowledge and experience of the world into the classroom and take what they learn in the classroom to their home and community contexts. Integration at all these levels is illustrated in the work of one Grade 4 classroom in Nova Scotia.

As the children learn about expository writing, they put together a book on the history of one small community in their area. The books are printed in paperback by a local publisher and sold in the community (Petite Rivière, 1993). The work involves both social studies and language learning, and the teacher combines the available time from both subject areas in order to maximize the time for the project. During the process, the children collect information from community members, learn how to search for material for the book, and make decisions about what to include and what to leave out, how to lay out pages, and how to select illustrations. They discuss what they have read and heard, including the meanings of words used in the past but no longer in common usage today. They write, read, conference, draft, edit, and generally engage in truly integrated learning activities that connect their own lives and experiences with life in the classroom.

Most of the chapters in this book are organized around the dimensions of language learning identified above. Chapter Two focusses on talking, Chapter Three on reading and writing, Chapters Four to Six on reading, Chapters Seven to Nine on writing, and Chapters Twelve and Thirteen on viewing and representing. Within these chapters, we draw links across dimensions when appropriate and, in the final chapter, tie the pieces together into an integrated language arts program.

## The Context of Language Learning

Children learn language in their homes, communities, schools, and broader society. Our primary focus throughout this section is on diversity within society and its implications for language arts learning and instruction.

We live in an increasingly diverse society. When children arrive at school, they bring with them a wide range of cultural, societal, and home influences that, taken as a whole, means each child views the world differently and interacts with others in unique and special ways. These differences involve gender, race, class, language, and culture.

A major challenge for public schools is to provide equal educational opportunities for all children. Studies suggest, however, that outcomes of schooling are far from equal. In Canada, a Southam News survey (1987) revealed higher rates of illiteracy in rural than in urban populations and among the poor and minorities than among other Canadians.

The latest available data reveal that 1 362 000 children in Canada (or one in five) are living in poverty (Hay, 1997). This is an increase of 46 percent since 1989. Poor children are twice as likely to have difficulties with academic achievement as children from mainstream homes, and are twice as likely to drop out of school. Low-income earners, the long-term unemployed, Aboriginal peoples, seniors, prisoners, people with disabilities, and racial and cultural minorities all have higher-than-average rates of under-education and poverty. Some Canadians interpret these results to mean that people are poor because they are illiterate. However, the National Anti-Poverty Organization (1992, p. 1) maintains that "It is poverty and other forms of inequality that create the barriers to good education for many Canadians." In his book entitled *Savage Inequalities*, Kozol (1991) points out large disparities in the United States in levels of funding for public education of middle-class and poor children. Put simply, less money is spent to educate children from poor than middle-class homes.

In recent years, it has become apparent that schools do not meet the needs of children from poor and minority homes as well as they do those from middle- and upper-income homes. To meet the needs of all the children in our classrooms, we need to be aware of diversity among the children and make a conscious effort to adjust instruction to reflect this diversity.

## Prior Knowledge

What is already known and what is already experienced form the basis for new knowledge that children develop. Most teachers are aware of differences in prior experiences that children from different backgrounds bring to language learning classrooms. For example, urban children will likely have far less knowledge about farm animals than will children who live on farms. And among the latter, those on mixed farms will have far more knowledge about farm animals than those on grain farms.

The prior knowledge we develop from past experience does not consist of a series of isolated facts or concepts, but is instead a mental framework that influences our expectations and imposes structure on the information we receive. Through relating new experiences and old ones, we build these organized frameworks that many theorists refer to as **schemata** (e.g., Rumelhart, 1980). Frank Smith (1975, p. 11) expresses this idea as a "theory of the world in the head."

These schemata, or theories of the world, develop through repeated experiences in a particular context. For example, children who are taken to McDonald's by their parents begin to develop a schema for going to a restaurant. They know that it is a place where they get food to eat, that they place an order at a counter, that someone at the counter takes the order, that the person at the counter puts the food on a tray, that the food is paid for, that one takes the food to a table to eat, and so on. When their parents take them to another restaurant where they sit down and someone comes to take their order, the children extend their schema for going to a restaurant to include features of that type of restaurant as well. Eventually, children who are taken to eat at a range of different restaurants will establish a schema that is sufficiently well developed to apply to most restaurants.

There are several implications of diversity in prior knowledge for classroom instruction:

- Teachers and children from different socio-cultural backgrounds often bring very different world views to the classsroom. In order to build on children's existing knowledge, teachers first need to find out and value what children know.
- By providing opportunities for children to relate new experiences to what they already know, teachers help them develop increasingly elaborate and complex schmata.
- Having children engage in activities such as writing definitions for new vocabulary will be far less effective than discussion, **semantic mapping**, or other activities that actively involve the children in building networks of ideas.

## Ways of Using Language

Closely related to diversity in prior knowledge are differences in language use, since it is through language that we make sense of experience and the world. Differences in language use were the focus of Heath's (1983) highly influential study of children from three communities in the Carolina Piedmont region of the United States who attended school together following desegregation. The teachers and parents wanted to find out why the children and teachers frequently could not understand one another. Specifically, they wondered why children who never stopped chattering at home rarely talked in class, and why children who were unable to answer simple questions in class could explain a rule for a ball game on the playground.

Heath found that the children from the three communities had experienced different ways of learning and using language at home. The experiences of some children matched the ways language was learned and used in the school better than did the experiences of other children:

- In "Maintown," a middle-class, school-oriented community, the focus of literacy-related activities was on labelling, explaining, and learning how to display knowledge. The children from this community were socialized into the interactional sequences that commonly occur in classrooms.
- Families in "Roadville," a white working-class community, also focussed on labelling and explanations, preparing children for literal comprehension tasks in the classroom. However, these children were unprepared for reading activities that involved reasoning or affective responses.
- In "Trackton," a black working-class community, the children were not taught labels or asked for explanations in their homes, but instead were asked to give reasons for and personal responses to events.

When children from all three communities arrived at school, the predominant type of questions asked by teachers involved having children name attributes of objects taken out of context, for example, "What colour is the horse in this picture?" The children from Trackton had not been asked these kinds of questions by their parents, and they thought these were dumb questions because their teachers already knew the answers. When teachers incorporated questions similar to those the Trackton children were asked at home, the children participated much more frequently and eventually responded to more school-based questions as well.

Again, the implications of diversity in ways of using language are obvious. By becoming aware of how language is used in the homes of children in their classrooms, teachers are able to adjust the ways language is used in the classroom to help bridge the gap between home and school.

## Ways of Telling Stories

Differences are also evident in the ways people tell stories and in what they think are good stories. This was highlighted in research by Michaels and Cazden, who listened to children and teachers during sharing time in kindergarten and Grade 1 classrooms (Cazden, 1988). Sharing time, sometimes called "show and tell," is a common activity in primary classrooms when children are invited to share a story or personal experience about their lives outside of school.

Michaels and Cazden found that teachers' reactions to children's stories revealed specific expectations about what the stories should be like. "Good" stories were those with a beginning, middle, and end, with all the ideas related to one topic. In one classroom, 96 percent of the stories told by white children met these criteria, but only 34 percent of those told by black children were topic-centred. Instead, many black children provided chains of loosely related actions or events, often with the topic left unstated. An example of these episodic stories follows:

> I went to the beach Sunday and to McDonald's and to the park and I got this for my birthday. [*Holds up purse.*] My mother bought it for me and I had two dollars for my birthday and I put it in here and I went to where my friend named Gigi. I went over to my grandmother's house with her and she was on my back and I and we was walking around by my house and she was heavy. She was in the sixth or seventh grade.... (Cazden, 1988, p. 13)

Teachers tended to react negatively to episodic stories, whereas they praised children who produced topic-centred stories. Michaels and Cazden believed that the difference in teachers' reactions was due to the match or mismatch between the narrative styles and themes of the children and the knowledge and expectations of their teachers.

To explore this further, they presented a selection of both topic-centred and episodic stories to black and white teachers and asked them to comment on how well-formed the stories were. Teachers were also asked to predict the probable academic success of the child who told each story. White teachers frequently rated episodic stories as hard to follow and predicted the children would be low-achieving, while black teachers rated both topic-centred and episodic stories positively.

Episodic stories are also common in Aboriginal groups. It is not that children from these communities cannot tell stories; it is that the stories they tell do not match their teachers' expectations. Many teachers are not aware of the mismatch between their socio-cultural backgrounds and those of the children in their classrooms. As Bernstein (cited in Cazden, 1988, p. 27) indicates, "If the culture of the teacher is to become part of the consciousness of the child, then the culture of the child must first be in the consciousness of the teacher." The first step in providing appropriate classroom instruction is awareness; the second is adjusting instruction so that children are entitled to tell their stories and to tell their stories their way (Bloome, 1991).

## Non-Standard English

So far, we have dealt with differences in people's stories and in the ways they use language in their homes. Many children also arrive at school using a non-standard form of English. For these children, one issue teachers face involves the extent to which children's oral language should form the basis for instruction compared with having them learn standard English. If teachers do not adjust instruction in relation to the language these children bring to school, the children frequently have difficulty learning to read and write. This occurs because of the discrepancy among their oral language, the language of books, and teachers' expectations of the children's writing.

However, if teachers introduce these children to reading using language written in their dialect, they may not learn the standard English necessary to succeed in mainstream society. According to Delpit (1988, p. 287), we do children who speak non-standard dialects of English no service to suggest, even implicitly, that standard English is not important. Children do need to learn to spell correctly and to use correct grammatical forms in order to gain access to higher education and jobs. The challenge for language arts teachers is to balance instruction that builds on the language children bring to the classroom with their need to communicate through standard English. It appears to be more a matter of when, rather than if, the standard form is introduced to children in elementary classrooms.

## Gender

To this point, we have dealt with differences related to socio-cultural backgrounds. In fact, gender differences are more pervasive—although in some ways more invisible—because of the way we are socialized into gender-based roles in our society.

Some differences are obvious. Most of us are aware, for example, that males and females perform differently in different subject areas (Wilkinson and Marrett, 1985). For example, girls tend to outperform boys in reading in the early grades, but by the secondary level, boys begin to pull ahead, particularly in mathematics and science. Several explanations have been given to account for differences between boys and girls in early reading achievement:

- Some educators focus on teachers' expectations. Teachers tend to expect that girls will be more successful than boys when they arrive at school.
- Others identify the feminization of elementary schools. They argue that since most teachers in elementary schools are female, boys have few male role models. However, boys are no more successful in reading in classrooms with male than with female teachers.
- Still others suggest that there is a "poor fit between the culturally prescribed male gender role and the student role that has become institutionalized in American elementary schools" (Brophy, 1985, p. 118). Boys are expected to be active, exploratory learners in our society, but schools traditionally have valued passive, recipient learners.

Another difference between boys and girls involves what they read. Surveys of reading preferences report that girls read more romance and horror, while boys opt for action and science fiction (Millard, 1997). In many cases, given a choice, boys do not read at all in school settings. Explanations for this vary. One view holds that these preferences are biologically determined—"that's the way boys and girls are!" In contrast, a more widely accepted view holds that gender is a social construct, with social interactions and group expectations shaping male and female roles and behaviours (Millard, 1997).

By the time children arrive at school in kindergarten, they have already been socialized into differentiated gender roles through their interactions with adults and older children in their homes and communities. In school they are likely to encounter a continuance of this sexual stereotyping, particularly as associated with literacy activities. For example, depictions of reading and writing in books are more likely to feature females than males. Boys who profess or demonstrate a preference for reading and writing over sports may be cast as "sissies," a pejorative term. However, girls who enjoy rough and tumble activities are called tomboys, a much more acceptable designation.

What happens at school to either reinforce or break down traditional gender roles and the pejorative notions associated with them? The short answer is not very much. Research consistently shows that teachers give more attention to boys than to girls (Brophy, 1985). While some of this attention is managerial and disciplinary in nature, boys engage in more verbal interactions of every type with teachers than do girls. Hence, the widespread belief that females talk more than males is not upheld in elementary school classrooms.

Even more interesting is the finding that it doesn't matter whether the teacher is male or female; both interact more with boys than with girls. This is not surprising when one considers that all of us, both males and females, have been exposed to the same gender role socialization pressures and, as a result, have come to share essentially the same expectations for how boys and girls will behave. Brophy (1985) argues that if gender inequalities are to be eliminated, we may need different, rather than identical, treatment of males and females in elementary classrooms.

The first step in dealing with diversity in language arts classrooms is becoming aware both of the knowledge and abilities children bring with them to school and of our own biases and preconceptions about the learning abilities of different children. Only with this awareness are we in a position to adjust learning expectations and experiences in the classroom to ensure that the learning environment is equitable for all children.

## Balanced Language Arts Programs

In the last section of this chapter, we revisit the great debate introduced earlier, to gain an understanding of the current focus of advocates of balanced literacy. We argue that while balance of phonics and meaning is important, there are many other aspects of balance to consider as well. Some of these are presented in Box 1.4.

## Phonics and Whole Language

We introduced this chapter by noting the current shift away from whole language to a renewed focus on phonics in beginning reading programs. Whole language is being vilified by the media (see, for example, the May 1998 issue of *Reader's Digest* for a vehement condemnation of whole language by Claudia Cornwall), parents, and educators alike. Many academics are rapidly distancing themselves from a movement they championed only a few years ago. Is whole language the villain so many people would now have us believe? First, let's consider what whole language is, and what it is not.

Most writers indicate that whole language is a philosophy or set of beliefs rather than an approach or technique. McKay (1993), for example, argues that whole language is a philosophy about learning, language, and the nature of relationships between children and adults. At the core of whole language is a focus on meaning as the essence of language learning and on children learning language through using it.

**Box 1.4  Variables in a Balanced Literacy Program**

**Phonics and Whole Language**

Focus on words            Focus on meaning
Teaching from parts to wholes    Teaching from wholes to parts

**Teaching and Use of Language**

Deductive        Inductive
Systematic       Incidental
Isolated         Contextualized

**Aspects of Language Arts**

Focus on reading    Focus on all aspects of language

**Level of Difficulty**

Common expectations               Different expectations
Relatively easy tasks for automaticity    Challenging tasks for new strategies
Independent learning              Scaffolding

**Ownership and Control**

Hierarchical relationships    Collaborative relationships
Teacher ownership             Student ownership
Competition                   Co-operation

Language is also seen as indivisible, with the whole always being greater than the sum of the parts (Goodman, 1986; McKay, 1993). In other words, the meaning a child constructs for a story is always more than the sum of the pronunciations and meanings of the individual words in the story. Hence, whole language advocates question activities in which children focus on individual skills in isolation from reading and writing. For example, rather than teaching spelling or phonics as isolated skills, whole language teachers help children learn how to use letter sound cues within the context of reading and writing connected texts. Teaching proceeds from whole texts to parts (such as words and letters) rather than from parts to the whole.

Language is viewed as personal, social, and cultural. "It is driven from the inside by the need to communicate and shaped from the outside towards the norms of the society" (Goodman, 1986, p. 26). What happens at school is based on what children already know and can do, and what children learn is used in their interactions in the home and community. The language arts program is connected with the rest of their school programs and their lives.

Advocates also recognize the political nature of language learning. Goodman (1986) writes about the empowerment of children as they make decisions about their own language use. McKay (1993) and Shannon (1989) write about children and teachers controlling the teaching and learning process.

While whole language has less to do with methods and practices than with philosophy and beliefs, some practices have been identified that are consistent with whole language (Altwerger, Edelsky, and Flores, 1987). In whole language classrooms:

- children engage in "real" reading and writing rather than exercises in reading and writing,

- children read more high-quality children's literature rather than working with material written to teach children how to read,
- children write regularly and for a variety of purposes, and
- assessment is based on observing children as they talk, read, and write rather than on **standardized tests**.

Froese (1990, p. 2) defines whole language as "a child-centred, literature-based approach to language teaching that immerses students in real communication situations whenever possible."

A major area of contention within the phonics/whole language debate concerns the teaching of phonics and spelling. Rather than providing a systematic set of planned lessons in these areas, whole language teachers believe that all skills are best taught incidentally in mini-lessons when they note a particular need in children's reading and writing. While this might be sufficient for some children, it is now generally recognized that others require direct teaching of skills in a sequential manner to become fluent readers and writers (Pressley and Rankin, 1994; Beck, 1998). However, does this mean that whole language philosophy should be rejected in its entirety and replaced by sequential phonics and spelling programs? Few academics or educators would go that far. As Cunningham and Allington (1999, p. xiii) point out, "Children do need phonics, but phonics is not all they need."

Most educators now recognize that no one way of teaching reading or writing will work for all children, nor will one way work for any particular child all the time. Children have diverse social, cultural, and economic backgrounds as well as different learning styles and abilities, and hence they do not all learn the same way. Part of what they need in literacy programs is balance between a focus on words and a focus on meaning. This idea has been championed in recent books on balanced literacy by Fountas and Pinnell (1996) and Cunningham and Allington (1999). As the authors of this text, we, too, recognize that this is critical and hence include suggestions for instruction on both words and meaning in our chapters on emergent literacy, reading, and writing. But the need for balance does not stop there. There is much more to balanced language arts programs than including work on both words and meaning.

## Teaching and Practice of Language

In the early days of whole language, it was not unusual to hear educators talking about children learning "naturally" by being immersed in rich literacy experiences with relatively little instruction at all. Today, few educators or parents would question Gaffney (1998) when she says that the key to children learning to read can be summed up in one word — teaching. It's the *how* of teaching that's currently open to debate.

### Deductive versus Inductive Instruction

One question in this debate involves whether instruction should be deductive or inductive. Deductive teaching is often associated with a transmission model of knowledge. Teachers present knowledge and have students use that knowledge in new situations.

In contrast, inductive teaching is more consistent with constructivist notions. Teachers begin with data and help students build generalizations about those data. For example, rather than teaching children the "final *e* rule," teachers present words that do (e.g., *kit, kite; fat, fate; cub, cube*) and do not (e.g., *love, give, some*) exemplify the pattern and ask children to figure out how the sounds and letters work. Proponents of inductive teaching maintain that because students are actively engaged in gathering and interpreting information, they more readily retain the knowledge they construct. This is highly motivational and leads to the development of self-directed learners. However, while inductive teaching might be more effective than deductive teaching, it is less efficient. Moreover, some children have great difficulty learning without direct instruction (Grimmett, 1994).

Constructivist teaching does not mean that children have to figure out how written language works all of the time, that they have to reinvent *everything* on their own. The question is not which is best — inductive or deductive instruction — but which will serve a child's needs at any specific point in time. Even when constructivist teachers decide to use deductive instruction, they know that no two children will develop exactly the same understanding of what's being taught.

### Incidental versus Systematic Instruction

Another major question faced by teachers is whether skills instruction should be provided incidentally in mini-lessons or sequentially in a systematic set of planned lessons. This question can certainly be asked about the practice of language arts skills and strategies. Should practice be provided on an occasional basis or on a continuous basis? The answer will depend, as it did for inductive and deductive teaching, on each child's daily needs.

Sometimes incidental instruction or occasional practice will be sufficient, but often it is not. Many times it is possible to teach strategies *as* children read and write, but again this is not always the case. Once more, balance is needed. By carefully observing children in the classroom, teachers decide when and how to provide instruction at any point in time. They also decide how much practice children need in order to generalize skills and strategies to other reading and writing contexts.

### Isolated versus Contextualized Instruction

Another question related to the "how" of teaching involves whether skills should be taught as separate components of the language arts program or in the context of real reading and writing as promoted by whole language proponents. Furthermore, should practice be provided with isolated words and tasks, or should it involve authentic language activities? (The latter is supported by thinking that says to become good at doing anything, whether it's riding a bike, swimming, or writing, we need to spend time actually doing it.)

Many children spend relatively little time at school actually reading. In the 1980s, Anderson, Hiebert, Scott, and Wilkerson (1985) reported that the average daily time children devoted to reading in the primary grades was only seven minutes. They found that most time allocated for reading consisted of the teacher talking about reading or the children completing worksheets. While there is little doubt that children need to spend time reading at home as well as in school, Stanovich (1986) has shown that this happens more frequently with good readers than poor readers. For many poor readers, their *only* reading is done at school.

## Dimensions of Language Arts

Until the past two decades, most language arts time was allocated to reading instruction and restricted largely to using one basal reading series. In the 1980s, the work of educators such as Graves (1983), Calkins (1986), and Atwell (1987) led to a sharp increase in the time children spent writing in elementary schools. Indeed, many educators appeared to assume that children would learn to read by reading their own writing and by reading and responding to the writing of their peers. Now, as the current reaction to whole language intensifies, there is a danger that a swing back to a renewed concentration on reading will result in minimal attention being paid to writing and other critical areas of language learning.

A balanced program does not mean that the same proportion of language arts instruction is devoted to speaking, listening, reading, writing, viewing, and representing every day. Rather, it means that children spend at least some time in each of these modes of language every day, and that over time they receive instruction to maximize their language growth in *all* areas.

## Level of Difficulty

Many children in language arts classrooms experience daily frustration because they are unable to complete tasks that are too difficult for them. Others are not sufficiently challenged to maximize their learning. Only by having a balanced program of language arts activities will children experience success *and* reach their potential. There are three major ways teachers can achieve this type of balance:

1. by adjusting their expectations for performance during the initial stages of learning something new,

2. by setting different expectations for different children on the same learning task, and

3. by providing different levels of materials and tasks for different children.

There is a marked contrast between how young children learn to talk at home and how they are later generally taught to read and write. Parents try to understand their children even when their oral language is far from the adult form. They reinforce their children's efforts to communicate by responding in a meaningful way. As Holdaway (1979) points out, no one expects a young child to speak in grammatically correct sentences with perfect pronunciation the first time he or she talks. In reading and writing, however, accuracy is often required from the beginning, both at home and at school. Teachers help children feel successful by having realistic expectations when they are learning something new.

Because children are not all at the same place in their language proficiency, teachers can also balance level of difficulty by expecting children to perform differently on the same learning task. For example, in a kindergarten class, the teacher might have very different expectations for what children will be able to do with a predictable book after it is read to them. That is:

- Some children will be able to identify words in the book as they reread it.
- Other children may point to the words as another child reads them, developing an understanding of the one-to-one relationship between words in oral and written language.
- Still other children may listen and chime in ("talk like a book" [Clay, 1972]), developing an understanding of how written language sounds.

In other words, different children do different things with the same book in order to achieve different objectives.

Sometimes, however, the teacher needs to adjust the level of materials and tasks for different children. For example, an important goal for all children is to become fluent, automatic readers. It is estimated that children need to read a minimum of three and one-half hours per week to achieve this goal (Rossman, 1987), and during this time, they need to be reading books that they can handle without assistance from others. In any classroom, books at a range of levels are required for this independent reading. The higher the grade level, the greater this range needs to be.

Although children need practice with reading and writing activities they can handle independently, they will not learn to their potential without activities that challenge them. At least some of the time, they need to be working in their zone of proximal development (Vygotsky, 1978). At this level, work is too difficult for them to complete independently, but they can achieve success with the support of their teacher or other students.

This support is frequently referred to as "scaffolding," a term used by Bruner (1975, p. 12) to refer to interaction between a young child and its mother, in which the mother supports the child "in achieving an intended outcome." The child decides to do something and the mother provides the assistance (such as a helping hand, gesture, or word) that allows the child to manage to do it. The concept of scaffolding highlights the importance of beginning with what children *can* do rather than what they cannot do, and viewing children as competent learners rather than deficient learners.

To plan instruction so that all children experience mastery and challenge on a daily basis, teachers need a great deal of information about their skills and interests. Later in this book, in chapters on oral language, emergent literacy, reading, and writing, we describe assessment techniques for obtaining this information.

## Ownership and Control

The notion of scaffolding raises questions about the ownership of learning and knowledge. Extending the scaffolding metaphor, Searle (1984, p. 480) asks the question, "Who's building whose building?" He believes that too often in schools it is the teacher who sets the agenda and then helps children to accomplish that agenda. Seldom do children adapt their own language resources to achieve purposes they set for themselves.

According to Edwards (1980), there is a sharp distinction in most classrooms between the teacher ("the one who knows") and the students ("the many who do not"). Because of this distinction, the major role of students is to listen and that of teachers is to tell. In addition, it is often the teacher who decides what counts as knowledge and who "owns" instructional talk. The teacher determines which students speak and then what they talk about, how long they talk, and how well they talked. In the end, it is the teacher who does most of the talking, and when he or she does ask questions, they nearly all require students to provide information that the teacher already knows.

The most common **discourse** pattern in classrooms is a three-part sequence of "teacher-initiation, student-response, teacher-evaluation" (the IRE pattern, Cazden, 1988). When children come to school, those from some homes are more familiar than others with this structure. The children from Trackton in Heath's study described earlier, for example, were far less familiar with this type of interaction than those from Maintown. The IRE pattern is consistent with a transmission model of knowledge and appropriate for some purposes (e.g., having children learn number facts), but it is far less consistent with constructivist views and inappropriate for supporting children's responses to literature. Although it is easy to imagine talk in which ideas are explored, it is much harder to make this a reality of daily classroom life. It is more than a matter of who talks when, involving a significant change in conceptions of knowledge and teaching and in how ownership is shared by children and teachers.

As Wells and Chang-Wells (1992) note, the important point is not whose vision — the teacher's or children's — will prevail, but rather what can be done to create a context in which meaning is co-constructed by the teacher and children together:

> In such a context, the teacher remains in charge, but his or her exercise of control is manifested not in a once-and-for-all choice between intervening with the correct answer or standing back and leaving the students to find their own solutions, but in the making of moment-by-moment decisions about how to proceed, based on knowledge of the topic, understanding of the dynamics of classroom interaction, intentions with respect to the task, and a continuous monitoring of the ongoing talk. (pp. 46–47)

Thus, the issue is not whether but *how* the teacher intervenes.

Clearly, the constructivist teacher assumes a different role from that of the traditional teacher who is "dispenser of information and authority on all things to be taught and learned in the classroom." And what might that role be, based on a social constructivist model of learning? The role is obviously a multifaceted one, including at least the following dimensions:

- The teacher is a *provider* of resources, and an *organizer* of space and time so that children have the opportunities and materials they need for learning (Lindfors, 1987).
- In the role of *demonstrator* (Smith, 1983), the teacher shows how something is done and demonstrates through actions that he or she is a reader, writer, and thinker.
- Learning is a lifelong activity, and it's important for children to see the teacher's own enthusiasm and questioning as a *learner*.
- The teacher is a *responder*. When we are learning something new, it is helpful to have someone respond to our questions, question us further, support our learning, and let us know how we are doing. That is not the same as judging our performance. Response is genuine and productive, and occurs as the teacher actively follows what children are trying to do and attempts to further that learning.
- In the role of *observer*, the teacher gains insight into the children's learning processes and comes to understand what children know and can do.

In the classroom incident described in Box 1.5, Linda Graves shares an experience in which she played all the roles described above. She was a provider of resources, demonstrator when she read her own writing, observer as she examined the leads Desira had written, and responder when she encouraged Desira to make her own choice. But most of all she was a learner. Her interaction with Desira helped her to more fully understand the importance of guiding children to gain control over their own writing.

Communicating teacher's roles to parents.

**Box 1.5    Teacher Roles: A Specific Example**

*Linda Graves shares an experience with a young student writer in her Saskatoon classroom.*

I remember a time when I was working with Desira in our Writer's Workshop. Desira had written a wonderful story about Fluffy, her cat. The lesson I had introduced to the students that morning was on leads. We looked at lots of books and discussed how the authors began their stories. Students were eager to share their favourite books and why they thought each lead was used to introduce each story. We also looked at our own writing and shared our leads. I read to the students my writing about our class cat, Kizmit. The children had lots of helpful suggestions on how I could "hook" the reader. I asked the students to think of two or three different ways they could write a lead on the story they were currently working on. Off they went to their special places in the classroom and hallway to weave more ideas on leads.

Desira was sitting quietly in a corner of the classroom hard at work. She had written three leads and was trying to decide which one she would like to use. I poured over her work with her, asking her to read me the leads.

- Once there was a cat who's name was Fluffy. he is potty trained. and he tears all the walls up. Sometimes he bites and scratches me and my sister but he thinks he's playing.
- there was a cat his name is Fluffy. he always crys for food. When we say no to him. he jumps in the Garbage can.
- Meaww Meaww Where's my Dinner cried Fluffy no food said Desira.

I loved them all, but my favourite was "Meaww Meaww." That is the one I wanted Desira to choose. With my teacher control finger poised on the start button, I almost said to her, "Desira, this is the best one. Why don't you lead your story with that?" But I stopped and told myself, "If you want these children to be the masters of their own writing, then you must allow them to make the choices they want." A rather tough thing for me to do. Regaining my composure, I then asked Desira what lead she was going to choose. She did not choose my preferred lead, but rather chose one that perhaps was more conventional and more like the leads she had read in other books. Desira was either not willing or not ready to take a risk that day and I had to support her decision, hoping a day would come when she would take a risk.

Desira learned something about leads that day, but perhaps it was I who learned the most. We must allow students to make choices for themselves if we truly want to empower them, to help them become masters of their own destinies. Desira went on from this day with the feeling that she had control over her writing, and that is exactly where the control should be. We must guide student writing, not take ownership for it. Thanks, Desira — you were my teacher that day!

Source: Linda Graves. Reprinted with permission.

As teachers' roles become more consistent with social constructivism, children take responsibility for more of their own language learning, and the relationship between teachers and children becomes more collaborative and less hierarchical (Vygotsky, 1962, 1978). By working collaboratively in classrooms, children develop a sense of ownership of both their knowledge and language. By making choices about their language learning, children begin to feel like readers and writers — they feel that they belong to the literacy club (Smith, 1988).

This last point emphasizes the social rather than individual nature of learning. Social constructivists place a focus on the social nature of language learning and on children working together, whereas transmission models tend to value individual learning and achievement. Although there is greater emphasis on co-operative learning and peer assessment in schools today than in the past, most schools continue to focus more on individual competition than on co-operation and assessment of group outcomes.

As we conclude this section, we return to the scenario at the beginning of the chapter in which Chad poses several questions about language arts instruction. The conclusion that both you and he have probably reached is that there are few simple answers. There is no one best way to facilitate children's language learning. In our discussion, we not only identified the need for a coherent theoretical framework, but also asked you to incorporate apparently irreconcilable approaches into a balanced language arts program that meets the needs of all children. Your most pressing question at this point is probably "But *how* do I do it?" Our main goal in the remainder of this book is to help each of you construct your own answer to this question.

## Summary

For the past century, educators and parents alike have engaged in a search for one best way to teach children to read and write. On one side of this "great debate" are those who believe that children need to learn a set of predetermined skills (the phonics approach). On the other side are those who believe that children learn to read and write without direct instruction (the whole language approach). Although many educators now realize that there is no one best way to teach reading or writing, programs are often driven by "best practices" rather than by a coherent theoretical framework.

There are three major theoretical perspectives on knowledge and learning: transmission, constructivism, and social constructivism. Skills-based instruction reflects a transmission model in which teachers have knowledge and transmit this knowledge to their students. Whole language instruction is more consistent with constructivism, where the focus is on actively making meaning, rather than on reproducing existing knowledge. But constructing meaning does not occur in a vacuum; social constructivism acknowledges the impact of the social context and social interactions on learning.

Elementary language arts programs generally include the following dimensions: listening, speaking, reading, writing, viewing, and representing. Through each of these dimensions, children construct concepts and principles and share those concepts, principles, and operations with others. Teaching language arts in an integrated way helps children transfer strategies from one language arts dimension to another, use developing language strategies in all subject areas, and link what they learn in the classroom to their home and community contexts.

A major challenge for schools is to provide equal educational opportunities for all children. This does not mean that all children should be treated the same, but that teachers need to take diversity into account when planning instruction. Children differ in the prior experience they bring to classrooms, in the ways they use language in their homes, in the stories they tell, in their proficiency with standard English, and in their gender. An important step in dealing with diversity in language arts classrooms is becoming aware both of the knowledge and abilities children bring with them to school and of our own biases and preconceptions about the learning abilities of different children.

Many educators argue that balance is crucial to meeting children's needs. The term "balanced literacy" is generally used to refer to programs that maintain a balance between work on words and work on meaning. Balance does not stop there, however. Another aspect of balance involves providing instruction in *all* aspects of the language arts rather than emphasizing one or two areas at the expense of the others. Still another aspect involves balance between the amount of time spent on teaching and that spent on using language strategies. Sometimes children learn inductively, whereas at other times they need deductive instruction. Sometimes incidental instruction is sufficient, whereas at other times direct, systematic instruction is critical to learning. And, to become good at any activity (including reading, talking, or writing), children need to spend time doing or practising it. Balance also relates to the difficulty level of tasks and materials. Children do not learn when tasks are too difficult, but they also do not learn unless they are sufficiently challenged. Teachers balance the level of difficulty by setting different expectations for different children and by varying the amount of teacher or peer support they provide to help children as they learn new strategies and establish mastery of these strategies. A final aspect of balance involves ownership and control. In social constructivist classrooms, children take more responsibility for their own learning, relationships between children and teachers become more collaborative and less hierarchical, and greater emphasis is placed on co-operation than competitiveness.

## Selected Professional Resources

Adams, M.J. (1990). *Beginning to Read: Thinking and Learning about Print.* Cambridge, MA: MIT Press. In this book, Adams provides teachers with a review of research on beginning reading instruction across most of the twentieth century, concluding that direct and systematic instruction in phonics is the most effective way to teach children to read. This book has significantly influenced current directions in language arts instruction for young children in North America.

Cunningham, P.M. and Allington, R.L. (1999). *Classrooms That Work: They Can All Read and Write* (2nd ed.). New York: Longman. Cunningham and Allington provide a compelling argument for combining best practices into a balanced literacy program. They also provide a practical guide for language arts teachers in the elementary grades.

## References

Adams, M.J. (1990). *Beginning to read: Thinking and learning about print.* Cambridge, MA: MIT Press.

Altwerger, B., Edelsky, C., and Flores, B.M. (1987). Whole language: What's new? *Reading Teacher, 41,* 144–154.

Anderson, R., Hiebert, E., Scott, J., and Wilkerson, I. (1985). *Becoming a nation of readers.* Washington, DC: National Institute of Education.

Atwell, N. (1987). *In the middle: Writing, reading, and learning with adolescents.* Portsmouth, NH: Heinemann.

Barnes, D. (1976). *From communication to curriculum.* Harmondsworth, UK: Penguin Books.

Beck, I.L. (1998). Understanding beginning reading: A journey through teaching and research. In J. Osborn and F. Lehr (eds.), *Literacy for all: Issues in teaching and learning* (pp. 11–31). New York: The Guilford Press.

Bloome, D. (1991). Anthropology and research on teaching the English language arts. In J. Flood, J.M. Jensen, D. Lapp, and J.R. Squire (eds.), *Handbook of research on teaching the English language arts* (pp. 46–56). New York: Macmillan.

Britton, J. (1970). *Language and learning.* Harmondsworth, UK: Penguin Books.

Britton, J., Burgess, G., Martin, N., McLeod, A., and Rosen, H. (1975). *The development of writing abilities, 11–18.* London: MacMillan Education.

Brooks, J.G. and Brooks, M.G. (1993). *In search of understanding: The case for constructivist classrooms.* Alexandria, VA: Association for Supervision and Curriculum Development.

Brophy, J. (1985). Interactions of male and female students with male and female teachers. In L.C. Wilkinson and C.B. Marrett (eds.), *Gender influences in classroom interaction.* Toronto: Academic Press.

Bruner, J.S. (1966). *Towards a theory of instruction.* Cambridge, MA: The Belknap Press of Harvard University.

Bruner, J.S. (1975). The ontogenesis of speech acts. *Journal of Child Language, 2,* 1–40.

Calkins, L. (1986). *The art of teaching writing.* Portsmouth, NH: Heinemann.

Cazden, C.B. (1988). *Classroom discourse: The language of teaching and learning.* Portsmouth, NH: Heinemann.

Chall, J.S. (1967). *Learning to read: The great debate.* New York: McGraw-Hill.

Clay, M.M. (1972). *Reading: The patterning of complex behaviour.* Auckland, NZ: Heinemann Educational Books.

Clay, M.M. (1993). *Reading Recovery: A guidebook for teachers in training.* Portsmouth, NH: Heinemann.

*Common curriculum framework for English language arts: Kindergarten to grade 12: Western Canadian protocol for collaboration in basic education.* (1996). Governments of Alberta, British Columbia, Manitoba, Northwest Territories, Saskatchewan, and Yukon Territory.

Cornwall, C. (May 1998). Scandal of our illiterate kids. *Reader's Digest,* 77–82.

Crawford, P.A. (1995). Early literacy: Emerging perspectives. *Journal of Research in Childhood Education, 10* (1), 71–86.

Cunningham, P.M. and Allington, R.L. (1999). *Classrooms that work: They can all read and write* (2nd ed.). New York: Longman.

D'Arcy, P. (1989). *Making sense, shaping meaning: Writing in the context of a capacity-based approach to learning.* Portsmouth, NH: Heinemann.

Delpit, L. (1988). The silenced dialogue: Power and pedagogy in educating other people's children. *Harvard Educational Review, 58,* 280–298.

Donaldson, M. (1978). *Children's minds.* New York: W.W. Norton & Co.

Edelsky, C. (1994). Education for democracy. *Language Arts, 71* (4), 252–257.

Edwards, A.D. (1980). Patterns of power and authority in classroom talk. In P. Woods (ed.), *Teacher strategies: Explorations in the sociology of the school* (pp. 237–253). London: Croom Helm.

Fountas, I.C. and Pinnell, G.S. (1996). *Guided reading: Good first teaching for all children.* Portsmouth, NH: Heinemann.

Frepon, P.S. and Dahl, K.L. (1998). Balanced instruction: Insights and considerations. *Reading Research Quarterly, 31* (2), 240–251.

Froese, V. (1990). *Whole language: Practice and theory.* Scarborough, ON: Prentice-Hall Canada.

Fulwiler, T. (ed.). (1987). *The journal book.* Toronto: Boynton/Cook.

Gaffney, J.S. (1998). The prevention of reading failure: Teach reading and writing. In J. Osborn and F. Lehr (eds.), *Literacy for all: Issues in teaching and learning* (pp. 100–110). New York: The Guilford Press.

Giroux, H.A. (1987). Critical literacy and student experience: Donald Graves' approach to literacy. *Language Arts, 64* (2), 175–181.

Goodman, K.S. (1986). *What's whole in whole language?* Richmond Hill, ON: Scholastic-TAB.

Gordon, C.J., Sheridan, M.E., and Paul, W.J. (1998). *Content literacy for secondary teachers.* Toronto: Harcourt Brace & Company.

Graves, D.H. (1983). *Writing: Teachers and children at work.* Exeter, NH: Heinemann Educational Books.

Grimmett, P.P. (1994). Induction and inductive teaching. In A.C. Purves (ed.), *Encyclopedia of English studies and language arts* (pp. 622–624). New York: Scholastic.

Halliday, M.A.K. (1975). *Explorations in the functions of language.* London: Edward Arnold.

Hay, D.I. (1997). Campaign 2000: Child and family poverty in Canada. In J. Pulkingham and G. Ternowetsky (eds.), *Child and family policies: Struggles, strategies and options* (pp. 116–133). Halifax: Fernwood Publishing.

Heath, S.B. (1983). *Ways with words: Language, life and work in communities and classrooms.* Cambridge, MA: Cambridge University Press.

Hiebert, E.H. (1991). *Literacy for a diverse society: Perspectives, practices, and policies.* New York: Teachers College Press.

Holdaway, D. (1979). *The foundations of literacy.* Gosford, Australia: Ashton Scholastic.

Kozol, J. (1991). *Savage inequalities: Children in America's schools.* New York: Crown Publishers.

Lauritzen, C. and Jaeger, M. (1997). *Integrating narrative through story: The narrative curriculum.* Albany, NY: Delmar Publications.

Lindfors, J.W. (1987). *Children's language and learning* (2nd ed.). Englewood Cliffs, NJ: Prentice-Hall.

McKay, R. (1993). Whole language: Defining our beliefs, examining our practices. In L.L. Stewin and S.J.H. McCann (eds.), *Contemporary educational issues: The Canadian mosaic* (pp. 482–504). Toronto: Copp Clark Pitman.

Millard, D. (1997). *Differently literate: Boys, girls, and the schooling of literacy.* London: Falmer Press.

Moffett, J. (1968). *Teaching the universe of discourse.* Boston: Houghton Mifflin.

Moffett, J. (1979). Integrity in the teaching of writing. *Phi Delta Kappa, 61 (4),* 276–279.

National Anti-Poverty Organization. (1992). *Literacy and poverty: A view from the inside.* Ottawa: National Anti-Poverty Organization.

Petite Rivière Elementary School. (1993). *History of Crousetown.* Lunenburg County, NS: Petite Rivière Publishing.

Piaget, J. (1972). *Insights and illusions of philosophy.* New York: Routledge and Kegan Paul.

Piaget, J. (1973). *The language and thought of the child.* New York: World.

Polanyi, M. (1969). Knowing and being. In M. Grene (ed.), *Knowing and being: The essays of Michael Polanyi* (pp. 123–137). Chicago: University of Chicago Press.

Pressley, M. and Rankin, J. (1994). More about whole language methods of reading instruction for students at risk for early reading failure. *Learning disabilities research and practice, 9 (3),* 157–168.

Richardson, V. (1997). Constructivist teaching and teacher education: Theory and practice. In V. Richardson (ed.), *Constructivist teacher education* (pp. 3–14). London: Falmer Press.

Rosenblatt, L. (1989). Writing and reading: The transactional theory. In J.M. Mason (ed.), *Reading and writing connections* (pp. 153–176). Boston: Allyn and Bacon.

Rossman, A.D. (1987). Reading automaticity: The essential element of academic success. *Principal, 67,* 28–32.

Rumelhart, D.E. (1980). Schemata: The building blocks of cognition. In R.J. Spiro, B.C. Bruce, and W.F. Brewer (eds.), *Theoretical issues in reading comprehension* (pp. 33–58). Hillsdale, NJ: Lawrence Erlbaum Associates.

Schön, D. (1987). *Educating the reflective practitioner.* San Francisco, CA: Jossey Bass.

Searle, D. (1984). Scaffolding: Who's building whose building? *Language Arts, 61 (5),* 480–483.

Shannon, P. (1989). The struggle for control of literacy lessons. *Language Arts, 66 (6),* 625–634.

Sinclair, D. (1996). Media literacy: Elementary, my dear TL. *Emergency Librarian, 24 (2),* 26–29.

Smith, F. (1975). *Comprehension in learning.* New York: Holt, Rinehart and Winston.

Smith, F. (1983). Reading like a writer. *Language Arts, 60 (5),* 558–567.

Smith, F. (1988). *Joining the literacy club: Further essays into education.* London: Heinemann.

Southam News. (1987). *Literacy in Canada: A research report.* Toronto: The Creative Research Group.

Stanovich, K.E. (1986). Matthew effects in reading: Some consequences of individual differences in the acquisition of literacy. *Reading Research Quarterly, 21 (4),* 360–406.

Vygotsky, L.S. (1962). *Thought and language.* Cambridge, MA: MIT Press.

Vygotsky, L.S. (1978). *Mind in society: The development of higher psychological processes.* M. Cole, V. John-Steiner, S. Scribner, and E. Souberman (eds.). Cambridge, MA: Harvard University Press.

Wells, C. G., and Chang-Wells, G.L. (1992). *Constructing knowledge together: Classrooms as centers of inquiry and literacy.* Portsmouth, NH: Heinemann.

Whipple, M. (1998). Let's go to the movies: Rethinking the role of film in the elementary classroom. *Language Arts, 76 (2),* 144–150.

Wilkinson, L.C. and Marrett, C.B. (1985). *Gender influences in classroom interactions.* Toronto: Academic Press.

# Chapter two

# Language Development and Oracy

**The Purposeful Nature of Language**
- Learning How to Mean
- Halliday's Functions of Language

**Language Structures**
- Semantics
- Syntax
- Phonology
- Pragmatics

**Perspectives on Language Acquisition**
- Behaviourist View of Language Learning
- Innatist View of Language Learning
- Interactionist View of Language Learning

**Language Development and the Social Context**
- Preschool Language Development
- Language Development in Elementary School
- Language at Home and at School
- Communicative Competence

**Language Development and Oracy**

**Oral Language in the Classroom**
- Listening
- Talking
- Assessing Oracy (Listening and Talking)
- Promoting Oral Language Growth in the Classroom
- Helping Children Become Effective Listeners
- Vocabulary Development

**Language in Learning**
- Language and Thinking
- Language across the Curriculum

Ms. Moorhouse has successfully taught reading and writing to her Grade 2 students for the last three years. Ms. Moorhouse, however, doesn't have a BA in English, and she is coming to feel that she needs to know more about the English language itself. Ms. Moorhouse listens to her students talking in class and on the playground, and she is aware that some of the children need help in refining their oral language abilities. She would like to know more about how to address children's nonstandard oral language habits so that her students will become more articulate as they share their ideas in class and with their peers and families at home. What do teachers need to know about language in order to be able to teach oral language skills to children? If children have learned the essentials of their language before they come to school, what is left to teach in school, other than reading and writing? ■

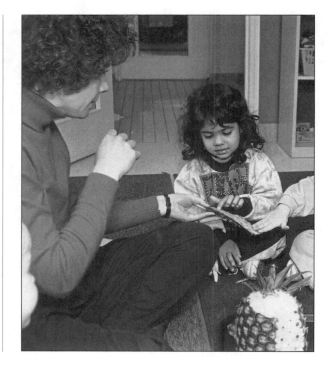

As they strive to help children express themselves clearly and in appropriate language, many teachers find themselves asking questions about language as well as about how children learn language in the years before they come to school. This chapter describes the basic elements of language and how children learn to construct meaning through language. It explores language development in children both before they enter school and during their years in the elementary grades. Teachers model appropriate language in their interactions with their students, and they make every effort to understand important concepts and principles about language development. They appreciate, like Ms. Moorhouse, that understanding the nature of language development also facilitates an understanding of the role of language in learning. In school, children do two major things in their language development: they continue to learn and refine their language abilities, both written and spoken, and they learn how to use language in order to learn.

## The Purposeful Nature of Language

In this section, we draw heavily on the work of Michael Halliday, a linguist and one of the most influential researchers and writers on language learning in the 1960s and 1970s.

In answering the question, "What is language?" Halliday (1969) maintained that the answer lies in the purpose or intention behind the language event. He believes that language is, for children, defined by its usefulness, by what language can do for them. Children learn language because there is something they need to *do*, and in order to do it, they need to communicate their intentions to another person. There is almost no limit to what children can do with language. From birth onwards, children develop the ability to communicate their intentions, and they develop that ability long before they develop language. Their gestures direct the behaviour of the adults around them: they hold up their arms to be lifted up, and they point when they drop a favourite toy. At other times they play, gurgling and repeating the sounds and rhythms they have learned, evoking playful responses from their caregivers.

### Learning How to Mean

Michael Halliday maintained that children know what language is because they know what language does. In other words, children learn about language through using it. Halliday explained that children come to understand the purposes of language from their own experiences of language in use. Children do not learn explicitly what a noun is, but they do learn to label. They do not understand what **grammar** is, yet they learn how to string words together into sentences that make sense to them and to the people with whom they intend to communicate. It was Halliday (1975) who coined the phrase "learning how to mean." Children learn language to express meanings to others and to construct meaning for themselves. A great deal of human thinking is done through language. It is difficult to imagine what it would be like to think without language, for although we think in feelings and images, we construct our most abstract thoughts through the vehicle of language.

Children learn language in real situations where something is being accomplished. That something may be the singing of a song at bedtime, the talk a mother engages in while she changes a child's clothing, the conversation that goes on around the dinner table, the choice of a television program, or the completion of a job in the yard. Frequently, children are invited to participate in conversations even when they are not yet capable of speaking in complete sentences — for example, when older siblings ask younger children what toys or books they would like to play with or what they would like to drink. At other times the language is being used in the world around the child. However, the **discourse** that contributes most to the growth of children's language capabilities and learning is the discourse that actively involves the child. Interaction, particularly with significant adults or more mature language users (Wells, 1986), is necessary for language development to occur. Watching television and being talked *at* are no substitutes for involvement. Genuine involvement and purposeful talk *with* children are the most important conditions upon which their language development rests.

## Halliday's Functions of Language

Michael Halliday identified seven "functions" of language (Box 2.1), which are summarized here. In everyday life we encounter *instrumental language* every time we ask another person to help us. Whether we are asking someone to pass the salt or ordering a meal in a restaurant, we are using the instrumental function of language. Closely related to this is the *regulatory function*. Sometimes it is difficult to tell these two functions apart, since when we regulate someone else's behaviour, it is often in order to meet our own needs. We encounter regulatory language in our lives at every turn. A "no smoking" sign, a handbook on how to make a kite, the requirements for an assignment for a university class — all are examples of this. *Interactional language* is simply the language we use to maintain and establish relationships (or to have an argument, which is another way of maintaining a relationship). It is the social chat we engage in over coffee, and the conversations we have with friends and colleagues. *Personal language* is used when we tell about ourselves—our feelings, thoughts, and beliefs. Our personal language lets the listener in on who we are, and often reveals part of our unique identity. ***Heuristic*** *language* is used when we explore and question and when we wonder and hypothesize. We hear it when a friend says, "I wonder what would happen if..." or when a child says, "Did Grandpa always have no hair?" The *imaginative* function of language comes into full play when we write stories or poetry, or when we daydream, make a wish list, or engage in play with a child. Jokes, riddles, and cartoons are part of this realm. *Representational language* is the language of reports, lectures, documentary programs on television, and textbooks. As teachers and students, we become very familiar with this type of language because it predominates in classroom discourse.

Of importance to teachers is Halliday's observation that each child develops language functions in unique ways and that the development of one or more functions may lag behind others. He added that probably the most useful functions of language in a classroom are heuristic and personal. However, he showed that the most common functions in classroom use, particularly those classrooms emphasizing a transmission model of knowledge, are representative and regulatory. In constructivist classrooms, teachers are aware that all language use has a purpose behind it. They also provide a wide range of experiences so that children have opportunities to use language in different functions across the school day.

Halliday's work suggests that children do not develop language in a haphazard or purposeless way. On the contrary, children develop language because they have needs

**Box 2.1**    **The Seven Functions of Language**

Based on his observations of young children's language development in the early years, Halliday (1969) proposed a model that categorized language use according to seven functions.

| Function | Example |
|---|---|
| 1.  Instrumental (language as a means of getting things, satisfying material needs) | "I want." |
| 2.  Regulatory (controlling the behaviour, feelings, or attitudes of others) | "Do as I tell you." |
| 3.  Interactional (getting along with others, establishing relative status and separateness) | "Me and you." "Me against you" |
| 4.  Personal (expressing individuality, awareness of self, pride) | "Here I come." |
| 5.  Heuristic (seeking and testing knowledge) | "Tell me why." |
| 6.  Imaginative (creating new worlds, making up stories, poems) | "Let's pretend." |
| 7.  Representational (communicating information, descriptions, expressing propositions) | "I've got something to tell you." |

Source: Based on M.A.K. Halliday (1969), "Relevant Models of Language." *Educational Review, 22* (1), pp. 26–37.

that must be fulfilled, and they quickly see that language enables them to make sense of and, to some extent, control their world. Through language, children can have their needs met, live in the world of the imagination, inquire, tell about who they are, tell what they know, and develop relationships. As children interact with others in classrooms, playgrounds, stores, and other public places, they use language with amazing proficiency. When children enter kindergarten classrooms, their language reflects an implicit knowledge of the rules of grammar and appropriate language usage. In their five years of life they have mastered the most complex learning task they will likely ever have to accomplish — the learning of language — and they can use that language to do a multiplicity of tasks. Most of this language is learned in a two-year period, between the ages of 2 and 4. At this age, children have often been called linguistic geniuses. By the time children are in school, they take language completely for granted.

# Language Structures

The next section of the chapter examines language itself. How do linguists describe language? What does language consist of? What do the terms "semantics," "syntax," and "phonology" mean? How do these systems connect to language arts in the elementary grades? These are the questions Ms. Moorhouse was asking as this chapter opened.

As adults, we do not usually remember exactly what facets of language we learned as children, but we are all aware that we did once learn language. We also teach language to our own children without having any training in how to do it, and usually without a conscious awareness that we are teaching it. We talk to children, listen to them, play with them, read and tell stories to them, and they seem to learn language without much effort or direct teaching. What is it that children learn and that adults take for granted?

Linguists describe language in terms of three systems: **semantics**, **syntax**, and **phonology**. In addition, we learn the **pragmatics** of language. The ability to manipulate the basic language elements of semantics, syntax, phonology, and pragmatics with relative ease and fluency is called **native speaker ability**. It is part of what we know when we understand the difference between "That mom is awesome" and "That, Mom, is awesome." It's what helps to create the humour in children's books such as *Amelia Bedelia* (Parish, 1963), when Amelia "checks the laundry," "dresses a chicken," and "draws the drapes." A whole array of cultural, social, and contextual factors influence native speaker ability. Although all of the systems of language are interrelated, for clarity we discuss them independently in this section of the chapter.

## Semantics

Semantics refers to the meaning component of language. A basic element of the meaning system of language is its **morphology**. *Morphemes*, the building blocks of meaning, are the smallest meaning units of language. Helping to create meaning within words and sentences, they consist of root words, or *free morphemes* (such as *ball*, *girl*, *play*, and *fast*) and *bound morphemes* (such as the *ed* suffix denoting past tense, the *s* suffix denoting plural, and the *er* suffix denoting "one who does"; e.g., a singer is one who sings). Prefixes are also examples of bound morphemes (e.g., *anti*, as in antihistamine or antiseptic). Bound morphemes do not stand alone, but have meaning only when attached to a free morpheme. The morphology of our language is extremely complex, yet children learn this aspect of language at the same time they learn the other systems that make up language.

*Idioms* and *compound words* are also part of the system of semantics that native speakers learn. These are phrases whose meaning is not related to the meanings of the individual words in the phrase. For example, "to kick the bucket" has nothing to do with either kicking or a pail: it means "to die." The meanings of idioms have to be learned in the same way as individual vocabulary items — they are unique and have to be understood in the context of their use.

In the same way, native speakers learn compound words, two separate words that together create a new, single meaning. Native English speakers understand what a houseboat and a housefly are, and know the difference between them. They know that a houseboat is "a house that is also a boat," and that a housefly is not "a house that is also a fly," but a fly that lives in houses. They know they can say that a plate broke or a briefcase handle broke, but they would not say that a sweater or a newspaper broke. These are examples of the colloquial restrictions that native speakers learn. All of this is part of our semantic knowledge.

More than simply the words and phrases we learn and use, semantics includes the highly cultural nature of language — how our language performs the job the culture requires it to do. Every culture has its own world view, which is encompassed in its language. All members of a culture tacitly agree on the meanings of words and phrases. In English we have a verb tense system that marks when an event occurs. Some languages, however, do not mark verb tenses in the same way as English. They might say, for example, to indicate that something happened in the past, "before now." The way in which a culture chooses to classify the world is arbitrary. The English language has many words for colour, whereas some languages make only a binary distinction (roughly equivalent to light and dark), although the physical perception skills of all people are the same. Similarly, the Inuktitut language has many words for snow, depending on the type and location of the snow, how it can be traversed, and what it is used for. In English we have a range of words for snow only if we ski or live in the North and need to describe road and ice conditions. Furthermore, many of the English words used in these instances are adjectives describing the snow, not substitutes for the word itself. Another example of language differences is in the Russian language, which makes an explicit distinction between alienable and inalienable possessions (e.g., respectively, my pen and my arm). The English language does not make this distinction overtly.

When teachers teach lessons on suffixes or on compound words, they are teaching the semantic system of language. Synonyms, antonyms, and homonyms are also examples of the semantics of language taught in elementary classrooms. These aspects of language are most effectively taught in the contexts of speaking, listening, reading, and writing, where they are likely to occur naturally rather than as isolated exercises or drills.

## Syntax

The basic unit in syntax is the sentence. Syntax refers to the way words are strung together to create meaning. Every language has its own syntax. In English, syntax and word order are almost synonymous: a change in the word order of a sentence almost always has an effect on meaning — sometimes minimally, sometimes drastically. "The dog bit the man" is very different in meaning from "The man bit the dog." Often a similar meaning is conveyed by two sentences that have different structures, as in "The child collected the books" and "The books were collected by the child." Rarely, however, do changes in syntax have *no* effect on meaning. To illustrate the role of syntax, take the sentence "I saw the kitten in the garden" and insert the word "only" at various points throughout to see the major shifts in meaning. For example, "Only I saw the kitten in the garden" is quite different in meaning from "I saw only the kitten in the garden," "I saw the only kitten in the garden," and "I saw the kitten only in the garden." Thus, the rules for ordering words in English are extremely important, because changes in syntax affect meaning. (And sentences following no rules of syntax — for example, "The I saw kitten the only garden in" — are clearly meaningless.) In elementary school classrooms, syntax is usually taught under the heading of "grammar."

As children mature, they have a growing capacity to embed more and more meaning into each sentence they speak or write by using clauses and phrases, making the sentence more compact and yet richer in meaning (Hunt, 1965). A young child may say in conversation with a partner, "I have a cat. He's called Sam. I like him. He's grey. He's my friend." An older person might combine these basic (or kernel) sentences and say something like, "I have a grey cat called Sam, whom I like very much because he's so friendly." The result is a more fluent language style as well as a more economic way of expressing meaning — in short, a more mature form of syntax.

Sentence combining and sentence building activities are often helpful to students because they demonstrate how language can be manipulated, and they provide alternatives for children in constructing sentences. They are also frequently enjoyable and playful activities with no right or wrong answers — just many alternatives. There are, for example, many ways of combining these four kernel sentences:

The puppy is black.
The puppy barked at the rabbit.
The puppy belongs to Janet.
Janet lives on Third Street.

Aternatives include "The black puppy belonging to Janet, who lives on Third Street, barked at the rabbit," or "Janet, who lives on Third Street, has a black puppy that barked at a rabbit." Clearly, there are many other combinations that students can create as they manipulate word order and come to a fuller understand of the role of syntax in the construction of meaning.

Although the words "grammar" and "syntax" are frequently used interchangeably, they do have different definitions. Syntax is a term linguists use to describe how human beings organize their language structures. Grammar is a term teachers have traditionally used to define a prescriptive set of rules. Syntax and grammar are both derived from the spoken language, but when grammar is taught in school, it usually pertains to writing. Educators and researchers (see Braddock, Lloyd-Jones, and Schoer, 1963) have long believed that grammar should not be taught in elementary schools in a formal manner. However, it is certainly helpful for children to know the difference between what is acceptable or appropriate and what is considered poor grammar. Unacceptable grammar is reflected in such commonly used sentences as "I borrowed him my pencil" and "I should've went earlier." The labels describing parts of speech (such as nouns, adjectives, adverbs, and so on) are also helpful to students, because they enable teachers and students to talk about language and how we use it, especially in the context of a writing workshop. Grammar is rarely studied as a set of rules in isolation today. There is a far greater interest in children being able to use these rules in their speech and writing rather than in identifying them. The focus is more on appropriateness in various contexts than on correctness. This aspect of language teaching and learning is dealt with in later chapters, notably in Chapter Nine.

## Phonology

The phonology of a language is its sound system. Every language has a set of sounds that enables its users to communicate meaning. The smallest units of sound in a language are *phonemes*. The English language has between 45 and 52 different phonemes (depending on the classification system and dialect). Phonemes are not the same in all languages, and what constitutes a phoneme in one language may not constitute one in another. English has the phonemes *l* and *r*, but these are not meaningful sounds in Japanese, for example. As a result, Japanese people who learn to speak English tend to confuse these sounds because they were not distinguishable in their first language. In the same way, English speakers have difficulty pronouncing many Swahili words beginning with *ng*, as in *ngoma*, which means "drum" (Lindfors, 1987, p. 55). Even though this sound is a separate phoneme in English (note the difference between "rim" and "ring"), English speakers do not hear it at the beginning of a word and hence have difficulty pronouncing it when it appears there. The nearest we have to this sound in English occurs in the words *ring* and *think*.

When the phonology of a language is transcribed into symbols, it is referred to as the **graphophonic** system. In English, these sounds are represented by the 26 letters of the alphabet. Understanding the sound–symbol relationship is one of the key learnings children accomplish in their literacy development. The manipulation of the graphophonic system forms the basis for children's reading and writing development in the primary years. It is important to note that the phonological system (sound system) and the orthographic system (written system) are two distinct systems of language, each with its own conventions. This is just one of the reasons why learning to read and write in English is a complex undertaking, especially where spelling is concerned.

A further element of phonology is intonation, which consists of stress, pitch, and juncture. Stress is the emphasis placed on different words, pitch is the level of the voice, and juncture is the pause that adds or emphasizes meaning. We provide intonation clues in writing through the use of punctuation.

The phonology of a language varies from one **dialect** to another. Dialect refers to variations in language based on social class, ethnic group, and geographic location. To some Canadians, the words *metal* and *pedal* rhyme, and the *t* in "congratulations" sounds like the *d* in "graduation." The words *cot* and *caught* are homonyms in Canadian English, but for some American or British speakers, the words have very different vowel sounds. *Calf* and *half* sound like *laugh* to most Canadian speakers, but like *scarf* (without the emphasized *r*) to British speakers. These differences in speech patterns can sometimes create difficulties for people in communicating meaning, but on the whole, we manage to communicate orally in English whether we are from India, South Africa, Australia, Pakistan, Wales, or Canada.

## Pragmatics

Pragmatics refers to the way in which speakers use language in context. For example, when a person says "the phone is ringing," it is usually a request for someone else to answer it, not simply a statement of fact. It is the speaker's intent that is of concern. Children do not learn language in isolation. The sounds, meanings, and grammatical principles learned are embedded in the social-interactive framework of the child's world. The rules governing how language is used in this social context make up the pragmatic component of language. As they become effective communicators, children learn to take both the speaker's and the listener's roles and perspectives into account at the same time. They learn how to modify the usage of words such as *here* and *there*, *this* and *that*. They learn how to say, for example, "I will put my cookie *here*. You can put your cookie *there*," or "I will have *this* one, and you can have *that* one." They also learn how to initiate a conversation, contribute to the topic, request clarification, create smooth changes in topic, provide both verbal and nonverbal feedback to keep the conversation going, monitor timing and pauses in the dialogue, and conclude the interaction appropriately.

Language use varies according to the social norm, an aspect of language known as *register*. Children, for example, learn a range of registers and styles that help them to function appropriately in situations ranging from formal (making a speech at high school graduation) to informal or nonstandard (playing in the park with friends, reading a comic book). Students who come from socio-cultural settings where nonstandard English is used are usually able to read textbooks and listen to television newscasts that are in standard English. They seldom have problems with comprehension. Competent speakers learn to control a range of registers that allow them to function in diverse situations in society. As they make the transition from student to teacher, some preservice teachers have to work at mastering standard English and a more formal register of language use. This is a necessary step if they are to be appropriate role models in the classroom and perceived as functioning professionals.

People who have strong pragmatics abilities are usually considered to be socially competent and confident (Mueller, 1983). These skills, together with linguistic competence, form what is known as *communicative competence*.

## Perspectives on Language Acquisition

The next section of this chapter addresses the various hypotheses proposed by researchers to account for children's language learning. The early acquisition of language by young children remains something of a mystery to educators and researchers alike. There is a great deal still to be learned about language acquisition. Teachers continue to be intrigued by the phenomenon, because language abilities are so very important to a child's later learning both inside and outside school.

### Behaviourist View of Language Learning

Until the 1950s, researchers believed that children learn language through the feedback they receive to their utterances. Children were seen as passive in their language learning — not initiating, but reacting and responding to the language of others. This was a behaviourist view of learning, postulating that children learn language as they are reinforced for their responses to a variety of stimuli (Skinner, 1957; Staats, 1971). The reinforcement could be either positive or negative, depending on the appropriateness of a given response. For example, if a child says "Ma-ma-ma-ma," there will likely be a positive response from the caregiver, just as when a child first waves a hand in a gesture of farewell. Children receive cuddles, smiles, frowns, angry retorts or soft verbal responses from their caregivers as they explore their environment and experiment with language. However, as researchers continued to explore children's language development, it became apparent that the behaviourist view of language acquisition could not account for all the things a child learns to *do* with language, nor for the vast amount of language a child learns or the unique utterances a child makes.

The behaviourist view subsequently gave rise to a plethora of language learning research with chimpanzees, mules, and other animals. Much of the research was carried out by Terrace (1979) who, after working in this field for five years, finally recognized that what the animals were learning was not a language in the sense that humans use language. The animals were responding to their trainers through printed and verbal symbols, but it was not language. Certainly, some of what children learn in their early years is attributable to behaviouristic responses from caregivers, but the majority of language learning is far too complex to occur solely as a result of this effect.

### Innatist View of Language Learning

In the 1950s, Noam Chomsky, a linguist at Harvard University, developed a completely new view of language learning that became known as the innatist view. He argued strongly that children have a predisposition for learning language, that some built-in device enables them to learn it quickly and easily. This device, which Chomsky labelled a Language Acquisition Device (LAD), has only to be triggered by language input of some kind and children will learn language. It is as though children have a custom-built software package that allows them to access language and use it after minimal "messing around" and "testing" of the program.

Shortly after the publication of Chomsky's major work (1957), Eric Lenneberg (1964) postulated that language must be learned in stages, such as those stages in children's physical development. Lenneberg pointed out some parallels between physical development and language development. He also maintained that there is a critical period for language development — from birth until about the age of 13, when the brain has largely matured. Lenneberg's work supported the innatist claim that genetic inheritance does not simply give human beings a mental ability for learning in general, but that it also provides a specific language learning ability. Lenneberg believed that exposure to language in the environment was a necessary and sufficient condition for language learning to occur, whereas Chomsky believed this capacity to be some kind of unconscious knowledge of language universals, built into the brain and activated when young children encounter a stream of meaningful language around them.

In a completely different approach to exploring language development, some researchers (including Donaldson, 1978) suggested that all children possess a general capacity for inference, a capacity that allows them to develop language. A child actively tests hypotheses and makes inferences in order to learn language.

All these approaches to language learning focus on the nature of the child's innate ability to learn language. It was not until the early 1980s that an approach to language learning was formulated based on a totally different set of principles or assumptions — an interactionist approach. In many ways this approach has at its base the old "nature versus nurture" controversy, for it involves the role of both the individual and the culture in the development of language.

## Interactionist View of Language Learning

The interactionist view of language development maintains that there must be a fully functioning human being (i.e., biologically intact, capable of developing language) and a fully functioning social system (i.e., an intact social environment) in place before language development can occur (John-Steiner and Tatter, 1983). In other words, language is contextualized; it happens in real situations for real purposes. If there is no intact social system in place, or if a child is disabled in some way, then normal language learning may not take place. If there is no interaction between the child and the social system, this will create a lack in language learning. Rather than seeing culture, society, and the child's psychological makeup and cognitive abilities as separate entities, the interactionist views all of them as interdependent, much like a woven tapestry. The child is part of the culture as much as the culture is part of the child. Language learning involves both learning *about* the culture and learning about being an individual who is a *part of* the culture. These facets of human life cannot be separated and examined in isolation. They are each part of the other, interacting and contributing to the unique development of all individuals. One of the most startling illustrations of the interactionist concept of language learning is embodied in the story of "Genie," which is presented in Box 2.2.

Researchers working from a behaviourist perspective on language learning believed that children's language acquisition was entirely a result of the reinforcement they received for their utterances. In the 1950s, Chomsky theorized that children possess some kind of language acquisition device, something like the hard-drive of a computer that pre-wires children for language learning. The LAD allows them to learn language after the device has been triggered by a minimal amount of language input

**Box 2.2   Genie: A Case Study**

In 1970, a 13-year-old girl named Genie (a pseudonym) and her nearly blind mother arrived at a social services office in Los Angeles asking for help (Rymer, 1992). The girl was stooped, could not talk, drooled uncontrollably, and was not toilet trained. She appeared to be about 6 or 7 years old. The child had been kept in one bare room, strapped to a potty chair during the day or tied into a crib with sides at night, and fed only soft food such as oatmeal, boiled eggs, and crushed bananas. As a result, she could not walk properly or chew food. Her father had forbidden the child to have contact with any member of the family, so she was never spoken to. The father took food to her, and when he did so he barked like a dog. Genie was terrified of dogs and cats.

In the years that followed, a number of researchers worked with Genie, attempting to socialize her and teach her language. Over a period of a few years, Genie experienced some success with language, first learning the labels for certain objects and speaking single words, often echoing what the researcher had said. Genie went on to two-word utterances, telegraphic speech, and sentences that were simple, yet meaningful, although she omitted all the little structure words of the English language. In short, she learned a vocabulary and a phonological system, but she never learned syntax.

As a young adult, Genie entered a hospital for the mentally ill, where she still lives. No one agency or person had custody of Genie, and as she grew up and lost her cuteness and appeal, various researchers and social services appeared to let go of any responsibility for her. Apparently, no other home could be found for her, though evidence of mental illness was never established.

It is difficult to determine whether Genie was mentally handicapped from birth, or whether the abuse and lack of social contacts in her first 13 years prevented her from developing her cognitive abilities. Certainly, Genie never developed fluent language ability, though she was apparently making excellent progress before she was placed in the mental hospital. Her story suggests that there might indeed be a critical period in language development, but since Genie's language education ended while she was still learning, it's not clear. The case of Genie is, fortunately, one of the only demonstrations of what might be the necessary and sufficient conditions for language development. From the evidence, it appears that her lack of language development was a result of the lack of care and social interaction she suffered as a child. A 1993 CBC radio documentary about Genie reported that today she hardly ever talks. She engages in repetitive behaviours such as filling a jug of water and drinking from it.

Source: Based on R. Rymer (1992, April 13), "A Silent Childhood—I," *The New Yorker*, pp. 41–81; and R. Rymer (1992, April 20), "A Silent Childhood—II," *The New Yorker*, pp. 43–77.

from caregivers. The most recent view of language learning is much more complex than either of these. The interactionist view postulates that children learn language as a result of the interaction of the human being, the social situation, and the culture. Language is contextualized and is learned through its use. This view of language development has powerful implications for teaching language arts and for using language in learning across the curriculum.

## Language Development and the Social Context

The next section of this chapter addresses the continuing development of children's language abilities from preschool through elementary school. In particular, attention is paid to the social context of language development and to the factors that influence the development of children's language.

## Preschool Language Development

Most caregivers talk to their infants as though they are equal participants in conversation. When a mother changes a baby's diaper she usually talks to the child, smiles, tickles the infant, and converses as though the infant understands the language and will respond. We hear a mother saying:

> Do you want your diaper changed? Oh, you're all wet! No wonder you were making a fuss. Let's see what we can do. There, does that feel better? Let's go see what Jennifer's doing.

This type of interaction is vitally important to young children, and before long they, too, begin to make sounds, to babble and coo and explore the sounds they are capable of making. By the time children are 9 or 10 months old, they can make all the sounds that are used in all the languages in the world. At this stage, children with normal hearing suddenly begin to stop making some sounds, continuing only with those they hear around them. They also adopt the intonation pattern and rhythm of the language they hear. By the time children are about 1 year to 18 months old, the sounds they make are more and more like words. Children who have hearing problems, however, will stop all the sounds they have been making and either not develop speech or be delayed in speech development, depending on the severity of their hearing problem.

The first stage of language development is that of the holophrase, or one-word utterance. Here a child uses one word to communicate a myriad of meanings. *Puppy* can mean anything from "Look at the puppy" to "I want to hold the puppy" to "That is a puppy." Children know what they mean, however, and if they don't get an appropriate response, they will let their conversational partners know. Halliday (1969) first identified his seven functions of language when he was exploring this very early stage of language development. Children learn to create words and string words together because they have things they want to *do*. They have needs, ideas, and relationships that are important and can best be expressed through language. It is the use of language that is the driving force behind its development.

Children speak their first words generally anywhere between the age of 10 months and 2 years. Their age when this happens does not seem to influence their language development in any significant way. The first words spoken are usually labels for items in the child's environment that he or she acts on, such as *cookie, milk, kitty, ball, sock,* and *daddy*. Words unlikely in that list are *crib* (unless the child has learned to let down its side!), *diaper, powder*, and any others used to label something in the child's world that he or she has no control over and that is not relevant to his or her intentions.

The second phase of development is the two-word utterance, where children string two words together to create more specific and detailed meanings. "Daddy gone," "More milk," "Cup fall" are examples of speech at this stage of development. The stage marks a breakthrough in language, because children move from simple labelling and the use of one word to a more sophisticated use of language. This stage is followed by telegraphic speech, where children string three or more words together to create meaning. Because they don't use structure words, their language sounds like a telegram. For example, a child might say, "Mummy go store" or "Nana come now." From here, children move on to creating complete sentences, and by the age of 4, their language is likely to sound very much like that of adults. Brown (1973) at Harvard University was one of the key researchers who described in detail the sequential development of children's speech. Brown studied the development of questioning and sentence combining, while researchers such as Clark and Clark (1977) studied children's early interactions with their caregivers. Research shows that although there are general patterns and trends in language development, every child passes through these stages and phases at different rates. However, the most important influence on the child's language development is the language and playful interactions that take place between him or her and the primary caregiver.

## Language Development in Elementary School

When children enter school at the age of 5 or 6, they have mastered the complexities of the language system. They understand syntax and phonology, and they can create a multitude of meanings from what they say and hear around them. They are aware of the printed symbols they see in their environment and can recognize print symbols, such as those on cereal boxes and in grocery stores and fast food restaurants. Most children know how to handle books by this age and take delight in being read to by a caregiver. They take pleasure in playing with language, and are beginning to understand the subtleties of language that underlie the creation of humour.

Early in the 1950s, Walter Loban (1963) undertook a longitudinal study of children's language development. He tracked one group of children in the Oakland area of California throughout their years of schooling from kindergarten to Grade 12. The study proved to be a landmark in our understanding of children's language development during the elementary years. Loban showed that children who enter school with low language ability are likely to remain lower than other children in their language ability throughout their schooling. Likewise, children who enter school with high language ability retain that advantage throughout their schooling. Not only that, but those children with high language proficiency make the greatest progress and improve their language ability the most, while children who have low language ability fall further and further behind their peers. This finding was one of the motivating forces that led to the development of Head Start programs in the United States in the 1960s (an initiative in which early intervention and support services are provided for poor preschool children and their families to try to break the poverty cycle). Loban also demonstrated that the direct teaching of grammar has little or no impact on the language development of elementary school children. Since this research was published in 1963, curriculum developers have struggled to create programs of study that balance instruction in the forms of language with the purposeful use of appropriate language in classrooms. A third major finding of Loban's study was that reading and writing abilities are related, and a fourth was that boys more than girls are more likely to have problems with language or, conversely, to appear in the group with the highest language ability. Overall, Loban showed that children learn language by using it, and that children's progress on this lifelong journey is strongly affected by what happens to them before they enter school.

Throughout the school years, children continue to develop and refine their language abilities in all areas, especially language structure, language use, and **metalinguistic awareness** (the growing ability to use language to talk about language as a formal code) (Lindfors, 1987). Metalinguistic awareness is part of children's thinking in general. Donaldson (1978) posited that young children's thinking is embedded; they make sense of language in the context of their everyday lives and experiences. In other words, children relate what they learn to what they know, and make sense of new experiences only in the context of what is familiar. A 6-year-old child, hearing that the family was going to Seattle, said that he didn't want to go to Seattle because "I don't even know who Attle is anyway." Donaldson showed that children also make sense of tasks they are asked to do in school in similar ways. If children are introduced to new concepts by working with concrete objects in the context of a familiar situation (for example, learning about fractions through cutting pizza or apples), they are more likely to understand the concept than if they are taught without concrete objects and in an unfamiliar context (learning about fractions through manipulating numbers on a whiteboard). As children get older they are able to understand language and thinking without embedding it in their everyday experiences. Donaldson maintains that by the age of 11 children are usually able to consider language outside the context of their own experiences. They can reflect on language as an entity separate from themselves, and hence manipulate it and learn about it with a new awareness.

## Language at Home and at School

From birth onwards, children creatively develop language in social situations. They actively figure out how language creates meaning by observing what it does. Children use forms of language they have never encountered before, which refutes a totally behaviouristic theory of language learning. From birth to age 6, children learn an astounding average of 21 new words a day (Miller, 1977). They attend to language selectively, however, using whatever is relevant to them. They speak and take note of how others respond, they notice how other people express meanings, they ask questions and imitate what other people say (and how they say it), and they use some general principles for figuring out how language works.

The primary social context for children's language learning is, of course, the home. Here, children first learn language in interaction with their caregivers. Slowly, the child's world gets larger. Children visit other homes, the daycare centre, stores, the playground, the doctor's office, and so on. When they enter school, they encounter a whole new social context, where adults' use of language is often different from what children have encountered in their homes. Generally, there is far less personal interaction in school than there is at home.

Some remarkable studies have explored the language environments of both home and school. Tizard and Hughes (1984) examined the language at home and at school of 4-year-old children in nursery schools in the United Kingdom. Their finding was that children do not encounter a richer language at school than at home (contrary to popular belief) primarily because of the nature of the interactions. Teachers have less time to devote to individual children, and are busy with the organizational aspects of teaching. They are not usually involved in doing things *with* children, which is when most language interactions occur with children at home (whether we are making dinner together or watching television together). Teachers speak *to* children but generally not *with* them.

Heath (1983) conducted a ten-year study (referred to in Chapter One) of language interactions in three communities in the United States that shared the same school. She found that language was used very differently in the three communities. When black working-class children went to school with mostly white middle-class teachers, the children from the black community had difficulties understanding and being understood. It was not only how they spoke that was the problem, but how language was used. The teachers had difficulty understanding "how and why the children used their language as they did" (Heath, 1983, p. 278).

An example of this was in naming practices. The black children often did not respond when the teachers called them by the name listed on the attendance register. When the teachers asked the children for their nicknames, they received no response.

When they learned the nicknames used in the community from parents and others, they felt they were unacceptable for use in school (e.g., "Frog" and "Red Girl"). But when they tried to develop new nicknames for the children, they received a negative response. The reason for all this was simple: In the black community the children were used to being addressed by their nicknames, and most of them were not even familiar with their legal first names. In addition, they had been taught not to respond to strangers or to white people asking questions about them or their families. Anything personal belonged only within the family. Naturally, the black children did not respond to the names the teachers gave them, since these names had no authenticity for them. The white children, on the other hand, had been taught to respond when called upon and to answer to their given names.

Similarly, how to define and show politeness differed between the two social groups. Black children would chatter freely with their neighbours and not pay attention when the teacher attempted to have circle time or story time on the rug. Their socialization had taught them to pay attention to their friends and neighbours rather than to an authority figure from outside the community. Once the teachers became aware of, and understood, the implications of the social differences in the use of language, they were able to accept the black children more readily and not simply label them as poor language users and slow learners.

Probably the most extensive study of language development completed in the social contexts in which children live is the Bristol Study conducted in England by Gordon Wells (1986). Wells followed 32 children from the ages of 2 to 9 years, tape-recording a number of fifteen-minute segments of their oral language interactions every day. The children were fitted with radio microphones, so the data were collected at various times and in a variety of contexts. The talk was analyzed for grammatical complexity and for the functions of language used. Wells challenged previous research findings (Tough, 1976) by showing that children from homes of low socio-economic status did *not* exhibit impoverished language use. At home, those children used language much the same as the children of high socio-economic status. However, what Wells also found was that the language of all 32 children was suppressed at school. He states, "For no child was the language experience of the classroom richer than that of the home — not even for those believed to be 'linguistically deprived'" (1986, p. 87). Wells discovered that teachers dominated conversation and that much of the talk children engaged in at school was inauthentic, lacking the purpose and spontaneity of real talk. These findings coincide with Tizard and Hughes's findings regarding the language of 4-year-olds. Clearly, there is a problem with oral language interactions in classrooms. These studies indicate that educators need to explore possibilities for expanding children's oracy in school, and determine the causes of the current failure to address this important area of language arts.

In the constructivist world of home, playground, street, shopping mall, club, and so on, children continue to expand their language strategies. As they interact with more people, and with people in different social contexts, they continue their efforts to make sense of language and to expand their phonological, morphological, syntactic, semantic, and pragmatic knowledge. In this capacity, the classroom is particularly important, as children learn language most effectively with teachers who support and stretch their efforts in language development. In constructivist classrooms, teachers and children learn and interact in language contexts that enable them to communicate and express their own thoughts and feelings. In other words, children develop language abilities most effectively when they use language in school for the same purposes for which they use language out of school. They write real letters to real people for real purposes, share their stories with people who are interested in hearing and responding to them, read books and magazines for pleasure and information, and generally engage in real-world language events, including listening and speaking.

Learning in a school context provides numerous opportunities for children to use language to solve problems and interact with the world, calling into play all of their linguistic knowledge and skills. Harste, Woodward, and Burke (1984, p. 9) suggest that "control of form is not a prerequisite to the language process." Unfortunately, much of school learning has, in the past, divorced meaning from form (Ferreiro and Teberosky, 1982). James Britton (1970) used the phrase "dummy runs" to describe many of the language experiences children are required to engage in at school. He maintained that

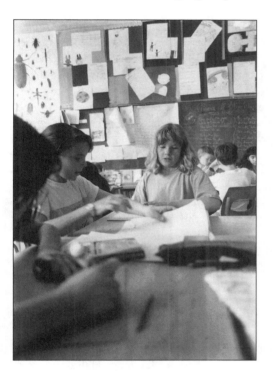

Children learning in a school context.

children must *practise* language in the sense that a doctor practises medicine and a lawyer practises law, and *not* in the sense that a juggler practises a new trick before performing it. When doctors practise medicine, they are totally engaged in problem solving with their patients in a professional capacity that calls upon all their knowledge and skills. When jugglers practise tricks, they repeat the same moves over and over as a rehearsal for the time when they will finally perform in front of an audience. Children do not need to rehearse language in school for a time when they will have to use it in the "real world." In a constructivist classroom, the activities children engage in across the curriculum are also activities that teach language. Children, as they use language in their learning, are encouraged to solve problems, make inferences, and express their own opinions and ideas. In such a context, children do not need rehearsals.

## Communicative Competence

"Communicative competence" is the ability to combine and use all aspects of language, including nonverbal communication, and to use them as a native speaker does. It is not simply linguistic competence, where a speaker knows the language and the rules of that language; it is the ability to make sense of the world through language, and to use language in diverse ways and situations to accomplish specific purposes.

Communicative competence, then, refers to language in use. A large part of communicative competence includes the pragmatics of understanding the appropriateness of interactions. Most interactions we encounter are comfortable and acceptable. When an interaction is neither of these, we are sensitive to it. Sometimes, we are face-to-face with our interlocutor and we can take note of the nonverbal aspects of the communication — for example, the expression on a person's face or the distance between ourself and our partner. But even if we are not in face-to-face communication, we might have the feeling that something is not appropriate. We might begin to question the interaction and ask, "What is really going on here?"

The following excerpt from a telephone conversation demonstrates a lack of communicative competence in Anne, one of the speakers:

| Anne: | You know what? |
|---|---|
| George: | No, I don't know, Anne. Tell me. |
| Anne: | You know what? |
| George: | No, Anne, tell me what you've been doing today. |
| Anne: | Are you there? |
| George: | Yes, I'm here, Anne. What have you been doing today? |
| Anne: | You know what? |

This exchange took place during a call between a resident of a group home and one of her caregivers. Anne, who initiated the call, appeared to lack social competence because she seemed to have difficulty in establishing the conversation with George. She violated basic rules of conversation (pragmatics), and it might have been difficult for George to know the purpose of her call. In fact, Anne did not have the communicative competence necessary to state her purpose and relay her message to George. The conversation continued only because George understood Anne's difficulty and was able to help Anne move into a conversation where she could narrate the day's events to him and share her excitement. The one essential element of communication is that it be purposeful. When the purpose of a conversation is not apparent, the whole event can become confusing and difficult.

Communicative competence includes the pragmatics of knowing how to open a conversation, establish rapport, take turns, get to the point, ask questions, clarify, check for understanding, be relevant, not talk for too long, supply all necessary information, and be truthful, clear, and comprehensible. If any of these elements is missing, a distortion in communication can occur. Usually, the conversational partner will correct the situation by asking relevant questions, focussing the speaker, paraphrasing, or stating directly that a problem exists (e.g., "I'm not sure what you mean by that. Are you saying that...?"). Naturally, we try to be as tactful as possible in a conversation to keep it focussed and flowing.

Children develop communicative competence when they are using language to achieve their own specific purposes. The seven functions of language Halliday (1969) noted in young children drive children to learn and to participate in language events as equal and demanding partners. The more they spend time with others, with an agenda of their own and freedom to explore their world, the more children will become competent communicators. (Note this lack of opportunity and experience in the story of Genie, narrated in Box 2.2.) The classroom, where there is a great diversity of background experiences, family lifestyles, and cultural mixes, provides a rich opportunity for developing communicative competence. Children learn to narrate, which is a fundamental way of making sense of the world (Rosen, 1984), to explain and inform, and to express their personal ideas and opinions. They also learn to adapt their communication to the situation, to the age and status of the conversational partner, to whether this is a family member or not, to their familiarity with their partner, and to the physical location of the communication. In short, a child speaks differently on the playground than in the classroom, in the doctor's office, or at church or temple. The development of these competencies at school is the focus of the remainder of this book.

## Language in Learning

> To this point, this chapter has focussed on how children learn language. The next part of the chapter focusses on how language helps children to learn, or how language influences cognition. Everyone has a theory of how the world works, and we develop that theory through our experiences of the world. Language plays a very large role in this process as we replay events to ourselves and others and, in doing so, make greater sense of them. We listen to or read others' opinions and ideas and clarify our own ideas, thus adding to our learning. We relate new experiences to old ones and continue to make sense of them all. The language we have at our disposal enables us, to a large extent, to perform this learning. Language allows us to shape our thoughts, to ask questions, to explore, to clarify, and to create meaning. Words allow us to put meanings together, and to create new understandings. In both children and adults, we can see the same processes taking place.

When Ms. Moorhouse was an undergraduate student in education, she read many chapters from textbooks and was later tested on the content. She learned the material well and answered the questions on the test to the satisfaction of the examiner. But how much had really made sense to her? How much of her learning was she going to be able to apply in her field experiences? In fact, Ms. Moorhouse didn't know what she knew until she engaged in conversations with her instructors and fellow students and was challenged by the learning needs of the children in her student teaching classroom. Only then were her understandings truly tested. What had those book chapters really been referring to? What had a specific phrase meant? How would this knowledge affect Ms. Moorhouse's planning for instruction? And how would her own learning relate to the learning accomplished by the students in her classroom? It was as these questions were raised and discussed that new understandings began to emerge for Ms. Moorhouse, and new ways of approaching learning and teaching became apparent.

## Language and Thinking

Information is not simply processed in isolation, but is shared, built on with peers, and discussed as it relates to real people and real contexts. This aspect of learning is one of the strongest reasons for having students engage in group projects, where they can study and work together, pooling information and helping one another to clarify and test out specific learnings. Through group interaction and exploratory talk, students question, make meanings more precise, and reinterpret past experience (which is why a personal story is often told to make a point). Interaction becomes crucially important as learners stretch their limits and move into areas that are uncertain, going beyond personal experience and specific situations. It is this concept of the role of language in the learning process that has caused educators to focus on processes such as collaboration, co-operation, group work, and the value of oral language in the classroom.

Sometimes we talk ourselves into understanding, and sometimes we write our way into understanding. Writing can create new worlds for the writer (and reader), but it may be that writing, even more than speech, "not only reflects our knowing ... but ... also causes our knowing" (Dillon, 1985, p. 9). We write letters, lists, papers, reports, and notes, and we also write for ourselves (poetry, stories, notes, diaries, logs). Journal writing is one of the ways in which we write for ourselves, as we attempt to recall and understand. Writing and then rereading our thoughts, pondering them, and revisiting them kindles personal and cognitive growth that we often cannot complete with other people. It is a task we have to accomplish alone. Writing encourages us to make our ideas separate from ourselves — putting our thoughts out there so we can examine them and hold on to them for future reference and ongoing reflection. This process is part of the decontextualization of thought (what Donaldson, 1978, calls "disembedded thought"). We can move into a more detached realm and see our thoughts as things to be played with and built on. Our thoughts, we find, are not only part of our self, but part of a larger world with more abstract and less personal meaning. We move from the contextualized (embedded) to the decontextualized (disembedded), and we move from the known to the unknown. We begin with our own experiences and our own ideas, but then we pass beyond them to a wider world, accommodating and assimilating the new.

## Language across the Curriculum

The work of Michael Halliday, James Britton, James Moffett, and Douglas Barnes has provided educators with valuable structures for analyzing, understanding, and creating language learning opportunities in diverse areas of the school curriculum. Now armed with a basis for developing language learning tasks that are meaningful, purposeful, and cohesive, many teachers have been helped to answer the critical question, "How can I help my students to learn?" The guiding principles outlined in this chapter can be applied to learning activities not only in language arts, but also in subject areas such as social studies, science, music, and health.

Halliday's functions of language have proved to be especially helpful to teachers because they focus the learning activity on a combination of knowledge about the topic *and* knowledge of how the form, purpose, sender, and receiver of a communication event interact. Box 2.3 contains examples of learning activities that one music teacher developed for her students in Grade 6. The theme was a study of two Romantic composers, Johannes Brahms and Robert Schumann. Box 2.4 presents a series of learning activities for a Grade 6 social studies unit on Ancient Greece. The activities illustrate the range of learning opportunities that can be generated in social studies.

## Oral Language in the Classroom

During the elementary school years, children continue to refine and extend all the language competencies that allow them to be full conversational partners in all walks of life, with many people, in many contexts. The research cited earlier in this chapter suggests that children learn these competencies most effectively when teachers talk *with* children on topics that are of interest to children, and in a manner that enables children to participate as *legitimate conversational partners.*

The term *oracy* was coined to refer to auditory and spoken language, just as "literacy" refers to written language. The study of oracy in classrooms is a relatively new development. Oral language skills form the foundation for literacy development. Children come to Canadian classrooms from a vast range of ethnic, racial, political, and social backgrounds. They bring with them a similar range of oral language abilities. Many children arrive with well-developed oral language. They ask questions, tell

## Box 2.3  Activities for a Grade 6 Music Class

### Heuristic and Interactional

It is the mid-1800s in Vienna, Austria. You and your friend have just attended an evening concert conducted by Brahms, who insisted on playing that very out-of-date music by Bach and Handel. You were bored to tears. It seems from the gossip that many others felt the same way. The evening, however, wasn't a complete loss, as you did enjoy the compositions that Brahms himself wrote. Take yourself to a mini-concert by listening to Bach's *Brandenburg Concerto #2 in F*, the second movement, and Brahms' *Piano Concerto #2 in B Flat Major, Opus 83*, the first movement. The music is on tape for you. After you have listened to the concert, role-play your conversation with your friend as you walk home from the concert. Share with each other what the differences in the music are, and why Bach's music sounds so old-fashioned to you.

### Representational and Regulatory

You are the editor of the magazine *Neue Zeitschrift fur Musik* (New Paths for Music). Brahms has asked you to draft an eye-catching advertisement to assist him in selling his sheet music. His bestsellers are his violin sonatas, trios, and string quartets.

### Interactional, Heuristic, and Representational

Robert Schumann has tried to commit suicide by jumping off a bridge. Fishers have pulled him out of the river. You are a reporter running along as Schumann is being carried home. By interviewing one of the fishers and some of the people in the street, you are trying to determine the circumstances leading up to the near-tragedy. You might even be able to arrange an interview with 13-year-old Marie Schumann, Robert Schumann's eldest daughter. Use a tape recorder for your interviews and the books provided in the classroom for your own research.

## Box 2.4  Activities for a Grade 6 Social Studies Unit on Ancient Greece

### Instrumental

*Oral:* The Delian League was a group of Greek city-states that banded together to protect each other from aggressive forces. Your class constitutes the members of the city-state of Athens, the largest and strongest member. Chios, also a member of the Delian League, has requested your help in battle against Persian aggressors. In a group debate, decide whether or not you should get involved in the war and help Chios.

*Written:* You are an accomplished athlete, but you have not been chosen to engage in the special training necessary to compete in the Olympic Games. You are unhappy and wish to participate in the games. Write a letter to the selection committee asking them to intercede on your behalf so that you can participate in the training.

### Regulatory

*Oral:* You, as citizens of Athens, are concerned about the civil rights of slaves in Athenian society. In small groups, discuss the present slave regulations and devise a new set of civil rights that will allow slaves the same rights as Athenian citizens. You will present these civil rights to the assembly.

*Written:* You are a rich Athenian citizen and, like all rich citizens of Athens, you buy and sell slaves regularly. You have just purchased a slave to help in the running of your household. Make a list of daily household chores for the slave to fulfil while she or he is living with your family.

### Interactional

*Oral:* You are citizens of Troy and are awaiting a message from the town crier (played by the teacher) after being summoned for an important meeting. The town crier arrives and says, "There is a giant wooden horse outside the city gate, left as a peace offering from Greece. We must decide among ourselves whether or not to accept this horse. We must also decide what to do with it, if we choose to accept it." As a class, discuss how you will make this decision. What will you as a group say?

*Written:* Women in Athenian society were confined to the home and denied the privileges of men. You are all Athenian women who feel you deserve the same rights as men. Discuss these issues among yourselves and write, for publication in the *Grecian Gazette*, individual editorials arguing the rights you desire.

*(continued)*

| Box 2.4 | Continued |

**Personal**

*Oral:* You are Athenian slaves waiting to be sold. A reporter (played by the teacher in role — see the chapter on Drama) interviews you to determine your emotional reactions to being sold.

*Written:* In Athens, many landowners frequently found themselves heavily in debt and often had to resort to selling their own children into slavery. You are a child who has to be sold into slavery. Write a diary entry that describes how you are feeling the night before you are to be sold.

**Heuristic**

*Oral:* Citizens of Ancient Greece believed in a direct democracy where all free adult males were equal and contributing members of the government. Some of you are members of the Athenian Assembly, while the rest are reporters who interview the assembly about why they have chosen a direct democracy rather than electing one leader.

*Written:* Imagine that the Olympic Games are coming to your country this year. You are chosen to make the public aware of how the first Olympic Games in Greece were conducted. Write a report that describes these games. Provide information on such topics as athletic events, opening and closing ceremonies, and prizes awarded. Your report will be published in the local newspaper.

**Imaginative**

*Oral:* You are in charge of entertainment at an Athenian banquet. To entertain your guests, you have decided to compose poetic "Who am I?" riddles based on mythical Greek gods. In groups of three, compose and audiotape these riddles.

*Written:* One of the mythical Greek gods of Mount Olympus has been killed in a fierce battle. You have been summoned by Zeus, ruler of the Olympic gods, to create a replacement. Write a story about a new god, and describe where and how your god originated, what he or she is the god of, and what powers he or she possesses. You may also want to give a physical description of your god. You will send your story to Zeus.

**Representational**

(The following task involves modern technology in the context of Ancient Greece.)

*Oral:* You are a member of the Athenian Tourist Bureau. Your job is to make a television commercial to entice people to visit Ancient Greece. In small groups, compose and dramatize a television commercial.

*Written:* You are the editor for *Ancient Greece Abroad*, a magazine for travellers. Design a brochure for these travellers that illustrates the culture of Ancient Greece. You may want to include aspects such as food, entertainment, and art.

*It is important to note that many of the above activities fulfil more than one language function. In (5), for example, the written task meets the representational function as much as it does the heuristic one. To complete a representational task, a certain amount of heuristic language must first be used. In (7), the activity draws on the heuristic, representational, and regulatory functions. All of the activities described here are examples of language arts tasks that also meet many of the objectives of the specific provincial programs in social studies. Such objectives include understanding that all people have similar physical, social, and psychological needs, and that Greek values, beliefs, and ideas have strongly affected Western civilization. In particular, these activities help to provide a fuller context for the communication skill objectives of writing a summary of the main points, collecting and organizing information into a short report, and sharing ideas through drama and role play.*

about themselves, engage in play, listen to and read stories, and know how to interact with teachers and other children in diverse situations. Other children may be shy or withdrawn, unwilling to participate, and unable to read. It may be that at home they have not been encouraged to ask questions, have not been exposed to books, or have different values about what is appropriate and acceptable from those of most children in white, middle-class classrooms. The studies by Loban, Wells, Heath, and Tizard and Hughes remind educators to examine their classroom practices, and to pay attention to listening and speaking and the ways in which these facets of language are facilitated by instructional programs.

# Listening

Of all the modes of language used in the elementary school classroom, listening is undoubtedly the most prevalent. The success of telling stories, providing instructions, organizing students and activities, and teaching concepts all depend on the abilities of the students to listen and to understand. Much of what students listen to in classrooms is not information as such, but directions about how to do something and what to do next. Children in the primary grades can easily be confused if they do not hear directions or do not understand the teacher's instructions. Being able to listen attentively and respond appropriately accounts for a large part of a child's success in a primary classroom. Even in the upper elementary grades, listening remains important in coping successfully with schooling.

Listening is probably the most used of the language modes from birth onwards. Infants listen in order to learn language, to communicate with others, and to construct meaning in their world. The need to listen continues in school and through adulthood. Many teachers today comment on what seems to be the short attention span of some children in their classrooms. These children, the teachers say, have difficulty in listening and paying attention to what is happening in class. At the same time, however, some research has demonstrated that in fact many teachers have poor communication skills: they talk too much, explain too much, and do not actively listen to their students (Cazden, 1988; Flanders, 1970; Berry, 1985). Thus, by modelling appropriate listening behaviours (among other strategies), it would seem that teachers can actually help children to listen effectively throughout the entire curriculum.

Listening is not the same as hearing. According to Freshour and Bartholomew (1989), listening consists of six components:

1. receiving — hearing the sounds in the environment,
2. attending — paying attention selectively to those sounds that are important,
3. understanding — creating pictures and mental images or making connections to concepts already understood,
4. analyzing — raising questions and interrogating the validity of what is heard,
5. evaluating — accepting or rejecting what is heard, and
6. reacting — responding to what has been heard, either emotionally, physically, or cognitively.

Listeners understand speech at about double the rate a speaker can produce it, and so the mind tends to wander away from the topic of conversation and onto something else. Research tells us the average length of time a listener can attend to one specific thing is only twenty seconds (Moray, 1969). To lengthen that attention span, most people learn how to listen actively by nodding, agreeing with the speaker, making notes on a paper, focussing on key words, formulating questions, and generally engaging in the stages noted above. When helping children to become active listeners, teachers can emphasize one stage at a time. Most importantly, teachers can help children to establish specific purposes for listening.

Wolvin and Croakley (1985) have distinguished five purposes for listening:

1. discriminative — to distinguish sounds, especially nonverbal communication,
2. comprehensive (or efferent) — to understand a message,
3. therapeutic — to allow a speaker to work through a problem,
4. critical — to comprehend and evaluate a message, and
5. appreciative (or aesthetic) — to enjoy a reader or speaker.

The purpose of listening to a message, as with any other language act, drives the way in which the listening takes place. If children understand why they are to listen to a message, a story, a poem, or a list of instructions, they are more likely to listen effectively and focus on the appropriate element of the communication. From the above list of purposes for listening, only three generally apply to the classroom: comprehensive (efferent), critical, and appreciative (aesthetic). When educators state reasons or purposes for listening and focus children's thinking on ways they can accomplish the task, children's listening skills are enhanced.

## Talking

In an increasingly oral society, success in interpersonal relationships, in learning, in the community, and in the workplace is closely related to oral communication skills. Research suggests that these skills are developed through modelling and through practice — that students learn about language and how to use it effectively through opportunities to interact with different people in different contexts to accomplish different purposes. (British Columbia Ministry of Education, 1988, p. 1.1)

For most people, talking is the primary means of communication. Through oral language and nonverbal gestures, we communicate most of our needs, fears, and dreams to the people we encounter in our day-to-day lives. Through oral language we frequently work out our ideas, "bounce" ideas off colleagues and friends, and communicate the most prosaic, yet necessary, messages to those closest to us. It is therefore of utmost importance that children's oral language abilities be fostered throughout elementary school. Oral language cannot be taken for granted or ignored.

Talk is a major part of classroom life every day, every year, in every grade. Oral language is used by students and teachers for all the purposes Halliday outlined—to have their needs met, to regulate the actions of others, to express who they are, to interact with peers and colleagues, to ask questions and wonder, to represent what is known, and to enter the world of the imagination. Students often need to talk their way into understanding before they begin a writing task. Sometimes, they also need to talk *while* they are writing, and they need to check out meanings and understandings with their peers. Speech facilitates thought, especially in the higher-level thinking required of problem solving (Vygotsky, 1962; Fillion, 1983; Wilkinson, 1984). The teacher's role in facilitating oral language development in the classroom is a crucial one. Research, as already noted, has demonstrated that teachers usually talk too much and do not listen to their students enough (Flanders, 1970; Berry, 1985). Teachers in constructivist classrooms ensure that students engage in small group work that will enhance oral language and thinking, and they facilitate oral language development whenever possible.

Much of the business of the classroom is conducted orally. Teachers give directions and instructions orally, present information orally, and organize classroom life orally. Students ask questions orally, and establish and maintain their social relationships orally. In the classroom, learning outcomes for oral language development include:

- varying speech to meet the needs of the situation (small group, whole class, one on one),
- speaking clearly (with good pronunciation) so that communication is enhanced, and
- speaking expressively and avoiding a monotone.

## Assessing Oracy (Listening and Talking)

Listening and talking usually occur together in any social or school situation. It is difficult to assess either one in isolation from the other. When teachers observe their students' listening strategies and abilities, it is likely to be in the context of group work the students are engaged in: a reader response group, a drama activity, a writing conference, a conversation with another student, a science activity, a parent–student conference, interactions on the playground, and physical education or art classes. Those are the same contexts in which they will also collect information about students' speaking abilities. Much of the information teachers collect about their students' oral language proficiencies is anecdotal — it occurs in everyday contexts and is noted as it occurs. Teachers in constructivist classrooms keep notebooks about their students' progress in all areas of the curriculum. These notes complement the students' portfolios of writing, artwork, and so on. The notes can help teachers make instructional decisions that affect their students' learning. If a child is experiencing difficulty in participating in a literature circle, for example, the teacher will want to observe the interactions more closely and decide how the student can be helped to participate more fully.

Teachers are becoming increasingly aware of their students' cultural backgrounds, and they understand that certain oral language behaviours considered appropriate and desirable in a European/Canadian context are not considered so in many other cultures. Some of these behaviours include:

- contributing without invitation to conversation or group discussions,
- sharing ideas and feelings,
- looking at the person being addressed,
- asking questions for clarification,
- inviting other people to contribute to the conversation,
- taking turns,
- assuming a leadership role,
- volunteering to begin the discussion,
- dealing with any conflict of opinion, and
- remaining courteous throughout.

Although teachers encourage these behaviours in their students in Canadian classrooms, they are also sensitive to the diversity of oral language values their students bring to the classroom.

The British Columbia Ministry of Education developed a resource package, *Enhancing and Evaluating Oral Communication in the Primary Grades* (1988), to assist teachers in developing and assessing children's oral communication skills. It is a comprehensive document that serves as a central source of information for this section of the chapter. Listed in the document are seven areas of communicative competence (detailed in Box 2.5):

1. affective behaviours
2. language awareness
3. listening comprehension
4. speech communication
5. critical/evaluative behaviour
6. interpersonal strategies
7. oral language codes

The authors suggest that these areas be assessed in three ways: through observing students as they communicate; through listening to what students say in conversations, group conferences, and other classroom activities; and through reading what students write.

A further resource for assessing language abilities is the *English Profiles Handbook*, which provides a series of assessment strategies for oral language.

---

**Box 2.5    Seven Areas of Communicative Competence**

*Affective behaviours* are those aspects of communication that reveal attitudes and values. They usually have to be inferred, but they can be uncovered by asking appropriate questions, such as: Did the students participate in a certain activity? Did they participate willingly and enthusiastically? Given a choice of activities, what do the students choose? Do they choose listening, speaking, or collaborative activities? What activities do the students remember? Do the students display emotional responses to specific experiences? Can they articulate these responses in a diverse range of media (writing, drawing, mime, puppetry, artwork, dance)?

*Language awareness* entails the actual knowledge students possess about their own language use and learning. This can best be uncovered by asking students direct questions about their learning, such as: How did they do something? Did they feel it was easy for them? How did they decide on certain strategies? What did they learn? What was the most important thing they learned?

*Listening comprehension* involves the students' abilities to construct meaning from what they hear. Teachers can assess students' abilities to construct meaning by listening carefully to their comments, by asking direct questions, and through observation. Children may sometimes give an inappropriate response if they do not understand the reason for doing something, and so it is essential that students know why they are listening and what they are listening for. Listening comprehension can be assessed according to whether or not the students meet the requirements of the task. Did they follow directions appropriately? Did they accomplish the task set out for them? How much support did the students need from the teacher or from peers? Can the students recall what they have heard? Can they recall the important features of what they have heard? Can they predict the unfinished parts of a message? How do they respond to literary material they hear? Do they ask questions about what they have heard? Are these questions relevant?

*Speech communication* is simply the assessment of how successful the students are in accomplishing the objectives of their speech. How much support do they need in order to accomplish their speech goals? How much control do the students have over their speaking strategies? Do they attempt to expand their repertoire of speaking strategies by experimenting with new forms?

*Critical/evaluative behaviour* involves the students' abilities to monitor their own speech and the messages they receive from others. Are they aware of whether their message has been understood? Are they able to question and clarify messages received from others? Are they able to self-question (e.g., "What was the best thing about my report to the class and did the students listen to me with interest?")?

*Interpersonal strategies* are those behaviours that allow students to create relationships with others. Children learn how to do this through their play and work in school. Interpersonal strategies include conversing, solving problems, sharing stories, and participating in drama activities — all of which reflect the interactional function of language identified by Halliday (1969).

*Oral language codes* are those aspects of language that allow us to communicate effectively to different people in different situations. Children learn a wide repertoire of language codes as they participate in relationships with a diverse group of people — grandparents, parents, friends, teachers, salespeople, and so on. Children have to learn to be aware of their audience, what must be communicated, and the most appropriate ways to communicate their thoughts and feelings. Children learn to pay attention to auditory perception and discrimination, voice skills (articulation and expressiveness), and vocabulary and syntax. Questions teachers can ask include: Do the students attempt to extend their range of language codes? Do the students pay attention to the aesthetic qualities of their speech? Do the students possess a range of language codes that work for them in different situations?

Source: Adapted from British Columbia Ministry of Education (1998), *Enhancing and Evaluating Oral Communication in the Primary Grades: Teacher's Resource Package*, pp. 2:5–2:9. Victoria, BC: British Columbia Ministry of Education.

Published by the Department of School Education in Victoria, Australia (1991), the document outlines nine "bands" of proficiency in oral language and provides descriptions and assessment practices for each. The handbook emphasizes the importance of talking with and listening to students, and of involving them in drama; listening to songs, poems, and stories; choral reading; sharing time; co-operative writing; group activities; instruction designing; readers' theatre; improvisation; co-operative "cloze" activities (discussed in Chapter Six); storytelling; role-playing; group discussions; cross-age tutoring; and reporting.

The assessment records in the handbook are organized into two categories: use of oral language and features of oral language. Spoken language "band D" (approximately Grade 4) lists the following attributes:

*Use of oral language*

- tells personal anecdotes, illustrating in a relevant way the issue being discussed,
- recounts a story or repeats a song spontaneously,
- retells scenes from a film or drama,
- offers predictions about what will come next,
- recites poems,
- asks questions in conversation,
- has a second try at saying something to make it more precise, and
- arouses and maintains audience interest during formal presentations (e.g., report to class, announcements).

*Features of oral language*

- uses a range of vocabulary related to a particular topic,
- maintains a receptive body stance in conversation, and
- speaks in a way that conveys feelings (while keeping emotions under control).

Teachers might want to make these lists of attributes into a checklist that could be augmented with comments on the oral language behaviours of each individual child. The assessment of oral communication abilities relies heavily on the teacher *listening* to children — not only listening to *what* children have to say and responding appropriately, but also listening to *how* children create and communicate meaning. Lists like those above can be helpful in tracking children's abilities and growth in this very important area.

One other source of information on assessing children's oral communication is *English in the National Curriculum*, published in 1990 by the Department of Education and Science in the United Kingdom. Attainment targets, statements of attainment, and examples are established for speaking and listening, for children ages 6 through 15. At age 9, for example, the statement of attainment is that children shall

- give a detailed oral account of an event, or something that has been learned in the classroom, or explain with reasons why a particular course of action has been taken (e.g., report to the class on a group science activity);
- ask and respond to questions in a range of situations with increased confidence (e.g., conduct an interview on a television program devised with other students);
- take part as speakers and listeners in a group discussion or activity, expressing a personal view and commenting constructively on what is being discussed or

experienced (e.g., contribute to the planning and implementation of a group activity); and

- participate in a presentation (e.g., describe the outcome of a group activity, or improvise a scene from a story or poem of the student's own devising).

When using rubrics such as this, it is helpful to teachers if they are familiar with the statements of attainment for children both younger and older than the grade level at which they teach. In any one classroom there will be a wide range of oral communication competencies. Familiarity with a broad range of abilities helps teachers to understand their own students' oral language development more clearly.

## Promoting Oral Language Growth in the Classroom

Many children talk with ease on the playground, but have difficulty expressing themselves adequately in the classroom or school office. Some children feel comfortable moving from one language register to another and speak easily to different people in different contexts. Other children are limited by their experiences of language use. While students are usually comfortable in using oral communication to get their needs met or to regulate the actions of others, they may not be as comfortable or as adept in using persuasive language, giving directions, or making inquiries in school. These functions of language can be taught through the everyday classroom interactions that occur among children, and between teacher and students, helping students to become more articulate, precise, and confident in their spoken language.

Thoughtful teachers and adults working with students nurture and support their oral language. If a child is having difficulty describing something, the teacher asks questions; if a child has difficulty explaining something, the teacher prompts and encourages. Activities that promote the functions of language, such as those outlined in Boxes 2.3 and 2.4, also promote the development of oral language. In addition, most drama activities enhance oral language development—both talking and listening. The teacher's role is to provide challenges to students in their oral language capacities, and also to support students in their oral language efforts. One of the conclusions reached by Loban after his longitudinal study of language development (1963) was that children who have well-developed oral language skills tend to learn to read more easily and become better readers than children who do not have strong oral language skills. It is clearly important that teachers understand the role of oral language in the classroom, and that they encourage children to use oral language effectively for a variety of purposes.

Many adults can remember being corrected in their language as children, or remember being told that their dialect was not appropriate and they should not speak in a certain way. Comments of this kind silence children and are equivalent to telling children they can sing in the choir, but must only mouth the words. Oral language is part of our familial and cultural heritage and an important part of who we are as human beings. Correcting a child's grammar or usage is not the same thing as facilitating oral language competency. The language students bring to school is to be accepted, and then it is to be built upon so that children can refine their knowledge and skills and become more articulate and confident speakers in a range of social situations.

In promoting oral language growth in classrooms, it is helpful for the teacher to give students opportunities to hold conversations with one another and with teachers, janitors, office staff, and visitors. Some of these situations will be unstructured, as when students play together at recess or chat while they set up activities. Other situations will be more structured, such as the talk that occurs when children are discussing science activities, creating dramatic episodes in social studies, sharing ideas in writing conferences, and participating in reading workshops. Purposeful talk includes that which surrounds journal writing, and the inevitable talk that provides much of the basis for written composition itself, particularly in the primary grades. In constructivist classrooms, oral language is the basis for much classroom learning as well as for the personal growth that occurs in children. All talk is purposeful to the speaker. Whether it is about last night's hockey game or a classroom project, an intention is being realized. Children grow and learn through their talk, and there is room in the classroom for many kinds of talk on different topics.

Box 2.6 contains an excerpt from a transcript of a social studies/drama class. The excerpt demonstrates how children use talk for many purposes and how they change register depending on the context. Clearly, the students in this class were actively engaged with the drama activity and were generally using language appropriate to the situation. They engaged in problem solving, brainstorming, and sharing their solutions. The students had to think as though they were pioneers themselves, and they quickly moved into role and took over the language and thinking of a family with a problem to solve. The students became more focussed, and the teacher observed that they seemed to learn more through these activities than they did through only reading and writing about the topic.

### Box 2.6   Purposeful Talk in a Drama Context

Jewel Bondar, a special education teacher, had taken her primary adaptation students on a field trip to Fort Edmonton Historical Park. In Alberta, children in an adaptation classroom are usually at least two years below the accepted standard of competency in at least four subject areas in school. The Alberta Grade 3 social studies curriculum requires that students study the history of their community. During a visit to the 1846 fort, one of the last students to leave the ice house had left the door open. The tour guide reprimanded the students for this and raised questions about the consequences of such forgetfulness for residents of the fort in 1846. On returning to the school, Jewel decided to engage the children in a group drama session about this action. She worked in role as the mother of a pioneer family.

**Jewel:** Are you ready to begin drama time?
**Children:** Yeh!
**Jewel:** When your father gets home he will whip you soundly—all of you!
[Silence]
**Jewel:** Was it you, John? Jake?
**Boy:** It was him. He got you, us all, in trouble.
**Jewel:** Do you have a name?
**Girl:** That guy there is Tom.
**Jewel:** And you?

**Girl:** Rebecca.
**Jewel:** Who did it?
**Children:** Did what?
**Jewel:** Look over there. What do you see?
**Girl:** Wolf tracks.
**Jewel:** What else?
**Girl:** Trees and a cookhouse and water.
**Jewel:** Good eyes, daughter. What else?
**Boy:** I see a door open over there.
**Jewel:** Look children! A door is open!
**Jewel:** I wonder what sort of person would go into someone else's ...
**Boy:** I told him not to, but he done it.
**Jewel:** What did he do?
**Boy:** A traveller came by in the night.
**Jewel:** How do you know?
**Jewel:** *[Out of role and into real life:] Do you want to be frightened by this?*
**Children:** *Nope, pioneers were tough, a kid done it.* [Back in role:]
**Boy:** Somebody forgot to lock it.
**Boy:** I told him where the food is, like when my brother tells me where the stuff, the good stuff is hid.
**Girl:** Look, mother, it is yucky. A door is open.
**Jewel:** What do you think is the problem? Why would that door be open?

*(continued)*

**Box 2.6    Continued**

| | |
|---|---|
| Boy: | He was hungry. |
| Jewel: | Who? |
| Boy: | The traveller, so he stole some food. |
| Jewel: | Oh no! The door to the ice house has been left open and our meat for winter is sure to spoil. |
| Boy: | I'll shoot a crow or somethin'. |
| Boy: | A crow would not even fill you up and we got no guns. |
| Girl: | There aren't no berries like we had for breakfast in winter. |
| Boy: | Nope and a lotta snow. |
| Girl: | Could we trap? |
| Boy: | Trap what? |
| Boy: | Buffalo. |
| Girl: | Ain't no trap big enough. |
| Girl: | I know, we could get beavers and rabbits and stuff. |
| Girl: | We'll starve on small things like that. Do we have to feed all of us all winter long? |
| Boy: | Of course, there ain't no Safeways. |
| Girl: | You dumby. |
| Jewel: | [Out of role and in real life:] Stop. Is this the way pioneer children would talk to one another? |
| Children: | Nope, they'd get beat, it's not appropriate, no put-downs remember? |
| Jewel: | Do you want to continue? |
| Children: | Yes, let's find out, come on you guys. I like this, yeah. |
| [Back in role:] | |
| Jewel: | Any ideas on what to do about the meat supply? What might we do? |
| Girl: | I got an idea. We could set a trapline like we did last day. |
| Boy: | We'll starve on small things like that. |
| Boy: | How much meat we got now? |
| Girl: | What meat? It stole and rotten, ain't it? |
| Children: | Pew! It stinks, there are bugs, it's green, yuk. |

| | |
|---|---|
| Jewel: | [In real life:] Stop. Put your head down on the table and close your eyes. I want you to think about the ice house. What is it similar to today? I want you to think what rotten meat would smell like, look like, taste like. What would the pioneers do for food in the winter if the meat spoils? In your tables, groups, I want you to help solve the problem. Somebody has left the ice house door open. The meat is warming and sure to rot if a solution or answer is not found soon. [Students brainstormed together for ten minutes and Jewel circulated among the groups. Table two needed assistance in focussing on the problem.] |
| Jewel: | Give me five! (Classroom control signal) |
| [Back in role:] | I don't believe someone has been so careless. Well, can any of you suggest what to do before your father comes home from his voyage? [Several hands go up.] |
| Jewel: | [Out of role and in real life:] I am going to ask each group to show the class how they think the ice house problem was solved. When I say freeze, I want you to stop like I expect in physical education class. In drama this is called a still image because it is similar to taking a picture, the people are in a pose. Kathy, can you stand over here, please? Brush your hair. Freeze — very good listening. Kathy brushed her hair and then when I said freeze, she gave a still image. Do you all understand freeze means to stop everything, not fall over or fall down? |
| Children: | Yes, we do. |

And so the drama continued. All the groups shared their tableaux, still image, and "thoughts in the head" (see Chapter Twelve).

Source: J. Bondar and J.B. Edwards (1995, Autumn), "Charting new territory: Pioneers in an adaptation classroom." *Ohio Journal of the English Language Arts, 36* (2), pp. 11–19.

To facilitate talk, classrooms can be organized so that children are able to talk to one another easily without having to move from their desks or speak in loud voices. Grouping desks together or seating children around small tables works effectively. It is also important to consider the purpose of the grouping, and to group children differently at different times. Most of the time, heterogeneous grouping is most effective, as it facilitates children's engagement in conversations, expressing what they know and asking questions of one another. Grouping of this kind enables children to help another and develop expertise independently from the teacher.

## Helping Children Become Effective Listeners

*The English Language Framework* (Ministry of Education, Victoria, 1988) makes the following suggestions for enhancing listening in the classroom. All the suggestions can be implemented by both teachers *and* students:

- Respect the opinions of others.
- Be a considerate listener.
- Negotiate rather than argue stubbornly.
- Share discoveries and queries.
- Interact in group discussions.
- Recall facts.
- Repeat instructions.
- Respond to what is heard.

Students can be encouraged to engage in active listening when they participate in writing conferences with their peers, engage in group projects, take part in drama activities, and read to each other in shared reading experiences.

As in any other area of the language arts, children learn best when they are provided with opportunities to listen in the context of their learning. They do not need exercises and drills on listening. Teachers can show children how to vary their listening according to the specific purpose for listening, and can help children develop specific listening strategies. Some students have only one strategy for listening no matter what the purpose—to listen hard and remember everything. Children can be helped to understand that once a purpose is established for listening, they can vary *how* they listen and hence be more effective listeners. Listening to a story such as *Baseball Bats for Christmas* (Kusugak, 1990) for pleasure (appreciative or aesthetic listening) allows a child to enter the world of the imagination; to create images of the setting, characters, and events; and to respond emotionally and intellectually to the narrative. Listening later to the teacher talk about the author, Michael Kusugak, requires a different kind of listening (comprehensive or efferent listening). Here the child attempts to understand information about Michael Kusugak, including his childhood in Repulse Bay, where Kusugak now lives and works; how he began writing for children; why he enjoyed listening to his grandmother's stories; and how he first learned English. Understanding this information helps the listener add richness to the story Kusugak wrote. Yet another kind of listening (critical listening) is required when the children and teacher talk together about how Michael Kusugak went by plane, at age 6, to a school far away from his home, returning only in the summers. As children ponder the dilemma of having young children stay at home versus providing them with an education, they are required to listen critically, assess what they have heard, make judgements about situations, and perhaps attempt to understand two sides of a debate.

Later in this book, in Chapter Eight, a Grade 4 oral history project is described. The students in this Grade 4 classroom tape-recorded interviews with local residents, searched archives and local libraries, and eventually wrote a history of one of the local communities. The project had a specific purpose. When the students were conducting the interviews, they were aware that they would later be using this information to write a book that would be sold in the community. Their listening was focussed on the information they could use in the book. The project is an example of the integration of all the language arts modes — listening, speaking, reading, writing, viewing, and representing. The students completed individual work, group work, and whole class work as they produced the history book. Clearly, listening played a large part in the success of the project.

## Vocabulary Development

Children learn new words both from reading and from listening to the constant stream of oral language around them. We each have a receptive and an expressive vocabulary. The receptive vocabulary is generally much larger than the expressive vocabulary—we can understand many more words than we actually use in speaking and writing. Young children's vocabulary development depends heavily on the oral language they hear around them, but as they get older, this development depends increasingly on their reading (McKeown and Curtis, 1987). Teachers in constructivist classrooms are aware that vocabulary develops most effectively when students are engaged in activities that stretch them to say new things in new ways. Thus, teachers play an important role in children's vocabulary development when they introduce new vocabulary in their classroom talk and draw their students' attention to those words.

New words generally enter our expressive vocabularies slowly, for users usually need to feel confident about the meaning and context of new words before they use them with ease in their oral or written language. When people hear or read a new word and pay attention to it, they might use the word in their speech, but only if they feel confident enough. Once a word is comfortably fixed in a speaking vocabulary, it is more likely to be used in writing, where it becomes more permanent. Some words become fashionable for a while and quickly move into the general lexicon. Words such as "viable," "interface," "cognizant," and "explicate" are all words that have appeared in common academic usage in the past twenty years and then have faded. Similarly, children have their own language (or slang) in which certain words attain powerful meaning before becoming outdated. Vocabulary generally cannot be taught through word lists and definitions, since words have to be used meaningfully. However, teachers can certainly help their students by showing them how to use a dictionary to check the meanings of any words they are unsure of and to cross-check the meanings against the context in which the words are used.

Maintaining a vital oral language curriculum means that classrooms cannot be quiet places. Teachers distinguish between the busy chat and movement of actively engaged children and the noise created by off-topic talking and irrelevant behaviour. Teachers in constructivist classrooms understand the need to develop learning activities that engage children's interests and stimulate oral language. They capitalize on activities such as literature circles, reader-response groups, and drama activities in an effort to enhance their students' abilities to articulate their thoughts and feelings clearly and with confidence.

At the beginning of this chapter, Ms. Moorhouse asked what it is she needs to know about language, and about children's learning of language, that will enhance her classroom instruction in the language arts. Understanding these concepts makes teaching the language arts more meaningful and purposeful. It is clear from the research conducted in this field that most of children's learning in school, including their reading and writing development, rests largely on oral language ability—the ability to listen and talk in a variety of registers and social contexts. Because this area of the language arts is so vital to children's success in school, it is important that they have the opportunity to talk in situations that encourage or challenge them to extend their talk repertoire. Since what is taught and valued in school contexts is normally assessed, it is important that children's oral language development be noted by teachers and feedback be provided to students and their parents.

## Summary

In constructivist classrooms, teachers make every effort to understand how children learn language, and to understand language itself. Language is probably the most complex and sophisticated of all human behaviours — many researchers maintain that it is the use of language that sets human beings apart from other animals. Language consists of four major elements: semantics, syntax, phonology, and pragmatics. Semantics refers to the meaning element of language; syntax to the organization of language; phonology to the sound system of language; and pragmatics to the ways in which language is used to communicate.

Over the years, theories of language acquisition have developed and changed. It was once believed that language was learned through the purely Skinnerian model of behaviourism: children make an utterance and learn whether or not it is correct through the reactive behaviour of those around them. It eventually became apparent that this explanation was not sufficient to account for the great range of words and sentence structures that children learn so quickly in the first four years of their lives. Behaviourist psychology cannot totally account for that kind of learning and thinking. In the 1950s, Noam Chomsky proposed the theory that language structures are innately present in children, and that when children encounter spoken language, these structures are activated and language learning progresses. Today, an interactional approach to language development prevails, whereby language acquisition is seen to be the result of a child's interaction with caregivers and the socio-cultural environment. From a balanced perspective, it is likely that some aspects of all three of these theories apply when children learn language.

The social context of language development has also received attention from researchers. Longitudinal studies by Loban, Heath, and Wells have demonstrated the effects of the social system, and especially the classroom, on children's language learning and language use. Although it was once believed that a school environment could provide a richer language environment for children than they were likely to experience at home, research has shown that this is not so. Children's language use in classrooms is generally suppressed and not as rich as children are likely to experience in their homes.

Language and learning cannot be separated. Much of what children learn, both in and out of school, takes place through the vehicle of language — both written and oral. The processing of thoughts cannot be separated from the use of language. How would we think if we didn't have language? Teachers in constructivist classrooms understand that children, to learn effectively, need the opportunity to work purposefully in groups, sharing ideas, questions, suggestions, and problem-solving strategies. As we talk through ideas, we think about them further, clarify them, refine them, and enhance our knowledge and understandings.

The oral language competencies of young children have been shown to be related to reading and writing abilities. Children entering school with strong oral language competencies are more likely to experience success in their literacy endeavours.

Although the focus of elementary language arts is generally on literacy development, a great deal of classroom communication occurs orally. Children can be helped to expand their listening and speaking skills so that they can maximize their learning opportunities. It is therefore important that oral language be nurtured and supported in classrooms so that children become effective listeners and speakers wherever they are. It is also important that children's oracy be assessed on an ongoing basis through informal observations and anecdotal records. Children need to know how strengthening their oral language abilities can improve their learning overall.

## Selected Professional Resources

British Columbia Ministry of Education. (1988). *Enhancing and Evaluating Oral Communication in the Primary Grades: Teacher's Resource Package.* Victoria, BC: British Columbia Ministry of Education. A comprehensive resource for teachers, these materials combine background information with specific, practical strategies. Resource packages are also available for the intermediate and secondary grades. The packages can be used by educators to help plan and monitor oral language learning across the curriculum, make decisions about the oral language development of students, plan instructional strategies, and develop evaluation formats.

Department of Education and Science. (1990). *English in the National Curriculum, 2.* London, UK: HMSO. The document outlines programs of study for children ages 6 to 15 and makes specific suggestions for implementation in the classroom. The document is not detailed, however, and needs to be supplemented with other resources.

Ministry of Education, Victoria. (1988). *English Language Framework, P–10: Language for Living.* Melbourne, Australia: Victoria Ministry of Education. The book lists goals for the oral language curriculum from kindergarten to Grade 9, and describes the teacher's role, the context, and specific learning activities in some detail.

## Children's Books Noted in Chapter Two

Kusugak, M. (1990). *Baseball Bats for Christmas.* Toronto: Annick Press.
Parish, P. (1963). *Amelia Bedelia.* New York: Harper and Row.

## References

Barnes, D. (1976). *From communication to curriculum.* Harmondsworth, UK: Penguin Books.

Berry, K. (1985). Talking to learn subject matter/learning subject matter talk. *Language Arts, 62* (1), 34–42.

Bondar, J. and Edwards, J.B. (1995). Charting new territory: Pioneers in an adaptation classroom. *Ohio Journal of the English Language Arts, 36* (2), 11–19.

Braddock, R., Lloyd-Jones, R., and Schoer, L. (1963). *Research in written composition.* Champaign, IL: National Council of Teachers of English.

British Columbia Ministry of Education. (1988). *Enhancing and evaluating oral communication in the primary grades: Teacher's resource package.* Victoria: British Columbia Ministry of Education.

Britton, J. (1970). *Language and learning.* Harmondsworth, UK: Penguin Books.

Brown, R. (1973). *A first language.* Cambridge, MA: Harvard University Press.

Cazden, C. (1988). *Classroom discourse: The language of teaching and learning.* Portsmouth, NH: Heinemann.

Chomsky, N. (1957). *Syntactic structures.* The Hague: Mouton & Co.

Clark, H. and Clark, E.V. (1977). *Psychology and language.* New York: Harcourt Brace Jovanovich.

Department of Education and Science. (1990). *English in the national curriculum, 2.* London, UK: HMSO.

Department of School Education. (1991). *English profiles handbook.* Melbourne, Australia: Victoria Department of School Education.

Dillon, D. (1985). Editorial. *Language Arts, 62* (1), 9.

Donaldson, M. (1978). *Children's minds.* New York: W.W. Norton & Co.

Ferreiro, E. and Teberosky, A. (1982). *Literacy before schooling.* Exeter, NH: Heinemann.

Fillion, B. (1983). Let me see you learn. *Language Arts, 60* (6), 702–710.

Flanders, N. (1970). *Analyzing teaching behavior.* Reading, MA: Addison-Wesley.

Freshour, F. and Bartholomew, P. (1989). Let's start improving our own listening. *Florida Reading Quarterly, 25* (4), 28–30.

Halliday, M.A.K. (1969). Relevant models of language. *Educational Review, 22* (1), 26–37.

Halliday, M.A.K. (1975). *Learning how to mean.* New York: Elsevier North-Holland Inc.

Harste, J., Woodward, V., and Burke, C. (1984). *Language stories and literacy lessons.* Portsmouth, NH: Heinemann.

Heath, S.B. (1983). *Ways with words: Language, life and work in communities and classrooms.* Cambridge, MA: Cambridge University Press.

Hunt, K. (1965). *Grammatical structures written at three grade levels.* NCTE Research Report Number 3. Urbana, IL: National Council of Teachers of English.

John-Steiner, V. and Tatter, P. (1983). An interactionist model of language development. In B. Bain (ed.), *The sociogenesis of language and human conduct* (pp. 79–97). New York: Plenum.

Lenneberg, E.H. (1964). The capacity for language acquisition. In J.A. Fodor and J.J. Katz (eds.), *The structure of language* (pp. 580–605). Englewood Cliffs, NJ: Prentice-Hall.

Lindfors, J.W. (1987). *Children's language and learning* (2nd ed.). Englewood Cliffs, NJ: Prentice-Hall.

Loban, W. (1963). *The language of elementary school children.* NCTE Research Report Number 1. Urbana, IL: National Council of Teachers of English.

McKeown, M.G. and Curtis, M.E. (eds.). (1987). *The nature of vocabulary acquisition.* Hillsdale, NJ: Lawrence Erlbaum Associates.

Miller, G. (1977). *Spontaneous apprentices: Children and language.* New York: Seabury Press.

Ministry of Education, Victoria. (1988). *English language framework, P–10: Language for living.* Melbourne, Australia: Victoria Ministry of Education.

Moffet, J. (1968). *Teaching the universe of discourse.* Boston: Houghton Mifflin.

Moray, N. (1969). *Listening and attention.* Baltimore: Penguin Books.

Mueller, S. (1983). An investigation in social competence using clinical and societal profiles. Unpublished master's thesis. University of California, Santa Barbara; as cited in C. Pratting and D. Kirchner (1987), A clinical appraisal of the pragmatic aspects of language, *Journal of Speech and Hearing Disorders, 52,* 105–119.

Rosen, H. (1984). *The importance of story.* Sheffield, UK: National Association for the Teaching of English.

Rymer, R. (1992a, April 13). Annals of science: A silent childhood — I. *The New Yorker, 68,* 41–81.

Rymer, R. (1992b, April 20). Annals of science: A silent childhood — II. *The New Yorker, 69,* 43–77.

Skinner, B.F. (1957). *Verbal behavior.* Englewood Cliffs, NJ: Prentice-Hall.

Staats, A.W. (1971). *Child learning, intelligence, and personality: Principles of a behavioral interaction approach.* New York: Harper & Row.

Terrace, H.S. (1979). How Nim Chimpsky changed my mind. *Psychology Today, 13* (6), 65–76.

Tizard, B. and Hughes, M. (1984). *Young children learning.* Cambridge, MA: Harvard University Press.

Tough, J. (1976). *Listening to children talking: A guide to the appraisal of children's language use.* Portsmouth, NH: Heinemann.

Vygotsky, L.S. (1962). *Thought and language.* Cambridge, MA: MIT Press.

Wells, G. (1986). *The meaning makers.* Portsmouth, NH: Heinemann.

Wilkinson, L. (1984). Peer group talk in elementary school. *Language Arts, 61* (2), 164–169.

Wolvin, A. and Croakley, C. (1985). *Listening instruction* (TRIP Booklet). Urbana, IL: ERIC Clearinghouse on Reading and Communication Skills and National Council of Teachers of English.

# Chapter three

# Emergent Literacy

**Perspectives on Early Literacy**
- Reading Readiness
- Emergent Literacy
- Summary and the Connectionist Perspective

**Emergent Literacy**

**Components of Emergent Literacy**
- Cultural Views and Functions of Written Language
- Nature and Forms of Written Language
- Speech–Print Relationship

**Assessing Emergent Literacy**
- Observing Children
- Interviews
- Collecting Samples of Children's Work

**Planning for Instruction**
- Rich Literacy Environment
- Daily Reading and Writing
- Control over Literacy Learning
- Acceptance of Approximations
- Differences among Learners
- Sequence of Instruction

**School Experiences That Facilitate Literacy Development**
- Reading to Children
- Shared-Book Experiences
- Shared Writing: The Language Experience Approach
- Writing
- Functional Interactions with Print

When the children arrive at Iris Li's kindergarten class each day, they meet together on the rug in one corner of the classroom and update the calendar and weather report. Iris has written the days of the week on cards, and the children select the card that shows what day it is, talking about what letter they see and what sound they hear at the beginning of the word. They describe the weather, and Iris prints what they say on a whiteboard. The children watch and listen to her say each word as she prints it. This type of activity has been taking place in kindergartens for decades. What is different now is that we are more aware of how this helps children construct knowledge about the connection between oral and written language.

There are other differences too. Rather than worksheets and visual discrimination activities with shapes and pictures, the children are engaged in a wide range of reading and writing activities. Every day Iris shares a story with the children, sometimes from a big book with print large enough so that all the children can see it as she reads. Iris carefully guides the discussion before, during, and after reading this book, focussing on both meaning and print. There is also a writing centre in the room where children go to write stories, letters, and recipes.

Print is everywhere in Iris's classroom. In one corner is a store centre with labelled cans and packages, as well as a cash register, pencils and paper for making grocery lists, and signs showing where different products are kept. As the children write grocery lists and identify products from their labels, they learn what print is for and how it relates to what they say. ■

Iris uses the term **emergent literacy** to describe her student's learning experiences. This term, which began to replace **reading readiness** in the late 1970s, signalled a significant change in the way literacy programs for young children were conceptualized and implemented. The two terms represent contrasting perspectives on how children learn to read and write.

- What are some images that you associate with these terms?
- What reading and writing activities do you think are appropriate for young children when
  they enter school?
- How can kindergarten and Grade 1 teachers figure out what types of instruction to provide for the children in their classes?

The purpose of this chapter is to help you construct answers to these and other questions you might have about the early stages of learning to read and write.

## Perspectives on Early Literacy

In this section, we present an overview of perspectives that have guided early reading and writing instruction in the twentieth century. Most of the discussion over the century has been focussed on reading, but the perspectives that have evolved also have implications for early writing.

### Reading Readiness

When Bill Clinton proclaimed in the 1990s that children should arrive at school ready to learn to read, he was using a construct with roots in the work of influential psychologists such as Stanley G. Hall near the beginning of the twentieth century (Durkin, 1983). Hall emphasized the impact of heredity on development and indicated that everyone went through the same stages of development in the same order. The term "reading readiness" first began to appear in the 1920s when educators, concerned about the number of Grade 1 children who had difficulty learning to read, applied maturationist notions to reading. They hypothesized that children who failed to learn to read were simply not yet at the appropriate stage of development. Since maturation rather than instruction was seen as necessary to move children to the next stage of development, the solution to reading problems was to delay instruction.

The notion that children needed to reach a certain age to be ready to learn to read received increased credibility through the results of an influential study by Morphett and Washburne in 1931. They examined the relationship between children's reading achievement and their mental age and concluded that children needed to reach a mental age of 6 ½ before they could profit from reading instruction. Although other researchers found that learning to read was more dependent on the nature of the reading program than the child's mental age (Gates, 1937), the maturationist perspective continued to prevail until the 1950s. By this point, another view was influencing how educators approached reading instruction for young children.

Rather than sitting back and waiting for children to get ready to learn to read, proponents of a developmentalist perspective believed that prereading experiences could hasten children's readiness. The reading readiness workbook was born. These workbooks were often part of basal reading programs and focussed primarily on three areas: language development, visual–motor abilities, and auditory discrimination (deHirsch, Jansky, and Langford, 1966). Typical activities in reading readiness workbooks involved colouring pictures of words that rhymed, choosing pictures of objects that faced the same direction, arranging pictures in order, and drawing lines between pictures of objects related in some way (e.g., mothers and babies or shoes and feet). Almost none of the activities involved written language, since the children were not considered ready for reading. Although some children already knew how to read when they arrived at school, it was common for all children in Grade 1 to complete reading readiness activities before beginning formal reading instruction. By the mid-1960s, however, constructivist views were beginning to affect the field of early literacy.

## Emergent Literacy

The term emergent literacy was first used by Marie Clay in 1966 (Crawford, 1995). She found that young children came to school with considerable knowledge about reading and writing and that they were able to use this knowledge in meaningful ways. The term "emerging" was used to indicate that learning to read and write involves growth along a continuum rather than mastery of prereading skills. The term "literacy" reflected a broader perspective than reading readiness, embracing both reading and writing. From an emergent literacy perspective, there is no sharp distinction between not being literate and being literate. Instead, literacy development is viewed as continuous, beginning with children's earliest experiences with print at home. Hence, in contrast to reading readiness, which was associated with kindergarten and the first few months of Grade 1, emergent literacy is seen as encompassing a considerable period of time. It begins very early in life for almost all children in a literate society (Teale, 1995) and continues to age 8 or 9 for some children (Sulzby, 1991).

Whereas in the past, parents had often been cautioned not to teach their children to read and write, proponents of emergent literacy view parents as playing a vital role in literacy development. They believe that young children sort out what print is for and how it works as they engage in a wide range of activities and experiences involving printed language. For instance:

- When they are read to by their parents, children not only experience the pleasures of a good story, but construct a schema for what stories are like and what book language sounds like.
- When they see their parents making lists to take to the supermarket and refer to these lists as they shop, children begin to understand that print carries ideas across time and space.
- In the morning as they eat breakfast, children become aware that there is a relationship between the words they say and hear and what is on the cereal box.

Today, emergent literacy is a term that pervades descriptions of early reading and writing development. Most educators who use the term hold a constructivist view of knowledge. They believe that children develop literacy by being actively engaged in meaningful literacy activities rather than being taught skills directly. They further believe that children need to be immersed in print-rich environments where they have opportunities to experiment with reading and writing. However, they still also feel that children develop literacy through a series of stages.

In contrast, social constructivists hypothesize that there are no qualitative differences in the processes of literacy used by readers and writers at different ages and levels of experience (Crawford, 1995). Rather than stages of development, social constructivists believe that literacy is specific to different cultures and that literacy learners construct meaning within their social context. Some social constructivists go even further, claiming that schools provide a more appropriate environment for some children to learn to read and write than they do for others. These educators maintain that a match between what children bring to school and what happens there is critical to literacy development. Purcell-Gates (1998) writes about the "terrifying mismatch" that often occurs between beginning reading instruction and children's entering knowledge about literacy.

## Summary and the Connectionist Perspective

Table 3.1 summarizes the similarities and differences among perspectives described so far in this section. From even a cursory examination of the comparisons provided, one can see the obvious relationship between the perspectives on early literacy development described above and the three major theoretical perspectives on language learning presented in Chapter One. Reading readiness perspectives tend to reflect transmission models, and emergent literacy perspectives tend to reflect constructivist and social constructivist models.

**Table 3.1**  Perspectives on Emergent Literacy

| Reading Readiness | | Emergent Literacy | |
|---|---|---|---|
| **Maturationists** | **Developmentalists** | **Constructivists** | **Social Constructivists** |
| • Readiness is discrete, separate from reading and writing development. | | • Emergent literacy is continuous, part of reading and writing development. | |
| • Reading and writing development begins at school. | | • Literacy development begins at home and occurs from infancy to age 8 or 9. | |
| • Children need time to mature before beginning formal reading and writing instruction. | • Nonprint activities develop readiness for formal reading and writing instruction. | • Literacy learning occurs in a print-rich environment where children are actively engaged in meaningful reading and writing. | |
| • Literacy development progresses through a series of stages. | | • Literacy development progresses through a series of stages. | • Literacy is culturally specific and there is no universal developmental stage. |
| • Question is how to prepare children for schools and literacy instruction. | | • Question is how to prepare children for schools and literacy instruction. | • Question is how to change schools and literacy instruction to meet the needs of the children |

While Table 3.1 captures the development of the most pervasive perspectives on literacy instruction across the century, it fails to reflect the diversity of current perspectives on beginning reading. In particular, it does not reflect the work of connectionists, who believe that, from the beginning, the focus should be on the code with direct, explicit instruction in phonics (Adams, 1990). Connectionists advocate a stage theory of reading development, breaking reading down into a series of skills that are, organized in a hierarchy and taught directly. Although connectionists acknowledge the need for print-rich environments for young children, they place priority on learning the code, which is seen as a means to fluent reading and comprehension.

> Our view of early literacy builds on a social constructivist perspective. However, like the connectionists, we believe that immersion in a print-rich environment is necessary but not sufficient for many young children to learn to read and write. Explicit instruction is necessary in literacy programs for young children. In contrast to the connectionists, however, we believe that early literacy development involves far more than learning sound–symbol relationships. In the next section, we provide a comprehensive model of the components of emergent literacy.

## Components of Emergent Literacy

Some writers have referred to what young children do with print as "reading-like" or "writing-like" behaviour to differentiate it from conventional reading and writing (Holdaway, 1979; Doake, 1988). However, as Harste, Woodward, and Burke (1984, p. 69) argue, even the term "emergent reading" implies that proficient language users engage in a process that is "psycholinguistically different from the process young children engage in." Working with young children from age 3, they found no compelling evidence that this is so. For example, when young children sit down to write, they use marks on a page to communicate a message. Although the marks may not yet be conventional spelling, the process of encoding meaning through symbols is similar to that used by the proficient writer.

Using terms such as "reading-like" or "writing-like" to describe what young children do with print raises the question of just when it is appropriate to label what the children do as "real" reading or writing. What percentage of words do children need to identify correctly in order to call what they are doing reading? What percentage of words must be spelled correctly before we say children are writing rather than engaging in writing-like behaviour? These terms create more questions than they answer.

We view reading and writing development as continuous, beginning with the child's earliest attempts to interact with print and progressing to proficient reading and writing. Hence, we refer to all young children's attempts to work with print as reading or writing (rather than as reading-like and writing-like behaviour), recognizing that over time these attempts will have more in common with the reading and writing of independent readers. Rather than discounting what young children do with print as inferior in some way (e.g., Downing, 1979), we agree with educators who recognize that the achievements of young children in literacy development are quite remarkable.

The following section, organized around major dimensions provided by Purcell-Gates (1998), attempts to capture the complexity of children's learning in the emergent stage of literacy development. An overview of these dimensions is presented in Box 3.1.

**Box 3.1**   Components of Emergent Literacy

**Cultural Views and Functions of Written Language**
- Expecting meaning from written language
- Engaging in purposeful reading and writing

**Nature and Forms of Written Language**
- Understanding that oral and written language are related
- Matching words heard with those in print (eye–voice matching)
- Internalizing the language of books

**Speech–Print Relationship**
- Differentiating between pictures and print
- Understanding how print works (conventions of print)
- Matching sounds and letters in words (alphabetic principle)
- Understanding terms related to books, reading, and writing

Source: Major headings extracted from V. Purcell-Gates (1998), "Growing Successful Readers: Homes, Communities, and Schools." In J. Osborn and F. Lehr (eds.), *Literacy for All: Issues in Teaching and Learning* (p. 54). New York: The Guilford Press.

# Cultural Views and Functions of Written Language

Children's views about the value and functions of written language are a direct reflection of their experiences within their family and the wider social context. In many families, children are read to from birth and literacy is a part of the very fabric of family life (Taylor, 1982). Although young children in these homes may not recognize letters and words as such, many do understand that what they see written in books, or written by parents as lists, memos, notes, and cards, contains meaning. From the age of about 2 onward, as soon as children can grasp a pencil or crayon, they become involved in representing and expressing meaning. As adults read books to them, children come to expect pleasure and that books will make sense. In turn, they try to make meaning as they interact with books independently.

Children in these types of homes see their mothers and fathers using reading and writing for a wide range of purposes. Their parents read manuals of directions to assemble new toys, furniture, and tools. They read items in the newspaper for both information and entertainment, and write letters for a wide variety of purposes. By talking to their parents about what they are doing and imitating or taking a reader/writer role alongside them, children learn why people read and write—for the fun of it, to find out something, to learn how to do something, or to communicate with someone.

However, not all children are born into or raised in literate environments. Studies by Taylor and Dorsey-Gaines (1988) and Purcell-Gates (1998) examined the literacy experiences of children in homes of low socio-economic status families. They found great variation in these homes in the extent to which people read and wrote and in the way they used reading and writing. Overall, many children from these homes came to school with either fewer or different types of print experiences than children from middle-class homes. Rather than labelling these children as deficient, social constructivists recommend that schools be prepared to provide for a wide range of individual differences when planning beginning reading and writing instruction.

## Nature and Forms of Written Language

A major understanding that children develop when they are read to involves the relationship or connection between oral and written language. Temple and Gillet (1989, p. 113) indicate that children need to know "that the talk that is inspired by a text is not a free-form commentary on the pictures, nor a story that changes a little with each telling, but rather a sort of frozen discourse that must come out just so every time the text is read." While this seems self-evident to adults who know how to read, few of us can remember when we reached this realization. One way children demonstrate an understanding that the story is a "frozen discourse" is by becoming intolerant if their parents do not read every word in the text exactly. They also demonstrate an understanding that spoken messages can be written down in their early writing when they produce scribbles or letters and ask that these be read back to them.

But children need to go beyond this general understanding of the relationship between oral and written language to a more specific understanding that each written word is related to one word they hear or say. By asking their parents to read the same book again and again until they have virtually memorized the text, children are able to begin matching words on the page with words in memory. This is frequently referred to as eye–voice pointing or speech-to-print matching. The child looks at each word at the same time as he or she is saying it.

It is not only experiences with books that contribute to awareness of the relationship between oral and written words. Torrey (1969) described a young boy who learned to read from exposure to advertisements on television, and others have documented the impact of **environmental print** on children's literacy development (Mason, 1984). In the supermarket, young children see products being named as they are selected, and they are frequently asked to find particular products. Television commercials, household products, and signs attract attention to print and help children become aware that each word they hear is linked directly to a word in written language. This is critical because it enables children to focus attention on the appropriate units of print as they attempt to read.

Through experiences with books, children also become aware that there are differences between the language in books and the spoken language they use in their daily lives. We rarely talk like the three little kittens who cried, "Oh Mother dear, we sadly fear, our mittens we have lost." Doake (1988) refers to this as learning the language of books, and Clay (1972, p. 28) refers to it as "talking like a book." Knowledge about the language of books is reflected in the stories children tell and in what they say when they read. Applebee (1978) examined the stories told by young children and found that even as young as 2 years, children who have been read to begin to differentiate storytelling from talking.

## Speech–Print Relationship

Perhaps the most basic knowledge children construct about print is that there is a difference between it and pictures. This is evident in children's writing when they begin to differentiate between what they write and what they draw (Harste, Woodward, and Burke, 1984). Understanding the difference between pictures and print is also evident when children point to print rather than pictures when reading a book from memory.

However, this is only the beginning of what children learn as they figure out how print works. In alphabetic languages, a few symbols are arranged in different orders to produce all the words in the language (referred to by Clay, 1975 as the "generating principle"), and these symbols are rarely repeated next to each other more than twice. Ferreiro and Teberosky (1982) studied the developing awareness of young children about this aspect of the printed language. As one task, they presented children with cards containing strings of printed symbols and asked the children to indicate which could be read and which could not be read. They found that the children tended to reject cards with fewer than three letters as not being readable (they were "too short"), as well as rejecting those with the same letter repeated several times ("it's all the same").

Early writing usually begins with scribble — large rounded gestures or scratchy straight lines. As the scribble evolves in form toward print, letters and familiar shapes emerge that children repeat as they perceive a likeness to models in their own world. Marie Clay (1975) has shown that this early writing plays a significant role in developing children's knowledge about how print works. Children come to understand that the same letter can be written in various ways (referred to by Clay as the "flexibility principle"). We see this when a child fills a piece of paper with different versions of the letter *A*, for example. We might see tall thin *A*'s, wide fat ones, ones that are upside down, and ones with no stroke across the middle.

Children also learn about directionality as they engage in early writing. They learn

- that print begins at the top of a page and continues to the bottom,
- that we read and write from left to right on the page,
- that the front of a book opens on the right, and
- that directionality is important to the identity of letters.

These directional principles are different for other languages, such as Hebrew and Mandarin. Many teachers and parents express concern when young children write their names backwards or confuse the letters *b* and *d*. However, until children encounter written language, they have an implicit understanding that directional orientation does not affect the identity of an object. For example, a cup is still a cup, whether the handle is turned toward the left or the right. We are still the same people whether we're lying down or standing on our heads. Directionality has not been used to differentiate objects in the child's environment, but with letters and numbers, all that changes. Nines and sixes are entirely different numbers, *b*'s and *d*'s are different letters, *on* and *no* are different words.

Perhaps the most critical understanding that young children construct about print involves the connection between letters and sounds. Many researchers hypothesize that a first step in developing this understanding involves awareness that words can be segmented into phonemes, or sound units. From her review of research on beginning reading, Adams (1990) concluded that **phonemic awareness**, or segmentation, is critical to success in learning to read. However, results of training studies indicate that "phonemic awareness training" by itself provides, at best, limited improvement in subsequent reading (Wagner, Torgesen, Laughon, Simmons, and Rashotte, 1993, p. 100). Whether phonemic awareness training results in reading growth depends on what else is done with the children while this training is being provided, and that "what else" seems to involve helping children make connections between letters and sounds. Many people refer to this as understanding the **alphabetic principle** — that letters in written words stand for sounds in spoken words (Muter, Hulme, Snowling, and Taylor, 1997).

Although largely an artifact of reading instruction, children also learn the terms we use to talk about reading and writing. They come to understand what teachers mean when they say, "Find the word 'cat,'" "What sound do you hear at the beginning of the word 'cat'?" and "Read the first sentence" (Mason, 1984). Many writers refer to terms about reading and writing as "metalinguistic knowledge" and note that young children frequently have quite different concepts from adults about terms such as *word*, *letter*, *sentence*, and *sound* (Reid, 1966; Downing, 1979). Other conventions they learn involve our use of punctuation and the associated terminology, as well as words we use to describe books (e.g., *front*, *back*, *author*, *cover*).

# Assessing Emergent Literacy

Some children arrive at kindergarten with very little understanding of what written language is for or how it works. Others come to school already reading and writing. Hence, right from the first day of school, children show considerable differences in their literacy development. As their teacher, you need to know what understandings your students have constructed about literacy in order to plan and provide appropriate experiences. In this section, we present suggestions for how you can informally assess the emergent reading and writing development of your students. But first, we provide a rationale for using informal as compared to formal assessment with young children.

Standardized reading readiness tests were widely used in the past to determine children's readiness to learn from formal reading instruction, and they are beginning to be used in some school jurisdictions again due to increased concern about accountability. These tests traditionally assessed areas often only peripherally related to reading achievement, such as vocabulary development and visual and auditory discrimination.

However, some readiness tests produced more recently, such as the Linguistic Awareness in Reading Readiness (LARR) Test (Downing, Ayers, and Schaefer, 1983), reflect concepts of emergent literacy rather than traditional notions of reading readiness. The LARR test provides indicators of children's ability to recognize literacy behaviour, their understanding of literacy functions, and their knowledge of the technical language of literacy. However, the major purpose of this test, like that of more traditional reading readiness tests, is to predict a child's readiness to learn from formal reading instruction.

While standardized readiness tests provide information about how a child ranks relative to other children, they tell little about the child's understanding of the connections between oral and written language or about his or her specific instructional needs. Informal assessment is generally recommended to teachers as a more appropriate means of deciding what children know about literacy and where they are in their literacy development.

Several advantages of informal assessment have been identified (Teale, Hiebert, and Chittenden, 1987):

- In contrast with formal testing, informal assessment is part of instruction. It is not separate from the teaching/learning process and, hence, does not take time away from instruction the way standardized testing does.
- Informal assessment is more broadly based than formal assessment. The focus is on all the literacy activities the child completes in the language arts classroom rather than what the child does on contrived test items.
- Informal assessment occurs continuously rather than at one or two points in the year.

As such, informal assessment provides a basis for daily lesson planning and responsive instruction.

Four major types of informal assessment have been described in the literature. The first three — observation, interviews, and samples of children's work — involve informal assessment by the teacher. The last involves student self-assessment.

A few years ago, Yetta Goodman coined the term "kid watching" to refer to the ongoing observation by teachers of children in classrooms. She suggests that kid watching is likely not as conscious as it needs to be for teachers to "gain the greatest insights from it" (1991, p. 58).

Teacher questioning has been a very common part of language arts instruction, and as Durkin (1978–79) has pointed out, this questioning has been primarily used to evaluate rather than to enhance children's understanding. In order to maximize insights from children's answers, however, it is crucial that we go beyond evaluating those answers as right or wrong and move on to determining what they tell us about children's literacy development. Interviewing generally refers to more structured interactions between teachers and children than those that occur in the classroom on a daily basis. Interview questions are usually organized around a specific topic or aspect of language learning, and the teacher may use the questions as prompts to gather information from children on an individual basis.

A third type of informal assessment involves gathering samples of children's work. This is not a new idea, but it has recently received considerable attention through the movement to "portfolio assessment." The term comes from artists' portfolios, in which they collect and display their best work. Portfolios of children's reading and writing are generally not restricted to their best work; instead, they are meant to contain samples across time. Valencia (1990), a strong supporter of portfolio assessment, maintains that portfolios are authentic, continuous, ongoing, multidimensional, and collaborative.

From a collaborative perspective, one of the major advantages cited for portfolio assessment is the potential it has for children to become involved in self-assessment. This is achieved by having children both select some of what goes into the portfolio and collaborate with their teacher in assessing what is there. Thus, portfolios have the potential to create a more democratic language arts classroom.

## Observing Children

As teachers, we gather information every time we interact with children, whether we are aware of it or not. However, even though these observations are often not recorded, they might still influence our instructional decisions. Some teachers keep anecdotal records, jotting down key observations of their students' reading and writing during or at the end of the day. For example, a teacher may note what books a child selected during free time or that a child was able to find the word *cat* in the language experience story that day. Teachers use these informal notes to track individual growth, ascertain the effectiveness of their instruction, and plan future class and small group activities.

Most beginning teachers find it useful to be more systematic in gathering and recording information. One way to do this is by using a checklist. Chittenden and Courtney (1989) recommend that observations be organized according to the contexts in which children learn language. The learning contexts described later in this chapter involve

- reading to children,
- shared-book experiences,
- shared writing (language experience approach),
- writing, and
- functional interactions with print.

Earlier in this chapter, we presented a comprehensive model of the components of emergent literacy, indicating the understanding that young children construct in the early stages of learning to read and write. The checklist in Table 3.2 is organized around attitudes and understandings related to literacy. For each attitude or understanding, behaviours are listed that indicate a child has developed an attitude or understanding in specific learning contexts.

The checklist can be used either as a general guide for unrecorded observations or in a more systematic way to record information on some or all of the children in the class. Used at regular intervals, it provides an indication of a child's progress toward

**Table 3.2   Emergent Literacy Checklist**

| Attitudes and Understandings | Learning Contexts | Behaviours | Comments and Examples |
|---|---|---|---|
| Positive attitude to books and print | Reading to children Shared-book experience | ___ enjoys story time ___ chooses books as free-time activity | |
| | Language experience | ___ rereads language experience stories in free time | |
| | Writing | ___ chooses to write during free time | |
| | Functional interactions with print | ___ shows interest in print around the classroom, school, community | |
| Written language is meaningful | Reading to children and shared-book experience | ___ makes comments or asks questions during story reading | |
| | Shared-book experience | ___ predicts meaningful words during completion reading or when words are covered | |
| | Shared-book and language experience | ___ reproduces meaning as a whole during rereading | |
| | Language experience and interactive writing | ___ contributes ideas during story writing | |
| | Interactive and independent writing | ___ produces meaningful message when reading what has been written | |
| | Functional interactions with print | ___ responds meaningfully to labels, calendar, charts in classroom | |
| Message stays the same | Reading to children, shared-book and language experience | ___ chimes in during reading ___ knows when teacher or another child makes a mistake during rereading | |
| | Functional interactions with print | ___ responds to labels/words same way each time | |
| How written language sounds | Shared-book experience | ___ memorizes favourite books ___ "talks like a book" when rereading | |
| | Language experience and writing | ___ "talks like a book" when dictating/writing stories | |

*(continued)*

**Table 3.2**    Continued

| Attitudes and Understandings | Learning Contexts | Behaviours | Comments and Examples |
|---|---|---|---|
| Story sense | Reading to children and shared-book experience | ___ predicts what will happen in a story | |
| | | ___ retells beginning, middle, and end of stories | |
| | | ___ is able to draw or dramatize stories | |
| | Language experience and writing | ___ includes beginning, middle, and end in stories | |
| Importance of print | Shared-book and language experience | ___ points to print during reading/rereading | |
| | Writing | ___ makes letters or letter-like forms when writing | |
| | Functional interactions with print | ___ points to print in classroom, school, and community | |
| Directional aspects of print | Shared-book and language experience | ___ begins reading at top of page | |
| | | ___ points from left to right when tracking print | |
| | Shared book | ___ reads left page before right page | |
| | Writing | ___ writes from top to bottom of page | |
| | | ___ writes left to right across page | |
| Speech-to-print match | Shared-book and language experience | ___ points to each word while saying it during reading/rereading | |
| Terms and concepts of print | Shared book and language experience | ___ uses terms *letters* and *words* while reading (e.g., "What's this word?") | |
| | Writing | ___ leaves a space between words | |
| | | ___ uses terms *letters* and *words* while writing (e.g., "How do you spell *on*?") | |
| | Shared-book experience, language experience, and writing | ___ uses terms *author, page, sentence* while reading and writing | |
| Decoding/ encoding strategies | Shared-book experience, language experience, and functional print | ___ identifies same word in different contexts | |
| | | ___ uses initial letter sound to help identify words | |
| | Writing | ___ verbalizes letter sounds while writing | |
| | | ___ bases spelling on letter names or sounds | |

constructing particular understandings and is a very useful component in the portfolios of children who are not yet reading independently. The right-hand column in the checklist is a space to record specific comments and examples. For instance, if the teacher has checked "chooses books as free-time activity," this column could include information on what types of books the child chooses (big books, animal books, familiar books), how frequently this happens (every day, once a week), and whether the child reads alone or with another child.

Information gathered on a checklist such as the one in Table 3.2 leads directly to instruction, since specific learning contexts are included as one organizer for the information collected. Consider the following examples of how information collected on this checklist might be interpreted:

- Children who are beginning to point globally at print as they read or reread books are showing that they understand the importance of print (as compared with pictures) in reading.
- When they point to words as the teacher reads, or they read a familiar book or language experience story as the teacher points, children demonstrate that they are ready for speech-to-print matching activities.
- Children who have achieved the speech-to-print match when rereading familiar books or language experience stories show that they are ready for instruction that involves identifying specific words, first in familiar books and language experience stories, and later in less familiar materials.

## Interviews

Parents have a great deal of information that can serve as a basis for planning instruction. Box 3.2 presents questions that teachers can use to solicit information from parents about the reading habits of family members in the home, as well as about the home reading and writing experiences of young children. The children themselves are also able to provide information about their home reading and writing experiences when asked questions such as those provided in Box 3.3.

Although teachers gain considerable information about an individual child's concepts and knowledge by observing them during shared-book experiences, there are times when further information is needed. Several people have developed interview schedules for this purpose. The one in Table 3.3 incorporates questions and concepts from book handling interviews suggested by Doake (1981), Alberta Education (1993), and Clay (1993).

Teachers use information gathered through interviews to supplement that gained as they observe a child's daily reading and writing in the classroom. This information helps the teacher ask a child to respond in ways during shared-book experiences that are consistent with the child's literacy concepts and knowledge. For example, it makes sense to ask a child to find a specific word on a page in a big book only if the child understands the significance of print and knows terms such as *word* and *letter*.

## Collecting Samples of Children's Work

### Emergent Writing

It is much easier to gather the artifacts of children's writing rather than their reading. Teachers often collect writing samples throughout the school year and keep them in a child's writing folder or portfolio. These samples are then analyzed to describe the development of the child's writing.

**Box 3.2**   **Parent Interview Questions**

**Reading and Writing Habits of Family Members**

1. Who reads and writes at home? (mother, father, siblings, others)

2. How much does X (repeat question for each person named in #1) read and write? (every day, twice per week, once per week)

3. What does X read and write? (newspapers, magazines, TV guide, children's books, cookbooks, letters, grocery lists)

4. Why does X read and write? (to learn, for pleasure, to accomplish a particular task)

**Reading to the Child**

5. How often is your child read to? (every day, once per week)

6. Who reads to your child? (mother, father, sibling, other)

7. What books are read? (titles or types of books)

8. What are some of your child's favourite books? (titles)

9. How many books does your child regularly have access to? (at home, the library)

10. How does your child feel about books and being read to? (positive, negative)

11. What does your child do when being read to? (mumbles along, asks questions, wanders away)

12. What does your child do independently with books? (nothing, looks at the pictures, reads aloud to him- or herself)

**The Child's Writing**

13. What types of writing behaviours does your child exhibit? (scribbling, using single letters for words, spelling some words phonetically)

14. How often does your child write? (every day, once per week)

15. What kinds of questions and comments does your child make when he or she is writing? (none, asks about spelling, talks about what he or she is writing)

**Box 3.3**   **Child Interview Questions**

**Family Reading and Writing Habits**

1. Who reads at home?

2. What kinds of things does X (mother, father, sibling, other person) read?

3. Why do you think X (repeat for each person named in #2) reads these things?

4. Who writes at home?

5. What kinds of things does X write?

6. Why do you think X writes these things?

**Child's Home Reading Experiences**

7. Who reads to you at home?

8. Do you enjoy reading? What do you like most about reading?

9. How often does X read to you?

10. Tell me the names of some of your favourite books.

11. Do you read to yourself at home? If so, how often? What do you read? What do you do when you read?

12. Do you write at home? If so, how often? What do you write? What do you do when you write?

**Table 3.3    Book-Handling Interview**

| Questions | Literacy Concepts and Knowledge | Comments |
|---|---|---|
| 1. *How books work* <br> Can you show me the front of the book? <br> Where is the title? What does it tell you? <br> Open the book so we can start reading at the beginning of the story. | ___identifies front of book <br> ___identifies title <br> ___identifies first page of story | |
| 2. *Importance of print* <br> Show me with your finger where to start reading. | ___points to print | |
| 3. *Directional aspects of print* <br> Show me the top/bottom of this page. <br> Show me which page to read first. <br> Show me with your finger which way I go as I read this page. | ___identifies top/bottom of page <br> ___reads left page before right <br> ___points left to right across line of print | |
| 4. *Speech-to-print match* <br> Point to the words as I read. | ___partial matching <br> ___exact matching | |
| 5. *Terms and concepts of print* <br> Point to one letter/word. <br><br> Point to the first/last letter in a word. <br><br> Point to an upper- or lowercase letter. | ___one letter <br> ___one word <br><br> ___first letter <br> ___last letter <br><br> ___uppercase letter <br> ___lowercase letter | |
| 6. *Letter/word identification* <br> Point to the letter __ (name two letters on the page). <br> Point to the word __ (name two high-frequency words on the page). | ___letter names <br><br> ___words | |
| 7. *Meaning in written language* <br> Tell me the story. | ___retells by naming pictures <br> ___retells part of story <br> ___retells beginning, middle, and end | |

Generally, the following stages can be used to describe young children's development of knowledge and concepts related to written language (Neuman and Roskos, 1993):

1. uses drawing for writing,

2. uses pictures and scribble for writing,

3. uses scribble for writing,

4. uses letter-like forms for writing,

5. uses letters (not based on sound) for writing,

6. uses letter names for invented spelling,

7. uses letter sounds for invented spelling, and

8. uses conventional spellings.

Not all children go through all these stages in this order, but a child who is still using scribble for writing is clearly not ready for a heavy focus on conventional spelling. Children also demonstrate growing awareness of directional principles in their writing, moving from scribbles placed in no particular order on the page, to some awareness of directional patterns, to the correct directional pattern (top to bottom, left to right, spaces between words).

Although much of the focus of research has been on the forms of emergent writing, it is important to look beyond these forms to determine children's understanding of the purposes of writing. Even when children scribble, they are indicating that they realize writing and drawing are different. As they begin to use letter or letter-like forms, they show an awareness that writers use symbols when they write. They begin to talk about what they have written (or ask someone to tell them what they have written), indicating that they are aware that written language holds meaning. As they continue to grow, they produce **invented spellings** and are aware that a message is encoded in the words they write.

David, a first-grader whose writing is presented in Exhibit 3.1, talked out loud to himself as he wrote, demonstrating clearly that he was aware he was encoding a message in print. He also reviewed what he had written at one point before writing more. In addition, his writing indicated that he was aware of the importance of directionality to letter identity and that he used letter sounds for spelling. At one point he printed the letter *d* at the top of the page and asked if that was right before writing a word in his story. However, he also used an arithmetic symbol to represent the word *plus* and needed help from his teacher to spell the words *trolls, live,* and *mushroom.*

**Exhibit 3.1** **David's Writing in Grade 1**

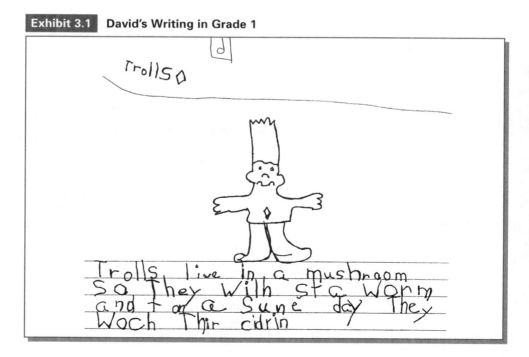

David's writing reflects a greater understanding of the nature of written language than that of another first-grade child, Jillian. When asked to write a story, she produced a labelled drawing (shown in the top part of Exhibit 3.2) for her friend, Ashley. She said that she did the same thing when asked to write at school. When asked to write all the words she could, Jillian produced the list at the bottom of Exhibit 3.2. Many of the same words appear on both lists, and several are the names of important people in her life, including her parents, friend, and sister. In relation to components of emergent literacy, Jillian showed that she was developing an understanding of how we use print to relate to other people. She also knew that words are used in writing, although her picture conveyed most of the message. She demonstrated only a beginning understanding of the alphabetic principle at this stage in her literacy development.

**Exhibit 3.2    Jillian's Writing in Grade 1**

Although general developmental patterns are useful to teachers in assessing children's progress in learning to write, Sulzby (1991) has pointed out that many children, even until mid- or late Grade 1, move between forms and understandings of writing. Whereas a child may write a short sentence using invented spellings and be able to read this sentence accurately on request, he or she might revert to scribbling on a more difficult task such as writing a whole book. From her research, Sulzby feels that this movement between more and less sophisticated writing is part of normal development. With this in mind, we recommend that teachers collect many samples in a variety of contexts rather than a single sample, to provide a more comprehensive picture of a child's literacy than might otherwise result.

## Emergent Reading

When children read orally or silently, no permanent record remains of their reading. While some teachers tape the reading of their kindergarten or Grade 1 children, it is not easy to use these tapes to assess growth. In addition, it takes a great deal of time to listen to tapes of children reading, and it is difficult to remember what the child did on one tape when listening to the next. A practical solution to this challenge is for the teacher to make a written record of a child's reading. Clay (1993) recommends that teachers take "running records" of their children's reading.

To take a running record, the teacher has a child read a book, and as the child does so, the teacher notes in writing what the child says and does. This can be done in one of two ways. In the first, the teacher makes a copy of the text the child will be reading and marks what the child says on that copy. Alternatively, the teacher can use a blank sheet of paper and put a mark for each word the child reads correctly and note any deviations from the text. These two options are shown in Box 3.4. For children in the emergent stage of literacy development, it is more appropriate to use books that they have some degree of familiarity with when taking running records, although it is useful at times to see what they do with a completely unfamiliar book.

**Box 3.4    Taking a Running Record**

Marking system for running records:
  A stroke (/) indicates word read correctly.
  A substituted word is written above the text word.
  An omission is indicated with a circle around the word.
  T indicates the word was provided by the teacher.
  SC indicates that a miscue was self-corrected.

Text: *Whistle, Mary, Whistle* by
Bill Martin, Jr.

Option 1: Making a copy of the text the child is reading

                                            T
"Whistle, Mary, Whistle, and you shall have a trout."

                                            fell
"I can't whistle, Mother, because my tooth is out."

"Whistle, Mary, Whistle, and you shall have a rabbit."

                                  I        my tooth
"I can't whistle, Mother, because I've lost the habit."

                                        dandy
"Whistle, Mary, Whistle, and you shall have a daisy."

                                            T
"I can't whistle, Mother, because it looks so crazy."

Option 2: Using a blank sheet of paper                   Coding

| Text | Coding |
|---|---|
| "Whistle, Mary, Whistle, | / / / |
| and you shall have a trout." | / / / / / T |
| "I can't whistle, Mother, | / / / / |
| because my tooth is out." | / / / fell /<br>         is |
| "Whistle, Mary, Whistle, | / / / |
| and you shall have a rabbit." | / / / / / / (used picture<br>cue for rabbit) |
| "I can't whistle, Mother, | / / / / |
| because I've lost the habit." | / I / my tooth<br>I've the habit |
| "Whistle, Mary, Whistle, | / / / |
| and you shall have a daisy." | / / / / / dandy<br>       daisy |
| "I can't whistle, Mother, | / / / / |
| because it looks so crazy." | / / / / T |

One way of analyzing children's reading is to examine their running records in relation to stages reported in the literature. The following stages are based on the work of Sulzby (1985) and Neuman and Roskos (1993):

1. pays attention to pictures, labelling objects rather than forming a story,
2. pays attention to pictures, making up a story from the pictures,

3. pays attention to pictures, telling a version of the story,
4. pays attention to pictures, and talks like a book,
5. pays attention to print, identifying some words and inventing the rest to produce a meaningful version of the story,
6. pays attention to print, focussing primarily on word identification, and
7. pays attention to both print and meaning cues, reading fluently.

All children do not go through all these stages, but it is clear that most begin by focussing on pictures and most need to spend some time internalizing and telling stories before they are ready to profit from a heavy focus on print. David, whose miscues are shown in Box 3.4, was paying attention to both print and meaning cues and was approaching reading fluency.

Another way of analyzing running records is to code deviations from the text in relation to what type of information the child used to produce these deviations. Goodman (1969) coined the word **miscues** to refer to these deviations rather than the word "errors" because he believes that they provide us with a great deal of useful information about how children read. As they read, he says, they are constantly using picture, print, and context cues to predict words, and their miscues provide insight into which cues they are using. Miscue analysis involves looking at each miscue the child has made and relating it to the information sources being used by the child. For classroom purposes, we recommend a simplified system for analyzing miscues, although more sophisticated systems may be necessary for children who have significant difficulty learning to read.

Children use two major sources of information as they read: print information and background knowledge. To become good readers, they need to integrate both sources of information so that what they read makes sense and is consistent with the print information. In our simplified miscue analysis, we recommend that you look at each miscue a child made and ask yourself two questions:

1. Does the word the child said look like the word in the text (thus indicating use of print cues)?
2. Does the word the child said make sense (thus indicating use of background knowledge)?

If the word the child says contains any of the letters in the text word, write the letter *P* above the word to indicate use of print cues. If the miscue makes sense up to that point, write the letter *M* above it to indicate use of meaning cues. Box 3.5 shows how David's miscues were coded using this simplified system of analysis.

Miscues are then interpreted as follows:

- Miscues with only a *P* above them indicate that the child uses print cues, but does not rely on his or her knowledge to make a meaningful prediction.

**Box 3.5   Coding of David's Miscues on a Predictable Book**

P: miscue contains at least one letter in the text word
M: miscue makes sense in relation to prior text

T
"Whistle, Mary, Whistle, and you shall have a trout."

M
*fell*
"I can't whistle, Mother, because my tooth is out."

"Whistle, Mary, Whistle, and you shall have a rabbit."

PM      M   PM
*I*        *my  tooth*
"I can't whistle, Mother, because I've lost the habit."

P
*dandy*
"Whistle, Mary, Whistle, and you shall have a daisy."

T
"I can't whistle, Mother, because it looks so crazy."

- Miscues with only an *M* above them indicate that the child uses his or her knowledge to predict a word that makes sense, but does not use print cues.
- Miscues with both a *P* and an *M* above them indicate that the child may be using both print cues and background knowledge.
- Miscues with neither a *P* or an *M* above them indicate that the child is unable to make effective use of either print cues or background knowledge.

A simple count of the number of miscues of each type in Box 3.5 shows that two were coded as meaningful, one as using print cues, and two as using both print and meaning cues. In addition, David waited for help from the teacher on two words, suggesting that he was focussing on print cues, even though he was unable to identify the words from these cues. Overall, this analysis of David's miscues shows that he is attending to both meaning and print cues but does not always use the cues together. He also does not correct any of his miscues, which suggests that either he is unaware that what he is reading doesn't make sense or look right or he has not yet developed enough facility with using print and meaning cues to self-correct.

In the actual classroom situation, we would want to analyze a larger sample of David's miscues to confirm this interpretation. However, from both the running record in Box 3.4 and the writing sample in Exhibit 3.1, it is clear that David has considerable knowledge about how books work. He also knows that written language is meaningful and is developing strategies for encoding and decoding words on the basis of print and sound cues. He has constructed many of the understandings involved in emergent literacy and is rapidly reaching independence in reading and writing.

As with writing, Jillian's stage of reading development is different from David's. When asked if telling and reading a story are the same, she answered, "Yes," and she also indicated that people can't read with their eyes closed because they can't see the pictures. When asked to read a familiar, predictable book (*A Dark, Dark Tale*), she was highly successful, relying primarily on memory of sentence patterns and picture cues. When introduced to an unfamiliar, predictable book, she was able to use her excellent auditory memory and language abilities along with picture cues to read the book with a high degree of accuracy after only two readings. When asked what kinds of books she read at school, Jillian proceeded to "read" one without the text in front of her. She used story book language and maintained a high degree of accuracy with the absent text, making a correction at one point to insert a line she had forgotten to include. Although Jillian knew a lot about books and book language, she was just beginning to develop an understanding of the forms of written language and of how written and oral language are related.

Finding out where children are in their literacy development is a necessary component of effective instruction, but it is clearly not enough. The biggest challenge is planning programs to meet the needs identified. The next two sections are designed to help you construct ideas to meet this challenge.

## Planning for Instruction

We begin by presenting some general guidelines for planning literacy instruction, and follow with a section on specific instructional strategies that facilitate young children's literacy development.

Parents are no longer told not to teach their children to read and write at home as they were in the middle of this century. Instead, it is now almost universally accepted that the home plays a crucial role in literacy development, and parents are being urged to read to their children from an early age. Children's literacy learning at home is frequently referred to as natural, and some educators argue that the developmental model used in the home should be extended to the school. These educators have done much to foster meaningful literacy programs for young children, and some of the principles outlined below are based on their work (e.g., Holdaway, 1979).

Other educators question whether the obvious lessons derived from home literacy can or should lead to prescriptions for the classroom (Sulzby, Teale, and Kamberelis, 1989). They contend that a heavy focus on natural literacy learning may lead to literacy programs devoted entirely to providing children with opportunities to read and write but little more. Most educators today agree that direct, explicit instruction is needed for most children learning to read and write. It is the focus of this instruction that is in question. The following general instructional principles reflect a range of perspectives as well as the recognition that children come to school from a wide variety of literacy environments.

## Rich Literacy Environment

Children who learn to read early are generally immersed in a literate home environment. They own books and are read to regularly by their parents. They are surrounded by print in their homes and communities, ranging from books to television commercials, signs, toys, newspapers, letters, and bills. They see their parents and other people in their home and communities reading and writing on a daily basis. Kindergarten and first-grade classrooms that are print-rich enable children to be involved daily in meaningful, purposeful literacy activities. When written language is used in authentic ways by their teacher and others, children are encouraged to view reading and writing as functional and worthwhile.

The following two examples help to distinguish between authentic literacy experiences and those that are more contrived. In one classroom, a teacher decides to increase the children's familiarity with signs in their community and to do so develops worksheets depicting frequently occurring signs such as stop signs, walk lights, restaurant signs, and signs on washroom doors. The teacher asks the children to say what they think the signs mean and what they should do when they see each sign. The teacher then puts the words on flash cards for the children to practise reading. Contrast this with another classroom where the children are planning to bake cookies and need to go to a local store to buy the ingredients. They first consult a recipe to determine what ingredients are needed, and then make a list to take to the store. On the way to the store, they talk about traffic signs. Once at the store, they locate the products needed. The major difference between these two classrooms is that, in the first, the goal is the reading of signs for their own sake. In the second, which involves more authentic learning, the goal is to get to a store to purchase products in order to make cookies.

## Daily Reading and Writing

Children do not learn to read and write by cutting out or colouring pictures, although this may develop their fine motor co-ordination. Similarly, children do not learn to read and write by working together to build a house out of blocks, although they may learn to work co-operatively and develop visual–motor perceptual skills.

In addition to being immersed in print-rich environments, we believe that children need to interact with books every day. For those who have been read to regularly by their parents before entering school, this will be a direct extension of home experiences, and they will know what to expect from and what to do with books. For other children, books and being read to will be less familiar. These children benefit from daily opportunities to play with and handle books, as well as from being involved in book-sharing activities. We also believe that children need to be involved in writing activities on a regular basis. Again this will be an extension of home experiences for some, but it will be relatively new for others. Through these activities, children have opportunities to see others write, to have their ideas written by someone else, and to experiment freely with their own writing.

## Control over Literacy Learning

Children who learn to read and write at home frequently have considerable control over their own literacy learning (Doake, 1981; Juliebö, 1985). They decide when and how long they write, and although they may not get their parents to read to them as often or as long as they would like, children often choose the book that will be read. These children frequently select the same book day after day and, by doing so, develop favourites that they practically memorize. As they reread the books independently, they have an opportunity to engage in eye–voice matching. They engage in as much practice as they want in order to develop control over whatever aspect of written language they are ready to handle. If parents attempt to involve children in some aspect they are not ready for, children often ignore the parents' questions or stop the activity. Essentially the children choose what they want to do or learn, and the parents help to facilitate their learning.

Parents are frequently surprised by how long their children are able to spend on a reading or writing activity. They are also often dismayed at how often their children want to have the same book read over and over again. Teachers frequently do not reread books to children, nor do they provide extensive opportunities for young children to reread the books that have been read to the class. But children need to achieve mastery over written language, and only by having numerous opportunities to practise will they develop this mastery and control.

Although children do not have as much control over what is read in the classroom as they do at home, teachers can certainly encourage their students to suggest books they would like to hear, particularly when rereading. In addition to group activities (such as compiling group language experience charts based on the experiences of several children rather than one), children benefit from opportunities to dictate stories or letters to guests or parents. Ownership is important for children as they learn how to read and write; it is even more critical to their becoming avid readers and writers.

## Acceptance of Approximations

Babies are given enthusiastic reinforcement by their parents the first time they say something that even remotely resembles "mama" or "daddy." Parents are not concerned that their child does not articulate every sound correctly. Similarly, when children are rereading their favourite books or pretending to write a letter to their grandmother, parents rarely insist on accurate reading or spelling, partly because they do not view these activities as real reading and writing. Doake (1988, p. 34) presents the following example of a mother reading *Brown Bear, Brown Bear, What Do You See?*

with her preschool daughter. Words the mother reads are presented in bold; what Adrienne says is in italics.

| Text | Adrienne and Her Mother |
|------|-------------------------|
| I see a blue horse. | **I see a** (mother pauses) ... **blue** (pauses) ... *horse* |
| Looking at me. | **looking** (pauses) |
|  | *look ... at me.* |
|  | *Tail!* (Adrienne points to the tail on the horse.) |
|  | **Yes.** (Mother responds and continues reading.) |
| Blue horse | **Blue horse** |
| Blue horse | *Blue horse* |
| What do you see? | **What do you see?** |
|  | *see?* |
| I see a gray mouse | **I see a** (pauses) |
|  | *gay mouse* |
| Looking at me | **Looking** (pauses) ... **at me**. |

Doake notes that the whole book was read in this manner, and not once did Adrienne's mother correct any miscues. Instead, she invited her daughter to participate in the reading activity, modelling correct responses when her daughter was unable to respond and accepting approximations of correct responses. In contrast, once a child is receiving language arts instruction at school, both parents and teachers often have a difficult time accepting approximate answers.

This reflects the traditional notion that children need to engage in word-perfect reading and letter-perfect spelling right from the beginning, a notion that has come under considerable criticism in recent years. Learning, when viewed from a constructivist perspective, involves exploring and actively constructing knowledge. The responses of children who learn to read and write before school entry gain closer and closer resemblance to conventional reading and writing. These children do not move from not being able to read and write one day to 100 percent perfect reading and writing the next (Doake, 1988). Children who are discouraged from reading or writing unless they can do it perfectly may become reluctant readers and writers. We are not suggesting that exact spelling and word identification are unimportant. Rather, we are arguing that this is not an appropriate goal until after a child develops an understanding of the components of emergent literacy.

## Differences among Learners

There is ample evidence that children arrive at school with differences in their knowledge about reading and writing. Heath's early study of children from different socio-economic environments (1983), referred to in Chapter One, still provides some of the best evidence we have in this regard. While children from all three communities in her study were immersed in literate environments, only the children from Maintown and to a lesser extent Roadville were involved in the kind of environment provided in schools.

The children of Roadville were read to by their parents and involved in other literacy activities, such as writing thank-you notes to relatives. They heard their parents talk about how important reading was, but rarely saw them reading and writing. The children were expected to answer specific questions about what they had read and, when retelling a story, to stay with rather than embellish the story line. Roadville children were tended to, encouraged, talked to, and generally prepared for dealing with everyday tasks such as making cookies, mowing the lawn, and fixing a bicycle. They were "given few occasions for extended narratives, imaginative flights of establishing new contexts, or manipulating features of an event or item" (Heath, 1983, p. 352). Thus, while they were ready for some aspects of school literacy and were successful in the initial stages of literacy instruction, they were not prepared for higher-level school literacy demands.

The children from Trackton had not been read to by their parents, and no stories had been told for them by parents or older children. Instead, the children observed numerous group debates over what letters, notices, or bills meant and listened to adults tell stories to one another. Stories were rarely reflections of what actually happened or retellings of a story read. Rather, good storytellers based their stories on actual events and real people but creatively fictionalized the details surrounding the real event. The primary message was of accomplishments, victories over adversities, or cleverness in the face of an enemy, and these stories had to be good in order to hold the audience's attention. This type of storytelling did not prepare children for the decontextualized story experiences of early schooling. Their "abilities to contextualize, to remember what may seem to the teacher to be an unrelated event as similar to another, to link seemingly disparate factors in their explanations, and to create highly imaginative stories" (Heath, 1983, p. 353) were suppressed in the primary classroom, and Trackton children fell quickly into a pattern of school failure. Parents from all three communities in Heath's study had a strong desire for their children to get ahead and depended on the school to play a critical role in their children's future. However, only the Maintown people were able to provide their children with home experiences that matched the expectations of the school.

What should schools do to ensure that all children learn to read and write? Purcell-Gates (1998) believes that we need to begin with the assumption that all children are learners:

> The notion that some children, because they hold different concepts about written language, are not ready to learn is nonsense. All children are not only ready to learn, they have been learning from birth. What this not-ready-to-learn dictum is really about is the fact that not all children are ready to learn from, or can make sense of, the curriculum presented to them in schools. Thus the issue becomes one of curriculum, not children. (p. 66)

From this perspective, Purcell-Gates recommends that teachers figure out where each child is in his or her literacy development and provide appropriate instruction. This does not apply only to children from different socio-economic environments, but also to children who have been labelled as having learning disabilities or mild mental handicaps. When teachers set appropriate goals and provide instruction to meet these goals, Purcell-Gates believes that the children will achieve success and not become discouraged.

There is considerable similarity in the literacy needs of children at the emergent stage of development regardless of whether they speak English as a first or second language, whether they have grown up in mainstream or other cultural environments, or whether they have been labelled as special needs learners or not. All benefit from being immersed in a meaningful, purposeful literacy environment and from having numerous opportunities for meaningful interaction with written language.

Teachers who have children from different cultural backgrounds in their classrooms recognize the importance of understanding and respecting the culture of all children. When teachers incorporate books and other experiences related to children's culture, the children are more likely to feel included in the classroom community. Similarly, when teachers are aware of differences in storytelling and interaction patterns in different cultural groups, they tend to accept all children's stories, and discontinuity between home and school is reduced.

Hough and Nurss (1992) believe that early childhood classrooms are generally well suited to the needs of ESL learners. Most early childhood classrooms provide numerous opportunities for concrete activities and small group interactions, and these types of literacy experiences are appropriate for both ESL learners and children whose first language is English. However, teachers of children with limited English proficiency often make two major adaptations. First, they ensure that input is comprehensible by making some changes in their language and using gestures and visual aids for the ESL learner. Second, as with all children from different cultures, the teacher takes conscious steps to ensure that ESL children feel they are part of the classroom group and that their culture is respected.

We are not suggesting that early childhood teachers can meet the needs of all children in their classrooms without assistance. Children with more severe learning problems, such as language delays, attention deficit disorders, and sensory impairments, need to be referred to appropriate specialists for assistance in planning appropriate programs.

## Sequence of Instruction

Although we do not believe that all children go through the same invariant stages in learning to read and write, some understandings do seem to come before others for most children. In relation to the components of emergent literacy delineated earlier in this chapter, children generally construct knowledge about the functions of written language (why people read and write) before they develop an understanding that oral and written language are related. Eye–voice matching is still a later development or construction. Similarly, for most children, being able to eye–voice match precedes understanding the alphabetic principle and being able to map letters onto sounds when spelling or to map sounds onto letters when reading (Morris, 1993).

The order of components presented in Box 3.1 provides a rough sequential order appropriate for many children. This is consistent with stages in the reading development of young children identified by Sulzby (1985) and Neuman and Roskos (1993), in which children move from a focus on pictures and meaning to a focus on print and finally to a focus on both at the same time. It is also consistent with the writing development of young children.

Harste, Woodward, and Burke (1984) have found that from the earliest stages of writing, children engage in intentional behaviour. They understand that people use "specific marks to sign specific meanings" (p. 108). Uses of written language generally precede forms in the writing development of young children. A heavy focus on form in the initial stages of learning to write often results in children becoming reluctant to write anything at all, as shown in the example presented in Exhibit 3.3. The school involved in this example is in an inner-city neighbourhood, and the first-grade child moved to the school when she went to live with her aunt and uncle at the end of September during Grade 1.

**Exhibit 3.3**  **Amber Learns to Read and Write**

When Amber arrived at Kathy Purkiss' Grade 1 class-room at the end of September, she appeared to have limited literacy background (Malicky, Purkiss, and Nugent, 1988–89). When asked to read predictable books (*Brown Bear, Brown Bear, What Do You See?* and *A Dark, Dark Tale*), she demonstrated a very positive attitude toward books generally and was able to "talk like a book." Her reading was meaningful although she was not yet able to match spoken to printed words or to rely on print cues to identify words. In sharp contrast with her reading, she viewed writing as a process of spelling words correctly and was very reluctant to write.

Amber was given one-to-one instruction for five months twice weekly using primarily shared reading, the language experience approach, and writing. Making steady progress in reading throughout the sessions, she was able to match spoken to printed words by mid-November and had begun to make use of print cues as she read. She also began to take familiar books and her language experience stories to her classroom to read to other children. This helped her to feel like a reader and gave her a sense of belonging to the "literacy club" (Smith, 1988) in her classroom.

Developing Amber's writing was more problematic. She was reluctant to write on her own and, when urged to try, produced short sentences of letters such as *I b swh* for "I like skipping." These written products were far less rich than the language experience stories she dictated, indicating that she thought she had to write and spell like adults do.

By late January, both of Amber's teachers were quite concerned with her progress in writing. Finally, the intervention teacher used a strategy recommended by Sulzby, Teale, and Kamberelis (1989). She assured Amber that her writing didn't have to be like grown-up writing, that no one else would read it. Tompkins (1997) has also indicated that "kid writing" is important for young children because it gives them permission to experiment with written language. Amber then began to write, generating the piece reproduced below.

When asked to reread what she had written, she read the alphabet first (the safe part) and then, pointing to the print line by line, read, "The elves made a castle for Santa to build his toys for the kids in the L. family. Santa likes to give out toys from the Christmas tree for all the kids." She smiled happily to herself when she finished reading. With reinforcement, Amber wrote another meaning-based story in the next session. She finally felt free to engage in the type of writing most young children do in the early stages of literacy development, and this appeared to be a necessary step in her writing development. By the end of January, she was beginning to include inventive spellings in her writing.

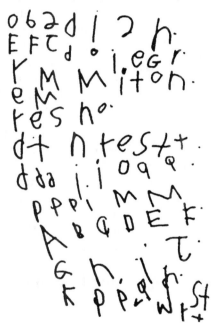

Although the development of reading and writing are not parallel, there are some similarities. Children initially approach both from a sense-making perspective, and they move from approximations of reading and writing to more conventional forms. Hence, while there is no fixed, hierarchical order to the components in Box 3.1, most children construct their understandings in approximately the order presented. Because learners are different, however, it is important that teachers continuously assess children's literacy development and base instruction on that assessment.

Purcell-Gates (1998) offers the following general suggestions. First, she notes that the literacy experiences provided at school must be appropriate for the emergent literacy component involved. For example, if we want children to learn to eye–voice match as they read, we need to use connected texts rather than isolated words. If we want them to learn the alphabetic principle, we need to have children listen to sounds in words as they write them and to look at words when they are reading. Second, Purcell-Gates recommends that, embedded in these activities, teachers give direct and explicit explanations to children. For example, when children are writing, she recommends that we point out and use labels for letters, words, and sentences. We also need to show children how to hear separate sounds in words and what letters go with these sounds. Third, Purcell-Gates recommends that some crucial constructs such as the alphabetic principle be taught systematically and explicitly. Overall, what she and many others are recommending is a balanced literacy program for young children, including a focus on all aspects of emergent literacy and involving both incidental and systematic instruction.

## School Experiences That Facilitate Literacy Development

In this section, we present a range of literacy experiences designed to help children construct knowledge about the components of emergent literacy outlined earlier in this chapter. These are organized according to teaching/learning contexts rather than emergent literacy components, because each type of context has the potential to develop several of the components. Table 3.4 presents an overview of teaching/learning contexts presented in this section, indicating emergent literacy components that can be developed in each context.

For each of the teaching/learning contexts described in this section, we present suggestions for instruction to help children develop specific understandings about literacy and strategies for dealing with print. We recommend that, in the initial stages of literacy development, most instruction on specific skills and strategies be presented within the context of reading and writing activities. Once children have developed basic understandings about the functions, nature, and forms of written language, systematic instruction about how print works is appropriate. Suggestions for this type of instruction are provided in Chapters Six and Nine.

### Reading to Children

Children's books provide the basis for a significant portion of the emergent literacy program. Young children benefit from a wide range of experiences with books, including hearing their teacher read books to them, reading with their teacher, reading in groups, and reading independently. They also need exposure to a wide range of books, including picture story books, **predictable books**, big books, nursery rhymes and poetry, information books, and ABC and counting books. Lists of books appropriate for reading to young children are presented in Chapter Ten.

While teachers have been reading to children for decades, many were not aware of all that this activity achieves, and it was often discontinued once children were able to read independently. In the past, teachers often told children to sit and listen quietly so as not to interrupt the reading. Thus, classroom reading was frequently very different from the interactive bedtime reading children experienced at home. Today, educators who hold a constructivist perspective recommend that teachers encourage children to talk about ideas in books before, during, and after the teacher reads (Mason, Peterman, and Kerr, 1989). The nature of the interaction varies depending on whether the teacher is reading a **narrative** or an informational book.

Before Reading  The major understanding children develop at this stage of the reading is that written language is meaningful. They also develop understanding of different purposes for reading as they talk about what to expect in different types of books. It is often the development of an anticipatory set that enables readers to track the meanings that are being created during reading. This set provides readers with a valuable source of information for identifying new words and self-correcting miscues.

- For all books, teachers draw children's attention to the picture on the cover and have them predict what they think the book is about. They encourage children to talk about their own experiences related to the topic or story. The children are also asked to predict whether the book will tell a story or tell about something.
- For informational books, teachers may need to demonstrate key concepts in the book if it becomes clear that several children have limited knowledge to bring to the topic.

During Reading
- While reading any book, teachers encourage the children to react to and comment on the story or ideas as they listen. Teachers also ask questions occasionally to monitor children's understanding of the story or ideas.
- For informational books, teachers may need to give demonstrations or examples of difficult ideas. These are based on the children's responses and teachers help by encouraging children to ask questions when they don't understand something.
- When reading story books, teachers rephrase the text when it is clear the children do not understand something. They also ask the children periodically to evaluate their earlier predictions and to formulate new ones. It is important for children to evaluate their own predictions rather than having the teacher do it for them.

After Reading
- For all books, children are asked to talk about what they have heard, relating the story or ideas to their own experiences.
- For stories, teachers often have children briefly retell the beginning, middle, and end in order to develop knowledge of story structure.

## Shared-Book Experiences

To emulate the reading experience young children have in literate homes, Holdaway (1979) recommends that teachers use enlarged or "big" books so that all children can see the print and that teachers read *with* rather than *to* children. Predictable books are particularly useful for this purpose, because the repetitive and rhythmic structure of the text supports early reading attempts. A list of predictable and big books is presented in Box 3.6. Other picture books suitable for shared-book experiences are listed in Chapter Ten.

Children construct different understandings about written language from shared-book experiences depending on the literacy backgrounds they bring with them. Children who have been read to a lot at home will likely construct understandings about the forms of written language and the nature of the print–speech relationship. However, for children with more limited book experience, the goal of instruction might be developing positive attitudes toward books or helping children understand the functions and nature of written language.

Although teachers sometimes group children according to literacy background, most of the time they provide shared-book experiences for the whole class. Because of

**Box 3.6** Predictable Books

*Ahlberg, J. and Ahlberg, A. (1978). *Each Peach Pear Plum*. New York: Scholastic Book Services.

Baum, A. and Baum, J. (1962). *One Bright Monday Morning*. New York: Random House.

Becker, J. (1973). *Seven Little Rabbits*. New York: Scholastic Book Services.

*Bonne, R. (1981). *A Dark, Dark Tale*. New York: Scholastic Book Services.

Carle, E. (1977). *The Grouchy Ladybug*. New York: Thomas Y. Crowell.

Carle, E. (1983). *The Very Hungry Caterpillar*. New York: Scholastic Book Services.

Carle, E. (1984). *The Very Busy Spider*. New York: Philomel.

*Cowley, J. (1980). *Mrs. Wishy-Washy*. Auckland, NZ: Shortland Publications.

*Cowley, J. (1983). *The Jigaree*. Auckland, NZ: Shortland Publications.

*Cowley, J. (1983). *Who Will Be My Mother?* Auckland, NZ: Shortland Publications.

Cranstoun, M. (1967). *1, 2, Buckle My Shoe*. New York: Holt, Rinehart & Winston.

Keats, E.J. (1971). *Over in the Meadow*. New York: Scholastic Book Services.

Martin, Jr., B. (1970). *The Haunted House*. New York: Holt, Rinehart & Winston.

Martin, Jr., B. (1970). *King of the Mountain*. New York: Holt, Rinehart & Winston.

*Martin, Jr., B. (1970). *Monday, Monday, I Like Monday*. New York: Holt, Rinehart & Winston.

Martin, Jr., B. (1970). *When It Rains, It Rains*. New York: Holt, Rinehart & Winston.

*Martin, Jr., B. (1972). *Brown Bear, Brown Bear, What Do You See?* New York: Holt, Rinehart & Winston.

Mayer, M. (1975). *Just for You*. New York: Golden Press.

*Melser, J. (1980). *Sing a Song*. Auckland, NZ: Shortland Publications.

*Morris, W.B. (1970). *The Longest Journey in the World*. New York: Holt, Rinehart & Winston.

Scheer, J., and Bileck, M., (1964). *Rain Makes Applesauce*. New York: Holiday House.

Sutton, E. (1973). *My Cat Likes to Hide in Boxes*. New York: Parents Magazine Press.

Tolstoy, A. (1968). *The Great Big Enormous Turnip*. New York: Franklin Watts.

Wing, H.R. (1963). *What Is Big?* New York: Holt, Rinehart & Winston.

*Available in "big book" form

differences in children's knowledge about literacy, however, teachers expect — and reinforce — different kinds of responses from different children. For example, while one child is developing an understanding of the alphabetic principle, another might be just beginning to internalize the language of books. A repetitive book is useful for both of these children, and they will both be able to predict words when teachers stop reading at predictable points during shared reading. However, only the first child will be able to respond to the teacher's invitation to point to the words in a line of print while it is being read.

Hough and Nurss (1992) believe that predictable books are well suited to the needs of children with limited English proficiency. These children can join in reading the repetitive parts of the story before individual words have become meaningful to them. Rereading both predictable and other picture story books is recommended for all children, including those learning English as their second language. This rereading provides ESL children with further exposure to written English and also helps them internalize the structure of stories written by authors who write from a Western cultural perspective. Having children dramatize familiar stories creates further opportunities for developing language and internalizing story structures. Picture story books with lots of action and repeated sequences, such as *The Three Billy Goats Gruff*, are particularly appropriate for this type of activity.

Holdaway (1979) outlines three basic steps in a shared-book experience:

1. discovery (initial reading of the book),
2. exploration (rereadings in the group), and
3. independent experience (individual and small group rereadings and follow-up activities).

Discovery  Holdaway argues that the most critical goal of the teacher when reading a new book is to provide an enjoyable experience for all children. This goal should not be sacrificed to any other purpose. The teacher encourages maximum participation of the children through talking with them about the book and asking and answering questions, as many parents do during bedtime reading. One way to encourage participation at this stage of the shared-book experience is to have children whisper a prediction to their partner once the teacher has set the stage. It is important for the teacher to organize the children so they can all see each page.

The guidelines presented above for story book interactions before, during, and after reading are also appropriate for predictable big books. In addition, teachers may ask some children to predict words in the title before they begin reading, drawing attention to both picture and letter cues to do so.

During reading of predictable books, teachers often point to words as they read, demonstrating for the children the one-to-one correspondence between oral and written words and emphasizing the left-to-right and top-to-bottom directional nature of print. They also encourage children to read along, sometimes stopping their reading at highly predictable places so that the children can fill in the text. The children are encouraged to use both context as well as letter cues to make and confirm their predictions. Teachers talk about aspects of the text using the terms children need to learn. For example, "The first word in this sentence is ... ," and "There is a question mark at the end of this sentence, so we need to sound as if we are asking a question when we read it."

Exploration  Various group activities provide further opportunities for children to interact with the book. These include

- rereadings,
- innovations on literary structures, and
- interpretations of the story through dramatization or art.

Children learn about the nature and forms of written language, and they begin to construct an understanding of the speech–print relationship through involvement in these activities.

Rereadings of predictable big books are often done at the request of children. With this type of book, children are encouraged to join in the reading as much as possible to learn the language of books. Teachers encourage group choral reading of the book, reading along with the children when they need support. By pointing to words as they read, teachers help children to hear the words as separate units and to match them with printed words on the page. By rereading the book several times, children are able to internalize the oral language they need in order to establish eye–voice matching when later reading the book independently or in a small group.

The teacher also uses the rereading time to focus on print and use of letter sounds to identify words. The teacher asks children questions such as "Where do I begin reading?" "Find words that begin with the letter *m*," and "What is this word?"

Reading nursery rhymes and other rhyming books and poetry to children helps focus their attention on the sounds in words. For many children, reading this type of material begins in the home, but teachers cannot assume children have knowledge of common nursery rhymes. Predictable books such as *1, 2, Buckle My Shoe* contain rhyming words, and children are encouraged to talk about which words rhyme. By seeing rhymes in big book format or on charts, children not only hear which words rhyme, but also learn that when words sound the same they often also look the same. When reading predictable rhyming books such as *Whistle, Mary, Whistle* to children, teachers often leave out the rhyming word so the children can predict them. For example, "Whistle, Mary, Whistle, and you shall have some bread. I can't whistle, Mother, because I'm standing on my _____."

The teacher also asks children to talk about the words that begin with a particular sound. In *1,2, Buckle My Shoe*, for example, "What words begin with the sound at the beginning of the word *fun*?" When children respond, *four*, *five*, and *fat*, they are directed to the book and helped to discover that these words also begin with the same letter. Teachers are cautioned here not to isolate sounds, because many are distorted when pronounced in isolation. While it is fairly easy to isolate sounds for letters such as *s*, *f*, and *m* without distorting them, it is far more difficult to produce isolated sounds for letters such as *b*, *d*, *g*, *p*, *t*, *k*, *j*, and *ch* without distortion. The sound for *b* often ends up with a schwa on the end and sounds a lot like *buh*.

Research shows that in the initial stages, it is easier for children to hear rhyming words and sounds at the beginning of words than sounds in the middle or at the end (Goswami and Bryant, 1990). To encourage children to begin using knowledge of letter sounds to identify words, the teacher might also cover all except the first letter of a word in a sentence and ask the children to predict the word using cues from sentence context and the first letter. We present more systematic ways to develop phonemic awareness and phonics knowledge in Chapter Six.

Bill Martin, Jr., who has written several predictable books, recommends that teachers have children innovate on literary structures to help them develop greater awareness of the language of books. For example, near Hallowe'en, the children can generate a Hallowe'en book based on the structure of *Brown Bear, Brown Bear, What Do You See?* It might go something like this:

White ghost, white ghost, what do you see?
I see a black cat looking at me.
Black cat, black cat, what do you see?
I see a green witch looking at me.

As the children dictate, the teacher writes this story on large chart paper for them to illustrate. The story can later be used both for group and independent rereadings.

A further and often deeper interpretation of stories is achieved through giving children the chance to dramatize or illustrate what they have read. Specific ideas for incorporating drama into literacy activities are presented in Chapter Twelve.

**Independent Experience** Big books that have been reread are placed in a reading centre for children to read independently or in small groups. Children reread the books as often as they wish, relying on meaning and print cues to reconstruct the text. They are encouraged to point to words as they read in order to more fully establish eye–voice matching.

To increase the exposure of young children to shared-book experiences and give them control over the number of times they hear favourite stories, a listening centre with taped books is invaluable. Tapes can be obtained commercially or produced by having volunteers or older children read and record stories.

Children's books are also now available in an interactive format for use on computers. *WiggleWorks* and *Living Books* are both highly interactive, providing children with an opportunity to listen or read along. These and other interactive books are described in more detail in Chapter Thirteen.

Perhaps most important to putting young children within easy and continuous reach of children's books is giving them regular access to a library. A classroom library is an important source of these books in kindergarten and Grade 1, but children also need to visit the school library often. This gives them an opportunity to use print to locate books and develop the habit of regular library use.

## Shared Writing: The Language Experience Approach

The language experience approach builds on children's own experiences and language as a source of material to be used for reading instruction. Children essentially tell a story or recount an experience, and the teacher acts as a scribe, writing what the children say. Although the language experience approach has been used in classrooms for several decades, understanding the nature of emergent literacy has led to an increased appreciation of its role in literacy development. As with shared-book experiences, the language experience approach is aimed at helping children construct understandings of many components of emergent literacy (see Table 3.4).

Teachers develop language experience stories with the whole class, with small groups, and with individuals. As with shared-book experiences, children at varying levels of literacy development can work effectively together on a language experience story, although the language learning will differ for each child.

**Table 3.4    A Balanced Emergent Literacy Program**

| Teaching/Learning Context | Emergent Literacy Component |
|---|---|
| **Reading to Children**<br>Teachers select quality children's literature and read to the whole class or small groups. They invite children to talk about ideas before, during, and after the reading. | • Positive attitudes toward books and reading<br>• Meaningful nature of written language<br>• Language of books<br>• Knowledge of text structure |
| **Shared-Book Experiences**<br>Teachers and children read "big books" together. The initial reading is followed up by group and individual readings of the same book. | • Positive attitudes toward books and reading<br>• Meaningful nature of written language<br>• Relationship between oral and written language<br>• Language of books<br>• Eye–voice matching<br>• Difference between pictures and print<br>• Terms related to books and written language<br>• Conventions of print<br>• Alphabetic principle |
| **Shared Writing (Language Experience Approach)**<br>Teachers and children write together; the children generate the ideas and the teacher does the scribing. The material generated is read by the whole class, small groups, and individuals and is also used for follow-up activities. | • Meaningful nature of written language<br>• Relationship between oral and written language<br>• Eye–voice matching<br>• Terms related to reading and writing<br>• Conventions of print<br>• Alphabetic principle |

*(continued)*

**Table 3.4    Continued**

| Teaching/Learning Context | Emergent Literacy Component |
|---|---|
| **Interactive and Independent Writing**<br>Teachers and children write together with a "shared" pen. Children also engage in daily independent writing. | • Positive attitudes toward writing<br>• Meaningful nature of written language<br>• Relationship between oral and written language<br>• Terms related to writing<br>• Conventions of print<br>• Alphabetic principle |
| **Functional Interactions with Print**<br>Teachers and children use print to get things done (e.g., organize the classroom, go on field trips, prepare food). | • Purposes of reading and writing<br>• Meaningful nature of written language<br>• Relationship between oral and written language<br>• Eye–voice matching<br>• Alphabetic principle |

The following description of the language experience approach has been adapted from ideas presented by Hall (1981). Teachers who use this approach place greater emphasis on the process of developing and using language experience stories, believing this to be more important than the final product itself.

1. *Experience.* Language experience stories begin with an experience. Trips, pets, classroom events, wordless picture books, pictures, and television provide springboards for discussion. When the children in one first-grade class visited another classroom in their school where chicks were hatching, their teacher, Susan Bennett, saw that this created an excellent opportunity to develop a language experience story.

2. *Discussion.* This is an essential step in the language experience approach, as discussion provides children with an opportunity to develop both the vocabulary and the sentence structures that will eventually be recorded. The teacher uses questions and prompts such as "I'm interested. Tell me more" to expand and clarify as well as to elevate the children's language beyond a listing of ideas. Susan Bennett had the first-grade children show how they would peck their way out of shells and asked them to imagine and talk about the first thing they might see.

3. *Recording.* As a group, children select the ideas to be recorded and provide an oral composition. This helps the children understand some of the basic differences between oral and written language. Then, as children dictate ideas, the teacher records them in large print on chart paper. As the teacher writes each word, the children watch to help them establish the link between oral and written words. The teacher makes comments and asks for help during this writing about where she or he begins writing, in what direction the print goes, about the use of capital letters and punctuation marks, and about special visual features of certain words (e.g., length, initial letter, and so on).

If the children have some awareness of letter names and sounds, the teacher has the children suggest which letters to include in some of the words being written to further develop phonemic awareness. For example, when the children in Susan Bennett's first-grade class dictated a sentence about the chicks pecking out of their shells, she asked, "What letters do we need to write the word *peck*?" One child said "p" and another "k." Susan printed these letters and added the *e* and *c* herself, slowly articulating the sounds so the children would hear them as she wrote. She also commented on the *ck* at the end of the word. She knew the children did not have enough knowledge of letter sounds to supply these letters without help.

A major dilemma teachers face when printing language experience stories is whether to write exactly what children say or to make changes. It is generally recommended that teachers use standard English spellings regardless of dialect (e.g., *going to*, not *gonna*) and use standard punctuation. However, controversy surrounds the question of whether or not to scribe ungrammatical sentences such as "I don't got no pencil." The answer depends on whether you are working with a group or an individual children and on the major purpose of the language experience activity. With individual children at early stages of emergent literacy development, most educators recommend scribing children's vocabulary and grammar to help them develop an understanding of the one-to-one correspondence between oral and written words. For example, if the child dictates "Me and another chick saw a cow" and the teacher changes it to "Another chick and I saw a cow," the child will likely reread the first part of the sentence as "Me and another chick," associating the wrong spoken words with what is written.

Preserving what children have dictated is also important when working with children learning English as a second language. The context, vocabulary, and language structures will be familiar to the children, and hence will support their initial reading experiences.

However, as a general guideline when working with groups of children whose first language is English, many teachers change non-standard English into the standard form. This practice is particularly prevalent when most of the children in the group use the standard form. This practice is also appropriate with children who are already able to match spoken and written words. One purpose of making changes to the standard form is to help children understand that there are differences between oral and written language. Children need to learn what book language sounds like to help them predict words as they read.

4. *Reading.* Immediately upon completing the story, the teacher reads it to the children, pointing to words as she or he does so. As a follow-up activity, the teacher may ask children if they want to make any changes, in order to engage them in revising what they have written. The teacher demonstrates revision by using carets and arrows, crossing out words, and writing in the margins. Once the children are happy with what they have dictated, the teacher and children read it together to ensure that their first reading will be successful. During subsequent rereadings, the children read more independently, with the teacher providing support as needed. Finally, when the children feel ready, individuals read the story alone.

5. *Follow-up activities.* A variety of follow-up activities are appropriate for both groups and individuals. Some examples follow:

   • During re-reading, the teacher asks children questions about where to begin reading, in what direction to read, how to know to stop at the end of a sentence, and so on, to develop concepts about print conventions.
   • Individual children are encouraged to read the story independently, pointing to the words as they read. Some teachers type the language experience story and make copies for the children to keep and read individually.

- Children are asked to find words containing a common letter (e.g., all the words that begin with the letter *m*). They talk about how all of these words begin with the same sound and the fact that some of the words begin with an uppercase *M* and others with a lowercase *m*.
- Sentences are cut apart, and children arrange the sentences in order, referring to the language experience chart if necessary. When the children are able to handle this task easily, individual sentences can be cut into words for them to put in order, again matching the words against an intact sentence strip if necessary.
- Selected words in the language experience story are covered, and the children are asked to predict words that make sense and sound right in the space. They then check their predictions by looking at the print.
- Poetry, songs, and other material are presented to children in large print on charts. By pointing to words on a chart as the children sing, further opportunities for eye–voice matching are provided. In addition, discussing words on the chart further develops knowledge of the forms of written language and of speech–print relationships.

## Writing

We include both interactive writing, where children and teachers write together, and independent writing in this section. These two types of experiences generally occur simultaneously in emergent literacy programs.

### Interactive Writing

Interactive writing is an extension of shared writing, with teachers and children sharing all aspects of the writing process, including scribing (Fountas and Pinnel, 1996). It generally involves a small group and can serve as a transition to independent writing or as a teaching/learning context for children beyond the emergent stage of literacy development in which more complex skills (such as paragraphing) are demonstrated. Fountas and Pinnell (1996) recommend the following five steps in interactive writing for emergent writers:

1. The teacher and a small group of children compose a piece together, sometimes innovating on the structure of a book they have read (see the section on shared-book reading on page 89). In the early stages of emergent literacy, Fountas and Pinnell recommend repeating the message several times and rereading it from the beginning each time a new word is completed.

2. The teacher and children share the pen. Sometimes the teacher writes the word and at other times invites children to come to the easel or whiteboard to fill in letters or known words.

3. To foster development of phonemic awareness and understanding of the alphabetic principle, the teacher selects some words and demonstrates how to articulate them slowly and connect sounds heard with letters. For example, "I stretch out the word *cat* like this, *cccaaattt*. Now I listen to the sound at the beginning of the word, *cccat*, and write the letter that goes with that sound." The teacher then invites the children to carry out a similar process, stretching words out and writing letters for the sounds they are able to hear.

4. Children quickly write known (sight) words. Others are analyzed, and different kinds of words are placed on a "word wall" to be used as a resource for further learning.

5. As the piece is written, the teacher draws the children's attention to print conventions such as spacing, punctuation, and directionality.

### Independent Writing

We recommend that young children have daily opportunities to write. Writing can be integrated with all the experiences described above. However, establishing a writing centre in the kindergarten or Grade 1 classroom will provide further opportunities and incentive to write. A writing centre contains a variety of writing implements and materials: paper, pencils, crayons, chalk, small chalkboards, erasers, markers, scissors, and glue.

Sulzby et al. (1989) believe that all kindergarten children reared in a literate culture can and will write if the following conditions are met:

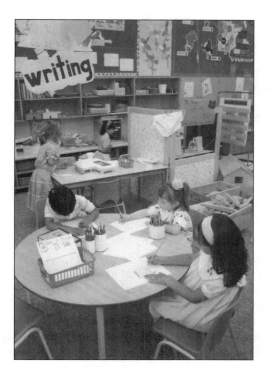

Children in a kindergarten writing centre.

• First and most important, they suggest that in order to encourage young children to write, teachers accept the forms of writing children use.

• Second, they recommend keeping requests simple, — for example, "write a story" or "write a letter to your mother" — and then asking children to read what they have written.

• Third, they recommend reassuring children that their writing "doesn't have to be like grown-up writing. Just do it your own way" (p. 70).

At the initial stages of children's independent writing, we recommend that teachers respond to the content or meaning of what children are writing, rather than placing a heavy focus on letter formation, spacing, and spelling. Proctor (1986) found that first-grade children in meaning-focussed classrooms scored higher on both mechanical and content measures than did children in traditional skills classrooms. Children in meaning-focussed classrooms wrote more and made fewer spelling errors, and their writing was characterized by a need to communicate ideas. They had a stronger sense of audience, and the ideas in their writing were more complex. Proctor concluded that when teachers focussed on meaning, children not only developed their ability to express ideas with clarity and vigour, but also mastered many of the mechanical aspects of writing.

This does not mean that teachers should not provide any spelling instruction at the emergent stage of literacy development. If children are trying to write phonetically, we recommend using this as an opportunity to further develop phonemic awareness and understanding of the alphabetic principle. There is considerable consensus in the literature about the need for young children to learn to hear individual sounds in words. What is not so clear is whether this is a prerequisite to reading and writing or if it develops as an outcome of children learning to read and write. Until this issue has been clarified, it is recommended that teachers include work on phonemic awareness as part of their language arts program for children in the early stages of literacy development.

One way we can help children hear sounds in words they are trying to spell is to slowly articulate each word as explained on page 96 and have the children repeat it slowly, listening for the sounds at the beginning, middle, and end of the word. By articulating words slowly rather than saying sounds separately, teachers are able to avoid distortion. It is also recommended that children be encouraged to represent each sound with one letter in the initial stages of writing. For example, the word *hammer* has four distinct sounds, and a young child who spells the word as *hamr* demonstrates the ability to hear all four of these sounds. As proficient readers, we need to listen closely to sounds in words to understand why young children spell words such as *hoped* as *hopt* and *dragon* as *jragn*. Like the spelling of *hamr* for *hammer*, these invented spellings indicate that children understand the alphabetic principle and that they are able to hear separate sounds in the words and map letters onto the sounds they hear. This is more important at the emergent stage of writing development than conventional spelling. In Chapter Nine, we describe stages children go through as they move toward conventional spelling, and we offer suggestions for spelling instruction.

## Functional Interactions with Print

Environmental print both inside and outside the classroom provides children with functional literacy experiences. Environmental print includes such things as signs, labels, calendars, charts, and lists that can be used to organize the classroom. Putting labels and signs up in the classroom is not, by itself, sufficient to help many children construct understandings of the components of emergent literacy. Children need to interact with print in meaningful ways to maximize their learning. Some examples of authentic experiences with environmental print follow:

- Teachers and child make labels to identify children's cubbyholes and show where things belong.
- Calendars are used to keep track of the day of the week and of children's birthdays. Teachers also use attendance charts to help children learn to read one another's names.
- Teachers present charts or lists on the blackboard to indicate the daily schedule, classroom jobs, and who will be at which centre. Schickendanz (1989) described how one teacher used these types of lists to foster children's literacy learning. The teacher put a list of activities the children could choose from on a chart and discussed them with the children, crossing each off after it had been discussed. If the activity was a familiar one, such as blocks, she asked, "Who knows what is next on my list?" When the children replied, "Blocks," she slowly said, "Yes, b-l-o-c-k-s" and ran her finger under the word as she did so (p. 98). Once all of the possibilities had been discussed, the children make their choices. (If several children chose the same activity, the teacher made a "turns" list.)

The children who chose the activity of making popcorn then consulted a recipe chart. At the top was written "things we need," and with the teacher's assistance, the children read and located the items on the list. The teacher then read the "what to do" part of the recipe, pointing to the words as she did so, and the children carried out the instructions. When the popcorn was finished, one child commented that they hadn't put salt on it, and the teacher referred her to the recipe, which didn't call for salt. The children decided that they wanted to use the next time, so one child put the word *salt* on the recipe chart.

- "Morning message" is a technique in which the teacher writes a brief message describing a significant event for the children that day. For example, "Today we are going to have a special visitor." Once the message is written and read, the children reread it (matching words heard to those in print as they do so) and discuss the day's upcoming events.

  After children have begun to read independently, these morning messages may be written in minimal-cues format to increase the focus on the speech–print relationship. In minimal-cues messages, the teacher leaves selected letters out of words, and the children predict what the message is on the basis of the remaining cues. For example, "We are go_ _ _ on a treasure hunt _ _ day." The children predict the words and, if they are able, tell which letters go in each blank.
- Play centres can support literacy-related activities. For example, a play post office involves a variety of props such as a mailbox, stationery, envelopes, pens, pencils, stamps, address labels, and signs about mailing. Other rich contexts for literacy learning include a cooking centre, store, doctor's office, and travel agent's office.
- Field trips provide opportunities for children to use written language for functional purposes. They might consult printed material when making plans for the trip, use environmental print to find their way around during the field trip itself, and write thank-you letters after they return.

## Summary

Until the last two decades, the concept of reading readiness influenced the type of reading instruction provided to young children when they arrived at school. Development was thought to proceed through stages, and during the first half of the century, many educators believed that a mental age of 6 1/2 was necessary to learn to read. By the 1950s, these views had changed, and children were given reading readiness activities to help them get ready for formal reading instruction.

In the late 1970s, the concept of emergent literacy began to replace reading readiness in program planning. From this perspective, literacy development is seen as continuous, beginning with children's earliest experiences with print at home. Components of emergent literacy include cultural views and functions of written language, the nature and forms of written language, and the speech–print relationship.

Children's emergent literacy is generally assessed using informal rather than standardized assessment tools. Four major types of informal assessment are used for this purpose: observation, interviews, samples of children's work, and children's self-assessment. Teachers constantly observe young children as they interact with print, and when they need a more organized record of their emergent literacy development, anecdotal notes and checklists are helpful. Interviews of both parents and children provide information about children's literacy experiences at home and about their understanding of why and how people read.

More specific information is obtained by giving children a story book and asking them to demonstrate their understanding of how books and print work, as well as their knowledge of terms such as *letter* and *word*. Samples of children's reading and writing also provide important clues to their literacy development. Early writing attempts are examined in relation to both form (e.g., drawing, scribbling, letters) and function. Samples of children's early reading may be collected by taking running records as they read. These records can be analyzed to describe children's use of picture, print, and meaning cues as they interact with print.

General principles for planning emergent literacy experiences have been based on the nature of literacy experiences children receive in literate homes. We recommend that young children be immersed in a rich literacy environment and involved in meaningful, purposeful literacy activities. We also recommend that children be involved in daily reading and writing, and that they be given the opportunity to have shared control of their literacy learning. Rather than requiring word-perfect reading and letter-perfect writing, it is important for teachers to reinforce children for producing approximate responses until they establish an understanding of most of the components of emergent literacy. It is also important for teachers to recognize that children come to schools from a wide range of different literacy environments and to take individual differences into account when planning instruction. All children are able to learn, and our task as teachers is to determine where they are in their literacy development and provide instruction appropriate to their needs. While all children do not go through the same invariant stages in learning to read and write, some understandings generally come before others for most children.

We recommend a balanced emergent literacy program for young children, involving a range of reading and writing experiences. Such a program includes reading to children, shared-book experiences, shared writing experiences, interactive and independent writing, and functional interactions with print. Children are encouraged to talk about ideas before, during, and after the reading of books by teachers and during shared-book experiences. Predictable big books are particularly useful for this latter activity. There are three steps in a shared-book experience: discovery or initial reading of the book, exploration or rereading, and independent experience.

The language experience approach provides the opportunity for shared writing experiences. The four stages in developing a language experience story are selecting an experience, discussing the experience to develop vocabulary and language, recording ideas as the children dictate them, and reading the story. Follow-up activities foster specific aspects of emergent literacy development. Interactive writing experiences provide opportunities for children and teachers to share both the generating and the scribing of these ideas, while independent writing gives children the opportunity to explore writing on their own and with other children.

Functional interactions with print are particularly useful for helping children understand functions of written language. Labels, calendars, charts, lists, morning messages, play centres involving print, and field trips provide opportunities for children to use written language in purposeful contexts.

## Selected Professional Resources

Morrow, L.M. (1997). *Literacy Development in the Early Years: Helping Children Read and Write* (3rd ed.). Boston: Allyn and Bacon. This edition of Lesley Morrow's book on literacy development from birth to Grade 3 provides a balanced approach to early literacy instruction, with a blend of constructivist ideas and explicit direct instruction approaches.

Ollila, L.O. and Mayfield, M.I. (eds.). (1992). *Emerging Literacy: Preschool, Kindergarten and Primary Grades*. Toronto: Allyn and Bacon. Experts from Canada and the United States present ideas to guide literacy development for children aged 3 through 9. Principles of literacy instruction and descriptions of classroom practices are included, as well as ideas on evaluation and working with parents.

## Children's Books Noted in Chapter Three

Ahlberg, J. and Ahlberg, A. (1978). *Each Peach Pear Plum*. New York: Scholastic Book Services.
Baum, A. and Baum, J. (1962). *One Bright Monday Morning*. New York: Random House.
Becker, J. (1973). *Seven Little Rabbits*. New York: Scholastic Book Services.
Bonne, R. (1981). *A Dark, Dark Tale*. New York: Scholastic Book Services.
Carle, E. (1977). *The Grouchy Ladybug*. New York: Thomas Y. Crowell.
Carle, E. (1983). *The Very Hungry Caterpillar*. New York: Scholastic Book Services.
Carle, E. (1984). *The Very Busy Spider*. New York: Philomel.
Cowley, J. (1980). *Mrs. Wishy-Washy*. Auckland, NZ: Shortland Publications.
Cowley, J. (1983). *The Jigaree*. Auckland, NZ: Shortland Publications.
Cowley, J. (1983). *Who Will Be My Mother?* Auckland, NZ: Shortland Publications.
Cranstoun, M. (1967). *1, 2, Buckle My Shoe*. New York: Holt, Rinehart & Winston.
Keats, E.J. (1971). *Over in the Meadow*. New York: Scholastic Book Services.
Martin, Jr., B. (1970). *The Haunted House*. New York: Holt, Rinehart & Winston.
Martin, Jr., B. (1970). *King of the Mountain*. New York: Holt, Rinehart & Winston.
Martin, Jr., B. (1970). *Monday, Monday, I Like Monday*. New York: Holt, Rinehart & Winston.
Martin, Jr., B. (1970). *When It Rains, It Rains*. New York: Holt, Rinehart & Winston.
Martin, Jr., B. (1970). *Whistle, Mary, Whistle*. New York: Holt, Rinehart & Winston.
Martin, Jr., B. (1972). *Brown Bear, Brown Bear, What Do You See?* New York: Holt, Rinehart & Winston.
Mayer, M. (1975). *Just for You*. New York: Golden Press.
Melser, J. (1980). *Sing a Song*. Auckland, NZ: Shortland Publications.
Morris, W.B. (1970). *The Longest Journey in the World*. New York: Holt, Rinehart & Winston.
Scheer, J. and Bileck, M. (1964). *Rain Makes Applesauce*. New York: Holiday House.
Sutton, E. (1973). *My Cat Likes to Hide in Boxes*. New York: Parents Magazine Press.
*The Three Billy Goats Gruff*. (1963). New York: Holt, Rinehart and Winston.
Tolstoy, A. (1968). *The Great Big Enormous Turnip*. New York: Franklin Watts.
Wing, H.R. (1963). *What Is Big?* New York: Holt, Rinehart & Winston.

## References

Adams, M.J. (1990). *Beginning to read: Thinking and learning about print*. Cambridge, MA: MIT Press.
Alberta Education. (1993). *Diagnostic teaching in a language learning framework 5*. Edmonton, AB: Student Evaluation Branch.
Applebee, A. (1978). *The child's concept of story*. Chicago: University of Chicago Press.
Chittenden, E. and Courtney, R. (1989). Assessment of young children's reading: Documentation as an alternative to testing. In D.S. Strickland and L.M. Morrow (eds.), *Emerging literacy: Young children learn to read and write* (pp. 107–120). Newark, DE: International Reading Association.
Clay, M.M. (1972). *Reading: The patterning of complex behaviour*. Auckland, NZ: Heinemann.
Clay, M.M. (1975). *What did I write?* Portsmouth, NH: Heinemann.
Clay, M.M. (1993). *An observation survey of early literacy achievement*. Portsmouth, NH: Heinemann.
Crawford, P.A. (1995). Early literacy: Emerging perspectives. *Journal of Research in Childhood Education, 10* (1), 71–86.
deHirsch, K., Jansky, J.J., and Langford, W.S. (1966). *Predicting reading failure*. New York: Harper and Row.

Doake, D.B. (1981). Book experience and emergent reading behaviour in preschool children. PhD dissertation, University of Alberta, Edmonton, AB.

Doake, D.B. (1988). *Reading begins at birth.* Richmond Hill, ON: Scholastic-TAB Publications.

Downing, J. (1979). *Reading and reasoning.* New York: Springer-Verlag.

Downing, J., Ayers, D., and Schaefer, B. (1983). *Linguistic awareness in reading readiness (LARR) test.* Windsor, UK: NFER-Nelson Publishing Company.

Durkin, D.D. (1978–79). What classroom observations reveal about reading comprehension instruction. *Reading Research Quarterly, 14* (4), 481–533.

Durkin, D.D. (1983). *Teaching them to read* (4th ed.). Boston: Allyn and Bacon.

Ferreiro, E. and Teberosky, A. (1982). *Literacy before schooling.* Exeter, NH: Heinemann.

Fountas, I.C. and Pinnell, G.S. (1996). *Guided reading: Good first teaching for all children.* Portsmouth, NH: Heinemann.

Gates, A.I. (1937). The necessary mental age for beginning reading. *Elementary School Journal, 37,* 497–508.

Goodman, K. (1969). Analysis of oral reading miscues: Applied psycholinguistics. *Reading Research Quarterly, 5* (1), 9–30.

Goodman, Y.M. (1991). Informal methods of evaluation. In J. Flood, J.M. Jensen, D. Lapp, and J.R. Squire (eds.), *Handbook of research on teaching the English language arts* (pp. 502–509). New York: Macmillan.

Goswami, U. and Bryant, P. (1990). *Phonological skills and learning to read.* East Sussex, UK: Lawrence Erlbaum Associates.

Hall, M. (1981). *Teaching reading as a language experience.* Columbus, OH: Charles E. Merrill.

Harste, J., Woodward, V., and Burke, C. (1984). *Language stories and literacy lessons.* Portsmouth, NH: Heinemann Educational Books.

Heath, S.B. (1983). *Ways with words: Language, life and work in communities and classrooms.* Cambridge, MA: Cambridge University Press.

Holdaway, D. (1979). *The foundations of literacy.* Gosford, Australia: Ashton Scholastic.

Hough, R.A. and Nurss, J.R. (1992). Language and literacy for the limited English proficient child. In L.O. Ollila and M.I. Mayfield (eds.), *Emerging literacy: Preschool, kindergarten, and primary grades* (pp. 137–165). Toronto: Allyn and Bacon.

Juliebö, M.F. (1985). The literacy world of five young children. PhD dissertation, University of Alberta, Edmonton, AB.

Malicky, G., Purkiss, K., and Nugent, B. (1988–89). Early intervention: A collaborative holistic approach. *Alberta English, 27* (1), 21–29.

Mason, J.M. (1984). Early reading from a developmental perspective. In P.D. Pearson (ed.), *Handbook of reading research* (pp. 505–544). New York: Longman.

Mason, J.M., Peterman, C.L., and Kerr, B.M. (1989). Reading to kindergarten children. In D. Strickland and L.M. Morrow (eds.), *Emerging literacy: Young children learn to read and write* (pp. 52–62). Newark, DE: International Reading Association.

Morphett, M.V. and Washburne, C. (1931). When should children begin to read? *Elementary School Journal, 31,* 496–508.

Morris, D. (1993). The relationship between children's concept of word in text and phoneme awareness in learning to read: A longitudinal study. *Research in the Teaching of English, 27* (2), 133–154.

Morrow, L.M. (1997). *Literacy development in the early years: Helping children read and write.* (3rd ed.). Boston: Allyn and Bacon.

Muter, V., Hulme, C., Snowling, M., and Taylor, S. (1997). Segmentation, not rhyming, predicts early progress in learning to read. *Journal of Experimental Child Psychology, 65,* 370–396.

Neuman, S.B. and Roskos, K.A. (1993). *Language and literacy learning in the early years: An integrated approach.* New York: Harcourt Brace Jovanovich College.

Ollila, L.O. and Mayfield, M.I. (eds.). (1992). *Emerging literacy: Preschool, kindergarten and primary grades.* Toronto: Allyn and Bacon.

Proctor, J.R. (1986). The effect of teacher's theoretical orientations on the writing produced by grade one students. MA thesis, University of Alberta, Edmonton, AB.

Purcell-Gates, V. (1998). Growing successful readers: Homes, communities, and schools. In J. Osborn and F. Lehr (eds.), *Literacy for all: Issues in teaching and learning* (pp. 51–72). New York: The Guilford Press.

Reid, J. (1966). Learning to think about reading. *Educational Research, 9,* 56–62.

Schickendanz, J. (1989). The place of specific skills in preschool and kindergarten. In D.S. Strickland and L.M. Morrow (eds.), *Emerging literacy: Young children learn to read and write* (pp. 96–106). Newark, DE: International Reading Association.

Smith F. (1988). *Joining the literacy club: Further essays into education.* London: Heinemann.

Sulzby, E. (1985). Children's emergent reading of favorite storybooks: A developmental study. *Reading Research Quarterly, 20,* 458–481.

Sulzby, E. (1991). The development of the young child and the emergence of literacy. In J. Flood, J.M. Jensen, D. Lapp, and J.R. Squire (eds.), *Handbook of research on teaching the English language arts* (pp. 273–285). New York: Macmillan.

Sulzby, E., Teale, W.H., and Kamberelis, G. (1989). Emergent writing in the classroom: Home and school connections. In D. Strickland and L.M. Morrow (eds.), *Emerging literacy: Young children learn to read and write* (pp. 52–62). Newark, DE: International Reading Association.

Taylor, D. (1982). *Family literacy: Children learning to read and write.* Exeter, NH: Heinemann.

Taylor, D. and Dorsey-Gaines, C. (1988). *Growing up literate: Learning from inner city families.* Portsmouth, NH: Heinemann.

Teale, W.H. (1995). Young children and reading: Trends across the twentieth century. *Journal of Education, 177* (3), 95–127.

Teale, W.H., Hiebert, E.H., and Chittenden, E.A. (1987). Assessing young children's literacy development. *Reading Teacher, 40* (8), 772–777.

Temple, C. and Gillet, J.W. (1989). *Language arts: Learning processes and teaching practices* (2nd ed.). Glenview, IL: Scott, Foresman & Company.

Tompkins, G.E. (1997). *Literacy for the 21st century: A balanced approach.* Columbus, OH: Prentice-Hall.

Torrey, J. (1969). Learning to read without a teacher: A case study. *Elementary English, 46,* 550–556.

Valencia, S. (1990). A portfolio approach to classroom reading assessment: The whys, whats, and hows. *Reading Teacher, 43* (4), 338–340.

Wagner, R.K., Torgesen, J.K., Laughon, P., Simmons, K., and Rashotte, C.A. (1993). Development of young readers' phonological processing abilities. *Journal of Educational Psychology, 85* (1), 83–103.

# Chapter four

# The Nature and Assessment of Reading

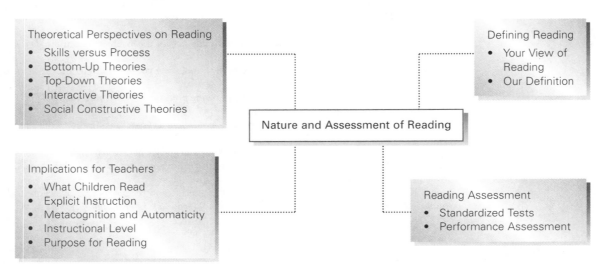

Theoretical Perspectives on Reading
- Skills versus Process
- Bottom-Up Theories
- Top-Down Theories
- Interactive Theories
- Social Constructive Theories

Defining Reading
- Your View of Reading
- Our Definition

Nature and Assessment of Reading

Implications for Teachers
- What Children Read
- Explicit Instruction
- Metacognition and Automaticity
- Instructional Level
- Purpose for Reading

Reading Assessment
- Standardized Tests
- Performance Assessment

Nearly every time you turn on the radio or television, you hear an advertisement for some kind of reading program. Some advertisers promise to increase your reading rate so you will be able to read one page per second. Others promise to dramatically increase children's level of reading achievement. Many claim to achieve immediate results, particularly for children who are experiencing difficulty with learning to read in school. Your neighbour knows that you are in a teacher education program and asks your opinion about one of these programs. Her fifth-grade daughter is having difficulty with reading, and she is considering spending hundreds of dollars on a commercial phonics program. What advice do you give your neighbour? ■

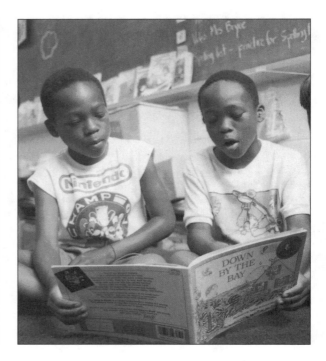

Thousands of parents each year are faced with this decision. The advertisers appeal to their hopes that their children will be successful in school and eventually get good jobs. The advertisers also appeal to the desire all of us have for quick-fix solutions. We would rather take a pill to lose weight than control our eating or exercise regularly. And we want easy, quick solutions to other complex problems, reading among them. From your understanding of what you read in the first three chapters of this text, you are likely dubious about the promises of the advertisers. However, before you will feel comfortable answering your neighbour's question, you probably need to construct answers to some of your own questions about reading — questions that you never needed to consider as a reader but that are crucial now that you are, or are planning to become, a reading teacher.

- How *do* people read?
- What are some of the basic issues facing reading teachers?
- How can teachers find the right reading experiences and instruction to provide  to individuals and groups of children?

We begin this chapter with a discussion of the nature of reading and of the general issues related to the teaching of reading. The rest of the chapter is devoted to strategies for assessing children's reading achievement and needs.

## Theoretical Perspectives on Reading

Psychology has dominated views on reading and on reading instruction in the schools since the beginning of the century (Huey, 1908). Behavioural psychologists focussed on reading as skill development, and cognitive psychologists focussed on the nature of the reading process. Only recently have theorists begun to recognize social aspects of the process. We provide a brief overview of theoretical perspectives on reading in this section, beginning with skills orientations and ending with social constructive perspectives.

### Skills versus Process

**Basal reading series** of the 1960s to 1970s were generally designed to develop a series of skills, often ordered hierarchically. For example, a certain number of sight words were introduced before letter sounds, and consonants were usually dealt with before work on vowel sounds. Comprehension was also broken down into component skills, with literal comprehension tasks assumed to be easier than those involving inferential and critical comprehension. Influenced strongly by behavioural theories, educators thought that reading could be taught by breaking it down into component skills to be learned one at a time, often through drill and practice.

In the 1970s, there was a major shift to a focus on reading processes rather than skills. Instead of asking what skills to teach, educators began to focus on how children read. This shift was reflected to some extent in basal readers used in Canada in the 1980s and early 1990s. For example, the Nelson Networks series included a *Reading and How* (Hughes and McInnes, 1983) book, focussed on reading processes, at each of Grades 4 through 6.

The emphasis of the process perspective is on how the child constructs meaning from print. The focus is on learning rather than teaching, the learner rather than the teacher, and the process rather than the products of learning (Malicky, 1991). Theorists who focus on the reading process hypothesize that there are three major variables in the reading process: the text, the reader's knowledge, and the process as readers interact with the text. The extent to which readers rely on the text as compared with their knowledge formed the basis for much of the discussion of reading processes in the 1970s.

## Bottom-Up Theories

Text, more specifically letters and words, has been the focus of theorists who view reading as bottom-up processing. According to this interpretation, readers begin with letters and, from them, identify words. As they identify words, they put them together to get the meaning of phrases, sentences, and passages. In other words, readers process information through a series of low-level to high-level stages. Gough (1972, p. 354), a strong proponent of the bottom-up view, stated that readers are not guessers. Although they appear "to go from print to meaning as if by magic," this is an illusion. Readers actually plod through sentences letter by letter. From a bottom-up perspective (Lipson and Wixson, 1991),

- reading is viewed as primarily a perceptual process,
- meaning resides in the text, and
- processing proceeds from parts to the whole.

Bottom-up theorists note that for readers to become proficient, processing of letter information must reach a level of **automaticity** so they can focus on meaning. Automaticity is the ability to carry out a process without conscious awareness, much like we steer a car on the highway without actively thinking about which way to turn the wheel.

## Top-Down Theories

While letters and words have been the focus of bottom-up theorists, those who view reading as top-down processing emphasize the key role that readers' knowledge plays in the reading process. A proponent of this view, Goodman (1970), called reading a "psycholinguistic guessing game." He maintained that readers use their knowledge about language and the world to generate hypotheses about meaning, which are then tested against the print. From this perspective, readers are seen as problem solvers, and a complete analysis of print is not considered necessary, or even desirable, for the construction of meaning. Before encountering text, readers have expectations about what they will read. As they read, they process text in relation to these expectations, and use this information to formulate predictions about what will come in the text. If the prediction sounds right and makes sense, readers continue reading, checking out the meaning as they read subsequent text. If the prediction does not sound right or make sense, readers reformulate their predictions and reread the text to check out these new predictions. Top-down processing can explain why many writers have so much difficulty proofreading their own writing. We have such clear expectations of what we will read that we do not see deviations from what we predict on the page.

From a top-down perspective, what readers know is more important than what they see. In top-down models of reading (Lipson and Wixson, 1991),

- reading is viewed as a language-thinking process,
- meaning resides in the reader, and
- processing proceeds from whole to part.

Top-down views of reading provided the basis for reading instruction in whole language classrooms during the 1980s and 1990s.

## Interactive Theories

In the late 1970s, writers such as Rumelhart (1977) and Adams, Anderson, and Durkin (1978) began to question whether either top-down or bottom-up models of the reading process were adequate. Bottom-up models were criticized for focussing on the minute analysis of words and for failing to account for either comprehension or the impact of meaning on word identification. The major criticism of top-down models was their vagueness in generating practical implications for teaching and their inability to account for research findings on the significant impact of word-level factors (such as phonemic awareness) on reading achievement. As a result of these criticisms, many educators began to consider how the two positions could be combined to produce a more adequate model of reading.

In Rumelhart's (1977) interactive model of reading, reading is viewed as neither top-down nor bottom-up, but rather as a process of synthesizing information from letters, words, sentences, and larger units of meaning. From an interactive perspective (Lipson and Wixson, 1991),

- reading is seen as a cognitive process,
- meaning results from interaction between the reader and text, and
- processing proceeds from whole to part and part to whole.

A major advantage of interactive models is that they help to account for different ways of processing information under different circumstances. For example, as good readers, we sometimes encounter material that is difficult to read, such as highly technical scientific material. When that happens, we adjust our reading to process the print information more carefully than we would when reading a novel or magazine article on a familiar topic.

## Social Constructive Theories

Psychologists have been concerned with reading since at least the turn of the century (Hiebert and Raphael, 1996), resulting in a heavy focus on the individual child and on reading as an individual achievement. The social, cultural, and political aspects of reading have largely been ignored. Hence, when a child has difficulty reading, many people believe that there is something wrong with the child rather than examining the child's home, school, or society. However, as indicated in Chapter One, we need to look beyond the child to explain differences in reading achievement.

Ironically, much of the impetus for a movement toward social perspectives on reading came from the work of Vygotsky (1978), a psychologist who theorized that the way we learn language is a result of our use of language in social contexts. Some theorists who have been influenced by Vygotsky's work recognize the impact of the classroom context on children's construction of meaning, although they continue to focus heavily on what is happening inside the child's head. Ruddell and Unrau (1994), for example, view reading as a socio-cognitive process. Their model of reading as a meaning-construction process includes the reader, text, classroom context, and teacher as major components. Meaning is negotiated through interaction and interchange among teachers, texts, and readers within specific learning environments.

Another major impetus to social views of reading came from literary theory, specifically from Rosenblatt's (1978) **transactional theory**. Rosenblatt sees the reader and text as having a circular rather than interactive relationship, with each affecting the other. Readers actively create meaning, relying on the text itself, their knowledge of language and the world, their background experiences, and their world view. The reader's response is conditioned by the context, depending on his or her purpose for reading a particular text. Further discussion of Rosenblatt's theory is presented Chapter Eleven.

According to Straw (1990), a major difference between interactive theories of reading and social constructive theories is that interactive theories are grounded in the basic assumption that reading is communication. Interactivists view reading as part of a larger language act that includes "the author as originator of meaning, the text as symbolic or representative of meaning, and the reader as receiver of meaning" (p. 171). In contrast, social constructive models perceive reading as a "more generative act than the receipt or processing of information or communication" (p. 171). In addition to the text and the reader's knowledge, meaning is constructed on the basis of the social background of the reader and the social context of the reading act, both within and outside of the school context.

By recognizing culture as "the fabric within which meaning construction occurs" (Hiebert and Raphael, 1996, p. 559), social constructivists are able to explain why more poor than rich children have reading difficulties and why girls tend to perform better than boys on measures of reading in the elementary grades. Who is regarded as a successful reader and whose meanings are regarded as "correct" are often more a matter of a child's race, class, and gender rather than of generic reading skills or strategies.

From a social constructive perspective,

- reading is seen as a socio-cultural process, and
- meaning is constructed as readers interact with texts, teachers, and peers within the classroom and broader social context.

From this perspective, reading is not only an individual achievement but also involves responding to texts in groups (Bogdan and Straw, 1993).

By now, you are likely more than a little aware of the similarity between this overview of theories of reading and the overview of theories of knowledge and learning presented in Chapter One. In Figure 4.1, we summarize the theories of reading included in this section and show how we link this set of theories with that presented in Chapter One.

## Defining Reading

Nearly everyone who is able to read has a view on what reading is and how it should be taught. As we noted at the beginning of Chapter One, most people's notions reflect their experiences of learning to read. You are likely no exception. We begin this section by asking you to articulate your views on reading, and then we present the definition we use as the basis for the remainder of our discussion of reading in this book.

**Figure 4.1**   **Theoretical Perspectives on Reading**

| Bottom-Up (transmission) | Top-Down (construction) | Interactive (transmission and construction) | Social Constructive (social construction) |
|---|---|---|---|
| Meaning ↑ Text ↑ Sentences ↑ Words ↑ Letters/Sounds | Knowledge and Expectations ↓ Print ↓ Meaning | Knowledge and Expectations ↓ Meaning ↑ Text ↑ Sentences ↑ Words ↑ Letters/Sounds | CONTEXT — Knowledge and Expectations ↕ Meaning ↕ Print |

## Your View of Reading

Because the construction of meaning always involves background knowledge and experiences, it is useful to bring this to the foreground as you continue to construct a more coherent theory of reading. To assist with this process, we have listed several statements about reading (some adapted from DeFord, 1985) in Box 4.1. Please read each of the statements and rate them from 1 to 5, with 1 indicating that you strongly agree and 5 that you strongly disagree.

**Box 4.1**   **Your Theoretical Perspective**

Rate each of the following statements about reading 1 (strongly agree), 2 (agree), 3 (no opinion), 4 (disagree) or 5 (strongly disagree).

____ 1. Children should master letter sounds before reading sentences and stories.

____ 2. When they come to a word they don't know, children should be encouraged to guess what would make sense and go on.

____ 3. Children should use both world knowledge and letter sounds to figure out unfamiliar words.

____ 4. Children should talk about why different people construct different meanings for the same story.

____ 5. Flashcard drill with sight words is necessary for children to learn to read.

____ 6. It is not necessary to introduce new words before children read them in stories.

____ 7. Children should predict what stories will be about before they begin reading, and revise these predictions using information in the text.

____ 8. It is useful for children to discuss texts in groups to negotiate meanings.

____ 9. It is a good practice to correct a child as soon as an oral reading mistake is made.

____ 10. Teachers should use good-quality literature rather than select material on the basis of word or vocabulary difficulty.

____ 11. Children need to develop strategies for both comprehension and the identification of words.

____ 12. Children should relate what they read in stories to what they see and do in their lives outside the school.

Source: Some of these items are based on D.E. DeFord (1985), "Validating the Construct of Theoretical Orientation in Reading Instruction." *Reading Research Quarterly, 20* (3), pp. 366–367.

After you have rated each statement, think about which theory each statement supports. Proponents of a bottom-up theory would strongly agree with statements 1, 5, and 9, whereas proponents of a top-down theory would strongly agree with statements 2, 6, and 10. Statements 3, 7, and 11 reflect an interactive theory of reading, and statements 4, 8, and 12 a social constructive view.

There are too few statements to clearly identify your theoretical orientation to reading. However, those of you who agreed or strongly agreed with all three statements in any of the four groupings delineated above have a leaning toward the theory associated with those statements. If you have a leaning toward one theory, think about how your school and home experiences might have led you to this view. Most likely, many of you are still in the process of developing a coherent view of reading, and as you work in classrooms you will refine this view on the basis of both your experience and your reading of the professional literature.

## Our Definition

In this textbook, we define reading as the active construction of meaning from cues in the text and from readers' background knowledge within a social context. We elaborate three major components of this definition below and draw implications for teaching and learning.

### Construction of Meaning

If we want children to view reading as a meaning-making rather than a meaning-getting process, we need to think carefully about what we say to them and the types of reading activities we ask them to complete. For example, if we constantly ask children literal questions such as "What colour was the girl's dress in this story ?" we may give them the incorrect impression that reading is a meaning-getting process and that the meaning is in the text. Similarly, unless we accept and discuss alternative interpretations of the same text, children will quickly learn that we do not really value their responses to literature and we think there is one "right" meaning — ours. A major portion of Chapter Eleven focusses on ways teachers can foster the development of children's responses to literature.

### Text Information and Knowledge

Our social constructive definition of reading supports the need for a balanced reading program. Children need to develop strategies for using both print cues and knowledge to identify words as they read. One way to do this is by presenting instruction on word identification strategies in a meaningful context. Otherwise, children may come to believe that the major purpose of reading is accurately identifying words and that meaning is secondary.

Teachers also need to take care that they present a balanced reading comprehension program that includes strategies for using both text cues and knowledge to construct meaning. A balanced program is one in which teachers encourage children to use a range of different cues as they engage in reading activities. In addition to asking "What sound does that word begin with?" when children encounter unfamiliar words, teachers also ask questions such as "What would make sense? What would sound right?" In addition to literal comprehension questions, teachers ensure that children have opportunities to respond to inferential and critical questions. Chapters Five and Six focus on instructional strategies for helping children learn to use both text-based and knowledge-based information to construct meaning.

## Social Context

Finally, our definition of reading leads us to view reading in relation to the child's home, community, school, and classroom contexts. The social nature of reading underlines the importance of social experiences and interactions in classrooms. Since knowledge is socially constructed, emphasis is placed on children and teachers talking and working together in groups rather than on individuals reading in isolation.

From a broader socio-political perspective, proponents of a social constructive reading theory acknowledge that classrooms are not neutral. They are inevitably more appropriate learning contexts for some children than others. The greater the discrepancy between the social background of the teacher and the children, the harder it will be to reduce discontinuities between home and school. Through instructional activities focussed on **critical literacy**, teachers help children critically examine inequities based on age, gender, and race to prepare them to engage in social action for change.

> What is important at this point is not that you have constructed a virtually identical definition of reading to the one we have shared, but rather that you have thought deeply about what you believe. This will provide you with a framework for examining the assessment and instructional strategies included in the remaining two and a half chapters devoted to reading.

## Implications for Teachers

> In the section you just read, we drew some general implications from our definition of reading, but teachers are faced with many other issues in reading as they make decisions about assessment and instruction. Most of these were introduced in Chapter One, but we revisit them here to draw specific implications for reading.

## What Children Read

There is considerable disagreement among both researchers and practitioners about what material children should read in classrooms, and this will likely increase as children gain access to the Internet. One area of controversy revolves around what types of texts are appropriate for children in the beginning stages of learning to read. Beck (1998, p. 22), for example, concludes from her experience as a teacher, mother, and researcher that "it is efficient for most children and essential for some children that the early textual material they read be developed using vocabulary that maximizes the regularity of the print-to-speech mapping system." Similar conclusions are reached by most proponents of bottom-up theories of reading who believe that phonic regularity of texts will make learning to read easier.

In contrast, proponents of top-down views of reading stress the importance of providing children with high-quality children's literature right from the beginning (Goodman, 1986). They recommend that teachers read these books to children, that the children read the books together, and eventually that the children read these books independently. In practice, many teachers who have adopted top-down theories make heavy use of books written with predictable and repetitive patterns (such as those listed in Chapter Three). In an examination of reading series used in Canada, Murphy (1991) found that a considerable amount of at the Grade 1 level was of this kind.

What nearly everyone agrees on is that children do need to read continuous text, although in recent years there has been an increase in suggestions that at least some work be completed with isolated words as part of a balanced literacy program (e.g., Pinnell and Fountas, 1998; Cunningham and Allington, 1999). Supporters of this position recommend that work be strategic and linked with reading and writing of real texts.

## Explicit Instruction

Some children seem to develop strategies for using text cues and knowledge to construct meaning with very little guidance from their teachers. Others benefit from explicit guidance from the teacher. The nature of this explicit instruction is an area of considerable controversy. Educators who hold bottom-up theories of reading recommend that reading be broken down into a myriad of subskills, with each taught in turn. Some children learn to read quite successfully in these types of programs, whereas others learn specific skills but have difficulty using them when they try to read.

Most educators who hold a top-down view of reading recommend that **strategy** instruction be provided when needed in mini-lessons, rather than according to a predetermined sequence. For example, if children are able to sound out most words but what they read does not make sense, teachers help them learn how to use **context cues** along with letter sounds to identify words. In these mini-lessons, teachers may model the strategy and then support a child in using the strategy, or they might deductively talk about the strategy and then provide the child with opportunities to use it.

Educators who hold interactive and social constructive views of reading recommend balanced programs focussed on the development of reading strategies for both word identification and comprehension (Pressley, 1998; Cunningham and Allington, 1999). Rather than mini-lessons, teachers provide systematic, explicit instruction on reading strategies. They give direct explanations of strategies, model use of these strategies, and assist students as they practise using strategies in meaningful and purpose-driven reading experiences (Pressley, 1998; Purcell-Gates, 1998).

There has been a resurgence of interest in guided reading in recent years. However, this is not the guided reading of the 1960s and 1970s, when teachers placed children in fixed ability groups, had them read short units of text, and then asked a series of questions before the children were allowed to continue reading. In the new guided reading, teachers explain or demonstrate for children the important things to be done while they read. Teachers follow the lead of their students, allowing them to do as much as they can and stepping in to support readers when needed. Much of what teachers do is to support "thinking" as students ask themselves what strategies they can use to solve the problems they encounter (Cunningham and Allington, 1999, p. 54).

## Metacognition and Automaticity

A major question related to explicit instruction is whether children need to become aware of reading strategies to become proficient readers. Awareness and control of reading strategies is generally referred to as **metacognition**.

Researchers have found that proficient readers have the following types of metacognitive knowledge:

- They have knowledge about *factors that affect reading* (Jacobs and Paris, 1987; Flavell, 1979). For example, a reader may know that he or she is good at figuring out hard words but has difficulty finding main ideas. A reader may also know that he or she is a better reader than most other children in the class, that there is a limit to how fast most people can read, and that it is generally easier to recall the gist of a story than to remember it word for word.

- They have knowledge about *reading strategies*. For example, they know how to figure out difficult words or how to study for a multiple-choice test.
- They know *when and why to apply particular strategies*. For example, they know they don't need to use a phonic strategy to identify a word they have already established as a sight word.

The regulative or control dimension of metacognition involves readers in planning and monitoring their reading. Proficient readers are able to plan what they will do as they read — for example, using the headings and subheadings to predict what a passage or chapter will be about before they begin reading. They evaluate their reading to determine whether what they read makes sense, and make corrections if it does not. For example, if you reached the end of this paragraph and decided that the meaning you constructed did not make sense, you might decide to reread the paragraph. Alternatively, you might decide to read to the end of the section to see if that helped you to make sense out of what you had been reading.

Researchers have generally found that young children are less likely to display metacognitive abilities than are older children (Paris, Wasik, and Turner, 1991). However, children's understanding and control of strategies increase with reading proficiency and age. Although some research tends to be more optimistic about the ability of young children to engage in metacognitive behaviour (Juliebö, Malicky, and Norman, 1997), there is still a question about the impact of metacognition on reading achievement. Ultimately, the aim of instruction is to help children achieve **automaticity** in their reading so that most of the time they do not have to consciously think about how to figure out words or to construct meaning. Brown (1980) refers to this as being on "automatic pilot." It is only when readers engage in a new reading activity or experience difficulty that they need to consciously think about what they are doing.

## Instructional Level

An area of controversy in the field of reading in recent years involves the notion of **instructional reading level,** which is similar to Vygotsky's (1978) **zone of proximal development**. This is the level just beyond the point at which children can construct meaning independently, the level at which they can construct meaning in an instructional context. If instruction is provided with materials below this level, the children practise existing strategies but do not develop new ones. If the materials are too difficult, the children struggle and become frustrated.

Some proponents of top-down theories recommend that one way to deal with this issue is to have all children work with the same material, but to have them receive different levels of support as they read. For example, a particular text might be appropriate for some children to read independently, for others to read with help from the teacher, and for others to listen to as the teacher reads. This is an acceptable practice as long as the children who do the listening also receive reading instruction using appropriate texts. Otherwise, some children may become good listeners but be denied the opportunity to learn to read.

How to match children with texts at an appropriate reading level is also an area of controversy. Proponents of bottom-up reading theories believe that the difficulty of a book can be determined by considering factors in the text, such as word and sentence length. In contrast, top-down theorists stress the impact of readers' knowledge and previous experience with texts on the meaning-making process. Some go so far as to ignore factors in the text, claiming that readability is determined almost entirely by children's interests and knowledge.

Proponents of interactive and social constructive reading theories disagree with both of these views. They maintain that regardless of how interested children are in a topic or how much background knowledge they have, factors in texts, such as word difficulty, sentence complexity, and text organization, directly influence the reader's meaning-making process. Conversely, these same educators say, no matter how short words or sentences are, children with no or very limited experience with the concepts in texts have difficulty constructing meaning. Social constructivists believe that text factors and children's experiences, knowledge, and interests need to be taken into account in selecting appropriate texts for them to read. Criteria and techniques for determining a child's instructional reading level are presented later in this chapter.

## Purpose for Reading

In her work on reader response, Rosenblatt (1978) pointed out that people read materials differently depending on their purpose for reading. When you were in elementary school, your teacher likely asked you to read both stories and informational material in a similar way. With both, you likely read and then answered a series of questions about what you had read. While this approach is appropriate for informational material — since **efferent** reading involves "taking away" information from what you have read — it is a questionable practice with narrative material. Rosenblatt maintains that children should be encouraged to read stories from an **aesthetic** stance, entering into and living through the stories rather than taking away information.

The distinction between efferent and aesthetic reading has implications for assessment and instruction. Perhaps most obvious from a social constructivist perspective is the need to include both narrative and informational materials in testing as well as instructional contexts. Even more crucial, however, is how we ask children to respond to these materials.

> Although this section dealt with only some of the issues facing reading teachers, from even this brief overview you can see that theory does have significant implications for practice. Reading programs based on bottom-up theories of reading contrast sharply with those based on top-down theories. Indeed, this difference has been at the heart of much of the great debate on reading touched on in Chapter One.

## Reading Assessment

> In this section, we begin with a focus on purposes for reading assessment and then move to a description of techniques that can be used to meet these purposes.

A major purpose of reading assessment is to obtain the information children and teachers need to optimize reading and learning. Children find out how they are doing and what they should do next. Teachers find out if what they are doing is working and what to have children do next. The ultimate goal in assessing any child's language learning is the improvement of instruction and of the child's reading. This sounds simple enough — figure out where the child is and go from there — but it becomes complicated by all kinds of other agendas from administrators, policy-makers, parents, and taxpayers. Assessment is also conducted to provide information to these stakeholders.

Parents have a right to know how their children are learning and functioning in schools, and administrators, policy-makers, and taxpayers have a right to know how effective reading programs are (Afflerbach, 1998). The central question in assessment, however, is what kind of information do teachers need to serve as a basis for program planning and for enhancing children's learning? And what are the best tools to gather this information?

## Standardized Tests

**Standardized tests** have been used in North American schools for many decades as one way to gather information about children's reading. Most of you will recall year-end reading tests when you were in school, and this practice continues today. In spite of changes in theories of reading, there has been little change in either the basic content or format of standardized tests since the 1930s. Most tests consist of word analysis, vocabulary, and comprehension subtests, and most comprehension subtests consist of numerous short paragraphs followed by multiple-choice questions (Hiebert and Raphael, 1996).

Standardized (sometimes called "norm-referenced") tests are developed by selecting items at a range of difficulty levels and administering them to children at various grade and age levels. Tables of norms are then developed, providing teachers with percentiles, grade equivalents, and/or standard scores corresponding to the number of items a child completes correctly. When a standardized test is administered, it determines how well the children in the class perform on the test in relation to the children in the standardization sample.

### Purpose and Use of Standardized Tests

The primary reason school systems and provincial governments administer standardized tests is accountability—to show that the programs provided in the school system are producing the desired results. Administrators compare the scores of one class, school, or system with those of the standardization sample and of other classes, schools, and systems. Sometimes scores are compared across provinces, states, and even nations.

To the extent that a standardized test is consistent with the curriculum of the language learning program in a particular school or classroom, it can provide one indication of the overall effectiveness of that program. The results indicate how the children in the program rank in relation to other children who took the test. Results can also be used to determine the relative strength of the children in a classroom in the areas measured by the test.

The results obtained on the *Gates-MacGinitie Reading Tests* (Canadian version, MacGinitie and MacGinitie, 1992) in a Grade 2 classroom are shown in Table 4.1. From these results, it appears that many children are achieving at a higher level in vocabulary than in comprehension. Their teacher may wish to examine the reading program and give greater emphasis to comprehension. This will be particularly important for those children who scored significantly lower on comprehension than on vocabulary. When children score low on the vocabulary subtest, the implications for instruction are less clear. Unless the teacher goes back over the test items with individual children, there is no way of knowing whether the low score reflects inability to identify the words or difficulty with word meaning. Results on standardized tests can also be used to indicate the need for more in-depth assessment for some children. From the results presented in Table 4.1, at least two children (3 and 25) are significantly below the others. However, it is highly likely that the teacher will have already identified these children as needing further assessment, from observing their work in class.

**Table 4.1    Results of a Grade 2 Class on the Gates-MacGinitie Reading Tests**

| Grade Equivalents* | | |
|---|---|---|
| Child | Vocabulary | Comprehension |
| 1 | 2.0 | 1.5 |
| 2 | 3.9 | 1.5 |
| 3 | 1.7 | 1.4 |
| 4 | 3.1 | 3.4 |
| 5 | 4.4 | 3.1 |
| 6 | 3.6 | 3.1 |
| 7 | 3.6 | 2.7 |
| 8 | 3.9 | 3.1 |
| 9 | 4.4 | 4.0 |
| 10 | 3.3 | 1.8 |
| 11 | 4.8 | 2.8 |
| 12 | 3.7 | 3.1 |
| 13 | 4.1 | 3.4 |
| 14 | 3.1 | 1.9 |
| 15 | 3.6 | 3.4 |
| 16 | 4.3 | 2.5 |
| 17 | 4.6 | 3.7 |
| 18 | 4.1 | 3.1 |
| 19 | 3.3 | 3.4 |
| 20 | 2.7 | 1.7 |
| 21 | 4.4 | 2.5 |
| 22 | 2.7 | 2.6 |
| 23 | 2.0 | 1.9 |
| 24 | 3.1 | 2.2 |
| 25 | 1.5 | 1.7 |
| 26 | 3.6 | 2.1 |

* A grade-equivalent score of 2.0 means that a child scored like the average child did in the standardization sample at the beginning of the Grade 2 school year.

## Critique of Standardized Tests

Standardized tests have come under considerable criticism in recent years (e.g., Pearson, 1998). One common criticism involves the extent to which items on standardized tests are consistent with the language arts programs being implemented. In particular, criticism is directed at the nature of the passages used to assess comprehension. They tend to be short and contrived rather than high-quality children's literature. The use of multiple-choice items leads opponents to contend that standardized tests fail to measure what really counts in reading — critical thinking, construction of meaning, collaborative learning. It is questionable whether the items on most standardized reading tests are appropriate for assessing the effectiveness of the type of language learning program being recommended in this textbook or those being implemented in many Canadian classrooms.

Rather than standardized tests measuring what is taught, the opposite is often the case — what is taught is determined by what is tested. Because of current demands by policymakers and taxpayers for accountability, the stakes are high. Hence, many teachers teach children what is measured on the tests. This narrows the curriculum and allows the tests to drive the curriculum, rather than the other way around.

There are other problems with standardized tests. Field (1990, p. 108) notes that test items are deliberately selected "to produce failure among some and success among others." How does this happen? When items are being selected for inclusion on a particular test, those items that all students get right or all students get wrong are eliminated because they do not help to differentiate among children. In other words, unless a set percentage of children fail an item, it is not included. And by linking scores on these tests to grade equivalents, it is predetermined that some children will be at grade level, some will be above, and some will be below. In other words, when norm-referenced tests are used, half of the children will succeed and half will fail. This leads to a basic contradiction between the goals of schooling and the use of standardized tests. On the one hand, most people believe that an appropriate goal of schooling is to ensure that all children are able to read at a level appropriate to their grade. On the other hand, the use of standardized tests means that this will never be achieved. Instead, some children are identified very early as reading below expectations, the emphasis being on what they cannot do rather than what they can do. This is by far the greatest concern with standardized tests of educators at all levels — the potentially negative impact that test results can have on individual children by marginalizing them and telling them that they are not good enough.

A relatively minor but widespread misuse of standardized test scores involves the way in which grade equivalents and other scores are interpreted. When someone says that a child is reading or writing at a particular grade level (e.g., 2.3), it is important to realize that this score should be interpreted as a range of scores around Grade 2.3. Every child's performance on a particular test will vary to some extent, depending on factors such as how the child feels, what the testing conditions are like, and how lucky the child is on the multiple-choice items that particular day. Variability in a child's performance on a test across time is referred to as the *standard error of measurement*. On the same test, an individual child might obtain a score of 2.3 on one day, 1.9 on another, and 2.6 on yet another. Because of this range, and also because of how grade equivalents are calculated (by comparing children with one another), grade equivalents can be used only in a very rough way to determine the appropriate level of materials for any particular child to read.

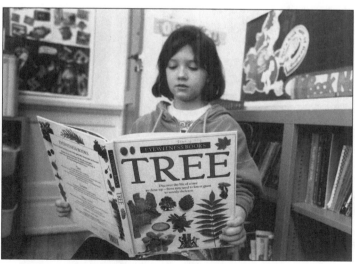

Upper elementary child reading a nonfiction book.

There are also misunderstandings surrounding the interpretation of percentile scores, largely because many people confuse them with percentages. Percentile ranks, which range from 1 to 99, indicate the proportion of students in the standardization sample who achieved raw scores higher or lower than a particular student. For example, a child with a percentile rank of 55 has performed as well as or better than 55 percent of the standardization sample. In other words, the child has performed better than over half of the children in the sample, and therefore is well within normal expectations for his or her grade and age level.

It is important to keep in mind that all these scores tell about an individual child is how he or she performed on one particular day compared with other children who completed that test. The scores tell little about how the child reads or about his or her specific instructional needs. With virtually no support among teachers for the use of standardized tests, many jurisdictions have moved to **performance assessment** instead.

## Performance Assessment

The essence of performance assessment is its emphasis on engaging children in the process about which the examiner wishes to draw inferences (Pearson, 1998). This type of assessment is viewed as providing teachers with the information needed for the daily planning of instruction, although there is less consensus that it provides an adequate basis for program evaluation at the school, system, or provincial levels. In performance assessment, the teacher observes children as they engage in daily reading activities in the classroom, asks children to talk about their reading, and collects samples of their reading for analysis.

### Observing Reading Behaviour

As noted in Chapter Three, teachers are continuously and implicitly assessing their students' reading each time they interact with them. The checklist provided in Table 4.2 is designed to help teachers observe and interpret children's reading behaviours during daily classroom reading instruction.

**Table 4.2    Reading Checklist**

| Aspects of Reading | Reading Strategy | Comments |
|---|---|---|
| Positive attitude to reading | ___ is able to name favourite books and authors<br>___ enjoys reading silently in class time<br>___ engages in extensive independent reading | |
| Integrates knowledge and text to construct meaning | ___ is able to set a purpose for reading<br>___ is able to predict what a story or text will be about from the title<br>___ is able to predict what will happen next in a story<br>___ uses both knowledge and text information to answer inference questions<br>___ retellings include inferences as well as text information | |
| Uses knowledge of text structure to construct meaning | ___ is able to answer questions about the setting, characters, events, and ending of stories<br>___ includes information from setting, events, and ending in retellings of stories<br>___ retells stories in sequence | |
| Uses knowledge of expository text structure to construct meaning | ___ is able to answer questions involving main idea, sequence, cause/effect, and comparison/contrast relationships<br>___ retellings reflect organizational patterns of informational texts (enumeration, cause/effect, sequence, comparison/contrast) | |
| Uses context cues to identify words | ___ oral reading miscues make sense and sound right in relation to prior text<br>___ gives real word rather than nonsense word responses when reading<br>___ corrects miscues that do not make sense | |

*(continued)*

**Table 4.2**   Continued

| Aspects of Reading | Reading Strategy | Comments |
|---|---|---|
| Uses print cues to identify words | ___ oral reading miscues look and sound like the words in the text | |
| | ___ most sounds are represented in inventive spellings | |
| | ___ identifies words by processing letter groups, syllables, or words within other words | |
| | ___ corrects miscues that do not "look right" | |
| Integrates context and print cues to identify words | ___ most miscues both make sense and sound right | |
| | ___ corrects most miscues that change the author's meaning | |
| Reads with automaticity | ___ identifies high-frequency words immediately | |
| | ___ reads fluently and at an appropriate rate | |
| | ___ completes silent reading assignments in a reasonable time | |

The headings in the left-hand column reflect those aspects of reading that are used to organize the teaching/learning techniques discussed in Chapters Five and Six. Hence, if a child does not display reading behaviours associated with a particular aspect of reading, you can go directly to the appropriate section in Chapter Five or Six to select the teaching/learning techniques to use with that child. For example, a child who is not yet able to include information from the setting, events, and endings of stories in retellings would benefit from work on narrative **text structure**. A child who is not yet representing most letters in inventive spellings and whose miscues bear little resemblance to words he or she is reading would benefit from work on phonemic awareness and letter sounds.

## Interviews

During classroom interactions, teachers can encourage children to talk about what they read, why they read, and how they read. The interview schedule outlined in Table 4.3 is designed to help teachers collect more specific information about a child's reading interests, habits, and knowledge about reading. A range of interview schedules were consulted in devising this one, including those of Atwell (1987); Goodman, Watson, and Burke (1987); and Lipson and Wixson (1991).

You will not likely ask any child all of these questions in one sitting. Instead, you will think about what you need to know about a particular child and select those questions that might help gather this information. For example, if a child rarely chooses books to read independently, you might ask the questions about interests and attitudes. If a child appears to have few strategies for making meaning as he or she reads, you might ask the last four questions in the reading strategies section.

## Reading Samples

As with emergent readers, you will want to save samples of children's reading throughout the school year to assess growth. Reading logs, which are commonly kept in children's reading portfolios, provide one type of information. In their logs, children keep a list of books they have read during the year, and make note of the amount,

**Table 4.3    Reading Interview**

| Area | Questions |
|---|---|
| Interests | • What kinds of things do you like to do in your spare time?<br>• What is your favourite subject at school?  Why?<br>• What kinds of books do you like to read?<br>• Name two books that you have read recently that you liked. |
| Attitudes | • If you could read a story or watch it on television, which would you choose? Why?<br>• How much time do you spend reading each day at home? at school?<br>• How many books do you own?  Do you go to the library to get books?<br>• How do you feel about reading? |
| Knowledge about Reading | |
| Functions of reading | • What is reading?<br>• Why do people read? |
| Reading strategies | • Think of someone who is a good reader.  How do you know he or she is a good reader?<br>• How would you help someone who was having trouble reading?<br>• What do you think about as you read?<br>• What do you do when you are reading and come to a word you don't know?<br>• What do you do when you are reading and something doesn't make sense?<br>• What do you do to help you remember what you read (e.g., in social studies)?<br>• Do you ever read something over again?  Why?<br>• Do you read some things faster than others?  Why? |
| Self-Appraisal | • How would you describe yourself as a reader?<br>• Is learning to read easy or hard?  Why?<br>• What's the easiest thing about reading for you?  What's the hardest thing?<br>• What kind of help do you think you need with your reading? |

genre, and level of material read. Wiseman (1992) suggests that the date each book was selected and completed also be recorded in the log, along with the child's comments about the book. These entries can help teachers determine children's growth in voluntary reading behaviour.

Another way to sample children's reading is through their written responses to literature. It is crucial to examine these responses in terms of the child's ability to reflect on the text and to relate it to his or her own life. Examples of children's responses to literature, as well as interpretations of these responses, are provided in Chapter Eleven. The responses illustrate how children interact with texts rather than their specific use of reading strategies. It is also important to keep in mind when examining responses that they are often as much a reflection of writing ability as reading comprehension.

Information on strategies and achievement can also be gathered by examining children's responses to reading comprehension assignments. Samples of written answers to questions can be included in the child's portfolio periodically throughout the school year. Again, however, it should be kept in mind that these may provide an underestimate of reading comprehension, depending on the child's level of writing proficiency. It is also useful to collect samples of children's oral reading to examine their growth in using meaning and print cues to identify words. As with young children, running records can be kept of children reading stories from basal texts, books, or passages specifically designed for this purpose. While it is more authentic to gather running records on materials actually being used in the classroom, at times teachers may wish to use informal reading inventories.

Informal Reading Inventories    Informal reading inventories usually consist of two components: a series of word lists, and a number of passages with comprehension questions at increasing levels of reading difficulty. The word lists included on the inventories are used to estimate the reading level at which to begin administering reading passages. That level is the one at which children can identify all or most of the words. This ensures that children do not spend time reading passages that are much too easy or much too difficult for them.

The teacher then has the child read passages orally and silently and answer the questions about them. The child continues to read passages of increasing difficulty until he or she is no longer able to identify 90 percent of the words or answer 70 percent of the questions correctly. As the child reads orally, the teacher keeps a running record of oral reading miscues and writes down the child's answers to comprehension questions. The marking system used for taking a running record with emergent readers is also an appropriate means of recording miscues for more independent readers. An adaptation of this system for use with independent readers is included at the top of Box 4.2.

Many teachers choose to use informal reading inventories because the passages and questions are all in one place and the teacher does not have to search out a series of books at a range of reading levels and design tasks to assess comprehension of passages in these books. Informal inventories are designed to be administered individually, so they are used primarily with children when the teacher is puzzled and needs more information to plan appropriate instruction. A wide range of informal reading inventories is available, including the *Informal Reading Inventory* (Burns and Roe, 1993), *Classroom Assessment of Reading Processes* (Swearingen and Allen, 1997), and the *Informal Reading–Thinking Inventory* (Manzo, Manzo, and McKenna, 1995). The last two inventories include both narrative and expository passages.

Interpreting Informal Reading Inventories    The teacher gets two major types of information from an informal reading inventory: achievement and diagnostic information. The child's level of reading achievement is the highest level at which the child meets the criteria set in the test for instructional reading level.

Although tests vary, the instructional reading level is generally the level at which the child is able to identify 90 percent or more of the words accurately *and* answer 70 percent or more of the comprehension questions correctly. The child is able to read material independently if word identification and comprehension are close to 100 percent. Material is too difficult for a child if he or she reads with less than 90 percent accuracy *or* less than 60 percent comprehension. It is important to remember that informal inventories provide only a rough indication of the level of material children can handle.

Children may be able to understand more difficult material if they know a great deal about it or are very interested in it. On the other hand, if the topic in a narrative or informational passage is unfamiliar, children may have difficulty with it even if it is at their instructional reading level as determined on an informal reading inventory.

Many informal reading inventories include an activity for children to do before they read each passage, to assess their background knowledge. On the *Qualitative Reading Inventory*, for example, children are asked to associate meanings with key concepts in passages to be read. On other inventories, they are asked to read the title and predict what passages will be about. Still others ask children to rate their knowledge about the content of the passage after they have finished reading it. From a social constructive perspective, a reader's knowledge is a critical component in the reading process.

How the reader uses this knowledge along with print and text information is even more important. Unfortunately, because we cannot get inside children's heads to see reading as it occurs, we have to rely on indirect evidence to interpret what they are doing. Two major sources of diagnostic data from informal reading inventories that provide this evidence are oral reading miscues and answers to questions.

**Miscues**  Oral reading miscues are analyzed according to the same two major **cuing systems** as for emergent readers — meaning and print. The major difference is that the criteria for coding miscues are more stringent. The criteria, as well as examples of miscues of a Grade 4 child, Paul, are presented in Box 4.2. The passage in this example is a goal-based narrative at the Grade 4 level from the *Qualitative Reading Inventory* (Leslie and Caldwell, 1990).

---

**Box 4.2    Oral Reading Miscues of a Grade 4 Boy**

Marking system for miscues

A substituted word or mispronunciation is written above the text word.
An omission is indicated with a circle around the word.
A *T* is written above words provided by the teacher.
An insertion is indicated with a caret.
*SC* indicates that a miscue was corrected.

Coding system for miscues

*M* (meaning-based): miscue makes sense in relation to prior text and the rest of the sentence as the child reads it.
*P* (print-based): miscue contains half or more of the same letters as the text word.
*I* (integrative, both print and meaning): miscue contains half or more of the same letters as the text word *and* makes sense in relation to prior text and the rest of the sentence.

Excerpt from a Grade 4 passage
            I                              I
Johnny                      for
John first gathered bags of apple seeds. He got

many of his seeds from farmers who squeezed apples to make a drink called cider. Then, in the spring, he left
                        P
                front tire SC
for the western frontier.
                    I
                trees
He planted seeds as he went along. Also, he gave them to people who knew how valuable apple trees were.
    John walked many miles in all kinds of weather. He had to cross dangerous rivers and find his way
                                        I
                                    cool
through strange forests. Often he was hungry, cold and wet. Sometimes he had to hide from unfriendly Indians. His clothes became ragged and torn. He used
        M
        his
a sack for a shirt, and he cut out holes for the arms. He wore no shoes. But he never gave up. He guarded his precious seeds and carefully planted them where they
                                        P
                                strange SC
had the best chance of growing into strong trees.

Source: Reading passage excerpted from B.B. Armbruster, C.L. Mitsakas, and V.R. Rogers (1986), *America's History*. Peterborough, NH: Schoolhouse Press. Copyright © 1986 by Schoolhouse Press. Reprinted by permission of the publisher.

It appears from the number of miscues on this passage that fourth-grade material is at Paul's instructional level. When asked to read material at the fifth-grade level, he made well over the acceptable number of miscues. When reading material at his instructional level, however, he showed that he was able to effectively use both print and context cues to predict words that made sense, sounded right, and checked out with the print. He was able to integrate print and knowledge-based cues to construct meaning as he read. Like many good readers, he corrected miscues when they did not make sense. He did not correct his substitution of *for* for *of* because this miscue was consistent with the meaning that he constructed. He was able to answer seven of the eight questions asked about this passage, confirming that he was able to effectively construct meaning when reading this passage.

The miscues for Kyla, a Grade 3 girl, are presented in Box 4.3. Kyla met the criteria for instructional reading level for both miscues and comprehension questions on the Grade 2 passage shown, but experienced frustration on more difficult passages. The most obvious thing about Kyla's miscues is the number she corrected. This shows that she was aware of when at least some of her miscues did not make sense or look right. Her self-corrections also indicate that she has developed some effective strategies for word identification. However, these strategies are not yet well enough developed to enable her to handle material at a third-grade level.

Effective readers use cues both in context and within words as they read. Miscues help teachers determine where to place the instructional focus at any point in time. For example:

- If children focus almost exclusively on print cues in material at their instructional level, they need less attention to cues within words for a while and a heavier focus on using context cues.
- If their miscues make sense but are not consistent with print cues, they need instruction on strategies for processing cues within words.

As soon as children begin to show more effective use of the cuing system that is the focus of instruction, however, it is crucial to provide a balanced program so that

---

**Box 4.3**    **Oral Reading Miscues of a Grade 3 Girl**

Excerpt from a Grade 2 passage

It was a Saturday morning. John looked at the toys in his room. They were all old and he wanted something new. John went to his mother. "All my toys are old," he said. "I want something new to play with." His

N
mother looked at (him) "John, we don't have the money
SC
All
to buy you anything new. You'll have to find a way to make something new." John went back to his room and looked around at the toys. There were many toys that were fun. But he had played with them so much
SC
They
that they weren't fun anymore. Then he had an idea.

M
one
His friend Chris wanted a truck just like his red truck.
SC
And John wanted a car like the (one) Chris got for his birthday. Maybe they could trade. John ran down the street to Chris's house. "Hey, Chris would you like to trade your car for my truck?" "Sure," said Chris. "I'll
P
They
trade. Later we can trade something else. That way
P    SC
well  away
we'll always have something new to play with."

Source: Reading passage excerpted from L. Leslie and J. Caldwell (1990), *Qualitative Reading Inventory*. New York: HarperCollins Publishers, p. 117. Reprinted by permission of Addison-Wesley Educational Publishers Inc.

children learn to use multiple sources of information to identify unfamiliar words. An analysis of Paul's miscues shows that he is able to use print and meaning cues, and that he can integrate them to construct a message consistent with that intended by the author. Kyla was also able to do this most of the time when reading a Grade 2 passage, but she needs to develop further strategies for dealing with both print and knowledge-based information so that she can handle material consistent with her grade placement.

**Questions**  Teachers use question data to determine what types of questions a child is able to answer. If children are successful in answering factual questions, they appear to be able to use text information to construct meaning. If they are successful in answering inferential questions, they appear to be able to integrate their world knowledge with text information to construct meaning as they read.

Children who are able to answer factual but not inferential questions may think reading is a meaning-getting rather than meaning-making enterprise, or they may not know how to use their knowledge along with text to construct meaning. They benefit from the teaching/learning strategies described in Chapter Five in the section on integrating knowledge-based and text-based information.

Children who are able to answer inferential questions better than factual ones may be relying too much on their background knowledge to construct meaning. Often, if they're asked to retell what they have read, they demonstrate limited processing of text information. They frequently benefit from teaching/learning strategies designed to help them use the structure of narrative and expository texts to construct meaning.

## Portfolios

Portfolios have been defined as "collections of artifacts of students' learning experiences assembled over time" (Valencia, Hiebert, and Afflerbach, 1994, p. 14). The reading portfolio provides information on children's reading, including strategies that they use in a range of everyday reading activities. The process of developing and discussing the portfolio is also intended to help children develop metacognition as they reflect on their reading (Wiener and Cohen, 1997).

Contents of a portfolio vary as a function of classroom events and the choices of teachers and students. In addition to information obtained from observations, interviews, and reading samples as outlined above, portfolios often include

- reading logs,
- responses to literature,
- reading and content area projects,
- self-assessments,
- family information, and
- (sometimes) the results on standardized reading tests.

A reading log is a record of what children have read. Responses to literature give an indication of how they interacted with literature. Projects reveal how effectively children used their reading strategies on an authentic reading activity, independently or in collaboration with their peers.

One of the arguments put forward in support of portfolio assessments is their potential for involving children in the assessment process. This involves much more than a change in how assessment is done. It suggests a fundamental change in the way power relationships are constituted between teachers and children. Children participate in decisions not only about what goes into portfolios, but also about what counts as "good" reading. The kinds of questions included in the self-appraisal section of the reading interview presented in this chapter provide a starting point. Many teachers ask children to select at least some of the reading samples included in their portfolios. They sit down with children periodically to look at and talk about the reading growth shown in their portfolio samples. Children are frequently invited to share their portfolios with their parents when they visit the school. When teaching a new reading strategy in the classroom, teachers invite children to comment on whether the strategy works for them and why or why not. These and other comments are included in some portfolios.

The content of reading portfolios reflects the reading theories of teachers, the reading programs in classrooms, and children's interests, goals, and strategies. Hence, there is considerable diversity in the nature of portfolios across children and classrooms. However, there remains a critical question. To what extent do portfolios reflect a real change from standardized tests in how reading is assessed? In our view,

- To the extent that teachers determine what counts as "good" reading, the collaborative potential of portfolios will not be achieved. When children are asked to participate in the assessment process, they are frequently asked to judge their progress toward goals set by the teacher.
- To the extent that performance assessment continues to focus on individual accountability and on reading as individual skill accumulation (Bloome, 1991), such assessment may not accomplish much more than standardized testing. Teachers may tell children that it is important for them to work together and may provide opportunities for them to work in groups, but if all assessment focusses on individual learning, children will know their teachers don't really value collaboration.
- To the extent that the focus is on how well children read rather than on how they read and use reading in their daily lives, there is not much difference between informal and standardized assessment.

Much of the pressure for standard criteria for evaluating material in portfolios comes from attempts to replace standardized testing with performance assessment. Both Pearson (1998) and Hiebert and Raphael (1996) note that research on portfolio assessment is not encouraging when it is used for high-stakes decisions regarding accountability or entry and exit of children from special programs. The major problem involves lack of consistency and comparability of teacher ratings across classrooms and jurisdictions.

It does not appear that one type of reading assessment can meet the needs of all stakeholders in education — students, teachers, parents, policy-makers, administrators, and the public. Standardized tests are more appropriate than performance assessment to answer the questions of policy-makers, administrators, and taxpayers about the effectiveness of reading programs. This does not mean that standardized tests cannot be improved, particularly in light of their mismatch with current theories and practices in reading. However, for performance assessment to achieve its potential, it does appear that we need to resist pressure to reduce the contents of portfolios to those pieces that answer the question of whether a child has met the standards for his or her grade level. Only when the information in portfolios is dedicated to describing children's reading will teachers have the information they need to plan appropriate instruction.

Reading assessment is not valuable for its own sake, but only if the information gathered is used to plan effective reading instruction and experiences for children in classrooms. Our goal as reading teachers is to match instruction and experiences with children's reading levels, interests, and strategy development in order to maximize their reading growth.

## Summary

Psychological theories have dominated the field of reading throughout most of this century. Behaviourist theories lead to skills models, in which reading is broken down into component skills to be learned one at a time. Cognitive theories place the focus on the reading process. In bottom-up theories of reading, the focus is on print, and processing proceeds from parts to wholes. In top-down theories, the focus is on readers' knowledge, and processing proceeds from wholes to parts. Interactive models of reading combine ideas from bottom-up and top-down theories. Meaning is viewed as resulting from interaction between the reader and text, and processing of parts and wholes occurs simultaneously.

Recognizing the importance of social interactions and social contexts in learning underlies social constructive theories of reading. These theorists see meaning as being constructed by readers during the act of reading, rather than being transmitted from authors to readers. We define reading in this textbook as the active construction of meaning from cues in the text and from the reader's background knowledge within a social context. This definition has implications for what children read, the nature of instruction in classrooms, the role of metacognition and automaticity in reading, the significance of instructional reading level, and the nature of purposes for reading.

A major goal of language learning assessment is to improve instruction in order to maximize children's reading growth. Two major types of assessment tools are standardized tests and performance assessment. Standardized tests measure a child's reading achievement in relation to other children's, and the primary purpose of this type of assessment is accountability. However, teachers need different information to serve as a basis for daily planning, and performance assessment is widely employed for this purpose. The focus of this type of assessment is on what children do as they read.

Checklists and interviews are used to assess how children use print-based and knowledge-based cues to construct meaning as they read. Reading logs are records of what children have read, and response journals provide an indication of how children interpret and react to literature. Samples of children's oral and silent reading are collected using informal reading inventories or as children engage in daily reading in the classroom. Examining answers to comprehension questions and oral reading miscues reveals further information on children's use of print-based and knowledge-based cues as they read.

## Selected Professional Resources

Cassidy, J. and Wenrich, J.K. (1998–99). Literacy research and practices: What's hot, what's not, and why. *Reading Teacher, 52* (4), 402–406. The authors present the results of interviews with literacy leaders from around the world on what's hot and what's not hot in the popular press and professional venues. Understanding which issues are influencing parents and policy-makers helps teachers influence policy and address parental concerns. It also provides a perspective from which to view, and possibly avoid, bandwagons.

Rhodes, L.K. (1993). *Literacy Assessment: A Handbook of Instruments*. Portsmouth, NH: Heinemann. Rhodes pulls together informal assessment tools from a wide range of sources, including interview schedules, checklists, miscue analysis, self-assessments, and observation schedules. These assessment tools focus on emergent literacy, reading, and writing.

# References

Adams, M.J., Anderson, R.C., and Durkin, D. (1978). Beginning reading: Theory and practice. *Language Arts, 55,* 19–25.

Afflerbach, P. (1998). Reading assessment and learning to read. In J. Osborn and F. Lehr (eds.), *Literacy for all: Issues in teaching and learning* (pp. 239–263). New York: The Guilford Press.

Atwell, N. (1987). *In the middle: Writing, reading, and learning with adolescents.* Portsmouth, NH: Heinemann.

Beck, I.L. (1998). Understanding beginning reading: A journey through teaching and research. In J. Osborn and F. Lehr (eds.), *Literacy for all: Issues in teaching and learning* (pp. 11–31). New York: The Guilford Press.

Bloome, D. (1991). Anthropology and research on teaching the English language arts. In J. Flood, J.M. Jensen, D. Lapp, and J.R. Squire (eds.), *Handbook of research on teaching the English language arts* (pp. 46–65). New York: Macmillan.

Bogdan, D. and Straw, S. (1993). Introduction. In S.B. Straw and D. Bogdan (eds.), *Constructive reading: Teaching beyond communication* (pp. 1–14). Portsmouth, NH: Heinemann.

Brown, A. (1980). Metacognitive development and reading. In R.J. Spiro, B.C. Bruce, and W.F. Brewer (eds.), *Theoretical issues in reading comprehension* (pp. 453–481). Hillsdale, NJ: Lawrence Erlbaum Associates.

Burns, P.C. and Roe, B.D. (1993). *Informal reading inventory.* Chicago: Rand McNally.

Cassidy, J. and Wenrich, J.K. (1998–99). Literacy research and practices: What's hot, what's not, and why. *Reading Teacher, 52* (4), 402–406.

Cunningham, P.M. and Allington, R.L. (1999). *Classrooms that work: They can all read and write* (2nd ed.). New York: Longman.

DeFord, D.E. (1985). Validating the construct of theoretical orientation in reading instruction. *Reading Research Quarterly, 20* (3), 351–367.

Field, J.C. (1990). Educators' perspectives on assessment: Tensions, contradictions and dilemmas. PhD dissertation, University of Victoria, Victoria, BC.

Flavell, J.H. (1979). Metacognition and cognitive monitoring: A new area of cognitive-developmental inquiry. *American Psychologist, 34,* 906–911.

Goodman, K.S. (1970). Behind the eye: What happens in reading. In K.S. Goodman and O. Niles (eds.), *Reading: Process and program* (pp. 3–38). Urbana, IL: National Council of Teachers of English.

Goodman, K.S. (1986). *What's whole in whole language?* Richmond Hill, ON: Scholastic-TAB.

Goodman, K.S., Watson, D.J., and Burke, C.L. (1987). *Reading miscue inventory: Alternative procedures.* New York: Macmillan.

Gough, P.B. (1972). One second of reading. In J. Kavanagh and J.G. Mattingly (eds.), *Language by ear and eye* (pp. 331–358). Cambridge, MA: MIT Press.

Hiebert, E.H. and Raphael, T.E. (1996). Psychological perspectives on literacy and extension to educational practice. In D.C. Berliner and R.C. Calfee (eds.), *Handbook of educational psychology* (pp. 550–602). New York: Macmillan.

Huey, E.B. (1908). *The psychology and pedagogy of reading.* New York: Macmillan.

Hughes, M. and McInnes, J. (1983). *Reading and how.* Scarborough, ON: Nelson Canada.

Jacobs, J.E. and Paris, S.G. (1987). Children's metacognition about reading: Issues in definition, measurement, and instruction. *Educational Psychologist, 22* (3 and 4), 255–278.

Juliebö, M.F., Malicky, G.V., and Norman, C.A. (1997). Metacognition of young readers in an early intervention program. *Journal of Research in Reading, 21* (1), 21–32.

Leslie, L. and Caldwell, J. (1990). *Qualitative reading inventory.* New York: HarperCollins.

Lipson, M.Y. and Wixson, K.K. (1991). *Assessment and instruction of reading disability: An interactive approach.* New York: HarperCollins.

MacGinitie, W.H. and MacGinitie, R.K. (1992). *Gates-MacGinitie reading tests* (2nd Canadian ed.). Scarborough, ON: Nelson Canada.

Malicky, G.V. (1991). Myths and assumptions of literacy education. *Alberta Journal of Educational Research, 37* (4), 333–347.

Manzo, A.V., Manzo, U.C., and McKenna, M.D. (1995). *Informal reading–thinking inventory.* New York: Harcourt Brace College.

Murphy, S. (1991). Authorship and discourse types in Canadian basal reading programs. *Reflections on Canadian Literacy, 9* (3 and 4), 133–138.

Paris, S.G., Wasik, B.A., and Turner, J.C. (1991). The development of strategic readers. In R. Barr, M.L. Kamil, P.B. Mosenthal, and P.D. Pearson (eds.), *Handbook of reading research,* Vol. 2 (pp. 609–640). White Plains, NY: Longman.

Pearson, P.D. (1998). Standards and assessments: Tools for crafting effective instruction? In J. Osborn and F. Lehr (eds.), *Literacy for all: Issues in teaching and learning* (pp. 264–288). New York: The Guilford Press.

Pinnell, G.S. and Fountas, I.C. (1998). *Word matters: Teaching phonics and spelling in the reading/writing classroom.* Portsmouth, NH: Heinemann.

Pressley, M. (1998). Comprehension strategies instruction. In J. Osborn and F. Lehr (eds.), *Literacy for all: Issues in teaching and learning* (pp. 113–133). New York: The Guilford Press.

Purcell-Gates, V. (1998). Growing successful readers: Homes, communities, and schools. In J. Osborn and F. Lehr (eds.), *Literacy for all: Issues in teaching and learning* (pp. 51–72). New York: The Guilford Press.

Rhodes, L.K. (1993). *Literacy assessment: A handbook of instruments.* Portsmouth, NH: Heinemann.

Rosenblatt, L. (1978). *The reader, the text, the poem: The transactional theory of the literary work.* Carbondale, IL: Southern Illinois University Press.

Ruddell, R.B. and Unrau, N.J. (1994). Reading as a meaning construction process: The reader, the text and the teacher. In R.B. Ruddell, M.R. Ruddell, and H. Singer (eds.), *Theoretical models and processes of reading* (pp. 996–1056). Newark, DE: International Reading Association.

Rumelhart, D.E. (1977). *Introduction to human information processing theory.* New York: John Wiley & Sons.

Straw, S.B. (1990). The actualization of reading and writing: Public policy and conceptualizations of literacy. In S.P. Norris and L.M. Phillips (eds.), *Literacy policy in Canada* (pp. 165–181). Calgary: Detselig Enterprises.

Swearingen, R. and Allen, D. (1997). *Classroom assessment of reading.* Boston: Houghton Mifflin Company.

Valencia, S.W., Hiebert, E.H., and Afflerbach, P.P. (eds.). (1994). *Authentic reading assessment: Practices and possibilities.* Newark, DE: International Reading Association.

Vygotsky, L.S. (1978). *Mind in society: The development of higher psychological processes.* M. Cole, V. John-Steiner, S. Scribner, and E. Souberman (eds.). Cambridge, MA: Harvard University Press.

Wiener, R.B. and Cohen, J.H. (1997). *Literacy portfolios: Using assessment to guide instruction.* Columbus, OH: Prentice-Hall.

Wiseman, D.L. (1992). *Learning to read with literature.* Boston: Allyn and Bacon.

# Chapter five

# Comprehension Strategies and Critical Literacy

Overview of Comprehension Instruction
- Questions
- Skills
- Strategies

Integrating Knowledge-Based and Text-Based Information
- Directed Reading–Thinking Activity
- KWL
- Question–Answer Relationship
- Reciprocal Teaching
- Think-Alouds
- Semantic Webs

Comprehension Strategies and Critical Literacy

Using Text Structure
- Narrative Texts
- Informational Texts

Studying
- Using Comprehension Strategies
- SQ3R

Critical Literacy
- Critical Reading
- The Nature of Multicultural Education
- Awareness and Understanding of Diversity
- Transformation and Social Action

A group of children in Grade 5 have just finished reading an informational text on the Caribou Gold Rush, and their teacher is leading a discussion to determine what meaning they have constructed. When she asks where gold was discovered in 1958, most of the children reply that it was near the junction of the Fraser and Assiniboine rivers, but Daniel says, "I think it was in Alaska. I heard about that in a TV program." Daniel is relying too heavily on his own knowledge at this point and not enough on the text. At another point in the discussion, the teacher asks the children to think about how the prospectors felt who did not strike it rich. Immediately, Heather answers, "It didn't say." In contrast with Daniel, Heather is not making enough use of her background knowledge. Other children begin to talk about what it might be like to be poor. ■

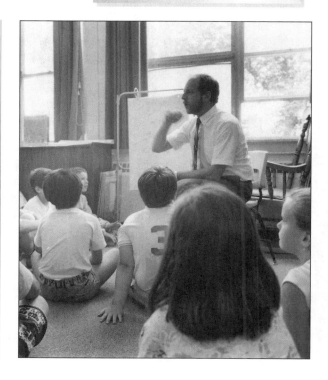

From a social constructive perspective, both text cues and background knowledge are crucial to constructing meaning while reading, and one important goal of reading instruction is to help children learn how to use these sources of information in an integrated manner. Another goal is to help children become aware of the impact of discrimination and inequities in society. Some of your questions as you prepare to teach reading likely include

- How can I help children make more effective use of cues in the text?
- How can I help children make more effective use of their background knowledge when reading?
- How can I help children integrate text cues and background knowledge when constructing meaning?
- How can I help children become aware of inequities in society?

The focus of this chapter is on instructional techniques to develop comprehension and critical literacy. Techniques for developing reading comprehension are organized according to information sources used by readers. Some techniques foster an integrated use of both knowledge-based and text-based information, whereas others focus on the use of text structure. Most of the techniques included in this chapter can be used to help children construct meaning from texts in social studies and science classes as well as in language arts classes. We begin, however, with a brief overview of how reading comprehension has been taught in the last few decades.

## Overview of Comprehension Instruction

Many of you received basic reading instruction in the elementary grades from a **basal reading series**. Two major techniques were recommended in these series for developing reading comprehension. In the first, the teacher asked questions while and after students read stories. In the second, children completed exercises (workbook, worksheet, and chalkboard) to develop specific comprehension skills. Both of these clearly reflect a transmission model of learning.

### Questions

Considerable research has been conducted on the questions teachers ask during reading instruction, and the results show that these questions generally test rather than teach reading comprehension (Durkin, 1978–79). Rather than teaching readers how to construct meaning while they read, the questions check whether the reader has constructed the teacher's meaning.

Researchers have also examined the level of questions teachers ask. Hierarchies of questions, such as those based on Bloom's taxonomy (1956), have been provided to reading teachers for decades. Although they vary, they commonly include at least three levels — literal, inferential, and critical — and are based on an assumption that meaning is a static reality that exists within the text.

- *Literal questions* require the reader to read the lines to comprehend what the author says.
- *Inferential questions* require the reader to read "between the lines" to infer relationships among ideas and draw conclusions intended but not explicitly stated by the author.

- *Critical questions* require readers to use their knowledge to make objective or subjective evaluations of the ideas in the text.

Research shows that teachers ask far more literal questions than ones involving inference, evaluation, or other higher-level thinking skills. A steady diet of factual questions may communicate to children that the meaning is on the page. It is little wonder that when asked an inferential question, some children such as Heather in the example at the beginning of this chapter respond, "It didn't say."

Questioning can be a powerful technique for helping children learn how to construct meaning as they read, and it is involved in many of the techniques described in this chapter. However, too often teachers ask most of the questions and the discourse falls into the pattern described in Chapter One: teacher-initiation, student-response, teacher-evaluation. Teacher questions also use up a lot of instructional time on testing rather than teaching, and they may communicate some unintended messages about reading if they are not carefully planned and formulated.

## Skills

Besides questioning, basal reading series have traditionally included exercises to develop comprehension skills such as finding the main idea, recalling details, and drawing conclusions. These exercises were generally presented in workbooks or on worksheets, often with little or no teaching beforehand of the skills needed to complete them. There is little support in the research for these types of skill-based exercises (Pearson and Fielding, 1991).

## Strategies

Researchers have found that instruction focussed on developing adaptable and flexible comprehension **strategies** helps children construct meaning. Instructional strategies that have proven their worth include activating prior knowledge, constructing mental images, analyzing stories into their story grammar components, generating questions, and summarizing. These strategies can be applied before (e.g., making predictions based on prior knowledge), during (e.g., mental imaging), and after (summarizing) reading. Students can also be taught repertoires of comprehension strategies through techniques such as reciprocal teaching (Pressley, 1998).

Overall, research has provided support for the following steps in the development of strategies:

1. direct explanation of strategies, including modelling,

2. teacher-supported practice of the strategies, and

3. independent application in a variety of contexts.

It is important to have children talk about why, how and when to use strategies during the first two steps if they are to develop metacognitive awareness and control.

Many instructional techniques foster strategy development. We have been very selective in this chapter, choosing strategies supported by research that are appropriate for helping children use both knowledge-based and text-based information in narrative and informational texts.

# Integrating Knowledge-Based and Text-Based Information

The focus of the techniques described in this section is on helping readers use what they know and what is on the page together as they read. An overview of the techniques and specific objectives for each technique are presented in Table 5.1.

## Directed Reading–Thinking Activity

The directed reading–thinking activity (or DRTA) is an instructional technique for use with narrative material. Students first predict what they will read, and then they check their predictions through subsequent reading. Formulated by Stauffer (1975), the technique helps students actively seek information from the material they read. The teacher acts as a catalyst to thought by asking such questions as

- What do you think?
- Why do you think so?
- How can you support it?

As readers predict what they will read, they rely on their knowledge, and as they check their predictions, they use cues in the text.

The DRTA is most appropriate for narrative material with a clearly defined plot that can easily be read in one sitting. Short mystery stories are ideal for this activity. The basic steps in the technique are outlined here and summarized in Figure 5.1.

**Table 5.1**  Instructional Techniques for Integrating Knowledge-Based and Text-Based Information

| Technique | Material | Helps Children |
|---|---|---|
| Directed Reading–Thinking Activity | Narrative texts with strong plot lines | • set purposes for reading narrative texts<br>• make and evaluate predictions during reading |
| KWL | Informational texts | • set purposes for reading informational texts<br>• ask and answer questions during reading |
| Question–Answer Relationship | Narrative and informational texts | • determine which information sources are required to answer specific questions<br>• answer text-based and knowledge-based questions |
| Reciprocal Teaching | Informational texts | • summarize text information<br>• ask questions<br>• clarify parts of texts that are confusing<br>• make predictions |
| Think-Aloud | Narrative and informational texts | • make predictions<br>• form visual images as they read<br>• link prior knowledge with text information<br>• monitor ongoing comprehension<br>• correct comprehension confusions |
| Semantic Webs | Narrative and informational texts | • activate knowledge before reading<br>• construct relationships among ideas<br>• relate text information with prior knowledge |

**Figure 5.1   Steps in a Directed Reading–Thinking Activity**

1. Based on the title and illustration or first paragraph of a story, the teacher asks students to predict what will happen by asking questions such as

   • What do you think this story will be about?
   • What do you think will happen in this story?
   • Why do you think so?

This last question is particularly important, because it gives children an opportunity to refer to both their knowledge and the cues in the title, picture, or first paragraph.

During the prediction process, the teacher's role is not to evaluate predictions, but rather to activate thought by asking students to defend their hypotheses. In Grade 1 classrooms, some teachers have the children whisper their predictions to a partner to ensure that all are engaging in the predicting process. The children then share their predictions in the group context, and the teacher writes them on the board for later reference. Once children are able to read and write independently, they can fill in prediction charts and share them with partners.

2. Students are then asked to read silently to a certain point in the material to confirm or disprove their hypotheses. It is particularly effective to have children stop at suspenseful points in the story.

3. After the students have read to the designated point, they discuss which of their hypotheses were confirmed. The teacher asks for evidence from the text to support the plausibility and accuracy of the hypotheses.

   • What do you think now?
   • Find the part in the text to confirm or disconfirm your prediction.

Students might read aloud a sentence or paragraph to provide this evidence. Again, this helps to focus attention on both text-based and knowledge-based information.

4. After students have completed the three-step process (predict, read, prove) with one segment of the material, they go on to the next segment. The process continues until they have read the entire text. Throughout, the teacher serves as a mentor to refine and deepen the reading–thinking process, but takes care not to evaluate the students' predictions. It is also useful to emphasize the importance of evaluating and finding proof in the text rather than deciding who is right or wrong. The DRTA is not a contest; it is a technique to make sure individuals start thinking before they begin to read.

Gillet and Temple (1994) suggest no more than five stops in one story in one sitting so as not to interrupt the students' reading too frequently. The DRTA is particularly helpful for those children who take a passive approach to reading and who appear to believe that the message is in the book. However, the technique will help these children become active, purposeful readers only if they know why they are doing it and how they can use a similar strategy when they read independently.

## KWL

The KWL technique helps children construct meaning when reading **expository writing.** Modelling the active thinking involved in reading for information (Ogle, 1986), the technique involves children using the following three basic steps:

1. accessing what they *know,*
2. deciding what they *want* to learn, and
3. recalling what they did *learn* as a result of reading.

The children use a group or individual chart like the one in Box 5.1 to guide them through these steps.

1. *K–What I know.* The children brainstorm information they know about the topic or a key concept in the material (e.g., wolves). The teacher records what the students brainstorm on the board or an overhead. The goal of this brainstorming is to activate whatever knowledge the readers have that will help them construct meaning as they read. Ogle (1986) suggests deepening students' thinking by asking questions such as

   • Where did you learn that?
   • How can you prove that?

To avoid implying a transmission model of knowledge, some teachers have children differentiate between ideas they are sure about (everyone agrees) and those they are not so sure about (some agree).

Some teachers also ask children to complete a second, optional part of this step—thinking about what general categories of information they are likely to encounter when they read. The children consider the information they have brainstormed and group it into more general categories (e.g., what wolves eat, where they live).

2. *W–What I want to learn.* As the children think about what they know on a topic and what categories of information might be included in what they read, questions emerge. After the group discussion, each child records his or her own questions in the W column to focus attention during reading. The children then read the material.

3. *L–What I learned.* After the children finish reading, they write down in the L column what they learned from reading. The role of the teacher is to have them locate cues in the text that they used to construct this information.

**Box 5.1** **A KWL Chart**

| Topic: | | |
|---|---|---|
| K | W | K |
| What I *know* | What I *want* to learn | What I *learned* |

Source: Adapted from D.M. Ogle (1986), "KWL: A Teaching Model That Develops Active Reading of Expository Text." *Reading Teacher, 39* (6), p. 565.

If not all of the children's questions are answered in the material, the children generate a list of "Questions I would like answered," and the teacher suggests further reading on the topic. This ensures that the children's desire to learn takes precedence over what the author has chosen to include.

## Question–Answer Relationship

Raphael (1986) presented this technique, the question–answer relationship (or QAR), for enhancing children's ability to answer questions. The technique is based on Pearson and Johnson's (1978) taxonomy of questions:

- textually explicit (answer in the text),
- textually implicit (answer involves use of both knowledge and text), and
- scriptally implicit (answer is in child's knowledge).

A QAR focusses on two major categories of information used for answering questions:

- *in the book* (text-based information), and
- *in my head* (knowledge-based information).

Each of these two categories is subdivided into two question types as shown in Table 5.2.

Raphael recommends introducing students to the two major categories — *in the book* and *in my head* — before having them deal with the four question types. In the initial stages of instruction, the students' answers to questions are less important than their being able to indicate which source of information is required. Raphael suggests the following steps in teaching QARs:

1. The teacher begins by explaining to the children that they are going to talk about questions and the best way to answer them. Some questions ask for information that the children can easily find in the book. Other times, they won't find it there and will need to use what they know to answer the questions. Each question can be answered by figuring out where to get the information needed for the answer.

**Table 5.2**   **Question–Answer Relationships**

| In the Book | In My Head |
|---|---|
| **Right There**<br>The words in the question and in the answer are "right there" in one sentence. Find the words used to make up the question, and look at the other words in that sentence to find the answer. | **Author and You**<br>The answer is not in the story alone. You need to think about what you know and what the author tells you and fit it together. |
| **Think and Search (Putting It Together)**<br>The answer is in the story, but you need to find it in more than one sentence or paragraph. The answer comes from more than one part of the text. | **On My Own**<br>The answer is not in the story. You need to use what you already know. |

Source: Adapted from T. Raphael (1986), "Teaching Question–Answer Relationships." *Reading Teacher, 39* (6), p. 519.

2. The teacher asks specific questions, and discussion focusses on where the children get information to answer each question.

3. The teacher gives the children short passages and questions for which both answers and QARs are provided for further discussion.

4. The teacher gives the children short passages with questions and answers, and the children indicate which QAR each belongs to.

5. The teacher gives the children passages and questions, and they identify both the QARs and the answers to the questions.

6. The children then move to the two questions for *in the book* and *in my head* categories and eventually to longer passages.

7. The teacher provides regular review and extends the use of QARs to content area texts.

The terms "in the book" and "in my head" can be confusing for primary children. Some teachers have found that substituting the terms "on the page" and "off the page" helps primary children gain a better understanding of the QARs involved in this instructional strategy.

## Reciprocal Teaching

Reciprocal teaching (Palincsar, 1986) is a dialogue between a teacher and children to jointly construct meaning as they read. It is designed to promote four comprehension strategies:

1. summarizing a passage in a sentence,

2. asking one or two good questions about the passage,

3. clarifying parts that are confusing, and

4. predicting what the next part will be about.

The teacher models these strategies using expository passages, and then the students assume the role of teacher using segments of the text.

1. *Modelling the strategy.* The teacher meets with a small group of students, each of whom has a copy of the same content area material, and models the four comprehension strategies while reading a paragraph from the material.

   a. The teacher summarizes the paragraph, and the students decide whether or not the summary is accurate.

   b. The teacher asks questions about the paragraph, and the students tell whether the questions involve important information in the passage and then answer the questions.

   c. The teacher identifies parts of the paragraph that could be confusing and, with the students' help, clarifies these parts.

   d. Finally, the teacher predicts what the next passage will be about, and the students judge whether the prediction is logical.

2. *Students assume role of teacher.* After the teacher has modelled the procedure with several segments of text, he or she asks a student to be the teacher. As the student teacher summarizes, asks questions, identifies confusing parts, and predicts what

will come next, the adult teacher provides feedback and coaches him or her through the strategies. The other students are asked to judge the adequacy of the summary, importance of the questions, and logic of the predictions, as well as to help clarify points and support the student teacher. The following steps indicate how reciprocal teaching is used when students assume the role of the teacher:

a. The teacher presents the children with the title of the material they will be reading and asks them to use background knowledge they have about the topic to predict what they will learn in the material. A student teacher is then appointed for the first part of the material, and the group reads it.

b. The student teacher asks a question that the other students answer, and then summarizes what has been read. The students judge the accuracy of the summary and the importance of the questions.

c. A discussion follows about clarifications that the student teacher and other students made while reading, or about points that they think still need to be made.

d. Finally, the student teacher and other students make predictions about the next segment of the material, and a new student teacher is appointed.

Throughout this dialogue, the adult teacher provides the students with feedback and instruction on how to use the four strategies more effectively. For example, the teacher might help the students to produce shorter summaries or to ask questions about main ideas as well as details.

At the end of each half-hour reciprocal teaching session, the teacher sometimes gives the children a passage they have not read before and asks them to summarize it or answer a few substantial questions about it. Reciprocal teaching is more appropriate for students at the upper elementary level than for primary children.

## Think-Alouds

"Think-alouds" are used to help readers clarify their views of reading and their use of strategies. Davey (1983) recommends the following four steps:

1. *Teacher modelling.* The teacher verbalizes his or her own thoughts while reading orally to provide a "model." The teacher selects a short passage that contains points of difficulty, contradictions, ambiguity, or unknown words. As the teacher reads the passage aloud, students follow silently, listening to how the teacher thinks through the reading. The following are examples of points that can be made during reading to help children develop metacognitive awareness and control (Davey, 1983):

   • Make predictions. (The teacher shows the children how to make predictions during reading.)
     "From the title, I predict that this story will be about a boy who wanted to fly."
     "In this next part, I think we'll find out why the boys got into a fight."
   • Describe the picture you're forming in your head from the information. (The teacher demonstrates how to develop images during reading.)
     "I have a picture of this scene in my mind. The boy is walking through a dark alley and there are no other people around."
   • Share an analogy. (The teacher links prior knowledge with new information in text. Davey calls this the "like-a" step.)
     "This is like a time we went to West Edmonton Mall and Sean got lost."

- Verbalize a confusing point. (The teacher shows children how to monitor their ongoing comprehension.)

  "This just doesn't make sense."

  "This is not what I thought would happen."

- Demonstrate fix-up strategies. (The teacher shows children how to correct their comprehension confusions.)

  "I'd better reread."

  "Maybe I'll read ahead to see if it gets clearer."

  "I'd better change my picture of the story."

  "This is a new word to me — I'd better check context to figure it out."

2. *Practice with student partners.* After several modelling experiences, children work together with partners to practise think-alouds. The partners take turns reading and thinking aloud with short passages.

3. *Independent practice.* Children practise independently with the use of checklists such as the one in Box 5.2.

4. *Use in other subject areas.* Teachers both model and provide opportunities for children to practise using think-alouds with content area materials. This helps children learn when and why to use certain strategies.

## Semantic Webs

A **semantic web** is a visual representation of relationships among ideas. These graphic arrangements (sometimes also referred to as semantic maps) show the major ideas and relationships in texts (Sinatra, Stahl-Gemake, and Berg, 1984) or among word meanings. A web consists of nodes containing key words, with connecting lines between nodes.

Joyce Bodell, an elementary teacher in Coquitlam, BC, uses prior and post-knowledge webs to achieve a number of significant purposes. Before beginning a new unit or theme, she has her students individually web everything that they already know about the topic. She writes the topic or idea on the board, reads it aloud, and then asks the children to take a minute or two to think of everything that they know about it and to record their ideas on a piece of paper.

This activity is completed individually for two reasons:

- First, Joyce wants to know what level of understanding each child is bringing to the unit of study. This informs her teaching and enables her to plan for content and lessons that will meet the children's needs most effectively.

---

**Box 5.2**   **Checklist for Think-Alouds**

|  | Not Very Much | A Little Bit | Much of the Time | All of the Time |
|---|---|---|---|---|
| Predicting | | | | |
| Picturing | | | | |
| "Like-a" | | | | |
| Identifying problems | | | | |
| Using fix-ups | | | | |

Source: Adapted from B. Davey (1983), "Think Aloud — Modeling the Cognitive Processes of Reading Comprehension," *Journal of Reading, 27* (1), p. 46.

- Second, it enables children to recognize for themselves how much they already know and to raise questions about particular ideas, facts, or aspects that they are not sure about.

After the webs are finished, Joyce collects and reads them, and then stores them away until the students have finished their unit.

At this point, Joyce usually does a whole-class brainstorming activity and records it on chart paper. This provides a written record of the children's combined knowledge, which Joyce leaves posted in the classroom. The children often refer back to it during whole-class lessons and discussions when they learn something that validates (or invalidates) what they thought they knew, or when they find an answer to a question that someone raised.

At the end of the unit, Joyce gives individual webs back to the children and asks them to use a coloured pencil to add their new knowledge to their webs and to cross out ideas that didn't really belong. The result is a two-colour web that provides the children with a powerful visual representation of all the learning they accomplished. Often, children ask for a second, larger piece of paper so that they can fit in all of their new ideas. They glue the original web in the centre and branch out onto the larger sheet. If a whole-class web was done, Joyce revisits this with the entire group, and together they build on their combined prior knowledge, adding all of the new information and understandings that they acquired. In the semantic web shown in Exhibit 5.1, the ideas within thick lines indicate the children's prior knowledge about Canada. The rest of the ideas indicate what they learned.

**Exhibit 5.1** **A Semantic Web of Canada**

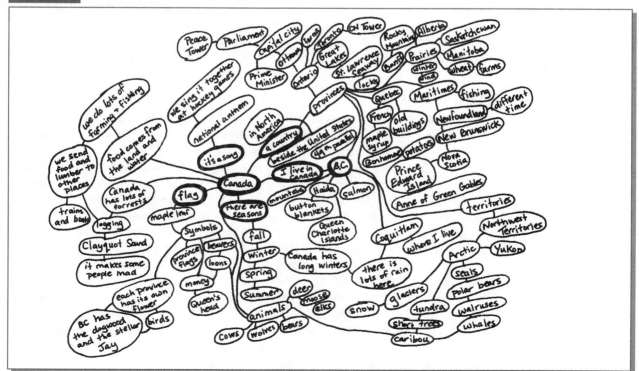

Source: Joyce Bodell. Reprinted with permission.

This second round of webbing offers the teacher a valuable assessment/evaluation tool. It demonstrates the breadth and depth of understanding that each student acquired. It can also be used to note what has not been learned, either by individuals or by most of the class. For example, if an important concept seems to be missing from most of the post-knowledge webs, it might indicate to the teacher that some additional instruction time needs to be spent on that area before the unit is drawn to a close.

All of the instructional techniques included in this section have the potential to help children develop awareness and control over their reading. This potential will only be achieved, however, if the teacher models strategy use and the children have opportunities to talk about and use the strategies being demonstrated. We also recommend having children evaluate which strategies work best for them in different contexts and for different purposes.

## Using Text Structure

This section deals first with helping children develop their knowledge of the structure of stories and then moves to informational texts.

As noted in Chapter Three, young children who have had stories read or told to them on a regular basis learn what stories are like, and the stories they tell reflect the structure of the stories they have heard. It's easier for children to construct meaning when reading stories if they are familiar with the structure of stories, because they will be able to relate ideas as they read and anticipate what comes next. Similarly, it's easier for children to construct meaning when reading informational texts if they know how authors organize and relate ideas in these texts. Since few parents will have read as much informational as narrative material to their children, fewer children come to school with an awareness of the structure of informational texts.

### Narrative Texts

*Story grammars* are attempts to delineate the basic elements of a well-formed story (e.g., Mandler and Johnson, 1977). Nearly all stories written in the Western tradition contain a setting, which introduces the main characters and tells where and when the story takes place, and a series of episodes. Although episodes are represented differently in different story grammars, common elements include a problem, attempts to resolve the problem, outcomes, and a resolution. Sometimes these elements are not presented in this order when authors use flashbacks in their writing.

There is considerable controversy about using story grammars with children. Stories written by authors from other cultures do not always conform to what these story grammars depict as well-formed stories. As children read more multicultural literature, story grammars will be less useful as a guide for their reading. Another problem is teaching story grammar for its own sake rather than to help children construct meaning. A related problem involves the often heavy focus on children learning specific terms related to story elements, such as characters, episodes, and so on. Rather than imposing this terminology on children, it is more useful for them to generate their own terms, such as *who* and *what happened*.

The best way to build knowledge of story structure is to provide children with experiences with stories on a regular basis. However, some explicit attention to story structure will benefit children with limited story experience and those who do not appear to reflect this knowledge in their storytelling or writing.

1. *Story maps.* The teacher prepares a chart, such as the one in Table 5.3, reflecting the structure of a typical story. Cochrane, Cochrane, Scalena, and Buchanan (1984) suggest that the best type of story to use for story mapping is a problem-centred one. The teacher reads the story to the children, and as a group, they analyze the story, filling in a large copy of the story map. This can be followed up with a range of activities, such as rearranging the parts of a well-formed story in order and filling in a missing story element.

2. *Questions based on story grammar.* Vacca, Vacca, and Gove (1991) suggest that teachers use story grammars to generate questions about stories. These questions can then be used to guide discussions both during and following reading. For example:

Setting

- Where did the story take place?
- When did the story take place?
- Who is the main character?

Problem/Internal Conflict

- What is the problem of the main character?
- What did _____ need?
- Why is _____ in trouble?
- What conflict does the main character have?
- What does _____ decide to do?
- How did _____ feel about the problem?

Attempts/Outcome

- What did _____ do about _____?
- What happened to _____?
- What will _____ do now?

**Table 5.3**    **Story Map**

| Setting |
| --- |
| When |
| Where |
| Who |
| **Events** |
| Problem/Internal Conflict |
| Attempts and Outcomes |
| Resolution/Reaction |

Resolution

- Was the problem solved? If not, why did the author do this?
- If so, how did _____ solve the problem?
- How did _____ feel at the end?
- What would you do to solve _____'s problem?

It is crucial that children understand why they are being asked these questions and how the information required to answer the questions relates to the overall structure of the story. Unless children are clear on the purpose for this activity, it will test their comprehension but not teach them how to construct meaning.

## Informational Texts

People read informational material to gain information. Authors generally use one of four types of organization to reflect different ways ideas are related, although they occasionally use narrative to inform as well. For example, although the purpose of this book is to inform, we occasionally share a short story about a child or classroom event to illustrate a point. Most of this book, however, uses informational text structures.

Three upper elementary children reading an informational book.

The four most common types of organizational patterns for informational material are enumeration, sequence, cause–effect and comparison–contrast. In the enumeration pattern, information about one topic is listed, but the order in which the information is presented is not important. (We used the enumeration pattern to write the paragraph you are currently reading. The topic is organization patterns for informational material, and the four types are listed and defined, with examples provided for clarification.) The sequence pattern, which presents information in time order, is commonly found in historical texts, recipe directions, and scientific experiments. We used this pattern to list steps in instructional techniques in the preceding section of this chapter. Cause–effect and comparison–contrast patterns appear in a wide range of content areas. We used the comparison–contrast pattern in Chapter Three when we contrasted concepts of reading readiness and emergent literacy. An overview of these four organizational patterns for informational texts, including characteristics, signal words, examples, and graphic organizers, is presented in Table 5.4.

### Enumeration Pattern

This is the pattern typically used in "main idea activities" in classrooms. Pearson and Johnson (1978, p. 89) state, "We know of no aspect of comprehension so universally accepted yet so often confused as the notion of 'Finding the Main Idea.'" The term *main idea* is variously used to refer to the most important idea, the topic, the title, or the theme. In fact, main idea–detail is a "logical relation between more general and more specific propositions" (p. 90). Main idea is the generalization arrived at by determining what the specific details have in common.

**Table 5.4**  Organizational Patterns for Informational Texts

| Pattern | Signal Words | Example Passage | Graphic Organizer |
|---|---|---|---|
| **Enumeration** Lists features, characteristics, and examples | *some, several, other, many, also, too, for example* | There are several good rules for bicycle safety. For example, always use hand signals. Another good rule is to ride on the right side of the street. Still others are not to go too fast and not to ride barefoot. (McGuire and Bumpus, 1973, A4, Level P) | Good Rules for Bicycle Safety — always use hand signals — don't ride barefoot — ride on right side of street — don't go too fast |
| **Sequence** Lists events or items in order | *first, next, last, finally, then, how to, directions* | Here are the directions for making a ham sandwich. First, take two pieces of bread. Then, put some ham on one piece. Finally, spread some mustard on it and cover. (McGuire and Bumpus, 1973, B2, Level P) | Directions for Making a Ham Sandwich ▼ take two pieces of bread ▼ put ham on one piece ▼ spread mustard on it ▼ cover |
| **Comparison–Contrast** Tells how people, places, things, and ideas are the same and/or different | *different, like, however, same, both, but* | Brian's new kite is different from Bill's new kite. Brian's kite is blue. It is shaped like a fish. Bill's kite is red. It is shaped like a diamond. (McGuire and Bumpus, 1973, A2, Level P) | Attribute / Brian's Kite / Bill's Kite; Colour / blue / red; Shape / fish / diamond |
| **Cause–Effect** Links one or more causes with one or more effects | *because, why, so, reasons, therefore, as a result* | "Why did you choose a goldfish for a pet?" asked Bruce. "Because they are easy to care for," said Cheryl. "They eat only a few times a week. You don't have to brush them, either. And they are fun to watch." (McGuire and Bumpus, 1973, B3, Level P) | Cause (Why?) Effect (What Happened?) easy to care for / eat only a few times a week / don't have to brush them / fun to watch → choose a goldfish for a pet |

Much nonfiction material is organized in this pattern, so being able to understand how ideas are related in these types of texts is crucial for content area reading. Authors provide "signals" (connective words) to readers to help them construct relationships among ideas. Signals to the enumeration pattern include words such as *several*, *other*, *also*, and *for example*.

**Classification of Words**  Pearson and Johnson (1978) note that children need to engage in the same kind of thinking to understand main idea–detail relationships as they use on classification tasks with words. For example, in the list of words

> *jump ropes*
> *kites*
> *toys*
> *dolls*

the word *toys* is the generalization, or the class, that all the others belong to. The following activities are useful for introducing this concept to children:

- The teacher presents to children word lists containing the classification label (such as the one above) and discusses the nature of the relationship among words in the lists (e.g., "How are these words the same? A jump rope, a kite, and a doll are all toys, so *toys* is the word that tells about all the others.").
- After children are able to describe relationships among words in lists containing the class label, the teacher presents lists of words without this label, for example:
  *screeching siren*
  *crash of thunder*
  *booming gun*

Discussing how the word or phrase generated by the children shows what the items in the list have in common (in this instance, something like *loud noises*) is essential so that students consciously think about the general–specific relationship.

**Passages**  When children understand the nature of the relationship between a generalization and specific ideas, they are ready to look for this pattern in passages. Some children need to work systematically through the steps outlined below. Others are able to move quickly into longer paragraphs that do not contain an explicitly stated main idea.

1. Well-organized passages are presented in which the author explicitly provides a generalization (main idea) in the first sentence. For example,

   > The chair was a great place to play games of make believe. Sometimes Miguel would pretend he was stunt flying. At other times he would make up games he called Hoopa Loopa and Twisto-Chairisto. Still other times he just sat very still and dreamed about things he might do someday. (McGuire and Bumpus, 1973, A4, Level I)

   Students read the paragraph and think about what all of the sentences have in common. They then determine whether one of the sentences reflects this shared meaning. The teacher also helps them see that authors use certain words to signal the way ideas are related. Signal words such as *sometimes* and *at other times* suggest that each sentence is a specific example of something. The objective of the discussion is to help children construct relationships among ideas rather than to label one sentence as the main idea. An example of the kind of discussion that teachers might use to help children understand how ideas are related in this type of paragraph is presented in Box 5.3.

2. Well-organized paragraphs where the author leaves the main idea unstated are then presented. For example:

   > Some seeds travel with the wind. Elm and Maple seeds do this. Other seeds are hitchhikers. Burrs stick to dogs, for example. Birds carry berry seeds, too. Still other seeds pop right out of their pods. (McGuire and Bumpus, 1973, B3, Level P)

**Box 5.3**    **Illustrative Lesson on Enumeration (Main Idea/Detail) Pattern**

1. The teacher provides students with copies of a short, well-constructed paragraph, such as:

   The moving ice did great things for Canada. It scraped a thick layer of topsoil off the Canadian Shield. This left the minerals near the surface where people could reach them. It carried good soil south to southern Canada where the climate is suitable for farming. Most interesting of all, it made Canada beautiful.

2. The teacher says, "Let's read this paragraph to find out the writer's main idea. We are going to underline the key words as we read. Let's look at the second sentence. What are the key words in this sentence?" Answers will probably be *scraped*, *topsoil*, and *Canadian Shield*. Students underline these words in the sentence. The teacher then asks the students to read on, underlining key words. When the children finish reading and underlining words, they share their underlined words with the group, and the teacher lists words

for each sentence on the board. Discussion will lead to a list something like the following:
   a. ice did things Canada
   b. scraped topsoil Canadian Shield
   c. left minerals near surface
   d. carried good soil southern Canada
   e. made Canada beautiful

3. The teacher then guides a discussion focussed on the nature of the relationships among the ideas in the five sentences. This discussion leads the students to conclude that sentences (b), (c), (d), and (e) are specific things ice did, while sentence (a) contains a general statement. Each of sentences (b), (c), (d), and (e) indicate one of the great things ice did for Canada. Sentence (a) is the general overall statement arrived at by determining what the specific ideas have in common. This is the main idea of the paragraph.

4. As a follow-up activity, students discuss the main idea of paragraphs selected from content area textbooks.

Source: Adapted from an illustrative lesson for upper elementary students presented in an unpublished paper by Phillis Sutherland, a teacher and remedial specialist in Edmonton Public Schools.

Again, the teacher guides children in a discussion of what these sentences have in common, underlining key words to focus on areas of similarity. They then construct a general statement that captures the common meaning of the sentences.

The paragraphs included in the examples to this point have been very well organized, with the authors using specific signal words to help readers construct relationships among ideas. Although this type of material is useful for helping children understand how ideas are related in the enumeration pattern, most material is not this tightly organized, nor do authors always provide so many cues to help readers construct relationships. Once children are familiar with the pattern and the relationships within this pattern, the teacher guides their reading of paragraphs in which ideas are not so clearly related and authors provide fewer cues (i.e., signal words or the explicit statement of main ideas) to help children construct relationships among ideas.

Outlining and Graphic Organizers   Pearson and Johnson (1978) suggest two techniques other than discussion to help clarify the relationship between main ideas and details: outlining and diagramming. Generally, the teacher models these techniques to visually show the relationships before asking students to generate their own outlines or diagrams. An example of a graphic organizer for the enumeration pattern is shown in Table 5.4.

Both outlining and diagramming can also be used for organizing ideas for written composition. Once a topic is identified, the children generate a number of ideas related to it through brainstorming. The children then organize these ideas using diagrams or outlines before they begin to write. Having children use diagrams for both reading and writing helps them understand how these language processes are related, and this in turn helps them transfer what they are able to do in one mode of language to the other.

## Sequence Pattern

Exercises on sequence patterns run a close second to those on main ideas for causing students difficulty. The most common type of exercise involves giving students sentences that are out of order. Students are asked to place a number beside each sentence to indicate what order they should be in. There are several reasons why this task is difficult, particularly for young children. One is that we generally use numerals (1, 2, 3) to indicate quantity rather than sequence. When numerals are used to indicate sequence, they are generally transformed to ordinals — *first, second*, and so on. As well, there is often no logical reason for one event to occur before another in the exercises given to children. In other words, the sequence is essentially arbitrary. Pearson and Johnson (1978, p. 116) point out that primary children find reversible relationships more difficult to understand than irreversible or logical relationships. For example:

> *John watched television before he ate dinner.* (reversible)
> *John closed the door. Then he bolted it.* (irreversible)

In addition, young children tend to pay attention to the order in which events are presented rather than to signal words (e.g., *then, before, after*) when sorting out the sequence of events. Hence, young children often interpret the sentence *Before Mary ate dinner, she read a book*, as first Mary ate dinner and then she read a book. Finally, many young children find that reordering sentences in their heads is too abstract.

We provide the following suggestions for planning instructional activities with texts written in the sequence pattern:

- Begin by having students understand the sequential relationships in familiar experiences before moving to unfamiliar material. Language experience stories are ideal for this.
- Present students with texts that illustrate irreversible events before reversible ones.
- Have students read material where the order of presentation matches the time order. Students need considerable instruction with temporal connectives before they can use them to aid comprehension.
- Have students recall the order in which events occurred rather than having them order sentences, unless the sentences can be physically moved to place them in order of occurrence.
- Have students use a time line or other type of graphic organizer (such as the one in Table 5.4) to show temporal relationships among ideas. Again, these types of graphic organizers can be used to generate ideas for written composition when the topic involves a sequence of events.

## Cause–Effect Pattern

Understanding the cause-and-effect pattern is crucial to constructing meaning from both narrative and informational material. Plots often revolve around cause–effect relationships in stories, and causality is important for understanding historical, social, and scientific issues.

Children need to learn several points about cause–effect relationships:

- One is the reciprocal relationship between cause and effect.
- Another is the chaining of causes and effects — that is, a cause produces an effect, which in turn causes another effect, and so on.
- A third is the meaning of causal connectives such as *because, since, therefore, why,* and *as a result.* Young children often use words such as *because* as if they were causes themselves rather than words to link causes and effects.

To help children construct causal relations as they read,

- Begin with texts that illustrate single cause–single effect relationships, then move to those that illustrate single cause–multiple effect and multiple cause–single effect relationships, and finally to those with chains of cause–effect relationships.
- Discuss the nature of cause–effect relationships with children. Throughout discussion, it is important to talk about the function of causal connectives, and to help children use these words in their own writing.
- Charting cause–effect relations helps many readers conceptualize the relationships among ideas. (Table 5.4 shows such a chart). These charts may also help children organize ideas involving causality for written composition.

## Comparison–Contrast Pattern

Comparison–contrast patterns are used by authors when they are describing characters and settings. They are also used in content area materials. We recommend using

- discussion focussed on common attributes of people, places, things, and ideas being compared, and on the features that differentiate those being contrasted,
- discussion to direct children's attention to specific words that indicate comparisons or contrasts, such as *however, on the other hand, both,* and *alike,* and
- charts to help children understand comparison–contrast relationships.

Teachers can give students a chart like the one in Table 5.4 before reading to guide their construction of comparison–contrast relationships as they read. Students can also use them after reading to guide recall or as a study guide, or to organize ideas when writing paragraphs comparing or contrasting places, people, things, or ideas.

We have included only a few possible instructional techniques for developing comprehension strategies in this section. Other techniques are described in the "Selected Professional Resources" listed at the end of this chapter. It is important to note, however, that these will not be effective unless children know why, how, and when to use strategies and are able to use the strategies before, during, and after reading.

## Studying

When asked how they study, many children say they just read the material again and again. Do you have a strategy for studying? If so, is it similar to any of the strategies described in this chapter?

Studying is a special kind of reading. As with all reading, the major goal is to construct meaning on the basis of text-based and knowledge-based information. However, individuals also need to organize information in order to enhance retrieval of the meanings they have constructed.

## Using Comprehension Strategies for Studying

Some of the instructional techniques described above can help children organize and retrieve information. For example, KWL helps children think about what they learned after they finish reading. The techniques included in the section on informational text structure help children to organize ideas in content area texts, and we know that it is easier to remember related ideas than isolated details. In addition, Standal and Betza (1990) suggest helping children develop the following strategies for both reading and studying:

- Scanning involves sampling the text. Readers rapidly search through the text to locate specific information or answer a specific question. They learn to focus on headings, pictures, summaries, illustrations, and key words rather than reading every word.
- Skimming is a quick survey of the text to get an indication of what it is about.
- Outlining helps children understand and retain relationships among ideas. Mapping can be used to teach outlining.
- Underlining and highlighting make it easier to refer to important points when reviewing information. (Because elementary children are rarely able to mark in their books, Cunningham and Allington, 1999, suggest that children use stickies to mark important points.)
- Note-taking can be introduced in the upper elementary grades.

These study skills are most effective when taught to children within the context of materials in the content areas.

## SQ3R

This classic technique, developed by Robinson (1961), continues to provide students with an organized, systematic approach to studying. Before beginning to read, students *survey* what they will read and ask *questions.* This ensures that when they do *read,* they are actively engaged in searching for answers. After they finish reading, they put what they have read into their own words *(recite)* or make notes about the questions generated from their survey of the material. Finally, they use these notes to *review* the major ideas and details in the passage. Throughout this process, they are continuously using information from both the text and their knowledge. Students can be given a guide such as the one that follows to help them apply the steps in SQ3R:

1.  *Survey.* Read the title and headings in the chapter to see the few main points. This should take no more than a minute and will show the three to six core items around which the rest of the ideas cluster. If the chapter has a final summary paragraph, this will also list the ideas developed. This orientation will help you organize the ideas as you read them later.

2.  *Question.* Turn the first heading into a question. This will arouse your curiosity and so increase comprehension. It will bring to mind information you already know, thus helping you understand that section more quickly. And the question will make important points stand out from details.

3.  *Read.* Read to answer the question. This is not a passive plowing-along-each-line exercise, but an active search for the answer.

4. *Recite.* When you have read the first section, look away from the book and try briefly reciting the answer to the question in your own words. If applicable, give an example. If you can do this, you know what is in the book. If you cannot, glance over the section again. Another way to recite is by jotting down key words and phrases in outline form in a notebook.

Repeat steps 2, 3, and 4 for each section.

5. *Review.* When you have read through the chapter, look over your notes to get a bird's-eye view of the points and their relationships. Check your memory about the content by covering up your notes and trying to recall the main points. Then expose each major point and try to recall the subpoints listed under it.

The balance of opinion among researchers is that SQ3R is effective, but this conclusion is by no means unanimous (Manzo and Manzo, 1997). Instruction on how to use SQ3R is most effective when given with materials students are actually studying for an examination. The teacher models the steps with part of one chapter from the text, thinking out loud. Students and teacher work through the next part together, with the teacher guiding students through the steps. Students then use SQ3R in small groups or individually.

One of the major obstacles to study strategy instruction is changing habits. Think about your own study habits and how easy it would be to incorporate the SQ3R steps into your study process. To be effective, study strategies need to become automatic so students are able to focus on the content of what they are studying rather than on the process of studying itself.

## Critical Literacy

Few language arts textbooks include information on critical literacy. With such broad availability of information through the Internet, it is becoming increasingly crucial that children critically examine what they read. In this section, we begin by discussing how critical reading has been treated in the past and then turn to the development of critical literacy.

## Critical Reading

Traditionally, critical reading has involved having children differentiate fact from opinion, good from bad, and reality from fiction. In addition, children have evaluated ideas as valid, invalid, or questionable, and detected and critiqued propaganda techniques (Irwin and Baker, 1989). Some of these activities, such as judging statements as fact or opinion, are based on the assumption that there is an objective truth against which to judge ideas (transmission model). However, others help children take different viewpoints. When critiquing advertisements, for example, children view the world both from the perspective of the salesperson trying to sell a product and from the perspective of a critical consumer.

One only has to watch television on Saturday mornings to find out how many advertisements are directed at children. Critical reading of advertisements helps children become aware of techniques used to convince, persuade, or get an individual to believe or buy something. Most educators who recommend work in this area provide a set of concepts to guide children's thinking and talking about these techniques. Typical of such lists is the one in Table 5.5 adapted from Manzo and Manzo (1997). Teachers provide advertisements for children to discuss in class, children find examples of different types of advertisements to discuss with their classmates, and children write advertisements individually or in small groups. The major purpose of these activities is to help children become critical consumers of ideas and advertisements, not that they learn to label propaganda techniques.

## The Nature of Multicultural Education

In the past few years, the term *critical literacy* has begun to replace *critical reading* in instructional materials. Critical literacy essentially means "arguing back with texts" (Gillet and Temple, 1994, p. 50) or, stated another way, "reading against the grain" (Temple, 1993, p. 89). As children construct meaning, they analyze texts for hidden biases, including those that suggest one gender, race, or social group is superior to another. The field of multicultural education provides a framework for planning and implementing instruction to develop critical literacy.

Multicultural education, according to Banks and Banks (1989), is the affirmation of equal opportunities for all children to learn regardless of gender, class, race, ethnicity, or culture. It also encompasses global awareness and recognition of racism, prejudice, discrimination, and equity. Multicultural education "begins with the child's understanding of self and the building of self-esteem, moves to an understanding and

**Table 5.5**  Propaganda Techniques

| Label | Description | Example |
|---|---|---|
| Bandwagon | Everyone is doing it; go along with the crowd. | "More people drink ___ than any other cola." |
| Testimonial | A famous person uses, believes, or does something. | "I use ___ shampoo every day to keep my hair shiny and beautiful." |
| Plain Folks | People that look like "you and me" suggest we use, believe, or do something. | "I've been washing clothes for many years and ___ really works." |
| Snob Appeal | This is the opposite of plain folks. | "If you want to be part of the in-generation, buy ___." |
| Name Calling | A person, thing, or movement is put down. | "Nerds like poetry." |
| Glittering Generalities | Using popular terms to describe an idea, person, or activity. | "It's time for a change. Vote ___." |
| Scientific Link | Scientific terms are used to make something seem better than it is. | "Four out of five doctors surveyed recommend ___." |

acceptance of others, and finally expands to a development of concern for larger problems and issues outside the child's immediate environment" (Finazzo, 1997). From this perspective, the focus of multicultural education goes well beyond issues of culture to include differences in family structure, ethnicity, gender, age, exceptionalities, values, socio-economic status, and ways of communicating.

To some educators, multicultural education means integrating artifacts and literature from other cultural groups into the curriculum. Banks and Banks (1989) refer to this as a *contributions approach*. Other educators use the multicultural materials they integrate into the curriculum in a different way. Through critical discussion during the meaning construction process, children learn that knowledge and understanding are influenced by assumptions, biases, and prejudices (the *additive approach*). Both the contributions and additive approaches are designed to help children develop knowledge and understanding of other groups and individuals, but neither approach necessarily involves social change.

Change, however, is at the heart of two other approaches to multicultural education. One of these involves critical pedagogy. Teachers use different materials and approaches to meet the needs of all learners, and the curriculum has a major focus on social equality. Banks and Banks refer to this as the *transformation approach*. The other approach involves *social reconstruction* or *social action*. In this type of multicultural education, children learn to take action against inequity and injustice and become involved in appropriate action at the local level and sometimes beyond.

## Awareness and Understanding of Diversity

In Chapters Ten and Eleven, we list several children's books written by authors from different cultures for use with children in elementary classrooms. Having children read and respond to this literature helps them become more aware of themselves and of others. This type of examination of literature gives children the opportunity to view realistically the diversity in their classrooms, communities, and beyond. They not only learn to identify and respect individual differences, they also develop an appreciation of what we all have in common.

Finazzo (1997) provides an even more comprehensive list of multicultural literature for elementary children. She also includes sample lesson plans for using children's literature to enhance their understanding of themselves and others. Two examples follow:

- In one example, Finazzo suggests using *Where the Wild Things Are* (Sendak, 1963) to help children realize that it is better to be themselves than to try to be someone they are not. The teacher begins by telling the class a story about something or someone she or he pretended to be and asks the children to indicate if they ever wished they were something or someone else. The teacher then reads and discusses the story with the children. At the point where Max leaves the wild things, the teacher asks the children why they think Max left and, at the end of the story, leads the children in a discussion of why Max may have wanted to be someone else for awhile. The children then brainstorm in writing or pictures what makes them happy to be themselves.

- In another example, Finazzo presents a lesson using the book *People* by Spier (1980) to expose children to diversity among people around the world and to help them identify diversity in their own classroom. The teacher begins by having the children talk briefly about how they are all the same (e.g., they are all wearing clothing, they all have shoes on.) The teacher then reads the book, and at the end asks the children to talk about what ways people in the world are alike. As the children share ideas, the teacher writes these similarities on a chart labelled *Alike*. Next, the children talk about differences, and the teacher writes these on another chart labelled *Different*. The teacher then asks the children to take off their shoes and put them in a pile. The children separate the shoes into different groups — shoes with laces, shoes with buckles, slip-on shoes, shoes with Velcro fasteners. Then they sort the shoes again by colour, and again by size. The same activity is repeated using other features for sorting — eye, hair, and skin colour, languages spoken at home, number of people in families. The children talk about the differences and similarities in the groups. The lesson ends by having the children create a collage from old magazines to illustrate diversity among people in the world.

A wide range of diversity is portrayed in children's literature, including differences in family structure, ethnicity, gender, age, exceptionalities, values, socio-economic status, and ways of communicating. This literature provides opportunities for children to see both themselves and their families portrayed by authors. However, some parents feel uncomfortable when children are exposed to family structures and values different from their own. As indicated in Chapter Eleven, parents and community groups are challenging the use of some books in schools and even their availability in school libraries. Examples include those books depicting same-sex parents and those portraying non-creationist beliefs.

In addition to the question of censorship, a major challenge teachers face in work on critical literacy is what to do when a child's meaning is quite different from their own. Lewis (1993) describes the difficulty she had with one boy's response to "The Pelican and the Crane" (Lobel, 1980). In this fable, a pelican comes to tea at the crane's house and is very sloppy and wasteful, all the time wondering aloud why nobody ever invites him anywhere. For example, when the pelican pours milk into his tea, he pours most of it on the table. When he is asked if he would like a cookie, he takes a large pile of cookies and stuffs most of them into his mouth, leaving a pile of crumbs. At the end of the story, the pelican says he hopes he will be invited back. The crane says, "Perhaps, but I am so busy these days," and calls for his maid to clean up the mess.

The moral given by the author is, "When one is a social failure, the reasons are as clear as day." But one child, Rick, felt sorry for the pelican because he was a klutz. Rick was critical of the crane for telling a lie and provided a very different moral for the story, "Give people a chance." What would you do if you were Rick's teacher? Lewis attempted to persuade Rick of her meaning because she felt it was her responsibility to help him understand texts in ways that match the expectations of those in power (the test-makers, for example). However, she had limited success and hypothesized the following:

> Perhaps Rick needed to know that he had formed a perfectly legitimate reading before he could listen for other voices as he read this fable. One way to legitimize his interpretation would have been to openly discuss differences between his moral and Lobel's [the author]. Before having Rick read the fable, I could have asked him to read for a moral that made sense to him. Afterward, we might have compared his moral to Lobel's and discussed ways that readers might interact with this text to arrive at different conclusions. Encouraging Rick to listen for other voices while legitimizing his own would help him to begin to understand that in literature, as in life, these different voices create a tension we all have to acknowledge before we can find a place for ourselves, before we can take a position. (Lewis, 1993, pp. 459–460)

How can teachers provide opportunities for children to listen for other voices, have their own voices legitimized, and learn to take a position on the meaning they construct as they read? John Proctor, a teacher and language arts consultant, shared the strategy outlined in Box 5.4 as one he finds helpful for these purposes.

## Transformation and Social Action

While the type of lessons described above are helpful, Edelsky (1994) believes that they do not go far enough. She stresses the need for teachers to "encourage a sustained look at the societal issues that are suggested by so many pieces of literature and that languish unexamined in personal responses" (p. 256). She urges teachers to move into a more transformative approach with children's literature.

Temple (1993, pp. 91–93) provides the following example of how one teacher did this with a group of second- and third-grade children. The teacher asked the following questions about *Beauty and the Beast* to help the children critically examine their assumptions about gender roles in society: "Suppose Beauty had been kind and clever but not prettier than her sisters. Do you think the author is suggesting that we should be more like Beauty or more like her sisters? Suppose Beauty had been a boy in this story, and the Beast had been a girl." As they discussed answers to these questions, the children dealt with issues such as the high value placed on outward appearance in our society, compared with inner qualities. One child said, "You don't judge people by how pretty they are. You judge them by how nice and kind and loving they are." The children also talked about how some of the time they themselves were like the "snotty" sisters and sometimes they were like Beauty, recognizing that there is good and bad in all of us. In relation to gender roles, one child summed it up with "What bugs me is that in the fairy tales, the guys are always doing things outside, and the girls are just basking around in their beautiful dresses."

| **Box 5.4** | **Dialogic Engagement** |
| --- | --- |

1. The children read a text with partners.

2. They pause at specified points and record

   - what they found out up to here, or what the key events were
   - the ideas their partner added
   - what they decided together

3. At the end of the reading, the partners record

   - what the moral was
   - what the story helped them to see

4. The children regroup into foursomes and discuss their conclusions. Each group records these conclusions on chart paper.

5. The groups pin their charts up at the front of the room, and as a class, they discuss common themes.

6. The class tries to arrive at a consensus, but also acknowledges the diversity of views.

7. The teacher's conclusion is also displayed as one voice in the discussion.

Contrasting *Beauty and the Beast* with a book such as *The Paper Bag Princess* by Robert Munsch provides further opportunities for children to examine the focus of our society on outward beauty. In this tale, it is the princess who saves the prince through courage and intelligence. Other books, such as *Tough Eddie* by Elizabeth Winthrop, examine stereotypic portrayals of males. *Tough Eddie* is about a young boy who acts tough but has a secret — at home, his favourite toy is a dollhouse.

Children also need opportunities to critically examine the texts they read in other areas of the curriculum. Edelsky (1994) writes about a teacher who has her fifth-graders look at the social studies materials on the Pilgrims and Indians provided for the school and ask themselves: Who wrote this? Whose idea is it? Do you think this is the way the Aboriginal people would tell it? Who benefits from this version of the story? How do they benefit from it? In the Canadian context, books about such topics as the Riel rebellion and exploration of the West by the French and English can be critiqued in a similar way.

The major goal of the examples provided in this section is transformation of the curriculum and of children's thinking. According to Freire (1970), the development of critical awareness of inequities and injustice is the first step in social change. Much of this change will be situated at the classroom and school levels, with both teachers and children taking responsibility for change. For example, in relation to gender equity, teachers ensure that learning materials are appropriate, representing the two genders fairly and equally so both boys and girls have appropriate role models. Learners of both genders are encouraged to be actively involved in the learning process. Teachers and children agree that stereotypical language referring to males and females is not acceptable in the classroom, and they are vigilant in their reading of other authors' work and in their own classroom interactions and writing to detect and exclude this type of language. In other words, teachers and children create classroom contexts and school communities in which all children are valued regardless of gender, age, race, exceptionality, or class.

> We are just beginning to figure out how to help children develop critical literacy in elementary classrooms. We know that children need to work in groups rather than individually, and that critique is at the heart of this type of reading instruction. And we know that the *what* and *why* of reading are as important as the *how*.

## Summary

Two major techniques have traditionally been used to develop reading comprehension — questioning and comprehension skill exercises. Teacher questions generally test rather than teach comprehension, and more are literal than inferential or critical. There is little evidence to support teaching a series of reading comprehension skills. Instead, this textbook presents instructional techniques to help children develop strategies for using both text-based and knowledge-based information as they read.

Several techniques can be used to help children integrate knowledge and text cues to make meaning as they read. Some of these include the directed reading–thinking activity, KWL, question–answer relationships, reciprocal teaching, think-alouds, and semantic webs. To help children use story structure to construct meaning, we suggest the use of story maps and questions focussed on story components. There are four major types of organizational patterns in informational texts: enumeration, sequence, cause–effect, and comparison–contrast. Discussion, charting, and diagramming can help children to construct relationships among ideas in these patterns. Many of these techniques are also useful as study strategies, although some children and teachers find specific study strategies useful as well.

Critical reading has traditionally been included in basal reading series. Although many activities designed to develop critical reading are based on a transmission model, some help children critique advertisements and other propaganda. Multicultural education provides a framework for going beyond critical reading to the development of critical literacy. Some approaches focus on developing awareness and understanding of diversity, including differences in gender, age, family structure, exceptionalities, social class, race, and ways of communicating. Others focus on transformation and social change.

## Selected Professional Resources

Finazzo, D.A. (1997). *All for the Children: Multicultural Essentials of Literature.* New York: Delmar. This text addresses current issues in children's literature, particularly cultural diversity and multiculturalism. The author provides a rationale for critical literacy activities, identifies children's books appropriate for this work, and presents sample lessons that have been used with elementary children in rural, suburban, and urban settings.

Manzo, A.V. and Manzo, U. (1997). *Content Area Literacy: Interactive Teaching for Active Learning.* Columbus, OH: Prentice-Hall. Manzo and Manzo describe a wide range of techniques to help children construct meaning from content area texts. They also include instructional techniques to help students learn how to study.

Tierney, R.J., Readence, J.E., and Dishner, E.K. (1995). *Reading Strategies and Practices: A Compendium* (4th ed.). Boston: Allyn and Bacon. A wide range instructional techniques to facilitate reading development are presented. The major focus is on comprehension, although attention is also given to study skills, word identification, assessment, and other aspects of reading instruction.

## Children's Books Noted in Chapter Five

Lobel, A. (1980). *Fables.* New York: Harper & Row.

Mayer, M. and Mayer, M. (1978). *Beauty and the Beast.* New York: Aladdin.

Munsch, R. (1980). *The Paper Bag Princess.* Toronto: Annick Press.

Sendak, M. (1963). *Where the Wild Things Are.* New York: Harper & Row.

Spier, P. (1980). *People.* New York: Doubleday.

Winthrop, E. (1985). *Tough Eddie.* New York: E.P. Dutton.

## References

Banks, J.A. and Banks, C.A. (eds.). (1989). *Multicultural education: Issues and perspectives.* Boston: Allyn & Bacon.

Bloom, B. (1956). *Taxonomy of educational objectives: Cognitive domain.* New York: McKay.

Cochrane, O., Cochrane, D., Scalena, S., and Buchanan, E. (1984). *Reading, writing and caring.* Winnipeg: Whole Language Consultants.

Cunningham, P.M. and Allington, R.L. (1999). *Classrooms that work: They can all read and write* (2nd ed.). New York: Longman.

Davey, B. (1983). Think aloud—modeling the cognitive processes of reading comprehension. *Journal of Reading, 27* (1), 44–47.

Durkin, D.D. (1978–79). What classroom observations reveal about reading comprehension instruction. *Reading Research Quarterly, 14* (4), 481–533.

Edelsky, C. (1994). Education for democracy. *Language Arts, 71* (4), 252–257.

Finazzo, D.A. (1997). *All for the children: Multicultural essentials of literature.* New York: Delmar.

Freire, P. (1970). *Pedagogy of the oppressed.* New York: Herder and Herder.

Gillet, J.W. and Temple, C. (1994). *Understanding reading problems: Assessment and instruction.* New York: HarperCollins.

Irwin, J.H. and Baker, I. (1989). *Promoting active reading comprehension strategies: A resource book for teachers.* Englewood Cliffs, NJ: Prentice-Hall.

Lewis, C. (1993). "Give people a chance": Acknowledging social differences in reading. *Language Arts, 70* (6), 454–461.

McGuire, M.L. and Bumpus, M.J. (1973). *Croft skillpacks.* Old Greenwich, CT: Croft Educational Services.

Mandler, J. and Johnson, N. (1977). Remembrance of things parsed: Story structure and recall. *Cognitive Psychology, 9*, 111–151.

Manzo, A.V. and Manzo, U. (1997). *Content area literacy: Interactive teaching for active learning.* Columbus, OH: Prentice-Hall.

Ogle, D.M. (1986). K-W-L: A teaching model that develops active reading of expository text. *Reading Teacher, 39* (6), 564–570.

Palincsar, A.S. (1986). Metacognitive strategy instruction. *Exceptional Children, 53* (2), 118–124.

Pearson, P.D. and Fielding, L. (1991). Comprehension instruction. In R. Barr, M.L. Kamil, P.B. Mosenthal, and P.D. Pearson (eds.), *Handbook of reading research,* Vol. 2 (pp. 815–860). New York: Longman.

Pearson, P.D. and Johnson, D.D. (1978). *Teaching reading comprehension.* New York: Holt, Rinehart & Winston.

Pressley, M. (1998). Comprehension strategies instruction. In J. Osborn and F. Lehr (eds.), *Literacy for all: Issues in teaching and learning* (pp. 113–133). New York: The Guilford Press.

Raphael, T.E. (1986). Teaching question–answer relationships. *Reading Teacher, 39* (6), 516–522.

Robinson, F. (1961). *Effective study.* New York: Harper & Row.

Sinatra, R.C., Stahl-Gemake, J., and Berg, D.N. (1984). Improving the reading comprehension of disabled readers through semantic mapping. *Reading Teacher, 38* (1), 22–29.

Standal, T.C. and Betza, R.E. (1990). *Content area reading: Teachers, texts, students.* New York: Prentice-Hall.

Stauffer, R.G. (1975). *Directing the reading–thinking process.* New York: Harper & Row.

Temple, C. (1993). Suppose Beauty had been ugly? Reading against the grain of gender bias in children's books. *Language Arts, 60* (2), 89–93.

Tierney, R.J., Readence, J.E., and Dishner, E.K. (1995). *Reading strategies and practices: A compendium* (4th ed.). Boston: Allyn and Bacon.

Vacca, J.L., Vacca, R.T., and Gove, M.K. (1991). *Reading and learning to read* (2nd ed.). New York: HarperCollins.

# Chapter six

# Word Identification and Fluency

Overview of Word Identification Instruction

Print Cues
- Issues in Teaching Phonics
- Phonemic Awareness Using Children's Names
- Hearing Sounds in Words
- Word Walls
- Word Families
- Making Words
- Word Sorting
- Word Parts

Context Cues
- Predictable Books
- Cloze Procedure

Word Identification and Fluency

Integrating Context and Print Cues
- Masking
- Minimal Cue Messages
- Oral Reading

Fluency/Automaticity
- Sustained Silent Reading
- Paired Reading
- Repeated Reading

Reading Intervention
- Characteristics of Effective Programs
- *Reading Recovery*
- Selecting Instructional Techniques

You have volunteered to go into your neighbourhood school to work with individual children in Grade 2 who have reading difficulties. The teacher has selected three children for you to help. He suggests that you spend the first day listening to them read orally to get a better idea of how they read. He selects a basal reader, designed for children at the beginning of the second grade, for them to read. Sarah begins to read quite smoothly, but before she gets to the end of the first line of print she stops and looks to you for help. "I don't know that word," she says. This happens several times before she completes the first page. Jason's reading is very different. He reads in a laboured manner, slowly sounding out words letter by letter, sometimes producing nonsense words rather than words that make sense in the sentence he is reading. He makes few corrections, plowing through the page and wondering aloud by the end what the story is about. Like Jason, Tyler reads very slowly, sounding out some unfamiliar words. However, he does not produce any nonsense words and is able to talk about what he has read at the end of the page. He tells you that reading is hard and that he doesn't read very much. ■

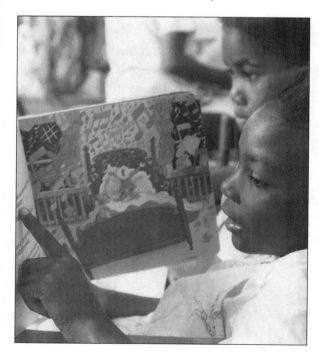

Although these three children are all experiencing difficulty reading material designed for the second grade, they have little else in common. Sarah knows some words by sight but appears to have developed few strategies for identifying unfamiliar words. Jason has developed some strategies for relating sounds to letters but has difficulty making sense as he reads. Tyler has developed some effective strategies for identifying words, but these strategies are not yet automatic and he finds reading laborious. What would you do with each of these children?

- How would you help Sarah learn to use print and sound cues to identify words?
- How would you help Jason produce meaningful words and correct miscues that don't make sense?
- How would you help Tyler achieve **automaticity** in his word identification so reading would be more enjoyable?

In this chapter, we focus primarily on instructional techniques to help children use both **context cues** and cues within words as they read. We also provide suggestions for developing automaticity and, in the final section, relate instructional techniques to common types of reading difficulties. The chapter begins with a brief overview of word identification instruction.

## Overview of Word Identification Instruction

Word identification has traditionally been taught from a skills perspective, with skills organized hierarchically into four major categories: sight vocabulary, phonics, structural analysis, and contextual analysis.

1. *Sight vocabulary* refers to words that occur frequently and that readers are able to identify automatically. As skilled readers, we recognize 99 percent of the words we read by sight.

2. *Phonics* is the identification of words through the relationships between speech sounds and letters, and it has been at the centre of the great debate about early reading instruction (e.g., Chall, 1967; Adams, 1990). Phonics has been broken down into more subskills than any other area of reading instruction.

3. *Structural analysis* involves identifying words by larger and more meaningful units such as prefixes and suffixes. Some people include syllabication as an aspect of structural analysis, while others consider it to be a component of phonics.

4. *Contextual analysis* involves using the context of sentences or of passages to predict unfamiliar words. Most educators include both grammatical cues (does it sound right?) and meaning cues (does it make sense?) under the rubric of contextual analysis.

Many language arts textbooks written in the 1980s and early 1990s included little information on instructional techniques for developing word identification strategies. For a time, as educators moved toward **whole language** programs, word identification became downright unpopular. Although most language arts educators recognized that print cues were an important source of information for readers, they did not feel that direct, systematic instruction was needed to help children make use of these cues. By the mid-1990s, however, concern that many children were not becoming proficient readers led many educators to abandon the whole language movement and reaffirm the importance of developing strategies for word identification. The danger now is not that word identification will be neglected, but rather that educators will go too far and word identification will become an end for its own sake, rather than a means of constructing meaning.

The following sections are organized in relation to cues that readers use for word identification — those within words, and those within sentence and passage contexts. In the final section, we present instructional techniques to help children integrate both types of cues. An overview of these techniques is presented in Table 6.1.

**Table 6.1**   **Instructional Techniques for Word Identification**

| Instructional Technique | Cue(s) | Helps Children |
|---|---|---|
| Children's Names | Print | • hear sounds at the beginning of words<br>• hear rhyming words<br>• relate sounds to letters<br>• differentiate upper- and lowercase letters |
| Hearing Sounds in Words | Print | • hear sounds in all word positions<br>• relate letters to sounds |
| Word Walls | Print | • identify common words as sight words<br>• hear rhyming words<br>• associate sounds with letters |
| Word Families | Print | • associate sounds with letters<br>• identify new words through analogy to familiar words |
| Making Words | Print | • associate sounds with letters<br>• use knowledge of letter sounds to spell words |
| Word Sorting | Print | • form generalizations about the sounds and visual features of words |
| Word Parts | Print | • use roots, affixes, and syllabication to identify words |
| Predictable Books | Context | • use meaning and language cues to predict words |
| Cloze Procedure | Context | • use meaning and language cues to predict words<br>• use meaning and language cues to monitor predictions |
| Masking | Print and context | • use context cues to identify words<br>• use letter sounds to identify words<br>• use word parts to identify words |
| Minimal Cue Messages | Print and context | • use context cues to identify words<br>• use knowledge of letter sounds and word parts to spell words |
| Oral Reading | Print and context | • use context and print cues to identify words<br>• use context and print cues to correct miscues |

# Print Cues

This section describes instructional techniques to help children use letters and word parts to identify words as they read. We begin with a discussion of issues teachers face when they teach phonics.

## Issues in Teaching Phonics

No area of reading instruction is as controversial as phonics. Many people view it as a panacea — the key to teaching all children to read. Others see it as a problem — an area of instruction leading to confusion and "word calling." We believe neither view is defensible on its own. Although it is helpful for children to be aware of the relationships between letters and sounds, particularly when spelling, knowledge of letter sounds is certainly not enough to make children good readers. It is more important that they be aware that reading is a meaning-making process and that mapping sounds onto letters is one strategy to use as they engage in this process. We do not want children to think that reading *is* sounding out words.

### Terminology

One of the issues teachers face when teaching phonics involves terminology. Nearly all of you are familiar with the terms *consonants* and *vowels*, although even this distinction is somewhat arbitrary (e.g., vowels are the letters *a, e, i, o, u,* and *y* — the latter when it is not the first letter in a word). The major difference between consonants and vowels is that there is one sound for most consonants, whereas there are several sounds for each vowel.

Most teachers' guides contain at least some terminology for describing consonants. *Consonant blends* and *consonant digraphs* are combinations of consonants. In blends, the two or three letters combined each retain their original sound (e.g., *bl, fr, sm, str*); in consonant digraphs, the letters that are combined produce a new sound (e.g., *th, sh, ch*). The letters *c* and *g*, meanwhile, are different from other consonants in that they have both hard (e.g., *car, go*) and soft (e.g., *city, gem*) sounds.

The terminology for vowels is even more complex than that for consonants. First, there are *long vowels* and *short vowels* (although there is nothing long about the sounds we call long; linguists call them "tense" instead). Whether a vowel is labelled long or short depends on its location in a word and the presence of other vowels in the same syllable. For example, when a vowel appears between two consonants, as in the word *can*, the vowel is generally short and the syllable is called a *closed syllable* (closed because there is a consonant at the end). On the other hand, a vowel at the end of a syllable, as in the word *go*, is usually long and the syllable is called *open*.

As with consonants, *vowel digraphs* are combinations of two letters that have one sound — generally the long vowel sound of the first letter in the digraph (e.g., *coat, meat, wait*). *Vowel blends* are called "diphthongs" and, as in consonant blends, each vowel in the blend keeps its sound (e.g., *oi, oy, ow, ou*). There are also vowels influenced by the consonants *r* and *l* (e.g., *a* influenced by *l* as in *fall* and vowels influenced by *r* as in *far, fir, for, burr, her*). These consonants are sometimes referred to as *vowel controllers*.

The terminology does not end there. *Phonograms* are letter clusters and often form the basis for *word families* (e.g., *at* — *cat, hat, mat, sat*). In phonograms, children map sounds onto larger parts of words rather than onto individual letters.

Although rarely used with children, other terms that frequently appear in teacher's guidebooks include phonemes (introduced in Chapter Two), graphemes, and the **graphophonic** system. The most common terms that children learn in phonics programs are consonants, vowels, and long and short vowels. Even these few terms, however, have limited utility. Rather than labelling sounds for the letter *a* short, long, and *r*-controlled, it is more important that children know three possible sounds (as in *can, cane,* and *car*) and that if one possibility does not result in a word that makes sense and sounds right, they should try another.

### Phonic Rules

Some people argue that labels and categories are necessary so that children can use phonic generalizations or rules. Some of you may recall phonic rules from your schooling, such as "When two vowels go walking, the first does the talking." One major problem with these rules is that they do not work often enough to make them worthwhile learning. There are many exceptions to the rule just given, including all the vowel diphthongs, (e.g., *join, about*). Consider as well the final *e* rule. Many common words, such as *give, love, some, come,* and *live,* do not follow that rule.

Another major problem with phonic rules is that children are often able to recite them but are unable to use them to identify unfamiliar words. For example, a child may be able to describe in detail how the *e* at the end of the word jumps over the letter in front of it and kicks the vowel to make it say its own name, but that same child then identifies the word *mate* as *mat.* We do not recommend rule memorization as an effective way to help children learn to map sounds onto letters.

### Letters or Larger Units

Another controversy about phonics concerns the size of unit children focus on — individual letters or larger units such as phonograms. Having children learn to associate sounds with individual letters and then blend these sounds into words is generally called *synthetic phonics.* A major problem with this approach was identified in Chapter Three. It is very difficult to isolate sounds for many letters without distorting them. Another problem involves using this approach with words of more than one syllable. It is not uncommon to hear young children attempting to identify words such as *hammer* by saying, "huh,a,muh,muh,eh,er," and then having no idea what the word is.

Having children identify words by mapping sounds to larger chunks of letters — phonograms — is often referred to as *analytic phonics.* The chunks generally consist of a vowel sound plus a consonant sound (e.g., -*ack*, -*ake*, -*eat*). These phonograms are used to create word families such as *back, pack, quack,* and *sack.* As Vacca, Vacca, and Gove (1991) point out, there are several advantages to this approach. Children find it easier to identify words using phonograms than rules, phonograms are fairly consistent, and a relatively small number of phonograms are found in many of the words in primary reading material. Still, children do come across words in which they do not recognize a phonogram and therefore need to map sounds onto smaller units of words.

### Separate or Integrated Instruction

Another controversy about phonics involves the extent to which it should be taught as a separate entity. A few years ago, it was not uncommon for phonics instruction to be scheduled in a separate time slot and taught in virtual isolation from the rest of the language arts program. Children who received this type of phonics instruction were often able to associate sounds with isolated consonants and vowels and to recite phonics rules, but they made almost no use of this knowledge when they read. Others were able to use the knowledge to identify words in lists, but when they attempted to read texts, they were unable to make effective use of their phonics knowledge.

Today, most children with reading difficulties do not lack knowledge of individual letter sounds (in spite of the fears of opponents of whole language). What they lack are strategies for using this knowledge to spell and figure out unfamiliar words. We recommend instruction that focusses on helping children use their knowledge of letter sounds to identify and spell words in the context of real reading and writing.

### Incidental or Systematic Instruction

A related controversy involves whether phonics should be taught through direct instruction in systematic lessons, or incidentally when children experience difficulty as they are reading or writing. The answer, like many others in the teaching of reading, is "It depends." Children at the emergent stage of learning to read need to figure out how letters and sounds are linked before systematic phonics instruction will make much sense to them.

As indicated in Chapter Three, letter sounds are best introduced to young children in conjunction with other activities, such as language experience stories and big books. The teacher talks about words and about the sounds associated with letters in words. When children are rereading, the teacher demonstrates and encourages the use of developing letter–sound knowledge and of other cues to identify words. During writing, the teacher encourages children to write words the way they sound.

Some children require specific instruction on the nature of the relationship between sounds and letters before they receive instruction on using cues within words to identify them. For these children, we recommend two instructional techniques that focus on phonemic awareness. Both techniques involve looking at written letters as well as listening for sounds, because researchers have found that phonemic awareness instruction is more effective when letters are included (Ball and Blachman, 1991; Byrne and Fielding-Barnsley, 1993; Hurford et al., 1994). Once children have figured out that letters and sounds map onto one another, most benefit from systematic instruction on letter sounds, how letter sounds work, and how to use this information as they read and write. Following a description of the phonemic awareness activities, we present several instructional techniques to help children learn to use cues within words to aid in their identification.

## Phonemic Awareness Using Children's Names

Cunningham and Allington (1999) suggest several activities to help build a foundation for work on word identification. The following one, involving children's names, is designed for children in kindergarten or early Grade 1.

The teacher writes the children's first names on sentence strips and cuts the names apart, with long names on long strips and short ones on short strips. Each day the teacher draws a name, and the child selected becomes "king" or "queen" for the day. His or her name becomes the focus of several language and literacy activities.

- The children interview the child, finding out what he or she likes to eat, play, and do after school, as well as how many brothers, sisters, dogs, and cats he or she has. The teacher writes this information on a chart and compiles a class book.
- The teacher focusses the children's attention on the child's name (e.g., *David*), pointing out that this word is David's name. The teacher indicates that it takes

many letters to write the word *David*, and the children count the letters. The teacher then says the letter names, *D-a-v-i-d*, and has the children say them with him or her. The teacher notes that the word begins and ends with the same letter and helps the children label one uppercase and the other lowercase.

- The teacher writes the child's name on another strip as the children watch and chant the spelling of letters with the teacher. The teacher cuts the letters apart, mixes them up, and has children come up and arrange the letters in the right order to spell the child's name, using the original sentence strip as a model.
- The children write the child's name on a large sheet of drawing paper and draw a picture of the child on the other side. The featured child takes these drawings home.
- As each name is added, the children compare them, talking about which names are longer or shorter and whether the names contain any of the same letters. When two names begin with the same letter, the teacher helps the children hear that they also begin with the same sound (e.g., *Luke* and *Linda*).
- When a single-syllable name such as *Sam* is selected, the teacher has the children listen for rhyming words. For example, the teacher says pairs of words (Sam — ham, Sam — big), and the children indicate whether the two words rhyme.
- When two names that begin with the same letter but different sounds are selected (e.g., *Caroline* and *Cynthia*), the teacher uses the opportunity to help children understand that some letters have more than one sound. The teacher writes the two names on the board and has the children say the two words several times, drawing out the first sound. The teacher then says several words beginning with the letter *c* but having different sounds (e.g., *cat, celery, candy, cookies, city, cereal, cut*). For each word, the children point to either *Caroline* or *Cynthia* to show which sound they hear, and the teacher writes the word under the name on the board.

Cunningham and Allington recommend using a similar technique with other concrete words, such as the names of colours or animals. The major focus is on hearing sounds at the beginning of words and associating these sounds with letters. The following technique is designed to help children hear sounds in all word positions.

## Hearing Sounds in Words

Marie Clay (1993) suggests a one-on-one modification of what is called the "Elkonin technique" to help young children hear sounds in words. The teacher begins by having children listen to figure out how many sounds there are in words, and eventually moves to having children link the sounds they hear with letters. This technique, originated by Daniil Elkonin (1973), is designed to help children make the connection between letters and sounds and to figure out how to map letters onto sounds when spelling, and sounds onto letters when identifying unfamiliar words. The steps in this instructional technique are presented in Box 6.1.

## Word Walls

Pinnell and Fountas (1998, p. 43) define a *word wall* as a systematically organized collection of words displayed in large letters on a wall. They use the term "interactive word walls" to emphasize that it is a tool rather than a display. Cunningham and Allington (1999) write about "doing a word wall" to connote the same thing. They recommend that teachers

**Box 6.1　Elkonin Technique**

1. The teacher prepares cards on which squares are drawn for each sound unit in words of two, three, and four sounds. For example:

m - e　　c - a - t　　j - u - m - p
i - t　　sh - i - p　　t - r - ai - n
　　　　b - oa - t

2. The teacher provides a selection of counters for the children.

3. The teacher articulates a word slowly. The child watches the teacher's lips and copies the teacher.

4. The child articulates the word slowly. (A mirror can be used if it helps children become more aware of what their lips are doing.)

5. The teacher articulates the word slowly, putting one counter in each box, sound by sound.

6. The child puts the counters in the boxes as the teacher says the word slowly, or the teacher puts the counters in boxes as the child says the word.

7. The child puts counters into boxes as he or she says the word.

8. Once the child is able to hear sounds in words, this activity is applied to spelling words as he or she writes.
   a. The child is encouraged to articulate slowly the word he or she wants to spell.
   b. The teacher draws a box for each sound segment and asks, "What can you hear? How would you write it? Where will you put it?"
   c. Initially the child writes the letters he or she is able to associate with sounds heard and the teacher writes the others. For example:

B　i　ll　　b　oa　t　　t　r　u　ck

9. After the child is able to hear and record most consonants and some vowels correctly, the teacher gives him or her a box for each letter. Clay suggests using broken lines initially when two letters do not represent distinct sounds. For example:

h　a　m｜m　e｜r

Source: Adapted from M.M. Clay (1993), *Reading Recovery: A Guidebook for Teachers in Training*, pp. 32–35. Portsmouth, NH: Heinemann.

- be very selective about the words on the wall, including only the most common words in children's reading and writing (e.g., *was, saw, of, for, from, they, that, what, with, will*),
- add words gradually—no more than five each week,
- make the word wall accessible to everyone, writing words in large clear letters,
- have children practise words by chanting or writing them, because many children can't just look at words and remember them,
- provide a variety of review activities so that children are able to identify and write words automatically, and
- make sure children spell word-wall words correctly in their writing.

Words are arranged alphabetically on the word wall, giving children an immediately accessible dictionary for the most troublesome words when they are reading or writing. The teacher and children complete several activities with words on the wall. For example:

- Children find words on the wall that rhyme with a word given by the teacher (e.g., "Find a word that begins with a *t* and rhymes with *walk*").
- The teacher writes a letter on the board and then says a sentence, leaving out a word that begins with that letter (e.g., "Write the word that begins with a *t* and fits into the sentence, *Paulo wants to _____ on the telephone*").
- The teacher thinks of a word on the wall and gives five clues, some related to visual

features ("It has three letters"), some to sounds ("It begins with the sound *s*"), and others to meaning ("It fits into the sentence 'I want to _____ the picture'"). The children write the word they think the teacher has selected after each clue.

## Word Families

As noted above, there are several advantages to having children use word families to identify words, particularly at the primary level (Vacca, Vacca, and Gove, 1991). The following steps are commonly used in the word family approach:

1. The teacher begins by teaching consonant sounds without isolating the letters and sounds. They have children listen to words that begin with the same sound (e.g., *bicycle* and *ball*), show them what letter goes with this sound, and then ask the children to say other words that begin with the same sound. The teacher often makes a key picture card for the sound being taught.

2. After the children have mastered several consonant sounds, the process of initial consonant substitution is used to present or analyze new words. For example, the teacher says and prints the word *cat*. Then the teacher changes the initial consonant and asks the children to identify the new word (e.g., *cat, bat*). When children encounter unknown words, the teacher encourages them to see if the word is similar to one they know and to use a process of substitution to identify the word.

3. The focus then shifts to final consonants and lastly to vowels, always dealing with sounds in word context and encouraging the children to use their developing knowledge of letter sounds to identify words as they read and to spell words as they write.

## Making Words

In this activity, developed by Cunningham and Cunningham (1992), teachers give children letters on cards, which they use to make words. During a period of about fifteen minutes, children make twelve to fifteen words, beginning with two-letter words and working up to longer words until they make a target word.

The teacher prepares a set of small letter cards for each child and one set of large cards to be used in a pocket chart or on the ledge of the board. Each card has the lowercase letter on one side and the uppercase letter on the other. The teacher begins planning a lesson with a target word (e.g., *winter*) that ties in with some aspect of the curriculum and contains letter–sound patterns the children need to learn. The teacher then generates a list of shorter words that can be made with the letters in *winter* (e.g., *in, tin, ten, net, wet, win, twin, went, rent, tire, wire, twine*). The teacher writes these words on index cards and orders the cards from shortest to longest and according to patterns. Once these materials are prepared, the teacher follows the steps outlined in Box 6.2 (Cunningham and Allington, 1999).

## Word Sorting

As children become more knowledgeable about letters and words, word sorting can be used as part of the making-words technique or separately for older children. This technique is designed to focus children's attention on particular cues in words. Children compare, contrast, and sort words according to specific print or sound features. Word sorts help children form generalizations about properties of words and also help them

## Box 6.2   Steps in a Making-Words Activity

1. The teacher places the large letter cards in a pocket chart or on the board ledge.

2. Each child has corresponding small letter cards. The teacher holds up the large letter cards, names each, and asks children to hold up their matching cards.

3. The teacher writes the number 2 or 3 on the board and says a word with this number of letters in a sentence. He or she asks the children to make the word using the small letter cards (e.g., "Take two letters and make the word *in*"). The children all say the word *in*.

4. A child who has made the word correctly using the small letter cards forms the word using the large cards in the pocket chart or on the ledge, and the other children check their word.

5. This continues for other words, with the teacher giving cues such as the following:" Add a letter to make the three-letter word *tin*. Many cans are made of tin." "Now change one letter and the word *tin* becomes *ten*." "Move the letters around in the word *ten* and make the word *net*." Before telling them the last word, the teacher asks if anyone has figured out what word can be made with all the letters. If they don't know, the teacher tells them the word, and they make it.

6. Once all the words have been made, the teacher places the word cards one at a time in the pocket chart or on the board ledge, and the children say and spell them. The teacher then picks a word and asks the children to find other words with the same pattern.

7. To maximize learning, the children use the patterns they have found to spell some new words dictated by the teacher.

Source: Based on P.M. Cunningham and R.L. Allington (1999), *Classrooms That Work: They Can All Read and Write* (2nd ed.), pp. 151–158. New York: Longman.

link new words to ones they already know how to identify and spell. Teachers and/or children begin by developing a word bank of known words for word sorting.

There are two types of word-sorting activities. In a closed sort, the teacher specifies the feature the children are to use to find words (e.g., all words with the same vowel sound, all words with two syllables, all words with a soft *g*). In an open sort, the teacher does not specify how words are to be grouped — the teacher asks the children to group words so that they are all the same in some way. In both types of sorts, it is important that children talk about words as they sort them, because this helps them better understand generalizations. It is also important that the teacher model the process several times so that the children understand what to do and why they are doing it.

Pinnell and Fountas (1998) recommend the following basic approaches to sorting words:

- *Sorting words by how they sound.* Children begin with initial sounds and move to ending and middle sounds.
- *Sorting words by how they look.* Children sort words that have double letters, double vowels, double consonants, and other common patterns.
- *Sorting words by connections between meaning units.* Children sort words in relation to root words, inflected endings, prefixes, suffixes, compound words, synonyms, antonyms, and so on.

## Word Parts

*Structural analysis* is the term traditionally used to refer to the identification of words using larger, more meaningful units than letters. It generally includes compounds, roots, affixes (e.g., *ly*), and syllabication. This area has not received the widespread attention of phonics, and much of the material available has the following types of limitations:

- First, material on compounds, roots, and affixes focusses almost exclusively on the association of their meaning to the words that contain such units, rather than on how knowledge of these units can be used to identify words.
- Second, the tasks children are frequently asked to complete, such as putting lines between syllables in polysyllabic words, don't involve reading or writing.
- Third, as with phonics, children are often required to learn terminology rather than to use word parts to identify words.
- Fourth, rules are frequently taught by memorization, particularly for syllabication. As with phonics, children may remember the rules but still be unable to identify the words to which those rules apply.

One way teachers help children learn to use structural units to identify words is by demonstrating how the children can organize difficult polysyllabic words into units. The teacher writes such a word in parts on the board (e.g., *but ter fly*), pronounces each part, blends the parts together, and checks to ensure that the word makes sense in its context. The teacher then encourages children to employ a similar strategy when they encounter other unknown words as they are reading. For many children, this is sufficient to help them develop an understanding of how structural analysis works and an intuitive ability to organize unfamiliar words into parts. Precise syllabication is generally not necessary, since context is available to check possible pronunciations. For those children who require more explicit instruction, activities such as the following are recommended:

1. *Compound words.* A common starting point to help children who have difficulty analyzing units larger than letters is compound words. Analyzing these words into two known real words is a concrete task. It also takes advantage of words that children already know how to identify. After a brief discussion of compound words, the teacher gives students a passage containing several compound words, with the compounds underlined. He or she asks the students to read the passage silently and be prepared to talk about what they have read. When difficulties occur, compound words are written in units on the board and discussed.

2. *Syllabication.* The goal of this instruction is to have children identify syllables by hearing and seeing places in words where structural breaks occur. This is a means toward identifying longer unknown words independently. Exact division in accordance with the dictionary is unnecessary until students reach the point where they begin to hyphenate words at the end of lines in their writing. Good advice to the reader is, "Break the word down to the point where you can see how to say it, say it and move on" (Gallant, 1970, p. 93). Box 6.3 presents steps for teaching syllabication.

3. *Affixes and inflectional endings.* We do not recommend systematically working through all affixes or inflectional endings, but rather recommend focussing on specific inflectional endings (e.g., *ed, es*) or affixes (e.g., *pre-, -ness, -tion*) when they cause difficulty. What works best is beginning with familiar words and then moving on to unfamiliar ones. Most instruction should involve words in context.

## Box 6.3    Steps for Teaching Syllabication

1. The teacher begins by helping children develop a concept of what syllables are in the words they hear. The teacher pronounces a polysyllabic word, accentuating the syllable breaks (*in for ma tion*). The teacher and children repeat the word together in syllables. Children who have difficulty hearing syllables in words often benefit from

   - clapping each time they hear or pronounce a syllable, or
   - putting their hand under their chin and feeling it move down for each syllable.

   The children then repeat the words in syllables without the teacher's aid. It is not important for the children to show how many syllables are in a word; rather, they need to be able to pronounce words in syllables.

2. To relate the concept of oral syllable to written language, the teacher presents familiar polysyllabic words to the children with syllable boundaries shown (e.g., *re port, fun ny*). Since the children already know how to identify these words, the focus is on syllables and how spoken syllables relate to the visual units. The children then learn the following visual clues that can be used to analyze words into syllables:

   - prefixes and suffixes form separate syllables,

   - double consonants or two consonants together are divided, except in the case of blends and digraphs,
   - a single consonant between two vowels often goes with the second vowel, and
   - the consonant before *-le* usually goes with it.

   The teacher selects one or two words to provide a visual reminder of each clue as they are introduced. He or she prints these on a chart (with syllable divisions shown) and places them where children can refer to them when a difficult word occurs in context. Eventually the children have models for all four visual clues.

3. The teacher has the children silently read texts containing polysyllabic words, reminding them to organize words into syllables if they have difficulty identifying them. They might lightly underline words that cause them difficulty, and these can be discussed after they finish reading. The teachers or students write selected words on the board in syllables for identification and discussion.

4. Finally, children use this strategy to identify polysyllabic words when reading independently. It is important that flexibility be stressed. If the word identified does not make sense, the children are encouraged to try it another way until they get a meaningful word.

This section focussed on helping children use cues within words to identify them. It's important that children know why they are learning these strategies. With the media's current heavy focus on phonics, you might feel considerable pressure to teach phonics for its own sake. Phonics is important, but it is best used in conjunction with other strategies for helping children identify unfamiliar words when they are constructing meaning. The next section focusses on helping children use cues beyond individual words.

## Context Cues

Whole language educators championed the use of context cues as a way for children to use their language and world knowledge to identify words as they read. Other educators have denigrated this approach as encouraging children to guess. We take the position that children need to use a range of strategies and cues as they read.

Context cues are one of several sources of information children have available to identify unfamiliar words. They need to use context cues *along with*, not instead of, print-based information.

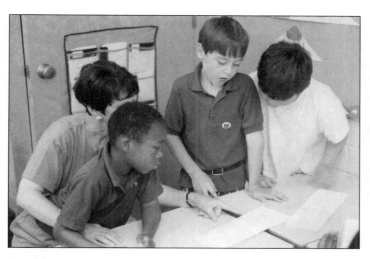

Three children identifying words in context.

# Predictable Books

One way teachers help young children make good predictions of words is by using highly predictable reading material. When reading predictable books to children, the teacher pauses at points in the text to provide opportunities for children to predict words that "make sense" and "sound right." When the teacher and children are reading together from big books, the teacher stops at highly predictable points to encourage the children to read on their own. When a child attempts to read a predictable book, the teacher encourages him or her to make predictions by asking, "What word would make sense? What word would sound right?"

Several series of predictable books are available, including the following:

- *Instant Readers* (Holt, Rinehart & Winston)
- *The Story Box* (Ginn)
- *Sunshine Books* (Ginn)
- *Literacy 2000* (Ginn)
- *Carousel Readers* (Dominie Press)
- *PM Starters and Books* (Scholastic).

In addition, many predictable trade books are available, some of them children's classics. A selection of these was presented in Chapter Three in Box 3.6.

# Cloze Procedure

In the "cloze procedure," words are deleted from a written passage and readers fill in the blanks using their knowledge of language and the world, along with clues available from the context. Although some educators recommend beginning with cloze activities in which the reader chooses from among several possibilities the word that best fills the blank, this detracts from the meaning-making nature of reading. We do not engage in a process of elimination, but rather one of meaning construction as we read.

Material at a wide range of reading levels, including both narrative and informational texts, can be used to make cloze passages. For early readers or those experiencing difficulty, the teacher initially deletes only a few words, selecting those that are highly predictable from the context. As readers begin to make more effective use of meaning and language cues to predict words, the teacher deletes more words, including those that are less predictable. An easy way to make cloze activities is to cut up pieces of self-adhesive notes to cover selected words in texts. An example of a cloze passage created from a story in *Ranger Rick* (October 1994) is shown in Box 6.4.

When introducing cloze activities, the teacher might begin with a whole class activity focussed on material presented on an overhead projector. The teacher models the process by reading through the entire passage with the students before they try to fill in the blanks. Once all students have read through the passage, a student volunteer

## Box 6.4   Sample Cloze Passage

The first paragraph (not shown here) is left intact so children will already have begun to make meaning by the time they get to the first blank. In that paragraph, Scarlett Fox and Ranger Rick Raccoon are in a picnic area near the ocean when they see a white shapeless form in the fog.

"Look, it's coming back!" Rick whispered in horror as the Thing came right toward them. Suddenly it _____ over their picnic basket and fell in a heap. Now Rick and Scarlett could see that the white thing was a _____ and out from under it crawled their friend Boomer Badger. He laughed gleefully between gulps of_____ as he tried to catch his breath.

Source: Reading passage excerpted from N. Steiner Mealy (1994, October), "Adventures of Ranger Rick." *Ranger Rick*, p. 40.

reads the first sentence and supplies the missing word. Other students who responded differently read the sentence and provide their responses. Class discussion centres on such questions as

- Why did you choose this word?
- What do you know about the topic in this passage that helped you predict this word?
- What in the passage helped you to make this prediction?
- Is there a difference in the meaning when we choose your word rather than X's?
- Why did different students predict different words?

Later, the teacher gives students cloze passages to complete individually. The teacher asks children to explain in small group discussions why they used particular words, again focussing on knowledge and text cues. The small group discussions might then lead to large group discussion of some of the more interesting or controversial items.

It is not important in cloze activities for children to predict the author's exact word. As long as the predictions make sense and sound right in relation to the rest of the passage, they are accepted. By insisting on exact replacements, the teacher would send the children the message that text cues are more important than knowledge when making meaning, and the task would be reduced to "guess what word the author used."

As with instructional techniques for using cues within words, it is important that children understand why they are reading predictable books and doing cloze activities. Otherwise they may not realize that they should use similar strategies to predict words when they come to unfamiliar words as they read.

## Integrating Context and Print Cues

We believe that in a balanced literacy program most instructional techniques on word identification should help children use *both* context and print cues, rather than one or the other. This section begins with a description of how one teacher provides this type of instruction. The remainder of the section presents instructional techniques designed to help children integrate strategies for using context and print cues as they read.

In Maureen Kelly's Grade 2 classroom, the first thing children do in the morning is read the morning message to find out what they will be doing that day. Maureen omits letters from some of the words, which encourages the children to predict what words will make sense and sound right and to associate letters with sounds in those words. When she notes that several children in the class are having difficulty with marking long vowel sounds in their writing, her minimal cues message includes several words containing the final *e* (e.g., "Today we will mak_ puppets and writ_ a story about something we lik_"). As the children predict the words, they discuss what letter needs to go on the end of each word and notice that in all the words, the sound of the vowel in the middle is the same as the name of the letter.

After the morning message has been completed and the children are working on group projects, Maureen calls together the six children whose writing reflects difficulty with final *e* and provides direct instruction. She tells them what she has noticed in their writing, beginning by noting what final *e* words they spelled correctly and then focussing on those spelled incorrectly. She gives the children word cards containing words with long vowel sounds, and they sort the words according to whether they contain the final *e* or not. Before they leave the group, the children revisit their writing and correct words containing the final *e*. When the children begin another writing activity later that morning, Maureen reminds them to think about the final *e* spelling pattern. The message the next morning again includes final *e* words for review, but introduces two vowels together as well.

The instruction in Maureen Kelly's classroom is explicit, systematic, and at the same time integrated. In the remainder of this section, we describe instructional techniques that teachers can integrate into their language arts program to help children use both print and context cues as they read.

## Masking

Holdaway (1979) describes how to use "masking" to help young children use context cues, structural units, and letter sounds to identify words. Working with either a transparency or a big book, the teacher uses a strip of paper to mask text lines and slides it aside to gradually expose parts of words, complete words, and phrases. Children read to the point where the next word is covered and predict what will come next. Then the teacher uncovers the word so the children can use print cues to check their predictions. Discussion focusses on how predictions are made and where cues come from.

## Minimal Cue Messages

The morning message in Maureen Kelly's classroom described above was presented in a "minimal cue" format. Such messages, a modification of the cloze procedure, are set up to encourage integration of print and meaning cues and to aid spelling. Teachers can develop minimal cue messages to focus on specific types of print cues (e.g., endings, vowel digraphs) when the teacher identifies this need.

The teacher writes a message to the children with some of the letters missing. Dashes are generally used to show how many letters are required. For example:

Tod_ _ is a _ery sp_cial d_ _. W_ are go_ _ _ to th_ m_seu_.

These messages work best when they are relevant to the children and the language is natural and predictable. It is important that teachers discuss with the children what cues they used in unlocking the minimal cue message. Discussion focusses on both meaning and print cues, such as "I knew the word had to be museum because you told us yesterday that we were going to the museum today. I also saw that the word began with the letter *m*."

Initially the teacher fills in the children's predictions, but gradually the children take over the writing. Children who have been exposed to this technique often begin to write minimal cue messages to other students or the teacher.

## Oral Reading

When children are reading orally, the way the teacher responds to their reading communicates a great deal about what cues and strategies the teacher thinks are important. If a teacher constantly says, "Sound it out" when the child has difficulty, the child may come to believe that reading equals sounding out. We recommend the following guidelines:

- If a child pauses during reading, wait to give the child time to use both context and print cues to identify the word. Encourage her or him to predict a word that makes sense, sounds right, and checks out.
- If a child makes a substitution while reading that is consistent with the author's meaning, ignore the miscue. Research shows that even good readers do not read with 100 percent accuracy; instead, they make some meaningful slips because of the constructive nature of reading. Ignoring such miscues communicates to children that making meaning is the essence of reading.
- If a child corrects a mistake, reinforce this by commenting on the appropriateness of the correction, rather than focussing on the error.
- If a child makes **miscues** that do not make sense, leave time for self-correction. If the child does not self-correct, ask whether what he or she read sounded right and made sense. Focus discussion on the meaning the child constructed from the reading.

For each instructional technique included in this chapter, we recommend having children talk about the strategies being used. Through discussion, they develop both metacognitive awareness of strategies and control of their reading. However, the ultimate goal is automatic application of word identification strategies most of the time so that children are able to focus their attention on meaning. The next section deals with helping children achieve automaticity.

## Fluency/Automaticity

Although there has been considerable criticism of sight word approaches (often referred to as "look and guess"), it is now clear that a crucial factor in skilled reading is the ability to recognize words effortlessly and automatically. In order to achieve automaticity, children need to read, read, and read some more.

Traditionally, sight vocabulary was taught using flash cards, word lists, and controlled-vocabulary materials. More recently, the focus has moved to reading connected texts. Rossman (1987) estimates that children need to read for a minimum of three and a half hours each week to achieve automaticity when reading material at their independent reading level.

One thing nearly all children with reading difficulty have in common is that they do not read very much. Research has revealed that children in high-level reading groups tend to spend more time reading than children in lower-level reading groups (Bloome and Green, 1984). The difference between good and poor readers in the amount of time they spend reading increases during their years in school. Good readers read more both at home and at school, while poor readers read very little in either context. Stanovich (1986) refers to this as a "Matthew effect"—the rich get richer and the poor get poorer. Since good readers are more likely than poor ones to read outside the classroom, it is imperative that time be set aside in school for all children to read.

Sustained silent reading is recommended for all children regardless of reading level. Many adaptations of sustained silent reading have appeared in recent years (e.g., DEAR—drop everything and read). Paired reading, on the other hand, is particularly appropriate for children who are experiencing difficulty learning to read or for those who are reluctant readers. Repeated reading is most helpful for children who read in a slow, laborious manner even when they are reading material below their instructional reading level.

## Sustained Silent Reading

This activity, developed by Hunt (1971), is becoming more prevalent in schools today. In addition to the opportunity it provides for increased exposure to reading, it helps create an atmosphere in which reading and books are extremely important. In the classroom, the child gains a positive image of reading by seeing the teacher and other children enjoying books.

The steps we recommend for implementing sustained silent reading (SSR) are presented in Box 6.5. Initially, the block of time should be short enough to ensure success, but gradually it can be increased to fifteen to twenty minutes per day. Sometimes teachers use a timer to indicate that SSR is over. Teachers also terminate the period depending on their observations. It is important that SSR end on a positive note while children are still interested in what they are reading. Interruptions are not permitted. A sign on the door indicating that SSR is in progress will minimize interruptions. Because of the power of modelling, it is essential that teachers also read during this time rather than catching up on other work.

| **Box 6.5** | **Steps to Implement Sustained Silent Reading (SSR)** |
| --- | --- |

1. The teacher discusses SSR with the children so they know what they will be doing, why they are doing it, what behaviours are expected of them, and how long they will be reading. For example, all students will read a book they have chosen, everyone will be quiet, and no one will move around the room.

2. Children are given advance notice so that they will have books chosen beforehand.

3. The teacher provides children with some background for choosing what to read by acquainting them with all kinds of books and by talking about books with them. The teacher "sells" books to children by reading parts of an interesting or exciting book to them to entice them to finish the book on their own.

4. Both teacher and children settle into comfortable spots in the classroom and read silently.

## Paired Reading

Paired reading, a technique developed in England by Topping (1987), involves a child reading with another reader from a book the child has selected. The other reader may be the child's parent, a volunteer, a teacher, or another child. The activity is done for ten to fifteen minutes on at least five days per week for eight to twelve weeks.

The steps in paired reading are presented in Box 6.6. Tutors praise children for appropriate signalling, self-correcting, and fluent reading. They also encourage children to talk about the meaning they have constructed both during and after reading.

**Box 6.6    Steps in Paired Reading**

1. The child chooses a book to read.

2. Beginning with a prearranged signal, the child and another reader read aloud together.

3. It is important for the child to read each word correctly. If he or she doesn't, the other reader reads the word correctly, the child repeats it, and they continue reading together.

4. Using another prearranged signal (e.g., a nudge or tap), the child indicates that he or she is ready to read alone. The other reader praises the child.

5. The child reads alone until an error is made or a word is encountered that he or she cannot read in five seconds.

6. The reader immediately rejoins the child by saying the difficult word and having the child repeat it, and then they continue reading together until the child gives the signal again and the procedure is repeated or the session ends.

Source: Based on A. Brailsford (1991), *Paired Reading: Positive Reading Practice*, pp. 3–4. Edmonton: Northern Alberta Reading Specialists Council.

# Repeated Reading

This technique is designed to develop sight vocabulary and self-concept as well as increased automaticity or fluency. The technique (Samuels, 1979) involves having the student read a short, meaningful passage several times until a satisfactory level of fluency is attained. Either the teacher or the student selects the material to be read, but it should be material the student is able to read independently and that he or she is interested in. If longer stories are chosen, short selections of 50 to 200 words are marked off for rereading.

The student reads the selection to the teacher, who records reading speed and number of word recognition errors on a graph. The teacher and student set a goal for both reading speed (e.g., 90 words per minute) and accuracy (no more than 5 errors in a 100-word passage). The student practises reading the selection until he or she reads at or above the goal set. Then the teacher and student select another passage, and the procedure is repeated. The graph provides a visual display of the student's increasing fluency. Samuels found that both the initial speed of reading passages and the number of rereadings required to reach the goal decreased over time.

Koskinen and Blum (1986) modified repeated reading so that two children work together rather than with the teacher, making the technique more practical for the classroom context. In paired, repeated reading, children read together for ten to fifteen minutes. Each child reads a short passage at his or her independent reading level three times and then evaluates his or her own reading as well as that of a partner. Paired repeated reading involves the following steps:

1. Children choose partners or are assigned partners by their teacher.

2. Children select their own passages of approximately 50 words to read. Some children need guidance to select material at their independent level.

3. The children read their passages silently and then decide who will be the first reader.

4. The first reader reads his or her passage to a partner three times, asking for help with words if needed. After each oral reading, the reader fills in a " How well did I read?" self-evaluation sheet. This sheet consists of a Likert scale ranging from fantastic to terrible (fantastic, good, fair, not so good, terrible). For young children, teachers use pictures to represent the points on the scale. The partner listens to the child read, and after the second and third reading, tells the reader how his or her reading improved. The listener never makes negative comments.

5. The children switch roles.

Teachers introduce and model the technique for children, helping them understand (1) the procedures involved, (2) how to listen and make positive comments (e.g., "I noticed you self-corrected," "read in phrases," "read more smoothly," "knew more words"), and (3) how to select material for reading. After teachers provide supervised practice, children are able to use the technique independently.

Although these techniques ensure that children spend at least some time reading, the ultimate goal of language arts programs is to create the context in which children *become* readers. The instructional techniques included in this chapter help children learn *how* to read. Purposeful reading experiences with a wide range of children's literature and other written material entice them into the world of readers.

## Reading Intervention

Many children — some estimates are as high as 25 percent — from mainstream homes have difficulty learning to read. Estimates are even higher for children from non-mainstream houses. In this section, we outline characteristics of successful intervention programs and suggest how to maximize the match between children's reading needs and instructional techniques.

## Characteristics of Effective Programs

Several articles appeared in the 1990s describing characteristics of effective reading intervention programs (Wasik and Slavin, 1993; Pikulski, 1994; Spiegel, 1995). Some of these characteristics are as follows:

1. *Early intervention.* Most educators agree that intervention needs to occur early. Children who are behind their peers fall further and further behind, widening the gap between good and poor readers across the elementary grades. Prolonged failure has negative consequences for children's self-concepts which, in turn, negatively affects their learning. By intervening in Grade 1, the cycle of failure can be prevented.

2. *Increased reading time.* Another characteristic of effective intervention is increased time spent reading. In many traditional remedial programs, children spend far more time completing workbooks or worksheets than reading books or other materials. It is through extensive reading of connected texts (not isolated words or letters) that children consolidate reading strategies and develop automaticity.

3. *Increased reading instruction.* Closely related to increased reading time is the need for teachers to devote more time to reading instruction for at-risk learners. As Spiegel (1995) notes, this enhances children's opportunity to learn. Rather than providing instruction in short time blocks once or twice per week, effective intervention involves consistent, daily reading instruction.

4. *Quality instruction.* Instructional time alone is not sufficient. For intervention to be most effective, quality of instruction is also important. In high-quality programs, ongoing assessment provides a foundation for instructional decisions. Rather than providing a prescribed program for all children, programs are designed around each child's needs and strengths. Direct instruction is required, focussing

on strategies and the *how to* of reading rather than specific bits of information presented in isolated ways (Pinnell, Fried, and Estice, 1990).

5. *Teacher training.* Intervention programs using certified teachers are more effective than those using para-professionals or volunteers. Indeed, the most effective programs, such as *Success for All* and *Reading Recovery*, include an ongoing professional development component.

6. *Individual or small group instruction.* The most effective intervention involves instruction for individuals or small groups (no more than four or five children). This type of intervention is expensive in the short term, but if children catch up with their peers and need no or little additional intervention, the long-term savings can be considerable.

7. *Coordination with excellent classroom instruction.* Finally, intervention is more effective when children's total reading program is taken into consideration. For maximum impact, children need to receive excellent and coordinated instruction both in their classroom and intervention programs.

## *Reading Recovery*

An intervention program that reflects most of the characteristics listed above and has been widely researched is *Reading Recovery*. This program was developed and trademarked by Marie Clay in the 1970s and has been implemented nationwide in New Zealand. Children making the slowest progress in reading after one year in school are identified, and in addition to classroom reading instruction, they receive one-to-one instruction for 30 minutes daily over a period of 10 to 20 weeks.

*Reading Recovery* consists of two components: an instructional component for children and a professional development component for teachers. The first step in *Reading Recovery* is a detailed assessment of the child's reading, followed by two weeks of instruction in which the child is engaged in reading and writing activities the teacher knows he or she can do. This is a time for confidence- and relationship-building. Then the teacher moves into instruction, and each 30-minute lesson includes the following activities:

1. The child rereads two or more familiar books.

2. The teacher takes a running record of the child reading yesterday's new book and teaches strategies.

3. The teacher and child work with letter identification (if necessary) and making and breaking words.

4. The child writes one or two sentences using the "hearing sounds in words" technique described earlier in this chapter.

5. The child rearranges the sentences that have been cut up by the teacher or child.

6. The teacher introduces and previews a new book with the child.

7. The child reads the new book with support as needed.

While reading and rereading books, teachers provide feedback on reading strategies being used or emerging. The goal of the program is to help children develop independent, self-generating systems for promoting their own literacy. The difficulty of new books increases gradually, ensuring that children experience success. Children are discontinued from the program when they have caught up to the average reading level of peers in their classrooms.

The professional development component of the program is an integral part of *Reading Recovery*. Clay has designed a three-tier system of professional development involving *Reading Recovery* trainers, teacher-leaders, and teachers. Teacher-leaders and teachers continue to receive professional development as long as they are involved in a *Reading Recovery* program.

*Reading Recovery* has expanded rapidly in both the United States (Hiebert, 1994) and Canada (Gregory, 1998) since the mid-1980s. Results of research generally show that the program works for most children, at least in the short term (Glynn, Bethune, Crooks, Ballard, and Smith, 1992; Pinnell, Lyons, DeFord, Bryk, and Seltzer, 1993; Center, Wheldall, Freeman, Outhred, and McNaught, 1995; Shanahan and Barr, 1995; Moore and Wade, 1998).

While ex–*Reading Recovery* children do continue to make progress after they complete programs, their rate of progress depends on several factors. One is clearly the nature of the program they are placed in. The other involves home and community factors. As Pinnell, Fried, and Estice (1990) point out:

> *Reading Recovery* is promising, but it is not *the* answer. There is no one answer to problems in education. Many of the children served by *Reading Recovery* remain in the potentially-at-risk category because of economic circumstances. Children may learn to *read* through *Reading Recovery*, but they do not turn into different children even though many adopt a much more positive attitude toward school. Poor children are still poor. Highly mobile families still move. (pp. 294–295)

## Selecting Instructional Techniques

As indicated above, one of the characteristics of effective intervention programs is individualized of instruction. This involves more than providing different types of instructional activities for good and poor readers. Research shows that instructional activities for poor readers tend to focus more on specific skill worksheets or management rather than on text comprehension (Johnston and Allington, 1991). There is little evidence that these types of programs are effective with poor readers. Indeed, they may do more harm than good. Pearson (1993, p. 505) notes that "the consequence of differentiated instruction for low-track students has been devastating, particularly for children of diversity."

What we need is differentiated instruction rather than one type of program for all children identified as having difficulties learning to read. The key is matching instructional techniques to the needs of specific children. Table 6.2 summarizes common reading difficulties and some techniques that are appropriate to use with children who display each type of difficulty.

As a teacher, you will be bombarded on a regular basis with people who claim to have found the answer to reading problems. It may be a diet, it may be exercises, it may be a specific commercial program, it may be listening or visual devices. But whenever someone presents one answer for all children with reading difficulties, alarm bells should sound. Reading is a complex process. Reading difficulties arise from a complex interaction of factors within the child, the school, and the broader

**Table 6.2   Matching Reading Difficulties and Instructional Techniques**

| Type of Difficulty | Recommended Techniques |
|---|---|
| • Child is a word caller and needs to make more effective use of background knowledge as well as text to construct meaning. | • Select techniques from "Integrating Knowledge-Based and Text-Based Information" (Chapter Five). |
| • Child relies too heavily on phonics knowledge to decode words and produces nonsense words when he or she reads orally. | • Begin with techniques from "Context Cues" and move quickly to those for "Integrating Context and Print Cues" (Chapter Six). |
| • Child has few strategies for using cues within words and constructs a different meaning from text information or little meaning at all. | • Begin with techniques from "Print Cues," and as soon as the child develops some of these strategies, move to those for "Integrating Context and Print Cues" (Chapter Six). |
| • Child can decode short words but has difficulty with longer ones. | • Select "Word Sorting" or "Word Parts" techniques from "Print Cues" (Chapter Six). |
| • Child uses strategies for processing cues within words but constructs a meaning that is not consistent with text information. | • Select techniques from "Integrating Knowledge-Based and Text-Based Information," emphasizing text-based information initially (Chapter Five). |
| • Child constructs meaning when reading stories but has difficulty with informational texts. | • Select techniques from "Informational Texts" in "Using Text Structure" (Chapter Five). |
| • Child appears to think the meaning is in the text and can deal only with factual questions. | • Select techniques from "Integrating Knowledge-Based and Text-Based Information" (Chapter Five). |

community. There are no simple answers. Each may be part of the solution for some children, but none will be the total solution for all children.

## Summary

Word identification has traditionally been taught from a skills perspective, with a focus on sight vocabulary, phonics, structural analysis, and contextual analysis. Recently, there has been an increased call for more attention to phonics in reading programs, but children need to learn strategies for using both print-based and knowledge-based information to be able to identify words as they read. Teachers are faced with several issues when planning phonics instruction, including how much terminology to use, how to deal with phonic rules, whether to focus on letters or larger units, whether to provide separate or integrated phonics instruction, and, finally, whether to teach phonics incidentally or systematically.

Instructional techniques to help children develop phonemic awareness are most effective when they involve printed letters as well as sounds. One effective strategy with young children involves having them hear and see similarities and differences among their names. Another effective technique involves using boxes to help children hear sounds in all parts of words and to link these sounds with letters. Techniques to help children make use of cues within words include word walls, word families, making words, word sorting, and word parts.

Context cues provide a way for children to use their language and world knowledge to predict words as they read. Predictable books support the use of context cues, particularly by young children. In the cloze procedure, words are omitted from passages and children use their language and world knowledge to predict words and monitor their predictions

The most effective instructional techniques for word identification involve using both print and context cues. Teachers integrate techniques such as masking and minimal cue messages into daily reading activities and are thoughtful as they respond to children's oral reading, reinforcing use of print, language, and meaning cues.

The ultimate goal of word identification instruction is to help children develop automaticity in using both print and context cues so that they are able to focus most of their attention on constructing meaning. Sustained silent reading, paired reading, and repeated reading are activities that enable children to reach this goal.

None of the instructional techniques described in Chapters Five and Six will meet the needs of all children. A major goal of teachers is to assess each child's reading needs and match the program as closely as possible with these needs. This is particularly critical for children who have difficulty learning to read. Intervention programs can break the cycle of failure when they occur early, provide increased time for reading and reading instruction, provide high-quality reading instruction, use certified teachers, involve one-to-one or small group instruction, and are coordinated with excellent classroom instruction.

## Selected Professional Resources

Cunningham, P.M. and Allington, R.L. (1999). *Classrooms That Work: They Can All Read and Write* (2nd ed.). New York: Longman. In this edition, Cunningham and Allington pull together what they believe works for classroom teachers. They discuss the components in a balanced literacy program, including activities teachers can use to increase children's word identification and fluency.

Pinnell, G.S. and Fountas, I.C. (1998). *Word Matters: Teaching Phonics and Spelling in the Reading/Writing Curriculum*. Portsmouth, NH: Heinemann. Pinnell and Fountas present a concept they call "word solving." Their goal is to help children learn to take words apart, to help them in their search for meaning when reading, and to construct words from letters and letter clusters when writing. They share instructional techniques for teachers to use in three contexts — reading, writing, and word study.

## Children's Material Noted in Chapter Six

Mealy, N.S. (October 1994). Adventures of Ranger Rick. *Ranger Rick*, 40–43.

# References

Adams, M.J. (1990). *Beginning to read: Thinking and learning about print.* Cambridge, MA: MIT Press.

Ball, E.W. and Blachman, B.A. (1991). Does phoneme segmentation training in kindergarten make a difference in early word recognition and developmental spelling? *Reading Research Quarterly, 26,* 49–66.

Bloome, D. and Green, J. (1984). Directions in the sociolinguistic study of reading. In R. Barr, M.L. Kamil, and P.B. Mosenthal (eds.), *Handbook of reading research* (pp. 395–421). New York: Longman.

Brailsford, A. (1991). *Paired reading: Positive reading practice.* Edmonton: Northern Alberta Reading Specialists Council.

Byrne, B. and Fielding-Barnsley, R. (1993). Evaluation of a program to teach phonemic awareness to young children: A 1-year follow-up. *Journal of Educational Psychology, 85,* 104–111.

Center, Y., Wheldall, K., Freeman, L., Outhred, L., and McNaught, M. (1995). An evaluation of Reading Recovery. *Reading Research Quarterly, 30* (2), 240–261.

Chall, J.S. (1967). *Learning to read: The great debate.* New York: McGraw-Hill.

Clay, M.M. (1985). *The early detection of reading difficulties.* Auckland, NZ: Heinemann.

Clay, M.M. (1993). *Reading Recovery: A guidebook for teachers in training.* Portsmouth, NH: Heinemann.

Cunningham, P.M. and Allington, R.L. (1999). *Classrooms that work: They can all read and write* (2nd ed.). New York: Longman.

Cunningham, P.M. and Cunningham, J.W. (1992). Making words: Enhancing the invented spelling-decoding connection. *Reading Teacher, 46* (2), 106–113.

Elkonin, D.B. (1973). USSR. In J. Downing (ed.), *Comparative reading: Cross-national studies of behavior and processes in reading and writing.* New York: Macmillan.

Gallant, R. (1970). *Handbook in corrective reading.* Columbus, OH: Charles E. Merrill.

Glynn, T., Bethune, N., Crooks, T., Ballard, K., and Smith, J. (1992). Reading Recovery in context: Implementation and outcome. *Educational Psychology, 12,* 249–261.

Gregory, D. (1998). The Canadian Institute of Reading Recovery national implementation data: 1996–97. Toronto: Canadian Institute of Reading Recovery.

Hiebert, E.H. (1994). Reading Recovery in the United States: What difference does it make to an age cohort? *Educational Researcher, 23,* 15–25.

Holdaway, D. (1979). *The foundations of literacy.* Gosford, Australia: Ashton Scholastic.

Hunt, L.C. (1971). Six steps to the individualized reading program (IRP). *Elementary English, 48,* 27–32.

Hurford, D.P., Johnston, M., Nepote, P., Hampton, S., Moore, S., Neal, J., Nueller, A., McGeorge, K., Huff, L., Award, A., Tatro, C., Juliano, C., and Huffman, D. (1994). Early identification and remediation of phonological-processing deficits in first-grade children at risk for reading disabilities. *Journal of Learning Disabilities, 27,* 647–659.

Johnston, P. and Allington, R. (1991). Remediation. In R. Barr, M.L. Kamil, P.B. Mosenthal, and P.D. Pearson (eds.), *Handbook of reading research,* Vol. 2 (pp. 984–1012). White Plains, NY: Longman.

Koskinen, P.S. and Blum, I.H. (1986). Paired repeated reading: A classroom strategy for developing fluent reading. *Reading Teacher, 40* (1), 70–75.

Moore, M. and B. Wade (1998). Reading and comprehension: A longitudinal study of ex-Reading Recovery students. *Educational Studies, 24* (2), 195–202.

Pearson, P.D. (1993). Teaching and learning reading: A research perspective. *Language Arts, 70* (6), 502–511.

Pikulski, J.J. (1994). Preventing reading failure: A review of five effective programs. *Reading Teacher, 48* (1), 30–39.

Pinnell, G.S. and Fountas, I.C. (1998). *Word matters: Teaching phonics and spelling in the reading/writing classroom.* Portsmouth, NH: Heinemann.

Pinnell, G.S., Fried, M.D., and Estice, R.M. (1990). Reading Recovery: Learning how to make a difference. *Reading Teacher, 43,* 282–295.

Pinnell, G.S., Lyons, C.A., DeFord, D.E., Bryk, A.S., and Seltzer, M. (1993). Comparing instructional models for the literacy education of high-risk first graders. *Reading Research Quarterly, 29* (1), 10–38.

Rossman, A.D. (1987). Reading automaticity: The essential element of academic success. *Principal, 67,* 28–32.

Samuels, S.J. (1979). The method of repeated readings. *Reading Teacher, 32,* 403–408.

Shanahan, T. and Barr, R. (1995). Reading Recovery: An independent evaluation of the effects of an early instructional intervention for at-risk learners. *Reading Research Quarterly, 30* (4), 958–996.

Spiegel, D.L. (1995). A comparison of traditional remedial programs and Reading Recovery: Guidelines for success for all programs. *Reading Teacher, 49* (2), 86–96.

Stanovich, K.E. (1986). Matthew effects in reading: Some consequences of individual differences in the acquisition of literacy. *Reading Research Quarterly, 21* (4), 360–406.

Topping, K. (1987). Paired reading: A powerful technique for parent use. *Reading Teacher, 40,* 608–614.

Vacca, J.L., Vacca, R.T., and Gove, M.K. (1991). *Reading and learning to read* (2nd ed.). New York: HarperCollins.

Wasik, B.A. and Slavin, R.E. (1993). Preventing early reading failure with one-to-one tutoring: A review of five programs. *Reading Research Quarterly, 28* (2), 179–200.

# The Process of Writing

**Models of Writing**
- Voices of Writing
- Levels of Writing

**Forms of Writing**
- Narrative
- Expressive
- Informational or Expository
- Persuasive
- Descriptive
- Poetry

**The Process of Composing**
- Rehearsal
- Drafting
- Feedback
- Presentation
- The Role of Audience

**The Process of Writing**

**Conducting a Writing Workshop**
- Guidelines for Conducting a Writing Conference
- The Students' Role in a Writing Workshop

**Social Interaction in the Writing Process**
- The Importance of Talk
- Peer Group Writing Conferences

*Dragon's Gaze*

As the dragon grew upon the land, his body changed
First his hand. The scales appeared
His face was true, like a dragon's face
Then everyone knew
A shimmering glass, pink and grey in his mouth —
a pearl lay
The dragon's eyes were looking at me
I looked away, towards my knee —
The river full!
The thunder crackled in the sky. The splashing water
on the grass
Rain!
Then I knew the dragon would be back — again ■

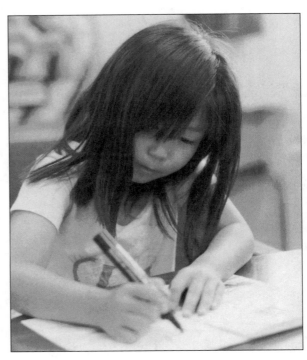

"D" ragon's Gaze" is a poem that was proudly shown to Monique during her first visit to her Grade 4 student teaching classroom. The writer explained to Monique that she had written it after their teacher had read Julie Lawson's book *The Dragon's Pearl* (1992) to the class. Monique was surprised to find that a student of this age could write such a vivid poem and immediately began to look forward to working with this group of student writers. Monique knew that writing instruction in elementary schools had changed dramatically over the last two decades, but she wasn't exactly sure of how the changes had affected classroom instruction. Monique's co-operating teacher was encouraging and reminded Monique that a good place to start would be to reflect on her own experiences as a writer and to think about what student writers need in order to develop their abilities to create and express their ideas. The teacher suggested that Monique consider the following questions as useful entry points:

- What do children need to know and be able to do in order to develop as writers?
- What role does the teacher play in helping young writers to grow?
- How can the teacher structure writing instruction to promote growth in both fluency of ideas and control of writing skills?
- How can the teacher balance the need for creative expression with the need for clear communication?
- What forms of writing are appropriate for elementary students?

This chapter is designed to help Monique answer the above questions. It provides an introduction to models of writing, defines the writing process, and describes how the process may be realized in classroom practice.

## Models of Writing

Not long ago, teaching writing meant teaching handwriting, or what was called "penmanship." Almost all the writing done by children in school was copied from the blackboard or from a book. Special teachers of penmanship circulated among the schools in a district, and children spent an hour or more each day working in their copybooks. The emphasis was on creating error-free, beautiful copy, not on composing and expressing ideas. Over the last two decades the emphasis has shifted from a preoccupation with the surface features of writing to an instructional perspective that balances the product with the process writers use to create, organize, and express their ideas.

The shift in orientation came about when teachers began to observe young writers in the act of composing (Graves, 1983; Calkins, 1986). They began to ask questions about the process that children used when writing: How do writers craft a piece of writing? How do they work on the ideas? How do they learn to shape the writing so that it is interesting and piques the interest of the audience? How do writers ensure that the piece says what they want it to say and that they have communicated the information and feelings they want to communicate? Teachers such as Graves and Calkins concluded that writing is a complex set of processes and skills that requires a command of the print code (**graphophonics**), grammar (**syntax**), and meaning-making devices (**semantics**), as well as of the physical act of creating print. It is a generative rather than a receptive process. Like all writers, the creator of "Dragon's Gaze" generated meaning using all the cuing systems of the language and culture. Pat D'Arcy

(1989), in her work as a language arts consultant, identified four elements of students' writing: processes (the thinking involved), products (the pieces of formatted writing), codes (spelling, punctuation, grammar, letters, words), and media (handwriting, word processing, notes, jottings, and so on). In a balanced instructional program, teachers help students to grow in each of these elements.

Today, we see writing as an act that is carried out with a specific purpose for a distinct audience. We use different voices, styles, and formats depending on the purpose and audience the writing is to serve. When student writers develop a sense of purpose and audience, they recognize that different formats help them to achieve their communication goals: letters, memos, poems, reports, editorials, invitations, journal entries, logs, diaries, essays, plays, filmscripts, textbooks, novels, short stories, lists, recipes, instruction manuals, and so on. As writers, we can never separate a piece of writing from its form, function, or audience. Each one affects the others and shapes the piece of writing. We learn much of this from the reading we do every day — in bus advertisements, television listings, mailbox coupons, letters to friends, application forms for jobs, cooking directions on packages of food, articles in magazines, and the novels we read. Each time we read, we learn more about writing and about what writers need to know and do to be effective.

## Voices of Writing

James Britton (1970) proposed a model of writing based on the voice of the writer. *Voice* refers to the combined effects of the writer's purpose, style, tone, and other intangibles, such as commitment, energy, conviction, and personality. Britton identified three voices of writing: expressive, poetic, and transactional. The expressive voice is used when we write in a journal, write a personal letter to a friend, or write in a notebook about ideas that have lingered in our minds. It expresses who we are and what we think and feel. In **expressive writing**, which usually tends to be informal, we articulate ideas that are close to us, that may not yet be fully shaped. Below is an excerpt from a piece of expressive writing by a boy in Grade 4, written as he thought about the book *On My Honor* by Marion Dane Bauer (1986):

> I hate it when my friends try to convince me to do things they want to do. I think Tony is being quite mean to Joel. I think that Tony just wants Joel to do what he wants to do. I can swim but not too good. But even if I was a professional swimmer I'd never swim in a river. I think it's a bad idea because the water is pushing you. It would just suck you up. A few minutes later you'd be dead.

**Poetic writing** is more literary and is used in stories as well as poems. Usually created for an audience other than the self, poetic writing often contains an aesthetic element not usually present in either expressive or transactional writing. "The Dragon's Gaze" is an example of poetic writing and so is the following poem completed by a child in Grade 3:

> *Cowboys*
> Brave and dirty,
> Hazing,
> Roping,
> Digging their spurs into the horses.

Riding,
Racing,
Branding the cattle —
Cowpunchers.

**Transactional writing** is used when the writer wants to convey information to others in a report, list, essay, or textbook. It is usually more formal than personal, focussing principally on the effective communication of content. However, transactional writing balances information with a personal perspective, as demonstrated in "About Seasons," presented in Exhibit 7.1. "About Seasons" was completed by a child in Grade 1 who visited the Cayman Islands with her family at Christmas time. When Tanya returned to Canada she suddenly understood the importance of seasons and realized that seasons exist all over the world, but that they vary in nature. Tanya was excited by her discovery and wanted to capture her ideas on paper so that she could present them to her classmates.

Britton noticed that young writers frequently move from one voice to another as they write. When writing a report on a pet, for example, they may add a personal anecdote about their own pet, and hence combine the expressive and transactional voices. Similarly, they may shift from the poetic to the expressive voice when writing a story, adding themselves as a character and writing in the first person. Britton terms this the *transitional voice*. In "About Seasons" (Exhibit 7.1), although it did not alter the voice of her writing, Tanya could not resist adding her address and phone number to the bottom of the page, thus ensuring her own personal stamp was placed on her piece. Usually, as writers mature, they are able to select an appropriate voice for their writing and remain consistently within that voice.

## Levels of Writing

James Moffett (1979) proposed a model of writing development that suggests a hierarchy according to the skills the writer needs and the purpose the writing is to serve. The first level is that of drawing or handwriting. This is the level at which children begin writing, as they struggle to make sense of the written language system and to replicate it. The second level is copying, where children are capable of copying from a model provided by someone else. At this point, the focus is on learning the correct form of letters and sentences rather than generating ideas. The third level is

**Exhibit 7.1   About Seasons**

About Seasons

It is almost spring. The weather changes to be warmer because the season is changing to be spring. After spring is summer which is very hot.
In some countries are even very hot during winter because they are closer to the equator, especially Africa. Some of Africa is on the equator. That's why giraffes live there.
After summer comes fall again. In the fall the leaves start to fall off the trees and get ready for winter.
Winter has a lot of snowstorms and people wear a lot of clothes because the weather is very cold and people think that if they wear a little more clothing they will keep warmer.
Each season is different every year.

transcribing or paraphrasing, where writers take someone else's ideas and write them in their own language and own words. The next level is crafting, where children generate meaning through writing in a conventional form. Here they focus on the structure of a piece and on communicating their meaning to the reader in the most effective way. The final level is what Moffett calls "the revision of inner speech." He claims this is the only true form of writing, for it involves expressing and shaping one's own thoughts. He also claims that it is rarely found in classrooms. An example of this final level is shown below. The piece was written just after the writer, in Grade 4, had read *On My Honor* (Bauer, 1986).

> Chapter eight confused me at the beginning. It didn't exactly say that Joel had gone home. When he was at home, I think I understood why and how he lied. Telling the truth in tough situations is very difficult. I would never lie at all, even in a problem like that. My friend's mom just moved here a little while ago and the apartment they lived in was allowed no children. Quite absurd! She only got to live there because she said she was a doctor. Stuff like that makes me very untrusting of the world. Taking a person by how much money they have etc. When I read that chapter I felt Joel's insecurity. He seems to be not acting normal with the problems he's having. A kid dealing with something like that is real scary!

In this piece, the writer is thinking through her feelings about lying. As she writes about the character in the book, she reflects on her own experiences with telling the truth and how, at times, people are moved to lie in order to survive. The writer struggles with the ambivalence she feels, knowing that lying is wrong, but understanding a little of why at times even good people might be dishonest.

Moffett (1979) maintains that children are more likely to be successful, thoughtful, articulate, and skilful writers when they engage in all five levels of writing in the classroom. He also maintains that all levels of writing should be *taught*. Moffett expresses concern that if instruction is confined to copying from the board, children will be less likely to develop the skills necessary for writing their own compositions. Likewise, if children are restricted to crafting polished pieces of writing with the aim of making them public in a writing workshop, they will be denied the opportunity of learning how to use writing as a way of exploring thought. Moffett's chief concern, in 1979, was that too much of the writing children were required to do in school was for the purpose of evaluating what they had learned. This is still a concern of many educators today.

In the 1970s, Donald Graves (1983) conducted research that led to a major shift in the teaching of writing in elementary schools, secondary schools, and colleges. His work, along with that of Lucy Calkins (1986 and 1991), Nancie Atwell (1998), and others, focusses on the process of writing and promotes a workshop approach to the teaching of writing. This means that children work with one another and their teachers, composing, drafting, revising, editing, and publishing their works. Graves's work enabled teachers to reconceptualize writing as a series of processes that a writer goes through when writing. When teachers take a workshop approach, they engage in writing themselves and so develop a fuller understanding of what a writer goes through to create a composition, making it clear and conventionally appropriate for an audience. The process requires time, thought, and the reworking of multiple drafts. The focus is on the process of composing and the thinking that must take place to develop a successful piece of writing. Graves's work has fundamentally changed the way educators think about the writing process and the teaching of writing in schools.

# Forms of Writing

## Narrative

**Narrative writing** links a series of events together either through a sequence in time or through cause and effect. It seems an almost natural way for human beings to make sense of the world. Barbara Hardy (1975) says that narrative is a "primary act of mind." We seem to think in narrative — retelling events to ourselves to see how the pieces fit together, or telling ourselves how something works as we try to figure out a problem. We even create lists in narrative, although we don't write the list that way. "I need mayonnaise because I want to make salad dressing on the weekend. I noticed the paper towel roll was almost used up. I don't want to run out while I'm working in the kitchen. I must remember to get chicken breasts for dinner." Narrative, then, is a way of linking thoughts so that they make sense to us. It's the story we tell ourselves that underlies whatever it is we are doing.

When writers develop a story they craft the narrative in a certain way. In Western culture a story is usually structured around an introduction, a middle section with a problem or conflict (sometimes a series of conflicts), and then an ending, which achieves some resolution of the problem. This structure is not common to all cultures; for example, Aboriginal Canadian and Caribbean stories often involve the same characters, who are familiar to the audience before the story begins. These stories, therefore, do not need the same kind of structure commonly used in most European stories. Applebee's 1978 study of the development of children's concept of story suggests that children have to learn to do two things simultaneously to successfully write or tell a story: chain events together, and focus on a theme, problem, or character. Applebee's research demonstrated that children begin to form stories from the age of 2 onward, but they learn to apply these two essential elements over time, mastering the story form (or "story grammar," as it is sometimes called) over a period of years.

As children mature, their stories become more complex and cohesive. Children become aware of an audience for their writing, and strive for clarity and an engaging text. A story written jointly by two Grade 5 girls is shown in Box 7.1. Unfinished at the end of the school year, the story was put "on hold" by the girls because they were not sure what to do with it next and they had another piece of writing they wanted to start. This story will be referred to again later in the chapter in the section about the importance of talk. At that point, the girls' struggle with crafting and ending the piece becomes more apparent.

## Expressive

Found in casual letters, diaries, and journals, this is the kind of writing we do informally as thoughts form in our mind. We rarely revise or craft expressive writing. (Britton's use of the word "expressive" to describe one of the three *voices* of writing differs from this use, though there is some overlap in meaning.) Expressive writing is done for an audience who knows the writer, and sometimes the audience is the self. Expressive writing is a means through which we present our ideas, thoughts, feelings, and interpretations of events. It may include responses to books we have read and movies we have seen. Expressive writing is essentially exploratory. In expressive writing, just as in expressive speech, we speculate, hypothesize, predict, and generally articulate our thoughts. Exhibit 7.2 illustrates a Grade 4 child's expressive writing.

**Box 7.1    The Wellington Story**

Written co-operatively by Sharon and Erica (Grade 5)

"Hi I'm home! Yvette have you started dinner yet?" called Margaret Wellington from down the hall. "Yes, Mrs. Wellington. Dinner will be served shortly," replied Yvette. Mrs. Wellington walked into the kitchen and dropped two packages on the dining room table. "The guests should be arriving soon. I'll go put my new dress on my bed for the upstairs maid to iron and then take these paints to my husband," said Mrs. Wellington and went upstairs. Later that evening, Mrs. Wellington came downstairs to help Yvette with dinner. Just then Mr. Wellington came downstairs. "I'll be out in the paint house while you girls fix dinner," he said and left.

Mrs. Wellington placed a bowl of cranberry sauce on the dining room table. Then she leaned over the bowl of cranberry sauce and put a candle on the center of the dining room table. "There," she said with a sigh.

Just then the doorbell rang. "Yvette, could you get the door please?" asked Mrs. Wellington. Yvette went to answer the door. "Good evening, Miss Murphy," said Yvette. "May I take your coat?" Miss Murphy handed Yvette her coat and went into the lounge.

After everybody arrived they all sat down for dinner. "Cheers to Mrs. Wellington for having this party," said Miss Murphy in a loud voice. Then they all lifted their glasses and clinked them together. "I'll go get my husband for dinner," said Mrs. Wellington and left. A few minutes later, Mrs. Wellington came back into the dining room. "My husband will be coming shortly," she said as Yvette started carving the turkey. After about ten minutes had passed Mrs. Wellington asked Yvette to go see where her husband was.

Yvette left the dining room and went to the paint house. There was a moment of silence and then Miss Murphy spoke. "The strangest thing happened to me yesterday," she said. I ... Ahhhhhh." Miss Murphy was interrupted (loud scream). Mrs. Wellington dropped her fork.

"It's coming from the paint house," said Mr. McGregor. They all rushed out to the paint house and saw Yvette shaking, with a knife in her hand. Mrs. Wellington gasped and walked into the paint house.

She saw her husband lying dead on the floor. "Yvette," she screamed.

"How could you?" Mrs. Landenburg walked into the room, looked at the body and fainted. "Somebody call the police," said Mrs. Hunt. Mrs. Wellington started to cry. Mr. McGregor called the police. About 5 minutes later they arrived. "We were in the neighborhood," they said. "Now what happened?" Mrs. Wellington explained the whole thing. "Then we walked in and saw her," she said pointing to Yvette, "standing there with a knife in her hand. She did it officer, I know she did."

"Why don't you go into the house and rest while we look around and take the body away," said the police officer. Mrs. Wellington went into the lounge with the other guests. "It's all right Margaret. It had to happen sooner or later being a famous painter and all," said Miss Murphy. "He was such a kind husband to me," said Mrs. Wellington and then started to cry. Meanwhile in the paint house officer McCarther was searching around the floor when he spotted a loose floorboard.

He pulled back the floor board and saw a white dress with a red wine stain on it. "Hmm," he said. Then he put on a pair of rubber gloves, picked up the dress and placed it in a plastic bag. Then he took a second look, and saw the top of a broken wine bottle. He picked up the wine bottle and put it into a plastic bag. Then he walked over to where Mr. Wellington was lying and picked up the knife that Yvette dropped and went into the lounge. "I'll have to take finger prints," said officer McCarther and pulled out a stamp pad in front of Mrs. Wellington. "Are you accusing me of killing my own husband? Why would I kill him?" asked Mrs. Wellington. "You might kill him for his money and besides everyone in the room is a suspect," said officer McCarther. "Why didn't I wait until he dies?" asked Mrs. Wellington.

*The girls ended the story with the following note to themselves:*

tired of story     change some parts
      Stop story for now
want to start cat by-law     not doing a play
      —yet at least!

Source: C. Lewis (1989), Partnership Writing: Ten-Year-Olds Talking and Writing Together. MEd thesis, University of Alberta, Edmonton, AB.

# Informational or Expository

Intended to explain or expose something, **expository writing** requires the writer to be well-organized, clear, and coherent. This writing is not meant to convey feelings or

**Exhibit 7.2    Grade 4 Child's Expressive Writing**

> *May 24*
>
> *I am okay in multiples I think multiples are fun, especaly in number numbers I understand multiples quiet lot. But with factors I don't understand. My dad does not either. My mom sort of does. So last night with the homework I was suck. But in the morning I got it easy figerd out I could do it. I need help on factors, not alot but*
>
> *Explaining about factors! let's tack the number 18 if you count up to 18 in 6's. you can get up to 18. Factors are when you can count in something and get the the number you are doing.*

personal observations, but to pass on information to an audience. Reports, textbooks, memos, and notices are examples of expository writing. The term paper is a form of expository writing with which most university students are familiar. Expository writing both informs the audience and demonstrates the role of the writer as an expert in the field. An example of a Grade 4 child's expository writing is shown in Exhibit 7.3.

**Exhibit 7.3    Grade 4 Expository Writing: Music in Crousetown**

The Anglican Church in Crousetown, has the oldest pipe organ in Nova Scotia. It is still used in 1993. Every Sunday music was a big entertainment in those days and it still is today.

Most of the music of long ago was made up for fun. Some children might take some spoons and clack them against their knees, or a little boy might put some beans in a can and shake the can.

At night some people might gather together in someone's house and listen to each other play fiddles and accordians.

In those days there were no heavy rock bands or electric guitars. In the old days some homes had pianos or pump organs and if there was someone who could play the piano or organ they would play for sing along songs. Instead of electric guitars some people would play wooden guitars.

They had just about the same fun the old fashioned way as we do with rock bands.

Source: Petite Rivière Elementary School (1993), *History of Crousetown*, p. 4. Lunenburg County, NS: Petite Rivière Publishing.

## Persuasive

**Persuasive writing** is used more often in our society than we realize. Advertising, editorials, political campaign literature, religious tracts, and much of the unsolicited junk mail that arrives in mailboxes consists of persuasive writing. Someone wants to persuade others to do something, buy something, or believe something. Children use persuasive writing when they do a poster presentation about a book or a book celebration. They write persuasively when they want something very much and have to convince an adult to allow them to have it. At school, for example, this can be channelled into writing to government agencies to request some kind of change. The writing might be part of a social studies or science project, and may involve a letter-writing campaign. An excerpt from a piece of persuasive writing by a Grade 6 child follows:

> I think instead of having a curfew we should have police patrolling the streets at night as a pair. I think we shouldn't have a curfew at night because there are a lot of people out that are not vandalizing the streets.
>
> I would like to talk about why there should be two policemen in each community and how they should work the streets. In my area we have different sorts of gangs. One kid that I know was riding his bike down the street and one of the gangs called Devil's Knights, one kid threw a knife and almost hit the kid. I think the police should talk to different people and ask questions about the gangs and where they meet. I hope we can get the perfect president to run a place like this.

## Descriptive

Descriptive writing is frequently part of a larger piece of prose, though descriptive pieces can stand alone. In descriptive writing the writer tries to create a verbal picture of a scene or event, and invites the reader to participate in the experience by providing rich sensory detail. Careful crafting of relevant detail can make a descriptive piece of writing particularly dramatic. Below is a piece of descriptive writing by a Grade 5 child, an excerpt from a story written in chapters:

> We'd been flying for almost an hour when a grotesque aroma floated from the back of the plane and filled the air. From experience, I knew that the meal was salmon and spinach paté. My stomach turned inside out at the thought of it. The old woman who I was sitting beside didn't help my stomach because she stank of Super Polly Grip, Efferdent and cheap perfume. The clickety-clack of her knitting needles was driving me insane as I tried to write a letter to my best friend, Brooke. I knew that she was going to be knitting for a long time because she had a pattern for a large sweater taped to the back of her tray and she was still on the first cuff!

A second piece of descriptive writing from a child in Grade 6 also came from a chaptered story:

> Then I saw her. She was massive, at least it seemed that way to me. Tall and sleek and black. I shut my eyes again until I felt soft breath on my back. She woofed softly and only then did I realize that she was my mother and meant no harm. I opened my eyes again and squinted as the light hit them. The interior of the

large foaling stall was dimly lit and quiet. The walls were made of dark, rough wood and a light rope hung across the doorway. This was all so new to me that I lay my head down and let my mother lick my tousled coat.

## Poetry

Poetry is a genre of writing and not a specific form such as narrative or persuasive writing. We are adding a short section on children's writing of poetry, however, because student teachers such as Monique, with whom we opened this chapter, frequently ask their instructors how they can go about teaching children how to write poetry.

Poetry is a genre of writing that attempts to capture feelings, events, places, and people in an aesthetically pleasing way. A few poetic words or phrases convey a whole set of meanings in a particularly striking manner. Poetry is not defined by a rhyming scheme or rhythm, but is uniquely artistic, although sometimes disconcerting. "The Dragon's Gaze," "Cowboys," and "Bad Luck" (presented in Exhibit 7.4) are examples in this chapter of poetry written by children in the elementary grades. The children who wrote these poems found the genre to be most effective for the meanings they wanted to convey. Children at all the elementary grade levels seem to find poetry a singularly effective genre for their writing.

Children in the elementary grades write much excellent poetry when they are encouraged to write, making each word do its "most effective job." It is not necessarily appropriate to provide children with a pattern for their poetry writing (such as haiku, cinquain, limerick, or diamante). When children are faced with fitting their words into an already established pattern, they frequently encounter difficulties because the constraints of the form are too limiting. Writing a good limerick, for example, is extremely difficult and takes a great deal of hard work, even for an experienced writer. Children can end up with a poorly written poem that has been created simply to fit the assigned form. Teaching children various forms of poetry and inviting them to attempt a poem of their own in that format is appropriate only in so far as they are being introduced to the form and are aware of its structure and its name.

Sometimes children can be effectively introduced to writing poetry when perceptive teachers help them to recognize the poem that is "hidden" in their writing. It is not unusual to find a poem submerged under a welter of "hitchhiker" words — words that are simply going along for the ride. The poem emerges as these "hitchhikers" are judiciously edited out. For example, Lucy, a Grade 2 student, wrote about a favourite memory. In her first draft she wrote:

**Exhibit 7.4**  **Grade 2 Poetry**

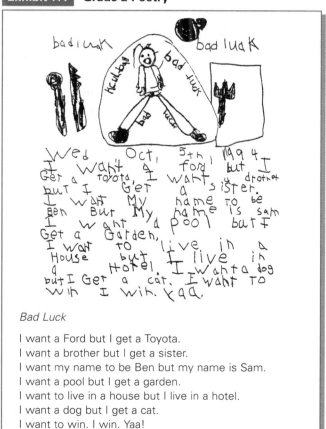

*Bad Luck*

I want a Ford but I get a Toyota.
I want a brother but I get a sister.
I want my name to be Ben but my name is Sam.
I want a pool but I get a garden.
I want to live in a house but I live in a hotel.
I want a dog but I get a cat.
I want to win. I win. Yaa!

> When I go to see my Grandma she always has the kettle boiling on the stove.
> When the steam comes hissing out she plops a teabag in the pot and makes a
> pot of tea. Then we sit down and have a family tea.

With her teacher's help she edited out the hitchhikers. Lucy ended up with the following poem, "A Visit with My Grandma":

> Kettle boiling on the stove
> Steam whistling out
> Here comes the teapot
> Plop — in goes the teabag
> Tea with Grandma.

Teachers can also prepare their students for writing poetry by encouraging them, as Lucy's teacher did, to use strong and colourful verbs and specific nouns in all of their writing, rather than decorating their writing with adjectives and adverbs. In addition, students can be encouraged to experiment with syntactical patterns to create particular effects. Notice how the effect of Lucy's poem can be changed if the last line becomes the first, or if the poem is simply entitled "A Visit." Sometimes, teachers may challenge their student writers to capture an event, scene, or idea by "saying the most with the fewest words possible." Thus, writing poetry helps students to focus their writing and to realize just how flexible and powerful written language can be.

## The Process of Composing

Most of what is known about composing comes from the observations of real writers and authors and the insights they provide. These writers often say there is no such thing as a finished piece of writing. As they write they think, and as they think and receive feedback, they revise, develop new ideas, begin new pieces, share old ones, and continue their development. As one aspect of thinking, writing both reflects and facilitates the exploration of ideas. The composition process is more spiral than linear, for writers do not stay in the same place for long when they write. They constantly anticipate what is needed and, in the process, develop new writing strategies, techniques, and ideas.

## Rehearsal

The first stage of composing is often called collecting, rehearsing, or pre-writing. At this point, writers collect ideas, memories, and experiences that help them to decide on a topic. They decide on what should be included in the composition, and what memories and recollections they can use to develop it. Writers use mixtures of people they have known, places they have visited, and their own experiences, whether real or vicarious. Writers of published works tell us that all their stories are about themselves, in some way. The American children's author Katherine Paterson tells of her feelings of loneliness and alienation during her Grade 1 year in the United States (Paterson, 1989). She had spent the first six years of her life in China, and on her first Valentine's Day in the United States she did not receive a single Valentine card. She maintains that all her books are about not receiving a Valentine, and that theme particularly pervades *The Great Gilly Hopkins*, *Bridge to Terabithia*, and *The Flip Flop Girl*.

We retain our memories and emotions, and these become the raw material of our writing. Children are just as capable as adults of choosing a topic and working with their experiences. They need help and encouragement, but the more they have ownership of their writing (i.e., assume responsibility for key decisions about topic choice, format, audience, and production timelines) and write about topics that interest them, the more they are likely to work at their writing and improve it. We learn to write by writing.

## Drafting

Once a topic has been determined, the writer begins to draft a text, putting onto paper the intentions developed in the rehearsing stage. The text may go through many drafts, and be modified and reworked, with the original intentions in mind. During the drafting stage, the writer becomes clearer about what can actually be done and what needs to be changed. The writer may play with the drafts, changing words here and there, adding to it, deleting parts that are not effective, and rewriting parts that simply don't work. It is during this stage that the writer asks, "Am I meaning what I say and saying what I mean?" Writers strive for clarity and try to maintain the interest and attention of the audience. Sometimes thoughts do not fall into place until the writer starts writing; the actual process of writing enables the ideas to flow. In a sense, writing seems to slow down thinking. As writers write, they have time and opportunity to capture their thoughts, reflect on them, and connect them to previous thoughts — a generative process.

As a draft takes shape, the writer revises it many times, moving parts around, editing it, and ensuring that it is ready for an audience. Much of this work used to be done with scissors and glue as writers cut and pasted parts to make a text more coherent. Now, that work is often done on a computer, which facilitates revision like no other writing tool. Many classrooms have computers, and children often learn how to work with a word-processing program, including using keyboarding skills, in Grade 3 or 4. Editing and revision skills still need to be taught. Much of this instruction can be delivered in mini-lessons or in the conferences that are an essential component of any writing workshop. When children are writing on paper, they can prepare for revision by writing on one side of the paper only and on every other line. These practices enable them to cross out, write over top, use carets to insert text, and make other changes without having to copy a whole piece over.

The writing shown in Exhibits 7.5 and 7.6 demonstrates the changes that Wendy, a Grade 2 student, made to her report on whales as she worked through the writing process. The two pieces presented are excerpts from the first draft and the final draft of the report. The children in Wendy's classroom were used to working through the writing process with their poetic and transactional writing.

## Feedback

Most writers need feedback while they are in the process of creating a composition. This is particularly so for children. Although some published authors, including Katherine Paterson, say they cannot share a piece of writing until it is completely finished because it is so close and precious to them, writing conferences are invaluable to most writers, whether they write at the elementary school level or for publication as adults. Peer conferences and group or one-on-one conferences with the teacher are necessary so that children can obtain feedback on their writing *when they need it*, and

**Exhibit 7.5** **Excerpt from the First Draft of Wendy's Report on Whales**

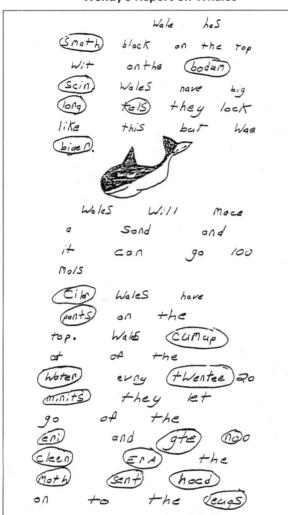

Source: F. Maaskant (1989), Children's Perceptions of Writing in a Grade One/Two Classroom, (Appendix). MEd thesis, University of Alberta, Edmonton, AB.

**Exhibit 7.6** **Excerpt from the Final Draft of Wendy's Report on Whales**

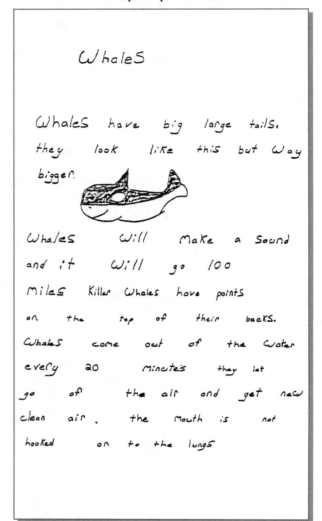

Source: F. Maaskant (1989), Children's Perceptions of Writing in a Grade One/Two Classroom, (Appendix). MEd thesis, University of Alberta, Edmonton, AB.

not when it is too late to make changes. It is during these conferences that children have the best opportunity to learn about writing. Guidelines for conducting writing conferences are presented later in this chapter.

## Presentation

The very last phase of the writing process is presentation, publication, or celebration. When a piece of writing is finished to an author's satisfaction, the piece can be shared with a wider audience. It might be read aloud to a whole class or group, made into a book and placed in the classroom or school library, sent to students at a nearby college, shared with residents of a seniors' home, or sent home to family. This is a time for celebrating the accomplishments of the writer. It is no longer a work-in-progress, and it is no longer appropriate for the audience to make critical comments or suggestions for change. The work will stand alone, ready for public scrutiny and the future enjoyment of reading audiences.

## The Role of Audience

Establishing an authentic audience for children's writing makes a difference in how children go about the process of composition and revision, as the following story illustrates. Fran Chalmers and her teaching colleague in Edmonton assigned a writing activity on the topic of dogs to their respective Grade 1 classes. The activity "bombed" in both classrooms. The two teachers shared their dismay and tried to figure out a reason for it. Had the students not had enough time to share their thoughts with a partner before beginning their writing? Did the children lack experience with dogs? Was there enough motivation in this activity? Was it relevant to the children's lives? Did the topic not interest them? As a result of their discussion, the teachers decided to return to their classes with the news that the children were going to share their stories with their buddies in the other Grade 1 classroom. The announcement had a profound effect. The children tackled the writing with renewed interest and enthusiasm. Only 30 minutes later, 27 pairs of children were excitedly reading their stories to each other. Awareness that a real audience was going to hear the stories made all the difference. This anecdote also demonstrates how being responsive to the students in their classes, and having a willingness to question their own teaching, helped Fran and her colleague to become more effective. To the benefit of their students, the teachers changed their plans at short notice when they realized the children were not fully engaged with the activity.

## Conducting a Writing Workshop

The teacher/researcher who had the most influence on the teaching of writing and on writing workshops in the 1990s was Nancie Atwell. In 1987, Atwell published her first book, *In the Middle*, and in 1998 she developed a second edition of the book, modifying her ideas after many more years of classroom teaching. In the second edition, Atwell lays out the expectations she has for writers' workshops and the guidelines she uses for her students' writing sessions. Although Atwell's suggestions are made largely with students in Grades 5 to 9 in mind, many of the ideas are modifiable for teachers and children in Grades 2 to 4. Box 7.2 lists some of Atwell's suggestions for conducting writing workshops in the classroom.

## Guidelines for Conducting a Writing Conference

Lucy Calkins (1991) and Nancie Atwell (1998) point out that young writers want to be listened to and want honest responses to their work. Sharing a piece of writing with an informed audience can be a most effective means of obtaining feedback. In the process, writers learn new ways of making meaning, building on their already existing writing skills. Teachers can teach or model feedback strategies that are productive and sensitive to the fact that every piece of writing is very special to its author. It is essentially a part of the writer, and as such, it must be respected by the audience. Students

## Box 7.2  Conducting a Writing Workshop

1. A writing workshop has a predictable format so that students know when it is to occur, what is expected of them, and what they can expect from the teacher and the situation. Teachers work out for themselves what feels comfortable and what seems to work in their classrooms. Time is provided for children to write, as well as respond to each other, and time is also provided for teachers to respond to individual students' work. Some teachers create a schedule so that they meet with a particular group of writers on a rotating basis. Group members give feedback to one another, and when the group finishes work together, the teacher is able to work with individual students who need help that day. Some teachers also try to build into their schedules time for their own writing so that children can see them modelling the writing process.

2. A writers' workshop is something like an artist's studio and has all the necessary resources. Young children need different colours and sizes of paper, scissors, tape, felt pens, pencils, pens, and staplers so they can create their own booklets for writing and drawing. Older children need dictionaries, a thesaurus, reference books, rulers, white-out liquid, and staples. If there are computers in the classroom, the students need easy and regular access to them, printing facilities, a safe place to store disks, and some degree of privacy (it is interesting how passersby do not feel awkward about reading what is on a computer screen, whereas they may hesitate to look over the shoulder of someone writing with a pen).

3. A writers' workshop can be noisy because children need to talk about their writing. However, teachers try to plan quiet times when all the students are writing. These times can be agreed upon by the class as the students begin to understand and articulate what they need as writers. Many children say that they cannot do any real writing or reading at school because it is too noisy. Teachers try to respect this need as well as the need for interaction. Teachers schedule quiet time that is used for writing only, and at that time any conversation must be in a whisper. They also schedule open time, when students can write or meet together in a response group on the floor in one corner of the room. In addition, some teachers schedule planned group conferences where they interact with the children in a more traditional way.

4. A writing folder is essential for each person in the classroom, including the teacher. The folder does not have to be specially purchased; children can design and make their own. The important thing is that the folder be expandable in some way so that it can hold a stack of writing. Ideally, the folder needs two or three sections — for pieces that are just being started, for works in progress, and for completed writing. Rather than have children keep these folders in their desks, it is usually easier and neater if all the folders are kept in a filing cabinet or large cardboard box that is accessible to the children at all times. A box can be decorated and kept in a prominent place.

5. All pieces of writing are dated with a draft number printed at the top. Students save all writings, even those that "don't work." This allows them to see how their work is changing. Sometimes a writer will go back to an earlier draft of a piece because it is better than a later one. When Sharon and Erica created "The Wellington Story" (Box 7.1), they were unsure what to do next. They had lots of thoughts, but needed time to distance themselves from the piece so they could return to it later with fresh ideas. The piece stayed in their writing folders with various dates on it at intervals as they worked on it over a long period of time. Eventually they agreed to abandon the story, but they each kept a copy of it. Perhaps one day we might see a variation of it in print!

6. Students can generate a list of possible writing topics and keep them at the front of the folder, either on the cover or stapled to the inside cover. They can add to the list on a regular basis as they discover new topics and experiences that will make good stories. Teachers often encourage children to take a few minutes every few weeks to update their list of possibilities, and discuss topics students have chosen to put on their own lists.

7. Writers are encouraged not to erase their work but instead to put a line through changes and insert new material above. Writing on every other line and on only one side of the paper faciliates this process and encourages children to make changes and insertions without having to rewrite the whole piece. When children compose on a word processor it is more difficult to separate drafts, as changes are made to a text on a continuing basis. However, it is helpful if children can print drafts at various stages of development, label them, and keep them in their folder.

(continued)

**Box 7.2** **Continued**

Alternatively, drafts can be saved on the computer, numbered in the same way.

8.  Writing conferences might focus on the content of a piece or on the topic or organization, clarifying the ideas and focussing the writing toward a more cohesive whole. A writing conference generally deals with only one of these elements at a time, since young writers cannot revise everything at once. The information given in a writing conference should be in small enough chunks that the writer can think about it and act on it.

9.  Lessons are taught as a result of specific points that arise in a writers' workshop, usually in the context of the children's writing. These lessons can be a vehicle for teaching many writing skills, such as capitalization, the use of commas and periods, particular spelling that is difficult for a large number of children, and clarification of ideas. The craft of writing can be taught in these lessons using a piece of student writing or a piece written by the teacher and displayed on the overhead projector. Grade 5 teacher Catherine Lewis often uses a piece of her own writing to demonstrate an idea to her students, and she will ask them to make suggestions about how the piece can be improved. The aim is always to improve the piece of writing, making it more interesting, effective, and enjoyable.

10. In writing conferences, teachers almost always invite the writer to read the work aloud. The teacher is then free to listen and to encourage the writer to lead the conference as much as possible. The writer can remain in charge of the piece. The role of the teacher and the other students is to make suggestions and share responses as interested listeners and co-writers. The conventions of writing can be attended to later in the process when the ideas and organization are firmly in place.

11. In order to be authentic and to model the writing process, teachers write themselves — either with the children or at some other time if they are too busy during the writers' workshop. In addition, teachers share their writing with their students. Children need to see that even adults struggle with creating good writing. Writing is hard work, and all authors labour over their compositions. Having published authors visit the classroom to speak about their work is a particularly effective strategy. Children find these visits inspiring as well as interesting, and they benefit from knowing that books come from real people, with editors who request many drafts and revisions before the book is ready to be published. Authors struggle with their work just as much as teachers and children struggle with their writing in elementary classrooms.

Source: Some of this material is based loosely on N. Atwell (1987), *In the Middle: Writing, Reading, and Learning with Adolescents*, pp. 83–84, 94. Portsmouth, NH: Heinemann.

can learn how to receive the work of others gently, how to give constructive feedback and positive comments, and how to make suggestions for future drafts and new pieces of writing. Teachers who model and promote a constructive and respectful process help to ensure that, when children share their pieces of writing with a group, they will feel safe and will be able to accept the feedback.

A well-structured conference is one in which students can predict or anticipate what will happen next. In a writing conference, the writer usually reads the piece to the teacher or to the group. This enables the listener (or listeners) to focus on the ideas, wording, and flow of the piece of writing. At the elementary school level, a three-part response system works well. First, children or teacher provide a positive comment about the piece — what works well or sounds good. Next, they ask questions about anything that is not clear in the piece. Finally, they make suggestions about what can be done to make the piece better. A conference might be very brief — just a few minutes of conversation with the teacher — or it can be a more formal and lengthy affair with a small group of students. In a conference, the teacher's goal is to provide feedback designed to improve the students' writing. The conference is effective when the teacher's responses provide strategic information that the writer can act on.

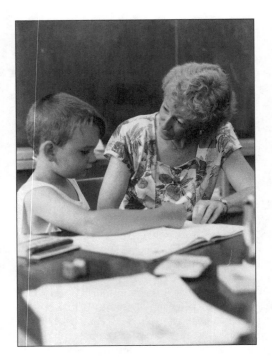

Teacher with primary child engaged in a writing conference.

Conferences can be conducted at a table in a quiet part of the room, or if the conference is one-on-one with teacher and student, it can be at the student's desk.

Atwell suggests that conferences be held about many different aspects of writing, including the ideas, information, audience, language, and format. She reminds us that the teacher and students act in conferences as mediators for learning, helping the writer to scaffold growth. Some educators maintain that it is best to focus on the content of a piece of writing during a writing conference, leaving writing conventions until much later in the process. Others feel that appropriate use of language conventions (correct spelling, punctuation, and capitalization) help in clarifying ideas and in making the piece flow more evenly. Certainly when a word processor is being used, the conventions of written language can be addressed throughout the writing process. Eventually, however, correct conventions have to be in place so that the meaning and feeling of the piece are communicated effectively to the audience. Frequent misspellings or other errors can detract from the effectiveness of a piece of writing, particularly when children have reached the age where these conventions are expected (around Grade 2 or 3) and invented spelling no longer adds to the personal voice of the writer. The conventions of language can be checked in an editing conference later in the writing process if necessary.

Just as writers need ownership of their piece of writing, they also need to feel ownership of the writing conference. Ownership can be facilitated by encouraging the writer to make decisions about the nature and the focus of the conference. Some teachers provide a box labelled "I need an editor" in which children can place their drafts when they are ready for the teacher to provide feedback or an editing conference. Before the conference, the teacher takes into account the student's writing stage and edits the draft for spelling and language conventions. In the process, a productive focus for the editing conference is identified. For example, the teacher may choose to review a particular spelling generalization or grammatical element with the student. During the conference, the teacher maintains this focus and encourages the student to note what was discussed for reference in future writing.

One of the key elements of a writing conference between student and teacher is response time. Most teachers find "wait time" difficult and frequently jump in with a suggestion before the student has had a chance to think and respond thoughtfully. One of the greatest challenges facing teachers in a writing conference is allowing the student time to think, not rushing in with a ready-made solution for the student writer. The writing belongs to the writer, and the teacher's role is to help the student become a better writer. This will not always mean that a perfect product is produced every time. Box 7.3 contains suggestions (from Atwell, 1998) for conducting writing conferences.

Writing conferences are not restricted to poetic writing, nor is poetic writing the only kind of writing that benefits from having an audience. Transactional writing also benefits from peer and teacher responses as it is created. In fact, any piece of writing we wish to do well may require input from others along the way. Letters to a business, letters to government agencies, reports, and play scripts can all benefit from feedback from others. Writers may work on their ideas and original drafts alone, but at some point they require feedback to clarify and present those ideas to a reading public.

| Box 7.3 | **Guidelines for Writing Conferences** |

1. Keep an eye on the time, and do not spend too long with one student.

2. Meet with as many writers as possible each day.

3. Circulate from one area of the room to another. Go to students' desks whenever possible.

4. Make a conference personal. It is a conversation. Kneel or sit next to the student.

5. Whisper and ask students to whisper when they confer with you. Do not distract other writers.

6. Build on what writers know and have done rather than telling them what they have *not* done.

7. Avoid generalized praise and moral evaluation, such as saying "good." Attending to the writer in a serious manner is more effective than giving a few words of praise.

8. Focus on one aspect of the writing in the conference, and don't try to "fix" everything or clarify all the "fuzzy" thinking.

9. Focus on meaning, and ask the questions you genuinely want to know about.

10. Invite students to note their intended actions at the end of the conference. You can add this to the conference record sheet.

11. At the end of the conference, ask the student to summarize the points discussed.

12. Be prepared to take notes — your questions and observations.

13. Don't take over the piece of writing, making it your own. Ask for permission (e.g., "May I show you a way to do this?").

Source: Some of this material is based loosely on N. Atwell (1987), *In the Middle: Writing, Reading, and Learning with Adolescents*, pp. 94–95. Portsmouth, NH: Heinemann.

## The Students' Role in a Writing Workshop

In addition to providing guidelines for teachers in conducting writing workshops, Atwell (1998) and others (e.g., Calkins, 1986, 1991) have provided suggestions for "rules" that will help students in working through drafts of their writing, eventually leading to pieces they feel proud of sharing with an audience. The rules set out in Box 7.4 are based on those Atwell provides for her students (1998, p. 115). These rules are appropriate for students engaged in poetic and transactional or informational writing, where a finished draft is important. Students who are engaged in journal writing or other forms of expressive writing may not need this structure. They do, however, need quiet time to write, assistance with the conventions of written language, and an opportunity to discuss their writing and their ideas with others.

## Social Interaction in the Writing Process

Although educators have long realized that learning to talk is a social process, it is only recently that we have acknowledged the importance of social interaction when writing. If, as Moffett (1979) maintains, true writing occurs only when we revise inner

## Box 7.4   Rules for Students in a Writing Workshop

1. Save everything. You never know when you might want to refer to a piece of writing again.

2. Date and label everything so you can keep track of what you have done. This is especially important when working on a word processor.

3. When a piece of writing is finished, clip all the drafts, notes, and brainstormings together with a copy of the final draft on the top.

4. Record every piece of finished writing in a log at the beginning of the writing folder.

5. Write on one side of the paper only, and always doublespace (write on every other line only).

6. Format your writing as you go (in paragraphs, lines, stanzas).

7. Try to attend to conventions as you write. Check spelling as soon as possible. Attend to punctuation as you write. Ask for help when you need it.

8. When working on a word processor, print every couple of days or every few pages of text. Read the piece through with pen in hand so that you can attend to the flow of the whole piece and not just chunks of the text as they appear on the screen.

9. Begin each writing session by reading over what you have already written. This allows you to establish where you are in the piece and creates momentum for the day's writing.

10. Writing is thinking. Don't interrupt other students while they are writing. Don't attempt to tell other people what to write.

11. If you need to talk to the teacher, speak in a whisper.

12. When you need to receive feedback from a student or teacher, move to the conference area and write down the comments as they are made. This way you will have a record of suggestions to take back to your writing.

13. Edit your work in a different colour from the text.

14. Always write as well, and as much, as you can.

Source: Adapted from N. Atwell (1998), *In the Middle: New Understandings about Writing, Reading, and Learning* (2nd ed.), pp. 115–116. Portsmouth, NH: Heinemann.

speech, then children need to become aware of what the revision of inner speech entails. Teachers can encourage children to make their inner speech explicit and to wrestle with the ideas they are attempting to articulate. Moffett says that teachers "have no choice but to work in the gap between thought and speech" (1979, p. 278). He also suggests that "writing cannot be realistically perceived and taught so long as we try to work from the outside in" (p. 279). In other words, true writing comes from within the writer, who must learn to articulate thought and put it into print. When children work collaboratively in the writing process, they have opportunities to explore the gap between thought and speech. When teachers listen to them, they can find out how children negotiate meaning and the structural elements of writing. The social context of writing in the classroom and the relationships among the students influence writing enormously. Through their talk, as Michael Halliday (1969) has said, they learn "how to mean."

## The Importance of Talk

As children talk together or with a teacher, continual scaffolding is evident. Through constant interaction, the students become teachers and learners interchangeably. The following excerpt is a planning session where Erica and Sharon, in a Grade 5 classroom, considered each other's opinions and incorporated them into a written debate about the city cat bylaws (Lewis, 1989).

Sharon:    Want to do a debate?

Erica:    Yes, then we can each have our own opinion.

Sharon:    What's yours about?

Erica:    My what?

Sharon:    Your issue you want to debate. I want to do the cat bylaw. OK?

Erica:    OK. I'll just put "Cat Bylaw" at the top of the page.

Sharon:    OK. If I was in charge of the world I'd change the cat bylaw.

Erica:    Do you want to do this one [pause] together? I don't have a cat, you do, so it makes a difference, doesn't it?

Sharon:    Cats should be able to walk around.

Erica:    And I'm going to write against that! Cats go to the bathroom everywhere and ...

Sharon:    Good, we disagree then — we agree on that. [Laughter.]

Erica:    And it smells! Write on the top of the page "Cat Bylaw" again.

Sharon:    Why?

Erica:    Because we're going to do it together.... We'll put my opinions and your opinions so we know whose is what.

Sharon:    I want to ask you a question. If you don't have a cat, would you still not like the rule as much? I still think it's dumb.

Erica:    Ya, but you wouldn't like it as much, like it wouldn't be.... Even if you had a cat would you still hate it more?

Sharon:    No, exactly the same.

Erica:    What! I'm writing against you, right?

Sharon:    Well, cats.... I agree that cats do that — go to the bathroom, I mean.

Erica:      I agree in a way. [Writes this down slowly.]

Sharon:    Don't write this next part down till I figure it out.

Erica:      But dogs — dogs do that too [still writes slowly, thinking, pausing]. Dogs do poop on our lawn.

Sharon:    Dogs usually have their owners with them.

Erica:      Not always. Some people let their dogs out 'cause we've had a lot of ...

Sharon:    Ya, but dogs don't come back.

Erica:      Yes, they do.

Sharon:    No, but cats always do — in the same place.

Erica:      Well, it depends on how far they go....

In their continuing negotiation of meaning, the two girls found that they became very aware of writing for an audience. They began to negotiate meaning and work out details, where each sentence, and at times each word, was important. Disagreements were common, and they questioned the logic of each other's ideas. The following excerpt, from a discussion Sharon and Erica held while writing a mystery story together, concerns the phrases *looked closer* and *looked again*.

Erica:      "He looked closer into the hole ..."

Sharon:    "He looked again" sounds better.

Erica:      Well, Sharon, if you looked closer, would you stick your head right into the hole?

Sharon:    It doesn't mean that.

Erica:      Well it does to me!

Sharon:    Closer isn't sticking your face into the hole, but "looked again" just sounds better.

Erica:      Sharon, you don't listen!

Sharon:    So, we don't use "closer" or "again." We say "he looked into the hole and saw the top of the wine bottle."

Erica:      No, "he looked closer" — a bit closer — know what I mean?

Sharon:    Why would he look closer to see the wine bottle?

Erica:      'Cause the dress might have covered it up, you know. Then "he looked again" doesn't mean "he looked closer."

Sharon:    Yes it does!

Erica:    Sharon, I don't know. It's the way — the sentence — the way ...

Sharon:    The way you put it sounds dumb.

Erica:    Well, where did he actually look?

Sharon:    Under the floorboards.

Erica:    Well, I don't think he needs to get closer to see under the floorboards — that's what I really mean.

Sharon:    When you say "looked closer," it doesn't necessarily mean you looked closely right in the hole — it means you sort of took a second look.

Erica:    Ya — that's it — he took a second look!

Sharon:    Oh, wow, we got it!

Erica:    Phew!

## Peer Group Writing Conferences

The following group conference was initiated and conducted by four students who relied on strategies their classroom teacher had taught them. The transcript, taken from Lewis (1989), shows how the students used these conferences to further their own writing development. Erica began by reading the unfinished "Wellington" story quoted in Box 7.1 earlier in this chapter.

Erica:    "'It's coming from the paint house,' said Mr. McGregor. They all rushed out to the paint house and saw Yvette shaking, with a knife in her hand."

Sharon:    That's as far as we've got.

Craig:    I have a question. Who's Yvette?

Erica:    The maid.

Craig:    What's her husband's name?

Erica:    The maid? She doesn't have one.

Dana:    No, Craig. Mr. and Mrs. Wellington.

Craig:    Oh, right.

Dana:    All of a sudden you brought in that Mr. McGregor. Who's he supposed to be?

Sharon:    One of the guests. When it says — well, we didn't want to just list them all.

Dana:     You could say, "Mr. McGregor, one of the guests...."

Erica:    Good idea.

Dana:     Where do you guys go from here?

Sharon:   Well, we're not sure. We have to have the loose floorboards so the police can find the ...

Erica:    We also think we want it to be a play and we talked about highlighting the speaking parts, except Sharon wants to write it all out so ...

Dana:     Hey, you guys, we forgot to say our favourite parts. The part about the paint house really catches my eye. Is this guy a painter—a famous one?

Erica:    Ya, and that's why Yvette kills him because he painted a picture of her and she is afraid that Mrs. Wellington will find out.

Dana:     Wouldn't it just be easier to destroy the painting than to kill the guy?

Sharon:   Well, another idea we had is that it's not Yvette. It's the wife and she kills him for his money. We aren't exactly sure about that part yet.

Craig:    I like the part where they find her holding the bloody knife.

Erica:    We didn't say it was bloody.

Craig:    Well, it would be, you know.

Because of the importance of talk and the amount of learning that takes place in group conferences, it is important to encourage and facilitate this kind of dialogue as part of the writers' workshop. Through interaction, students become more aware of their covert writing processes and of the conventions necessary for effective communication with an audience. Sharon said,

> I like to talk about all my ideas and I like to figure it all out with someone else. It got kind of hard, you know, because I get really excited and I yelled at Erica —she's so picky, though, you know. [Smiles.]

The following statements illustrate the students' thoughts on writing conferences:

Dana:     Some days it's easy—all goes well, and some days it's bad—it's really hard.

Erica:    Well ... it's both actually—easy and hard. Maybe at different times it's harder....

Craig:    It helps me—I love talking to someone.

Sharon:   She helps me about quotations and ... other things, too.

The extensive use of expressive language enables students to clarify and extend their thoughts as they write. Children benefit from talking through their understanding at every stage of the process. Some days, there is more talk than writing, but it is through this talk that children make explicit their understandings of what writing is and what writing can do. They also articulate their understandings of literary structures and what it is that makes a piece of writing work. In "The Wellington Story" (see Box 7.1), Sharon and Erica demonstrated a command of the mystery story genre and of the conventions of story writing. Carefully crafted with an audience in mind, their story undoubtedly reflects some of the reading they have both completed.

## Summary

Writing is both an art and a skill, an activity that can give enormous pleasure to the writer as well as to the reader. Most people need to write on a daily basis, either in their jobs (a phone message, a technical report) or in their personal lives (a letter to their child's school, a grocery list, a diary, a poem). Writing instruction in the past tended to emphasize the development of competency in the surface features of language. With the advent of the process approach to the teaching of writing, teachers now help their students to develop both composition and presentation skills. Writing instruction, as a process, stresses the purpose for writing, the audience for the writing, and the relationship of these to form and function.

As they compose, students are encouraged to write for a variety of audiences and for particular purposes. James Britton (1970) pointed out that written composition can be distinguished according to purpose and intended audience. Expressive writing is written either for the self or for an audience close to the writer, and records or captures personal thoughts, feelings, and intentions. Transactional writing takes place when the writer wants to convey information to others in a formal report, list, essay, or textbook. Poetic writing is usually created for an audience other than the self. It contains aesthetic or literary elements and is the voice used in stories as well as poems. Teachers teach skills that range from drawing the letters and words (handwriting), to transcribing, paraphrasing, crafting, and revising inner speech (Moffett, 1979). In a balanced program of writing instruction, all of these voices and levels of writing are taught. Students can then learn to be effective writers who are able to write for a range of audiences and purposes.

When composing and crafting a piece of writing, young writers need a structure in the classroom that will allow them to have large chunks of quiet writing time, conferences that provide feedback from an interested and informed audience, and the opportunity to share finished pieces with "the public." Writing conferences help writers to draft and revise their thoughts until they are sure they are saying exactly what they want to say. It is in the writing conference that most teaching occurs, and it is the entire process of drafting, revising, editing, and sharing that helps children to become better writers.

Teachers now recognize the important role that children's talk plays in their development as writers. When children are on-task and are engaged fully in a shared writing experience, they learn a great deal from one another through exchanging and negotiating ideas. The quest for clarity and appropriateness of language, the response of the readers, and the power of words to evoke images and feelings are the elements young writers learn about as they write together in the classroom.

## Selected Professional Resources

Atwell, N. (1998). *In the Middle: New Understandings about Writing, Reading, and Learning* (2nd ed.). Portsmouth, NH: Boynton/Cook. Atwell's book is a superb resource to help in organizing writing workshops in the classroom. The book establishes rules of conduct and processes of interaction. Although Atwell describes organizational structures and procedures for reading and writing workshops for middle grade students, her book is also appropriate for elementary grade teachers who wish to organize writers' workshops in their classrooms. In detail, Atwell describes how to prepare for a writing workshop, how to get started, how to respond to writers and their writing, and how to conduct mini-lessons in writing.

Tompkins, G. (1999). *Teaching Writing: Balancing Process and Product* (3rd ed.). Toronto: Maxwell Macmillan Canada. One of the most comprehensive books on teaching writing in the elementary school grades, this text provides an overview of the writing process, illustrated throughout with examples of children's writing. Specific chapters are devoted to journals, narrative, poetry, letters, informational or expository text, descriptive pieces, and biographical writing. There is a chapter on writers' tools (spelling, handwriting, grammar, editing) and one on assessing student writing. The book is well laid out and easy to read. It makes an excellent resource for any teacher's professional library.

## Children's Books Noted in Chapter Seven

Bauer, M.D. (1986). *On My Honor*. New York: Bantam Doubleday Dell.

Lawson, J. (1992). *The Dragon's Pearl*. Toronto: Stoddart.

Paterson, K. (1977). *Bridge to Terabithia*. New York: HarperCollins.

Paterson, K. (1978). *The Great Gilly Hopkins*. New York: Thomas Y. Crowell.

Paterson, K. (1994). *The Flip Flop Girl*. New York: Lodestar Books (Dutton).

## References

Applebee, A. (1978). *The child's concept of story*. Chicago: University of Chicago Press.

Atwell, N. (1987). *In the middle: Writing, reading, and learning with adolescents*. Portsmouth, NH: Heinemann.

Atwell, N. (1998). *In the middle: New understandings about writing, reading, and learning* (2nd ed.). Portsmouth, NH: Boynton/Cook.

Britton, J. (1970). *Language and learning*. Harmondsworth, UK: Penguin Books.

Calkins, L. (1986). *The art of teaching writing*. Portsmouth, NH: Heinemann.

Calkins, L. (1991). *Living between the lines*. Toronto: Irwin.

D'Arcy, P. (1989). *Making sense, shaping meaning: Writing in the context of a capacity-based approach to learning*. Portsmouth, NH: Heinemann.

Graves, D.H. (1983). *Writing: Teachers and children at work*. Exeter, NH: Heinemann.

Halliday, M.A.K. (1969). Relevant models of language. *Educational Review, 22* (1), 26–37.

Hardy, B. (1975). *Tellers and listeners: The narrative imagination*. Dover, NH: Longwood.

Lewis, C. (1989). Partnership writing: Ten-year-olds talking and writing together. MEd thesis, University of Alberta, Edmonton, AB.

Maaskant, F. (1989). *Children's perceptions of writing in a grade one/two classroom*. MEd thesis, University of Alberta, Edmonton, AB.

Moffett, J. (1979). Integrity in the teaching of writing. *Phi Delta Kappa, 61* (4), 276–279.

Paterson, K. (1989). *The spying heart: More thoughts on reading and writing books*. New York: Lodestar Books.

Petite Rivière Elementary School. (1993). *History of Crousetown*. Lunenburg County, NS: Petite Rivière Publishing.

Tompkins, G. (1999). *Teaching writing: Balancing process and product* (3rd ed.). Toronto: Maxwell Macmillan Canada.

# Writing across the Curriculum

Writing and Learning

Think Books and Journals
- Writing in Science
- Writing in Math

**Writing across the Curriculum**

Dialogue Journals

Writing to Consolidate What Is Known

Research Projects
- Guiding the Research Process
- Writing Relevent Research

When Jean-Pierre was placed in a combined Grade 2/3 classroom for a full term of student teaching, the teacher, Mr. Pettigrew, told him the students wrote in almost every subject area. Jean-Pierre was unsure of how this could be done. He recalled that, when he was in elementary school, any writing that he did in a subject area consisted mainly of copying notes from the board and answering his teacher's questions. Jean-Pierre was curious about what this writing across the curriculum might look like. He was intrigued by the notion of writing for learning, but he had many questions. Did Mr. Pettigrew encourage his students to write poems in science, or stories in math? How can children effectively write about their learning when many of them are only just learning how to write? Doesn't the process take a lot of class time that could be better spent on learning the content? What do the children gain from putting their learning into their own words? Considering the amount of time it takes for

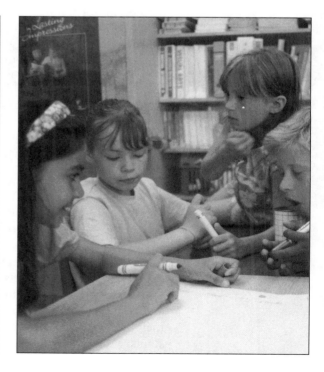

students to write, is it possible for a teacher to also adequately cover the prescribed curriculum? This chapter attempts to answer Jean-Pierre's questions, and explores what teachers and researchers know about learning and the importance of students talking and writing as they learn. ■

## Writing and Learning

In constructivist classrooms, students and teachers write as a means of engaging in ongoing dialogue about learning. Sometimes the students' dialogues are internal, with themselves, and sometimes they are with their peers and teachers. In these classrooms, teachers and students write to explore topics, ideas, and subject area content, as well as to demonstrate their understandings. This is in sharp contrast to transmission-oriented classrooms, where writing in the curriculum areas is primarily used as a means for students to demonstrate what they have learned — teachers teach the content, and the students provide written evidence that they can recall it. This change in perspective, from transmission to construction, has been motivated in part by research findings that indicate that writing is a powerful tool that can help students to make sense of their learning as they engage in it (D'Arcy, 1989). As Donald Murray points out, "when we write we discover what we know" (1984, p. 7).

In the mid-1960s, when James Britton and the team of researchers from the London Institute for Education collected their data on *The Development of Writing Abilities, 11–18* (1975), they found that the majority of the samples of children's writing they collected had been done by students to demonstrate what they knew. As D'Arcy says of the practice at the time, "Writing was unquestionably regarded as a mode of expression chiefly to indicate *what had been learned*, not as one to learn through" (D'Arcy, 1989, p. 105). Writing to make sense of the students' own world, perceptions, or feelings was rare. Little more than a decade later, however, Fulwiler (1987) outlined five basic assumptions about language and learning that were approved by the National Council of Teachers of English. Three of these assumptions are particularly important to teachers with regard to writing across the curriculum:

1. When people articulate connections between new information and what they already know, they learn and understand that new information more effectively (Bruner, 1966).

2. When people write about new information and ideas— in addition to reading, talking, and listening — they learn and understand them better (Britton et al., 1975).

3. When people care about what they write and see connections to their own lives, they both learn and write with greater efficacy (Moffett, 1968).

These findings have led teachers in constructivist classrooms to become acutely aware of how they can help their students to make their thinking visible, to develop confidence in their ability to think, and to value their own thoughts. Thus, writing for learning is not restricted to particular forms or formats. Journals, notes, letters, diaries, scripts, commercials, brochures, invitations, reports, and posters all provide opportunities for students to demonstrate the meanings that they have constructed. In addition, dialogue journals, think books, and learning logs allow children to share their thinking with their teacher or peers in a supportive environment that encourages students to expand and explore their ideas further.

After conducting research into young children's non-narrative writing, Thomas Newkirk (1987) concluded that the early elementary years need not be a time when "narrative must do for all." He showed that in active writing programs, the early years are a time when children make considerable advances toward mature expository writing. From labelling and list-making through to creating basic paragraphs, children demonstrate the capacity they have for writing in a variety of forms to meet a range of purposes. Their writing demonstrates, in particular, their abilities to organize their thinking and record it on paper.

Newkirk concluded from his study that "the abilities shown by the students are probably closely tied to the knowledge they possess on their topics and to the collaborative community in which they work" (1987, p. 141). Teachers building collaborative learning communities, where students develop their abilities to write in a variety of genres, attempt to ensure that their students

- are interested in the topic,
- have questions they want to answer, and
- are motivated to share their learning with others.

The power of the collaborative community cannot be underestimated. As Jean-Pierre observed the classroom interactions in his student teaching placement, he became aware of how Mr. Pettigrew strove to maintain an atmosphere where children's interests were piqued and their thinking and writing were challenged. It was a community of learners that supported one another in asking and answering questions, and where the children respected one another's ideas.

Newkirk (1987) also concluded from his study that writers should not suddenly be expected to write expository prose in upper elementary school. They should first be encouraged in the early years of schooling to label, write lists, and generally sort and make sense of what they know. He maintained that young children learn most effectively when they write in their own voice in ways that are meaningful to them. Tanya's writing about seasons, presented in Chapter Seven (Exhibit 7.1), certainly supports Newkirk's findings in this regard. Newkirk's data also suggest that young children develop organizational skills *as they write*. Newkirk believes that children learn and organize their ideas through writing about the world they know. Once they are comfortable with doing that, they can begin to represent their understandings of the world more abstractly. What they need is the opportunity. Tanya's winter vacation in the Caribbean prompted her to think about seasons across the world. The piece suggests that although Tanya usually experiences winter as being very cold, she now understands that in some parts of the world even winter is warm. Thus the teacher encourages students to record and examine their immediate experiential world before they move on to more formal and abstract writing. Overall, it is clear that children can write in many forms, and for many purposes, from the very beginning of schooling.

## Think Books and Journals

Pat D'Arcy (1989) writes that think books and journals provide the space for learners to reflect, rehearse, reshape, and redraft what they know. She quotes the Children's Learning in Science Group in the United Kingdom when she says, "If a pupil's own picture of how the world works is ignored, her ability to make sense of someone else's picture, the teacher's or the textbook writer's, is seriously impeded" (p. 3). The writing learners do as they learn — writing about emerging ideas, insights, thoughts, and reflections—is part of their own picture of how the world works. Because that picture is constantly changing, the writing is not moving toward a finished product, but is part of the process of helping learners clarify their thinking and develop new understandings. Journal writing acts as a platform on which other ideas can be built. Students can go back to the writing and re-examine the ideas captured there, reflect upon them, refine them, and build on them as they integrate new knowledge with the old. In the past, educators have frequently thought of writing as something that is done when the ideas are fully formed, but writing for learning is an intrinsic part of the total learning process. It makes learning personally meaningful and creates what we might call "action knowledge" rather than "book knowledge" (Barnes, 1976).

While academic prose tends to be logical, formal, conventional, organized, assertive, and objective, the writing in a journal is conversational in tone and reads much like talk. Journal writers begin with what they know and build their understandings as they write (Shuy, 1987). The journal entry in Exhibit 8.1, written by Jasmin, a student in Grade 4, provides an example of what is meant by writing to understand. It contains emerging ideas, or exploratory statements and reflections, and shows the student actively making meaning from new learning. Douglas Barnes (1976, p. 76) says that writing is a means by which writers can take an active part in their own learning: "As pupils write they can — under certain circumstances — reshape their view of the world, and extend their ability to think rationally about it." James Britton (1982) refers to this same process as "shaping at the point of utterance." The advantage of students writing about their ideas as they are processing them is that they are forced to focus on them to a far greater degree than when they simply talk about them. Talked-over ideas are often lost; we may be distracted and lose the thread of our thoughts. But writing provides a record of where we have journeyed in our thinking, and points to where we might travel next.

**Exhibit 8.1**  **Jasmin's Math Journal Entry**

> Multiples of 2,3,4,5,9,10                    Dec.20
>
> All multipels of 2 are even - 2.4 6.8.10 12 14,16,18 and so on, multipels of two can be put into groups. The last dight of multpels of two are even.
>
> Multipuls of 3 are odd for exampel 3x7 = 21 and 21 is odd.
>
> the last Multipels of 4 can be formed by the 2 digits that are divisble by 4.
>
> divisabelt is just Eaxtact.

# Writing in Science

MacAlister, Kydd, and Jones (1988, p. 3) explored the value of writing in science. They write:

> The chances are that most teachers think of science notes in terms of lab write-ups, diagrams and graphs, and specialized vocabulary.... They all have a place in science, but there are other kinds of writing that can be useful in an activity oriented classroom.... The idea of science notebooks that blended expressive writing with occasional forays into poetic writing appealed to us. We had already agreed that "worksheet science" was detrimental to developing complete thoughts. It tended to fragment concepts as well as demanding little original writing from students. We also agreed that the formal lab write-ups required of students in higher grades were too abstract for young learners.

In constructivist classrooms, teachers encourage students to write and share anticipatory questions and predictions (**heuristic** or exploratory writing) before they engage in any science activity. Students are then encouraged to write observations in their notebooks as the activity proceeds. In *Writing and Primary Science*, MacAlister, Kydd, and Jones (1988) suggest that the pieces of writing children complete in science, and the drawings and charts that accompany them, can provide a rich source of evaluative and diagnostic information for teachers. "Reading an explanation written in a child's words tells the teacher more about their level of concept development than any multiple choice test" (p. 27). The specialized vocabulary of science (really, of any discipline) becomes much more important and relevant to children when they understand the concept embedded in the language. The talk that takes place when learners write in a think book, learning log, or notebook, as well as the actual writing, provides a forum for sharing and clarifying ideas that leads to understanding the concept and internalizing the specialized vocabulary. Exhibits 8.2 and 8.3 present science notebook entries from children in Grade 1 (Ozdoba, 1992).

| Exhibit 8.2 | Thomas's Writing in Science |

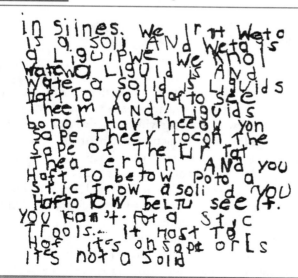

In science we learned what is a solid and what is a liquid. We know what a liquid is and what a solid is. Liquids have to, you have to see them and liquids do not have their own shape. They take on the shape of the jar that they are in and you have to be able to put a stick through. A solid you have to be able to see it. You can't put a stick through it. It has to have its own shape or it's not a solid.

Source: A. Ozdoba (1992), *Writing to Learn: Science Journals in Year One*, p. 100. MEd thesis, University of Alberta, Edmonton, AB.

**Exhibit 8.3**    **Grade 1 Science Notebook**

We made ice-cream using a baby food jar, and ice and salt and chocolate milk and the way we did it. And coffee container. And the way we used it. (1) One person puts milk in the jar (2) and then put the lid on (3) put some ice then salt (5) baby food jar in the ice (6) put more ice in (7) put more salt (8) put the lid on and shake. And when we opened it, it was ice cream.

We maDe ice-cream
Useing A Baby food Jar
And ice And salt
And choclate milk
And the way We Did it
And coffe Con tanre
And the way we useD it
aone Person puts milkonte
Jar And then put the liD on
put some ice then salt
BADy in the ice put mo
ice in put More salt
put the lid on And Shake
And when we open it
it was ice cream

Source: A. Ozboda (1992), Writing to Learn: Science Journals in Year One, p. 95. MEd thesis, University of Alberta, Edmonton, AB.

## Writing in Math

Much has been written about the role of talk in mathematics learning at the primary grade levels (see Mathematical Association, 1987). Linda Wason-Ellam (1987) studied journal writing in mathematics with one group of children in Grade 1. She discovered that the journals fulfilled four distinct purposes for the children:

1. self-questioning,

2. organizing information,

3. assimilating new learning, and

4. making guesses or hypotheses.

From her work, Wason-Ellam concluded that writing is a worthwhile venture that enhances children's mathematical abilities and understandings. She says of what she observed: "Writing to learn demands a view of learning which is active and personal. The students created their own language through interaction with mathematical experiences.... Knowledge was a personal possession based on the knower's experience. This was different from memorizing, transcribing and reciting" (p. 22).

Further research by Edwards (1992) on the use of learning journals or think books in mathematics in Grades 2, 4, and 6 showed that journals can be a safe and challenging environment where students can enjoy knowing that they do indeed know what they know, and they can come to comfortable and fruitful terms with what they do *not* know. Jasmin, for example (see Exhibit 8.1), would often discover when writing in her journal that she was not as clear about her mathematics learning as she had expected. Sometimes she expressed confusion and asked for help, and at other times her partner would point out inconsistencies in her reasoning. Edwards found that learning journals took the focus off other students' learning and away from marks and correct answers, and focussed instead on what individual children understood and could clearly articulate. For most of the children *and* the teachers, writing in math journals provided an opportunity to discover the learning they had under control and to consider a focus for future learning. The writing also allowed the students to open up to other people's ideas, experiences, and understandings. Journalling provided opportunities for the teachers to recognize the children as individuals in the classroom with unique learning needs and areas of expertise. The journal writing also encouraged children to write in their own style of language, while at the same time pushing the boundaries of that language and challenging them with the language of the discipline, the textbook, the teacher, and other children — a kind of language with which they may not have felt totally comfortable before writing in the journals.

When the children in Edwards' study wrote in their journals, they reshaped and redrafted as they engaged in learning (D'Arcy, 1989). It was also evident that some of the children seriously reflected on their learning and through that *reflection*, engaged again in *reshaping* and *redrafting* — what D'Arcy calls the "three Rs of learning" — a cycle of learning that people repeat throughout their lives. Shared meaning remained at the heart of these learning journals (which were also dialogue journals), and this "stream of meaning" (Bohm, 1990) flowed among children and teachers as all learned from one another. The journals not only proved to be beneficial learning experiences for the children, but were powerful vehicles that encouraged teachers to examine their teaching and knowledge base in mathematics education. As teachers read the student journals, they learned much about how they could improve their own practice. They reflected on

- the complex mathematical questions children ask,
- their own knowledge and understandings of mathematics and how these could be improved,
- the need for extremely clear and explicit teaching of mathematics,
- the effectiveness of journals as informal assessment tools,
- the clues the students' writing provides as to what they understand and what they do not understand, and
- how all of this information could be used to adjust and adapt specific teaching content, methodology, and student groupings in the classroom.

Working with personal learning journals requires a considerable commitment of time and energy. Writing in the journals takes up a great deal of class time, and a teacher who embarks on such a project must be willing to devote sufficient time to guiding the children through the process in order for it to be successful. Teachers have found that math journals can be used effectively from Grade 1 onward. Gradually, communication skills will improve, especially in the area of **expressive writing**, which in turn leads to **expository writing**. The teachers in Edwards' study realized that they needed to be flexible enough in their planning to encourage the children to use the journals at odd moments in the week, sometimes when the teacher least expected it. D'Arcy (1989, p. 150) says, "I have a hunch that some of us need to verbalize our understandings of a non-verbal system like maths if we are to pin down patterns of significance." Children, especially, must feel their way through the concrete world of the known before they can begin to represent their understandings abstractly. Learning journals provide one vehicle through which children can do this.

# Dialogue Journals

Dialogue journals are sometimes referred to as "response journals," but we use that term only for those journals where the students are writing in response to their learning—such as about a piece of literature or a science activity—not in response to one another. Where children are writing to a partner (whether a parent, teacher, or peer), we call those journals dialogue journals. (A journal can be both a dialogue journal and a response journal, but the two terms are not synonymous.)

When teachers and students engage in writing dialogue journals, a partnership is created with the person being addressed, a partnership based on compassion, acceptance, and a sincere interest in the other (Roderick and Berman, 1984). Bohm (1990, p. 1) adds to this:

> *Logos* means "the word," or in our case we would think of the "meaning of the word." And *dia* means "through"—it doesn't mean two. A dialogue can be among any number of people, not just two. Even one person can have a sense of dialogue within himself.... This derivation suggests ... a stream of meaning flowing among and through us and between us. And this shared meaning is the "glue" or "cement" that holds people and societies together.

Bohm (1990, p. 2) maintains that in a **dialogue**, unlike in a debate, nobody is trying to win. "In a dialogue, there is no attempt to gain points, or to make your particular view prevail. Rather, when a mistake is discovered on the part of anybody, everybody gains.... In a dialogue everybody wins." However, as we noted in the introduction to this chapter, in transmission-oriented settings the learner is most often a passive receiver, waiting to be told. Dialogue is not common. But, as Carswell (1988) noted, studies on the role of language in learning have emphasized the need for learners to find meaning in the world through the use of language as a tool of exploration. Vygotsky (1962), Polanyi (1969), Britton (1970), and Halliday (1975) have all argued for the use of language in a heuristic or exploratory way, by students as well as teachers, so that they may make greater personal sense of their learning. Dialogue, either spoken or written, is one way for students to pursue inquiry and create personal meaning in their learning, two critical features of a constructivist approach.

Students may write dialogue journals with the teacher, parents, or a peer. The aim of a dialogue journal is to enable the learner to clarify and explore meanings in collaboration with a partner. The adage "two heads are better than one" pertains in this situation. When students work in a small group to discuss an issue or try to solve a problem, it may take longer, but they usually learn from the experience. Adults know what happens when they discuss a book or movie with a group of friends. Their original responses are often modified, and they may find their understandings changing as they challenge themselves to expand the meaning created. The result of such dialogue is often a broader or deeper interpretation of their experiences. Teachers sometimes provide prompts for journal entries (see Atwell, 1990), while others provide a specific structure for the entry. One suggested format for a notebook or journal entry is presented in Table 8.1. This format is designed for students working in pairs. It provides prompts to help the students focus their thoughts.

In the math project cited previously (Edwards, 1992), the children wrote in dialogue journals and responded to each other regardless of their level of writing ability or mathematical understanding. Enthusiasm for the process was maintained through-

**Table 8.1**   **Model for a Science Notebook Entry**

| 1. My observation: | |
|---|---|
| 2. My conclusion: | 4. My partner's conclusion: |
| 3. What it meant to me: | 5. What my partner added: |
| 6. When we talked it over, our conclusion was: | |

Two children reading a dialogue journal.

out the year. In Grade 6, the children often made a number of entries back and forth on one topic with their partner before the dialogue ended. On other occasions, there was only one entry and one response. The children enjoyed the opportunity to write to, and get responses from, many different people, and the process was structured so that they changed partners every few weeks. Jasmin (whose work was presented in Exhibit 8.1) would read her partner's responses and consistently understand them, whoever that partner was. However, she frequently needed additional oral dialogue with her partner to become totally clear about a concept. She would have many questions to ask before she and her partner were satisfied that she really had understood. At that point Jasmin would then be able to articulate the process, either orally or in writing, much more clearly herself. Whether it was the peer explanation that made more sense than the teacher's, or whether it was simply the dialogue, we do not know. Margaret Donaldson (1978) speaks of the distance between learner and teacher and says that it is often more difficult to teach when the gap between the two is wide. In this case, the gap between teacher and learner was small — a point in favour of co-operative learning. The teachers reported positive class dynamics — the students were caring, compassionate, and genuinely engaged in a process of learning together.

In the Grade 2 class, the students left spaces in their math journals so that the teacher could provide feedback or answer a question. Frequently, the children drew a line on which the teacher was expected to respond. For example, Julia wrote, "I get up at 7:30. What time do you come to school? ___." A further journal entry from this class is shown in Exhibit 8.4. The children in this classroom made connections with their prior learning and were consolidating it into a more holistic understanding of the world. For example, children noticed that words used in one context could be used in a completely different context. Billy related his new knowledge of temperature and thermometers with prior knowledge in science, and observed a rule of capitalization:

Today we learned about temperature and Celsius and Mr. Celsius. A thermometer is something that tells the temperature. Do you know what the grey stuff is in a thermometer? It is called mercury. There is a planet named Mercury. The grey stuff in a thermometer is spelled with a smaller m and the planet is spelled with a big M. Mr. Celsius is now dead. He was called Mr. Celsius! He invented the thermometer! He named the thermometer after him.

**Exhibit 8.4**    **Grade 2 Math Journal Page**

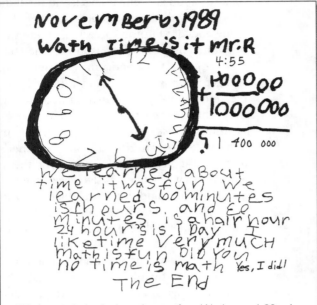

We learned about time. It was fun. We learned 60 minutes is 1 hour and 30 minutes is a half hour. 24 hours is
1 day. I like time very much. Math is fun. Did you know
time is math?

The process of writing in a dialogue journal is not always smooth. Experience has shown that teachers play a very important role in the success of dialogue journals even if they are not directly engaged in the dialogue. In one Grade 6 class, problems arose with motivation and with the meaningfulness of the journals. In that instance, the teacher gave very little guidance to the students other than telling them to write. Often, a child's entry did not receive an appropriate response from the partner. For example, Marianne wrote,

> The only part I don't get is when Mrs. Armstrong told us that when you have a question like this:
>
> $$40.8$$
> $$\times\ 80.4$$
>
> that the numbers in the ones place make up two decimal places. Then the decimal is two spots from the end.

This was met with a response from Marianne's partner about something entirely different. In the next entry, Marianne repeated her question:

> Math is pretty easy, but I still don't understand why, when you have a question like this
>
> $$40.8 \times 19.9 = 811.92$$
>
> why the decimal would be two places after the decimal in the answer.

This time her partner did respond, and said:

> I don't really understand why there has to be a two decimal place in the answer either. I wish I could do my social report on a typewriter....

Marianne was remarkably persistent, and in her third entry she again came back to the same question. Once again, she did not receive an appropriate response. However, as a result of reading Marianne's math entries above, Mrs. Armstrong completed three carefully planned lessons on the topic, including guided practice for the children, helping to clarify a very important math concept that many of the children in the classroom had not fully understood.

When teachers use learning logs or journals in their classrooms they

- read the student journals regularly to see how they might adapt their instruction and further facilitate their students' learning,
- encourage students to look at any questions their partners pose and consider them thoughtfully,
- provide "talk time" for pairs of students to figure out their answers to questions as well as their problem-solving strategies (some students need as long as ten minutes to read their partner's responses and discuss them),

- teach children what constitutes an appropriate response, and
- model responses on the overhead projector to help children become comfortable with a dialogue journal (not to tell children what to say, but to demonstrate a variety of ways in which they might respond to each other).

So that students can accept their partners' responses and not be hurt by a critical response, everyone in the class can be encouraged to begin their responses with a positive remark followed by a comment or recommendation. This is a response pattern many children are familiar with in writing conferences. It makes sense for children to follow this pattern in their dialogue journals as well. The following example demonstrates this twofold response pattern:

> Jeremy, I like the way you explained it. It really makes sense. I also liked the way you showed an easy and a hard problem. You should talk about the remainder and tell people about estimating.

Edwards' study (1992) found that in some situations children preferred to take their partner's journal home with them and make their responses there. The teachers in the study ensured that children who took a journal home with them understood that this was a privilege, and that taking someone else's private work home involves trust and respect.

Dialogue journals are an extension of co-operative learning. Each child becomes a teacher as well as a learner. Students learn together and from one another. Most children feel good about writing and responding in dialogue journals. With carefully established procedures and regular reading by the teacher, dialogue journals are an effective and enjoyable means of learning across the curriculum.

## Writing to Consolidate What Is Known

Many forms of writing serve to consolidate what a person knows, including journal writing and writing in notebooks. As we drafted the manuscript for this book, we rethought our understandings, worked through difficult ideas, consolidated what we knew about teaching and learning in language, and raised more questions. The writing of this book is part of our own continuing search for understanding. We went through all the stages that D'Arcy (1989) outlines:

1. recollecting
2. reflecting
3. reshaping
4. redrafting.

Writing that consolidates what a person knows is meeting the representational function of language that Halliday (1975) identified, and it uses what Britton (1970) has termed the expository or transactional voice. Writing that consolidates knowledge is a reflection of what the writer knows *at the time of writing*, and it acts as a kind of summary of the learning journey.

Exhibit 8.5 demonstrates how a student in Grade 3 consolidated her knowledge of homesteading on the Prairies.

Understanding can be consolidated at key junctures in the learning process, not only as a final activity. Students record what they have learned, with specific reference

| Exhibit 8.5 | **Homesteading** |

> GETTING A
> HOMESTEAD
>
> Many people came to ALBERTA to get a homestead. A homestead is peace of land you can farm on. To make the homestead yours you had to live on it six month of three years. You got the peace of land free but you had to pay $10.00 for the registration fee. After you pay while. you live on the peace of land you had to get thirty acres planted into crops. You also had to build a house worth at least $300.00 dollars. By the way the people looking for homesteads look for water near by. They also look for people near by too. THAT'S HOW THEY GOT HOMESTEADS 100 YEARS AGO.

to content and processes (such as measuring or estimating in mathematics). After teaching a Grade 6 unit on scale and its uses, Ms. Redfern asked her students to write a consolidating entry about scale in their math journals. Here is a selection of the class's entries:

"What I know about scale!

Scale is used for maps, to tell you how far it is from one place to another. Scale tells you the distance and how many kilometers or miles it takes to get from one place to another."

"The first thing you need to know how to work on scales you need to have the mm. and the cm. in order because then you can go from cm. to km. and then you can get all your answers right. When you have a test it's not hard when you go one space up like 2m.=20cm. by adding the zero in the order.

I'm not finished…"

"1.  Measure the length and width of tables in nearest metres because we want to find the actual measurement.
2.  We have to decide what the scale will be because we have to shrink it.
3.  We look at the graphing paper because we have to find out how many centimetre squares there are."

"Scale is anything that you can measure in linear instead of drawing the real size of whatever it is! You have to do this because if you don't it could take the rest of your life to draw it the real size!"

"I know scale a little better now because I know some questions I didn't know before like who does scaling? People who build houses and cartographers. Now I know that you can measure scale with anything. What do you measure money and time with?"

These five entries reveal the range of meanings children created from the unit on scale, and the ways in which they were able to apply that knowledge to the world. The writing shows how some children grasped the concept of scale very well, while others were limited to trying to manipulate numbers to make scale work for them. The writing provided excellent feedback for Ms. Redfern (who did much reteaching as a result) and also enabled the children to discover for themselves what they knew and how well they knew it. The children who were struggling to articulate their learning began to realize that they did not fully understand the concept, and some were more open to revisiting the topic as a result.

# Research Projects

In adult life, research reports are frequently written in areas of engineering, law, medicine, social services, business, and academia, to name just a few. Reports in these contexts are always predicated on a question or line of inquiry. Researchers essentially gather data to help them answer questions. When children are required to complete research reports in school contexts, the purpose is often unclear. Children are asked, for example, to write reports on a Canadian province, an animal, or a community. But the first step in any research endeavour is to formulate questions that guide the study and provide the intrinsic motivation to complete the project. When students are required to conduct research and write a report in school, it is essential that they formulate the questions, have a genuine interest in the topic, and be motivated to discover answers to their questions. Teachers play a key role in establishing interest and motivation, in guiding students to formulate their questions, and in helping students learn relevant research strategies.

To conduct research and write research reports in school, students need to develop the ability to write exposition. As Newkirk has demonstrated (1987), children's early writing is usually in the expressive voice, but as they pursue questions that are of interest and relevance to them, they learn to organize their ideas and begin to write in a variety of forms and voices. This was evident in Tanya's piece, "About Seasons", in Exhibit 7.1. However, children still benefit from instruction in expository writing, as well as in the research process. The challenge for teachers is to help students make the transition from expressive to expository writing in an interesting and enjoyable way.

Children may find expository writing challenging because it is intended for a distant rather than an immediate audience. For many children, the only audience for expository prose is the teacher (and that means the teacher as evaluator). But children learn by doing—they learn as they write, and through their writing they can acquire the transactional or expository voice. Exhibit 8.6 demonstrates Kelly's transactional voice in an excerpt from her report on the solar system completed in Grade 5. Kelly's teacher ensured that her students knew the audience for their writing (in this case, their peers in the classroom), and she encouraged her students to write specifically for that audience on a topic of their own choice. Kelly's writing is well-organized and includes information that she found to be personally intriguing as well as challenging. Kelly was fascinated by the notion that stars are born and die. Her illustration for this section of the report shows her playfulness with the idea, and, at the beginning of each page, Kelly posed the question to her classmates, "Is this fact or fiction?" Kelly's research not only started with a question, but posed a question throughout the text.

Many children have only a vague understanding of the research process. These children have a much greater chance of successfully completing a project if the teacher provides direct and specific instruction for them. Effective teachers teach their students how to

- use library resources,
- use the table of contents and index of a book,
- locate information in books, encyclopedias, and magazines,
- interpret information from pictures, charts, graphs, videotapes, and audiotapes,
- use the Internet effectively,
- paraphrase what they read, make notes, and put what they read into their own words,

**Exhibit 8.6    Fact or Fiction? The Solar System**

True. Stars are born in clouds of gas and dust called nebulas. Millions of years later the dust particles and gas are pulled together so they can heat up. When the gas is hot enough, a nuclear reation, like a bomb, sets off and it is born. Changes occur as the star gets older. Some keep growing and then shrink. Other stars project gas into space. When the stars are quite old they start to shrink and they are called white drawf stars. When they start to cool off they become black drawf stars and then the star is dead.

- translate information into visual form on charts, graphs and diagrams,
- conduct interviews,
- search archives, and
- organize their findings into a report.

These strategies are best taught in the context of the research process, presenting the various strategies at times when the students need them. An example is using an overhead from a page in an encyclopedia at the same time as working with a set of encyclopedias in the classroom. Teachers may begin by helping students to develop a report collaboratively. Introducing young children to conducting library research and writing exposition is usually much more effective when teacher and students find information together as a class than if they work independently. The more children are shown *how* to do research and the more they are actively *involved* in doing it themselves, the more effective the learning will be.

## Guiding the Research Process

Teachers in Grades 1 to 4 sometimes provide students with an outline, matrix, or web to help them organize information once they have located it. These devices help students make decisions about which information is relevant and which is not. Some devices have room for children to make their own notes in the spaces provided.

These outlines, matrices, or webs are not like the typical outlines many of us were required to write in high school. Rather, they are graphic organizers that help children make sense of their research. Not all children will need such a device; however, graphic organizers do provide a sense of direction for those children who need some structure and guidance in putting together a report. An example of one graphic organizer — a data collection chart — is shown in Figure 8.1. Another form of graphic organizer is that used at the beginning of each chapter in this textbook to help the reader see the "big picture" as well as how the sections of the chapter relate to one another.

When a Grade 3 class was learning about animals, they focussed on the concept of adaptation. The guiding question was "How do animals survive?" A class case study was created around the polar bear. Once the children began locating resources for the study, they zeroed in on the research question and found relevant information that helped them answer it. Thus, their reading was conducted from a specific perspective. Information was noted through words, phrases, charts, diagrams, and so forth as the students collected their data. The following headings emerged as the students compiled their findings:

- physical appearance
- habitat
- food
- enemies
- migratory patterns
- conclusions (how the research answered the question)

These headings were not meant to dictate how the research report was to be written. Instead, they provided structures that guided the children's developing sense of organization.

As part of the research process, children need individual conferences with the teacher if they are to have their individual learning needs met and be assured that they are on track with their research. An anecdote here demonstrates the importance of individual writing conferences during the process of report writing.

Jared, in Grade 4, was completing a research report on fish. The report was to be made into a book to be placed in the classroom library. Jared had chosen to focus on the Mating Ritual Fish. The teacher, Mr. Johnson, felt quite sure there was no such fish, but Jared was adamant about his findings. Because of his concern, Mr. Johnson sat

**Figure 8.1**   **Data Collection Chart, Community Services, Grade 2**

with Jared as Jared went over the books he had used as resources in his study. There, on one page, was a photograph of a school of fish and beneath it the caption "mating rituals." Jared and Mr. Johnson together carefully reread this section of the book, but it took some intense discussion before Jared could recognize that this was not a breed of fish, but a process that fish engage in to reproduce themselves. Jared wrote his report on tropical fish, and was pleased with the outcome.

Because of Mr. Johnson's careful monitoring of the children's research, Jared's misinterpretation was discovered well before the report was already in progress. It would not have been helpful to Jared's self-esteem, his understanding of fish, or his confidence about library research to produce a report based on a misreading of the resource material. In this anecdote, Jared made a very reasonable meaning construction. In his interactions with Mr. Johnson that meaning was adjusted through discussion, providing an example of how meaning is socially constructed and negotiated.

Traditional report formats often give way today to more interactive, visual, or imaginative presentations of research. Chapter Thirteen discusses the role of technology in language arts and provides information on working with Hyperstudio and other software packages in creating multimedia presentations as alternatives to the paper research report. Children also develop new ideas for research reports from reading nonfiction books. Many current nonfiction materials available for children employ formats and strategies that are compelling and exciting. Expository prose can be full of the enthusiasm and excitement we feel when we discover something new and want to share it with a wider audience, as demonstrated in the excerpt from Kelly's report shown in Exhibit 8.6.

## Writing Relevant Research

As already noted in earlier chapters, a fascinating research project completed for many years by Grade 4 children at Petite Rivière Elementary School in Lunenburg County, Nova Scotia, was a series of books about the local area. Each year the children, who were bussed to the school from a wide area, selected a community within the county and pursued the questions "What makes this community unique?" and "What makes this community such a special place to live?" The project involved more than library research. The students went into the community to interview residents and business-people, complete correspondence, and search archives in order to answer their guiding questions. Once the research was completed, they wrote and presented the material in a final bound form that was accessible and interesting to the general public. The books were printed (complete with ISBN number) and bound by a local company and sold by the school. Stories, drawings, biographies, history, lists, poems, recipes, directions for games, minutes from meetings, maps, and posters were all included. One excerpt from *History of Crousetown* (1993) is shown in Exhibit 7.3, and a further excerpt is presented in Exhibit 8.7.

Before researchers begin the process of writing a research report, they try to understand their subject as much as possible so that they can communicate their findings clearly and interestingly. The children of Petite Rivière Elementary School became "experts" in their local history before they embarked on the writing. They knew they were going to publish a book that would be sold in the community they had written about, as well as in the county as a whole. They therefore began to develop an awareness of the clarity required of their writing if it was to make sense to readers who

**Exhibit 8.7**    **Stores in Crousetown**

The first store in Crousetown was owned by Beechum Crouse. It used to be attached to the house that Robert Crouse is living in today. Beechum Crouse's Store sold pipes, tobacco and many different things.

Robert Crouse's father (Merle Crouse) opened a store in 1936.

Later Arthur Bolivar ran Merle Crouse's store. Merle sold the business, but he wouldn't sell the building. Arthur Bolivar then retired from the store in the early 1970s.

Johnny Himmelman had a store and a post office in Crousetown at the same time as Merle Crouse's store. John Himmelman's store is still standing across from the Community Cemetery.

Source: Petite Rivière Elementary School (1993), *History of Crousetown*, p. 24. Lunenburg County, NS: Petite Rivière Publishing.

might not know them personally and likely did not know the details of the story to be told. Their teacher, Mrs. Haché, writes:

> The oral history projects in Grade 4 at Petite Rivière Elementary School involved the students in researching the history of a local community and then writing and publishing a history book and companion storybook about that community.
>
> Each student chose several topics that would become part of the history book. They researched their topics in the following ways: I took a group of students to the Public Archives in Halifax to research the old newspapers of that community. People from the community brought in artifacts and information to our classroom museum (a collection of old items from the community). I took the students, four at a time, after school to interview older citizens in the community (the students were prepared for the interview with questions from the whole class and a release form for each person interviewed). These interviews were videotaped and used for reference in the classroom by the students as they wrote their reports. The students checked these reports for grammar, spelling, and punctuation. The students then discussed their finished report with the teacher and proceeded to put their information and artwork together in the format for the history book.
>
> The storybook is different from the history book in that it is written collaboratively. For the storybooks, the children wrote their own versions of each chapter. I then read all the chapters and underlined in red the best sentences and paragraphs in each child's writing. We then started writing the story collaboratively with the children enthusiastically discussing each sentence. All the students focused on making sure they had some of their own sentences in the finished chapter. I wrote the story on the blackboard and then, in pairs, they typed each chapter or story on the computer. After it had been typed, the story was photocopied and an overhead transparency made. Then the class collaboratively edited and revised it. At this point, the dictionary and thesaurus were

in constant use. The stories were reviewed several weeks later and final revisions, including decisions about which artwork to use and where to place it, were made before the storybook was published.

The final stage of the project was an evening presentation in the community hall for everyone in the community. The children sent special invitations to the people they interviewed and they presented their finished books to them that evening. They prepared an evening of entertainment based on the project (readings, drama, and an old-fashioned singsong) and then served food prepared by their parents. The importance of this celebration for the community, and its impact on all the people gathered together for this special evening, cannot be overemphasized.

Mrs. Haché integrated many aspects of the language arts into this project each year. The children interviewed, discussed, listened, made notes, read, and wrote as part of the project. They worked collaboratively in some areas and individually in others. Mrs. Haché provided guidance and structure, while at the same time giving the children the opportunity to make the books truly their own. All the students had parts of their work included in the final books, and the purpose of the project was clear to the children from the very beginning (as it was to the community and to the final audience in the community hall). It was through their involvement in this personally and socially relevant project that the students were able to develop their ability to write effective exposition. In addition, the students learned to write for a more general audience than the immediate one they were familiar with in their classroom and homes.

The Grade 4 oral history project at Petite Rivière became a tradition. Each year's class looked forward to it, and as the children moved into Grade 5, they took care of marketing and promoting the book and handling the accounting required for publication and sales. Mrs. Haché and the children selected a different local community to study each year, so the books and the project remained unique and interesting for both the children and their teacher, as well as for community members.

Children frequently find visual depictions of their learning, such as designing and drawing posters, satisfying vehicles for representing what they have learned about a topic. Children at the beginning of the twenty-first century are particularly visual in their learning. They watch television and movies, play video games, and use the Internet to a much greater degree than children did in past generations. When children combine their artwork and writing, they provide striking demonstrations of what they know. Frequently, these integrated presentation formats are more appealing to children than more traditional forms. Similarly, charts, graphs, maps, and diagrams often provide children with opportunities to share their understandings more fully. The importance of report writing lies in the fact that it remains a major format for organizing and presenting information to others. In addition, research reports provide opportunities for children to organize their thinking and learning about the world.

## Summary

In constructivist classrooms, writing across the curriculum is much more than copying notes from the board or writing reports to demonstrate what has been learned. It is an opportunity for learners to write as they are learning, and to process that learning, making greater sense of what they know. It is a time for questioning, hypothesizing, predicting, and sometimes consolidating knowledge. Writing across the curriculum can be done from Grade 1 onward, as shown by the samples of young children's writing presented in this chapter. Writing for learning is best taught when it is modelled by teachers or developed in collaborative efforts with students and teacher working together. In addition, research and study skills are taught with the aim of helping children to become independent learners who feel confident in locating and using library resources and in accessing primary sources through such means as interviews and archival searches. Many of the skills needed to conduct research involve organizing information. This important ability can be taught collaboratively in the early grades as children become familiar with the use of webs, grids, and charts to facilitate their learning.

Being able to write thoughts on paper is one way in which people remind themselves of what they know and think. It is also a way to communicate those thoughts to others. As students develop their abilities to read and write for multiple purposes and for varied audiences, they take greater control of their own learning. The ability to recount, recapture, and reflect on their experiences and emerging understandings is a critical life skill. Most importantly, the skills students develop as they write in learning logs, think books, response journals, and dialogue journals, and the research inquiry and reporting they complete, provide them with a repertoire of powerful learning strategies. Through employing these strategies, students articulate connections between new learning and what they already know, making personal sense of their learning and becoming better writers.

> This chapter opened with Jean-Pierre as he was about to begin a student teaching placement in a Grade 2/3 classroom. Jean-Pierre raised many questions about writing for learning and had some concerns about the value of his students spending time writing and talking in subject areas across the curriculum. It didn't take long for Jean-Pierre to discover that the students wrote in learning logs, math journals, and science notebooks, as well as in their writing folders. The idea that writing actually helped them to learn made complete sense to the students in Mr. Pettigrew's classroom. The students wrote to explore what they were learning, to ask questions when they were unsure, and to figure out meanings with a partner. The students each had a personal record of what they had learned, and they had an opportunity to receive feedback on their learning from their peers and from Mr. Pettigrew. In turn, Mr. Pettigrew had evidence of what his students were learning — and he knew which students needed help in specific areas of the curriculum. As a result of his experiences in the Grade 2/3 classroom, Jean-Pierre found that his own writing in his student teaching journal gained importance and relevance to his practice, especially when he shared some of his entries with Mr. Pettigrew and with the students in the class.

## Selected Professional Resources

Atwell, N. (ed.). (1990). *Coming to Know: Writing to Learn in the Intermediate Grades*. Portsmouth, NH: Heinemann. A practical approach to writing across the curriculum, this book, edited by Nancie Atwell, consists of chapters written by classroom teachers (Grades 3 through 6) who asked their students to write as scientists, historians, mathematicians, and literary critics do — to use writing-as-process to discover meaning. The book describes specific classroom activities and is an excellent reference for beginning teachers. Suggestions for unit planning and for ways of incorporating writing across the curriculum are provided. In particular, the volume addresses writing reports, conducting interviews, recording observations, taking notes, and using learning logs. The book contains many examples of children's work, teachers' responses, and lists of classroom resources.

D'Arcy, P. (1989). *Making Sense, Shaping Meaning: Writing in the Context of a Capacity-Based Approach to Learning.* Portsmouth, NH: Heinemann. This British book explores and describes the many different types of writing children in an elementary school can do. The book is rich in samples of children's writing and comments on the writing process. D'Arcy focusses on writing across the curriculum, and she particularly examines the writing–thinking connection and the role writing plays in stimulating thought as well as capturing it on paper.

# References

Atwell, N. (ed.). (1990). *Coming to know: Writing to learn in the intermediate grades.* Portsmouth, NH: Heinemann.

Barnes, D. (1976). *From communication to curriculum.* Harmondsworth, UK: Penguin Books.

Bohm, D. (1990). *On dialogue.* Ojai, CA: David Bohm Seminars.

Britton, J. (1970). *Language and learning.* Harmondsworth, UK: Penguin Books.

Britton, J. (1982). *Prospect and retrospect: Selected essays of James Britton.* G. Pradl (ed.). Montclair, NJ: Boynton Cook.

Britton, J., Burgess, G., Martin N., McLeod, A., and Rosen, H. (1975). *The development of writing abilities, 11–18.* London: MacMillan Education.

Bruner, J.S. (1966). *Towards a theory of instruction.* Cambridge, MA: The Belknap Press of Harvard University.

Carswell, R.J.B. (1988). Journals in a graduate curriculum course. *English Quarterly, 21* (2), 104–114.

D'Arcy, P. (1989). *Making sense, shaping meaning: Writing in the context of a capacity-based approach to learning.* Portsmouth, NH: Heinemann.

Donaldson, M. (1978). *Children's minds.* New York: W.W. Norton & Co.

Edwards, J. (1992). Dialogue journals in math: Grades two, four and six. *Reflections on Canadian Literacy,* 10 (1), 2–12.

Fulwiler, T. (ed.). (1987). *The journal book.* Toronto: Boynton/Cook.

Halliday, M.A.K. (1975). *Explorations in the functions of language.* London: Edward Arnold.

MacAlister, S., Kydd, G., and Jones, G. (1988). *Writing and primary science.* Calgary: Calgary Board of Education.

Mathematical Association (UK). (1987). *Math talk.* Cheltenham, UK: Stanley Thornes.

Moffett, J. (1968). *Teaching the universe of discourse.* Boston: Houghton Mifflin.

Murray, D. (1984). *Write to learn.* New York: Holt, Rinehart and Winston.

Newkirk, T. (1987). The non-narrative writing of young children. *Research in the teaching of English, 21,* 121–145.

Ozdoba, A. (1992). Writing to learn: Science journals in year one. MEd thesis, University of Alberta, Edmonton, AB.

Petite Rivière Elementary School. (1993). *History of Crousetown.* Lunenburg County, NS: Petite Rivière Publishing.

Polanyi, M. (1969). Knowing and being. In M. Greene (ed.), *Knowing and being: The essays of Michael Polanyi* (pp. 123–137). Chicago: University of Chicago Press.

Roderick, J.A. and Berman, L.M. (1984). Dialoguing about dialogue journals. *Language Arts,* (61) 7, 686–692.

Shuy, R. (1987). Research currents: Dialogue as the heart of learning. *Language Arts,* 64 (8), 890–897.

Vygotsky, L.S. (1962). *Thought and language.* Cambridge, MA: MIT Press.

Wason-Ellam, L. (1987). Writing across the curriculum. *Canadian Journal of English Language Arts,* 11 (3), 5–23.

# Chapter nine

# Assessment and Conventions of Writing

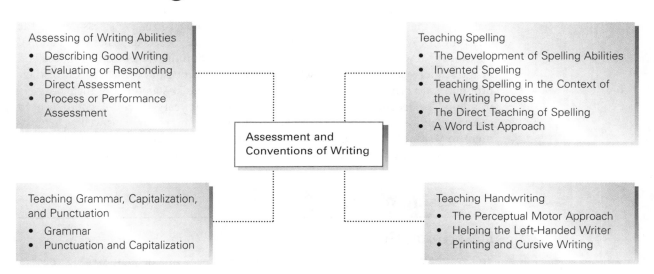

**Assessing of Writing Abilities**

- Describing Good Writing
- Evaluating or Responding
- Direct Assessment
- Process or Performance Assessment

**Teaching Spelling**

- The Development of Spelling Abilities
- Invented Spelling
- Teaching Spelling in the Context of the Writing Process
- The Direct Teaching of Spelling
- A Word List Approach

Assessment and Conventions of Writing

**Teaching Grammar, Capitalization, and Punctuation**

- Grammar
- Punctuation and Capitalization

**Teaching Handwriting**

- The Perceptual Motor Approach
- Helping the Left-Handed Writer
- Printing and Cursive Writing

Asha is completing her fifth week of student teaching in Grade 5. Her first student teaching placement was in a Grade 1 classroom, and so Asha has been particularly conscious of the progress students make in the elementary school years. She cannot help but comment to her co-operating teacher, Ms. Hwang, how much children learn and grow in those years. The sheer amount of information they have processed is astonishing to her, but so is the development of their abilities in writing and reading. Asha asks Ms. Hwang how she records the progress the students make. How does Ms. Hwang plan for report cards and student/parent conferences? How does she know what to teach to individual students? How do the students become competent spellers? How do they learn appropriate grammar? Does Ms. Hwang teach handwriting? How did she learn to write neatly on the chalkboard? How does Ms. Hwang gather and sort information about her students into useful "chunks" that

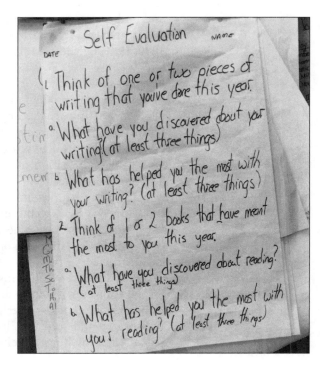

will provide feedback for her instruction in the classroom, help the children to understand their learning, and provide information to parents and a measure of instructional success for the school board? ∎

Asha's observations and questions are important. Having taught students in Grade 1 as well as in Grade 5, she is aware that individual students require different methods of instruction depending on their varying needs. Sometimes children learn best in small groups, sharing their writing, receiving feedback, and receiving instruction through their teacher's comments and advice. At other times, they learn more effectively in individual writing conferences. And on occasion students need direct lessons in specific areas. Assessing student writing abilities is a crucial part of the planning and instruction cycle. Ongoing, formative assessment in the classroom provides teachers with the information they need to make instructional decisions that will enhance their students' learning. Summative assessment at the end of the school year provides the school district with a measure of the success of their programs and provides individual children with a regular statement of their progress in school. To become well-rounded writers over their years in school, children need assistance in learning correct spelling, punctuation, and grammar, as well as involvement in writing and reading workshops. This chapter addresses the areas of assessment of writing and the direct instruction of the conventions, or tools, of writing.

## Assessing Writing Abilities

## Describing Good Writing

To describe and assess children's writing, teachers need an adequate writing vocabulary and explicit knowledge of what constitutes good writing. Current instructional and evaluation practices among teachers of elementary school writing are informed by research that recognizes writing as a complex cognitive process (Flower and Hayes, 1980; 1981; Berthoff, 1981) that "is as variable and unique as the individual's personality" (Graves, 1975, p. 237). In their instruction and evaluation of student writing, teachers show respect for the idiosyncratic nature of the writing process and value both the written products and the writing processes of individual students. However, while the writing of a text appears to be an expression of personal emotions and ideas, it is in fact a "learned social practice" (Gilbert and Taylor, 1991, p. 41) Similarly, teachers' readings of student writing are influenced not only by individual differences, but also by the application of different reading frames that have been socially learned. This means that teachers' assessments of pieces of writing are, either consciously or unconsciously, strongly influenced by the socially learned expectations of the teachers — by the ways in which both the author's and the reader's cultural experiences and views of the world are reflected in the writing. In other words, it is not possible to objectively assess any piece of writing. Every reading of a text is culturally and socially constructed.

Professional educators involved in designing of broad-based evaluations of student writing, however, generally advocate an individualistic cognitive approach to writing. Evaluation methods are designed "to suppress or displace value-laden and political readings of student papers by putting the locus of evaluation outside the individual reader, situating it instead either in the text itself or in a supposedly community-wide set of standards" (Schwegler, 1991, p. 205). Hence, provincial ministries of education in Canada attempt to train the teachers who mark provincial writing tests to be as objective as possible, minimizing reader bias and ensuring that scoring is consistent. Reliability checks are conducted regularly throughout the marking sessions. Readers of student writing are viewed as authorities who shrug aside their social values and histories when engaged in the evaluation process. However, an examination of scores assigned to the narrative writing of elementary and middle grade students on large-scale examinations in Canada, Great Britain, and the United States reveals consistent patterns in the distribution of scores assigned to girls' and boys' writing (Applebee, Langer, and Mullis, 1986; Stobart, Elwood, and Quinlan, 1992; Alberta Education, 1992; 1995; U.S. Department of Education, 1995). Repeatedly, greater percentages of scores at the high and medium levels for the grade are assigned to girls' narrative writing, and greater percentages of scores at the lower levels are assigned to boys' narrative writing. Does this mean that boys do not write as well as girls, or do educators describe their expectations of "good writing" in terms of the kinds of writing completed by girls?

In a constructivist classroom, teachers focus on evaluating a wide range of writing abilities. Wide use of a process approach to writing has helped many teachers understand writing more fully. Yet, teachers are still trying to come to terms with the cultural and social nature of writing and accept that differences in writing exist between genders and from one social group to another (Peterson and Bainbridge, 1999). Although most teachers have an internalized set of criteria that tells them when they have read a good piece of writing, they may still have problems articulating *why* they would describe that particular piece as "good." It is important for teachers to be aware that there is no *one* way to evaluate children's writing, generating one mark or grade that represents the child's level of development in writing as a whole. The primary focus of assessment is on helping children to increase their learning and on helping teachers to plan for instruction. As a result, a range of scales and methods of assessment are necessary depending on what the student and teacher need to know.

## Evaluating or Responding

The method of writing assessment teachers choose in their classrooms is related to the purpose of the assessment and to the teachers' beliefs about their roles as teachers of language. As Wilkinson, Barnsley, Hanna, and Swan (1983, p. 872) put it:

> If one seeks to develop only the skills of writing, one chooses a marking scheme focusing on that. But if one is concerned with the growth of individuals, for whom language is a means to that end, then one's scheme of assessment is conceived to perceive that growth and to further it.

Searle and Dillon (1980) found that when teachers responded to student writing, they focussed mainly on form, and their written comments to students consisted almost exclusively of evaluative and instructional points. The teachers in the study generally attempted to correct all the errors in the conventions of written language. This study took place twenty years ago, and the major finding was that teachers did not focus on the meaning and purpose of language, but rather promoted the belief that what a child has to say matters *less* than how it is said. Since that time there have been enormous changes in the teaching of writing and in how teachers respond to student writing.

Educators now know that the ways in which teachers respond to student writing shape the student's writing behaviours by providing indications of teacher expectations. Teachers teach writing explicitly through their written responses and through the writing conferences they hold with their students, and implicitly through time allocation and instructional emphasis (writing time is no longer a "filler" for Friday afternoons!). When it comes to assessment, teachers make every effort to collect evidence of their students' growth in writing, record that growth, and present the evidence to parents, children, and administrators.

At one time, writing abilities were assessed through **standardized tests**, but a more effective and more common evaluation strategy today is the use of student writing samples and the **direct assessment** of them. Direct assessment is used by teachers in their own classrooms and also in large-scale province-wide or state-wide assessment projects.

## Direct Assessment

### Writing Samples

When reading students' writing samples, teachers are mindful that writing is not a single skill: syntax, organization, and word choice vary according to the purpose and audience for the writing. The purpose and intended audience for a piece of writing shape the piece. Expressive writing is writer-oriented: its purpose is to reveal feelings, attitudes, and perceptions. Expository writing is subject-oriented: it is meant to explain or present information on a subject. Persuasive writing is audience-oriented: the writer takes a position on a topic and tries to convince others about it. The stimulus, or prompt, for a writing task also frames the piece of writing and influences the piece considerably. Therefore, when teachers read and score student writing samples, they take all of these factors into consideration, varying their reading of the piece according to the purpose and the stimulus.

Direct assessment focusses on children as communicative beings who are developing their abilities as writers. The development of children's writing progresses from simple to complex, from literal to metaphoric, and from a preoccupation with self to an awareness of the psychological characteristics of others (Wilkinson, Barnsley, Hanna, and Swan, 1983). Thus, children's writing reflects growth in empathy, social cognition, personal perception, and self-awareness, as well as in language skills. It is therefore possible to see a developmental process in children's writing. Taking account of the thinking and feeling involved in creating a piece of writing provides useful insights into children's cognitive processes and shows how young writers may use the world of imagination as a means of understanding their own reality. Learning to write is very much like learning to think, for only through writing can we examine the actual meaning of our words and the logic—or lack of it—that leads from one statement to another.

Many teachers and language arts consultants develop their own rubrics for assessing writing in the classroom. Frequently, the rubrics are developed in collaboration with the students. This process facilitates three things:

1. As the students and teacher together develop the rubric, they explore what constitutes a good piece of writing.

2. The students become aware of the criteria on which they will be evaluated.

3. Students remain in control of all aspects of their writing from onset to completion.

The collaborative nature of the process demonstrates the teacher's respect for the students and recognition of their contributions in the classroom. Alberta language arts consultant John Proctor has developed many rubrics for assessing writing in his work with children in schools. One of his rubrics for assessing Grade 6 persuasive writing, developed collaboratively with a class of students, is presented in Table 9.1.

The assessment requirements of most school districts and provincial governments are frequently at odds with the needs of students and teachers. Where students want to know how they can improve their writing, and teachers want to inform the planning they do in order to meet their students' learning requirements, school districts and provincial governments (and sometimes parents) want to know how their students' abilities compare with the abilities of students in other jurisdictions. They also want a measure of how much their students know and can do—and the more objective, the better. As a result, teachers learn how to complete a wide range of assessment procedures, some demonstrating accountability to the general public and others designed to provide feedback to individual students and input to instructional planning.

**Table 9.1**   Rubric for Assessing Persuasive Writing — Grade 6

| If you are going to mark my argument, here's what to look for: | Marks Possible | My Mark | Peer Mark | Teacher's Mark and Comments |
|---|---|---|---|---|
| **A. What I said and how I said it:** | | | | |
| I made a strong first impression | 2 | | | |
| I presented both sides of the issue | 5 | | | |
| I presented my points in order | 4 | | | |
| I proposed a solution | 2 | | | |
| My argument was clear and made sense | 3 | | | |
| **B. How I presented my ideas for my reader:** | | | | |
| I checked my spelling | 2 | | | Spelling words to work on: |
| I made sure my ideas were in sentences with correct capitals and punctuation | 2 | | | |
| My handwriting, neatness, and presentation were the best I can make them | 2 | | | |
| **C. Working for bonus marks:** | | | | |
| I took out the garbage by taking out words (such as "I feel" and "In my opinion") | 2 | | | |
| I made a real effort to persuade you that my argument was a good one | 1 | | | |
| **Total marks** | **25** | | | |
| **Comments:** | | | | |

Source: Reprinted with permission of John Proctor, University of Alberta.

## Holistic Scoring

> Holistic evaluation of writing is a guided procedure for sorting and ranking written pieces. The rater takes a piece of writing and either 1) matches it with another piece in a graded series of pieces or, 2) scores it for prominence of certain features important to that kind of writing or, 3) assigns it a number or letter grade. The placing, scoring, or grading occurs very quickly and impressionistically, after the rater has practiced the procedure with other raters. (Cooper, 1977, p. 3)

In **holistic scoring** students are evaluated on what they do *well* rather than on what they fail to do. This method encourages teachers to focus on the specifics they have in mind for rating essays and stories before reading them. These specifics may include

- the students' attention to purpose and audience, and the ability to organize ideas according to the needs of communicating with that audience, whether through poetic, persuasive, expressive, or informative modes,
- the students' attention to the visual and verbal cues of the assignment (for example, "give at least one reason ..."),
- the students' developmental capabilities, allowing for the general language characteristics of children of a similar age (for example, the invented spelling of children in the primary grades), and
- constraints of the evaluation situation — that is, the context or setting where the writing takes place (in many evaluative situations, for example, children do not have time to revise, edit, or ask for peer or teacher assistance).

A number of different methods for conducting holistic assessments have been established. Two of the best known are general impression marking and the essay scale. *General impression marking* is one of the simplest forms of holistic assessment. The rater scores the paper by deciding where it fits in the range of papers produced for that assignment on that occasion. Although there is no analysis of specific features and no summary of scores, this method has high reliability (Cooper and Odell, 1977) because experienced raters use an implicit list of features in much the same way as classroom teachers. If teachers were to spread out in front of them a set of writing from all the children in their class, written on the same day and on the same topic, it would be fairly clear which were the "best" pieces of writing and which were the least well developed. The middle-ranked pieces would be more difficult to arrange in some kind of order, but eventually a teacher would be able to make the decision based on an implicit or internalized set of criteria. The use of this method for scoring or assessing writing can be facilitated in a school setting by a second teacher working collaboratively on the assessment. On such occasions, the teachers' implicit criteria are made explicit as problematic pieces of writing are discussed and a grade is decided upon.

The *essay scale* is a series of complete pieces arranged according to quality. At one end of the scale is an exceptionally good example, and at the other end is one providing insufficient writing on which to base a judgement. A rater attempts to evaluate a new piece of writing by matching it on the scale with the piece of writing most like it. This procedure is frequently undertaken in large-scale assessment projects, such as those at the provincial, state, or school district level.

## Analytic Scales

Analytic scoring breaks the writing performance down into component parts, such as organization, wording, and ideas. It takes longer to accomplish than holistic scoring, but provides more specific information and is usually regarded as being more objective. The list of features assessed may range from four to twelve, with each feature described in some detail and with high, mid, and low points identified and described along a scoring line for each feature.

Criteria-based assessment of writing has been used by the Alberta Department of Education since 1983 in the Grades 3, 6, and 9 provincial tests of written language. A modified version of these criteria is still used in the provincial tests and has proven useful to teachers in developing a vocabulary for discussing and conducting formal writing assessment, and in developing an explicit sense of what might constitute good writing. In the provincial tests, the students are required to produce two writing samples: one a narrative piece prompted by a story starter, and the other a functional piece prompted by a specific purpose for a specific audience. In recent years, the test has provided some choice of topic and includes time for planning and discussion with peers. The functional piece may be a business letter, for example, and is assessed according to "content" (development and organization, fulfilling the purpose, tone of the piece, and awareness of audience) and "content management" (accuracy and effectiveness of words and expressions, control of sentence structure, usage, mechanics, and format). Content and content management are equally weighted in the assessment.

The pieces of narrative writing are assessed according to five criteria: content (context, plausibility, details, awareness of audience), organization (introduction, sequencing, cohesion, and closure), sentence structure (type, length), vocabulary (specific, image-creating, accurate, and effective), and language conventions (capitalization, spelling, punctuation, format, usage, clarity, flow). The reporting category of content for Grade 6 narrative and functional writing (1998) is shown in Tables 9.2 and 9.3. Each category is scored from INS (Insufficient) through 1 to 5.

Below are the Grade 6 descriptors for a piece of writing that "approaches the standard of excellence":

### Content

- The context is clearly established and sustained.
- The events and/or actions are consistently appropriate for the established context.
- Supporting details are specific and consistently effective.
- The writing captivates and holds the reader's interest and is creative and/or original.

### Organization (or development)

- The introduction is purposeful; interesting; clearly establishes events, characters, and/or setting; and provides direction for the writing.
- Events and/or details are arranged in paragraphs in a purposeful and effective order, and coherence is maintained.    *Grade 6*
- Connections and/or relationships among events, actions, details, and/or characters are consistently maintained.
- The ending ties events and/or actions together.

### Sentence structure

- Sentence structure is effectively and consistently controlled.

**Table 9.2**    Alberta Education Grade 6 Descriptors for Content (Narrative Writing)

**Focus**

When marking CONTENT appropriate for Grade 6 narrative writing, the marker should consider how effectively the writer

- establishes a context
- uses events and/or actions that are appropriate for the established context
- uses specific details (of characters, setting, actions, events, etc.)
- demonstrates an awareness of audience

| | | |
|---|---|---|
| 5 | Meets the Standard of Excellence | • The context is clearly established and sustained. |
| | | • The events and/or actions are consistently appropriate for the established context. |
| | | • Supporting details are specific and consistently effective. |
| | | • The writing captivates and holds the reader's interest and is creative and/or original. |
| 4 | Approaches the Standard of Excellence | • The context is clearly established and generally sustained. |
| | | • The events and/or actions are appropriate for the established context. |
| | | • Supporting details are specific and generally effective. |
| | | • The writing engages and generally holds the reader's interest. |
| 3 | Clearly Meets the Acceptable Standard | • The context is established but may not be sustained. |
| | | • The majority of the events and/or actions are appropriate for the established context. |
| | | • Supporting details are appropriate, general, and may be predictable. |
| | | • The writing generally holds the reader's interest. |
| 2 | Does Not Clearly Meet the Acceptable Standard | • The context is vaguely established and may not be sustained. |
| | | • Some of the events and/or actions are appropriate for the established context. |
| | | • Supporting details are few and/or may be repetitive. |
| | | • The writing does not hold the reader's interest. |
| 1 | Clearly Below the Acceptable Standard | • The context may be unclear and/or not sustained. |
| | | • There are few events and/or actions. |
| | | • Supporting details are scant. |
| | | • The writing is confusing and/or frustrating for the reader. |
| INS | INSUFFICIENT | • The student has written so little that it is not possible to assess the content. |

Note: *Content* and *Organization* are weighted to be worth twice as much as the other categories.

Source: Alberta Education (1998), *Information Bulletin, 1998–99: Grade Six*. Edmonton: Alberta Education, Student Evaluation Branch. Reprinted with permission of the Minister of Learning, Province of Alberta, Canada, 1999.

**Table 9.3**    Alberta Education Grade 6 Descriptors for Content (Functional Writing)

| Focus | |
|---|---|
| When marking CONTENT appropriate for Grade 6 functional writing, the marker should consider<br><br>• effectiveness of development and organization of the topic<br>• how the purpose of the assignment is fulfilled with complete and appropriate information<br>• appropriateness of tone and awareness of audience | |
| 5  Meets the Standard of Excellence | • The development of topic is clearly focussed and effective.<br>• Complete information is presented, and this information is enhanced by precise and appropriate details that effectively fulfil the purpose.<br>• An appropriate tone is clearly and effectively maintained. |
| 4  Approaches the Standard of Excellence | • The development of topic is generally focussed and effective.<br>• Complete information is presented, and this information is substantiated by appropriate details that fulfil the purpose.<br>• An appropriate tone is clearly maintained. |
| 3  Clearly Meets the Acceptable Standard | • The development of topic is adequate.<br>• Sufficient information is given, and this information is supported by enough detail to fulfil the purpose.<br>• An appropriate tone is generally maintained. |
| 2  Does Not Clearly Meet the Acceptable Standard | • The development of topic is vaguely focussed and ineffective.<br>• Essential information may be missing. Supporting details are scant, insignificant, and/or irrelevant. The purpose is only partially fulfilled.<br>• An appropriate tone is evident but not maintained. |
| 1  Clearly Below the Acceptable Standard | • The development of topic, if present, is inadequate.<br>• Essential information and supporting details are inappropriate or lacking. The purpose is not fulfilled.<br>• Little awareness of appropriate tone is evident. |
| INS INSUFFICIENT | • The marker can discern no evidence of an attempt to fulfil the assignment, or the writing is so deficient in length that it is not possible to assess content. |

Note: *Content* and *Content Management* are equally weighted.

Please advise students that their work must be related to the assignment. Writing that is completely "off topic" will be awarded an Insufficient.

Source: Alberta Education (1998), *Information Bulletin, 1998–99: Grade Six*. Edmonton: Alberta Education, Student Evaluation Branch. Reprinted with permission of the Minister of Learning, Province of Alberta, Canada, 1999.

- Sentence type and length are consistently effective and varied.
- Sentence beginnings are varied.

*Vocabulary*

- Words and expressions are used accurately and effectively.
- Specific words and expressions are used to create vivid images and/or to enrich details.

*Conventions*

- The quality of the writing is enhanced because it is essentially error-free.
- Errors, if present, do not reduce the clarity or interrupt the flow of the communication.

As a demonstration, Box 9.1 presents an excerpt from a piece of writing by a Grade 6 student, together with an evaluation of the piece based on the above criteria.

---

**Box 9.1    Zulu**

They came over to me talking in soft mumbling sounds that I couldn't understand. I backed into the corner of the stall and watched as they brought out a small harness. The creature reached out a hand and stroked my neck.

"He's a big one Alana, are ya still sure you want 'im?" One asked, obviously refering to me.

"Yes, the bigger they are the higher they jump."

The first speaker stepped forward and held out the soft leather thing, which they called a halter, for me to smell. It had no scent but I drew my head back and turned away. I looked for my mother, she was watching, but did nothing. The one they called Alana took the halter and slipped it over my head. I shook my head, not liking this thing tight on my face. I ran around the stall and rubbed my face on the rough wood of the wall.

"He's a spirited one alright." Henry said (The first one)

"Yeah, I don't intend to break that." Alana commented

"What are you going to call him?"

"Well his sire is Zulu Royaal and then his mother is Gotoit, so his name is Go to it Zulu. A pretty good name I think."

Henry came over, took hold of the halter and rubbed my ears. His hands were strong and gentle, I now knew why my mother was kind to these creatures.

A week passed. I got used to the halter and lead rope. I saw Henry and Alana each day. I asked my mother about them. She told me that Alana was her master and mine too. She said that I was to do what Henry and Alana wished me do and never to kick or bite. They have big plans for you, she would say, you will become great one day, till then you must do as they say.

When they came into the stall I could tell that there was something different about them. Not as happy. Alana came over to me right away and rubbed my nose and ears. I sniffed at her pockets as I had seen my mother do. She patted my side and slipped the halter over my head. I had grown much stronger over the last few days and loved to play tug'a'war with the shank. I looked at my mother, who I still would not move far from, Henry had put a halter on her too. I knew something was different today.

**Analysis**

*Content.* The piece of writing demonstrates a strong voice. Written as a first-person narrative, its details and description create an immediate engagement with the central character, a horse. The vivid description is enhanced by the use of dialogue. Rather than telling the reader that Zulu is a large horse, the writer demonstrates it in Henry's comment: "*He's a big one Alana, are ya still sure you want 'im?*" The reader is also forewarned of coming events through Alana's response: "*Yes, the bigger they are the higher they jump.*" The entire excerpt from the story is focussed on the events in the stall, and the early breaking of the young horse and his introduction to the harness. There are no extraneous details, no irrelevant content. The reader's interest is captivated and sustained.

*Organization.* The introduction is interesting and clearly establishes a setting and a point of view. The events of the story are arranged in paragraphs in a coherent sequence and are clearly connected, creating a cohe-

*(continued)*

**Box 9.1   Continued**

sive piece of writing. The unfolding of events reveals the horse's character and situation, and the ending ties events together, as well as foreshadowing the events of the next chapter.

*Sentence structure.* The sentence structure is effectively controlled, with a variety of sentence lengths and types from co-ordination (*"I backed into the corner of the stall and watched as they brought out a small harness"*) to subordination (*"The first speaker stepped forward and held out the soft leather thing, which they called a halter, for me to smell"*). There are no sentence fragments or run-on sentences. The sentence beginnings are varied (*"When they came into the stall, ..."*).

*Vocabulary.* Words and expressions such as *halter, shank,* and *lead rope* are used accurately. The vocabulary is varied and colourful. Words such as *mumbling, creative, scent,* and *spirited* create vivid images and add to the rich detail presented in the piece.

*Conventions.* The conventions of written language are of a high standard and the piece is enhanced because it is vitually error-free. Quotation marks are used appropriately, as are question marks and periods. Paragraphs are well-formed, and the indentation of paragraphs and direct speech is formatted correctly. Occasionally dialect is used, and appropriate punctuation is used to mark this (as in *'im*). There are numerous commas where periods or semicolons would have been more appropriate, but this does not reduce the clarity or break up the flow of the text (*"I looked for my mother, she was watching, but did nothing"*). This usage is likely connected to the reading the student has done. The writer's favourite book was *Black Beauty* by Anna Sewell, originally published in 1877. *Black Beauty* uses a more old-fashioned style, with the frequent use of commas to break up the text, rather than periods or semicolons.

## Process or Performance Assessment

The shift in teaching writing, from a product to a process orientation, has created a similar shift in assessment strategies. Educators understand that when children's writing is assessed, observations of the general writing behaviours of the students are to be included, not only of the written products.

### Profiles and Checklists

One of the most thorough and useful guides to performance assessment is in the *English Profiles Handbook* published by the Department of School Education in Victoria, Australia (1991). In this book (p. 65), nine "bands" of writing development have been identified to include Grades 1 through 9. The bands range through the following levels:

a) Knows that you say something when you write. Is curious about print and beginning to find out what it means.
e) Able to plan, organize, and polish own writing. Can write in paragraphs using vocabulary and grammar suited to the topic. Writes convincing stories.
i) Is a skilled writer, able to produce text in many forms. Writing can be powerful and evocative.

Each band is then described in more detail, with suggestions as to how data can be collected through writing conferences, writing sessions, discussion with parents, samples in writing folders, written conversations, the publishing and presenting of writing, proofreading, editing, and note-taking. A collection of

Teacher reviewing and discussing a child's writing.

observations about each child can be organized under the headings of "what the writer does," "what the writing shows," and "use of writing." A companion volume from the Ministry of Education, Victoria, Australia, and a most useful book to have in any professional library, is *The English Language Framework P–10*, (1988) which clearly outlines growth points in writing.

Teacher Stephen Leppard (1991) developed a reading–writing continuum designed to record the developing writing abilities of children as they pass from kindergarten to Grade 3. A copy of the continuum for each child is passed along from the teacher of one grade to the next throughout the primary years. The list of descriptors can be read, and any that pertain to an individual child at that time can be highlighted. Each assessment period (three to four months) is noted in a different-coloured highlighting pen. Thus, over a period of time, the child's progress is revealed as the different colours flow through the continuum. An excerpt from the continuum is presented in Table 9.4. The continuum is easy to use and convenient for teachers, since the observations have only to be recorded by highlighting certain characteristics.

McKenzie and Tompkins (1984) developed a writing process checklist that covers all the phases of writing, as shown in Table 9.5. The checklist can be modified by individual teachers to reflect aspects of the writing process that they believe are important or that better meet the needs of the children in their classrooms.

**Table 9.4    Writing Continuum**

**Individual Writing Stages**

**1. Take-Off Stage**

- Can write name.
- Excited about writing.
- Wants to write (stories, lists, letters, or ideas).
- Need not rely on patterning.
- Invented (temporary) spelling becomes closer to standard.
- Writing is more meaning-centred.
- Can pick out words that are spelled incorrectly.
- Understands that each letter is a representation of a sound (phonetic understanding).
- Use of characters is moving closer to standard form.
- Sound correspondence more complete.
- Sound features of words are represented according to the child's hearing and articulation (leads to omission of pre-consonant nasal, e.g., *NUBRS — numbers*).
- Realizes that print can conserve a thought statement permanently.

**2. Independent Writing**

- Writes stories with some sense of story structure.
- Awareness of grammar and language conventions.
- Spelling is near standard OR spelling deteriorates because more complex words are being used.
- Understands that vowels are included in every word.
- Understands that vowels are included in every syllable.
- Vowels may be used inappropriately (e.g., *MEAK — make*).
- Developing a sense of punctuation.
- Developing an ability and desire to self-edit some corrections (spelling, simple sentence structure).
- Written work can be carried over, or continued, the next day.
- May begin to understand the inconsistencies within the English language.

Source: S. Leppard (1991), "A Reading–Writing Continuum." In *Program Continuity: The Positive Link.* @ Access: The Education Station. Reprinted with permission.

**Table 9.5**    Checklist of Writing Processes

| Student | Dates | | | | | |
|---|---|---|---|---|---|---|
| **Prewriting** | | | | | | |
| Can the student identify the specific audience to whom he/she will write? | | | | | | |
| Does this awareness affect the choices the student makes as he/she writes? | | | | | | |
| Can the student identify the purpose of the writing activity? | | | | | | |
| Does the student write in a topic that grows out of his/her own experience? | | | | | | |
| Does the student engage in rehearsal activities before writing? | | | | | | |
| **Drafting** | | | | | | |
| Does the student write rough drafts? | | | | | | |
| Does the student place a greater emphasis on content than on mechanics in the rough drafts? | | | | | | |
| **Revising** | | | | | | |
| Does the student share his/her writing in conferences? | | | | | | |
| Does the student participate in discussions about classmates' writing? | | | | | | |
| In revising, does the student make changes to reflect the reactions and comments of both teacher and classmates? | | | | | | |
| Between first and final drafts, does the student make substantive or only minor changes? | | | | | | |
| **Editing** | | | | | | |
| Does the student proofread his/her own papers? | | | | | | |
| Does the student help proofread classmates' papers? | | | | | | |
| Does the student increasingly identify his/her mechanical errors? | | | | | | |
| **Publishing** | | | | | | |
| Does the student publish his/her writing in an appropriate form? | | | | | | |
| Does the student share this finished writing with an appropriate audience? | | | | | | |

Source: G. Tompkins (1990), *Teaching Writing: Balancing Process and Product*, p. 211. Columbus, OH: Merrill. Reprinted with permission. Originally published in L McKenzie and G. Tompkins (1984), "Evaluating Students' Writing: A Process Approach," *Journal of Teaching Writing, 3*, pp. 201–202.

## Portfolio Assessment

**Portfolio assessment** is a form of process or performance evaluation. The aim is not to take one piece of writing in isolation, but to look at a collection of children's writings in many forms and voices. A portfolio might include stories, poems, letters, journal entries, lists, semantic maps, responses to literature, book reviews, artwork associated with the language arts, puppets, and writing from across the curriculum. In this way, children can see their writing as more than separate, isolated pieces. Portfolios also give children the opportunity to self-evaluate in choosing what they wish to put into the portfolio. A portfolio is not the same as a writing folder. A writing folder contains work-in-progress, some finished work, and topics that might be the bases for future pieces. A portfolio should be carefully put together to show what a student can do. The portfolio might be a flat-bottomed paper bag that the child has decorated, or it might be a concertina folder that expands to accommodate objects other than sheets of paper. Published books and reports might go into the portfolio, as well as comments from peers who have read or heard pieces written by the student.

Farr and Tone (1994) provide many suggestions for developing and assessing portfolios. Among them is that teachers look at the volume of work in the portfolio, the interest and attitudes of the writers, and, of course, the development and growth of the writing. Here the criteria outlined earlier in this section on content, organization, vocabulary, sentence structure, and conventions will be useful. Farr and Tone also suggest how teachers can use portfolios to aid them in their instruction. An example of one teacher's comments on a child's portfolio is presented in Table 9.6.

**Table 9.6**   **Assessing the Contents of a Portfolio**

| What the Teacher Notices in Portfolio | What That Suggests |
|---|---|
| Hillary's writing compares her little brother to the little brother in Judy Blume's *The Pain and the Great One*. | She likes stories that relate fairly directly to things that are happening in her life. |
| There is little fluency and connection in pieces of writing in Keith's portfolio. | There is very little evidence that Keith thinks much about a topic before he begins writing. |
| This fifth-grade boy reads one comic book after another and does not record them all on his logs. Most are the funny type; many are about Garfield. | I will look for some humorous stories about cats for him to read — perhaps with a character as ornery as Garfield. |
| Anders has a note attached to two mysteries he has written, saying they are his favourites. He also has indicated on his log that an adventure story he wrote is his best because "it is exciting." There is not a large amount of writing in the portfolio, though. | I need to develop more opportunities for Anders to write. The adventure is a good story; perhaps if he shared it with some fellow students and saw how they enjoyed it, he would be encouraged. |
| Tad doesn't write a lot, but he draws well and his classmates consider him the best artist in the class. His journal, which is spotty, is mainly about sports heroes. He also writes reviews about scary movies he has seen. | I will ask Tad if he wants to be the sports editor on the next issue of the class newspaper. He could also illustrate one of his friend Adam's stories and perhaps write a sequel to it. I will see if he might like to read *Joe Montana and Jerry Rice* by Richard J. Brenner and the mystery *Is Anybody There?* by Eva Bunting. Another book I can recommend to him is *Scary Stories to Chill Your Bones* by Alvin Schwartz. He could review the ones he reads for the paper and/or for the bulletin board. |
| Heriyadi's story "A Pizzaman's Adventure" is a string of events that happen to a delivery person. It uses the same character names as in his story "The City Street." Both of these stories have stringy plots but are very rich in details that build and build are offering the reader a complete picture of the character. | There is keen evidence that Heriyadi is thinking about what he writes and its impact on his reader. It's as if he keeps wanting to ensure that the picture is really complete enough for his viewers to see it as he does. |

*(continued)*

**Table 9.6**   Continued

| What the Teacher Notices in Portfolio | What That Suggests |
|---|---|
| There are no obvious sources for Benny's writing about bats and Thanksgiving. There are numerous accurate details about bats. He details the familiar feast in describing Thanksgiving. | Benny appears to have used background knowledge in writing.<br><br>The student uses familiar things. |
| The student wrote "Ghost Story" about witches and cats because it was Halloween and he wanted something appropriate. He also has many cats at home.<br><br>Harold's "Snow Day" is about sledding, eating snow, and building a snowman. It ends with a question asking readers what they remember about snowy days. | He seems to be very audience-conscious in this piece. He anticipates that the things he likes about snow will also be what the audience likes, but he has to ask to check it out. |

Source: R. Farr and B. Tone (1994), *Portfolio and Performance Assessment: Helping Students Evaluate Their Progress as Readers and Writers.* ©1994 by Harcourt Brace & Co.. Reprinted by permission of the publisher.

A general assessment of the portfolio can also be made using the organizational outline adopted by the Department of School Education in Victoria, Australia (1991). An example of how this might be done is demonstrated below (p. 73):

*What the writer does:* Shaun edits work to a point where others can read it. He corrects common spelling errors, punctuation, and grammatical errors, especially when he reads his pieces aloud to peers. He develops ideas into paragraphs and uses a dictionary or thesaurus to extend and check his writing vocabulary.

*What the writing shows:* Sentences have ideas that flow. Paragraphs have a cohesive structure. Shaun shows the ability to argue and persuade. The messages in his expository and persuasive writing can be identified by others, but sometimes information is omitted. Brief passages are written with clear meaning, accurate spelling, and appropriate punctuation. Shaun can shift appropriately from first to third person in his writing. He consistently uses the correct tense in his writing. He uses compound sentences with conjunctions. His vocabulary is appropriate for a familiar audience such as peers, younger children, or adults, but he occasionally chooses an inappropriate word. Shaun has a consistent handwriting style, and when using the word processor, he uses a variety of fonts and print styles appropriate for the task.

*Use of writing:* Shaun creates characters from his imagination and makes appropriate use of narrative and other forms of writing. He writes properly sequenced narratives with convincing settings.

Robert Piccott, a Grade 6 teacher at Michael Wallace School in Dartmouth, Nova Scotia, describes how he uses portfolio assessment:

Portfolio assessment assists me in evaluating student progress, but most importantly, it challenges students to research their own learning. The students keep a photocopy box, which they use to house their portfolios. These boxes are divided into subject areas. Each week we have a portfolio update time, when students are asked to select from their works and add to their portfolio. I developed a form that the children must complete before including selections in the portfolio. I also include other reading and writing inventories, which the children re-do from time to time so they can assess how their reading and writing behaviours are changing. Each box has a chart on the cover showing all the different activities we do in our classroom. I ask the students to try to add a wide variety of items to their portfolios, and they use the chart on the cover as a guide in doing this.

The students include only those items they feel are their best work. They may include anything, so long as they can justify why they chose it. Periodically, I hold a conference with each student to help them reflect and set goals for the coming weeks.

Twice each year I conduct parent–teacher–student conferences that last between thirty minutes and one hour. The onus is on the child to demonstrate progress through discussion of the work in the portfolio. At this time, we set goals for the coming months. These goals are specific in nature and based on what the students feel they need to work on. The students identify an assessment component so we know how they are moving toward fulfilling the goals. Highly positive in nature, these conferences are a time to celebrate student-perceived successes.

Through discussion, writing, and reflecting, portfolio assessment helps children become better thinkers and communicators. More importantly, they learn to take responsibility for their own learning.

The last sentence captures the essence of portfolio assessment. It is not something teachers do *to* children but rather *with* them. Portfolio assessment in Robert Piccott's classroom is a reflection of holistic, constructive language learning and teaching in action.

The assessment strategies we have discussed are designed to provide teachers with information about all major aspects of children's writing. In constructivist classrooms such as Robert Picott's or Ms. Hwang's, instructional decisions are based primarily on this information. In general, teachers use a variety of instructional contexts to respond to their student writers. Table 9.7 presents an overview of three of those contexts and the learning outcomes associated with them.

**Table 9.7** Instructional Contexts and Learning Outcomes

| Context | Outcomes |
| --- | --- |
| Writing Conference | • extend or focus ideas<br>• clarify and organize thinking<br>• support productive ideas and directions<br>• extend vocabulary |
| Editing Conference | • strengthen sentence structure<br>• improve spelling, punctuation, and capitalization<br>• enhance format and presentation<br>• self-correct grammar and usage |
| Direct Instruction (whole class or small group) | • improve spelling<br>• refine presentation skills (handwriting, formatting)<br>• extend organizational schema<br>• reinforce grammar and usage |

The major categories of writing composition identified and assessed by large-scale assessments (content, organization or development, sentence structure, vocabulary, and conventions) provide a useful framework for instruction. They give teachers a lens through which they can view student writing *and* their own instruction. The areas of content and organization or development are best taught through the process of writing, through the interactions that occur during the writing conferences conducted in a writing workshop (see Chapter Seven).

Vocabulary and sentence structure are areas of the language arts that are also most effectively taught and learned in the context of a child's talking, reading, and writing. There are occasions, however, where direct teaching of sentence structure is helpful to students. Chapter Two of this text addresses the development of vocabulary as well as the development and refinement of sentence structure. Sentence structure and word usage are addressed again under the teaching of grammar later in this chapter. The teaching of spelling, capitalization, and punctuation is directly addressed in the next sections of this chapter.

## Teaching Spelling

### The Development of Spelling Abilities

No aspect of the school curriculum is more researched and tested than spelling ability. Some of the very first educational research was conducted in spelling— whether children could spell specific words correctly or not, and which method of instruction was the most effective. Loomer (1978) compiled an impressive overview of research in the teaching of spelling, describing studies dating back to 1913, none of them particularly conclusive. During the 1970s, a major shift occurred in research in the teaching of spelling, moving away from measuring children's spelling abilities and the efficacy of a chosen instructional method, to exploring how children develop the ability to spell correctly and the factors that affect their development. Is correct spelling tied to reading ability? Do word lists and frequent spelling tests help children become better spellers? Do children learn correct spelling as they read and write?

### Invented Spelling

Children's very early writing attempts demonstrate what is known as "invented spelling." Much research has been conducted in the area of invented spelling (Beers and Henderson, 1977; Gentry, 1978, 1981; Templeton, 1979; Zutell, 1979), particularly on how children move from invented to more conventional spelling. Invented spelling was a controversial aspect of language arts education for many years, mainly because some educators felt that invented spelling should not be encouraged in classrooms. It is now known that invented spelling is part of the developmental progression children make as they journey toward mastering orthodox spelling. What remains controversial is how long children should be encouraged to use invented spelling, and just when and how teachers should begin to teach conventional spelling. Children's use of invented spelling occurs as a result of children listening acutely to the spoken language they hear around them. Young children are particularly sensitive to the sounds of words, and as they attempt to encode words into print, they try to put the sounds they hear into symbol form (Read, 1975).

During the process of acquiring orthodox spelling abilities, children generally move through five major stages of invented spelling. The process can last from age 3 or 4 through to age 11 or 12 (the Grade 5 or 6 level) and even into adulthood for some people. Before the age of 3, most children draw and make letter shapes, but their attempts are not usually referred to as spelling, though it is recognized that these young learners are indeed "writing."

The five stages of invented spelling are

1. *Prereading or precommunicative spelling.* This stage of invented spelling consists of the random orderings of whatever letters children can draw. There is no awareness of sound–symbol relationship, and so strings of letters such as Beth's writing (in Exhibit 9.1) of *REaEoEfa aogrt NOCe baEONOEOLE* might appear on the page. Children may have their own "meaning" to go along with the letters, and may tell a coherent story to accompany them. An adult might transcribe this story onto the same page as the child's print. In Beth's case, her mother transcribed the message "I like Santa's mustache. I got my Christmas tree up last night." At this stage, Beth has no knowledge that specific configurations of letters and words are needed to create meaningful print. However, she does have a firm grasp of the message concept — that what is written on a page signifies a particular meaning.

**Exhibit 9.1    Beth's Prereading Spelling**

2. *Prephonetic or semiphonetic spelling.* In this stage, children have a primitive concept of the alphabet and of letter names, and so letter names are used as clues in spelling. Children in this stage might write *NHR* for "nature," or represent a whole word with one letter, usually an initial consonant. Rarely are vowels used; a child's spelling in this stage consists almost entirely of consonants. Ian's writing, shown in Exhibit 9.2, is moving into the **phonetic** stage, but much of his spelling still reflects semiphonetic elements, as in his spelling of *GRL* for "girl" and *JWP* for "jump."

3. *Phonetic spelling.* This is the stage most commonly seen in students from kindergarten through Grade 3. Children have an understanding of sound–symbol correspondence, but they represent the features of words according to how they themselves hear and articulate the words. This often leads to the omission of preconsonant nasals, such as the *M* in *NUBERS* or the *N* in *SWIMIG*. Exhibits 9.3, 9.4, and 9.5 illustrate children's spelling during this stage.

4. *Transitional spelling.* In the second through fourth grades, children generally include a vowel in every syllable and use familiar spelling patterns, though they are frequently used incorrectly. The word "make" may be spelled as *maek,* or "was" as *whas.* Rules are overgeneralized, and the aspects of spelling a child is currently learning become obvious through error patterns in the writing. In Exhibit 9.6, the writer spells "witch" as *wich,* and in Exhibit 9.7, "came" is spelled *caem.* Children also use the meanings of words to help them spell. One child wrote a note to his mother who was attending university at the time: "I hope you have a good time at youknowvursdy." There is no

**Exhibit 9.2**    Ian's Prephonetic Spelling

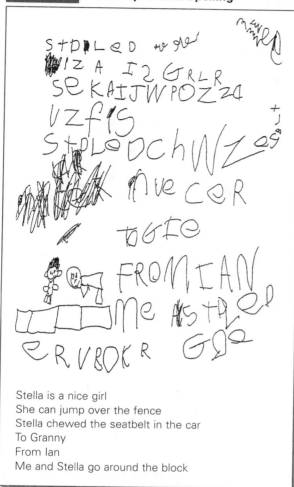

Stella is a nice girl
She can jump over the fence
Stella chewed the seatbelt in the car
To Granny
From Ian
Me and Stella go around the block

**Exhibit 9.3**    Omar's Phonetic Spelling

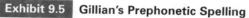

The one with the spider and the turtle.

**Exhibit 9.4**    Hannah's Phonetic Spelling

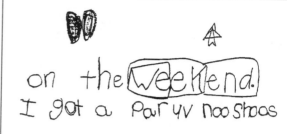

On the weekend I got a new pair of shoes.

**Exhibit 9.5**    Gillian's Prephonetic Spelling

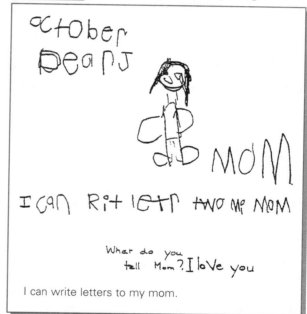

I can write letters to my mom.

doubt that he understood that university is a place where people come "to know." Exhibits 9.6, 9.7, and 9.8 show the transitional spelling of writers in Grade 2. These students are exploring the nature of spelling conventions such as the use of *ch*, the *ed* suffix, *ck*, and silent vowels (*caem* for "came") and are developing a core vocabulary of standard spellings (*I, my, the, on*).

5.  *Standard spelling.* Generally, at about Grade 5 or later, children demonstrate a more sophisticated understanding of spelling. They understand the constraints of syntax and morphology on their spelling (i.e., the conventions of spelling), and they use dictionaries to assist in correct spelling. Children at this age have learned

| Exhibit 9.6 | April's Transitional Spelling |
| --- | --- |

My favourite part was when the witch kissed Thistle.

| Exhibit 9.7 | Zak's Transitional Spelling |
| --- | --- |

When pig blew up and the family came out of pig's stomach.

| Exhibit 9.8 | Michael's Transitional Spelling |
| --- | --- |

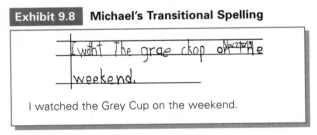

I watched the Grey Cup on the weekend.

that correct spelling is a courtesy to the reader, as well as necessary for expressing meaning clearly to an audience.

Although these stages appear to be a natural progression for most children, the question remains as to how and when conventional spelling should be encouraged or required in classrooms. The answer is that spelling always counts, and conventional spelling can always be encouraged — but young children must first of all be helped to compose their own texts before they are *required* to adhere to the conventions of written language. In addition, it is important that teachers and caregivers focus on the words children use in their writing most frequently — words such as *I, was, and,* and *but.*

Much standard spelling can be taught during editing conferences, but some children need a more structured approach to learning conventional spelling. When adults write in journals or write letters to friends, even their spelling may not be 100 percent correct. What is important in these cases is that they make an effort to spell correctly so they can communicate with themselves (through the journal) or friends (through letters). When focussing on spelling in children's writing, it is helpful for teachers and parents to keep in mind the audience and the purpose for the writing. There are many occasions when the message to be conveyed is more important than correct spelling, especially if the piece is to be read by a limited audience.

Teachers and parents can, however, help students to become better spellers by being mindful of the things that *good* spellers do, emphasizing these behaviours in their children. Most of the time good spellers do the following:

- Recall spelling patterns and generalizations they have learned through their reading and writing.
- Know about words and how to use them.
- Have a repertoire of spelling strategies to choose from and do not rely only on one or two strategies.
- Know which is the best strategy to apply in which situation.
- Do not rely on sounding out words (too unreliable).
- Do not rely on spelling "rules" (again, too unreliable).
- Use visual memory in conjunction with other strategies.

In summary, good spellers *think* about their spelling and do not rely on rote memorization.

## Teaching Spelling in the Context of the Writing Process

Many children develop competency in standard spelling entirely through reading, writing, and sharing their writing with an interested audience. However, standard spelling does require effort to master; it is a discipline to be learned. An awareness of the need for correct spelling can be taught from Grade 2 onward. It is easy for any writer to become lazy about spelling, but it is essential for a committed writer to adhere to conventional forms. Habits formed in childhood often persist into adulthood, though usually adults have only one or two major error patterns in their spelling. For some, the error pattern will be confusion over double consonants (words such as *embarrass*); for others it will be problems with reversing letters, or omitting letters in a word (e.g., *contain* spelled as *contian* or *cotain*). Once adult writers become aware of the nature of their spelling difficulties, they can make efforts to learn the specific words they have difficulty with, usually words such as *embarrassment* or *containment*.

Teachers can help their students learn conventional spelling by conducting regular brief lessons using the overhead projector, focussing attention on common misspellings, and encouraging children to watch for these specific words in their spelling that particular week. More idiosyncratic misspelling can be addressed in writing conferences, but usually not until a piece is ready for a final draft unless the word is an unusual one for the child to write (e.g., *cornucopia* and *satellite*). This also applies to errors in capitalization, punctuation, and grammar. In elementary school, teachers rarely focus lengthy language arts lessons on these aspects of writing, nor do they provide worksheet exercises for the students to complete. The skills are more likely to be addressed in the context of the students' current writing, and through brief lessons interspersed with other activities.

Lessons of ten minutes' duration are usually more effective than drills and worksheet pages of exercises. It is the context of the usage and the relevance to the child that make an impact on their learning. Skills learned out of context are rarely transferred to writing completed in workshops or to writing done across curricular areas. If a number of children in the class have problems in one specific area, a group can be formed so that the teacher can give direct instruction to those who need it. There is no point in teaching to a whole class if only a few children really need to learn that skill. Through reading children's writing, and through listening to the talk children engage in while they write, teachers can gain much useful knowledge about who needs to be taught certain skills and who has already mastered them.

The presence of spell-check tools on computer word-processing programs provides both advantages and disadvantages for students. Before working with the tools, students need guidance in using them effectively and appropriately. Students can be encouraged to use the tool as a first step in eliminating typographical errors and in identifying misspelled words. Following this, students must check for homonyms and homophones. Which word did they actually intend to use? The computer does not make distinctions of this nature and will not catch such misspellings. Here, the spell-check tool provides an interesting focus for instruction, teaching students an awareness of homonyms and homophones as spelling items *and* teaching young writers not to rely on computer spell-checkers completely. Many spell-check tools have an "auto-correct" feature that individual children (or the class as a collaborative whole) might want to program with their own frequent misspellings. Again, this process provides a vehicle for instruction as students identify their common misspellings and focus their attention on them.

Following are some specific strategies for aiding students in their spelling development:

- Ask students to write on every other line of a paper so that they can make changes without rewriting or erasing.
- Encourage writers to leave blank spaces for words they do not know how to spell. It is important that thoughts continue to flow; omitted words can be inserted later. Students can be encouraged to write the first few letters of the omitted word so they will have a greater chance of remembering which word they had intended to use.
- Note spelling errors by putting an asterisk in the margin of students' writing. Ask the students to find the errors themselves. Children can frequently recognize incorrect spelling, and in doing so they are reminded of the words they have difficulty in spelling.
- Encourage children to have paper at their desks so that words they are unsure of can be written down for them.
- Refrain from providing only an oral spelling of a word; always accompany it with a written model. Spelling is essentially a visual memory activity that is only conducted in writing. It is therefore important that students *see* the word they need help in spelling.
- Teach students how to use a dictionary, thesaurus, and other word books effectively, and encourage their use. A spelling dictionary is usually more effective for elementary school students than a conventional dictionary. A student who needs to spell *rein* will usually look under *ra* in a conventional dictionary, thus meeting with little success.
- Alphabet games help students to understand how dictionaries and encyclopedias are organized. Activities such as lining up in alphabetical order according to last name or first name also help children understand how to use telephone books and other reference aids.

## The Direct Teaching of Spelling

Research studies have demonstrated that new and different words enter the language on an ongoing basis. Dictionaries are updated regularly, but many of the new words they contain will appear in children's writing first. Ves Thomas (1979) showed that *more* words were used in children's writing in the late 1970s than were used 40 years before that time. Since 1979, language has changed enormously, largely through the advent of personal computers and video games. Children and adults use a whole new vocabulary every day; words such as *mouse, windows, Internet, microchip,* and *search engine* have new meanings. At the same time these words have entered the lexicon, there has been a shift in the way writing is taught in elementary schools. Children are encouraged to write about what they do and what they think, so more of the child's personal world has entered the classroom. Characters from video games appear in stories, and reference is frequently made to these games and to various computer programs that children have access to at home or at the video arcade. Teachers have to contend with a vocabulary in children's writing that is expanding and changing. This expanding vocabulary obviously causes an equal increase in the number of words children must learn to spell correctly. It may appear that children do not spell as well today as they did in the past, but it is also probable that children are using more words, are writing more, and are attempting to spell a greater range of words than in earlier times.

As mentioned previously, spelling is one of the most heavily researched areas of the curriculum, with research dating back to the very first part of the twentieth century. Spelling competence is easy to test; a word list can be dictated to a student, and the examiner can check to see whether or not the words are spelled correctly. However, it has been discovered that words spelled correctly on a word list do not necessarily transfer to a piece of writing created in a different context. It appears that unless the words have been internalized and become part of the stored knowledge a writer possesses, the spelling remains in doubt. Spelling a word correctly on a test list is no guarantee that the same word will be spelled correctly in a shopping list, a journal entry, a letter, or an essay.

One of the chief findings of this body of research (well documented by Loomer, 1978) is that teaching words through a spelling program in a textbook is generally ineffective. It is not the use of a word list, as such, that is ineffective, but the selection of words included on the list and the activities suggested for learning the words. In four different spelling series examined by Edwards (1983), words appeared at different grade levels in the four different books. For example, the word *party* was placed at a different grade level in each of the series, and ranged from placement at Grade 3 to Grade 6. Today, there is a tendency toward grouping words according to their spelling pattern or generalization (see the *Nelson Spelling Series*, De Sousa, 1998). There is still no research evidence, however, that this strategy is any more effective than grouping words according to frequency of use.

Spelling textbooks generally do not present the teaching of spelling in ways that are consistent with research findings about learning in general. The activities in spelling textbooks do not encourage risk-taking, a critical component of learning, and they encourage students to rely on rote memorization. Many of the activities are repetitious and rarely help poor spellers become strong spellers; the books often contain "busy" pages with mixtures of cartoon graphics, bold colours, and many different fonts. There are frequently so many different activities on one page that it is difficult to tell what is being taught. Activities range from crossword puzzles to "Alphaspell," "Noun Hunt," "Syllable Count," "Letter Ladders," and "Word Chains." Research has shown many times that the only real way to become an effective speller is to do lots of writing for audiences other than oneself, read widely, and check spelling in a dictionary or word book whenever there is doubt. Even the most recent spelling textbooks do not focus on *teaching* spelling, but focus instead on children's word games. Teachers must ask, "What am I teaching by doing these activities, and what else could I do with this time that would be more beneficial to my students in learning how to be good spellers?"

A number of good resources are available to assist teachers in helping their students become strong and independent spellers. These include *Spelling Strategies You Can Teach* by Mary Tarasoff (1990), *Spelling Instruction That Makes Sense* by Jo Phenix and Doreen Scott-Dunne (1991), and *Spelling: Sharing the Secrets* by Ruth Scott (1993).

Children are more likely to become effective spellers if their motives for using correct spelling stem from communicative needs rather than a desire to please the teacher. If children have something important to say, and they have an audience they wish to address, correct spelling will help them convey their message clearly to the reader. Correct spelling is a courtesy to the reader, and is also important in transmitting a clear message. Correct spelling adds to the writer's credibility. This is especially important for teachers, who are generally perceived as role models. Teachers are expected to spell every word correctly (if a word is spelled incorrectly on a wall chart or on the chalkboard, one can almost guarantee that a visiting teacher or parent will notice it!), and certainly teachers should not send to parents or the public any of their writing that has not been carefully checked for correct spelling.

## A Word List Approach

When employing a word list approach in the direct teaching of spelling, teachers ensure that they use

- a reliable word list created from either the words children in the classroom have difficulty spelling or from a reliable resource book such as Thomas (1979),
- a self-corrected pretest of ten to twelve words,
- a study procedure to ensure that children learn effective strategies for memorizing words,
- "check tests" with a buddy throughout the week,
- a mastery test of the entire list of words originally provided on day one, and
- a record of spelling achievement (on a chart at the back of the spelling scribbler).

### Word Lists

When a teacher has observed children's writing and has identified those students needing direct spelling instruction (which would rarely be more than half the class), a word list approach is usually effective. The word list compiled by Ves Thomas, found in his book *Teaching Spelling: Canadian Word Lists and Instructional Techniques* (1979), remains one of the most reliable and thorough resources for teachers today. The word lists in the book are based on the frequency of usage of words in children's writing in Canada, so that the most frequently used words are on the word list for the youngest children (Grade 2), and so on up through the grades. It is suggested that word lists and study procedures *not* be used with children before Grade 2.

If teachers choose to create their own word lists, they may base them on the spelling errors they notice in the students' writing in their classroom. The use of either a pre-existing list or a teacher-compiled list should provide an effective vehicle for students to study the correct spelling of words. It is not suggested that children learn spelling from lists of words compiled from current units of study across the curriculum. Words on such lists are usually used for only a short period of time, when the unit is being studied, and the words are not usually the most frequently used words in the students' writing in general. The most important factors in creating a word list are that the words be relevant to children's lives and be used regularly in their writing.

Many studies have been conducted on the most frequently used words in both adult and children's writing. It has been found that the most common 100 words used by elementary school children in their writing make up about 60 percent of all the words children write. The most common 500 words make up 70 percent of all words written, and the most common 2000 words make up 83 percent of all words written (Simpson, 1980). The average elementary school program teaches between 3500 and 4500 words over a five-year period. It is therefore essential that the words taught on those lists form part of a child's *core* spelling vocabulary. The remainder of the words children use in their writing have to be learned by memory from the simple experience of writing them and checking for correct spelling in dictionaries and other word books. Thomas's research finding (1979) that Canadian children are using an increasing number of words in their writing has implications for the teaching of spelling, since it is not possible to teach all these words by memory in the five years of an elementary school spelling program. Table 9.8 displays one well-known list of the 100 words most frequently written by children in elementary school (Carroll, Davies, and Richman, 1971).

## Self-Corrected Pretest

A word list is most effectively used when it is preceded by a self-corrected pretest. All the children in a spelling group are given a test *before* the words are presented to them in list form for study. This procedure allows children to identify which words they actually have difficulty spelling correctly. As children self-correct the pretest, they

**Table 9.8**    **The 100 Most Frequently Used Words in Children's Writing**

| | | | | |
|---|---|---|---|---|
| a | find | like | over | up |
| about | first | little | people | use |
| after | for | long | said | very |
| all | from | made | see | was |
| an | has | make | she | water |
| and | have | many | so | way |
| are | he | may | some | we |
| as | her | more | than | were |
| at | him | most | that | what |
| be | his | my | the | when |
| been | how | no | their | where |
| but | I | not | them | which |
| by | if | now | then | who |
| called | in | of | there | why |
| can | into | on | they | will |
| could | is | one | this | with |
| did | it | only | through | words |
| do | its | or | time | would |
| down | just | other | to | you |
| each | know | out | two | your |

Source: J. Carroll, P. Davies, and B. Richman, (1971), *American Heritage Word Frequency Book*. Boston: Houghton Mifflin. Adapted and reprinted by permission of the publisher.

become aware of the spelling errors they have made, and this feature alone allows most children to correctly spell the word the next time they use it. The self-corrected pretest is probably the single most effective strategy for improving spelling ability. It provides each child with an individualized list of words that need to be studied, because the words spelled correctly can be put aside until the end of the week. At that time, a mastery test will be given that includes all the words on the original list.

It is very important that children correct their own pretest, for much learning occurs while they check their spelling. Sometimes only two or three words might be incorrectly spelled, and at other times there may be as many as five or six. If a child is presented with more than five or six words to study in one week, it is usually too many to be learned effectively. Children who experience difficulty in spelling need to work with small amounts of material and short lists of manageable words. In the early grades, a pretest of ten words is usually sufficient. In upper elementary school, the list may include from ten to twelve words.

## Study Procedure

Words spelled incorrectly on the pretest are written out correctly and are used as a model for the study procedure (see Box 9.2). On the day following completion of the study procedure, students can work in pairs, giving each other buddy tests of their own personal spelling words. All students can benefit from learning a study procedure for spelling. There are many variations of study procedures, and if children do not have success with one version, they can try a modified version. For most children, the study procedure is a "key to the door" where successful spelling is concerned. Spelling is a visual memory task, and a good study procedure provides weak spellers with a concrete structure for their learning. A suggested study procedure is outlined in Box 9.2.

A sound study procedure eliminates the irrelevant and time-consuming activities sometimes found in spelling textbooks. It focusses the energies of the students on the direct learning of specific words that the individual finds difficult. There are likely to be occasions in the classroom when other methods of teaching spelling are necessary. For example, children with special needs may require alternative strategies that more specifically meet their learning requirements.

| **Box 9.2    Spelling Study Procedure** |
|---|
| 1. Look at the word, pronounce it, and say the letters (auditory and visual stimulation). |
| 2. Listen to the sounds and notice how they are represented (sound–symbol relationship). |
| 3. Close your eyes and try to see the word as you pronounce it (recall–visualization). |
| 4. Keep your eyes closed and say the letters in order. |
| 5. Open your eyes and check. |
| 6. Write the word without looking at the model. Check writing (kinesthetic recall). |
| 7. Write the word a second time and check it. |
| 8. Write the word a third time. If it's correct, consider it learned. |

## Mastery Test

A final mastery test given at the end of the week consists of the complete pretest list originally provided to the students at the beginning of the week. Spelling scores can be recorded on a chart at the back of a spelling scribbler so that children can track their own progress.

## Spelling Practices to Avoid

Over the years, educators have become aware that some teaching strategies have not proven helpful in assisting children with improving their spelling:

- Pointing out the "hard spots" in words may be helpful only to a small number of children, and the hard spots are likely to be different from one child to another.
- Teaching spelling rules is not effective, since very few spelling rules can be applied regularly. Sayings such as "*i* before *e* except after *c*" may be very useful to most writers, but if they are taught as rules, then words that do not follow the rules must also be pointed out (such as *weigh* and *neighbour*). It is more effective to teach how to add suffixes (e.g., *baby* becomes *babies*) than it is to teach specific spelling rules. Most rules have almost as many exceptions as adherents (Clymer, 1963).
- Avoid having students copy spelling lists as a punishment, which establishes a negative attitude toward spelling that is not helpful to children's feelings about writing in general. Educators strive to promote enthusiasm for writing and try not to detract from the joys of writing by making writing, or any other school activity, abhorrent to children.

## Teaching Grammar, Punctuation, and Capitalization

### Grammar

As discussed in Chapter Two, educators often use the terms "**grammar**" and "syntax" interchangeably. Syntax is the term linguists use to describe the organization of language structures. Grammar is a term teachers usually use to define a prescriptive set of rules to be followed. Syntax is derived from the spoken language, but when it is taught in schools, it usually pertains to writing and is labelled "grammar." Educators and researchers (such as Braddock, Lloyd-Jones, and Schoer, 1963) have long believed that grammar should not be taught in elementary schools in a formal manner. However, children need to know the difference between what is acceptable or appropriate and what is considered poor grammar. They also need a vocabulary to be able to talk about language if they are to engage in writing conferences and develop an awareness of the writing techniques good writers use. Three basic perspectives on grammar are presented in Box 9.3.

The teaching of grammar, usually based on the traditional, prescriptive model, was once perceived as a core feature of the elementary school curriculum. Today it is relegated to a somewhat minor role. Only a few decades ago, memorizing grammar rules, as well as poetry and quotations from plays, was believed to be good for the mind. The mind was conceptualized as a muscle, and memorization as good exercise for that muscle. Today, however, grammar is not taught as an end in itself, but as one of the tools to be used in the process of writing. Knowledge and control of grammar enables writers to strengthen their writing and clarify meaning, facilitating effective and precise communication. Correct and appropriate grammar also enables people to speak in a manner approaching "standard English," the form of English that conforms to established educated usage and is generally considered correct.

Studies in language development have shown that many concerns voiced by teachers about "grammar" are mostly concerns about usage, and usage depends on the dialect learned when children are young. A person's dialect can change when he or she moves from one area to another, or works among people speaking a closer approximation of standard English. However, the basic rules of grammar learned in childhood usually persist throughout life, and the majority of those rules are correct. By the age of 6, when most children enter school, they have already mastered most of the grammar of the language, as described in Chapter Two.

## Box 9.3     Three Perspectives on Grammar

Linguists describe the structure of language in three ways, and all three ways influence the way grammar is taught.

1. The best known is *traditional* or *prescriptive grammar*, which provides rules for socially correct usage. This perspective dates back to the Middle Ages and has its roots in the study of Latin. The major contribution of traditional grammar is in the terminology it provides for students and teachers to talk about language. Because this form of grammar is based on Latin, it is not entirely appropriate for use with the English language, as it cannot adequately explain how language works. However, the three elements of grammar continue to be taught and prove useful to writers as they work their craft—types of sentences (declarative, interrogative, imperative, exclamatory); parts of sentences (simple, compound, complex, compound–complex); and parts of speech (nouns, pronouns, verbs, adverbs, adjectives, prepositions, conjunctions, and interjections).

2. *Structural grammar* attempts to describe how language is used. Structural grammar is not prescriptive, but descriptive, and it highlights the differences between written and spoken language patterns. The study of structural linguistics has provided detailed information about language in use, but it focusses on form and does not attempt to relate meaning to usage. Seven basic sentence patterns are identified, and it is the variations and combinations of these seven patterns that make up all the sentences people speak or write.

3. *Transformational grammar* is the most recent approach to the study of grammar. Transformational linguists attempt to describe both the way language works *and* the cognitive processes used to produce language. They refer to two levels or structures of language (the surface structure and the deep structure) to describe how meaning in the brain is transformed into the actual sentences people speak. Much research and development work was conducted during the 1960s and 1970s to make this approach viable for use in classrooms.

A thorough exploration of grammar and its teaching can be found in G. Tompkins and K. Hoskisson's (1995) *Language Arts: Content and Teaching Strategies* (3rd ed.). Englewood Cliffs, NJ: Prentice-Hall.

Controversy has arisen in the past about whether dialect is part of a child's cultural heritage, and therefore to be protected and respected, or whether educators have the responsibility to teach children standard English so that all children will have a greater opportunity for success in higher education, business, and the professions. It is generally agreed, however, that grammar should be taught in school so that children learn to become effective writers and have the opportunity to move between dialect and standard English in speech.

It has been acknowledged for many years that teaching grammar in isolation from a child's actual writing is ineffective (Elley, Barham, Lamb, and Wyllie, 1976). Creating teaching units and providing worksheets on grammar have little effect on children's writing and speaking. More effective learning occurs when grammar is taught as part of the editing process of composition, and in brief lessons, when necessary. Children can sometimes detect grammatical errors in their compositions, especially if the flow of the language or the meaning is disturbed by the error. However, much of the time, children cannot detect their own grammatical errors because the writing makes sense to them.

As members of language communities, we accept certain phrases and incorrect usage as the norm, and it is difficult to teach children to change that usage. This is where a direct lesson is useful, because the whole group can focus on that particular item of usage and there is more likelihood that children will retain an awareness of it. One caution: students should, at no time, be embarrassed by their language usage. Language is an idiosyncratic part of every human being, and children (as well as adults) feel belittled if their language is criticized or faulted. Effective teachers handle this issue sensitively, aware that one dialect is not better than another, but different. Children can be taught that although it may be appropriate to say "I should've went" when they are playing with their friends, when they are in school their writing and oral language is expected to more closely adhere to standard English, and "I should have gone" is correct and appropriate.

A lesson on the differences in usage between *taught* and *learned*, *lent* and *borrowed*, or *seed* and *saw* might, for example, be necessary in some classrooms. A lesson on misplaced participles can be fun for children in the elementary years, as they can see the humour in sentences such as "I saw the lady walking down the hill with purple hair," and they enjoy figuring out why the sentence is ambiguous as well as how to fix it. It is through meaning that grammar can be taught most effectively, not through parsing sentences or learning definitions of parts of speech. Shelley Peterson has provided high-quality teacher resource material to support the Western Canada Protocol for the English Language Arts in her two books, *Becoming Better Writers* (1995) and *Teaching Conventions Unconventionally* (1997).

Knowledge of labels and definitions of parts of speech allows writers and speakers to talk about the language they are using. It is in this context that these items can be taught in school. In writing conferences and during the editing process, labels such as noun, adverb, and clause can be used. Through direct lessons they can be taught to the entire class. A brief ten-minute presentation, using examples on an overhead projector and involving the children in discussion, can be effective in reminding children about grammar and usage and in introducing certain concepts to children for the first time. Lengthy lessons with exercises on worksheets are generally not necessary. It *is* necessary, though, for children to learn these labels and their meanings so they can talk about their writing and hence improve it.

## Punctuation and Capitalization

Punctuation and capitalization are the "mechanics" of written language, just as intonation is of oral language. Writing conferences and short lessons are the most effective and appropriate vehicles for teaching the skills of punctuation and capitalization. As with grammar and word usage, worksheets of drill and skill exercises are not effective. During instruction, it is useful to refer children to the literature they are currently reading. Novels provide a quick reference for checking how direct speech, paragraphing, and the capitalization of names and places are addressed. Children often remember rules of capitalization and punctuation for a short time after they have been taught, but then forget to use them when they are composing and focussing on ideas.

Lessons are enhanced when teachers make them directly relevant to situations that affect the students—for example, through using samples of children's writing or questions children have raised themselves. It is a good idea to refer to these questions and honour their intent. Children who ask questions are the ones who want to learn. A lesson on using quotation marks might begin, for instance, with a problem raised by a student. Anne is writing a story and wants to use dialogue for two of the characters. She stops in her writing at "Who's going to run for help and who's going to stay here she asked." Anne does not know where to place the quotation marks. An overhead transparency of a comic strip can be used to demonstrate how quotation marks are used. Whenever the actual words spoken by a character are shown in a comic strip, they are inside a balloon. In a story, quotation marks are used instead of a balloon. Only the actual words spoken belong inside the quotation marks. The teacher can demonstrate this with a section of a story that includes dialogue printed on an overhead transparency (an overhead can easily be made of a page from a novel the children are familiar with). Working through Anne's original piece of student writing, the class can work with the teacher, putting in the quotation marks where they belong. As in many other learning situations, a collaborative approach is usually helpful for students, since they can engage with the problem as a group rather than in isolation. Instead of a follow-up exercise to see if the children have understood, it is more effective to observe the children's writing and remind them, when necessary, about the lesson. Lessons can be repeated, using different examples, whenever appropriate.

## Teaching Handwriting

It might appear, in the early years of the twenty-first century, that handwriting is a lost art. Certainly, the fine penmanship recognized in our grandparents is not evident in the handwriting of most students in today's classrooms. In fact, the focus of instruction has shifted from penmanship to composition. Yet legible handwriting is essential in today's world of computers just as much as it was 50 years ago. Although much writing is completed on a word processor, a great deal of what we write on a daily basis is still done by hand. Notes, jottings, journal entries, memos, and letters to friends are usually handwritten. Therefore, the need to teach handwriting in elementary school is still there, so that children can produce legible script with a minimum of *time, effort,* and *concentration* (the three criteria that are key to teaching handwriting). Students need to be able to read their own handwriting, and we all need to be able to read the handwriting of others.

Some points for teachers to remember:

- Students are greatly helped if they are taught to write in a way that is fluent, easy, routine, and comfortable.
- A teacher who pays little attention to handwriting is suggesting to students that handwriting is not important.
- The true test of handwriting is in situations where it is used on a day-to-day basis, doing such regular jobs as making lists, writing notes, leaving messages, and writing letters.
- In handwriting instruction, good teaching and modelling are essential, not just in the early grades, but throughout elementary school.
- A teacher's handwriting on the chalkboard, on wall charts, and on student work is a model for students of how letters are formed and what good writing looks like.

## The Perceptual Motor Approach

Handwriting is more than simply a motor skill, fine muscle co-ordination, and practice. Children have to remember letter forms, somehow internalizing them. This is where the term "perceptual motor skill" originates. Each child has to build a perception or mental image of each letter form. It is a thinking process as well as a fine motor process. The research in this area goes back to the 1960s, to the work of Bea Furner (1969).

Furner believed that a child must first have a clear concept of how each letter appears, saying out loud how each letter is formed, while at the same time drawing it.

**Box 9.4**  **Steps in Teaching the Perceptual Motor Approach to Handwriting**

- The teacher models handwriting instruction on the board (or an overhead projector). Clear lines are drawn on the board so that children can see the spacing of letters and the lines on which they are positioned.
- The teacher uses a consistent writing vocabulary such as *baseline, midline, headline,* and *tail-line.*
- As the teacher draws a letter on the board, he or she describes where the letter begins, the direction in which the hand moves, and the place where the letter ends.
- The children describe aloud the strokes the teacher is using as the teacher draws the letter again.
- The children draw the letter, saying aloud the description as they write, while being guided by the teacher.
- After the letter is completed, the children compare the letter they have drawn with a model already on paper at their desks.

The same process is used in teaching **cursive writing**, as well as for **manuscript printing**. Steps in the instructional process are described in Box 9.4.

A guided practice of the manuscript letter *d* might go as follows:

Pencil on the midline, go counterclockwise, round to the baseline, back up through the midline, up to the headline, retrace down to the baseline. Stop.

This would be repeated a number of times until the children begin to master the letter. A model on each child's desk provides immediate feedback as the child compares the written letter with the model. An example of one model is presented in Exhibit 9.9. The teacher attends to the number of strokes, the starting and stopping points, the direction of the strokes, and the size of the letters. The process should not be repeated more than five times during each practice session, or handwriting will lose quality — one good reason for not having children write lines or copy tedious work as a punishment.

**Exhibit 9.9**  **Model of Writing: S for Snoopy**

"S" starts like "c" c c c c

S S S

Words with "S."

Snoopy

Snoopy

Sentences with S

In the intermediate grades, children may not need handwriting lessons every week, but they do need them from time to time, when the teacher can see that some children are having difficulty with a certain letter or letter combination. A lesson on the overhead projector can result in improvements in children's awareness of their handwriting and in penmanship legibility. These lessons are sometimes referred to as "maintenance lessons."

Evaluation of handwriting considers

- the form and size of the letters,
- the spacing of letters and words,
- alignment according to headline and baseline, and
- uniformity of slant.

Many handwriting scales are available for evaluating handwriting, but most do not allow for individuality in writing style. The criteria listed above are usually sufficient for providing feedback to a student and for talking about ways in which handwriting can be improved.

## Helping the Left-Handed Writer

Approximately 10 percent of children in North America are left-handed. Although educators no longer insist that children write with their right hand (as was once the case), learning to write can still pose challenges for children who are left-handed. These children have unique instructional needs because of the nature of writing in the English language. English is written from left to right, thus creating a movement of the arm away from the body for right-handed children. Left-handed children physically move their arm toward their body as they write. In addition, as left-handed writers move their arm, they cover up what they have just written. Not only do they have no clear visual image of what they have written, but in covering up their writing they are also more likely to smudge their work and have further difficulty in rereading their script. Since the writing is covered by their hand, left-handed children cannot read their writing as they go, but have to stop and move their arm to reread their script.

Teachers can help left-handed children to write clearly and legibly without discomfort, developing a hand that requires a minimum of time, effort, and concentration. This is particularly important because, in order to produce clean copy and be able to read their work as they write, left-handed children frequently develop a "hooked" motion, curling their wrist over the top of the page and distorting the motions necessary to form letters. Left-handed writers may therefore require more one-on-one instruction from the teacher than right-handed writers, but sensitive teachers understand that this is necessary if the students are to be given the opportunity to develop handwriting that is legible, well-formed, evenly spaced, and with a uniform slant.

Here are some suggestions to help left-handed children at school and at home:

- Make sure the child is holding the pencil correctly — about 3 to 4 cm from the point and with the correct grasp by the fingers (i.e., farther away from the point than right-handed writers).
- Position the paper so that it is tilted downward at the right-hand side. This allows for an even slant and lets the child see what he or she has already written. Some teachers have found it helpful to place a piece of masking tape on the student's desk to indicate an appropriate tilt.
- Try to prevent the development of a "hooked" wrist — the habit of hooking the wrist around the writing — so as not to cover up what has been written.
- Seat the child so that light comes over the *right* shoulder and therefore the shadow of the hand does not fall on the writing.
- Provide children who need it with a lower desk surface to write on, or a cushion so that they can be higher in their seat and have a clearer view of their work.
- Do not insist on a slant to the right in letter formation. Many left-handed children write more effectively with a vertical formation.

## Printing and Cursive Handwriting

Two styles of handwriting are taught in elementary school: printing (also called manuscript writing) and cursive writing. Children generally begin with printing and toward the end of second grade or the beginning of third grade move into a cursive hand. The specific styles of each vary according to region and country. In North America there are a number of popular cursive styles, including D'Nealian (described below). Box 9.5 presents a comparison between traditional manuscript and cursive forms and D'Nealian script. While many provincial and state curricula have a model of handwriting to be followed, increasingly provincial departments of education are not providing a model script. Curriculum guides and programs of study should be consulted before any handwriting style is taught, as it is important that students have a consistent style across the grades.

Toward the end of Grade 2 many children are eager to begin cursive handwriting and will begin to make the transition on their own. Other children will not be comfortable with cursive script until well into Grade 3. Many children today are expressing a preference for continuing to print, some reverting to manuscript printing in the later grades. There is no particular reason why they should move into cursive handwriting other than that it is an accepted adult convention. One of the advantages of D'Nealian script is that it was developed specifically to make the transition from printing to handwriting easier for children. A simplified form that flows from manuscript to cursive with little change in letter forms, this script is extremely legible and easy to use. Most other styles of writing are more difficult for children, and specific lessons on individual letters have to be taught. Children working with D'Nealian or similar scripts usually move into using cursive writing toward the middle of Grade 2.

The perceptual motor approach can be used for teaching cursive writing in much the same way as outlined earlier with printing. However, a new vocabulary has to be used to describe the strokes necessary. Children beginning cursive writing become familiar with terms such as undercurve, overcurve, downcurve, and horizontal curve. These are the strokes necessary for linking letters to create a fluid handwriting style. The most difficult aspect of learning cursive handwriting for most children is forming capital letters. This is the area in which children generally need most guidance and

**Box 9.5    D'Nealian Script**

With D'Nealian, the formation, size, slant, and rhythm learned in first grade are continued and built upon in Grades 2 and 3. As a result, second and third graders don't have to "start all over" when they begin learning cursive forms.

Source: D'Nealian ® ALPHABET. Copyright © 1993, 1999 by Scott, Foresman. Reprinted by permission of Addison-Wesley Educational Publishers Inc.

practice. It is not unusual for adults to use a simplified version of cursive capital letters (and often they print them).

Handwriting habits formed in the early years of schooling frequently persist into adulthood. It is therefore essential that handwriting be taught effectively in the elementary school, with emphasis placed on legibility and comfort in writing. The example teachers set in their own handwriting has a great impact on children. Teachers' writing on the chalkboard should therefore be clear and legible, for just as with spelling, teachers are the primary models.

> The questions Asha posed to Ms. Hwang during her Grade 5 field experience provided a focus for her as she completed her final supervised teaching before embarking on her career. Critical aspects of Asha's learning included teaching the conventions of written language, helping students develop positive habits in their writing, and knowing how to assess student writing so that it could inform her instructional practices as well as inform students of their own learning. All teachers are required to assess student progress in school and keep a record of it. Even more valuable for teachers is knowing how to use that evaluative feedback to plan and implement instruction, tracking individual student needs and progress. Asha began to focus on the details of teaching: developing her handwriting on the chalkboard, monitoring her own spelling, listening to students talk about their writing, following individual compositions through the writing process, talking with students about their story ideas, and observing their journals and literature response books. Asha also began to develop her own writing folder, sharing one of her pieces with the students, understanding the power of collaboration in a learning community.

## Summary

Writing is a complex cognitive process. The criteria for determining *good* writing varies according to gender, personality, social group, and culture. In their instruction and evaluation of student writing, teachers generally show respect for the idiosyncratic nature of the writing process and value both the written products and the writing processes of individual students. In constructivist classrooms, teachers focus on a wide range of writing abilities and recognize that there is no one way to evaluate children's writing, nor one mark or grade that adequately represents a student's writing development or abilities.

Writing assessments, both large-scale and classroom-based, are usually conducted using samples of student writing (direct assessment). Direct assessment involves either a holistic procedure or an analytic scale (criteria-based assessment). Holistic scoring is a guided procedure for sorting and ranking pieces according to general criteria, such as matching them with other pieces from the same class or assessing the prominence of certain features of the writing (e.g., strength of argument). Analytic scoring breaks the writing down into component parts such as vocabulary, sentence structure, and organization.

Performance or process assessment attempts to record the writing behaviours and attitudes of the student as well as the written product itself. Data is collected through writing conferences, conversations with parents, writing sessions, and pieces of writing from the student's writing folder. Checklists have been developed by individual teachers and by researchers so that they can handle the wealth of information effectively. Portfolio assessment is a type of performance assessment. The teacher makes generalizations based on reviewing a collection of student writing samples in different forms and voices—poetry, essays, reports, stories, letters, and response journal entries. Students usually select most of the pieces that go into the portfolio, as the aim is to demonstrate what the student can do.

Although regular student assessments meet the requirements of school jurisdictions and form a measure of accountability for teachers, they are most important in providing feedback to students and their families on an individual's learning and development. A second major function is in providing teachers with directions for their classroom instruction. As teachers assess their students' writing abilities, they gain direct information as to what they need to teach and reteach and how they might conduct that instruction. Teachers who notice that a large number of their students have difficulty using quotation marks or commas immediately plan direct instruction on those topics, either with a small group of students or with the entire class. Students who demonstrate a lack of organization in their writing are candidates for a lesson in organizing ideas, perhaps through the use of a story board. Appropriate assessment of student writing provides invaluable feedback to teachers on what students need to learn and what teachers need to teach.

Many students learn to use the conventional tools of writing (including spelling, punctuation, capitalization, and grammar or usage) as they engage in the writing process or as teachers provide feedback during editing or writing conferences. Alternatively, these skills can be taught through direct instruction based on the children's own writing and their questions and challenges. Many students will require multiple lessons using direct instruction: demonstration, guided practice, individual application, and assessment. Teachers use a range of strategies to reteach a concept or skill until they are reasonably certain the students have successfully learned it. Children in kindergarten through Grade 2 continue to use invented spelling as they explore the written symbol system and the graphophonic system. Sound–symbol relationships are complex in the English language, and most children take a number of years to move entirely into standard spelling. Direct instruction in spelling is advised for children who experience particular difficulties in the area, but only in Grade 2 or later. Word lists with a study procedure and mastery test remain the most effective means of direct instruction.

Handwriting is taught regularly and often in the primary grades, but students in the intermediate grades also require maintenance lessons occasionally. A perceptual motor approach can be used throughout the grades, with children verbalizing letter descriptions or saying them silently as they draw the letters. A handwriting model at each student's desk is invaluable. Teachers' own handwriting, particularly their writing on the chalkboard, has a major influence on how students value handwriting and strive to achieve a legible hand. The aim of handwriting lessons is for each student to achieve legible handwriting with a minimum of time, effort, and concentration.

Young children bring to school a vast store of knowledge about language and how it is used. Teachers plan programs that allow children to use this knowledge to communicate with a wide range of audiences for a variety of purposes. An integral component of that writing program is teaching the conventions of written language. Without a working knowledge of these conventions, compositions cannot be as effective as their writers would wish. Much of the empowerment of writing comes from its precision, clarity, and imagery, whether in a novel, journal, poem, or report.

## Selected Professional Resources

Alberta Education. (1998). *Information Bulletin, 1998–99: Grade Six*. Edmonton: Alberta Education, Student Evaluation Branch. (Available at http://ednet.edc.gov.ab.ca/studenteval.) Since 1984, the Student Evaluation Branch of Alberta Education has compiled an annual publication outlining the assessment procedures, timelines, formats, and standards used that year for evaluating writing across the province in Grades 3, 6, and 9. The booklets include the story starter or prompt for the writing tasks (both narrative and functional), as well as the instructions teachers are to provide to students as the task is presented. The detailed scoring rubric is helpful to teachers in their classroom instruction.

Hodges, J., Whitten, M., Brown, J., and Flick, J. (1994). *Harbrace College Handbook for Canadian Writers* (3rd ed.). Toronto: Harcourt Brace and Company. This handbook is a standard reference guide for students and individual writers. It is also used as a textbook for college classrooms. The book summarizes the principles of effective writing and provides a quick and handy reference. Reflecting the Canadian context, the book contains examples from Canadian writers and the Canadian milieu. It follows MLA style (Modern Language Association), citing rules and examples for grammar, punctuation, and usage, as well as providing the formats for documents such as business letters. It contains a glossary of terms and sections on "the whole composition" and "writing the research paper" and on the paragraph and the sentence. Information on sentence sense, parts of speech, verb forms, clauses, capitalization, spelling, and hyphenation can be found in this reference book.

Myers, M. and Spalding, E. (1997). *Assessing Student Performance Grades K–5. (Standards Exemplar Series)*. Urbana, IL: National Council of Teachers of English. This book grew out of the work of thousands of teachers in the United States who worked together to select and design on-demand tasks and portfolios to assess student writing competencies. On-demand tasks are those to be completed in the classroom within a specified time limit. The portfolios include a combination of assigned and freely chosen projects, both timed and untimed. The book consists mainly of selections of children's writing, along with rubrics and commentaries, that demonstrate children's wide-ranging abilities in writing across the grades from K to 5. The framework for assessment is based on three ways of knowing the language arts: knowing that, knowing how, and knowing about.

Peterson, S. (1995). *Becoming Better Writers*. Stettler, AB: F.P. Hendriks; and Peterson, S. (1997). *Teaching Conventions Unconventionally*. Stettler, AB: F.P. Hendriks. The first of the two companion volumes by Shelley Peterson is a recommended resource for the Western Canada Protocol for English Language Arts. The book contains practical information to assist teachers in passing on successful fiction-writing techniques using sample lessons, overheads, ideas for wall charts, and annotated bibliographies. The second book focusses on revision and editing strategies. It includes mini-lessons with samples of student writing, suggestions to help in planning writing conferences, and instructional strategies for teaching grammar, punctuation, and spelling. Assessment tools are included in both books, as are ideas for using literature to teach writing.

Phenix, J. and Scott-Dunne, D. (1991). *Spelling Instruction That Makes Sense*. Markham, ON: Pembroke. This Canadian resource provides useful alternative strategies for teaching spelling in the context of a balanced literacy program. The authors trace a brief history and explain the "logic" of spelling. They include sections in the book on the developmental nature of learning to spell and suggest many learning activities for use in elementary classrooms. An especially helpful chapter suggests ways in which spelling development can be assessed and recorded, as well as ways in which parents can be kept informed about spelling itself and their children's progress.

Thomas, V. (1979). *Teaching Spelling: Canadian Word Lists and Instructional Techniques*. Toronto: Gage. Thomas's book remains one of the best sources of word lists and strategies for teaching spelling. Thomas summarizes previous research findings and presents them in an accessible format. He develops a historical background for the direct teaching of spelling and presents a rationale for teaching only a core spelling vocabulary. Thomas discusses the grade placement of words on word lists and lists the 3000 most commonly used words in children's writing, breaking them into grade levels. The book also lists the 200 most frequently misspelled words in children's writing (from *about* to *writing*). The teaching strategies, activities, and record-keeping devices included in this book are of direct use to classroom teachers.

# References

Alberta Education. (1992). *Achievement testing program provincial report.* Edmonton: Alberta Education.

Alberta Education. (1995). *Achievement testing program provincial report.* Edmonton: Alberta Education.

Alberta Education. (1998). *Information bulletin, 1998–99: Grade Six.* Edmonton: Alberta Education, Student Evaluation Branch.

Applebee, A.N., Langer, J.A., and Mullis, I.V. (1986). *The writing report card: Writing achievement in American schools.* (Report No. 15-W-02). Princeton, NJ: Educational Testing Service.

Beers, J.W. and Henderson, E.H. (1977). A study of developing orthographic concepts among first graders. *Research in the Teaching of English, 11,* 133–148.

Berthoff, A.E. (1981). *Making meaning: Metaphors, models and maxims for writing teachers.* Montclair, NJ: Boynton/Cook.

Braddock, R., Lloyd-Jones, R., and Shoer, L. (1963). *Research in written composition.* Champagne, IL: National Council of Teachers of English.

Carroll, J., Davies, P., and Richman, B. (1971). *Word frequency book.* Boston: Houghton Mifflin.

Clymer, T. (1963). The utility of phonic generalizations in the primary grades. *The Reading Teacher, 4,* 252–258.

Cooper, C.R. (1977). Holistic evaluation of writing. In C.R. Cooper and L. Odell (eds.), *Evaluating writing: Describing, measuring, judging* (pp. 3–31). Urbana, IL: National Council of Teachers of English.

Cooper, C.R. and Odell, L. (eds.). (1977). *Evaluating writing: Describing, measuring, judging* (pp. 3–31). Urbana, IL: National Council of Teachers of English.

Department of School Education. (1991). *English profiles handbook.* Melbourne, Australia: Department of School Education.

De Sousa, D. (1998). *Nelson spelling series.* Scarborough, ON: ITP Nelson, Thomson Canada.

Edwards, J. (1983). Knowledge of spelling research, instructional methods and spelling ability. EdD dissertation, University of Northern Colorado, Greeley, CO.

Elley, W., Barham, I., Lamb, H., and Wyllie, M. (1976). The role of grammar in a secondary school English curriculum. *Research in the Teaching of English, 10,* 5–21.

Farr, R. and Tone, B. (1994). *Portfolio and performance assessment.* Fort Worth, TX: Harcourt Brace College.

Flower, L. and Hayes, J. (1980). The dynamics of composing: Making plans and juggling constraints. In L.W. Gregg and E.R. Steinberg (eds.), *Cognitive processes in writing: An interdisciplinary approach* (pp. 31–50). Hillsdale, NJ: Erlbaum.

Flower, L. and Hayes, J. (1981). A cognitive process theory of writing. *College composition and communication, 32,* 365–387.

Furner, B. (1969). Recommended instructional procedures in a method emphasizing the perceptual motor nature of learning in handwriting. *Elementary English, 46* (8), 1021–1030.

Gentry, J.R. (1978). Early spelling strategies. *Elementary School Journal, 79,* 88–92.

Gentry, J.R. (1981). Learning to spell developmentally. *The Reading Teacher, 34,* 378–381.

Gilbert, P. and Taylor, S. (1991). *Fashioning the feminine: Girls, popular culture and schooling.* North Sydney, Australia: Allen & Unwin.

Graves, D. (1975). An examination of the writing processes of seven-year-old children. *Research in the Teaching of English, 9,* 227–241.

Hodges, J., Whitten, M., Brown, J., and Flick, J. (1994). *Harbrace college handbook for Canadian writers* (3rd ed.). Toronto: Harcourt Brace and Company.

Leppard, S. (1991). A reading–writing continuum. *Program continuity: The positive link.* Calgary: Alberta Educational Communications Corporation.

Loomer, B. (1978). *Educator's guide to spelling research and practice.* Iowa City, IA: Iowa Department of Public Instruction and the University of Iowa.

McKenzie, L. and Tompkins, G. (1984). Evaluating students' writing: A process approach. *Journal of Teaching Writing, 3,* 201–212.

Ministry of Education, Victoria. (1988). *English language framework, P–10: Language for living.* Melbourne, Australia: Victoria Ministry of Education.

Myers, M. and Spalding, E. (1997). *Assessing student performance Grades K–5. (Standards Exemplar Series)*. Urbana, IL: National Council of Teachers of English.

Peterson, S. (1995). *Becoming better writers*. Stettler, AB: F.P. Hendriks.

Peterson, S. (1997). *Teaching conventions unconventionally*. Stettler, AB: F.P. Hendriks.

Peterson, S. and Bainbridge, J. (1999). Teachers' gendered expectations and their evaluation of student writing. *Reading Research and Instruction, 38* (3), 255–271.

Phenix, J. and Scott-Dunne, D. (1991). *Spelling instruction that makes sense*. Markham, ON: Pembroke.

Read, C. (1975). *Children's categorizations of speech sounds in English*. Urbana, IL: National Council of Teachers of English.

Schwegler, R. (1991). The politics of reading student papers. In R. Bullock and J. Trimbur (eds.), *The politics of writing instruction: Postsecondary*. Portsmouth, NH: Heinemann.

Scott, R. (1993). *Spelling: Sharing the secrets*. Toronto: Gage.

Searle, D. and Dillon, D. (1980). The message of marking: Teacher written responses to student writing at intermediate grade levels. *Research in the Teaching of English, 14* (3), 233–242.

Simpson, C. (1980). *The Scott, Foresman word study for spelling*. Glenview, IL: Scott, Foresman & Company.

Stobart, G., Elwood, J., and Quinlan, M. (1992). Gender bias in examinations: How equal are the opportunities? *British Educational Research Journal, 18* (3), 261–276.

Tarasoff, M. (1990). *Spelling strategies you can teach*. Victoria, BC: Pixelart Graphics; Active Learning Institute.

Templeton, S. (1979). Spelling first, sound later: The relationship between orthography and higher order phonological knowledge in older students. *Research in the Teaching of English, 13*, 255–265.

Thomas, V. (1979). *Teaching spelling: Canadian word lists and instructional techniques*. Toronto: Gage.

Tompkins, G. (1990). *Teaching writing: Balancing process and product*. Columbus, OH: Merrill.

Tompkins, G. and Hoskisson, K. (1995). *Language arts: Content and teaching strategies* (3rd ed.). Englewood Cliffs, NJ: Prentice-Hall.

U.S. Department of Education. (1995). *Windows into the classroom: NAEP's 1992 writing portfolio study*. Washington, DC: Office of Educational Research and Improvement.

Wilkinson, A., Barnsley, G., Hanna, P., and Swan, M. (1983). More comprehensive assessment of writing development. *Language Arts, 60* (7), 871–881.

Zutell, J. (1979). Spelling strategies of primary grade school children and their relationship to Piaget's concept of decentration. *Research in the Teaching of English, 13*, 69–79.

# Chapter ten

# Children's Literature for the Classroom

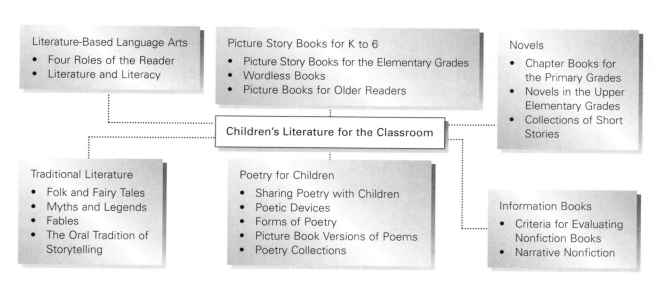

**Literature-Based Language Arts**
- Four Roles of the Reader
- Literature and Literacy

**Picture Story Books for K to 6**
- Picture Story Books for the Elementary Grades
- Wordless Books
- Picture Books for Older Readers

**Novels**
- Chapter Books for the Primary Grades
- Novels in the Upper Elementary Grades
- Collections of Short Stories

Children's Literature for the Classroom

**Traditional Literature**
- Folk and Fairy Tales
- Myths and Legends
- Fables
- The Oral Tradition of Storytelling

**Poetry for Children**
- Sharing Poetry with Children
- Poetic Devices
- Forms of Poetry
- Picture Book Versions of Poems
- Poetry Collections

**Information Books**
- Criteria for Evaluating Nonfiction Books
- Narrative Nonfiction

Jennifer is about to begin a full term of student teaching and would like to incorporate novels and literature circles into her teaching of reading, balancing the reading series generally used in the classroom. Jennifer has compiled a list of books appropriate for novel studies, but she wants to add to that list and help the teacher to develop a larger classroom collection of books for her students' selection during DEAR (Drop Everything and Read) time. Which new novels would make interesting novel studies? Should she choose novels or a combination of novels and picture books? Which poetry anthologies are available for her to use, and which nonfiction literature can she include in her reading program? How can she go about selecting high-quality nonfiction books to support the topics she will be teaching in science and social studies? ■

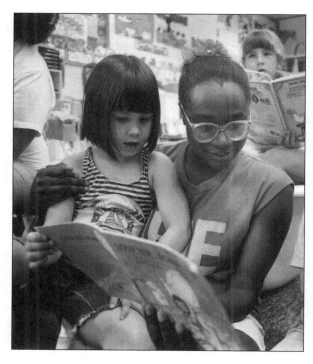

The questions Jennifer asks about suitable reading materials for her student teaching classroom demonstrate her commitment to providing the best possible learning opportunities for her students. One of the the most exciting developments in language arts instruction over the last twenty years has been the shift in focus from the use of a "reading series" approach to that of incorporating **children's literature** and **trade books** into reading instruction. **Reading series** certainly have a place in elementary classrooms and can provide a range of reading experiences for children. However, the explosion of exciting trade books written and illustrated for children has made it increasingly possible to create reading and language arts programs that are literature-based. Researchers, scholars, and many classroom teachers have discovered that children's literature is an essential component of teaching children both how to read and how to appreciate reading as a pleasurable aesthetic experience.

If you take a few moments to look back on your own reading history, you may remember learning how to read. Some of the experiences might have been in school, others at home. Some might have involved teachers, while other memories may be of grandparents, older siblings, and parents sharing stories and books with you. Many people can remember the moment when they *knew* they could read by themselves. Others feel they could always read and have very few specific memories. What are some of the earliest stories you recall? Where did you read? Did you visit a library? Did your family subscribe to book clubs or to magazines? These are important questions to keep in mind when designing a literacy program, because we know that literacy learning is complex and multifaceted.

Not long ago, "children's literature" connoted an elite canon of "quality" books that largely included the classics, both old and contemporary, from *Anne of Green Gables* (Montgomery, 1908) to *Angel Square* (Doyle, 1984). In this textbook, children's literature refers to those books, both fiction and nonfiction, that are acknowledged by critics to be of high quality and well written, and that provide children with pleasurable and challenging reading experiences. The term "trade books" has a broader definition, including all books that are published for preschoolers, young readers, and young adults, but *not* as part of a basal reading series or as textbooks for use in schools. Trade books encompass many genres of literature, including comics, series books such as R.L. Stine's Goosebumps (e.g., *Welcome to the Dead House,* 1992), and magazines. The term "reading series" refers to a set of materials specifically designed for teaching reading and language arts. These used to be referred to as "basal readers" because they frequently formed the basis for an instructional program in reading. Many of the current reading series are anthologies of materials taken directly from published works of literature by well-known authors. These series generally consist of teacher guides, student anthologies, workbooks, and supplemental materials such as assessment materials, big books, correlated trade books, audiovisual aids, and computer software.

**Genre**, a word borrowed from French, means "literary species" or "literary form." The epic, tragedy, comedy, essay, biography, novel, and poetry are traditional genres. New forms have been added to this list over the years, and now the term is used as a convenient (and somewhat arbitrary) way of classifying literary works. Today, genre refers to a body of literature that has certain common elements. The genres usually referred to in children's literature are picture books, wordless books, concept books, biographies, classics, legends, myths, folk tales, fairy tales, fables, historical fiction, contemporary realistic fiction, fantasies, science fiction, poetry, and nonfiction—and each of these may in turn be subdivided into a number of different categories or sub-genres.

Competent and avid adult readers often recollect with fondness their visits to the bookmobile in the city, the arrival of the *Star Weekly* in the mailbox, comics, their first library card, favourite books, and endless series books, from the Bobbsey Twins to the Babysitter's Club. Learning from this, and from all that has been written about teaching reading and the language arts, educators have embraced the concept of literature-based reading instruction, and many have created language arts programs based on trade books of many genres. There's no question of the respect that teachers have today for the power of children's literature and for the authors and illustrators who create literary works for children. This is demonstrated by such events as the locally organized Children's Literature Round Table groups that meet across Canada and the excellent children's literature conferences such as Kaleidoscope, held every four years in Calgary (sponsored by the Learning Resources Council of the Alberta Teachers' Association), and Canadian Images Canadien held every four years in Winnipeg (sponsored by the Manitoba School Libraries Association). These conferences also underscore the recognition that children's literature is receiving in language arts education programs across all the grades, from kindergarten to high school.

Reading good books connects us with the rest of the human race and lets us know that our feelings and experiences are not unique, but part of what makes us human. Children who learn to appreciate literature are at an advantage in society and in life, not the least because good books give them a context within which to better understand the place they hold in the scheme of things.

## Literature-Based Language Arts

In this section of the chapter, we explain the importance of children's literature in language arts programs, and the role literature plays in teaching children how to read and to become lifelong readers. This section of the chapter demonstrates why Jennifer has decided to incorporate more literature into her language arts program.

With a careful choice of books and appropriate instruction, children can learn to read from interesting and well-written, well-illustrated trade books as well as from reading series. Literature-based language arts instruction does, however, call upon increased knowledge and skill on the part of teachers. Not only must teachers know children's books (including their titles, authors, themes, plots, characters, and structures), but it is also helpful if they understand how books work and what the various literary techniques used in the books are teaching young readers. Literature-based instruction is important because it incorporates *all* of the language arts and may involve such activities as novel studies, shared reading, drama work, art activities, puppetry, journals and other kinds of writing, and book talks by children. It thus requires a good deal of organization and knowledge of strategies (e.g., literature circles and response groups). It also demands that teachers read the books their students are reading and be prepared to participate with children as they generate shared meanings from the works they read.

## Four Roles of the Reader

What is the advantage of working with literature in the classroom? If children learn to read from trade books, will they lack any of the basic skills required in the early stages of independent reading? Reading is more than matching written symbols with sounds, more than acquiring a reading vocabulary, more than understanding word meanings. Reading ability is more than being able to answer someone else's questions about a text. Freebody and Luke (1990) describe four roles of a reader: code breaker, text participant, text user, and text analyst. They maintain that successful reading means being able to accomplish all four of these roles simultaneously.

- Being a *code breaker* involves understanding the sound–symbol relationship and the alphabetic principle.
- Being a *text participant* means developing the resources to engage the meaning systems of discourse (i.e., "the processes of comprehension call upon the reader to draw inferences connecting textual elements and background knowledge required to fill out the unexplicated aspects of text," p. 9).
- Being a *text user* means knowing how to use a variety of texts in real social contexts throughout daily life (i.e., knowing what to do with a text in a given social context).
- Being a *text analyst* means reading critically, or having "conscious awareness of the language and idea systems that are brought into play when a text is used" (p. 13) (i.e., being able to recognize the ideological perspective of a text and to stand outside that perspective and question it).

We already know that, before they enter school, many children learn to read from the reading materials they have in their homes, usually magazines and books. Scholars, researchers, and teachers have learned that children's literature has a greater likelihood of encouraging children to take on the four roles of the reader proposed by Freebody and Luke. The more contrived or artificial stories sometimes found in reading series are generally designed to encourage code-breaking rather than any of the other three roles. Works of children's literature are more likely to challenge readers not only to be code breakers, but also to make inferences, to analyze the text, and to predict events and outcomes.

In *Come Away from the Water, Shirley* (Burningham, 1977), for example, the reader is encouraged not only to decode the text and read the words, but also to read the pictures that, at first glance, appear to have nothing at all to do with the words on the page. In order to construct a meaningful story, the reader has to engage with the book as a text participant, text user, and text analyst. There is more than one story being told in these pages. Participating only as a code-breaker would create a limited story with little appeal to children. *Rosie's Walk* (Hutchins, 1969) provides a further example of this phenomenon.

There are times today when a reading series can be very useful to teachers. If a large and varied collection of children's reading material is not available, or when a student has a particular learning need, then a reading series may provide the resources necessary for instruction. In general, however, most children will learn more about reading from children's literature than from a reading series. Children clearly need to learn code-breaking skills early in their lives, but they also deserve to learn how to be text users, text analysts, and text participants if they are to become independent readers capable of constructing meaning from the texts they read. Thus, from children's literature, children are provided with the opportunity to learn both how to read *and* how to appreciate the ways in which texts work. The combination of the two creates rich possibilities for reading for pleasure and reading for information throughout life.

## Literature and Literacy

Research in language learning and literacy development has consistently shown that one of the most important factors in a child's early literacy development is the amount a child is read to (and with) in the preschool years. Wells's (1986) longitudinal study of language development, conducted in Britain during the 1970s, showed that the single most important factor in reading development is the amount a child is read to during the preschool years. The study also demonstrated that

- children who are read to from infancy onwards have an enormous advantage when they begin formal schooling (this finding has significant implications for teaching those children who come from situations where reading is not common and is not regarded as a pleasurable or satisfying endeavour),
- early reading experiences affect writing as well as reading abilities, and are also influential in developing children's listening and comprehension skills, and
- the more children read and are read to, and the more children talk about what they are reading and writing, the more successful they are likely to be in school and in their literacy endeavours.

Many preschool children love books. They are fascinated by the pictures on the page and by the shared experience of reading on a caregiver's lap. This pleasurable anticipation of books provides parents and educators with the opportunity to provide quality works of literature for the young. *Each Peach Pear Plum* by the Ahlbergs (1978) is a contemporary extension of traditional literature that has become a classic. *Each Peach Pear Plum* contains illustrations rich in the detail of the nursery rhymes, folklore, legends, and fairy tales of western Europe. It is a book that can be read on a range of levels. The very young child, who is still unable to follow the plots of traditional stories, can enjoy the repetition of "each peach pear plum" and the rhyming patterns, as well as the predictability of the language. Older children enjoy the humour derived from their prior knowledge of the fairy tales and nursery rhymes alluded to in the book.

Children learn from books such as this that reading is an active experience. In addition to what children learn about values, culture and life, they learn about handling and "reading" books—much of what Holdaway (1979) refers to as "literacy set." Children learn directionality: the front and back of a book, which way is the right way up, and which way the story moves through the book—in the case of *Each Peach Pear Plum*, with text on the left, pictures on the right, and a "cuing" picture above the text. Children learn that books can be actively responded to, and that books are a way into a pleasurable experience.

Children's early experiences with books such as *Each Peach Pear Plum*, and the experiences they have with reading in school, affect how they perceive themselves as readers and how they perceive reading: whether it is a relevant activity or not, whether it is a pleasurable activity or not, and whether books are worth the time and effort needed to have a truly *satisfying* reading experience. Teachers who use literature as a basis for their reading instruction demonstrate to children that books *are* worth the time and effort required of a reader, and thus children are more likely to become readers as adults. Teachers who clearly enjoy reading—and who demonstrate this joy in their daily life in classrooms—invite children into the world of books with enthusiasm and excitement.

## Picture Story Books for K to 6

This section suggests the titles of a selection of picture books for children across the elementary grades, including some books that deal with complex and difficult issues.

Every genre of literature is represented in **picture books**. The label "picture book" refers to a general category of books having the same basic format and way of communicating a message. Some books may more appropriately be called "illustrated books." True picture books involve a partnership between text and pictures, with the pictures and text *together* telling the story or presenting information. The most common genres of picture books are wordless books, concept books (such as counting and alphabet books), predictable books, easy-to-read books, and picture story books. There is often overlap among the genres within picture books. This section of the chapter focusses on picture story books rather than on the other picture book genres such as alphabet or counting books.

## Picture Story Books for the Elementary Grades

Picture story books are a powerful vehicle for teaching children both *how to read* and *how to become readers*. It is understood that reading should be taught in the context of real texts, but it is not until we look in detail at books such as *Come Away from the Water, Shirley* (Burningham, 1977), *Tuesday* (Wiesner, 1991), and *Zoom Upstream* (Wynne-Jones, 1992), that we fully understand the reading lessons children are receiving from picture books. Meek (1988) refers to these as "private lessons," the lessons good readers learn about reading *without* formal instruction. *Come Away from the Water, Shirley* tells one version of the story through the pictures (and through Shirley's eyes) and another version of the story through the text (and through the parents' eyes). In *Zoom Upstream*, Wynne-Jones's simple adventure story about a cat is remarkably extended by Eric Beddows's detailed and imaginative illustrations of the "catacombs" of ancient Egypt.

An example of a picture book that can be read on many levels is *Rosie's Walk* (Hutchins, 1969). It contains 1 sentence, 32 words, and 27 pages of pictures. *Rosie's Walk* is a story that, if told in words alone, would take many paragraphs and lose much of its allure. *Rosie's Walk* contains at least two stories: the story of Rosie the hen and her barnyard walk, and the story of the fox who silently follows her but is not even mentioned in the text (though he is prominent in the illustrations). The reading lesson, which transfers directly to adult books such as *The Englishman's Boy* by Guy Vanderhaeghe (1996), is an important one — there is more than one story in any book, and there is more in any book than is written on the page.

Young readers understand the way picture books work because they attend to multiple cues, not only to text. They focus on visual cues much more significantly than do adults. These young readers are engaging in completely different reading experiences today than previous generations of children did, because they have access to picture story books that are more challenging and interactional than before. Books such as *Rosie's Walk* and *Tuesday* are often called "writerly" texts because readers must use their imaginations to fill in the textual gaps and thus "complete" the writing of the story. Barthes (1970) used the term "scriptable" to describe texts such as these and the term *lisible* to describe what are now commonly called "readerly" texts — those in which the writer has provided most of the information for the reader, and the writer's meanings tend to be clear and direct.

Early readers need experiences with both writerly and readerly texts, and teachers can provide the instructional support children need to be able to move from one to the other. As a result of their early reading experiences with writerly texts such as *Rosie's Walk* and *Come Away from the Water, Shirley*, more children are likely to enjoy novels such as Vanderhaeghe's *The Englishman's Boy* when they grow up. They are also more likely to continue reading for pleasure as well as for information as adults.

Box 10.1 lists some picture books that are appropriate for children in the elementary grades, and Box 10.2 lists specifically Canadian picture books.

**Box 10.1**    **A Selection of Picture Story Books**

Ahlberg, J. and Ahlberg, A. (1986). *The Jolly Postman*. London, UK: Heinemann.
Brett, J. (1989). *The Mitten*. New York: Scholastic.
Briggs, R. (1975). *Father Christmas Goes on Holiday*. Harmondsworth, UK: Puffin Books.
Browne, A. (1983). *Gorilla*. New York: Alfred A. Knopf.
Carle, E. (1974). *The Very Hungry Caterpillar*. Harmondsworth, UK: Puffin Books.
dePaola, T. (1975). *Strega Nona*. New York: Prentice-Hall.
Fox, M. (1990). *Possum Magic*. New York: Harcourt Brace & Company.
Hodges, M. (reteller). (1984). *Saint George and the Dragon*. Boston: Little, Brown & Company.
Keats, E. (1964). *The Snowy Day*. New York: Viking.
Kellogg, S. (1979). *Pinkerton, Behave!* New York: Dial Books.
Kent, J. (1971). *The Fat Cat*. Harmondsworth, UK: Puffin Books.
Lionni, L. (1963). *Swimmy*. New York: Pantheon.
McKee, D. (1980). *Not Now, Bernard*. London: Anderson Press.
Martin, R. (1992). *The Rough-Face Girl*. New York: G.P. Putnam's Sons.
Ross, T. (1993). *The Three Pigs*. London: Arrow Books.
Rylant, C. (1982). *When I Was Young in the Mountains*. New York: Dutton Books.
Steptoe, J. (1987). *Mufaro's Beautiful Daughters*. New York: Lothrop.
Van Allsburg, C. (1985). *The Polar Express*. Boston: Houghton Mifflin.
Wagner, J. (1978). *John Brown, Rose and the Midnight Cat*. New York: Bradbury.
Wiesner, D. (1990). *Hurricane*. New York: Clarion Books.
Wild, M. (1990). *The Very Best of Friends*. New York: Harcourt Brace & Company.
Wood, A. (1987). *Heckedy Peg*. New York: Harcourt Brace & Company.
Yolen, J. (1987). *Owl Moon*. New York: Philomel Books.

**Box 10.2**    **Canadian Picture Books**

Andrews, J. (1985). *Very Last First Time*. Vancouver: Douglas & McIntyre.
Bourgeois, P. (1986). *Franklin in the Dark*. Toronto: Kids Can Press.
Cumming, P. (1993). *Out on the Ice in the Middle of the Bay*. Toronto: Annick Press.
Eyvindson, P. (1996). *Red Parka Mary*. Winnipeg: Pemmican.
Gilman, P. (1992). *Something from Nothing*. Richmond Hill, ON: North Winds Press.
Gregory, N. (1995). *How Smudge Came*. Red Deer, AB: Red Deer College Press.
Harty, N. (1997). *Hold On, McGinty*. Toronto: Doubleday Canada.
Hutchins, H. (1995). *Tess*. Toronto: Annick Press.
Jam, T. (1997). *The Fishing Summer*. Toronto: Groundwood Books.
Khalsa, D.K. (1986). *Tales of a Gambling Grandma*. Montreal: Tundra Books.

*(continued)*

**Box 10.2　Continued**

Lunn, J. (1988). *Amos's Sweater*. Toronto: Groundwood Books.
McFarlane, S. (1991). *Waiting for the Whales*. Victoria: Orca Book Publishers.
McGugan, J. (1994). *Josepha: A Prairie Boy's Story*. Red Deer, AB: Red Deer College Press.
Morck, I. (1996). *Tiger's New Cowboy Boots*. Red Deer, AB: Red Deer College Press.
Muir, S. and Muir, M. (1987). *Albert's Old Shoes*. Richmond Hill, ON: North Winds Press.
Munsch, R. (1980). *The Paperbag Princess*. Toronto: Annick Press
Nichol, B. (1997). *Dippers*. Toronto: Tundra Books.
Simmie, L. (1995). *Mr. Got to Go*. Red Deer, AB: Red Deer College Press.
Thompson, R. (1993). *Who*. Victoria, BC: Orca.
Tibo, G. (1988). *Simon and the Snowflakes*. Montreal: Tundra Books.
Vaage, C. (1995). *Bibi and the Bull*. Edmonton: Dragon Hill Press.
Wallace, I. (1984). *Chin Chiang and the Dragon's Dance*. Toronto: Groundwood Books.
Wynne-Jones, T. and Nutt, K. (1985). *Zoom Away*. Toronto: Groundwood Books.

## Wordless Books

Children in preschool and kindergarten enjoy sitting alone or in small groups reading wordless books. In actively encouraging emerging readers to engage with books, it is appropriate for teachers to share such books with the class, especially "big-book" versions that enable all the children to see the pictures. It is also important that teachers take a close look at the pictures before the book is shared with children (part of the preparation required in these circumstances), for children will ask many questions and make observations about the illustrations. Children focus heavily on the illustrations in books and can be particularly insightful about the details included. In their early reading experiences, children rely heavily on pictures in order to create meaning from the page. As teachers acknowledge the observations children make and the questions they ask, they enhance the children's response to the book and help expand their understanding through discussion and interaction. Box 10.3 lists wordless books that are appropriate for children from preschool to Grade 3.

## Picture Books for Older Readers

Picture books are not only for pre- and beginning readers, just as wordless books, such as *Sunshine* (1981) and *Moonlight* (1982) by Jan Ormerod, are not only for children who cannot yet read. Similar to *Each Peach Pear Plum* in its intertextual references (to *Red Riding Hood* and many other folk tales and fairy tales) is *The Tunnel* by Anthony Browne (1989). Intended for children in the upper elementary grades, this book requires many readings to unravel its multi-layered (**polysemic**) text and illustrations. There is a great deal of reading to be done in the gaps in the turn of a page, or between text and picture. It is in these gaps that readers are invited to take an *inferential walk* (Eco, 1978) or, in other words, to read between the lines. Thus, readers learn the key role that inferencing plays in reading and in constructing meaning. Some readers may encounter difficulty in following the story depicted in *The Tunnel* and feel that Browne has omitted too much, has left too many inferential gaps, and in general has created

**Box 10.3   Wordless Books**

Aliki. (1995). *Tabby: A Story Told in Pictures*. New York: HarperCollins.
Anno, M. (1970). *Topsy-Turvies*. New York: Walker/Weatherhill.
Aruego, J. (1971). *Look What I Can Do*. New York: Scribner.
Baker, J. (1991). *Window*. New York: Greenwillow Books.
Banyai, I. (1995). *Zoom*. New York: Viking.
Blades, A. (1989). *Fall*. Vancouver: Groundwood Books.
Collington, P. (1997). *A Small Miracle*. New York: Knopf.
Dupasquier, P. (1988). *The Great Escape*. Boston: Houghton Mifflin.
Falwell, C. (1991). *Clowning Around*. New York: Orchard Books.
Goodall, J. (1988). *Little Red Riding Hood*. New York: M.K. McElderry Books.
Hoban, T. (1988). *Look! Look! Look!* New York: Greenwillow Books.
Hutchins, P. (1971). *Changes, Changes*. New York: Macmillan.
Keats, E.J. (1974). *Kitten for a Day*. New York: Four Winds Press.
McCully, E. (1988). *New Baby*. New York: Harper & Row.
Mayer, M. (1974). *Frog Goes to Dinner*. New York: Dial Press.
Tafuri, N. (1990). *Follow Me!* New York: Greenwillow Books.
Tanner, J. (1987). *Niki's Walk*. Melbourne, Australia: MacMillan.

too writerly a text. These readers want the story to be laid out for them more explicitly, so that they receive a direct message from the author and don't have to create the meaning themselves. (Many adults also struggle with the story in the book and with the nature of the illustrations, because Browne manages to create allusions to several of the more disturbing aspects of relationships and growing up, leaving readers to relate their own experiences to the story and perhaps respond at deeply personal levels.) In such books, then, teachers play an important role, through dialogue and discussion groups, in helping children take inferential walks, draw inferences, make educated guesses, and understand overall that there is no correct answer when "gap filling" in texts.

Many picture books are aimed at an audience of older children, children who can already read well and who have a rich experience in working with text. Sixth-grade children respond powerfully to books such as *Black and White* (Macaulay, 1990) and *June 29, 1999* (Wiesner, 1992). *Black and White* is an adventure in **metafiction**, a constant and deliberate reminder that a book is something an author and reader create together — something that is not real and is open to many interpretations and structures. The book consists of four narrative strands, each making use of different narrative and pictorial techniques. Each double-page spread is divided into four sections so that the four narratives unfold at the same time. On the title page of the book there is a warning from the author: "This book appears to contain a number of stories that do not necessarily occur at the same time. Then again, it may contain only one story. In any event, careful inspection of both words and pictures is recommended."

In *June 29, 1999*, a very different story, student Holly Evans develops an ambitious and innovative project for her science assignment. While her classmates are sprouting seeds in paper cups, Holly launches seedlings into the sky on tiny air balloons. Although her teacher and fellow students are skeptical, only five weeks later giant vegetables begin to fall from the sky, landing in various parts of the United States. The book displays Wiesner's unconventional artwork and the same dry humour he uses in *Free Fall* (1988) and *Tuesday* (1991).

These picture books, and others created for older readers, are not necessarily easy-reading books. Many of them deal with mature themes and contain illustrations that provide powerful messages supporting and adding to the text. Two books set in Europe during World War II are *Rose Blanche* (Innocenti, 1985) and *Let the Celebrations Begin!* (Wild, 1991). In Canada, the latter book is published as *A Time for Toys* by Kids Can Press. Where *Rose Blanche* is a story about the darkness of war, *Let the Celebrations Begin!* is a story of hope. It is a tribute to the human spirit and to the survival of so many innocent people who lived for years in horrific conditions in concentration camps. In addition to these books about Europe during World War II, there are a number of powerful picture books about the dropping of the atomic bomb on Hiroshima on August 6, 1945. These include *Hiroshima No Pika* (Maruki, 1980), *My Hiroshima* (Morimoto, 1987), *Sadako* (Coerr, 1993), and *Shin's Tricycle* (Kodama, 1995).

Although the books noted above are of a serious nature, many others for older readers are entertaining, playful, and clever, stimulating the imagination and stretching our notions of reading. Picture story books aimed at older readers include *Night in the Country* (Rylant, 1986), *Piggybook* (Browne, 1986), *The Widow's Broom* (Van Allsburg, 1992), and *The Mummer's Song* (Davidge and Wallace, 1993). Each of these books creates a sense of wonder and provides challenging perspectives on the reading event and on the nature of the picture book. Additional titles of picture books suitable for older readers are presented in Box 10.4.

---

**Box 10.4    Picture Books for Older Readers**

Barbalet, M. and Tanner, J. (1992). *The Wolf.* Toronto: Doubleday.

Baylor, B. (1986). *I'm in Charge of Celebrations.* New York: Charles Scribner's Sons.

Blake, W. (1993). *The Tyger.* (Neil Waldman, illustrator). New York: Harcourt Brace Jovanovich.

Bouchard, D. and Vickers, R.H. (1990). *The Elders Are Watching.* Tofino, BC: Eagle Dancer Enterprises.

Briggs, R. (1982). *When the Wind Blows.* New York: Schocken.

Carrier, R. (1985). *The Hockey Sweater.* Montreal: Tundra Books.

Eyvindson, P. (1994). *The Night Rebecca Stayed Too Late.* Winnipeg: Pemmican.

Goble, P. (1984). *Buffalo Woman.* New York: Aladdin, Macmillan.

Hutchins, P. (1980). *The Tale of Thomas Mead.* London: Macmillan.

Lewis, J. (1993). *How I Got My Dog Sled.* Waterloo, ON: Penumbra Press.

Macauley, D. (1979). *Motel of the Mysteries.* Boston: Houghton Mifflin.

Noyes, A. (1981). *The Highwayman.* (Charles Keeping, illustrator). London: Oxford University Press.

Noyes, A. (1983). *The Highwayman.* (Charles Mikolaycak, illustrator). London: Oxford University Press.

Oberman, S. (1993). *The Always Prayer Shawl.* Honesdale, PA: Boyd Mills Press.

Polacco, P. (1988). *The Keeping Quilt.* New York: Simon & Schuster.

Scieszka, J. (1995). *Math Curse.* New York: Viking.

Sendak, M. (1981). *Outside Over There.* Harmondsworth, UK: Puffin Books.

Thurman, M. (1993). *One Too Many.* Toronto: Viking Kestrel.

Turner, A. (1985). *Dakota Dugout.* New York: Macmillan.

Valgardson, W.D. (1996). *Sarah and the People of Sand River.* Toronto: Groundwood Books.

Van Allsburg, C. (1984). *The Mysteries of Harris Burdick.* Boston: Houghton Mifflin.

Yee, P. (1996). *Ghost Train.* Toronto: Groundwood Books.

Zhang, S.N. (1993). *A Little Tiger in the Chinese Night.* Montreal: Tundra Books.

Picture books, then, have the potential to teach important concepts about reading that can come only from working with real texts, and they are important in forming the attitudes of young children toward books in general. There is a wealth of high-quality picture books available for children in the elementary grades today, books containing artistry, excellent writing, and vivid imagery.

Take the time to locate one of the books mentioned in this section of the chapter, and see if the comments made here match the meanings you create from the book. Did the comments in this chapter help you see the book or the experience of reading in a new light? What does this experience demonstrate to you about your role in teaching reading and in mediating texts with children?

## Novels

In the following section, we suggest a number of novels for children in Grades 2 to 6, including many Canadian titles.

## Chapter Books for the Primary Grades

As children become more familiar with picture books and with story structures, and as their reading abilities become more sophisticated, they move from using pictures as a primary means of creating meaning to an increased reliance on text. Many beginning novels are available for young readers (which children in Grades 2 and 3 frequently refer to as **chapter books**), and they fall into all of the major genres. It seems that the movement from reading picture books to reading books with chapters denotes a transition in an individual's growth as a reader. This is not to suggest that children are no longer interested in reading picture books or that picture books cannot continue to capture their interest and imagination.

The reading levels of many beginning chapter books range from Grades 2 to 4 (i.e., a level calculated by the application of a readability formula). Readability does not depend on the complexity of language alone, however, but has much to do with the structure of the book and the background experience the reader is required to bring to it. Often, beginning chapter books contain illustrations, and these assist readers in the transition from picture books to novels. The content and writing style of numerous beginning chapter books are equally appropriate for older elementary students whose reading level is below grade level, and for those who simply wish to read a "good" (albeit easier) book.

There are many well-known "entry-level" novels, among them Mordecai Richler's three titles about the character Jacob Two-Two: *Jacob Two-Two Meets the Hooded Fang* (1975), *Jacob Two-Two and the Dinosaur* (1987), and *Jacob Two-Two's First Spy Case* (1995). These books are a combination of fantasy and realistic fiction, and are suitable for reading aloud to the class as well as for independent reading. There are also many recommended beginning novels of realistic fiction, including novels written by Canadian authors Ken Roberts, Budge Wilson, Jean Little, and Sylvia McNicoll.

In *Hiccup Champion of the World* (Roberts, 1988), Maynard Chan gets the hiccups and none of the cures generated by his family, friends, and peers are successful. However, just before Maynard is about to appear on a television show, his hiccups cease — temporarily. Budge Wilson's story, *Harold and Harold* (1995), is about a young boy named Harold whose friendship with a beautiful blue heron also named Harold assists him in being accepted by his new coastal community. Jean Little's *Lost and Found* (1985) narrates the story of Lucy, who moves to a new town and is concerned about making friends. Lucy finds a dog she names Trouble, and the dog helps ease Lucy's loneliness. In the novel *The Big Race* (1996), McNicoll tells the story of a Grade 3 boy's constant competition with a female classmate who excels at everything she does. Various events, including a broken nose, eventually bring the characters together in friendship.

A selection of beginning novels is presented in Box 10.5.

---

**Box 10.5   Beginning Novels**

Bjornson, H. (1997). *Raymond's Raindance*. Burnaby, BC: Skoal House.
Blume, J. (1971). *Freckle Juice*. New York: Bantam Doubleday.
Blume, J. (1981). *The One in the Middle Is the Green Kangaroo*. New York: Bantam Doubleday Dell.
Choyce, L. (1998). *Famous at Last*. East Lawrencetown, NS: Pottersfield Press.
Cleary, B. (1984). *Ramona Forever*. New York: Bantam Doubleday Dell.
Corbett, S. (1960). *The Lemonade Trick*. New York: Scholastic.
Croteau, M. (1996). *Fred and the Stinky Cheese*. Translated by S. Cummins. Halifax: Formac.
Dahl, R. (1970). *Fantastic Mr. Fox*. New York: Knopf.
Dahl, R. (1980). *The Twits*. New York: Bantam Skylark Books.
Dahl, R. (1981). *George's Marvelous Medicine*. New York: Bantam Skylark Books.
Elste, J. (1996). *True Blue*. New York: Grosset & Dunlap.
Fleischman, S. (1986). *The Whipping Boy*. New York: Greenwillow.
Fox, P. (1967). *A Likely Place*. New York: Aladdin Paperbacks.
Gardiner, J.R. (1980). *Stone Fox*. New York: Crowell.
Gauthier, G. (1995). *Mooch Forever*. Translated by S. Cummins. Halifax: Formac.
Gravel, F. (1992). *Mr. Zamboni's Dream Machine*. Translated by S. Cummins. Toronto: James Lorimer & Company.
Hutchins, H. (1997). *Shoot for the Moon, Robyn*. Halifax: Formac.
Korman, G. (1997). *Liar, Liar, Pants on Fire*. Richmond Hill, ON: Scholastic Canada.
Little, J. (1985). *Lost and Found*. Markham, ON: Viking Kestrel.
MacLachlan, P. (1985). *Sarah, Plain and Tall*. New York: Harper & Row.
MacLachlan, P. (1994). *Skylark*. New York: Harper Trophy.
Manes, S. (1982). *Be a Perfect Person in Just Three Days*. New York: Bantam Skylark Books.
Manuel, L. (1997). *The Cherry-Pit Princess*. Regina: Coteau Books.
Park, B. (1982). *Skinnybones*. New York: Alfred A. Knopf.
Park, B. (1987). *The Kid in the Red Jacket*. New York: Alfred A. Knopf.
Paterson, K. (1992). *The King's Equal*. New York: HarperCollins. (originally published in picture book format)
Richardson, G. (1997). *A Friend for Mr. Granville*. Edmonton: Hodgepog Books.
Roberts, K. (1990). *Crazy Ideas*. Vancouver: Douglas & McIntyre.
Roberts, K. (1991). *Nothing Wright*. Vancouver: Douglas & McIntyre.
Roberts, K. (1994). *Past Tense*. Vancouver: Douglas & McIntyre.
Roy, R. (1982). *Where's Buddy?* New York: Clarion Books.
Smith, D. (1973). *A Taste of Blackberries*. New York: Crowell.
Smith, R.K. (1972). *Chocolate Fever*. New York: Bantam Doubleday Dell.
Smucker, B. (1987). *Jacob's Little Giant*. Toronto: Puffin Books.
Steele, M. (1993). *Featherbys*. Victoria, BC: Hyland House.
Wishinsky, F. (1998). *Crazy for Chocolate*. Richmond Hill, ON: Scholastic Canada.

As children begin to move from picture books to chapter books, their book selection will be determined largely by the encouragement of their teacher, their peers, and their own interests. Teachers help children to grow by making book suggestions based on each child's interests and reading ability. Children benefit because a novel requires a greater investment of time and effort than a picture storybook. At the same time, children need to know that a book they select has the potential to engage their interests as well as being at an appropriate reading level. In general, reading materials of high personal interest are more fully comprehended than materials of low interest. A reader's strong interest in a topic can transcend his or her reading abilities (Hunt, 1970). Research also shows the importance of teachers reading the books their students are reading, so they can discuss the books with their students (Pantaleo, 1994). Through these discussions, teachers may challenge students to extend their interpretations and to add new dimensions to the meanings they create.

## Novels in the Upper Elementary Grades

Many children begin their foray into novels with **contemporary realistic fiction**, perhaps because it is one of the avenues through which they can, on the one hand, come to know the world in which they live and, on the other, explore issues of which they have little personal experience. This genre continues to be the most widely read of them all in the upper elementary grades. In the Canadian novel *Jasmin* (Truss, 1982), Jasmin's parents seem to be unaware of the burdens their 12-year-old daughter is shouldering in helping to raise a family of six children. Jasmin is not succeeding in school and so decides to run away from the possibility of repeating Grade 6 and from the responsibilities of being the oldest of a large family. Spending time alone in the wilderness and meeting some new friends helps Jasmin in her search for independence, and brings assistance for her family.

*Finders Keepers* (Spalding, 1995) tells the story of two boys in Fort McLeod, Alberta, who become unlikely friends. Danny, a Ukrainian child, and Joshua, a Peigan boy, find ways to help each other after Danny discovers an 8000-year-old arrowhead. Together they uncover the origin of the arrowhead and in doing so become great friends, learning how to deal with their respective difficulties and differences (including a learning disability).

In *The Onlyhouse* (Toten, 1995), set in the 1960s, Lucija, a recent Croatian immigrant, moves to a new neighbourhood and tries to make friends. She finally discovers the joys of true friendship, but also experiences the neediness of her new friend, Jackie, and the problems of Jackie's mixed-up family. Other recommended titles of contemporary realistic fiction that focus on relationships include

- *Philip Hall Likes Me. I Reckon Maybe* (Greene, 1974)
- *The Daring Game* (Pearson, 1986)
- *Afternoon of the Elves* (Lisle, 1989)
- *Maniac Magee* (Spinelli, 1990)
- *Walk Two Moons* (Creech, 1994)
- *The Watsons Go to Birmingham, 1963* (Curtis, 1995)

Novels such as these encourage students to explore personal and social issues that may help them attain an increased understanding of themselves and others.

A genre much enjoyed by children in the upper elementary grades is that of mystery. These stories challenge children to become actively engaged in problem solving.

Young readers enjoy putting the pieces of the puzzle together, hypothesizing, and making inferences as they act as detectives in solving the mystery. Well-formed mystery stories can be difficult to find, however, so that when children discover series books such as the Hardy Boys, Nancy Drew, or Encyclopedia Brown, they frequently read all the books in the series in their desire to remain engaged with the genre. As they become familiar with a particular series' pattern, they also become increasingly better at predicting solutions and fitting clues together. The result is that children tend to grow out of these rather predictable plots and patterns, becoming ready for something more demanding and more sophisticated. In the 1990s, children turned to the genre of horror stories in addition to mysteries. The Goosebumps series by R.L. Stine was extremely popular for a number of years, and many parents and educators expressed concern over children reading these books (see, for example, Perry and Butler, 1997; Dickson, 1998). Not unexpectedly, readers soon outgrew the books, wanting a greater challenge and a new thrill in reading.

There are, however, numerous well-written mystery stories to recommend. Betsy Byars has authored a series of mystery books about a character named Herculeah Jones. *Dead Letter* (1996) and *Death's Door* (1997) are two titles in the series. In Bunting's *Is Anybody There?* (1988), 13-year-old Marcus is certain that someone other than a family member is regularly coming into his house. Marcus has evidence to support his belief — a key to the house is missing, food is disappearing, and other items are vanishing from the house — but he needs proof to confirm his suspicions. In *Secrets in the Attic* (York, 1984), Jodie must unravel a mystery to prove her father's innocence in a crime. Jodie's father was killed in a car accident, and rumours circulated in the town implicating him in the theft of some money. Through her explorations in her Aunt Winifred's attic, Jodie is able to expose the real thief. *The Dragon Children* (Buchan, 1975) involves two mysteries occurring concurrently. One day, while John is in the woods near his house, an unknown boy appears and informs John about a crook in town who is swindling elderly people out of their money. John eventually learns the identity of the boy, and the two work together in catching the criminal. Other recommended titles are

- *The Treasure of Alpheus Winterborn* (Bellairs, 1978)
- *Who Stole the Wizard of Oz?* (Avi, 1981)
- *The Kootenay Kidnapper* (Wilson, 1983)
- *Lucy Forever & Miss Rosetree, Shrinks* (Shreve, 1987)
- *Megan's Island* (Roberts, 1988)
- *The Mystery at Wolf River* (Shura, 1989)
- *The Chinese Puzzle* (Brouillet, 1996)

**Historical fiction** is a genre that presents new challenges for many young readers, for it typically presents fictional characters in a historically accurate context. The genre often requires that the reader have some prior knowledge of the time period in which the story is set. Rosemary Sutcliff is a British author who has written many books of historical fiction for children. Her books are superbly crafted, thoroughly researched,

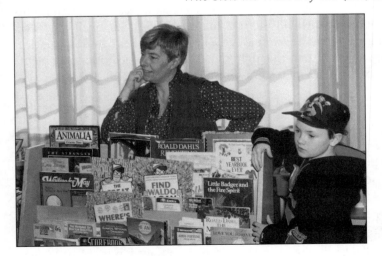

Teacher and primary boy with book display.

and extremely well written. *Warrior Scarlet* (1958), for example, is set in the Bronze Age in Great Britain, a period for which there is no written record and which is not connected to the real lives of most Canadian children. Readers savour her descriptive passages, and once into the story, a reader is hooked, for the book addresses issues that are as relevant today as they probably were hundreds of years ago. Historical fiction is a particularly suitable genre for teachers to share with their classes as a read-aloud. It also helps in creating a context and a deeper understanding of many social studies topics, and can inspire themes for work across the curriculum.

Books of historical fiction about Canada and by Canadian authors have become more plentiful over the last few years. Examples include *Underground to Canada* by Barbara Smucker (1977), dealing with slavery; *A Very Small Rebellion* by Jan Truss (1977), about the Riel rebellion; *The Sky Is Falling* by Kit Pearson (1989), about World War II; and *Rebellion: A Novel of Upper Canada* by Marianne Brandis (1996).

A list of Canadian historical fiction is provided in Box 10.6.

| **Box 10.6** | **Canadian Historical Fiction** |
| --- | --- |

Attema, M. (1996). *A Time to Choose*. Victoria, BC: Orca. (young adult)
Bellingham, B. (1985). *Storm Child*. Toronto: James Lorimer & Company.
Clark, J. (1977). *The Hand of Robin Squires*. Toronto: Clarke, Irwin.
Duncan, F. (1976). *Cariboo Runaway*. Don Mills, ON: Burns & MacEachern.
Greenwood, B. (1984). *A Question of Loyalty*. Richmond Hill, ON: Scholastic.
Lottridge, B. (1992). *Ticket to Curlew*. Toronto: Douglas & McIntyre.
Lunn, J. (1986). *Shadow in Hawthorn Bay*. Toronto: Lester and Orpen Denys.
McNaughton, J. (1996). *To Dance at the Palais Royale*. Toronto: Tuckamore Books.
Martel, S. (1980). *The King's Daughter*. Vancouver: Douglas & McIntyre.
Pearson, K. (1991). *Looking at the Moon*. Toronto: Viking.
Pearson, K. (1993). *The Lights Go on Again*. Markham, ON: Viking/Penguin.
Reynolds, M. (1993). *Belle's Journey*. Victoria, BC: Orca Books.
Yee, P. (1989). *Tales from Gold Mountain*. Toronto: Groundwood Books.

Other high-quality books of historical fiction (from outside Canada) include

- *Snow Treasure* (McSwigan, 1942)
- *Sing Down the Moon* (O'Dell, 1970)
- *The Upstairs Room* (Reiss, 1972)
- *The Summer of My German Soldier* (Greene, 1973)
- *The Slave Dancer* (Fox, 1973)
- *Journey Home* (Uchida, 1978)
- *The Sign of the Beaver* (Speare, 1983)
- *Number the Stars* (Lowry, 1989)
- *Letters from Rifka* (Hesse, 1992)
- *Thunder Rolling in the Mountains* (O'Dell and Hall, 1992)
- *Zlata's Diary: A Child's Life in Sarajevo* (Filipovic, 1994)

**Time-slip fantasy** is a genre that has become popular in recent years, though it has its roots in *Tom's Midnight Garden* (1958) by Philippa Pearce. The story usually begins in the present, and then, through some artifact from the past, the protagonist is transported into a different time, typically a specific period in history. *The Castle in the Attic* by Elizabeth Winthrop (1985) fits into this category of novel, and so does

Janet Lunn's book *The Root Cellar* (1981), which is about the American Civil War. A well-known Australian time-slip fantasy is *Playing Beatie Bow* (1980) by Ruth Parks. Three Canadian time-slip fantasy books were published in 1987: *The Doll* by Cora Taylor, *Who Is Francis Rain?* by Margaret Buffie, and *A Handful of Time* by Kit Pearson. In *Who Is Frances Rain?* a pair of spectacles takes Lizzie back into the isolated pioneer times of rural Manitoba in the early part of the twentieth century. Through her experiences in a different time, Lizzie is able to deal with her life in the present in a more effective and positive manner.

**Fantasy** literature engages the reader's imagination and gives free rein to endless possibilities. The reader is taken to worlds where animals and toys can speak, and where people can travel across time and into completely fictional worlds. The genre is popular in all the elementary grades. Young children, for example, enjoy *Charlotte's Web* (White, 1952) and *James and the Giant Peach* (Dahl, 1961). Older children enjoy *The Dark Is Rising* (Cooper, 1969) and *The Indian in the Cupboard* (Banks, 1980). Although fantasy literature has a devoted following in Grades 5 and 6, it can be a challenging genre for children *and* teachers alike because of the complexity and sophistication of the ideas embedded within it. Many books of **high fantasy** (usually quest stories), such as *The Hobbit* (Tolkien, 1937) and *The Golden Compass* (Pullman, 1996), are read by both children and adults. Much modern fantasy has its roots in ancient myths and legends, especially in the *Tales from the Mabinogian*, which is a collection of Welsh myths dating back many hundreds of years. Both Susan Cooper and Alan Garner (*The Owl Service*, 1967) refer to the *Mabinogian* in their writing, and it is useful if readers have at least a nodding acquaintance with this material when reading these authors' books. A modern children's version by Gwynn Thomas and Kevin Crossley-Holland (1985) is a wonderful addition to any classroom library.

Additional examples of fantasy literature for children are

- *The Wind in the Willows* (Graham, 1908)
- *The Velveteen Rabbit* (Williams, 1922)
- *The Borrowers* (Norton, 1952)
- *A Wrinkle in Time* (L'Engle, 1962)
- *Tuck Everlasting* (Babbit, 1975)
- *Redwall* (Jacques, 1987)
- *The Giver* (Lowry, 1993)

Box 10.7 lists a selection of Canadian novels suitable for students in Grades 4 to 6.

**Box 10.7    Canadian Fiction for Upper Elementary Readers**

Bradford, K. (1996). *Shadows on a Sword*. Toronto: HarperCollins.
Clark, J. (1995). *The Dream Carvers*. Toronto: Viking.
Doyle, B. (1979). *You Can Pick Me Up at Peggy's Cove*. Toronto: Douglas & McIntyre.
Ellis, S. (1991). *Pick-Up Sticks*. Toronto: Groundwood Books.
Fairbridge, L. (1995). *Stormbound*. Toronto: Doubleday.
Godfrey, M. (1994). *Just Call Me Boom Boom*. Richmond Hill, ON: Scholastic Canada.
Horrocks, A. (1996). *Breath of a Ghost*. Toronto: Stoddart Kids.
Hughes, M. (1983). *My Name is Paula Popowich!* Toronto: James Lorimer & Company.
Hutchins, H. (1997). *The Prince of Tarn*. Toronto: Annick Press.

*(continued)*

**Box 10.7**  **Continued**

Little, J. (1969). *One to Grow On.* Toronto: Puffin Books.
Little, J. (1997). *The Belonging Place.* Toronto: Viking Press.
Lottridge, C. (1992). *Ticket to Curlew.* Toronto: Groundwood Books.
McLaughlin, F. (1990). *Yukon Journey.* New York: Scholastic.
Matas, C. (1995). *The Primrose Path.* Winnipeg: Blizzard Publishing.
Pearson, K. (1993). *The Lights Go On Again.* Toronto: Viking.
Pearson, K. (1996). *Awake and Dreaming.* Markham, ON: Viking.
Sherman, G. T. (1997). *Grave Danger.* Richmond Hill, ON: Scholastic.
Woodbury, M. (1997). *Jess and the Runaway Grandpa.* Regina: Coteau Books.

## Collections of Short Stories

The short story, as a literary form, has existed only since the middle of the nineteenth century. Although it has its roots in ancient tales and narratives, it was Edgar Allan Poe and Nathaniel Hawthorne, among others, who developed the short story as an art form. They were followed by writers such as Katherine Mansfield and Somerset Maugham in Britain and by Ernest Hemmingway in the United States. A short story is a brief fictional narrative (though it can be anything from 500 to 15 000 words) that consists of more than just a mere record of an incident. It has a formal structure with unity of time, place, and action. Generally, a short story reveals the true nature of a character.

Today, there are a growing number of high-quality collections of short stories for children in Grades 3 to 6. These are delightful and frequently thought-provoking stories that are well-crafted pieces of writing. Readers familar with Tim Wynne-Jones's picture books will be especially appreciative of his three books of short stories: *Some of the Kinder Planets* (1993), which won the **Governor General's Award** and the Boston Globe–Horn Book Award for Children's Literature, *The Book of Changes* (1994), and *Lord of the Fries* (1999). Kit Pearson has edited an anthology of short stories and excerpts from works of Canadian children's literature titled *This Land* (1998). *The Back of Beyond* (Ellis, 1998) is another collection of short stories suitable for the upper elementary grades.

## Traditional Literature

Traditional literature remains a staple of the elementary language arts curriculum from kindergarten to Grade 6. Today there are many beautifully illustrated retellings of traditional stories, originating from around the world. This section presents a sampling of these books.

The genre of traditional literature, which is sometimes referred to as "folk literature," includes fairy tales, folk tales, Mother Goose rhymes, legends, myths, proverbs, epics, fables, and more. These are mostly short stories that reflect the values and dreams of a society, and through which societies and their cultures come alive. Traditional literature is, in general, a body of work that was originally passed from generation to generation orally. Scholars and educators agree that traditional literature is a most important genre for children, and it is frequently the first genre with which children become truly familiar. "Once upon a time" is a phrase that young children all over the Western world associate with the telling of a story. It signals the beginning of a narrative designed to take the child into the world of imagination. The classic fairy tale has a structure that has become ingrained in the Western psyche. Jean Little's book, *Once Upon a Golden Apple* (1991), plays with children's internalization of the structure of fairy tales, and the humour in the book is based on children understanding these "rules" and knowing they are being manipulated.

## Folk and Fairy Tales

Many traditional versions of folk and fairy tales are available today. Some author–illustrators have become well-known for their renditions of these stories, people such as Laszlo Gal, Leo and Diane Dillon, Jan Brett, Trina Schart Hyman, Jane Yolen, Paul Galdone, Robert San Souci, and John Steptoe. Galdone's version of *Little Red Riding Hood* (1974) is particularly appropriate for young children, while Hyman's rendition of *Little Red Riding Hood* (1983) is more appropriate for older readers. *The Twelve Dancing Princesses* has been retold by Janet Lunn (1979, illus. by Laszlo Gal), Ruth Sanderson (1990), and Marianna Mayer (1989, illus. by Kinuko Craft). Jan Ormerod has retold *The Frog Prince* (1990 illus. by David Lloyd), and Glen Rounds has produced a version of *The Three Billy Goats Gruff* (1993).

There are also parodies of well-known tales in books such as *The Three Little Wolves and the Big Bad Pig* (Trivizas, 1993) and *The True Story of the Three Little Pigs* (Scieszka, 1989). Both of these books are based on the traditional story *The Three Little Pigs* and depend on intertextual connections for their humour and impact.

In a number of clever retellings of fairy tales, the texts deviate little from the original version, but the illustrations create a powerfully different meaning to the story. *Hansel and Gretel*, retold by Anthony Browne (1981), is one such book where the traditional story is retold in a modern setting. Ian Wallace's (1994) rendition of *Hansel and Gretel* also places the story in a contemporary setting, this time in Atlantic Canada.

Modern fairy tales such as *The Tough Princess* by Martin Waddell (1986, illus. Patrick Benson) and *The King's Equal* by Katherine Paterson (1992, illus. Vladimir Vagin) play with readers' expectations and knowledge of the fairy tale genre. These books raise questions about traditional gender roles and the messages implicit in most fairy tales (for example, that a woman must be rescued by a man and is then dependent on him for living happily ever after). *The Tough Princess* manages to do this in a humorous way that questions traditional expectations from the first page. Paterson's book, *The King's Equal*, raises the same questions as *The Tough Princess*, but in a different manner, and the book accomplishes much more than a reversal of traditional gender roles. Paterson has created a story in which all the participants learn from their actions, and the presence of the mysterious wolf adds a mystical element. As teachers and students read and interact with these modern versions of fairy tales, readers may discover deeper meanings in the traditional tales. They may also be moved to question them, given the context of current societal beliefs and values.

## Myths and Legends

Many novels for children and adults are based on the patterns, characters, and plots of the best-known myths and legends, and certain recurring themes in literature can be traced back to myths. As a result, it is helpful for young readers to be introduced to myths and legends as part of the repertoire of elementary school reading. Greek, Roman, Celtic, and Norse myths are the better known of these stories, though many books now available are devoted to Aboriginal American, Chinese, and South American myths. Joseph Campbell (1988) argues that myths are powerful literature that should be read by everyone to help us understand ourselves as human beings and as social and spiritual creatures.

One such recent retelling of a Chinese myth, *The Dragon's Pearl* by Julie Lawson (1992), is beautifully illustrated by Paul Morin. The book won the **Amelia Frances Howard-Gibbon Award** for illustrations in 1993. Also illustrated by Paul Morin is Tololwa Mollel's Tanzanian myth *The Orphan Boy* (1990), which won the 1990 Governor General's Literary Award for illustration. Priscilla Galloway has retold a number of Greek myths, including *Aleta and the Queen: A Tale of Ancient Greece* (1995), *Atalanta: The Fastest Runner in the World* (1995), and *Daedalus and the Minotaur* (1997). All are illustrated by Normand Cousin. It is interesting to note that myths and legends have spawned many phrases in the English language. Greek myths in particular have generated phrases such as "the Midas touch," "Pandora's box," "Herculean effort," and "a Trojan horse."

Legends are stories told about real people and their feats or accomplishments. Usually the narratives are mixed with superstition, and they expand and enhance the actual exploits of their heroes. Legends are closely related to myths, but they do not contain supernatural deities as myths do. The stories of Beowulf, King Arthur, Robin Hood, William Tell, Davy Crockett, and Johnny Appleseed are legends. From reading myths and legends, children are encouraged to seek explanations for the phenomena in their lives — to ask questions about modern "legendary" figures and heroes and perhaps relate them to the possibilities inherent in their own lives.

## Fables

The origin of the fable is thought to reside with a Greek slave named Aesop, who lived in the sixth century B.C. Experts, however, believe there were many sources of the fable, since it is found worldwide. Fables are fictional tales that are meant to entertain though they also contain a moral. They usually have only two or three characters, frequently talking animals who possess human-like characteristics. Fables are popular with young children today largely because of the presence of the talking animals and the humour the stories contain. Fables such as "The Town Mouse and the Country Mouse" and "The Tortoise and the Hare" remain particular favourites with children. There are also many variations of "The Lion and the Mouse" and "The Raven and the Fox."

## The Oral Tradition of Storytelling

True storytelling calls upon stories that are part of the tradition of oral literature, stories that have many versions and can be modified to suit audience and purpose. These are the stories that are handed down within families or within cultural groups. The Aboriginal peoples of Canada, the United States, Australia, and New Zealand have a rich fund of stories, some of which are ritual stories that may not be shared with the general public. Families also have their stories and storytellers — stories of early settlement in homesteads on the prairie, stories of great-grandfathers who worked on the trans-Canada railway, stories of great hardship, illnesses, long journeys at sea, family treasures, and great adventures. These are the stories that cannot easily be written down and neatly illustrated. They are stories that have a special significance to the listener and frequently appeal to a small audience. This is the difference between storytelling and "performing" a text.

Children in the elementary grades generally enjoy a good storyteller. They enjoy hearing a senior citizen speak of times past in a small community, and they enjoy collecting the stories of community members. True storytelling demands discipline so that a story is captured and shaped to suit the audience and the purpose for its telling. A rambling recollection of an event that occurred a number of years ago is not the same thing as a story. Thus, teachers who wish to engage in storytelling, or to have their students tell stories in the classroom, should hone their storytelling skills. This includes perfecting the nuances of chosen vocabulary, intonation, facial expressions, and hand gestures, as well as ensuring that stories have cohesion, development, and appropriate closure, just as a good written tale does. Storytelling must also be rehearsed in the same way that any performance is rehearsed before it is shared with an audience.

Teachers can make full use of storytelling in their classrooms and help children develop as storytellers by having them read many different versions of a traditional story and then retell it in their own way. In this way children can invest the oral story with their own thoughts and feelings, story and storyteller becoming one. Two excellent resource books for teachers are *And None of It Was Nonsense: The Power of Storytelling in the Classroom* by Betty Rosen (1988) and *Stories to Tell* by Bob Barton (1992). Rosen describes her thinking, preparation, follow-up work, and lessons. The book also includes selections of her students' work. Barton has put together a set of resource materials for storytelling, and draws on his experiences as a Canadian storyteller/teacher/writer. He encourages teachers to tell their own stories, including the songs, rhymes, jingles, chants, and sayings they remember. Barton connects the worlds of storytelling, drama, games, movement, and role play in the creation of new stories, reminding us that stories can be revisited and remade again and again. In *Stories in the Classroom*, Bob Barton and David Booth (1990) collaborated in furthering their work on storytelling, drama, and response to literature. It provides another valuable resource for teachers.

## Poetry for Children

The nursery rhymes, songs, and jingles of their infancy constitute a core of literature for most children. Poetry has a major role to play in the language arts curriculum. This section presents selections of poems, poetic forms, and poetic devices appropriate for the elementary grades.

Many adults remember clearly the nursery rhymes, jingles, skipping songs, and playground chants they heard when they were preschoolers. Opie and Opie (1963) refer to these oral rhymes as "the true waifs of our literature in that their original wordings, as well as their authors, are usually unknown" (p. 7). Many of these rhymes, now considered suitable only for the nursery, were not originally intended for children. They stem from old ballads, political lampoons, and "wordly songs." The Opies spent more than twenty years collecting and researching nursery rhymes, and the section of incidental notes at the back of their collection, *The Puffin Book of Nursery Rhymes*, provides fascinating insights into the history of many rhymes in the book. Young children continue to enjoy nursery rhymes, with their unusual words, frequent nonsense, and compelling rhythms.

As adults we also remember the deeply meaningful and emotive poems read to us by family members and teachers, poems such as "Meg Merrilies" by John Keats and

"The Highwayman" by Alfred Noyes. Refrains and particularly humorous stanzas from poems such as "The Adventures of Isabel" by Ogden Nash also remain fixed in our memories. We may remember writing poems in school or responding to poems in response journals or through drama activities. Huck, Hepler, Hickman, and Kiefer (1997, p. 390) write that

> Poetry can both broaden and intensify experience, or it might present a range of experiences beyond the realm of personal possibility for the individual listener. It can also illuminate, clarify, and deepen an everyday occurrence in a way the reader never considered, making the reader see more and feel more than ever before. For poetry does more than mirror life; it reveals life in new dimensions.

Poetry communicates experience by appealing to both the thoughts and feelings of the reader. Each word is carefully chosen by the poet for the nuances and emotive meanings it conveys. Children usually need to experience poetry as being pleasurable and often amusing before they can experience its more beautiful and philosophical aspects. Poetry should be as much a part of the literary world of children as contemporary realistic fiction or picture books are. Learning to understand and appreciate poetry is an ongoing process, as it is with other forms of literature. Children are more likely to enjoy poetry if they have experienced it from their earliest days, through nursery rhymes, jingles, and songs. Nursery rhymes and skipping rhymes cannot be considered poetry, but they do lay the foundation for later journeys into poetic language.

Defining poetry is a challenge, for many contemporary poets are breaking the traditional expectations of poetry, both in content and form. Words are placed across the page, at angles, and in bunches. Contemporary poetry is written about subjects not previously dealt with (taking the garbage out, watching father eat mashed potatoes at dinner time, listening to a fight between parents). However, poems continue to make children laugh, ponder, imagine, remember, and see the world in new ways. Indeed, poetry helps to develop insights and new understandings.

As Booth and Moore (1988) write, "Children's poetry has a special appeal: the form and language of poetry speaks directly to the child, to their senses, their imaginations, their emotions, their feelings, their experiences of childhood" (p. 22). Experience tells us that children are not interested in static poems that describe the seasons, weather, or events in nature. Rather, they are interested in poems of action, rhythm, rhyme, and energy that invite them to participate and relate to their everyday experiences. Children are naturally rhythmical. From the earliest nursery rhymes to the poems of Dennis Lee, a musical rhythm pervades the text. Children are generally intrigued by the sound of language as they play with it and learn its melody.

## Sharing Poetry with Children

Children become readers and appreciators of poetry by experiencing poetry with adults who enjoy, read, and share poetry with them. Hearing the skillfully crafted arrangement of the sounds of a poem read aloud is one of the primary pleasures of poetry. Although enunciation is a fundamental component of any kind of oral sharing of poetry, it is also vital that poetry be read interpretively. This means that a reader must learn to focus on the emotive meanings conveyed by a poem, whether those meanings are playful or wistful. When children hear Sheree Fitch read her poems aloud, they are entranced by her sheer energy and engagement with the words:

> I've a yearning
> That is burning
> A desire for Higher learning
> I would like
> To go to college
> To improve upon
> My knowledge ...
> (From *If You Could Wear My Sneakers* by Sheree Fitch [poetry] and Darcia Labrosse [illustrations] © 1977 Sheree Fitch and Darcia Labrosse. Reprinted with the permission of Doubleday Canada Limited.)

Readers of poetry, whether adults or children, consider the mood they wish to set when reading a poem aloud. The interpretation of a poem is greatly influenced by how a reader varies its tempo, volume, rhythm, pitch, and juncture. Briefly,

- *tempo* refers to how slowly or quickly words or lines are read,
- *volume* refers to loudness,
- *rhythm* describes emphasis or stress,
- *pitch* refers to the lowering or raising of the voice, and
- *juncture* describes the location and length of pauses.

Teachers and students may vary these elements when reading poetry and then discuss if and how the changes affected their interpretations of the poems.

Choral reading and implementing of drama strategies enhance children's understanding and awareness of poetry. Sound effects, mime, puppets, shadow-plays, and role-playing are dramatic techniques that can be used when working with poetry in the classroom.

## Poetic Devices

*Rhyme* is a very common element of poetry. Indeed, some children believe rhyme to be the sole determining feature of poetry. The poems of Michael Rosen, Dennis Lee, Jack Prelutsky, and Shel Silverstein are contemporary works whose use of rhyme, rhythm, and playfulness forms part of their appeal. Although rhyme is a popular device of poets, children may need to expand their definition of poetry if they are to enjoy more sophisticated poems in later years.

*Comparison* is another device used by poets. The use of *similes*, explicitly comparing one thing with another using the words "like" or "as," and the use of *metaphors*, comparing two things by implying that one is like the other, are two common comparison techniques used by poets. A beautifully illustrated picture book of similes is *As Quick as a Cricket* (Woods, 1982). A tongue-in-cheek collection of similes for older readers is *As: A Surfeit of Similes* (Juster, 1989). A further poetic device used by writers is *alliteration*. Alliteration is the repeated use of the same initial consonant in consecutive words or the use of words that are close in proximity and that produce a pattern of the same or similar sounds. Chris Van Allsburg used alliteration in his alphabet book *The Z Was Zapped* (1987). *Some Smug Slug* (Edwards, 1996) is another example of the use of alliteration to tell a tale.

*Onomatopoeia* is a device wherein writers use sound words (e.g., splash, slurp, boing) to make the writing more vivid and sensory. The elements of tempo, volume, stress, and pitch can be manipulated in ways to assist in conveying the meaning and imagery of sound words. *Machine Poems* (Bennett, 1993) and *Click, Rumble, Roar: Poems about Machines* (Hopkins, 1987) are collections of poems that contain many examples of onomatopoeia. The repetition of words and phrases is another device used by many poets. For example, in the book *A Dark Dark Tale* (Brown, 1981), the author repeats the words "dark, dark." As the poem continues, each location described in the text as "dark, dark" progressively decreases in size. The poem begins, "Once upon a time there was a dark, dark moor" and the next dark, dark location is a wood, and the next one a house, and then a door, and so on.

*Imagery* and *figurative language* are other important poetic elements that play a role in poetry for children. Langston Hughes's poem "City" (1950) creates the image of the city as a bird, and Carl Sandburg (1944) likens the fog descending on a city to a cat in his poem "Fog." The language, imagery, and rhythm of poetry interact in creating the emotional force of a poem. Langston Hughes's poem entitled "Poem" (1960) evokes a powerful emotional response in most readers, as does "Listening to Grownups Quarrelling" by Ruth Whitman (1968).

## Forms of Poetry

One of the most popular forms of poetry with children is *narrative poetry*, poetry that tells a story. One narrative poem that has been reproduced in picture book format is *The Cremation of Sam McGee,* written by Robert Service and illustrated by Ted Harrison (1987). *Lyric* and *free verse* are two other forms of poetry enjoyed by children. Lyric poetry frequently describes a mood or feeling and elicits strong emotions about the subject of the poem. Although free verse poetry generally lacks rhyme, this type of poetry allows poets great freedom in creating their own rules of rhythm. Emotional language and imagery are important elements of free verse. The topics of free verse poetry are often abstract or philosophical.

*Haiku* and *cinquain* are forms of poetry that have prescribed structures. Haiku, a form of poetry originating in Japan, is a three-line poem with the first and last lines each having five syllables and the middle line having seven syllables. Traditionally, haiku dealt with topics associated with nature or the seasons, but modern haiku is written about a much broader range of subjects. Cinquain, a five-line stanza, is structured around 22 syllables in a 2-4-6-8-2 syllable pattern.

Rhyme, rhythm, and sound are important poetic elements that influence students' opinions of poems (Tompkins and Hoskisson, 1995). Edward Lear popularized *limericks*, now a favourite form of poetry among children and adults alike, in his book, *The Complete Book of Nonsense* (1846, 1946). Limericks are usually humorous or silly five-lined verses, with the first and second lines rhyming with the fifth line and the shorter third and fourth lines rhyming with each other. Often the fifth line is a repetition of the first line. Two books of limericks are *The Book of Pigericks* (Lobel, 1983) and *The Hopeful Trout and Other Limericks* (Ciardi, 1989).

*Concrete poems* are arranged in a particular manner on a page in order to create an image or visual shape of the poem's subject. For example, in the poetry collection *A Hippopotamusn't* (Lewis, 1990), Lewis has written a concrete poem about the flamingo, cleverly arranging the words in a flamingo shape. Concrete poetry is meant to be seen even more than heard. This form of poetry often lacks a rhythm or rhyming pattern. *Seeing Things: A Book of Poems* (Froman, 1974) and *Concrete Is Not Always Hard* (Pilon, 1972) are two collections of concrete poetry.

## Picture Book Versions of Poems

There are many picture book versions of single poems, including Robert Frost's "Stopping by Woods on a Snowy Evening," illustrated by Susan Jeffers (1978), and Eugene Field's "Wynken, Blynken & Nod," also illustrated by Susan Jeffers (1982). Jan Brett (1991) has illustrated a picture book version of "The Owl and the Pussy Cat" by Edward Lear, and Ed Young (1988) has illustrated Robert Frost's poem "Birches." Ted Rand has illustrated two poems: "My Shadow" (1990) by Robert Louis Stevenson, and "Arithmetic" (1993) by Carl Sandburg.

In the picture book *In Flanders Fields: The Story of the Poem by John McCrae* (1995), Linda Granfield not only presents "In Flanders Fields" but also shares information about the poet and his experiences working in a field hospital. She describes the living conditions and daily routines of the soldiers and provides information about World War I. She also explains the origin of the symbolic gesture of wearing a poppy. The illustrator, Janet Wilson, travelled to Flanders to do research for her paintings because she wanted them to be as accurate as possible.

Canadian poet sean o huigin has written many poems for children. Much of o huigin's work is traditional humorous light verse. Two serious works written by o huigin and published in picture book format are *Atmosfear* (1985), an anti-pollution poem with a cautionary message, and *The Ghost Horse of the Mounties* (1983), a poem based on an event that took place in 1874 when a violent thunderstorm stampeded the horses of the first Mounties in Manitoba. In 1983, *The Ghost Horse of the Mounties* became the first children's poetry book ever to win the Canada Council Children's Literature Prize.

## Poetry Collections

Many books of poetry are collections of one individual's works. Examples include

- *Dogs and Dragons, Trees and Dreams* (Kuskin, 1980)
- *A Light in the Attic* (Silverstein, 1981)
- *The New Kid on the Block* (Prelutsky, 1984)
- *Roomrimes* (Cassedy, 1987)
- *Day Songs, Night Songs* (Priest, 1993)
- *Demi's Secret Garden* (Demi, 1993)
- *Beast Feast* (Florian, 1994)
- *If You Could Wear My Sneakers* (Fitch, 1997)

Byrd Baylor, David McCord, John Ciardi, Dennis Lee, and Myra Cohn Livingston are also known for collections of their poetry.

Many poetry books are specialized collections of poems related to a single theme or topic — for example, snow, dinosaurs, monsters, dragons, magic, festivals, machines, Hallowe'en, and nightmares. General anthologies of poetry are useful for teachers to have on hand. Notable anthologies include *The Oxford Book of Poetry for Children*, compiled by Edward Blishen (1963); *The Random House Book of Poetry* by Jack Prelutsky (1983); *The New Wind Has Wings: Poems from Canada*, compiled by Mary Alice Downie and Barbara Robertson (1984); *Til All the Stars Have Fallen* by David Booth (1989); and *Images of Nature: Canadian Poets and the Group of Seven* by David Booth (1995). A number of poetry anthologies suitable for use in elementary school classrooms are listed in Box 10.8.

**Box 10.8**  **Poetry Resources**

Balaam, J. and Merrick, B. (1989). *Exploring Poetry: 5–8*. Sheffield, UK: National Association for the Teaching of English.

Bouchard, D. (1993). *If You're Not from the Prairie*. Vancouver: Raincoast Books.

de Paola, T. (ed.) (1988). *Tomie de Paola's Book of Poems*. New York: G.P. Putnam's Sons.

de Regniers, B.S., Moore, E., White, M.M., and Carr, J. (comp.) (1988). *Sing a Song of Popcorn: Every Child's Book of Poems*. New York: Lothrop, Lee & Shepard Books.

Fleischman, P. (1985). *Joyful Noise: Poems for Two Voices*. New York: Harper and Row.

Goldstein, B. (ed.) (1993). *Birthday Rhymes, Special Times*. New York: Delacorte.

Harrison, M. and Stuart-Clark, C. (comp.) (1995). *The New Oxford Treasury of Children's Poems*. Toronto: Oxford University Press.

Larrick, N. (ed.) (1991). *To the Moon and Back*. New York: Delacorte.

Lee, D. (1974). *Alligator Pie*. Toronto: Macmilllan Canada.

Lee, D. (1977). *Garbage Delight*. Toronto: Macmillan Canada.

Merrick, B. (1991). *Exploring Poetry: 8–13*. Sheffield, UK: National Association for the Teaching of English.

Prelutsky, J. (1993). *The Dragons Are Singing Tonight*. New York: Greenwillow Press.

Rosen, M. (1984). *Quick, Let's Get Out of Here*. New York: Dutton.

Silverstein, S. (1974). *Where the Sidewalk Ends: Poems and Drawings*. New York: Harper.

Steig, J. (1988). *Consider the Lemming*. New York: Farrar, Straus, and Giroux.

Willard, N. (1981). *A Visit to William Blake's Inn*. San Diego: Harcourt Brace Jovanovich.

Wood, N. (1993). *Spirit Walker*. New York: Doubleday.

Worth, V. (1987). *All the Small Poems*. New York: Farrar, Straus, and Giroux.

# Information Books

Nonfiction or information books are an important learning resource for use across the curriculum. Nonfiction books must be current, accurate, and appealing to children. This section presents various types of nonfiction books, as well as criteria for evaluating nonfiction materials.

Information books (also known as nonfiction literature) play a major role in every elementary classroom, for it is this genre that provides the resource material for most teaching across the entire curriculum. Through reading about a topic from many sources and from a number of different perspectives, students are able to construct a fuller understanding of the topic. Each piece of information and each point of view helps to create a broader picture in the mind of the student and provides the fertile ground for new meanings to develop. Meaning, after all, resides in the individual learner. Many children in the primary grades (and earlier) thoroughly enjoy reading nonfiction materials, and it is this genre that caters to the special interests of students and provides them with the resources they need for pursuing their avocation. However, it is only recently that educators have recognized children's interests and pleasure in reading nonfiction materials and have begun to teach children how to read expository texts as well as narrative texts.

Doiron (1994) comments that "the primacy of fiction in our literacy programs" is being challenged, and Pappas (1991) maintains that a lack of exposure to nonfiction text translates into a lack of opportunity to write nonstory compositions. The result, Pappas believes, is that most children are unprepared for the expository writing of secondary school. Clearly, children need both narrative and non-narrative reading and writing experiences. Now, with children in even the primary grades being encouraged to write reports and projects using nonfiction materials for information, educators are teaching youngsters how to use the index of a book, the glossary, and the table of contents, as well as how to browse through a book quickly to see from the pictures and the headings if the book is going to be helpful or interesting.

There are at least eight major types of nonfiction books:

1. photo-documentaries

2. "how-to" books

3. question and answer formats

4. experiment and activity books

5. sequential explanation (survey) books

6. field guides

7. biographies

8. narrative nonfiction

There are also specialized books such as picture songbooks. Some of these nonfiction books are designed to be used as reference materials and have a typical expository format. Others are intended to be read from beginning to end, more like a work of fiction, and consist of narrative text.

Nonfiction material has improved a great deal in quality and presentation over the last ten years. Many of the nonfiction materials still on library shelves from the 1970s look dull and uninviting compared with more recent publications. The explosion in technology, allowing for the superb reproduction of photographs, maps, and other graphics and a more interesting and accessible page layout, has created a splendid new age of nonfiction, especially for young readers.

Many awards have been specifically created for nonfiction books. These include the Information Book Award sponsored by the Children's Literature Round Tables of Canada, the Orbis Pictus Award for Outstanding Nonfiction for Children established by the National Council of Teachers of English (in the United States), the Boston Globe–Horn Book Award established jointly by the *Boston Globe* and *The Horn Book Magazine* (United States), and the *Times* Educational Supplement Information Book Awards (UK). The designation of these awards is a mark of the increasing recognition accorded nonfiction books, as well as a recognition of children's strong interest in informational materials. It is also an indication that the quality of nonfiction materials has improved sufficiently to merit awards specifically for the genre.

## Criteria for Evaluating Nonfiction Books

The information available in any subject area grows rapidly over time. Keeping a nonfiction collection up to date is a major challenge and a major expense for any school or library. Books published on a topic ten or fifteen years ago are likely to be out of date today. It is therefore important that nonfiction books be purchased for the school or classroom library with discrimination, and with the aid of library selection tools such as *The Horn Book Magazine, School Library Journal, Emergency Librarian,* or *Booklist.* It is also important that the books made available to children be current, and that they not be allowed to remain on the shelves for years without being reviewed. A list of evaluation criteria for nonfiction books is presented in Box 10.9.

The *accuracy* and *authenticity* of material is probably the most difficult criteria for educators to assess. The first thing to look for in any nonfiction book is an indication from the author(s) that either they have the expertise themselves (as with Beatty and Geiger, 1992, in *Buried in Ice: Unlocking the Secrets of a Doomed Arctic Voyage),* or they have consulted with experts in the creation of the book (as in the Starting with Space series from Kids Can Press). The latter series contains excellent illustrations, clear explanations, and interesting activities for readers to complete either at home or at school. The books in the series have a glossary, an index, a table of contents, *and* an acknowledgement of the assistance provided by the scientists at the Royal Ontario Museum (McLaughlin Planetarium). This last piece of information tells the reader that the information contained in the book has come from a reliable source. Whatever is provided for the reader, however, the main criteria for selecting a book must be compatibility with the reader's own background knowledge of the subject. Teachers play a crucial role in assisting their students to select books that are appropriate in content — books that are neither too simple nor conceptually overloaded.

**Box 10.9    Criteria for Evaluating Nonfiction Books**

**Format**
- Is the book well made so that it will stand up to wear?
- Is the page design uncluttered?
- Is the book visually appealing? Does it invite the reader to browse through it?
- Does it pique the reader's interest?
- Are there enough visuals and enough colour to make the book appealing?

**Organization and Style**
- Is the material presented in a clear and unambiguous way?
- Does the book create a feeling of reader involvement and convey a positive tone?
- Does the author use vivid and interesting language?
- Is the content structured clearly and logically, with appropriate subheadings?
- Are there reference aids such as a table of contents, index, bibliography, glossary, and appendix?

**Content**
- Is the content presented in a manner that allows children to connect it with their own experiences?

- Where content has been simplified, does it retain accuracy?
- Does the book include the author's sources as well as additional information for keen readers who want to learn more?
- Is the book current and does it reflect (and mention) current research activity in the field?
- Are the qualifications and experiences of the authors presented?
- Does the book avoid stereotypes and present differing viewpoints?
- Is a distinction made among fact, theory, and opinion?
- Does the book foster a scientific method of inquiry?

**Graphics and Illustration**
- Are there appropriate and sufficient maps, charts, and diagrams to add to the reader's understanding of the text?
- Are the graphics and illustrations an appropriate size?
- Are the graphics and illustrations clearly understandable and well-labelled?
- Do the maps, charts, and diagrams contain appropriate detail?

Source: Based on F. Smardo Dowd (1992), "Trends and Evaluative Criteria of Informational Books for Children." In E. Freeman and D. Person (eds.), *Using Nonfiction Trade Books in the Classroom: From Ants to Zeppelins,* pp. 34–43. Urbana, IL: National Council of Teachers of English.

The *format* of nonfiction books is an especially important area to evaluate. Some nonfiction books are too "busy" in their layout for young readers. The visual effect is one of overload, as the reader has to attend to too much input at one time. A pleasing book in terms of content and format is *Light Magic and Other Science Activities about Energy* (Rising and Williams, 1994), a book readers will likely pick up and read in occasional short bursts rather than use as a reference book or for a sustained read. Many activities are included in the book, which children can complete themselves, and the illustrations are generally of high quality. This book is suitable for a classroom collection, and it covers a large number of broad topics related to energy. *Light Magic* is one of the better books of its kind.

Unfortunately, many science books are printed without colour photographs and diagrams. These may contain lots of interesting information and ideas for children, but they are not laid out or planned in ways that make them accessible for young readers. The books usually contain black-and-white drawings that, in combination with the black-and-white text, do little to help children stay focussed on the various units of meaning presented on each page. Too much information is presented in the same format for readers to be able to easily pick out which information belongs together. Children can become overwhelmed by the amount of information, even if it is in the form of a diagram or drawing, and they may close the book and move on to something else. Colour photographs and drawings help young readers move their eyes and their attention around the page from one unit of meaning to another more easily. *The Disaster of the Hindenburg* (Tanaka, 1993) is well-formatted, allowing the focus of attention to move smoothly from text to diagram to photograph and back to text. The format provides the reader with the help necessary to take in the information and make sense of it.

## Narrative Nonfiction

Some of the most fascinating nonfiction materials published recently are narrative texts that incorporate details and explanations into a story. These books are not easy to come by. David Suzuki sought to use narrative in his Nature All Around series. Some of the books in the series work better than others, but all remain blatantly didactic, consisting of what is basically a lecture-tour by a mother, father, or other character in the story. The aesthetic experience afforded by these books does not meet the informative value.

*Anastasia's Album* (Brewster, 1996) is a most interesting Canadian work of narrative nonfiction consisting of photographs, watercolours, and hand-decorated pages capturing the life of Tsar Nicholas's youngest daughter. The story of the Romanov family is told from the perspective of Anastasia herself, and includes excerpts from her diaries and letters as well as the recollections of family friends. The book makes interesting and compelling reading for adults as well as children, and does not "talk down" to a child audience.

One of the best-known books of narrative nonfiction for young children is the award-winning Australian book *Where the Forest Meets the Sea* by Jeanie Baker (1987). It is an innovative picture book that chronicles the reflections of a young boy exploring the rainforest of northern Queensland with his father. The illustrations (also done by Baker) consist of relief collage constructed from a mix of natural materials, including lamb's wool, fabric, and leaves. The effect is stunning—a rich three-dimensional perspective on the rainforest that invites the reader to explore the secrets of the rainforest and the majesty of nature. The boy plays, imagines, wonders, and questions: "Will the rainforest still be here when we come back?" No answers are provided, no didacticism. It is left to the reader to ponder the question.

*Theodoric's Rainbow*, written by Stephen Kramer (1995) and illustrated by Daniel Mark Duffy, tells the story (much of it through pictures) of Theodoric of Freiberg, a German philosopher and theologian who was one of the first people to experiment in science (rather than philosophize). Theodoric discovered how drops of water reflect and refract light. He then went on to develop the first geometrically correct explanation of the rainbow. There is far more text in this book than in *Where the Forest Meets the Sea*, but the text is straightforward and well-written. Children from Grade 3 onwards (and possibly earlier) will find this beautiful book fascinating.

*Thunderstorm!* (Tripp, 1994) is a book that describes the large and small changes that take place in the atmosphere when weather fronts move. Such changes warn animals and humans to seek shelter from the explosive force of a storm. The book, illustrated by Juan Wijngaard, tells in narrative style how a thunderstorm develops over one farm, building in intensity and transforming quiet farmland into nature's most spectacular sound and light show.

These and other well-written, well-illustrated nonfiction books for children have moved the genre into a new era. Many may truly be termed literature for the pure pleasure, as well as the information, that they offer. Ultimately, though written for children, they make compelling reading for all ages.

> At the beginning of this chapter, Jennifer wondered how she could include nonfiction literature in her reading program. This last section of the chapter has provided examples of books she might suggest to her students. These books provide educators with opportunities for teaching and creating new meaning for students, and provide children with opportunities to reflect on and appreciate the artistic presentation and well-crafted texts of this genre.

## Summary

Scholars such as Meek (1988) and Wells (1986) have demonstrated how children who are read to in their preschool years and who learn to appreciate literature are much more likely to experience success in their literacy development and in their learning in school. They are also more likely to read for pleasure when they are adults. Learning from this, educators have embraced the concept of literature-based reading instruction, and many have created language arts programs based on the many genres of trade books available. Consequently, children's literature is incorporated into most language arts programs in Canada, whether it is used to balance a basal reading series or used as the foundation for the literacy program.

A wide range of top-quality literature is available for children in the elementary grades. The picture book genre is growing most rapidly in terms of scope and quality. Many picture books are produced for students in upper elementary and junior high schools. Likewise, most novels for children are available in paperback and include fantasy, contemporary realistic fiction, historical fiction, time-slip fantasy, mystery, and horror. Modern classics — books such as *Charlotte's Web* (White, 1952) and *Angel Square* (Doyle, 1984) — are part of the cultural heritage of youngsters. Traditional stories, poetry, and storytelling all play a role in the repertoire of literary materials and activities with which children engage. Books of all genres continue to create opportunities for children to take on the four roles of the reader as described by Freebody and Luke (1990): code breaker, text participant, text user, and text analyst. Mastering these four roles not only enhances a child's reading ability, it also contributes to the lifelong pleasures he or she will have from reading.

The quality and number of nonfiction books available for the classroom have increased markedly over the last fifteen years. Current technology has helped to create colourful, interesting, and understandable diagrams, charts, and maps. Graphics are generally appealing, and photographs are reproduced with greater clarity than ever before. Authors of nonfiction material for children must write intelligently for an audience that has access to more information than was ever previously available. Such materials must therefore be current, accurate, well-designed, and interesting, for they are competing with the Internet, television, and movies as sources of information for students. However, good nonfiction literature for children must also be aesthetically appealing to a wide audience, including adults. This is especially the case in books of narrative nonfiction where information is embedded in a contextualized narrative. Frequently such stories are accompanied by illustrations rendered by well-known artists.

As language arts programs increasingly incorporate works of children's literature as instructional resources, teachers are finding they must be knowledgeable about books, authors, and illustrators, and must be able to talk with children about the books they are reading. Teachers regularly recommend books of all genres to children. This means that teachers increasingly read books written for children and are familiar with the reading interests of their students. If teachers enjoy books and welcome children into the world of literature, their students are also likely to enjoy books and become lifelong readers.

## Selected Professional Resources

Huck, C., Hepler, S., Hickman, J., and Kiefer, B.Z. (1997). *Children's Literature in the Elementary School*. (6th ed.). Dubuque, IA: Brown & Benchmark. This American text remains one of the most encompassing of resources on children's literature. It is an excellent source of information on the different genres of literature, the history of children's literature, author and illustrator profiles, and planning for instruction in the elementary school. The book provides a wealth of background information, and is a useful reference tool for classroom teachers.

Kiefer, B. (1995). *The Potential of Picturebooks: From Visual Literacy to Aesthetic Understanding*. Englewood Cliffs, NJ: Prentice-Hall. This textbook is devoted to examining the many issues associated with picture books, including children's responses to them and the development of contexts that support and encourage these responses. Kiefer devotes the second section of her book to discussions about the history of picture books, the process of creating them, and their artistic styles. In the third section of the book, "Picturebooks in the Classroom," she explores the art of the genre, provides suggestions for studying an illustrator, and discusses bookmaking and publishing. Kiefer provides many classroom suggestions and also identifies numerous titles throughout her book.

Tomlinson, C. and Lynch-Brown, C. (1998). *Essentials of Children's Literature* (3rd ed.). Needham Heights, MA: Allyn & Bacon. Chapters 1 and 2 discuss many issues related to children and literature, including defining children's literature, identifying the value of children's literature, describing the elements of fiction, and exploring the visual elements, artistic styles, and media of books. The authors devote an entire chapter to each of the following categories of literature: poetry, picture books, traditional literature, modern fantasy, realistic fiction, historical fiction, biography and informational books, and multicultural and international literature. As well as discussing various issues related to each category, the authors provide extensive references to authors and books for each category of literature. The remaining two chapters of the book describe organizational structures and teaching strategies for literature-based programs. The text also includes an extensive appendix of children's book awards and another appendix of professional resources.

## Children's Books Noted in Chapter Ten

Ahlberg, J. and Ahlberg, A. (1978). *Each Peach Pear Plum*. London: Kestrel Books.

Avi. (1981). *Who Stole the Wizard of Oz?* New York: Alfred A. Knopf.

Babbitt, N. (1975). *Tuck Everlasting*. New York: Farrar, Straus and Giroux.

Baker, J. (1987). *Where the Forest Meets the Sea*. New York: Greenwillow Books.

Banks, L.R. (1980). *The Indian in the Cupboard*. New York: Avon Books.

Beatty, O. and Geiger, J. (1992). *Buried in Ice: Unlocking the Secrets of a Doomed Arctic Voyage*. Mississauga, ON: Random House.

Bellairs, J. (1978). *The Treasure of Alpheus Winterborn*. New York: Dial Books for Young Readers.

Bennett, J. (1993). *Machine Poems*. Don Mills, ON: Oxford University Press.

Blishen, E. (comp.). (1963). *The Oxford Book of Poetry for Children*. London: Oxford University Press.

Booth, D. (1989). *Til All the Stars Have Fallen*. Toronto: Kids Can Press.

Booth, D. (1995). *Images of Nature: Canadian Poets and the Group of Seven*. Toronto: Kids Can Press.

Brandis, M. (1996). *Rebellion: A Novel of Upper Canada*. Erin, ON: The Porcupine's Quill.

Brett, J. (illus.). (1991). *The Owl and the Pussy Cat*. (Poem by Edward Lear.) New York: Putnam.

Brewster, H. (1996). *Anastasia's Album*. Toronto: Penguin Books.

Brouillet, C. (1996). *The Chinese Puzzle*. Charlottetown: Ragweed Press.

Brown, R. (1981). *A Dark, Dark Tale*. New York: Scholastic.

Browne, A. (1981). *Hansel and Gretel*. London: Julia MacRae Books.

Browne, A. (1986). *Piggybook*. New York: Alfred A. Knopf.

Browne, A. (1989). *The Tunnel*. London: Julia MacRae Books.

Buchan, B. (1975). *The Dragon Children*. Richmond Hill, ON: Scholastic-TAB.

Buffie, M. (1987). *Who Is Frances Rain?* Toronto: Kids Can Press.

Bunting, E. (1988). *Is Anybody There?* New York: Harper & Row.

Burningham, J. (1977). *Come Away from the Water, Shirley*. London: Cape.

Byars, B. (1996). *Dead Letter*. New York: Viking.

Byars, B. (1997). *Death's Door*. New York: Viking.

Cassedy, S. (1987). *Roomrimes*. New York: Thomas Crowell.

Ciardi, J. (1989). *The Hopeful Trout and Other Limericks*. New York: Houghton Mifflin.

Coerr, E. (1993). *Sadako*. (E. Young, illustrator). New York: Putnam.

Cooper, S. (1969). *The Dark Is Rising*. New York: Collier Macmillan.

Creech, S. (1994). *Walk Two Moons*. New York: HarperCollins.

Curtis, C. (1995). *The Watsons Go to Birmingham, 1963*. New York: Delacorte.

Dahl, R. (1961). *James and the Giant Peach*. New York: Puffin Books.

Davidge, B. and Wallace, I. (1993). *The Mummer's Song*. Toronto: Groundwood Books.

Demi. (1993). *Demi's Secret Garden*. New York: Henry Holt & Co.

Downie, D. and Robertson, B. (comp.). (1984). *The New Wind Has Wings: Poems from Canada*. Toronto: Oxford University Press.

Doyle, B. (1984). *Angel Square*. Toronto: Douglas & McIntyre.

Edwards, P. (1996). *Some Smug Slug*. New York: HarperCollins.

Ellis, S. (1991). *Pick-Up Sticks*. Toronto: Groundwood Books.

Ellis, S. (1998). *The Back of Beyond*. Toronto: Groundwood Books.

Filipovic, Z. (1994). *Zlata's Diary: A Child's Life in Sarajevo*. New York: Penguin.

Fitch, S. (1997). *If You Could Wear My Sneakers*. Toronto: Doubleday Canada.

Florian, D. (1994). *Beast Feast*. New York: Harcourt Brace.

Fox, P. (1973). *The Slave Dancer*. New York: Bradbury.

Froman, R. (1974). *Seeing Things: A Book of Poems*. New York: Thomas Y. Crowell.

Galdone, P. (1974). *Little Red Riding Hood*. New York: McGraw-Hill.

Galloway, P. (1995). *Aleta and the Queen: A Tale of Ancient Greece.* (N. Cousin, illustrator). Toronto: Annick Press.

Galloway, P. (1995). *Atalanta: The Fastest Runner in the World.* (N. Cousin, illustrator). Toronto: Annick Press.

Galloway, P. (1997). *Daedalus and the Minotaur.* (N. Cousin, illustrator). Toronto: Annick Press.

Garner, A. (1967). *The Owl Service.* London: William Collins & Sons.

Graham, K. (1908). *The Wind in the Willows.* New York: Scribners.

Granfield, L. (1995). *In Flanders Fields: The Story of the Poem by John McCrae.* (J. Wilson, illustrator). Toronto: Lester.

Greene, B. (1973). *The Summer of My German Soldier.* New York: Bantam.

Greene, B. (1974). *Philip Hall Likes Me. I Reckon Maybe.* New York: Bantam Doubleday Dell.

Harrison, T. (illus.). (1987). *The Cremation of Sam McGee.* (Poem by Robert W. Service.) New York: Greenwillow.

Hesse, K. (1992). *Letters from Rifka.* New York: Puffin Books.

Hopkins, L.B. (1987). *Click, Rumble, Roar: Poems about Machines.* New York: Thomas Y. Crowell.

Hughes, L. (1950). "City." In *The Langston Hughes Reader.* New York: Harold Ober Associates.

Hughes, L. (1960). "Poem." In *Don't You Turn Back: Poems by Langston Hughes.* L.B. Hopkins (ed.). New York: Knopf.

Hutchins, P. (1969). *Rosie's Walk.* London: Bodley Head Press.

Hyman, T.S. (1983). *Little Red Riding Hood.* New York: Holiday House.

Innocenti, R. (1985). *Rose Blanche.* Mankato, MN: Creative Education.

Jacques, B. (1987). *Redwall.* New York: Philomel.

Jeffers, S. (illus.). (1992). *Wynken, Blynken and Nod.* (Poem by E. Field). New York: E.P. Dutton.

Jeffers, S. (illus.). (1978). *Stopping by Woods on a Snowy Evening.* (Poem by Robert Frost.) New York: Dutton Books.

Juster, N. (1989). *As: A Surfeit of Similes.* New York: William Morrow.

Kodama, T. (1995). *Shin's Tricycle.* New York: Walker.

Kramer, S. (1995). *Theodoric's Rainbow.* (D.M. Duffy, illustrator). New York: W.H. Freeman & Co.

Kuskin, K. (1980). *Dogs and Dragons, Trees and Dreams.* New York: Harper & Row.

Lawson, J. (1992). *The Dragon's Pearl.* (Paul Morin, illustrator.) Toronto: Stoddart.

Lear, E. (1946 [1846]). *The Complete Book of Nonsense.* New York: Dodd, Mead.

Le Guin, U. (1971). *A Wizard of Earthsea.* Harmondsworth, UK: Penguin.

L'Engle, M. (1962). *A Wrinkle in Time.* New York: Farrar, Straus and Giroux.

Lewis, J.P. (1990). *A Hippopotamustn't.* New York: Dial Books for Young Readers.

Lisle, J.T. (1989). *Afternoon of the Elves.* New York: Orchard Books.

Little, J. (1985). *Lost and Found.* Toronto: Penguin Books Canada.

Little, J. (1991). *Once Upon a Golden Apple.* Markham, ON: Viking.

Lobel, A. (1983). *The Book of Pigericks.* New York: Harper & Row.

Lowry, L. (1989). *Number the Stars.* New York: Houghton Mifflin.

Lowry, L. (1993). *The Giver.* Boston: Houghton Mifflin.

Lunn, J. (1979). *The Twelve Dancing Princesses.* (L. Gal, illustrator.) Toronto: Methuen.

Lunn, J. (1981). *The Root Cellar.* New York: Scribners.

Macaulay, D. (1990). *Black and White.* New York: Houghton Mifflin.

McNicoll, S. (1996). *The Big Race.* Richmond Hill, ON: Scholastic Canada.

McSwigan, M. (1942). *Snow Treasure.* New York: E.P. Dutton.

Maruki, T. (1980). *Hiroshima No Pika.* New York: Lothrop, Lee & Shepard Books.

Mayer, M. (1989). *The Twelve Dancing Princesses.* (K. Craft, illustrator.) New York: Morrow.

Mollel, T. (1990). *The Orphan Boy.* (P. Morin, illustrator.) Toronto: Oxford University Press.

Montgomery, L.M. (1908). *Anne of Green Gables.* London: L.C. Page & Company.

Morimoto, J. (1987). *My Hiroshima.* Sydney, Australia: Collins.

Norton, M. (1952). *The Borrowers.* San Diego: Harcourt.

O'Dell, S. (1970). *Sing Down the Moon.* New York: Bantam Doubleday Dell.

O'Dell, S. and Hall, E. (1992). *Thunder Rolling in the Mountains.* New York: Bantam Doubleday Dell.

o huigin, s. (1983). *The Ghost Horse of the Mounties.* Windsor, ON: Black Moss Press.

o huigin, s. (1985). *Atmosfear.* Windsor, ON: Black Moss Press.

Ormerod, J. (1981). *Sunshine.* Harmondsworth, UK: Puffin Books.

Ormerod, J. (1982). *Moonlight.* Harmondsworth, UK: Puffin Books.

Ormerod, J. (1990). *The Frog Prince.* (D. Lloyd, illustrator.) New York: Lothrop, Lee & Shepard Books.

Parks, R. (1980). *Playing Beatie Bow*. Ringwood, Australia: Penguin Books Australia.
Paterson, K. (1992). *The King's Equal*. (V. Vagin, illustrator.) New York: HarperCollins.
Pearce, P. (1958). *Tom's Midnight Garden*. London: Oxford University Press.
Pearson, K. (1986). *The Daring Game*. Markham, ON: Puffin Books.
Pearson, K. (1987). *A Handful of Time*. Markham, ON: Viking Kestrel.
Pearson, K. (1989). *The Sky Is Falling*. Markham, ON: Viking Kestrel.
Pearson, K. (1998). *This Land*. Markham, ON: Viking.
Pilon, A. (1972). *Concrete Is Not Always Hard*. New York: Xerox Education.
Priest, R. (1993). *Day Songs, Night Songs*. Toronto: Groundwood Books.
Prelutsky, J. (1983). *The Random House Book of Poetry*. New York: Random House.
Prelutsky, J. (1984). *The New Kid on the Block*. New York: Greenwillow Books.
Pullman, P. (1996). *The Golden Compass*. New York: Knopf.
Rand, T. (illus.). (1990). *My Shadow*. (Poem by Robert Louis Stevenson.) New York: Putnam.
Rand, T. (illus.). (1993). *Arithmetic*. (Poem by Carl Sandburg.) New York: Harcourt Brace.
Reiss, J. (1972). *The Upstairs Room*. New York: Scholastic.
Richler, M. (1975). *Jacob Two-Two Meets the Hooded Fang*. Toronto: Puffin Books.
Richler, M. (1987). *Jacob Two-Two and the Dinosaur*. Toronto: Puffin Books.
Richler, M. (1995). *Jacob Two-Two's First Spy Case*. Toronto: McClelland & Stewart.
Rising, T. and Williams, P. (1994). *Light Magic and Other Science Activities about Energy*. Toronto: Owl (Greey de Pencier Books).
Roberts, K. (1987). *Pop Bottles*. Vancouver: Douglas & McIntyre.
Roberts, K. (1988). *Hiccup Champion of the World*. Vancouver: Douglas & McIntyre.
Roberts, W.D. (1988). *Megan's Island*. New York: Macmillan.
Rounds, G. (1993). *The Three Billy Goats Gruff*. New York: Holiday House.
Rylant, C. (1986). *Night in the Country*. New York: Bradbury Press.
Sandburg, C. (1944). "Fog." In *Chicago Poems*. New York: Harcourt Brace & Co.
Sanderson, R. (1990). *The Twelve Dancing Princesses*. New York: Little, Brown & Co.
Scieszka, J. (1989). *The True Story of the Three Little Pigs*. New York: Scholastic.
Shreve, S. (1987). *Lucy Forever & Miss Rosetree, Shrinks*. New York: Alfred A. Knopf.
Shura, M.F. (1989). *The Mystery at Wolf River*. New York: Scholastic.
Silverstein, S. (1981). *A Light in the Attic*. New York: Harper & Row.
Smucker, B. (1977). *Underground to Canada*. Toronto: Clarke, Irwin.
Spalding, A. (1995). *Finders Keepers*. Victoria, BC: Beach Home.
Speare, E.G. (1983). *Sign of the Beaver*. New York: Bantam Doubleday Dell.
Spinelli, G. (1990). *Maniac Magee*. Boston: Little, Brown & Co..
Stine, R. L. (1992). *Welcome to the Dead House* (Goosebumps Series). New York: Scholastic.
Sutcliff, R. (1958). *Warrior Scarlet*. Harmondsworth, UK: Puffin Books.
Tanaka, S. (1993). *The Disaster of the Hindenburg*. Richmond Hill, ON: Scholastic/Time Quest.
Taylor, C. (1987). *The Doll*. Toronto: Douglas & McIntyre.
Thomas, G. and Crossley-Holland, K. (1985). *Tales from the Mabinogian*. New York: Overlook Press.
Tolkien, J.R.R. (1937). *The Hobbit*. Boston: Houghton.
Toten, T. (1995). *The Onlyhouse*. Red Deer, AB: Red Deer College Press.
Tripp, N. (1994). *Thunderstorm!* (J. Wijngaard, illustrator.) New York: Dial Books.
Trivizas, E. (1993). *The Three Little Wolves and the Big Bad Pig*. London: William Heinemann.
Truss, J. (1977). *A Very Small Rebellion*. Edmonton: J.M. Lebel Enterprises.
Truss, J. (1982). *Jasmin*. Vancouver: Douglas & McIntyre.
Uchida, Y. (1978). *Journey Home*. New York: Aladdin Paperbacks.
Valgardson, W. D. (1997). *Garbage Creek*. Toronto: Groundwood Books.
Van Allsburg, C. (1987). *The Z Was Zapped*. New York: Houghton Mifflin.
Van Allsburg, C. (1992). *The Widow's Broom*. New York: Houghton Mifflin.
Waddell, M. (1986). *The Tough Princess*. (P. Benson, illustrator.) London: Walker Books.
Wallace, I. (1994). *Hansel and Gretel*. Toronto: Douglas & McIntyre.
White, E.B. (1952). *Charlotte's Web*. New York: Harper and Row.
Whitman, R. (1968). "Listening to Grownups Quarrelling." In *The Marriage Wig and Other Poems*. New York: Harcourt Brace & Co.
Wiesner, D. (1988). *Free Fall*. New York: Lothrop, Lee & Shepard Books.
Wiesner, D. (1991). *Tuesday*. New York: Clarion.
Wiesner, D. (1992). *June 29, 1999*. Boston: Houghton Mifflin.

Wild, M. (1991). *Let the Celebrations Begin!* (J. Vivas, illustrator.) Adelaide, Australia: Omnibus Books.

Williams, M. (1922). *The Velveteen Rabbit.* New York: Doubleday.

Wilson, B. (1995). *Harold and Harold.* Porters Lake, NS: Pottersfield Press.

Wilson, E. (1983). *The Kootenay Kidnapper.* Don Mills, ON: Collins.

Winthrop, E. (1985). *The Castle in the Attic.* New York: Bantam Skylark.

Woods, A. (1982). *As Quick as a Cricket.* New York: Child's Play International.

Wynne-Jones, T. (1992). *Zoom Upstream.* (E. Beddows, illustrator.) Toronto: Douglas & McIntyre.

Wynne-Jones, T. (1993). *Some of the Kinder Planets.* Toronto: Douglas & McIntyre.

Wynne-Jones, T. (1994). *The Book of Changes.* Toronto: Douglas & McIntyre.

Wynne-Jones, T. (1995). *The Maestro.* Toronto: Douglas & McIntyre.

Wynne-Jones, T. (1999). *Lord of the Fries and Other Stories.* Toronto: Douglas & McIntyre.

York, C. (1984). *Secrets in the Attic.* New York: Scholastic.

Young, E. (illus.). (1988). *Birches.* (Poem by Robert Frost.) New York: Henry Holt & Company.

## References

Barthes, R. (1970, trans. 1974). *S/Z: An essay.* New York: Hill & Wang.

Barton, B. (1992). *Stories to tell.* Markham, ON: Pembroke.

Barton, B. and Booth, D. (1990). *Stories in the classroom.* Markham, ON: Pembroke.

Booth, D. and Moore, B. (1988). *Poems please! Sharing poetry with children.* Markham, ON: Pembroke.

Campbell, J. (1988). *The power of myth.* New York: Doubleday.

Dickson, R. (1998). Horror: To gratify, not edify. *Language Arts, 76* (2), 115–122.

Doiron, R. (1994). Using nonfiction in a read-aloud program: Letting the facts speak for themselves. *Reading Teacher, 47* (8), 616–623.

Eco, U. (1978). *The role of the reader.* Bloomington, IN: Indiana University Press.

Freebody, P. and Luke, A. (1990). "Literacies" programs: Debates and demands in cultural contexts. *Prospects, 5* (3), 7–16.

Freeman, E. and Person, D. (eds.). (1992). *Using nonfiction trade books in the classroom: From ants to zeppelins.* Urbana, IL: National Council of Teachers of English.

Holdaway, D. (1979). *The foundations of literacy.* Gosford, Australia: Ashton Scholastic.

Huck, C.S., Hepler, S., Hickman, J., and Kiefer, B.Z. (1997*). Children's literature in the elementary school.* (6th ed). Dubuque, IA: Brown & Benchmark.

Hunt, L.C. (1970). The effect of self-selection, interest and motivation upon independent, instructional and frustration level. *Reading Teacher, 24* (2), 146–151.

Keifer, B. (1995). *The potential of picturebooks: From visual literacy to aesthetic understanding.* Englewood Cliffs, NJ: Prentice-Hall.

Meek, M. (1988). *How texts teach what readers learn.* Stroud, UK: Thimble Press.

Opie, I. and Opie, P. (1963). *The Puffin book of nursery rhymes.* Harmondsworth, UK: Penguin Books.

Pantaleo, S. (1994). Teacher influence on student response to literature. PhD dissertation, University of Alberta, Edmonton, AB.

Pappas, C. (1991). Fostering full access to literacy by including information books. *Language Arts, 68* (6), 449–461.

Perry, L.A. and Butler, R.P. (1997). Are Goosebumps books real literature? *Language Arts, 74* (6), 454–456.

Rosen, B. (1988). *And none of it was nonsense: The power of storytelling in the classroom.* Richmond Hill, ON: Scholastic-TAB.

Tomlinson, C. and Lynch-Brown, C. (1998). *Essentials of children's literature* (3rd ed.). Needham Heights, MA: Allyn & Bacon.

Tompkins, G. and Hoskisson, K. (1995). *Language arts: Content and teaching strategies.* (3rd ed.). Englewood, NJ: Prentice-Hall.

Vanderhaeghe, G. (1996). *The Englishman's boy.* Toronto: McClelland & Stewart.

Wells, G. (1986). *The meaning makers.* Portsmouth, NH: Heinemann.

# Chapter eleven

# Responding to Literature

**Reader Response**
- Learning through Response
- Response Groups
- Literature Response Journals
- Readers' Workshop
- Literature Circles
- Novel Studies
- Alternative Modes of Response
- Dependent Authorship

**Book Selection**
- Guidelines for Appropriate Selection of Children's Literature
- Censorship of Children's Materials
- Issues and Controversies

**Responding to Literature**

**Canadian Literature**
- Why Canadian?
- Books by Aboriginal Canadians

When Shawn began his student teaching in a Grade 5 classroom, the teacher told him he would be working with the students as they engaged in response groups. She invited him to suggest a few novels the students might enjoy. Shawn wanted to choose some Canadian books but wasn't sure which titles would be most appropriate. He also wanted to suggest books the children would enjoy, but not something controversial that might run the risk of offending the school community. Shawn began researching current titles and began to think about how the language arts teaching strategies he had learned in his course work would fit into response group activities. How, for example, could Halliday's functions of language (1969) help him? Where would dramatic response be most appropriate, and in what ways could he help the children to become involved in writing response journals? ∎

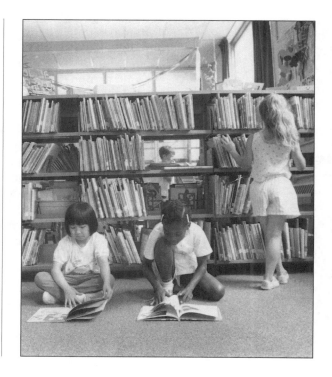

This chapter addresses Shawn's questions about how teachers can facilitate literary response and how they can go about selecting literature for the classroom. As an introduction to these topics, cast your mind back to your own early reading instruction. What and where did you read in school? Was more than one reading series or more than one grade level of material used in your classroom? Did you visit the school library regularly and check out books to take home? Did the classroom have its own collection of books? Were you allowed to read some books and not others? Who decided what you could and could not read? Did you participate in response activities such as group discussions, puppet shows, or journal writing about the books and stories you were reading? Did your teacher read books aloud to the whole class regularly, and talk with the class about well-known authors and illustrators and their work? These same questions are important for teachers to consider when planning a balanced literacy program for their own classrooms. The decisions they make about these items will deeply affect the literacy programs they develop and implement with their students.

## Reader Response

The first section of this chapter explains what is meant by reader response and what that response "looks like" in a classroom. As well, many activities are described for use in the elementary language arts program.

*Reader response* refers to the events that occur within a reader when a piece of text is read. Rosenblatt (1978) maintains that text is simply squiggles on a page until a reader reads it. When a reader reads the print, *something* happens within the reader. That "something" is often labelled "response." The response might be boredom, confusion, interest, sadness, empathy, or joy, but a reading event is never undertaken without a variety of responses. People respond to all kinds of events in their everyday lives — a menu read in a restaurant, a movie seen at the cinema, news from a friend, a television show, international news on the radio, a song, a play, an editorial in the newspaper. Response is part of the human condition, part of our interactions with the people and the world around us. It is part of the meaning-making process, and as such, response to literature is an important component of a language arts program.

Rosenblatt (1978) refers to the reading experience as a transaction between *text* and *reader*, a transaction that creates the *poem*, or what Rosenblatt terms the "lived-through experience with the text." Readers respond to the "poem" (a term used broadly by Rosenblatt to mean the transactional experience) as they read, after they read, and when they reflect on or recapture their reading experience. Rosenblatt maintains that a response is dictated to a considerable extent by the purpose for reading or, in other words, by the *stance* from which the reader approaches the text. A stance can be anywhere on a continuum from efferent at one end, where the reader seeks information of some kind, to aesthetic at the other, where the reader focusses on appreciating what is read. Response fluctuates along this continuum as we read. At one moment a reader may be reading for the pure pleasure and appreciation of a work, and the next moment might be noticing something interesting and memorable in the text, or something that relates to a piece of information received from a different source in the recent past. For example, when reading *The Doll* (Taylor, 1987), a reader may first be appreciating the artistry of the language and the tantalizing nature of time-slip fantasy. Then, suddenly, his or her attention might shift to a focus on prairie fires and the devastation they can cause to farmland and livestock—a thought that can be connected with a newspaper article he or she read the previous day. The reading experience thus moves from an aesthetic stance to a more efferent stance.

The extremes of response on this continuum can be demonstrated by two quite different reading events. When someone is reading a first-aid manual to treat an injury, the reading has a very pragmatic purpose—to allow the reader to gain essential information that will directly affect his or her behaviour in the immediate future. The reading of a first-aid manual is *efferent reading*, at the far end of the continuum. When that same person is reading a novel, however, the purpose is likely to be to allow him or her to gain a deeper understanding of the human experience. As readers engage with a novel, they enter into the space of the novel and disconnect themselves from the time of their own existence as well as their own ongoing or chronological time. This is where Rosenblatt (1978) uses the term "lived-through experience with the text" to describe an *aesthetic reading* (Cooper, 1985, p. xiv). A good book is almost certain to evoke a deep personal engagement, whether that turns out to be one involving angst or one involving pleasure.

Rosenblatt maintains that when teachers provide opportunities for children to respond aesthetically to a text, either in a basal reader or in a trade book, the text "can become the object of reflection and analysis, according to the various critical and scholarly approaches" (Farrell and Squire, 1990, p. 106). In other words, a text first evokes an aesthetic or "lived-through" response and then evokes a more efferent response as the reader consciously thinks about the text and the reading experience. For example, a short story such as "Tashkent" (in *Some of the Kinder Planets*, by Tim Wynne-Jones, 1993) may be read in such a way that the reader enters the story's time, identifying with the protagonist's illness and recuperation, and leaving behind the more immediate concerns of the world. When reflecting on the story, however, the reader constructs meaning (based on the text) that may relate to other stories or poems, to geographical facts, to information the reader already possesses, or to the reader's own life or that of a friend. When readers reflect in this way, they re-enter ongoing chronological time and engage in a more efferent response. A *totally* efferent response to "Tashkent" might include summarizing the story as we retell it to a friend, locating in an atlas the place names mentioned in the story, or comparing the story with a poem that has a similar theme. These transactions form the cornerstone for the creation of possible meanings, as well as for coming to understand how texts work.

What is seen of response to literature in a classroom is like the tip of an iceberg: much of it remains out of sight (Purves and Rippere, 1968). Teachers can keep the following points in mind as they engage students with literature:

- The extent to which students show their responses in a classroom context depends very much on the reading abilities of the individual children.
- How much of their responses students show depends very much on the level of trust they feel in the classroom environment.
- People in general do not share feelings and thoughts if they don't feel safe.
- If children are taught that there is one "right" response to a piece of literature (usually the teacher's response or interpretation), they are less likely to express their own responses.
- Through sharing and discussing responses, students discover that meaning can be negotiated and constructed in a multitude of equally valid ways.

- When students are encouraged to respond to texts and to engage in dialogue with themselves, their peers, and teachers about books, they are more likely to see that meaning is created by the learner, and that multiple ways of knowing and responding to literature are valid and necessary.
- Students who share their responses to literature and have their responses accepted respectfully are likely to become more thoughtful and critical readers than those students who do not experience a fair exchange of responses.

## Learning through Response

In encouraging children to respond to texts, teachers must understand *why* response is encouraged and what is being *learned* through the activity of responding. Both points are connected. By reading trade books and responding to them, children discover how texts work, what constitutes a good book, how language can be used in different ways to create different meanings and effects — in short, how to become readers, not just people able to read. As a result of active responding, children are likely to take ownership of the reading process and to come to understand that there is no right "answer" to literature (although, as Rosenblatt, 1978, says, some responses are more legitimate or appropriate than others). Learning to respect and honour their own interpretations of what they have read, they gain the confidence to become more critical in their thinking about texts, more creative in their own writing, and much more capable in their ability as language users and language learners. In effect, they take on the four roles of the reader (Freebody and Luke, 1990) described in Chapter Ten: code breaker, text participant, text user, and text analyst.

Literature can be the basis for an entire language arts program in the elementary classroom, for the nature of reading and response encourages children to integrate their knowledge, make personal sense of it, and express it through movement, the visual arts, music, drama, writing, and dialogue. Thomson (1987) reminds us that "the development of a mature response to literature involves a progressive movement from close emotional involvement to more distanced reflective detachment, and from an interest in self to an interest in other people and the human condition" (p. 153). This means that the process of response almost always begins with an aesthetic, personal experience of the text — the very experience that a response activity in the classroom aims to encourage and facilitate.

## Response Groups

One important vehicle for exploring a text is the response group. Adult readers have discovered the pleasures of reading clubs, where members read a book in their own time and then come together as a group to discuss the book and explore interpretations of it. A reading club is a response group. Such groups play a valuable role in the elementary language arts classroom.

Teachers and researchers have discovered that children benefit from *orally* sharing and shaping their responses to books. As they share their own responses and listen to the ways in which other readers have responded to a book, children become aware that no two readers read in the same way or create meaning in the same way. In the process of discussion, their attention is drawn to details they might have missed, and they are called to think about things that, as individual readers, they might not have thought about.

Taking part in a response group can be a fascinating experience. It can also be a frustrating experience if readers want everyone in the group to respond to a book in the way in which *they* have responded to it. Research conducted by Eeds and Wells (1989) formed the foundation for *Grand Conversations* (Peterson and Eeds, 1990), a book that underscores the importance of dialogue in constructing meaning from a text. Peterson and Eedes (1990, p. 21) write: "The lecture model places knowledge outside the students for them to passively receive; dialogue recognizes that knowledge is something students actively construct." The authors provide many suggestions and insights for teachers who work with response groups, including ideas for selecting books, facilitating literature study, and evaluating responses to literature. They also reiterate that children need time in class just for reading, and that children should not be expected to do all of their reading outside class time.

Critical in response groups is that teachers respect each child's ideas and not impose their own ideas on the class. There are many occasions when teachers have to put their own feelings and opinions aside to listen to the students' voices. Ms. Rahime, for example, teaching Grade 4, had chosen a popular book for a read-aloud. Daniel made an initial response of "I don't think this is a very good story." Ms. Rahime took the utmost care to receive Daniel's response, respect it, and further Daniel's thinking by asking questions about his comment. Daniel continued his response by saying that the author had not told the whole story and that a lot of information was missing. As a result of that observation, Ms. Rahime moved her students into a "hot-seating" activity in groups of three. Hot-seating involves one student taking on the role of one of the characters from the story in an interview-type situation. The character is on the hot seat and answers questions put to him or her by the other students in the group. The character answers the questions within the context of the story as written, but depends on personal interpretation and inference to fill in any missing details. Within half an hour of their original discussion, Daniel and the other students had created many versions of the story, each group developing the "missing" pieces. Thus, these students engaged in a deeper and more expanded reading of the text by making inferences and interpretations together. At the end of the session the students were so eager to reread the story that at least half the class went straight to the library looking for a copy of the book and for other titles by the same author.

Discussions such as the one in Ms. Rahime's classroom can be extremely enlightening for a teacher and can provide a springboard for choosing and creating alternative ways of responding to books. The role of the teacher in literature response groups is that of sensitive guide, helping to create links from the text to actual life experiences and to other texts, and inserting literary insights at appropriate moments. Peterson and Eedes (1990) maintain that comments such as "Let's think more about that" can help children reflect on their reading and deepen their responses to the reading. Talking with students about a book is likely to be a more effective teaching strategy than asking direct questions such as "What was your favourite part of the story, and why?" because it immediately creates a possible connection to the child's own life and demands a personal engagement with the text.

Stanley Fish (1980) says, "Not only does one believe what one believes, but one teaches what one believes, even if it would be easier and safer and more satisfying to teach something else" (p. 364). If we believe that teaching reading means asking children questions, requiring them to provide a retelling of almost every story they read, or picking out the main ideas from a chapter in a book, then our teaching of reading will betray those beliefs. Langer (1994) writes: "The thought-provoking literature class is an environment where students [and teachers] are encouraged to negotiate their own meanings by exploring possibilities, considering understandings from multiple perspectives, sharpening their own interpretations, and learning through the insights of their own responses" (p. 207). She goes on to remind us that response is based as much on the reader's own personal and cultural experiences as it is on the particular text and its author. In closing, Langer says, "In instructional contexts of this sort, that treat all students as thinkers and provide them with the environment as well as the help to reason for themselves, even the most 'at-risk' students can engage in thoughtful discussions about literature, develop rich and deep understandings, and enjoy it too" (p. 210).

## Literature Response Journals

Literature response journals provide children with opportunities for reflection on what they are currently reading. The journals are usually intensely private and personal, for they may depict exactly how a reader interprets a text and responds to it. When teachers read children's response journals, they try to be sensitive to the nature of the writing and aware of the privileged position they hold in accessing this material. They do not correct grammar or spelling errors, but try to respond to the content, reading in the role of "fellow reader," not as an "authority" on the text. The Grade 2 children who wrote the following entries in response to *Miss Rumphius* by Barbara Cooney (1982) certainly were not focussing on correct spelling as they completed their entries. In this peer dialogue journal approach, they wrote an entry, exchanged journals with a partner, and then wrote a response to their partner's entry. The teacher did not draw attention to their invented spelling, but instead complimented the pair on their interesting exchange and added a comment about her own dislike of some aspects of gardening.

Melissa: This story reminds me of me becos I alwiys wanted to plant a garden over in they emtey lot acros from us but my mom sade it wood be to mush work, but I'm saving my alowince for some plants and flowers so I can plant some ther.

Stuart: I like planting flowers and vegebals but I hate it when I have to take a slug off a flower there so slimy and ugly but I kind of have a indoor green house that I got from Scholastic books.

In response to *Two Bad Ants* by Chris Van Ahlsburg (1988), the two wrote:

Melissa: This reaminds me of wen I went to the mountins and I fownd a wered object it looked like a melted tin but it was verry hard to bend. at ferst I thot I wood end up richer than my parentes but I endied out not beaing rich atole. Do you think the ants were beaing gready or wanted to try their musteyris cristels that we know is sugar. It also reaminds me of the time my brother fownd a white rock and thot it was a cristel and he came in yelling mom - mom I fownd a white crustel.

Stuart: The rock your brother found probely had shiny minirels in it but doase your brother still have the rock.

Melissa: he still thinkes ther cristeles so he heas got tuns.

Literature response journals work most effectively when they are open-ended and unstructured. It appears that the more structure is provided for these journals, the more contrived they can become and the less fluent and cohesive the responses

(Pantaleo, 1994). As Melissa and Stuart demonstrated in their exchange above, a journal entry consists of personal writing in the expressive voice. Useful questions to ask in regard to any teaching activity are "What are we teaching, and what do we want children to learn?" Teachers have discovered from experience that most children will eventually work through many of the structures and elements of literature if they are given the opportunity to ask questions and search for answers themselves.

In the journal entry below, Cathie, in Grade 6, summarizes the ending of *Jasmin* by Jan Truss (1982), and in doing so revisits the text to synthesize meanings and explore her reasons for enjoying the book. Most importantly, Cathie captures the theme of the book, noting that Jasmin undergoes a "rite of passage" that allows her to have a new, more mature understanding of her life and her identity as a teenager.

> I think that the end of this book was excellent because everything wrapped up well. Jasmin's clay animals were put in a box that had home-made forest surrounding them. She won second prize at the Science Fair. Her teachers decided Jasmin could go to grade seven as they were giving her another chance. Her parents talked to a family counsellor advising them to give Jasmin her own room. They also advised Leroy to be moved to a special home because he was getting too big for them to be looking after anymore. The good thing was that he could visit them on weekends. While Jasmin had run away, her whole family began to realize how much they needed her and when she was found, they showed love for her again. Jasmin realized she was pretty (someone had painted a picture of her) and could do useful things with her hands (example, clay animals). Best of all she liked who she was!

Directing children to focus their responses on some specific aspect of the text such as plot, setting, characters, or theme does *not* appear to be as effective as leaving the response options totally open to the students, providing suggestions only where necessary. Response writing, like any other type of writing, is learned. Children who are not used to writing in the expressive voice (see Chapter Seven) may need some time to get used to the idea that this is an acceptable form of writing. It is not a matter of learning *what* to write, but rather of learning *how* to write a response.

Any response to literature is shaped by the text itself. Some texts, such as *Gorilla* by Anthony Browne (1983) or *Julie* by Cora Taylor (1985), invite immediate responses, though the responses will differ significantly from one reader to another. Most readers readily identify with the protagonists of these two stories and can empathize with the situation in which the characters find themselves. Other texts, such as *The Golden Compass* by Philip Pullman (1995), may at first appear strange, complex, or even baffling. The text may generate many questions before a reader can shape a response to it, and the response is likely to change as the reading progresses.

Whether the reader's response to a book is tentative and questioning, or confident and fully engaged, teachers and researchers have found that the written responses of children to books demonstrate what the children know, what and how they think, and just exactly how they have comprehended a text. Thus, there is little need for having a child retell the story to ascertain whether he or she has understood a book or not. It is clear, for example, that Ron, in Grade 5, not only enjoyed *The Dragon Children* (Buchan, 1975), but understood the complex plot:

> I really liked this book because there were two mysteries in the whole book. One of the mysteries was if the crook would make it out of town in time, and

if John, Scott, Cathy and Steven would get the crook or not. The other mystery was to find out who or what Steven really was. I figured out what Steven was by putting all the clues together. At the end of the book I found out who Steven was. At first I thought that Steven was a ghost (even though he was) that the crook had drowned in the river. I was half right about that.

It was a surprise to me when John, Scott, and Cathy found out that the crook wasn't who they thought he was. It surprised me because when Steven told John that the crook was driving a green car with a license plate number 5K-206 it wasn't the crook driving it. Instead it was the man who had come with his family for their vacation. The man did seem like a crook though because when he was walking through the woods with his son, it looked like he had kidnapped the child.

My favorite part, though, was when Scott sneaked up behind the real crook and poked the needle in his back-end. I liked it because it really made me laugh.

Ron wrote this response about how he played detective as a reader in order to fit all the pieces of the story together, making meaning and unravelling the two mysteries. The response demonstrates how Ron engaged with the text, and how he experienced a more distanced response to the book rather than a personal identification with the characters and their actions.

Mitch, in Grade 5, wrote the following dialogue journal entry in response to Chapter 3 of *The Iron Man* (Hughes, 1968), which the teacher had read aloud to the class:

I think the Iron Man will be like the machine in the scrap metal yard that gets rid of the metal. The Iron Man will be happy, the farmers will be happy and Hogarth can visit the Iron Man all the time. Who were the people that had the picnic on the hill and will they show up again? If the Iron Man is controlled by something, who or what is it and what will it think of the Iron Man being so happy? If there is more Iron Men does the Iron Man we know about keep in touch with them? If he does, maybe our Iron Man will tell the others and they will come too. I like how the author called all the metal delicacies. I can see how the chain is spaghetti and maybe the knobs on the bed were chocolate covered candy. Brass covered iron. I don't understand how different kinds of metals have different kinds of tastes. What do you think the Iron Man's favorite kind of metal is? ... What will happen when the Iron Man runs out of food at the metal scrap yard? Will they bring him food from other towns? Do you think the Iron Man will ever go back to the sea? Maybe if he leaves the scrap yard all the townsfolk will look for him at the sea. Do you know if the farmers filled up the hole? I sure hope so. It would be disastrous if somebody fell down the hole. If somebody did fall down the hole, maybe the Iron Man will help them out and then he might not be hated so much. Is the Iron Man hated? I think it starts out in the story that the Iron Man was hated but now I think maybe he is more liked.

Mitch's response is like "stream of consciousness" writing. He has put onto paper the many questions raised for him as he listened to this chapter of the story, and has highlighted some of the images in Hughes's writing. The response demonstrates the engagement Mitch experienced as he listened to the story, processing the thoughts that went through his mind about this chapter. Mitch moved quickly from one idea to another, not stopping long to reflect on any one aspect of the chapter, but trying to capture the excitement and wonder evoked by this modern fairy tale. Mitch makes predictions about the fate of the Iron Man, accurately foretelling the Iron Man's role in the community and the shift in the populace's perceptions as the Iron Man becomes an ally of the people instead of an enemy to be defeated.

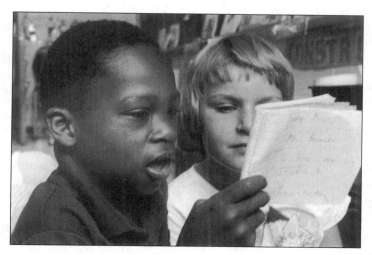

Two children reading a literature response journal.

Literature response journals provide opportunities for the teacher to deliver instruction and feedback to students that is student-oriented as well as text-oriented. Response journals provide a place for children to slow down their thinking and reflect on their reading, asking questions, wondering, predicting, and synthesizing. Here children can genuinely work at seeking to understand how literature weaves its magic, how reading is accomplished, and how books work.

## Readers' Workshop

*Readers' workshop* was a term made popular by Nancie Atwell in the 1980s. The second edition of her book *In the Middle: New Understandings about Writing, Reading and Learning* (1998) continues her exploration of children's reading and response. A complaint frequently voiced by children is that they are given very little time in school to actually *read*. Instead, they are required to devote most of their time to activities *about* reading (Pantaleo, 1994). Like Peterson and Eeds (1990), Atwell suggests that if children are to truly enjoy the reading experience, time for reading as well as for learning about reading must be established in school. She maintains that because children read magazines, TV guides, and other such material out of school, teachers play an important role in encouraging students to broaden their reading repertoire by selecting novels, poetry, plays, biography, and works of nonfiction when they are in school. The books, however, should be of interest to the students and, where appropriate, self-selected.

Atwell proposes a readers' workshop format where most of the in-class time is spent reading, and mini-lessons are used for what Purves (1993) suggests is schooling in the teaching of reading and literature. Atwell offers the following guidelines for conducting a readers' workshop:

- Have children come to the workshop prepared with a book in their possession that they are ready to read or are already in the process of reading. The book should be self-selected from either the classroom or the school library. Readers' workshop is not a time for making book selections.
- Regardless of grade level, ensure that students have a sustained and uninterrupted time for reading. Suitable timelines for readers' workshops vary from grade level to grade level. Grades 5 to 7 require 20–30 minutes for reading. Younger students

require much less, depending on their ability to sustain silent reading. Thus in Grades 1 and 2, the reading time might be only ten minutes.

- Encourage children not to talk or disturb others during reading time, though they may sit or recline anywhere, depending on the physical constraints of the classroom.
- Help students understand that quiet time is important when reading. Most readers cannot read fluently if there is noise around them, or if they are trying to attend to more than one activity at once.

Mini-lessons, whether planned or spontaneous, should usually be brief (say, between five and fifteen minutes), and designed in response to the students' needs. A mini-lesson may be

- a discussion of a topic (e.g., the need for quiet time during reading, the procedures and agendas for response groups, how the classroom library is organized, classroom literary resources, organizing a reading folder and keeping a record of books read, self-assessment procedures, and goal setting);
- a book-share by the teacher (reading part of a book to the class), a book talk by the teacher or a group of students, or some other presentation of activities completed by students *in response* to a book they have read;
- a presentation on a particular author, where the teacher shows the class a number of books by that author (information about authors is available in libraries in publications such as *Meet Canadian Authors and Illustrators* [Gertridge, 1994] or the book series *Something about the Author* [edited by Commaire, annual]); or
- a further exploration of a book in response groups, journal writing, or alternative response activities.

The key role of the teacher in a readers' workshop is to facilitate students' learning as they progress from personal interpretations and understandings ("My question is ...," "It reminds me of ...," "I don't understand why...") to shared meanings ("This story is about ...") and on to negotiated meanings ("We think the writer wanted us to understand that ..."). The readers' workshop is a place where students can read, take ownership of their reading, and respond in their own language to the material they have selected to read. They discuss their ideas about a text with other readers and come to shared and negotiated understandings of the meanings of the stories, poems, and plays they are reading.

Purves (1993) has emphasized that reading in school can never be like reading out of school, because in school it is the teacher's job to facilitate children's growth in book selection, reading skill, confidence, fluency, and ability to express thoughts and opinions and to engage in critical and creative thought. As Purves writes: "I urge us to see our task in schools as helping students read literature and understand the culture, to speculate on the ideas and the imaginative vision, and to speculate on the nature and the use of the language that is the medium of the artistic expression" (p. 360). Much of this can be achieved, we believe, in well-handled readers' workshops.

## Literature Circles

In his book *Literature Circles: Voice and Choice in the Student-Centered Classroom*, Daniels (1994) writes, "Literature circles are small, temporary discussion groups who have chosen to read the same story, poem, article or book. While reading each group-determined portion of the text (either in or outside of class) each member prepares to take specific responsibilities in the upcoming discussion, and everyone comes to the group with the notes needed to help perform that job" (p. 13). In other words, literature circles are student-led discussion groups. Each literature circle in a classroom is likely to be reading a different book, but the groups meet regularly according to a schedule. The teacher acts as a facilitator for the groups. Role sheets guide the students in the roles they agree to take on. Roles include

- discussion director
- illustrator
- summarizer
- connector
- literary luminary
- travel tracer
- investigator

Daniels's system is highly organized, and can be both interesting and enjoyable for students. Teachers need to be aware, however, that literature circles can become mechanistic and, if due care is not taken, can function from an efferent stance. The greatest learning is likely to take place when students also write in response journals and engage in the unstructured "grand conversations" described by Eeds and Wells (1989). Literature circles provide teachers with a well-organized and interesting structure for beginning group work with students in response to literature.

## Novel Studies

The term *novel study* is used to describe a range of group activities that encourage and facilitate students' reading and responding to novels. At the elementary school level, novel studies provide a vehicle for children to experience a novel in a small group setting, much like a book club or response group. Novel studies can be conducted with a whole class of children, though they can usually be separated into small groups for many of the discussions and activities. Novel studies can also be conducted in small groups of four to six students, as in a literature circle.

Multiple copies of novels are necessary for a novel study, so it is most economical to involve no more than five or six children with one novel at any one time. Prepared novel study sets are usually prepackaged in groups of six books. Many teachers complete one whole-class novel study at the beginning of the year to set out the expectations for novel studies and to establish guidelines and procedures for novel study activities. After the initial whole-class study, teachers usually work with small groups, as in a literature circle.

Successful novel study requires creating a classroom community where reading is important and students and teachers behave like "real readers." As highlighted by both Atwell (1998) and Daniels (1994), children benefit from opportunities to self-select reading material and from having substantial time to read independently. Students can be assigned to groups based on their approximate reading speeds, or they can self-select a reading group based on their interest in the novel. The group chooses a book to read, and the group members meet regularly to discuss the book and complete response activities. The activities can be designed by the students or suggested by the teacher.

In preparation for the group activity, the students agree to achieve specific goals for each meeting. The goals may include reading a certain number of pages before the meeting, or accomplishing certain tasks such as answering questions raised in the previous meeting. This is a way of "thinking back and thinking ahead." It provides students with a means of synthesizing their reading, making predictions, asking questions and negotiating meaning with the group. During the discussion time, the teacher circulates about the room, listening to the ongoing conversations and participating where appropriate. Once the discussions are complete, each group sets a new reading goal that can be recorded on a small chart posted at the front of the classroom. The teacher can monitor the reading goals to ensure they are appropriate for the various groups. The students spend the rest of the period reading their novels, writing in their response journals, or engaging in alternative response activities. The teacher can either read silently during this time or assist individual students with their responses.

Journal responses can be written at any time during the reading of a novel: the midpoint, on completion of the texts, or (as more frequently happens) during the reading. The students can decide on the content of their responses (there is no particular structure or format for the entries), but they are encouraged to select and write in depth about one or two ideas, images, feelings, memories, or thoughts they experienced during or after their reading. This helps the students to explore, extend, or develop their reading experiences. Some students relate the story to other books, movies, or experiences in their lives; some evaluate a situation or a character, or put themselves in a character's position in the book and discuss what they would feel or do and why; and others discuss the author's writing purpose, style, or techniques.

Reading instruction also occurs in a novel study when individual students or groups of students require assistance in dealing with comprehension difficulties, selecting novels, or organizing themselves to meet their goals. Because students in this activity are largely independent in their work, they need to be aware of the expectations for novel studies, such as when it is appropriate to write in their response journals and when to hand responses in to the teacher. It is also important that children know where to find the novels they are interested in reading, the procedures for signing out books, and any other classroom routines related to this study activity.

As mentioned above, a number of prepackaged novel studies are available for use in classrooms. A word of caution: Many commercial novel studies are not of high quality and include exercises more like the ones found in old-fashioned reading series (formerly called "basal readers"). This approach has been referred to as the **basalization** of children's literature — turning the work of literature into skill-building exercises (or "dummy runs" as Britton, 1970, called them). Teachers use their professional judgement when assessing the value of such resources for their own classrooms. They keep in mind their own objectives in working with literature in the classroom, and the needs of the students they teach.

A set of 27 novel studies has been developed by Edmonton Public Schools (1998) for use across Canada. These are well-developed studies that provide teachers and students with support in examining some outstanding works of fiction for children. The published novel studies in the series include *The Doll* (Taylor, 1987), *Ticket to Curlew* (Lottridge, 1992), *Julie of the Wolves* (George, 1972), *The Golden Aquarians* (Hughes, 1994), *Anne of Green Gables* (Montgomery, 1908), and *The Root Cellar* (Lunn, 1983). Each novel study consists of a spiral-bound teacher's guide and a computer disk. The teacher's guide provides background on the book, a bibliography, suggested relevant Web sites that students might access, a summary of the novel, information about the author, and suggested student activities. The student activities are, in most instances, accompanied by blackline masters and, for *The Doll*, range from questions intended to prompt journal writing to enrichment activities including poetry writing, letter writing, an author profile, a crossword puzzle, drama activities, a rubric for conducting an interview with grandparents, collecting and exploring family expressions, creating a family tree, and guidelines for writing a field guide for plants and for writing a recipe book. The computer disk contains many of the activities from the teacher's guide and provides additional capabilities for developing classroom databases. These particular novel studies are a sound resource for student teachers and for beginning teachers who have not previously conducted a novel study. Many of the suggested activities can be generalized to a broader range of novels.

## Alternative Modes of Response

As children begin to read, continue reading, and finish reading a novel, they can engage in many interesting activities that will help them explore, interpret, and more fully understand the text. Chapter Twelve on drama strategies includes examples of activities that might be part of a novel study. Benton and Fox (1985) also provide a rich source of activities for promoting children's explorations and meaning-making from books. Their suggestions for working with *Tuck Everlasting* (Babbitt, 1975) include

- creating a timeline,
- drawing portraits of the characters,
- "hot-seating" the characters,
- writing character sketches,
- interviewing characters for a talk show,
- making wanted posters for Mae Tuck (a character in the book),
- creating a map of the story's setting, and
- writing an imaginary diary entry as the character Winnie.

These activities encompass the full spectrum of response, from aesthetic to efferent. Halliday's (1969) functions of language (discussed in Chapter Two of this text) also provide a solid foundation for creating a diverse range of purposeful language activities for children as they respond to and explore novels. Many children find it difficult to write in a response journal or may be shy of speaking up in a response group. Fortunately for them, and indeed for all readers, there are alternative and enjoyable ways of representing response to literature. In the rest of this section, more than a dozen examples of response activities are described, using *Awake and Dreaming* by Kit Pearson (1996) as the sample novel.

*Awake and Dreaming* is the story of a young girl named Theo and her "flower child" mother, Rae. Theo dreams of being part of a stable, loving family with her own room and brothers and sisters to play with. She loves reading and often loses herself in a book, the school library being her only source of pleasure. Rae is an immature and irresponsible parent who lives in poverty and moves from one apartment to another regularly. She and Theo live on welfare and supplement their income by begging on the streets of Vancouver. When Rae moves in with her new boyfriend, Cal, Theo must go to live with her Aunt Sharon in Victoria. While on the ferry, Theo falls asleep and awakens to find herself in a house in Victoria — part of a family at last. But is it real?

Here are a number of drama strategies that could be used to facilitate response to the story:

**Hot-seating**  Rae has arrived home from panhandling in downtown Vancouver. Theo is exhausted from dancing to recorded music. In groups of three, students take turns "hot-seating" the characters from this chapter of the book (Chapter Three). The teacher will likely need to model this strategy first if the children are not familiar with it. In the role of Cindy (or one of the other characters) the teacher can take questions from the students about Cindy's thoughts and feelings about Rae and her lifestyle. Following this, the students take turns "being" Theo, Rae, or Cal (Rae's boyfriend) and entertain questions from the other two students in the group. Students draw on their own experiences and previous knowledge to create answers to the questions that will fit the context of the story.

**Tableaux**  Theo is sitting in a seat on the ferry watching the other children in the lounge playing. Theo notices a woman in a baggy tweed coat watching her. A girl speaks to Theo and invites her to join their group. They go outside onto the deck together, playing and "flying" in the wind. Rae reappears, and Theo panics. The next thing Theo hears is a steady dripping of rain as she awakens in a soft warm bed. In groups of four to six, students can create tableaux—still pictures of these scenes. Each group first decides what it wants to include in its tableau, and plans who will take the role of each character. Once this is determined, the students take up their positions, perhaps by acting out a brief portion of the story and freezing the action at a given moment. The children then orchestrate the tableau so that it becomes an artistic and aesthetically pleasing portrayal of the scene. Students can imagine this as either a photograph or as a diorama exhibit in a museum. Rereading Chapter 6 will help the students discover the details of the situation and portray their interpretations of it. Each group is given the opportunity to show its tableau to the rest of the class.

**Thoughts-in-the-head**  While engaged in their tableaux, the teacher touches each character gently on the shoulder. At the touch, the students, *in role*, say what thoughts are going through their minds at that moment. If any students do not wish to speak, they may remain silent and the teacher moves on to the next character.

**Puppets**  Many different kinds of puppets can be created to put on a play of some part of the story. From paper lunch-bag, sock, or paper plate puppets to more elaborate creations, students generally enjoy this activity. Some groups of students may want to script the play first; others may simply create the dialogue as they go. Either way, all groups should have the opportunity to rehearse before sharing their work.

**Readers' theatre**  Readers' theatre is a form of oral presentation in which scripts are read aloud rather than memorized. Participants read their parts expressively and use their voices, gestures, and facial expressions to communicate images, events, and actions in the minds of audience members. In readers' theatre, the characters may sit on stools or a high bench to read their parts. Often, to identify themselves, the participants wear an item of clothing typical of the character they are "reading." Thus, Theo might wear a tattered sweatshirt or jacket. For this dramatic activity, the teacher may need to rewrite or script portions of the original text or provide students with instructional assistance as they create the readers' theatre script themselves.

**Character profile**  Students select a character from the book and dress as that character. Each student enters the classroom donned in appropriate attire and tells the other students about him or herself. Drawing on the novel, the student describes the character and the significant events that have happened to him or her (as the character). Classmates may ask the character questions.

These activities represent only a few of the many drama strategies that can be used in a literature or language arts program. More drama strategies for use in reader response are presented in Chapter Twelve. Drama activities frequently take longer than planned and should not be rushed. Throughout their drama work, students are encouraged to talk with one another about their interpretations, opinions, likes and dislikes, and personal "pictures" of the characters and setting. This oral processing enhances the students' personal engagement with the text, and can help them have a more satisfying and memorable experience with a book. Only one or two of the above activities should be selected for use with any one text. A common option is to have groups of children in a classroom work on different activities, which makes sharing the sessions with one another all the more interesting. Readers are usually curious about other readers' interpretations of the work under consideration.

Visual art activities have the same appeal as the drama strategies suggested above, allowing children to become actively involved in creating an artifact representative of their responses. Drawing, painting, and making models, dioramas, wall charts, and portraits are just a few of the activities that give children the opportunity to display their responses to a text. For the book *Awake and Dreaming*, the following activities could be considered:

**Photograph album**  Students create a "photograph album" of the Caffrey family during Theo's early life and later when she and Rae move to Vancouver. "Photographs" can consist of pictures taken from magazines, or they can be created by the children themselves, either with a camera or with art supplies. A caption can be added beneath each image. The students can explain why they chose to include the images they did in their albums.

**Scrapbook**  In a similar manner to the photograph album, students make a scrapbook of the mementos of Theo's families—both the Caffreys and the Kaldors. Students can make notes, menus, pet paw prints, and other such memorabilia from Theo's life and her encounter with the character Cecily Stone.

**Mapping**  Students create large and colourful maps of the area of Victoria where Theo lived with the Kaldors and where she eventually met Cecily Stone. The map is not necessarily intended to be a realistic depiction of Victoria, but can be created from the description provided in the text. Alternatively, students could map the journey Theo took from Vancouver to Victoria. If students wish to locate a real map of the area and base their renditions on it, this will also extend their learning.

**Silhouettes**  Individually or in small groups, students draw on transparencies a silhouette of a character from the story. The finished drawings can be displayed using the overhead projector. What features have the artists given the various characters? Why are these features important?

**Drawings**  After reading parts of the book or the entire book, students draw scenes, characters, or various aspects of their own interpretation of the story. Drawing can elicit some insightful responses from students that might not otherwise be captured. Students may also want to write about their drawings.

**Book covers**   Students usually have very definite ideas about the appropriateness of a book cover. Some students may want to design an alternate cover for *Awake and Dreaming*. The graphics used, the positioning of the title and author's name, and the colours are all important elements in creating a book's initial appeal. A book cover can invite a reader into the text or be a factor in dissuading him or her from reading the book. An important facet of a student's response to a book can be found in the alternate cover he or she might design. Covers created by students can be displayed along with other items profiling the novel.

**Dioramas**   Any setting from a book can be used as the starting point in creating a diorama. A number of settings in *Awake and Dreaming* lend themselves to this kind of interpretation (e.g., the cemetery). Dioramas are frequently made from large shoe boxes, and many odds and ends of materials can be carefully put together to create an effective representation of the setting and atmosphere of the novel as a whole. Dioramas can provide an enticement for other students to read the book.

**Advertisements**   If a reader had to create a poster advertising *Awake and Dreaming*, what would it be like? What would a publishing company look for in a poster? What would a prospective reader want to know about the book? What ambiance could be created through a poster? What colours would be most effective in portraying this story? After students have read a novel, an advertising poster can be an exciting way to share their responses to the book with the rest of the class.

**Wall charts**   There are many kinds of wall charts students can develop to help themselves understand a book. For *Awake and Dreaming*, students might consider creating a family tree to show the relationships noted in the story, or a timeline that tracks the story's events or records Theo's moves from one apartment to another.

Benton and Fox (1985) suggest that teachers, when considering various oral, dramatic, visual, and written response activities, ask themselves two fundamental questions: "Will this activity enable the reader to look back on the text and to develop the meanings he has already made?" and "Does what I plan to do bring reader and text closer together, or does it come between them?" (p. 108). Activities that meet the criteria set by Benton and Fox will extend students' reading transactions, enhance students' meaning-making from the text, and avoid any unnecessarily lengthy examination of the text that may detract from the reading experience.

## Dependent Authorship

Adams (1987) coined the phrase "dependent authorship" to describe activities that invite students to write from within the world of the literary text. The writing depends on the original text, since it is based on knowledge and understanding of that text. Meyers (1997) suggests a number of dependent authorship activities, including writing

- a dream that a character in the book may have,
- a flashback that illuminates a character and some aspect of the chararacter's personality,

- a flashforward that extends the story,
- a continuation of the work, picking up where the author left off,
- an interior monologue that captures the unspoken thoughts of a character,
- a poem or song that could appear in the work,
- a diary entry for one of the characters,
- a new passage that incorporates a character from another story into this work, and
- letters a character might have written.

Children have also written diary entries by Theo after she met Cecily Stone; a letter from Theo to the character Anna, ten years after the story ended; a report by the social worker, Ms. Sunter, after her conversation at school with Theo; a poem by Rae after her move to Victoria; a dream of Sharon's; a biography about Cecily Stone; and a new passage incorporating Polly from Sarah Ellis's book *Pick-Up Sticks* (1991), wherein Polly helps Theo settle into her new life with her Aunt Sharon in Victoria.

Dependent authorship activities can be generated by teachers when they have a thorough knowledge and understanding of Halliday's seven functions of language (1969). Keeping in mind the primacy of the purposes of language enables teachers to develop learning activities that are authentic language acts. Dependent authoring is conducted from "inside" the literary work, and always takes the student into a deeper understanding of it. It also underscores the intertextual elements of any piece of writing, "recognising that every literary work is a wellspring for others" (Meyers, 1997).

> This section of the chapter has provided both a theoretical perspective on reader response and a demonstration of how these elements can be woven into learning activities for children. Response groups, journals, literature circles, novel studies, and dramatic and visual responses all hold possibilities for enhancing children's meaning-making in relation to the literature they read and hear in the classroom.

## Book Selection

> This section of the chapter explores the definition of good literature and who has the right to make that determination. Which awards are devoted to children's literature? Which books should be selected for use in the classroom, and how are decisions made?

The confounding question facing most elementary school teachers is who decides what constitutes a "quality" book for children?

Over the years, it has generally been accepted that children, parents, teachers, and librarians are all involved in making the decisions. In fact, however, many of the most prestigious awards for children's literature are made by library and other associations whose awards committees consist solely of adults. (Examples include the **Amelia Francis Howard-Gibbon Award** and Governor General's Award in Canada, the Caldecott and Newbery Awards in the United States, and the Kate Greenaway and Carnegie Medals in the UK.) We know that children's choices of "good" literature frequently vary from adult choices (Pantaleo, 1995). Children enjoy books that involve mystery, excitement, humour, and adventure. Teachers, on the other hand, think it is more important that the reader be interested in, and able to identify with, the characters in a story (elements, not surprisingly, ranked much lower by children). Thus teachers and librarians often recommend books to children that may be good for the adult reader even though they hold no particular appeal for children. The result is that children often learn to ignore these book suggestions.

A number of **Children's Choice Awards** do exist, usually at the regional level in Canada and at the state level in the United States. Voting for these awards is conducted through the schools, providing children with a chance to show their support for the books they like. Unfortunately, these awards are not generally given high regard. This has prompted many observers to question the perceived significance of children's interests and opinions about books, and the intended purpose of the more prestigious awards.

We have to ask: If a book is good, what is it good *for*? Is it a challenging reading experience that will delight readers and help them become *better* readers by showing them something new? Is it a good book for taking on vacation and reading on the beach? Is it a good book for teaching more about language arts skills, or for helping readers learn how to do something of special interest to them, such as keeping a successful tropical aquarium? Is it a good book because it enables the reader to escape from real life and see life differently? In trying to answer questions such as these, teachers, librarians, and even scholars of children's literature are coming to realize how difficult it is to describe the specific characteristics or features of "quality" literature. A book that demonstrates how to create a healthy tropical aquarium will differ enormously from a book of short stories. A book that a person finds so notable that he or she wants to keep a copy for a long time is likely to be very different from the pocket book picked up as reading material for a long plane trip. Clearly then, describing quality in each of these cases must vary according to the format of the book, the purpose of the author, and the purpose, interests, and reading experiences of the reader.

## Guidelines for Appropriate Selection of Children's Literature

When selecting materials to include in a classroom or school library, teachers and teacher–librarians make every effort to choose books that meet the needs of both children and the curriculum. Knowledge of child development and the literary quality of books, as well as knowledge of the provincial programs of study and of curriculum expectations, help teachers make appropriate selections. Critics might say that "book selection" is simply a code for a librarian's own brand of censorship, but as Roberts (1996, p. 19) asserts, there are distinct differences between selection and censorship:

> Selection is a positive process that supports intellectual freedom when the selector considers resources in a holistic manner with the intent of including as many as possible in the library collection. Resources are selected objectively, according to set criteria, without regard for a selector's personal biases. Conversely, censorship is a negative process in which the censor searches for reasons, either internal or external, to exclude a resource.

Sound selection decisions are guided by the quality of reading and learning, even when, as Booth (1992, p. 9) says, "reading reveals unpleasant truths or viewpoints opposed to those of a particular parent or child, as long as the child is deemed capable of dealing with such ideas."

The selection of print materials for use in schools is a complex issue, for it is difficult to say in a public education system who should decide what children should and should not read. The debate involves freedom of expression and beliefs about what is appropriate for children, what is moral and what is immoral, and what is acceptable and not acceptable in society. It is highly likely that most children will confront difficult and disturbing ideas as they grow up. Reading and discussing a broad range of literature can help children become critical thinkers and thoughtful human beings capable of making sound judgements, both as individuals and as members of society.

The selection debate relates directly to the discussion of emancipatory or critical constructivism presented in Chapter One of this textbook. It is a compelling and difficult issue, and one that teachers are frequently required to address.

In 1974, the Canadian Library Association issued a statement on intellectual freedom that was subsequently adopted by the Canadian School Library Association. Two parts of that statement are of particular relevance for educators. The first asserts that it is a person's fundamental right to have access to all expressions of knowledge, creativity, and intellectual activity and to be able to express one's thoughts publicly. The second states that libraries must guarantee and provide access to all expressions of knowledge and intellectual activity, including those elements that conventional society might deem unacceptable or unpopular (Canadian Library Association, 1974). Thus, anyone who endorses this statement, and who thereby advocates selection as opposed to censorship of materials, still has the right to object to certain books if he or she so chooses, but not to insist on their removal from library shelves so that others are denied access to them. Advocates of book selection also respect the child's intellectual freedom (and innate common sense) and believe that adults have an obligation to be honest with children. This approach to selection does not argue that all books for children are of equal quality and equal value, or that they are even appropriate for children of all ages, but it does assert that children have the right of access to the best literature and learning resources available.

The most important things teachers can do when engaged in selecting of reading materials are to be aware of their own biases and values; to stay current with issues, themes, and book publications and reviews; and to maintain files of policy statements, useful resources, procedures for dealing with challenges to materials, and guidelines from recognized authorities. ("Challenges" are those occasions where books or other materials are considered by an individual or group to be inappropriate for the audience, and a request is made for the material to be removed from the classroom or library.) Many professional resources and tools are available to aid teachers and librarians in selecting books. By far the best resource for this is professional journals. For example, *Canadian Children's Literature*, published by the University of Guelph in Ontario, provides reviews of Canadian publications as well as articles about Canadian children's literature. It is the most prominent children's literature journal in Canada. *Teacher Librarian Today*, published by the Learning Resources Council of the Alberta Teachers' Association, contains book reviews, author/illustrator profiles, and well-informed articles on school librarianship in Canada. *Emergency Librarian*, published jointly in Canada and the United States (out of Vancouver and Seattle), presents articles that reflect literature-related concerns common to both countries. Other worthy professional journals include *Language Arts*, *The Reading Teacher*, and *The Horn Book*.

In addition to the journals, a variety of other resources are available to help teachers with book selection. One of these is the *Our Choice* catalogue, issued annually by the Canadian Children's Book Centre in Toronto. It lists recommended materials published each year in Canada, including fiction and nonfiction books, videos, CD-ROMs, and audio cassettes and CDs. Another is *Children's Book News*, which is issued four times a year by the Canadian Children's Book Centre and contains book reviews, articles, news, and information about children's literature events held across the country. Also helpful is the *Canadian Book Review Annual*, an evaluative guide to Canadian-authored, English-language publications. It reviews the year's scholarly publications, reference materials, and publications for children. The emphasis is on analyzing and evaluating materials, with brief descriptions also provided of the books reviewed.

As this section has shown, many book selection tools are available in Canada for students such as Shawn (introduced at the start of this chapter), and for inservice teachers who want to engage their students with the very best of children's literature. Information about book censorship is also available. Since censorship and challenges to books and periodicals in school libraries are unpredictable and usually emotional, it is critical that teachers try to remain up-to-date and well-informed about processes for dealing with book challenges. We discuss these issues in the next section.

## Censorship of Children's Materials

As already noted, there is a clear difference between selecting materials for use in schools and censoring these materials. Where book selection uses positive criteria to determine which books to place in a collection — what Nodelman (1992) calls the "books we approve of" — censorship seeks to remove, suppress, or restrict books *already present* in a collection. Censorship is generally ineffective in ensuring that only the most "appropriate" of books are read by students, yet it can be extremely disruptive to the life of a school. Occasionally, a **challenged book**, removed from library shelves, will become a best-seller and read more widely than if it had not been challenged.

School libraries and classrooms encounter far more challenges to books than do public libraries in North America (Schrader, 1996). This makes it imperative that teachers and librarians be informed on the issues and prepared to debate the relative merits of the materials selected for use in their schools. Educators have a responsibility to fulfil their professional obligations to learners by providing students with the very best in children's literature, meaning material that challenges children to think critically and explore new ideas and perpectives. Teachers have a further role, however, which is to help their students become more thoughtful and critical about their own choices of reading materials, and to help them develop their abilities to think for themselves and make sound judgements.

Teachers are often surprised to see what children's books and textbook series are commonly challenged. *Bridge to Terabithia* (Paterson, 1977), *The Paper Bag Princess* (Munsch, 1980), *Thomas's Snowsuit* (Munsch, 1985), *Who Is Frances Rain?* (Buffie, 1987), the Impressions series (Booth, Phenix, Pauli, and Swartz, 1984–88), and *Harry Potter and the Sorcerer's Stone* (Rowling, 1998) have all had censorship threats in recent years. Jenkinson (1994) found that challenges to books increased in Manitoba in the ten-year period between 1983 and 1993. The authors challenged most often in Jenkinson's study were Robert Munsch (*Giant: Or, Waiting for the Thursday Boat*, 1989, and *A Promise Is a Promise*, 1988), Roald Dahl (*Revolting Rhymes*, 1982, and *The Witches*, 1983), Alvin Schwartz (*Scary Stories to Tell in the Dark*, 1981), and William Steig (*The Amazing Bone*, 1976). Jenkinson also identified the top ten reasons for challenges. These were that the work in question

1. concerned witchcraft or the supernatural (24 percent),

2. contained or concerned violence (18 percent),

3. contained material inappropriate for an immature audience (12 percent),

4. described or showed explicit sex (10 percent),

5. contained questionable morality (9 percent),

6. described or showed nudity (9 percent),

7. contained obscenities (8 percent),

8. contained profanities (7 percent),

9. contained sexism or role stereotypes (6 percent), and

10. contained beliefs contrary to those of a particular religious ideology (5 percent).

In addition to challenges are the indirect instances of censorship, in which books simply go missing, have pages removed, or are ripped up or defaced. For example, in one case we know of, Mickey in *In the Night Kitchen* by Sendak (1970) had a diaper drawn on his naked body by a K–8 teacher who was upset by his nudity. Censorship can also be an attempt by special-interest groups to protect themselves against ideas or beliefs that may threaten their status. *Maxine's Tree* by Diane Leger-Haskell (1990), for example, was challenged in 1992 by members of the IWA-Canada on British Columbia's Sunshine Coast as being "emotional and an insult to loggers" (Nodelman, 1992, p. 132).

Explicit procedures detailing how book complaints will be received and reviewed can be set up by school boards or by individual schools. Information about past legal rulings, groups behind challenges, and approaches to resisting challenges is available from organizations such as the Book and Periodical Council (Toronto), the Canadian Library Association (Toronto), the National Council of Teachers of English (Urbana, Illinois), and the International Reading Association (Newark, Delaware). An extremely useful publication is *The Students' Right to Read*, published by the National Council of Teachers of English (1982). The book includes sample forms for collecting a statement of concern from a complainant, a sample letter to a complainant, instructions for establishing an evaluating committee, and suggestions for evaluating the complaint.

The National Council of Teachers of English and the International Reading Association have recently developed a CD-ROM resource, *Rationales for Challenged Books* (National Council of Teachers of English, 1998), which includes more than 200 rationales for over 170 commonly challenged materials for kindergarten through Grade 12 (though the emphasis is on publications for Grades 7 to 12). Publications are listed both by title and author on this Web-type resource, and information is provided about book challenges and what can be done by schools and libraries to counter challenges.

Very few books for children deal themselves with the topic of book selection and censorship. One of the few is *Maudie and Me and the Dirty Book* by Betty Miles (1980). Kate and Maudie, students in Grade 6, volunteer to read to first-grade children in a nearby primary school. They make careful book selections with the help of their teacher and based on the interests of the children in the class. Unfortunately, Kate's selection causes a furor among the parents, and soon the school and the community is caught up in censorship issues — much to the dismay and incomprehension of Kate and Maudie. The book presents the various concerns related to book selection in a comprehensive manner, and demonstrates the emotional responses that literature can evoke, particularly in a school setting with young children.

## Issues and Controversies

The greatest flurry of censorship activities lately has been over picture books depicting same-sex family relationships (gay and lesbian couples), such as *Daddy's*

*Roommate* (Willhoite, 1990) and *Heather Has Two Mommies* (Newman, 1989). The 1998 banning in Surrey, BC, of books about same-sex parents (notably *Asha's Mums* by Rosamund Elwin, 1990, *Belinda's Bouquet* by Leslea Newman, 1998, and *One Dad, Two Dads, Brown Dad, Blue Dad* by Johnny Valentine, 1994) underscores the unpredictable nature of censorship. In our view, it is regretful that children living in same-sex families are denied the right to read about children living in the same social contexts. Perhaps those who would try to censor such a topic need to remember that only fifteen to twenty years ago, books featuring single-parent families or divorced parents were considered unsuitable for young readers.

No less controversial has been the issue of discrimination in literature. In the middle to late twentieth century, it was not uncommon to find books for children that were explicitly racist in their treatment of blacks or Native North Americans. When many of these books were originally published, however, society in general was not as aware of the appalling discrimination portrayed in them. Since the 1948 Universal Declaration of Human Rights by the United Nations General Assembly, book publishers and educators have fought hard to prevent the publication of books that are clearly discriminatory.

In the first edition of *The Bobbsey Twins* (Hope, 1904), for example, the reader was told what a good mother Flossie was to her dolls, for she protected them from a black doll given to her by one of the servants. Flossie told her friends that the doll didn't really belong in the family. However, since Flossie's mother explained that there were "no asylums for black orphans," the doll was allowed to stay with the others — separated from them by a piece of cardboard. Given the nature of American society at that time, it was hardly surprising to see such blatant racial discrimination in a book for children. Today's readers cannot expect that such a passage would have been edited out of the book in 1904. What is surprising, however, is that the piece was not removed from the book until the 1950s.

One of the earliest "multicultural" books in North America was *The Story of Little Black Sambo* (Bannerman, 1899), set in India but with illustrations depicting black characters. Although Bannerman's book has received much criticism for its racial stereotyping, the story has remained hugely popular. It has been retold numerous times, and was recently published in two new editions. *The Story of Little Babaji* (Bannerman and Marcellino, 1996) contains the original text, except that the characters are given authentic Indian names. Fred Marcellino's illustrations place the story clearly in India. *Sam and the Tigers: A New Retelling of Little Black Sambo*, written by Julius Lester and illustrated by Jerry Pinkney (1996), depicts black characters but the fantasy setting (Sam-sam-sa-mara) removes it from any specific geographic location.

Stereotypical images abound in literature, from the works of Shakespeare to *Anne of Green Gables* (Montgomery, 1908) and *The Adventures of Huckleberry Finn* (Twain, 1885, 1963). For instance, the central feature of many of the American classics containing racist stereotypes was the presence of "indolent, happy-go-lucky slaves" (Miller-Lachmann, 1992). Other books, such as *The Five Chinese Brothers* (Bishop, 1938), seemed to promote the stereotype that all Chinese people look alike. Books such as these now provide a springboard for discussing issues such as racism, slavery, social class, and stereotyping in general.

Literature portrays all aspects of human nature, and children's literature is no exception. Through the library collections that teachers make available in schools, students can learn to appreciate the human condition, to discriminate good from bad and just from unjust, and to make sense of the world and their feelings toward it in a new and deeply personal way. As they select literature for children, teachers face the challenge of putting their own feelings and biases aside and presenting a balanced and equitable view of our diverse global community.

## Canadian Literature

In this section, we address the reasons why it is important for Canadian children to read Canadian literature as well as international literature, and suggest many book titles that are specifically Canadian in context.

Over the years, Canadians have become accustomed to receiving media largely from the United States and Britain. Children's print materials are no exception. Most professional books currently available for teachers, especially those about multicultural literature, are from the United States, and they largely (and sometimes entirely) refer to American books. However, the stories and experiences of Hispanic Americans, African Americans, Chinese Americans, and other ethnic and cultural groups are not necessarily parallel to those of Canadians.

It is well accepted that children need to see their own culture represented in the books they read. In the 1980s, Canadian publishing companies increased their publication of Canadian trade books for children and young adults. Today, many excellent children's books are being written and produced in Canada. The Canadian Children's Book Centre in Toronto (CCBC) publishes lists of books, information about authors, and the *Children's Book News* newsletter. More information about CCBC is presented in Box 11.1.

**Box 11.1  The Canadian Children's Book Centre**

The Canadian Children's Book Centre (commonly referred to as the CCBC) is located in Toronto. It contains a collection of Canadian children's materials that is available for browsing by members of its society, and extensive files on Canadian authors, illustrators, and the Canadian book publishing industry. The CCBC produces the newsletter *Children's Book News* four times each year, which contains book reviews, information about authors and illustrators, lists of book awards and current winners, as well as information about author and illustrator visits to schools and libraries across Canada during Canadian Children's Book Week (held annually in November). The CCBC also annually publishes a catalogue of books (and videos) that have received the "Our Choice Award." Both the catalogue (*Our Choice: Your Annual Guide to Canada's Best Children's Books and Videos*) and the newsletter can be obtained from the CCBC by writing to 35 Spadina Road, Toronto, Ontario, M5R 2S9, or e-mailing ccbc@sympatico.ca. For more information, you can also visit the CCBC Web site: http://www3.sympatico.ca/ccbc/.

## Why Canadian?

Literature can be a powerful vehicle for the transmission of national culture anywhere in the world. Diakiw has written that in "most culturally homogeneous countries, children grow up hearing and learning the stories that define their culture ... and these shared stories lie at the heart of a culture's identity" (1997, p. 37). He argues that there are powerful commonplaces in Canada's culture and identity — shared values that most Canadians can identify with — and that school is an important place to explore, discuss, and debate these. One way to uncover these is through Canadian stories and literature. "Literature, arts and crafts, music, dance, film, and poetry blend together over time to crystallize an image that says, 'This is who we are'" (Diakiw, 1997, p. 37).

Canada prides itself on its "cultural pluralism" and the importance of accepting different races, ethnicities, languages, and cultures. Nieto describes this as "a model based on the premise that all newcomers have a right to maintain their languages and cultures while combining with others to form a new society reflective of all our differences" (1992, p. 307). Yet, Bissoondath (1998) warns that Canada's policy of multiculturalism could lead to a reinforcement of stereotypes and a "gentle marginalization" of those who accept and display their ethnic heritage. He maintains that Canadian multiculturalism has emphasized difference and has retarded the integration of immigrants into the Canadian mainstream. A 1991 national survey found that, in general, "Canadians identify most strongly with being Canadian, rather than identifying with their ethnic origins" (Esses and Gardner, 1996, paragraph 21). Bissoondath writes that "we need to focus on programs that seek out and emphasize the experiences, values and dreams we all share as Canadians, whatever our colour, language, religion, ethnicity or historical grievance. And pursue acceptance of others —not merely tolerance of them" (1998, p. 22).

If children are to know themselves and the country in which they live, opportunities for them to read about Canadian people and Canadian places in the literature they encounter is essential. As they read stories that take place in regions of the country other than their own, children become familiar with that part of the country and can begin to identify with it. Likewise, when children read stories that take place in foreign countries, those countries becomes less "foreign" to them. Researchers understand that when children read aesthetically, they may identify with the characters, setting, or events of a story. However, until the last twenty years or so, Canadian children had little they could identify with. Most Canadian children grew up with a canon of British literature, partly because Canada was a Commonwealth country, but also because very little children's literature was published in Canada.

Today, a wide range of high-quality children's literature is published all across Canada, and some of that literature is published by school districts and by relatively small publishing houses. This has had an impact on children's reading across the country, for now students can read about Canadian people and places, from Peggy's Cove and Saskatoon to Ungava Bay and Yellowknife. When they read Canadian materials, children can imagine the prairie, mountains, or seacoast, and they learn more about Canada and who they are as Canadians. Many scholars and writers have suggested that the land, the actual environment or physical landscape of Canada, characterizes the Canadian short story and perhaps even Canadian literature in general. *Mr. Got to Go* by Lois Simmie (1995) is a charming picture book set at the Sylvia Hotel in Vancouver, *The Doll* by Cora Taylor (1987) is a time-slip novel set in Fort Carlton, Saskatchewan, and *Rebellion* by Marianne Brandis (1996) is a novel set in historical Toronto. Each of these books provides different insights into Canada and what it means to be Canadian, and each is profoundly reliant upon the landscape in which it is set. Perhaps through reading Canadian literature, children can develop pride in being Canadian and an appreciation and understanding of Canada's role in the global community. Defining our identity as Canadians is a continuing process and one in which our students have a role.

From Canadian books such as those noted above, children not only learn about Canada and being Canadian, they also learn that Canadian people can be authors and illustrators, and that authors and illustrators live in places where the students might also live. Authors become real people, and writing and illustrating become possible professions. Well-known authors and illustrators now visit schools on a regular basis, and some of the hard work and the craft of writing and illustrating are demonstrated to children as they listen to artists speak about and read their published work. Several organizations across Canada, such as the Young Alberta Book Society (see Box 11.2),

<table>
<tr><td>Box 11.2</td><td>The Young Alberta Book Society</td></tr>
</table>

The Young Alberta Book Society is an advocate for the literary arts and a year-round resource for information on Alberta authors and illustrators and their works. The organization provides displays of Alberta children's books at relevant conferences throughout Alberta and organizes *Chrysalis*, an annual celebration of children's books that involves readings in schools and public libraries across the province. The Young Alberta Book Society is also the regional liaison office for the Canadian Children's Book Centre. The society's mailing address is 2nd Floor, Percy Page Centre, 11759 Groat Road, Edmonton, Alberta, T5M 3K6; its e-mail address is yabs@compusmart.ab.ca; and its Web site is http://www.yabs.ab.ca.

exist for the sole purpose of enhancing literacy development and introducing Canadian authors and illustrators to children in schools. Box 11.3 presents a list of Canadian fiction suitable for children in Grades 4 to 7.

In addition to fiction materials, good nonfiction books about Canada have been written and published by Canadians. *Buried in Ice: Unlocking the Secrets of a Doomed Arctic Voyage* (Beatty and Geiger, 1992) is a book about the Franklin expedition, which most children find to be an intriguing tale. The authors tell a fascinating story, explore Canadian history, and describe what Canadian scientists and journalists do in their work. The discoveries made about the expedition received international attention, and it allowed Canadians to take pride in their accomplishments and in their Canadian heritage. A list of recent Canadian nonfiction books is presented in Box 11.4.

## Books by Aboriginal Canadians

In recent years, many excellent books for children have been created by Aboriginal Canadian authors and illustrators. The works of George Littlechild, Leo Yerxa, C.J.

<table>
<tr><td>Box 11.3</td><td>A Selection of Canadian Literature for Grades 4 to 7</td></tr>
</table>

Bedard, M. (1990). *Redwork*. Toronto: Lester & Orpen Denys.
Bedard, M. (1994). *Painted Devil*. Toronto: Lester.
Bly, D. (1993). *The McIntyre Liar*. Edmonton: Tree Frog Press.
Brouwer, S. (1993). *The Accidental Detectives:* Shortcuts. Wheaton, IL: Victor Books.
Buffie, M. (1987). *Who Is Frances Rain?* Toronto: Kids Can Press.
Burnford, S. (1963). *The Incredible Journey*. Toronto: Little, Brown and Co.
Calvert, P. (1993). *Picking Up the Pieces*. Toronto: Maxwell Macmillan Canada.
Doyle, B. (1982). *Up to Low*. Toronto: Groundwood Books.
Eyvindson, P. (1987). *The Wish Wind*. Winnipeg: Pemmican Publications.
Godfrey, M. (1987). *It Seemed Like a Good Idea at the Time*. Edmonton: Tree Frog Press.
Godfrey, M. (1988). *Send in Miss Teeny Wonderful*. Richmond Hill, ON: Scholastic TAB.
Houston, J. (1979). *River Runners*. Toronto: McClelland and Stewart.
Hudson, J. (1984). *Sweetgrass*. Edmonton: Tree Frog Press.
Hughes, M. (1982). *Hunter in the Dark*. Toronto: Clarke, Irwin.
Little, J. (1984). *Mama's Going to Buy You a Mockingbird*. Toronto: Penguin Books.
MacKay, C. (1979). *Exit Barney McGee*. Richmond Hill, ON: Scholastic.
Mowat, F. (1956). *Lost in the Barrens*. Toronto: Little, Brown and Co.
Pearson, K. (1987). *A Handful of Time*. Markham, ON: Viking Kestrel.
Reynolds, S. (1991). *Strandia*. Toronto: HarperCollins.
Smucker, B. (1979). *Days of Terror*. Toronto: Clarke, Irwin.
Smucker, B. (1989). *Jacob's Little Giant*. Toronto: Puffin Books.
Taylor, C. (1985). *Julie*. Saskatoon: Western Producer Prairie Books.
Weiler, D. (1993). *RanVan the Defender*. Toronto: Groundwood Books.

**Box 11.4  A Selection of Canadian Nonfiction for Children**

Beatty, O. and Gieger, J. (1992). *Buried in Ice: Unlocking the Secrets of a Doomed Arctic Voyage*. Misissauga, ON: Random House.

Bondar, B. (1993). *On the Shuttle: Eight Days in Space*. Toronto: Greey de Pencier Books.

Brewster, H. (1996). *Anastasia's Album*. Toronto: Penguin Books Canada.

Chase, E.N. (1993). *Waters*. Richmond Hill, ON: North Winds Press.

Dudley, K. (1997). *Wolves: The Untamed World*. Calgary: Weigi Educational.

Granfield, L. (1993). *Cowboy: A Kid's Album*. Toronto: Groundwood Books.

Hill, L. (1993). *Trials and Triumphs: The Story of African-Canadians*. Toronto: Umbrella Press.

Kenna, K. (1995). *A People Apart*. Toronto: Somerville House.

London, J. (1993). *The Eyes of Grey Wolf*. San Francisco: Chronicle Books.

Owens, A. and Yealland, J. (1996). *Forts of Canada*. Toronto: Kids Can Press.

Raskin, L. and Pearson, D. (1998). *52 Days by Camel*. Toronto: Annick Press.

Reevers, N. and Froman, N. (1992). *Into the Mummy's Tomb: The Real Life Discovery of Tutankhamen's Treasures*. Richmond Hill, ON: Scholastic.

Shell, B. (1997). *Great Canadian Scientists*. Vancouver: Polestar.

Shemie, B. (1997). *Houses of China*. Montreal: Tundra Books.

Swanson, D. (1994). *Safari Beneath the Sea*. Vancouver: Whitecap Books.

Swanson, D. (1997). *Bug Bites*. Vancouver: Whitecap Books.

Tanaka, S. (1997). *Discovering the Iceman*. Richmond Hill, ON: Scholastic.

Tanaka, S. (1998). *The Buried City of Pompeii: What It Was Like When Vesuvius Exploded*. Richmond Hill, ON: Scholastic.

Thornhill, J. (1991). *A Tree in a Forest*. Toronto: Greey de Pencier Books.

Zhang, S.N. (1995). *The Children of China: An Artist's Journey*. Montreal: Tundra Books.

Taylor, Michael Arvaarluk Kusugak, Thomas King, and Jordan Wheeler have become particularly popular. Jordan Wheeler's short stories for elementary age children are superbly crafted and immensely enjoyable. His work can be found in the collection *Achimoona* (Campbell, 1985) and *Adventure on Thunder Island* (King and Wheeler, 1991). Leo Yerxa's (1993) illustration of *Last Leaf First Snowflake to Fall* won the Amelia Frances Howard-Gibbon Award from the Canadian Library Association in 1994. The artwork in this book is exceptional.

George Littlechild's book *This Land Is My Land* (1993) is a particularly stunning introduction to Aboriginal literature, with personal stories about Littlechild's family members and ancestors. The short narratives are unforgettable in their intensity and poignancy. Littlechild writes and paints about his experiences in boarding school and recalls memories, many of them tragic, of family members. He speaks excitedly about his first visit to New York City, and describes the development of his artwork. The book ends optimistically, with Littlechild telling about the current revival of Aboriginal culture and traditions and emphasizing the pride he feels in his ancestry.

*Two Pairs of Shoes* by Esther Sanderson (1990) is a picture story book about a girl named Maggie and two special gifts she receives for her eighth birthday. Maggie's mother gives her a pair of shiny, black patent-leather shoes, and her *kokom* (grandmother) gives her a pair of hand-made beaded moccasins. Grandmother tells Maggie, "From now on you must remember when and how to wear each pair." The author has dedicated the book to "all children who walk in two pairs of shoes."

Michael Kusugak has produced many well-received picture books, most of them illustrated by Vladyana Krykorka. One of the best known is *Northern Lights: The Soccer Trails* (1993). The book embodies the life and spirit of the Inuit people of the North. Each double-page spread consists of a full-page illustration on one side and the text, adorned with a beadwork flower or motif set above or below, on the other. The children's toys, the dogs, and the landscapes are depicted by Krykorka in dazzling colours that capture the tones of the Arctic and the unique flavour of the Inuit culture. *Hide and Sneak* (1992) by the same author–illustrator team also captures the traditional culture and way of life in the Arctic. The book contains illustrations surrounded by Inuit script opposite each page of English text. It is a celebration of the mythology and traditional symbolism of Inuit culture.

A selection of books by Aboriginal Canadian authors and illustrators is provided in Box 11.5.

The chapter began with Shawn, a preservice teacher beginning a student teaching experience in a Grade 5 classroom. This section of the chapter has attempted to answer Shawn's questions about a teacher's role in engaging children with books. By now, Shawn understands the valuable role played by children's encounters with literature in helping them understand themselves and their world. By providing multiple ways for children to respond to literature, the teacher clearly demonstrates the many options a reader has when constructing personal and shared meanings. In a democratic society such as Canada's, a reader is free to make informed choices about reading material. As a teacher guides children in their

**Box 11.5    Children's Material by Aboriginal Canadians**

Bouchard, D. and Vickers, R.H. (1990). *The Elders Are Watching*. Tofino, BC: Eagle Dancer Enterprises.

Campbell, M. (ed.). (1985). *Achimoona*. Saskatoon: Fifth House.

Clutesi, G. (1990). *Stand Tall, My Son*. Victoria, BC: Newport Bay.

King, E. and Wheeler, J. (1991). *Adventure on Thunder Island*. Toronto: James Lorimer and Company.

King, T. (1992). *A Coyote Columbus Story*. Toronto: Groundwood Books.

Kusugak, M. (1990). *Baseball Bats for Christmas*. Toronto: Annick Press.

Kusugak, M. (1993). *Northern Lights: The Soccer Trails*. Toronto: Annick Press.

Littlechild, G. (1993). *This Land Is My Land*. Emeryville, CA: Children's Book Press.

Loewen, I. (1986). *My Mom Is So Unusual*. Winnipeg: Pemmican.

Loewen, I. (1993). *My Kookum Called Today*. Winnipeg: Pemmican.

McLellan, J. (1989). *The Birth of Nanabosho*. Winnipeg: Pemmican.

Oliviero, J. and Morrisseau, B. (1993). *The Fish Skin*. Winnipeg: Hyperion Press.

Pachano, J. (1985). *The Changing Times: Baby William*. (one of a series of four books) Chisabi, QC: James Bay Cree Cultural Education Centre.

Paul-Dene, S. (1992). *I Am the Eagle Free (Sky Song)*. Penticton, BC: Theytus Books.

Plain, F. (1993). *Amikoonse (Little Beaver)*. Winnipeg: Pemmican.

Sanderson, E. (1990). *Two Pairs of Shoes*. Winnipeg: Pemmican.

Slipperjack, R. (1987). *Honour the Sun*. Winnipeg: Pemmican.

Taylor, C.J. (1994). *Bones in the Basket*. Montreal: Tundra Books.

Weber-Pillwax, C. (1989). *Billy's World*. Edmonton: Reidmore.

Yerxa, L. (1993). *Last Leaf First Snowflake to Fall*. Toronto: Groundwood Books.

book selections, demonstrating respect for multiple viewpoints and lifestyles is a key consideration.

## Summary

"Reader response" refers to the events that occur within a reader when he or she reads a piece of text. That response is part of the meaning-making process, and as such, it is an important component of a language arts program. Rosenblatt (1978) maintains that a response to literature is dictated to a considerable extent by the purpose for reading or the *stance* from which the reader approaches the text. A stance can be anywhere on a continuum from efferent at one end, where the reader seeks information of some kind, to aesthetic at the other, where the reader focusses on appreciating what is read. A text first evokes an aesthetic or "lived through" response, and then evokes a more efferent response as the reader consciously thinks about the text and the reading experience.

Through reading works of literature and responding to them, children come to understand how texts work, what constitutes a good book, how language can be used in different ways to create different meanings and effects — in short, how to become readers, not just people able to read. Children are more likely to take ownership of the reading process and to understand that there is no right "answer" to literature when they are invited to respond to a text (though, as Rosenblatt says, some responses are more legitimate or appropriate than others). Responses to literature can be captured and represented in a written, oral, visual, or dramatic form.

An important vehicle for exploring a text is the response group, which works very much like a reading club. Teachers and researchers have discovered that children benefit from orally sharing and shaping their responses to books, and successful group work can enhance the enjoyment children experience in their reading. Literature response journals provide children with opportunities for written reflection on what they are currently reading, as do literature circles, novel studies, readers' workshops, and drama and art activities. There are also many "dependent authoring" activities that enhance children's enjoyment and understanding of literature.

When selecting materials to include in a classroom or school library, teachers and teacher–librarians must make every effort to choose books that meet the needs of children as well as the needs of the curriculum. The selection of print materials for use in schools is a complex issue, for it is difficult to say in a public education system who should decide what children should and should not read. There is, however, a clear difference between selecting materials for use in schools and censoring these materials. Where book selection uses positive criteria to determine which books to place in a collection, censorship seeks instead to remove, suppress, or restrict books already present in a collection. Guidelines for handling complaints about books can be established by school boards or by individual schools, and many agencies provide guidelines for creating such processes.

Educators understand that when children read aesthetically, they may identify with the characters, setting, or events of a story. However, until the last twenty years or so, Canadian children had little they could identify with in the literature available to them. Most Canadian children grew up with a canon of British and American literature. Today, a wide range of high-quality children's literature is published across

Canada, some of that literature is published by school districts and relatively small publishing houses. Canadian literature for children is now noted and characterized by its multicultural nature, and there are many excellent Aboriginal Canadian authors and illustrators creating books for children. Perhaps through reading Canadian literature, children can develop pride in being Canadian and an appreciation and understanding of Canada's role in the global community. Defining our identity as Canadians is a continuing process and one in which our students have a role.

## Selected Professional Resources

Commaire, A. (ed.). (published annually since 1971). *Something about the Author.* Detroit: Gale Research. Information about most published authors in North America and Britain can be found in this series of books. Only a few Canadian authors are included. The information is invaluable for novel or author studies and is easily accessible. The entries include reviews of each author's work.

Egoff, S. and Saltman, J. (1990). *The New Republic of Childhood: A Critical Guide to Canadian Children's Literature in English.* Toronto: Oxford University Press. Egoff and Saltman's classic text (originally published in 1967) provides a history of children's literature in Canada and an overview, genre by genre, of the rich diversity of Canadian titles available for children in the elementary and middle years. The authors provide insightful discussion of books, topics, themes, issues, illustrators, and authors. The book is an excellent resource for Canadian teachers, with a detailed index and complete bibliographies of the materials referenced in each chapter.

## Children's Books Noted in Chapter Eleven

Babbitt, N. (1975). *Tuck Everlasting.* New York: Farrar, Straus and Giroux.
Bannerman, H. (1899). *The Story of Little Black Sambo.* New York: Frederick A. Stokes and Company.
Bannerman H. and Marcellino, F. (1996). *The Story of Little Babaji.* New York: Michael di Capua Books (HarperCollins).
Beatty, O. and Geiger, J. (1992). *Buried in Ice: Unlocking the Secrets of a Doomed Arctic Voyage.* Mississauga, ON: Random House.
Bishop, C. (1938). *The Five Chinese Brothers.* New York: Coward, McCann & Geoghegan.
Brandis, M. (1996). *Rebellion: A Novel of Upper Canada.* Erin, ON: The Porcupine's Quill.
Browne, A. (1983). *Gorilla.* New York: Alfred A. Knopf.
Buchan, B. (1975). *Dragon Children.* Richmond Hill, ON: Scholastic-TAB.
Buffie, M. (1987). *Who Is Frances Rain?* Toronto: Kids Can Press.
Campbell, M. (ed.). (1985). *Achimoona.* Saskatoon: Fifth House.
Cooney, B. (1982). *Miss Rumphius.* New York: Viking Penguin.
Dahl, R. (1982). *Revolting Rhymes.* London: Jonathan Cape.
Dahl, R. (1983). *The Witches.* New York: Farrar, Straus and Giroux.
Ellis, S. (1991). *Pick-Up Sticks.* Toronto: Groundwood Books.
Elwin, R. (1990). *Asha's Mums.* Toronto: Women's Press.
George, J. (1972). *Julie of the Wolves.* New York: Harper & Row.
Hope, L.L. (1904). *The Bobbsey Twins.* New York: Grosset & Dunlap.
Hughes, M. (1994). *The Golden Aquarians.* Toronto: HarperCollins.
Hughes, T. (1968). *The Iron Man.* London: Faber and Faber.
King, E. and Wheeler, J. (1991). *Adventure on Thunder Island.* Toronto: James Lorimer and Company.
Kusugak, M. (1992). *Hide and Sneak.* (V. Krykorka, illustrator.) Toronto: Annick Press.
Kusugak, M. (1993). *Northern Lights: The Soccer Trails.* (V. Krykorka, illustrator.) Toronto: Annick Press.
Leger-Haskell, D. (1990). *Maxine's Tree.* Victoria, BC: Orca Books.
Lester, J. (1996). *Sam and the Tigers: A New Retelling of Little Black Sambo.* (J. Pinkney, illustrator.) New York: Dial Books for Young Readers.

Littlechild, G. (1993). *This Land Is My Land*. Emeryville, CA: Children's Book Press.

Lottridge, C. (1992). *Ticket to Curlew*. Toronto: Groundwood Books.

Lunn, J. (1983). *The Root Cellar*. Toronto: Lester & Orpen Dennys.

Miles, B. (1980). *Maudie and Me and the Dirty Book*. New York: Avon Camelot.

Montgomery, L.M. (1908). *Anne of Green Gables*. London: L.C. Page & Company.

Munsch, R. (1980). *The Paper Bag Princess*. Toronto: Annick Press.

Munsch, R. (1985). *Thomas's Snowsuit*. Toronto: Annick Press.

Munsch, R. (1989). *Giant: Or, Waiting for the Thursday Boat*. Toronto: Annick Press.

Munsch, R. and Kusugak, M. (1988). *A Promise Is a Promise*. Toronto: Annick Press.

Newman, L. (1989). *Heather Has Two Mommies*. Boston: Alyson Wonderland Publications.

Newman, L. (1998). *Belinda's Bouquet*. Anola, MB: Blue Heron Enterprises.

Paterson, K. (1977). *Bridge to Terabithia*. New York: HarperCollins.

Pearson, K. (1996). *Awake and Dreaming*. Toronto: Puffin/Penguin.

Pullman, P. (1995). *The Golden Compass*. New York: Ballantine Books.

Rowling, J.K. (1998). *Harry Potter and the Sorcerer's Stone*. New York: A.A. Levine Books.

Sanderson, E. (1990). *Two Pairs of Shoes*. Winnipeg: Pemmican.

Schwartz, A. (1981). *Scary Stories to Tell in the Dark*. New York: HarperCollins.

Sendak, M. (1970). *In the Night Kitchen*. New York: Harper & Row.

Simmie, L. (1995). *Mr Got to Go*. Red Deer, AB: Red Deer College Press.

Steig, W. (1976). *The Amazing Bone*. New York: Farrar, Straus and Giroux.

Taylor, C. (1985). *Julie*. Saskatoon: Western Producer Prairie Books.

Taylor, C. (1987). *The Doll*. Toronto: Douglas & McIntyre.

Truss, J. (1982). *Jasmin*. Vancouver: Douglas & McIntyre.

Twain, M. (1963 [1885]). *The Adventures of Huckleberry Finn*. New York: Washington Square Press.

Valentine, J. (1994). *One Dad, Two Dads, Brown Dad, Blue Dad*. Boston: Alyson Wonderland Publications.

Van Allsburg, C. (1988). *Two Bad Ants*. Boston: Houghton Mifflin.

Willhoite, M. (1990). *Daddy's Roommate*. Boston: Alyson Wonderland Publications.

Wynne-Jones, T. (1993). *Some of the Kinder Planets*. Toronto: Douglas & McIntyre.

Yerxa, L. (1993). *Last Leaf First Snowflake to Fall*. Toronto: Groundwood Books.

# References

Adams, P. (1987). Writing from reading: "Dependent authorship" as a response. In B. Corcoran and E. Evans (eds.), *Readers, texts, teachers*. Portsmouth, NH: Boynton/Cook.

Atwell, N. (1998). *In the middle: New understandings about writing, reading and learning* (2nd ed.). Portsmouth, NH: Boynton/Cook.

Benton, M. and Fox, G. (1985). *Teaching literature: Nine to fourteen*. London: Oxford University Press.

Bissoondath, N. (September 1998). No place like home. *New Internationalist*, 20–22.

Booth, D. (1992). *Censorship goes to school*. Markham, ON: Pembroke Publishers.

Booth, J., Phenix, J., Pauli, W., and Swartz, L. (1984–88). Impressions, K–7 [series]. Toronto: Holt-Harcourt Brace Jovanovich.

Britton, J. (1970). *Language and learning*. Harmondsworth, UK: Penguin Books.

Canadian Library Association (1974). *Statement on intellectual freedom*. 29th Annual Conference, Winnipeg, MB.

Commaire, A. (ed.). (published annually since 1971). *Something about the author*. Detroit: Gale Research.

Cooper, C. (1985). *Researching response to literature and the teaching of literature*. Norwood, NJ: Ablex.

Daniels, H. (1994). *Literature circles: Voice and choice in the student-centered classroom*. York, ME: Stenhouse.

Diakiw, J. (1997). Children's literature and Canadian national identity: A revisionist perspective. *Canadian Children's Literature, 23* (3), 36–49.

Edmonton Public Schools. (1998). *The Doll: A novel study*. Edmonton: EPSB, Resource Development Services.

Eeds, M. and Wells, M. (1989). Grand conversations: An exploration of meaning construction in literature response groups. *Research in the Teaching of English, 23* (1), 4–29.

Egoff, S. and Saltman, J. (1990). *The new republic of childhood: A critical guide to Canadian children's literature in English.* Toronto: Oxford University Press.

Esses, V. and Gardner, R. (1996). Multiculturalism in Canada: Context and current status. *Canadian Journal of Behavioural Science* [on-line], *28* (3). Available at http://www.cpa.ca/cjbsnew/1996/ful_edito.html [1998, March 11].

Farrell, E. and Squire, J. (eds.). (1990). *Transactions with literature: A fifty year perspective.* Urbana, IL: National Council of Teachers of English.

Fish, S. (1980). *Is there a text in this class? The authority of interpretive communities.* Cambridge, MA: Harvard University Press.

Freebody, P. and Luke, A. (1990). "Literacies" programs: Debates and demands in cultural contexts. *Prospects, 5* (3), 7–16.

Gertridge, A. (1994). *Meet Canadian authors and illustrators.* Richmond Hill, ON: Scholastic Canada.

Halliday, M.A.K. (1969). Relevant models of language. *Educational Review, 22* (1), 26–37.

Jenkinson, D. (1994). The changing faces of censorship in Manitoba's public school libraries. *Emergency Librarian, 22* (2), 15–21.

Langer, J. (1994). Focus on research: A response-based approach to teaching literature. *Language Arts, 71* (3), 203–211.

Meyers, D. (1997, Fall). Dependent authorship: A dependable teaching activity for reading and writing critically and creatively. *Statement,* 20–22.

Miller-Lachmann, L. (1992). *Our family, our friends, our world.* New Providence, NJ: R.R. Bowker.

National Council of Teachers of English. (1982). *The students' right to read.* Urbana, IL: National Council of Teachers of English.

National Council of Teachers of English. (1998). *Rationales for challenged books* [CD-ROM]. Urbana, IL: National Council of Teachers of English.

Nieto, S. (1992). *Affirming diversity.* New York: Longman.

Nodelman, P. (1992). We are all censors. *Canadian Children's Literature, 68,* 121–133

Pantaleo, S. (1994). Teacher influence on student response to literature. PhD dissertation, University of Alberta, Edmonton, AB.

Pantaleo, S. (1995). Students and teachers selecting literature: Whose choice? *Illinois English Bulletin, 82* (2), 33–46.

Peterson, R. and Eedes, M. (1990). *Grand conversations.* Richmond Hill, ON: Scholastic-TAB.

Purves, A. (1993). Toward a re-evaluation of reader response and school literature. *Language Arts, 70* (5), 348–361.

Purves, A. and Rippere, V. (1968). *Elements of writing about a literary work: A study of response to literature.* NCTE Research Report No. 9. Urbana, IL: National Council of Teachers of English.

Roberts, E.A. (1996). A survey of censorship practices in public school libraries in Saskatchewan. MLIS thesis, University of Alberta, Edmonton, AB.

Rosenblatt, L. (1978). *The reader, the text, the poem: The transactional theory of the literary work.* Carbondale, IL: Southern Illinois University Press.

Schrader, A. (1996). Censorproofing school library collections: The fallacy and futility. *School Libraries Worldwide, 2* (1), 71–94.

Thomson, J. (1987). *Understanding teenagers' reading: Reading processes and the teaching of literature.* Norwood, Australia: Australian Association for the Teaching of English.

# Chapter twelve

# Drama in the Elementary Classroom

By Patricia A. Payne

Drama and Literacy Development
- Scenario I
- Scenario II
- Scenario III

From School Time to Drama Time
- Using Pictures
- Transforming Text
- Representing New Ideas
- Scenario IV
- Scenario V
- Scenario VI

Classification of Drama
- Drama as Playing
- Drama as Context for Learning
- Drama as Interpretation of Literature
- Drama as Theatre

Drama in the Elementary Classroom

Planning and Teaching Drama
- Teaching Drama: Interpretation of Literature
- Teaching Drama: Contextual Drama

Teacher Concerns Related to Drama
- Learning the Language of Drama
- Using Role
- Management
- Time
- The Concert
- Evaluation

## Drama and Literacy Development

The chapter begins with a description of three classroom scenarios. The discussion following each example serves to highlight

- the power of drama for literacy development, and
- issues facing teachers as they begin their drama journey.

The remainder of the chapter outlines the different forms of dramatic activity that support literacy development.

### Scenario I

Teacher: I would like you to get into small groups and practise your parts for the play. Today we will practise reading our lines, and tomorrow you will have time to act them out.

During the next few days the students rehearse their plays for a performance to another class. Some children forget their lines, the shy students find it difficult to project their voices, the audience becomes more restless and inattentive. Classroom management becomes more problematic, and the teacher becomes more frustrated. She re-evaluates the educational merits of this type of drama activity and wonders how she can improve her strategies to facilitate the implementation of drama.

This scenario mirrors the school experience of many preservice teachers. It reflects the view of drama as performance: performing a play to peers or to a larger, unknown audience—at the school concert, for example. When I announce to my students in the introductory language arts class, "Next class will be a drama workshop," trepidation is written across their faces. This initial apprehension is reflected in their learning log comments. For example:

> In elementary school, drama was a word I hated to hear. It was only done occasionally and was worth many marks, which put a great deal of stress in the situation, especially for someone like me who was shy. (Lynne De Boyle, 1999)

> Drama meant the school concert — I did not enjoy "being on show." Drama as a tool for learning rather than performance sake — this is pretty much a new way for me to look at drama. (Danielle Couillard Fash, 1999)

> In my education I didn't do drama until junior and senior high, so when you said that we'd be doing drama today, my heart began to beat quickly. I was afraid to do anything for fear that I would make a fool of myself. (Christine Ventura, 1999)

A slightly different perception of drama is revealed by inservice teachers who choose to participate in the senior drama methods course. These teachers are exploring new ways to enhance their teaching of language arts. Like the teacher in Scenario I, they have often tried to implement some form of drama because they value active learning, but — also like that teacher — they have had less than satisfactory experiences. "To me, incorporating drama into my teaching meant painful, time-consuming preparations" (Flynn and Carr, 1994, p. 39).

Some teachers have a tendency to blame themselves for their lack of success, so they take a drama course to improve their strategies. They expect to learn ways of helping their students act out plays. The trouble is, these preservice and inservice teachers have (from their own experience) developed a concept of drama that is difficult to implement in elementary school: **drama as performance.** What they first need, therefore, is a different understanding of what drama is and what it involves.

New theories about language and language learning bring forth fresh insights and require new concepts and labels. For example, "reading readiness" has been replaced by the term "emergent literacy." The first label represents a behaviouristic perspective, the second a developmental one. Such new terms represent new understandings, and these in turn shape classroom practices. The *Memory Box* drama, which is described in the next section, is an example of drama practices that have been shaped by a new understanding of drama. Here, drama is used to provide a context for learning — specifically, a context for the purposeful use of language. This form of drama is referred to as **contextual drama.**

## Scenario II

Mr. Hughes, a teacher at Florence MacDougall Community School, High Level, Alberta, has read Mary Bahr's story, *The Memory Box*, to his Grade 3 class. This story tells of a young boy's visit to his grandparents' cottage during the summer holidays. During this visit his grandfather gets lost. His grandmother explains to her grandson that his grandfather has Alzheimer's disease. Together they make plans to assemble a memory box. The teacher uses this story idea for the following dramatic activity.

### Episode I

**Teacher-in-role as friend of the grandfather. He is talking to the whole class, which is seated around his chair.**

Well, friends, you all know my dear buddy has Alzheimer's and I think you all know that he has a special birthday coming soon. So, I'd just like to read this letter I received from his grandson and see what you think. [Reads the letter from the grandson requesting help from friends and family to help with a birthday celebration.] Well, what do you think? Can we do it?

**Student:** We could bring photos to help him remember.

**Teacher-in-role:** That's a great idea! [The discussion continues and the class contributes several possibilities.]

**Teacher-in-role:** Well, you seem keen to help, so I'll write and tell him we'll get organized for this party. [Moves from the chair and "re-enters" as teacher.]

**Teacher:** You certainly had lots of great ideas. We will work on these tomorrow.

### Episode II

**Teacher:** Let's see if we can use some of your suggestions to organize this celebration. [Through the teacher's questioning, the more general ideas from Episode I are shaped into concrete, specific details. "We need to think about Grandpa's life," "What did he do?" "What events will we celebrate?" "How?" "What is our relationship to him?" and "How will we help him remember?" are a few of the key questions that focus the drama.]

**Teacher:** Let's chart these ideas so we don't forget them. [Chart developed, as shown here.]

| Examples from the Planning Chart | | | |
|---|---|---|---|
| What did Grandpa do? | How old was he? | Who was he with when it happened? | Represented by |
| (a) Caught the biggest fish in the tournament | 35 years | Friends Jim and Tom | Picture of a fish, certificate, news article reporting the event. |
| (b) Invented a special beaver trap | 45 years | Colleagues Bill and Jack from Fisheries and Wildlife Department | Diagram of the trap. Oral descriptions, a beaver story, reasons for the invention. |
| (c) Great teller of stories | 22 to present | Children, grandchildren | Book, picture of a character from the story. |

| | |
|---|---|
| Teacher: | We have all these ideas, so ...? What do we need to do next? |
| Student: | We need to decide who we are going to be. I want to be his fishing buddy, I love fishing! |
| Student: | We have to make up our memory and then make something to help Grandpa remember. |

[Plans are negotiated, and the students complete the activities outlined in Episode III.]

Episode III
Students choose their role and create their memory, first orally, then in writing. Students are then grouped according to roles and shared events. For example, all the fishermen collaborate on the same story. Some stories are modified to avoid repetition and contradictions. Finally, memory objects are assembled.

Episode IV

| | |
|---|---|
| Teacher-in-role as Grandpa's friend: | All sit quietly until I bring our dear friend to this celebration. We have the birthday cake? When he walks in the door, sing "Happy Birthday." [Teacher exits the circle and re-enters slowly as Grandpa, signalling the change with a pair of spectacles, a walking stick, and slow steps. Keeping his eyes down, he enters, muttering.] |
| Teacher-in-role as Grandpa: | What day is it today? I know it's supposed to be something important.... Who are all these people? |
| Students-in-role: | Happy Birthday! [The memories are shared with Grandpa. After the last object is presented, the teacher places his stick and glasses on the chair, steps out of the circle, and becomes the narrator.] |
| Teacher-as-narrator: | Grandpa treasured the memory box: it gave him so much pleasure. His grandson is grown up now and he too treasures that box. It reminds him of all the happy times he spent with his grandparents at the cottage. [Pauses a moment, and then steps back into the circle as teacher.] |
| Teacher: | The drama went very well today. You all stayed in role and there was no giggling. Well done! [The students reflect on this imagined experience and compare it with their personal experience of dealing with elderly and sick people.] |

This new understanding of drama stems from the pioneering work of Dorothy Heathcote, a British drama educator. (See, for example, Heathcote, 1972.) Working with students in this way has been labelled "group drama," "process drama," "drama as a medium for learning," "drama for understanding," "role drama," and, as used in this chapter, "contextual drama." Each one of these labels signifies a critical attribute of this new understanding of drama. As Neelands (1992, p. 5) says, this way of working with students involves using drama as "an important means of constructing and experiencing the social contexts within which the different functions and uses of language can be identified and developed."

Once teachers have participated in a contextual drama, they quickly see that this strategy can easily become part of their regular teaching and that time-consuming preparations are not required. They recognize the potential of contextual drama to support learning in all areas of the curriculum, and they have no difficulty grasping the new insights about drama. The teachers try out these ideas with their classes and share their experiences enthusiastically with other teachers in drama workshops. Through sharing, they receive further support and reinforcement from their peers, which encourages them to continue implementing contextual drama in all areas of the curriculum. Listening to one of them speak, you would hear comments such as, "This writing is amazing for this child. She has hardly written anything all year. The drama provided an excellent prewriting activity," and "This child, in role, spoke in front of the whole class for the first time."

However, once the drama workshop ends, so does a lot of this support. What happens then? Drama is still not used extensively in elementary schools, even though research demonstrates that it supports student learning (Schaffner, 1985). It seems a good thing to do, but few teachers do it. Why? The teacher's insights following the next scenario illuminate this paradox. In my role as a language arts consultant, I was requested by Nicole McGillivray, a first-year teacher, to teach a lesson that demonstrated how **drama strategies** support literacy development. It was January of the school year, and these Grade 1 students were just beginning to write. The time available for the lesson was 40 minutes.

## Scenario III

I chose to use the following poem by A.A. Milne (1928, p. 30) as a stimulus for oral and written language development.

*The More It Snows*

The more it
SNOWS-tiddely-pom,
The more it
GOES-tiddely-pom
The more it
GOES-tiddely-pom
On
Snowing.

And nobody
KNOWS-tiddely-pom,
How cold my
TOES-tiddely-pom
How cold my
TOES-tiddely-pom
Are
Growing.

The poem was recited in a variety of ways:

- I read the poem, modelling expressive intonation.
- I read the poem while the class tapped out the beat of "tiddley-pom" as they said the words.
- I divided the class in half and had them use an antiphonal arrangement:
  Group I:　　The more it SNOWS
  Group II:　　Tiddely-pom
  Group I:　　The more it GOES ...

- Each group had the opportunity to recite the other group's lines.
- We said the poem together as we tapped out the rhythm.

After the choral work had been completed, most of the students had memorized the poem and shared their accomplishment. The poem was recited in unison once more and was followed by the *narration* described below.

**Teacher-narration, imaging:** Close your eyes. [Waits for quiet and slowly continues.] You are tucked in your bed. In a moment you are going to get out of bed and go to the window. [Pauses.] See yourself getting out of bed, move over to the window, and open the drape. You are so happy.... It's been snowing! What can you see? [Pauses.] You get dressed quickly and go outside to play. [Pause.] Keep your eyes closed and imagine playing in the new snow near your house. [Pause.] I am going to come round and tap you on the shoulder, and I want you to speak out loud and say what you are doing. [The teacher moves to first child, taps the shoulder.]

**Voice-in-the-head:**

| | |
|---|---|
| Child I: | I am making a snow angel. |
| Child II: | I am shovelling the path. |
| Child III: | [No response. Teacher moves to the next child.] |
| Child IV: | I am making footprints. I make my name. [The process continues until the students have had an opportunity to respond.] |

After this activity, the students transformed their images and oral sentences into written form. Many of the students wished to share their efforts, so their work was folded into the poem.

I then divided the class into small groups and gave each group an opportunity to present. The group lined up facing the front of the class. The students recited the poem using the antiphonal arrangement. At the end of the poem, each person stepped forward and read a sentence while displaying a picture. Each presentation of the picture was punctuated by the refrain "tiddely-pom." To complete the presentation, the class created an additional line that was recited in unison, "Oh! I do-o-o-o hope it keeps on snowing!" This informal presentation was shared with another class at the Grade 1's request.

In planning this lesson, I selected strategies that I thought Nicole might be able to incorporate into her own teaching repertoire: *imaging* and *voice-in-the-head*. I also needed to demonstrate how these strategies supported literacy development. Nicole's analysis suggests that these intents were realized.

**Nicole:** The way you focussed the class was great. Getting them to close their eyes and then slowly and quietly providing them with cues to help them create a picture in their head really helped. They had no trouble sharing their ideas. I could use that. What's it called?

**Pat:** Imaging.

**Nicole:** Yes, I could use imaging. It is more effective than saying, "Pretend you have just woken up, it's been snowing. What do you see?" Imaging gives the students more time to think, and the activity of walking around the classroom and tapping them on the shoulder as a signal to share their ideas was also effective. It did not stop the flow of the lesson, and those students who needed more thinking time could take it. They were also encouraged by other students' ideas. That way of doing it —

Pat:   Voice-in-the-head.

Nicole:   — voice-in-the-head allowed them to stay with their image.

Pat:   They did well reciting the poem. You have obviously done some choral work with them.

Nicole:   Yes, but I usually have them chant repetitious phrases from poems and stories. "Fee, fie, fo, fum" from "Jack and the Beanstalk," "I'll huff and I'll puff and I'll blow your house down" from "The Three Little Pigs"—chants like that. I do it spontaneously and the kids enjoy it. What I liked was the way these activities supported the writing process. I had no one saying, "I don't know what to write."

Pat:   Yes, imaging, voice-in-the-head, and chanting are three drama strategies that are fairly easy to implement, particularly in this lesson. Although the children were seated at their desks, they remained actively involved.

Nicole:   Yes, they were involved. I would not have counted those activities as drama. I thought drama meant active ... active in the sense of physical activity. I know you don't mean that here. [Points to another poem.] I could use similar strategies with this nursery rhyme.

Nicole's analysis of this lesson highlights several important points. First, the connections between the general teaching strategies familiar to most teachers and the less familiar drama strategies need to be made explicit. Second, the shift that is required of the teacher to move a class from school time to drama time, from the here and now of the classroom to the "as if" world of drama, demands closer scrutiny. (Examples illustrating this transition are described later in the chapter.) Nicole recognized the shift that was required. "Yes, I could use imaging, instead of saying, 'Pretend you have just woken up, it's been snowing. What do you see?' She also articulated the other benefits of using such strategies — there is more time to think, the flow of the lesson is not interrupted, activities are connected to help the students compose. She was able to identify how the drama strategies were part of the writing process.

Later, chatting with the teacher of the class who had viewed the poetry presentations, Nicole had further insights.

Teacher:   My kids enjoyed the presentation. Thanks for sharing. My Grade 1's love to do *choral speech*.

Nicole:   Yes ... and my class loved the drama strategies.

Teacher:   Choral speech is drama?

Nicole:   [Provides a synopsis of the lesson.] So you see the drama strategies, imaging and voice-in-the-head, were used to help the students compose their sentences, but these strategies were not part of the presentation of the poem.

Teacher:     You could use imaging and voice-in-the-head to help with reading comprehension, too.

Nicole:      Yes?

Teacher:     For example, imaging. Let's say you were going to read the story of Goldilocks. You could take the sentence, "She went through the wood!" The students could image the scene, and then their oral responses could be translated into a collective picture. The class picture could be compared with the illustration in the story book. I could also see using these strategies with illustrations to develop predicting skills.

Nicole:      How?

Teacher:     [Points to a picture of the three bears returning to find their house in disarray. Consternation is reflected in their faces.] "You are the father bear ... say out loud what you are thinking." When the students have had an opportunity to respond as the three characters, you can continue the story to verify or modify the students' thinking in role.

Nicole:      Great idea! I think I could do that kind of drama.

Nicole McGillivray shared this lesson idea with another Grade 1 teacher, Anna McAskile, who provided a number of writing samples after she had taught the drama lesson. Exhibits 12.1 and 12.2 were composed as a result of the imaging and voice-in-the-head strategies. Exhibits 12.3 and 12.4 represent the elaboration of these ideas completed in another lesson.

**Exhibit 12.1**   **Brittany's Representation of Her Imaging**

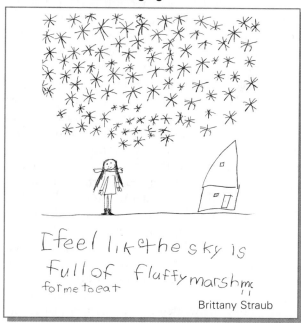

I feel like the sky is full of fluffy marshm
for me to eat

Brittany Straub

**Exhibit 12.2**   **Kyle's Representation of His Imaging**

I feel like I'm flying in the ske.

Kyle Didzena

**Exhibit 12.3**   Brittany's Elaboration of Story Idea from Imaging Activity

One day I wakeup I saw the snow falling. I putc on my close and whent outside And I saw the snow falling. I liked the snow it was beutful. It looked like marshmallows it was a beutful. white. The snow cuvered the groud.

Brittany Straub

**Exhibit 12.4**   Kyle's Elaboration of Story Idea from Imaging Activity

One day I wock up and I drest up and wet outside and I toucka jump wen I touck th jump I feel like I'm flying in the ske. I was on my toboggan I wet down the big hill

Kyle Didzena

In Scenario III, imaging, voice-in-the-head, and narration were strategies that were part of the composing process. When the product, the poem, was presented, these processes were not visible. Many teachers are using similar strategies in their daily teaching but don't count them as "drama," because their conception of drama is equated with performance. Like Nicole, once they are aware of this misconception of drama and are cognizant of the slight shift required to use these strategies in a more conscious manner, they feel "I can do that!" When drama is incorporated as part of the writing process, it can be efficient and effective — it does not have to be time-consuming and painful.

Similar insights were gained by preservice teachers who recently participated in a one-hour drama workshop as part of the introductory language class at the University of Alberta. The students listened to a traditional folk tale, *The Three Sillies*, in which a man, woman, and daughter behave stupidly. A young gentleman refuses to marry the daughter until he sees three sillies sillier than these three. Of course he does, and in true folk tale fashion, the young gentleman and the daughter live happily ever after. After hearing the story, the class was instructed to work in a small group to create a frozen picture, or *tableau*, of one scene from the story. First, voice-in-the-head was added to this tableau, which then led to a short *improvisation* of the scene. After the story was enacted, each group created a new silly situation and shared the improvisation with the class.

The culminating activity of the workshop was for each group to share its new version of the story in written form. Boxes 12.1 and 12.2 are two examples from the same improvisation, one written as a newspaper article, the other as a narrative piece.

**Box 12.1**   A Silly Story: Sink or Drink

If you're at the brink of sinking, why not try drinking! Drinking the water in the boat that is! It's an odd response, but that is exactly what a group of tourists did when they discovered a hole in their boat while on a zoo cruise in the swamps of Louisiana. Tourists along the shore of the alligator-infested waters could be heard shouting "Jump, jump!" The gang onboard the boat, however, countered these nasty directives with "Drink, drink." They used whatever they could find on the boat — straws, teacups, and their hands — to literally drink the water away. Luckily, a passing patrol boat saw their desperate situation and came to the rescue. Wouldn't Mark Twain have made a good story out of this!

Source: Katherine Weber, workshop participant (1999). Reprinted with permission.

### Box 12.2    A Silly Story: There's a Hole in the Boat!

It was a hot July day. Sharlene and her friends watched the sun dance off the clear blue water as they rowed the boat in unison. As the sun beat down on their golden shoulders, they felt as though the world could not be more perfect than it was at the exact moment. Suddenly, one of the girls in the back screamed, "There's a hole in the boat!"

Sure enough, water came pouring in the boat from a hole as large as a tennis ball. No one knew how the hole came to be.

"What should we do?" one girl cried. Several suggestions were made and each one was tried in its turn.

"Make juice out of it and drink it," Angie suggested.

"Use your shoe to scoop it out," exclaimed another.

"Soak it up with a rag," offered Mary.

"Stuff Lisa in it," Angie said with a nervous giggle.

"Make another hole so the water can seep back out!" Jane cried.

The girls tried in vain to stop the water, but it kept oozing in. Finally, the most sensible idea came up, "Let's all jump out of the boat!" And so they did. The girls splashed wildly in the blue water while the boat slowly sank.

Source: Yvonne Mik, workshop participant (1999). Reprinted with permission.

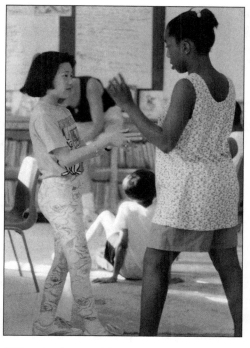

Girls going into a tableau.

The following learning log comments indicate that the preservice teachers understood how drama can support literacy development:

> I didn't realize (until today) that drama fits into the language arts curriculum. Now, though, it seems very obvious to me! (Yvonne Mik, 1999)

> As I am such a hands-on learner, I can see how this process will internalize the learning for students. When you explained the writing process — brainstorming ideas, putting ideas together, and writing the first draft—it was easy to see how this same process happened in our group when we were creating our tableau of another silly solution. (Danielle Couillard Fash, 1999)

Table 12.1 highlights the connection between drama and literacy by analyzing the two drama lessons ("The More It Snows" and *The Three Sillies*) in relation to the writing process.

### Table 12.1    Drama and Writing

| Writing Process | Grade 1 | Preservice Teachers |
|---|---|---|
| Idea generation | | |
| 1. Stimulus | Poem, "The More It Snows" | Story, *The Three Sillies* |
| 2. Method of presentation | Choral work by teacher and students | Storytelling by the teacher |
| 3. Drama strategies | • imaging<br>• voice-in-the-head | • tableau<br>• voice-in-the-head<br>• improvisation |

*(continued)*

**Table 12.1   Continued**

| Writing Process | Grade 1 | Preservice Teachers |
|---|---|---|
| First draft | Picture and sentence | Dramatization of a new silly solution |
| Second draft | Elaboration of picture and sentence | Dramatization transformed into writing. |
| Revision | Not completed | Peer conferencing |
| Edit | Not completed | Final copies produced |
| Publication/celebration | Presentation of the poem to another class | Display |

The scenarios in this introduction provide you with a glimpse of the range of activities we label "drama." The discussions have outlined some of the benefits and perceived difficulties associated with implementing drama in the elementary classroom, and three major ideas were noted:

1. Our understanding of drama shapes our classroom practices.
2. Our understanding of the connections between the drama process and the reading and writing processes eliminates time-consuming preparations, as drama is seen as part of, not apart from, literacy instruction. Drama is viewed not as a curricular frill — something to be done if there is time — but as a medium for learning. Drama provides a context for meaningful literacy activities.
3. Our understanding of the similarities between familiar, generic teaching strategies and less familiar drama strategies supports a change in teacher stance. This change of stance from "expert/I am in charge" to "negotiator/storyteller" is a prerequisite if the teacher wants the class to explore the "as if" world of drama. This change in stance — reflected in the language and gestures of the teacher — enables the teacher to use appropriate drama strategies to implement the various dramatic forms.

When teachers' actions are shaped by this knowledge, their apprehension about using drama in the classroom diminishes, and they begin their drama journey. The remainder of this chapter provides further elaboration of these insights, with examples of classroom practice.

## Classification of Drama

Our understanding of drama shapes our classroom practices.

Drama is like language in that one uses it to learn about events, issues, and relationships. Drama is taught not so students become better at doing it, but as a way of helping them understand the world. It can be used across the curriculum. As students become engaged in drama activities and become familiar with a variety of strategies, their drama skills do improve. Like language, drama skills are taught in context as the students explore meanings of stories, poems, issues, and events. The term "drama" applies to a wide range of activities, from the informal dramatic play of a young children's tea party or the informal classroom presentation of a puppet play, to the more formal production of a school play with an audience. Table 12.2, a modification of Bolton's 1979 **classification of dramatic forms**, highlights the differences among these various concepts of drama.

**Table 12.2   Drama As ...**

|  | Playing | Context for Learning | Interpretation | Theatre |
|---|---|---|---|---|
| Critical attributes | • spontaneous<br>• no specific end<br>• no practice required<br>• duration of the play determined by students | • context is created through negotiation by students and teacher, who take roles to explore an event, issue, or relationship<br>• dramatic tension is necessary to move drama forward<br>• it appears spontaneous but the language and actions are prompted by the demands of the situation, which is carefully structured by teacher<br>• reflection is crucial | • author's ideas are represented<br>• a variety of different modes of expression are used: dramatization, story theatre, readers' theatre, choral speech, puppetry | • parts are assigned<br>• lines are memorized and rehearsed for an audience |
| Examples | Playing at castles (p. 342) | Planning a celebration (p. 332) | Dramatization of stories and poems (p. 334) | High school drama performances |
| Age | Young children, 3 to 6 years | All ages | All ages | Older students |
| Teacher's role | • provides space and time in the classroom for playing to occur | • negotiator — helps students create the context<br>• facilitator — helps students understand their roles<br>• provides tension<br>• guides students to seek a solution | • selects literature to be interpreted<br>• teaches specific drama skills<br>• coaches students to improve skills | • director — chooses the play, auditions, organizes rehearsals to polish students' skills to performance level |
| Educators | Vygotsky (1978) | Bolton (1979), Booth (1986), Heathcote (1972), Neelands (1992), O'Neill et al. (1977) | McCaslin (1996), Moffett (1983), Stewig (1983) | Sporre (1993) |

## Drama as Playing

**Drama as playing** is a very important type of activity, because it fosters the social and intellectual development of the young child. As Vygotsky (1978, p. 102) says, "Children at play are always above their average age, above their daily behaviour; in play, it is as though they were a head taller than themselves." This type of drama places the least demand on the teacher, who simply provides time and space for the play to occur. The students decide how long they will play, with whom, and what the play will be about.

This type of drama as playing should be encouraged in young children. Classrooms in kindergarten that support this activity will have a designated space and props box for dramatic play. Sometimes teachers will structure this space to support the themes the class is studying. The space may become a house, restaurant, hospital, post office, or store. Dramatic play fosters social skills, verbal abilities, co-operation, and symbolic representation, as illustrated in the following example:

### An Example of Dramatic Playing

(Two children in a kindergarten class are playing with large interlocking construction blocks.)

Richard:    Let's make this into a castle. [Points to the structure he has built.]

Marilyn:    Yes, and this [placing skipping rope around the structure] can be the water and this [placing large block over the rope] can be the bridge.

Richard:    What are you going to be?

Marilyn:    I'm going to be the bridge keeper.

Richard:    I'm going to look after the castle. [They continue planning their play.] Come and let's eat.

Marilyn:    Okay. I have to put up this bridge first ... a dragon might come. [Makes the noise of the bridge going up as she imitates a winding action.]

Richard:    Dinner is ready. [Uses the rest of the blocks to create a table.]

Marilyn:    Hey, I want those blocks for my bridge.

Richard:    No, they're mine.

[The squabble terminates the co-operative dramatic play.]

For young children's dramatic play to work, they tacitly agree to abide by certain rules related to time, space, and people. These rules shape the dramatic play. The rules of this situation are "We agree to be in a castle" (space); "Our story happened a long time ago" (time); "We agree to take on the roles of drawbridge keeper and castle keeper" (people); and "We agree to do and say what we think those people did and said in that time and place" (space, time, and people). The first part of this dramatic play is concerned with negotiating the rules of the drama game so the play can begin. In order to sustain belief in their play, the children use a variety of strategies. The play terminates when a rule is broken. The drawbridge keeper comes out of role, and the young child demands ownership of the blocks.

The analysis of drama as playing in Table 12.3 illustrates some of the strategies used by young children in spontaneous play. The strategies used in the *Memory Box* drama described earlier are more structured versions of the ones that have their genesis in children's play. Table 12.4 illustrates the structured drama strategies used in this drama.

**Table 12.3**    Emerging Drama Strategies: Drama as Playing

| Strategy | Examples |
|---|---|
| 1. Use of objects to build belief | Use of interlocking blocks. "Let's make this into a castle." |
| 2. Defining space | Skipping rope represents water. "This can be the water and this can be the bridge." |
| 3. Use of role | "I'm going to be the bridge keeper." |
| 4. Narration | They did their work and then it was time for supper. |
| 5. Movement | Act out making the supper, winding the drawbridge. Imitates the noise of the bridge being lifted. |
| 6. Soundtracking | • Dialogue to negotiate rules: "Let's make this into a castle." |
| 7. Dialogue | • Dialogue in role: "I have to put up this bridge." |

**Table 12.4**    Structured Drama Strategies: Drama as Context

| Strategy | Examples |
|---|---|
| 1. Use of objects to build belief | Glasses and a walking stick used to support the teacher in role as Grandpa. |
| 2. Defining space | Children seated in a circle to define the drama space. |
| 3. Use of role | Participants decide on a specific role in relation to the main character (friends, family members). |
| 4. Narration | Teacher: "Grandpa treasured the memory box. It gave him so much pleasure." |
| 5. Movement | A group of friends enact the catching of the prized fish to remind Grandpa of the event. |
| 6. Soundtracking | Not used in this drama. |
| 7. Dialogue | • Dialogue for negotiation: Teacher: "Can we do it?" Student: "We could bring photos to help him remember." |
| | • Dialogue in role: "What day is it today?" "I Teacher as know it's supposed to be Grandpa: something important." |

Contextual drama appears outwardly spontaneous, like drama as playing, but it is carefully structured by the teacher to help students achieve new insights and understanding.

## Drama as Context for Learning

In **drama as a context for learning**, the teacher often works in role and facilitates the action from within the dramatic context. For example, in Scenario II, the teacher-in-role as Grandpa's friend worked with his friends and relatives (students) to plan an appropriate celebration. Rather than acting out a story with a defined beginning, middle, and end, this form of drama is more concerned with creating dramatic contexts within which teacher and pupils explore themes, issues, and relationships. As in dramatic play, the participants first construct the meaning of the dramatic situation so they can work within it.

## Drama as Interpretation of Literature

The choric presentation of A.A. Milne's poem "The More It Snows" described earlier is an example of **drama as interpretation of literature**.

Transforming text into a drama presentation is a means of helping students understand, interpret, and compose stories and poems. This form of drama is used as a way of representing ideas from a story or poem. Students are encouraged to interpret literature through a variety of **dramatic forms** of expression: *dramatization, puppetry, readers' theatre, choral speech,* and *choric drama*. Most often, these forms are shared with classmates. When they are polished and rehearsed for a general audience — such as a school assembly or school concert — they move toward drama as performance.

## Drama as Theatre

**Drama as theatre** places great demands on students as actors and the teacher as director. A great deal of time and energy is spent in rehearsing, and the educational gains may be minimal, although such an enterprise probably strengthens home and school relations. This chapter does not address this form of drama.

It is important to understand the differences among these four classifications of drama, because our understanding shapes what we do in classrooms. As illustrated in Figure 12.1, "I did drama today" could represent a range of activities, depending on the teacher's interpretation of the term "drama."

---

**Figure 12.1**    **Different Conceptions of Drama**

**Drama as Playing**
The teacher sets up the play area as a restaurant. The children play at being cooks, waiters, customers.

**Drama as Interpretation**
Teacher selects a story and guides the children through a series of procedures until the dramatic product is complete.

"I did drama today."

**Contextual Drama**
Teacher selects a story, decides on a focus, and adopts a role to create a context for problem solving.

**Drama as Theatre**
Parts are assigned, and students practise a scene. The teacher directs.

## Planning and Teaching Drama

Consider the statement "I did drama today using Bahr's *The Memory Box*." For a teacher who views drama as interpretation of literature, this sentence summarizes certain strategies and procedures: dividing the story into scenes, assigning characters, practising the scenes, and then sharing the presentation with peers. For a teacher who equates drama with contextual drama, this statement would mean selecting the type of strategies and procedures outlined in Scenario II. Drama as interpretation of literature places the teacher outside the play as director, guide, and coach. The contextual approach places the teacher inside the drama as he or she takes on various roles to support the work.

The next section of this chapter provides specific lesson ideas for teaching these two types of drama. Important to keep in mind, however, are the following points:

- All of these lessons have been taught to elementary children by either university students as part of a drama project or by me in response to a teacher's request for strategies to support literacy development. The selection of strategies presented in these lessons is limited to ones that beginning drama teachers could appropriate more readily.
- All of these lessons were part of, not apart from, the language arts curriculum. The teachers saw drama as a context for language learning, because in "doing drama," all the six language arts were included. When children complete a play for reader's theatre, they have an opportunity to repeat and practise their part. Such opportunities for oral interpretation develop fluency in reading in a purposeful context. Listening, talking, viewing, and representing are used throughout the dramas. When children are representing their ideas through tableau, the rest of the class is viewing and interpreting the meaning. In creating a tableau, students need to talk and listen to one another to shape their representation. Not all drama activity involves writing, but the examples described earlier illustrate the drama–writing connection.

Our understanding of the connection between the drama process and the reading and writing processes eliminates time-consuming preparations, as drama is seen as part of, not apart from, literacy instruction. Drama is viewed not as a curricular frill — something to be done if there is time — but as a medium for learning. Drama provides a context for meaningful literacy activities.

## Teaching Drama: Interpretation of Literature

### Dramatization

This dramatic form involves transforming stories and poems using improvisation. The students are guided and coached by the teacher.

Primary Level:
*Caps for Sale* (Slobodkina, 1947)

The teacher reads the story, which involves a peddler and monkeys, to the class. While the peddler rests in the forest, monkeys, hiding in the trees, steal his caps. When the peddler finds out, he gets angry. He shakes his fist, stamps his foot, and throws his own cap on the ground. The monkeys then imitate him, so he is able to retrieve his caps. As a literature response activity, the teacher dramatizes the story with the whole class.

| | | |
|---|---|---|
| *Narration:*<br>*Movement:* | Teacher: | So the peddler went to sell his caps, he packed his tray.<br>[All the children portray the peddler and enact the story, adding limited **dialogue** as the teacher narrates.] |
| | Teacher: | The peddler went back to town shouting ... |
| *Chant:* | Children: | Caps for sale! |

Primary Level:
*Three Billy Goats Gruff*

| | | |
|---|---|---|
| *Storytelling:*<br><br>*Chant:* | | The teacher has read the story to the children before the lesson. The class sits around her in a circle. She invites them to help her retell the story by joining in the refrain, "Who's that trip trapping over my bridge?" This invitation to join in the story is signalled by the teacher's posture, voice, tone, and pause. "Class, when I raise my hand like this, you say, 'Who's that trip trapping over my bridge?'" When the students have listened to the retelling of the story, the teacher moves into the *dramatization*. |
| | Teacher: | Find a space. Lie on the floor. As I count to ten, you become more and more relaxed. Eyes closed. One ... two ... [Teacher moves around the room to see if the children are following directions and then continues with the story.] |
| *Relaxation:* | Teacher: | You are beginning to wake ... stretch ... put on your trousers ... [The teacher narrates the process of getting dressed, and children mime the actions.] |
| *Movement:*<br>(parallel action) | Teacher: | You walk slowly and heavily out of your house. You are so, so big.... [When the teacher sees the children have attained the movement quality of a giant she continues.] |
| *Narration:*<br>*Chant:* | Teacher:<br>Class: | Stop Mr. Troll and listen. Trip-trap-trip-trap. Troll, you say ...<br>[Teacher signals, and class responds in unison.] Who's that trip-trapping over my bridge?<br>[This dramatic sequence is repeated for the three goats. The combination of narration by the teacher and parallel action by the students can be used for any story. As the teacher narrates, all students assume the same role simultaneously. These strategies are well-suited to younger students, who require more active participation.] |
| *Role:*<br>(as the big billy goat) | Teacher: | Mr. Troll, I am going to butt you with these horns. [Moves out of role, which is signalled by change in posture and voice.] On the count of three you are butted in the stomach and fall into the river. Let's practise that part. [When the students have practised, the teacher moves back into role.] Move, Mr. Troll, I am warning you. I have very dangerous horns. I will count to three: one, two, ... three. [The children collapse on the floor, and the teacher moves out of role and narrates the ending of the story.] The goat joined the other goats, and they lived happily ever after. |

Upper Elementary Level:
*King of the Cats* (Jacobs, 1973)
Story synopsis: The sexton's wife is sitting by the fire with her big black cat, Tom. Her frightened husband returns home from work. He tells her that while he was digging a grave he saw six black cats carrying a coffin covered with a purple pall with a crown on top. As the sexton watched the service, the leader of the cats turned to him and said, "Go, tell Tom Tildrum that Tim Tildrum is dead." When the sexton spoke these words

to his wife, their cat Tom flew up the chimney, never to be seen again. The teacher selects one scene from the story to begin the drama.

| *Tableau:* | Teacher: | The sexton was digging the grave, and when he looked up, he was so scared. If he had taken a picture of that scene, what would it look like? I would like you to get into groups of seven and create that picture. [Students create two tableaux: one depicts the cats entering the churchyard, the other shows the cats kneeling around the grave.] |
| | Teacher: | Let's look at these different frozen pictures. Look at the tableaux and tell me one thing you really liked. Give one suggestion for improvement. |
| | Sally: | They are not being silly. All their faces and bodies are sad, like this [demonstrates]. They could make it better by all holding the coffin at the same height. |
| *Reflection on the drama:* | Teacher: | Can you try Sally's suggestion? You did well to stay so serious for so long. Well done! We've really improved at staying in drama time. [The process continues, and the teacher reinforces the improvement in drama skills and helps the students to incorporate the suggestions. The improvement in the movement quality of the frozen pictures reinforces the commitment to the drama.] |
| *Voice-in-the-head:* | Teacher: | Move into your tableau. As I come around and tap you on the shoulder, tell me one thought. If you can't think of anything to say, just put your head down and I'll move on. [The teacher moves to the tableau depicting the grave scene and taps Mary on the shoulder.] |
| *Individual memory:* | Mary: | I'll miss you Tim. [Her response is inaudible to the rest of the class. Rather than spotlight the child by asking her to repeat the sentence in a louder voice, the teacher encourages a choral response. "Excellent Mary. Say after me, class, 'I'll miss you, Tim.'" The process continues and the students contribute their individual memories of Tim. "I'll remember the time you helped me win the alley fight." "You looked after me when I was sick." "You helped me find Dick Whittington, my master. Thank you, Tim."] |
| | Teacher: | Some very interesting thoughts, lots of great stories there. Let us now add *movement* and *dialogue*. You will begin in tableau, come alive for a few seconds, and then freeze again. |
| *Improvision, action, and dialogue:* | | [The Grade 4 students practise their short improvisations and share them with the class. The sharing is important, since drama skills are taught in context. The students practise the skill (such as slowly picking up the coffin) in order to clarify the meaning of the story. Shaping the movement quality deepens the aesthetic experience for the students.] |

The dramatization of such folk tales can be extended in a variety of ways, as Table 12.5 illustrates.

When dramatizing stories with students, the key to success is to select a small part of the story with strong action qualities. Many folk tales have this characteristic. With primary children, *parallel action* is more appropriate than tableau. Young children like to move, and tableaux are too static. In the stories *The Three Billy Goats Gruff* and *Caps for Sale*, the same strategies were used. The teacher

- selected a story with a strong line of action,
- chose one or two short scenes to be enacted,
- analyzed the movements of the characters and included these descriptions in the narration: (e.g., "Troll, you walk very slowly to the bridge"),

**Table 12.5** Extension Activities from *King of the Cats*

| | |
|---|---|
| Music | • One class focussed more on dramatic movement and music, and the story became a dance drama. |
| Writing | • Another class folded in different literacy activities, including stories, eulogies, résumés for the position of king. |
| Drama | • One class moved into contextual drama and had a meeting to decide the next heir apparent. |
| Drawing | • One class, at Hallowe'en, made the story into a shadow play. They used cutouts placed on the overhead projector and recorded the dialogue and sound effects. |

- gave all children the same role and chose scenes in which the characters were clearly defined, and
- folded in simple dialogue, such as "Caps for sale!" and "Who's that trip-trapping over my bridge?"

These same principles can be applied in transforming text into a puppet play.

## Puppetry

When using puppetry in the classroom, it is important to simplify puppet construction. The puppets help the students move into the imaginary world of drama. Many shy children find security in this form of drama. They can hide behind the puppet theatre as attention is focussed on the puppet. Puppet plays should not be scripted, because students find it difficult to read scripts and manipulate the puppets at the same time. To organize students for puppetry, consider these guidelines:

- Provide guidance and materials for puppet construction.
- Help students select an appropriate part of the story. Select a small part with strongly defined action.
- Provide practice time. Put a time limit on the practice and then evaluate. At this point, the first attempt can be appreciated and improved. Group process skills can be reinforced. It is often these procedural concerns that deter teachers from drama work — "It takes too much time and energy" (Edwards and Payne, 1994).
- Celebrate puppet plays by inviting another class to watch the polished performance.

## Readers' Theatre

Readers' theatre is a form of oral interpretation in which a group of readers performs written texts using a script. This activity provides a meaningful context for practising reading aloud. Commercially printed scripts are available, but students can prepare their own scripts. Guidance from the teacher is needed to facilitate this task, since children need assistance with

- *Choosing a story.* The story needs to be short, with lots of dialogue and a variety of characters.

- *Organizing the cast.* The class needs to be grouped according to the number of characters involved in the story.
- *Transforming the story into a script.* Initially, the teacher may model this process with the whole class.

As the students become more proficient at transforming story into play, they can create their own scripts. This transformation of text to script involves students in a close reading of the text, which is an excellent context for developing comprehension abilities. Readers' theatre is more akin to a radio play, except that the readers are visible and can use gestures and facial expressions to portray meaning. This form is more appropriate for older students (Grades 3 to 6).

Readers' theatre gives students practice in reading aloud and making oral interpretations. Oral interpretation is also a major focus of choral speech and choric drama.

## Choral Speech

Choral speech is the art of interpreting text as a group. The following nursery rhymes have been selected to demonstrate the variety of ways they can be interpreted. Older students can use these same strategies with more age-appropriate poems. Choral work can be as informal as students chanting repetitive phrases while the teacher reads a story, or as formal as students performing a poem for an audience, to be judged at a drama festival. For more formal presentations, there are four basic ways that text can be approached for choric work to achieve variety.

**Line-by-Line Arrangement**   Scenario III, in which the poem "The More It Snows" was used, is an example of arranging poetry line by line. Each child, or group of children, chants one line.

**Antiphonal**   The class is divided into two groups: one group recites the first verse, and the other group recites the second verse. This process is continued throughout the poem. For example:

Group 1:   Pussy Cat, Pussy Cat
Where have you been?

Group 2:   I have been up to London
To visit the Queen.

Group 1:   Pussy Cat, Pussy Cat
What did you there?

Group 2:   I frightened a little mouse
under the chair.

**Cumulative**   One voice begins and others are added throughout the poem.

Student 1:   For want of a nail a shoe was lost.

Students 1 and 2:   For want of a shoe a horse was lost.

| Students 1, 2, and 3: | For want of a horse the general was lost. |
| Students 1, 2, 3, and 4: | For want of a general the battle was lost. [Pause] |
| Student 1: | All for the want of a nail. |

**Unison**  All students say all parts. Unison is not very appropriate for elementary children because the meaning of the text is obscured by the singsong pace of the group. It takes practice to effectively interpret a poem in unison. Students prefer to spend time adding action, dialogue, and props to their choral interpretation. With these additions, choral speech becomes *choric drama*. Choric drama is a combination of dramatization and choral speech. For example, John Ciardi's "Mummy Slept Late and Daddy Fixed Breakfast" (1962) lends itself to this form of drama. A group of children can improvise Daddy preparing breakfast while the rest of the class recites the poem.

All these forms of drama can be used in the elementary classroom to help students develop an appreciation of literature. In the process of transforming text into drama, students use many skills that support the comprehension and composition of stories. As Moffett (1983, p. 114) says, "For any narrative, what improvisation does is to translate what happened into what is happening, thus making the abstraction of the story come alive in the present moment."

Transforming a text into a dramatic improvisation involves students moving between these different levels of abstraction, from what happened to what happens. This process becomes internalized by the students and shows up in their written stories as dialogue (present tense) and narration (past tense).

Contextual drama also supports literacy development through the exploration of text. This exploration is not concerned with transforming written text into a dramatic form, but rather with using drama to understand the text more fully.

## Teaching Drama: Contextual Drama

A brief overview of contextual drama was provided earlier in this chapter. It was noted that, while contextual drama outwardly appears to be spontaneous (like dramatic playing), in fact it is structured through careful planning (unlike dramatic playing). Planning for this structured spontaneity can benefit from some of the recent insights generated by a number of drama educators, notably those included in the References section of this chapter.

The 1972 film *Three Looms Waiting* illustrates very effectively some of the principles that are fundamental to contextual drama. Although somewhat dated, the film shows Heathcote, the pioneer of this work, demonstrating the powerful affective quality of this kind of drama. This intensity can be akin to that experienced by small children who are deeply absorbed in dramatic play. Following is an example of a contextual drama in which the students involved achieved this kind of intensity. Their work had the spontaneous quality of dramatic play, but this spontaneity was achieved through careful planning and the use of several drama strategies.

### Contextual Drama: An Example

The story *Old Henry*, by Joan Blos (1987), deals with a social studies theme. This drama was used with a Grade 2/3 class and represents three hours of instruction. Old

Henry is a new resident in the village. He is very untidy, and the villagers try to help him. Old Henry refuses help, and conflict ensues.

*Phase 1 — Establishing the life and activity of the village*

| | |
|---|---|
| *Read story:* | The teacher reads the story up to the episode where the men try to help Henry. |
| *Imaging:* | Children are asked to close their eyes and imagine what Henry's house might look like. |
| *Discussion:* *Drawing:* | They share their ideas, and the teacher draws Henry's house as they provide the detail. [The class begins to concretize context as a way of building belief, as a way of stepping into the imaginary world of Old Henry.] |
| *Imaging:* | The teacher continues the imaging exercise. "Close your eyes. You also live in this community. Who are you? What does your house look like? Draw your house." |
| *Imaging:* (students are encourged to adopt the role) | The teacher rolls out a large piece of paper, places Mr. Henry's house at one end, and asks the students to place their house on the map and draw the other important buildings. As the children are working on the activity, the teacher walks around feeding information and giving suggestions "I wonder who lives here?" |
| *Mapping:* *Subtle questions and responses:* | "Maybe I can find information about Mr. Henry from the shopkeeper?" As children begin to accept the lures, the teacher reinforces their roles. Child says: "Mr. Henry comes into my shop for his parrot seed." The teacher: "Oh, so you know something about him then?" |

*Phase 2 — Establishing the community*

| | |
|---|---|
| *Gossip strategy:* (building the character of Mr. Henry, giving the students a chance to move into role) | The teacher asks the class to sit around the map. "There seem to be a lot of stories going around our community about Mr. Henry. Maybe we could share these? It may help us to know how to deal with him. Please introduce yourself and share a story if you have had dealings with Mr. Henry. I am the mayor and I know he's honest because he pays his taxes." Students share their stories about Mr. Henry. |
| *Teacher-in-role:* | The mayor calls a town meeting. |
| *Defining space:* | Chairs are set up in a formal manner. A child is selected to role-play the clerk of the court. |
| *Use of ritual:* (slows down the drama and gives students time to deepen belief) | The mayor asks all the "citizens" to introduce themselves and say what they do. This process is done very formally. The teacher uses the role as mayor to control: "Order, please." |

| | |
|---|---|
| *Teacher-in-role:*<br>(formal manner represents authority figure) | The mayor says, "Clerk of the court, please read out the charges." |
| *Use of documents:* | The clerk reads, "City bylaw 99: Failure to keep town tidy. City bylaw 11: Failure to shovel snow. City bylaw 63: Failure to pay fines." [These documents can be prepared by the teacher alone or with the children out of drama time; use of formal language sustains belief.] |
| | The mayor states, "I, the mayor of this town, am hereby opening the floor for discussion." |
| *Storytelling:* | Children provide eyewitness accounts. |
| *Mantle of the expert:*<br>*Meeting:* | The mayor closes the meeting with the following statements: "I am hereby appointing special community task forces to find a solution to our problem." [The class is divided into groups, and the groups discuss their ideas. Students become "experts" on solving problems as members of the task force.] The mayor continues with his speech: "Please have a full written report to present at the next council meeting." |
| *Teacher-in-role:* | Town meeting — the groups present their solutions [reports written out of drama time]. [Teacher/mayor leaves the room and comes back as Mr. Henry.] |

*Phase 3 — Injecting the tension*

| | |
|---|---|
| *Improvisation:* | Mr. Henry rejects all proposals. He tells the community members they are intolerant and informs them of his departure. |

*Phase 4 — Seeking a solution*

| | |
|---|---|
| *Writing:*<br>(these documents are written out of drama time but help to consolidate ideas) | The community members modify proposals and generate other solutions in the form of news reports, letters to Mr. Henry, and diary entries. |

During the reflection on the drama, the students discussed the impact of their solutions on themselves and Mr. Henry. The class reflected on the similarities of the dramatic situation to a local political issue. "We've done our best; we've been responsible. Mr. Henry needs to co-operate. It's just like what's happening with our hockey team. Let them go, the hockey team and Mr. Henry." This example once again illustrates the generalization of experience from one situation to another. After the reflection on the drama, the class compared their handling of the situation with that of the author, Joan Blos.

In this drama, the planning was broken down into four phases (Littledyke and Baum, 1986). These phases overlap and the boundaries are not rigid.

Phase 1:    Establishing the life and activity of the village
   •    creating the context and roles

Phase 2:    Establishing the meaning of village life
   •    villagers share stories about Mr. Henry
   •    villagers cope with the problem

Phase 3:   Injecting the tension
- Mr. Henry rejects the village proposals and calls the citizens intolerant

Phase 4:   Seeking a solution
- villagers modify proposals
- villagers decide Mr. Henry has to take some responsible action

In the first phase, the emphasis is on building belief in the drama through tasks—imaging, drawing, and mapping. In the second phase, the tasks become less important and the students are asked to reflect on village life. They share their stories about Mr. Henry and review his status using a variety of strategies, teacher-in-role, gossip, defining space, ritual, documents, storytelling, meeting, eyewitness accounts, and news reports. In phase 3, the villagers' suggestions are rejected and Mr. Henry leaves. Sometimes the tension in the drama is introduced gradually. For example, one villager says, "I hope Mr. Henry accepts our proposal because his art shop brings many new people to the village. They spend a lot of money." In phase 3 of this drama, the element of surprise is used: the teacher switches roles from being the mayor to being Henry instantly. Phase 4 follows the logic suggested by the students. Students put their own solutions into operation, writing letters, news reports, and diary entries, setting them into the context of their own lives during the reflection phase. In each of these phases, the teacher plans for certain events to occur. However, the outcome of these events is not so predictable, as the students create their characters and make suggestions. It is this unpredictability that gives this work its energy. The students feel empowered when their suggestions are translated into action. It is the teacher's use of a variety of strategies to structure the students' suggestions that makes this succeed.

## From School Time to Drama Time

What does the teacher need to understand, do, and say to transport students from the "here and now" of the classroom to the imagined world of drama?

In the planning phase, the teacher has to understand the differences among the four major types of drama (see Table 12.2) in order to select the type most suited for the purpose. It is at this point that confusion often arises about the connection between a dramatic form and a drama strategy. Is the strategy of tableau a part of dramatization, choric drama, or contextual drama? Is chanting a refrain (choral speech), a dramatic form, or a drama strategy? To clarify this confusion, I compare writing and drama to highlight the connection between form and strategy. Teachers understand that a variety of forms (poems, stories, reports) can be developed by using a common strategy—brainstorming, for example—to generate ideas for writing. They also realize that some strategies are more appropriate for specific forms. Using the pattern of a familiar story to compose a new story or using an interview to gather data for a report are examples of form-specific strategies. Likewise, some drama strategies, tableau and voice-in-the head, can be used to develop a variety of dramatic forms, whereas a strategy like teacher-in-role is more specific to contextual drama. Understanding the relationship between strategy and form permits teachers to maximize the use of a few strategies to access a variety of dramatic forms. Following are several descriptions of the use of tableau and voice-in-the-head. The following examples are ordered from simple to complex in terms of organization and classroom management.

## Using Pictures

In the first example, the teacher provides each group in the class with a picture depicting a scene of pioneer life. The students are asked to select one character and imagine what he or she is thinking. These thoughts are shared, and the teacher identifies the drama strategy as voice-in-the-head. In the second example, the teacher provides each group in the class with a new set of pictures and the instruction to "be like waxworks in a museum to represent the people in the picture." The groups share the representations, and the teacher names this drama strategy as tableau. Tableau is an efficient strategy for representing information quickly.

## Transforming Text

In the fourth example, the teacher reads a story and instructs students to "create a tableau with voice-in-the-head" of one scene from the story. And in the third example, the teacher provides a general statement — for example, "The people leave." The students create a tableau that illustrates this idea. Headlines from the newspaper can also provide many ideas for this kind of activity.

## Representing New Ideas

In the fifth example, students listen to part of a story and are asked to create an ending using tableau. These endings are compared with the one in the text. The students can also use tableau and voice-in-the-head to create new stories. Sixth, students use these strategies in social studies to represent life in the past and present. Each group of students presents two tableaux, one showing an aspect of life in pioneer times (farming, for example), and the second representing farming in the present day.

As these drama strategies are presented, they are not extended into a particular dramatic form. Rather, they are providing an alternative way of representing ideas related to different learning outcomes in different curriculum areas. Tableau and voice-in-the-head require additional strategies to create a particular dramatic form. However, students can move easily from the static tableau to improvisation. "Your tableau comes alive for 30 seconds. What will you do or say?" or "Now add movement and words to your tableau to explain what is happening." Such guidance moves students smoothly into drama time.

The decision to extend these activities depends on the comfort level of the teacher. Some teachers require more controlled and gradual ways of moving from school time to drama time. The social health of the class also influences such decisions. These activities provide possible ways of making this transition, and with additional strategies, the teacher can access a variety of dramatic forms. Table 12.6 outlines some additional drama strategies that could have been used to extend the drama described previously in this chapter. These examples include dramas based on Bahr's *The Memory Box*, Galdone's *The Three Sillies,* and Milne's poem "The More It Snows".

In *The Memory Box* drama described earlier in this chapter, the teacher chose to employ a class discussion to generate ideas that were chanted and then used to plan the drama. The same outcome could have been achieved through the tableau strategy.

**Table 12.6**    **Forms and Strategies**

| Form | Strategy | Activity |
|---|---|---|
| Dramatization (*The Three Sillies*) | 1. Tableau<br>2. Voice-in-the-head<br>3. Narration | Students create a scene from the story using strategies 1 and 2. The teacher uses narration to link the scenes. |
| Choric drama ("The More It Snows") | 1. Tableau<br>2. Voice-in-the-head<br>3. Antiphonal arrangement | The class is divided into three groups. Two groups recite the poem using strategy 3; the other group creates the tableau of each verse and incorporates strategy 2. |
| Contextual drama (*The Memory Box*) | 1. Tableau<br>2. Voice-in-the-head<br>3. Use of role | "Let's imagine I have a photo-graph album of Grandpa's life. Create a tableau of one of these photos." The ideas presented are used to move into role. |

There would have been more talk in less time, and the ideas would have been shared very effectively and efficiently.

> Our understanding of the similarities between familiar, generic strategies and less familiar drama strategies supports a change in teacher stance. This change of stance from "expert/I am in charge" to "negotiator/storyteller" is a prerequisite if the teacher wants the class to explore the "as if" world of drama. This change in stance—reflected in the language and gestures of the teacher—enables the teacher to use appropriate drama strategies to implement the various drama forms.

Once teachers have experienced the efficiency of using drama, they are encouraged to incorporate more drama strategies into their teaching repertoire. As already noted, drama is another way of learning, not an additional curriculum subject. The following teacher scenarios illustrate drama strategies that achieve similar learning outcomes to the more familiar language arts strategies. The crucial difference between the two types of strategies is the stance and language of the teacher. Using drama generally encourages more student participation than the non-drama approaches.

## Scenario IV

Let's examine the drama strategy "gossip" to illustrate these points just discussed. Mr. Henry, a story character from *Old Henry* by Joan Blos (review the example of contextual drama detailed earlier) has moved into the village and is creating problems for all the residents. The teacher asks the students to form small groups and take the role of the villagers. She directs them to "share the rumours and gossip you have heard around the village." After the gossip session, one student from each group shares the rumours discussed, and these are listed on a chart by the teacher. In this way, all the possible ideas for the drama can be examined more critically out of drama time. Because students understand that gossip is not necessarily "true," they know that their responses will not be wrong.

This drama strategy encourages uninhibited participation and uncritical acceptance of responses. The goal of this activity is to generate a quantity of ideas — in effect, it is a form of brainstorming. The shift required is a change in teacher stance from "I am in charge" to "we are in this together," which is manifested in tone, gesture, and language. This shift involves a change in the language of the teacher from "Get into groups and brainstorm as many ideas as you can and then we will chart them on the board," to "You are all a little upset at Mr. Henry's behaviour. He's bothered you, and you've heard lots of rumours and gossip about other things he has done. You meet your friends in the village, and you begin to share the rumours you have heard." The first example is the typical language of instruction, the second is the language of the storyteller. The brainstorming activity engenders a more impersonal response ("He is a litterbug"), whereas the gossip strategy promotes a narrative response ("I saw him at the park and he threw his litter on the grass").

## Scenario V

Mr. Hughes, a second-year teacher at Florence MacDougall Community School in High Level, Alberta, begins by reading articles and stories to his class about the life of Houdini, the magician. After the reading is completed, he moves into role as Houdini's press secretary:

> Welcome. I am Mr. Brown, Mr. Houdini's press secretary. You must be the newspaper reporters. Now as you can imagine, Mr. Houdini has a very tight schedule and his time is limited. In order to make this conference efficient, I would like you to prepare some questions before he arrives so there is no repetition. I will have to limit the time so he can make his next appointment.

Rather than giving explicit instructions, Mr. Hughes chooses his words very carefully. The students know their role and task; the press of time adds creative tension to the drama. Out of role, the teacher monitors the group discussions, and when he thinks the students are prepared, he moves back into role as Houdini.

> Good morning. My press secretary tells me you have some questions for me?

The press conference is completed, and Houdini leaves before all questions are answered. The "reporters" are disappointed, so, out of role, Mr. Hughes gives his students time and resources to find the answer to these questions on their own. Their reports are published in the school newspaper. In his comments about the lesson, Mr. Hughes said, "I like this story because I *am* a magician and I can demonstrate a few tricks. I did this story last year, but I used the KWL strategy [see Chapter Five]. It worked well, but the class was more engaged this time; it showed in their writing." When asked what had prompted him to incorporate drama, he explained it this way: "In my first year of teaching I needed more control. When you use drama, you give the students more decision-making power — but there is always the anxiety they may not come up with anything! After teaching for a year, I realize I can take back the control by saying, "Let's stop. This drama is not working. What can we do?" After I had used role in the *Memory Box* drama, I felt more confident to try it with this story. The students had no difficulty relating to me as teacher, Houdini's press secretary, and Houdini. My change in posture and language keyed them to these role changes."

The control issue is very important, particularly in contextual drama. The teacher is part of the drama and has to guide the students from within the role. If students are unco-operative, it does not work and it is important to hand back the responsibility to the class—saying, for example, "We need to fix this. Any suggestions?" Because our notion of drama as performance is so embedded in our consciousness, we tend to equate stopping a lesson with interrupting and spoiling a play. But this shouldn't be so. Just as we examine and practise group process skills in other situations (such as writing conferences and literary response groups), so we should have no hesitation in applying the same procedures to drama situations.

## Scenario VI

The students read the story "Red Riding Hood" and, guided by teacher questions, they create a story grammar (see Chapter Five). The purpose of this strategy is to help students understand the structure of a story. This same learning outcome can be achieved by using tableau and improvisation along with narration. The students act out the problem and the solution; the teacher connects the scenes through narration.

Not only can narration act as a link between different scenes, it can also help teachers focus the attention of students on smaller pieces of a whole text. For example, the story *King of the Cats* uses narration very effectively. Compare the following samples of teacher language: "Make a tableau of the part where the cats come to the grave and scare the sexton" and "The sexton was digging the grave and, when he looked up, he was very, very scared. Make a tableau of what he saw." The first example is the language of instruction, the second is the language of storytelling. Narration provides the same information, but it has more affective resonance: if narrated with appropriate expression, it can create a dramatic tension or provide an appropriate atmosphere that deepens the students' belief in the drama. It can also be used to summarize an end to a drama to effect closure. For example, in the *Memory Box* drama, the teacher moves out of role as Grandpa and moves into the role of narrator to bring the drama to a satisfying closure: "Grandpa treasured the memory box: it brought him so much pleas-ure." These uses of narration — introducing, linking, or closing dramatic action — save time because they eliminate unnecessary repetition of text. To use narration successfully, the teacher adopts the language of the storyteller to create an atmosphere appropriate to the dramatic context.

These last three scenarios demonstrate the links among the more familiar language arts strategies—brainstorming, KWL, story grammar (see Chapter Five)—and the less familiar drama strategies of gossip, teacher-in-role, improvisation, and narration. All of the scenarios illustrate what teachers might do and say to help students move from school time to drama time.

## Teacher Concerns Related to Drama

Edwards and Payne (1994) studied teachers in a drama support group for two years. During that time, many concerns about implementation were raised. Some of those concerns are described here.

## Learning the Language of Drama

The teachers reported experiencing the most difficulty with terms used to label strategies in the contextual approach to drama. This issue was addressed earlier in this chapter in the section starting on page 340. Throughout this chapter, the labels of the forms and strategies have been referred to often so that the reader can learn the labels in the context of the dramatic situation.

## Using Role

Initially, the teachers in Edwards and Payne's 1994 study had some difficulty stepping into role. They found it helpful to pattern their role on a character from literature (Mr. Henry, Houdini) or to take on a role endowed with authority (such as a mayor or press secretary). These roles have a similar stance as the teacher role and permit the teacher to have some degree of control over the dramatic events.

Some teachers have found it helpful to step into role by using a hand puppet. They speak to the class as if they are the puppet. Other teachers step into role for only a few minutes and then step out of role to continue the drama. Mr. Hughes's use of role in the *Memory Box* drama on page 332 exemplifies this way of working. As teachers become more at ease with this strategy, they find it more efficient to use a variety of roles to move the drama along quickly. This was Mr. Hughes's choice as he took on the role of Houdini and the press secretary in his later drama. Other teachers jump right into role and are able to fold in a variety of strategies to accomplish their learning out-comes. *Old Henry* is an example of a more complex drama. If you examine the plan-ning phases in that example, you will notice that Mr. Hughes did not go through all of them using drama. The context, roles, and tension (phases 1, 2, and 3) were provided by the story. His use of narration and the letter from the grandson on page 332 moved the class quickly to phase 4 — seeking a solution. The drama strategies associated with contextual drama enable teachers to integrate drama as part of the curriculum. These smaller episodes, such as the ones previously described, are easier to manage than a drama that is continued over several lessons. The decision to use role depends on the teacher's comfort level and control needs.

## Management

For the teachers in Edwards and Payne's study, management issues arose when they initially introduced drama into their classrooms. The following rules alleviated these concerns:

- Have a signal for stopping. This can be a verbal command, such as "freeze," or some other signal.
- Clarify the boundaries of the drama space. Avoid the gym.
- Establish co-operation. Review the classroom rules.
- Use a drama "eye." This term represents the rule "we agree to enter this 'as if' world of drama." Following is one teacher's description of how she developed this rule:

  I role-played a short sequence and then asked the students to describe my actions and to explain how they arrived at their meaning. Through discus-sion these young students could articulate the difference between using your real eyes and using your "drama eyes" — between school time and drama time. The students practised using their drama eyes by demonstrating vari-ous activities, for example, eating their favourite food. They also practised identifying my actions as being in school time or drama time. It is important to remind students, particularly young students, of this distinction. At times, the emotions experienced in drama seem very real, and it is imperative that students can step out of drama time into school time to reflect on these feelings. Obviously, I want my students to be involved with, but not overwhelmed by, the drama experience. My students always have the choice of stepping out of drama time. I usually place a chair outside the boundary of the drama space and the students can go there if they feel uncomfortable during the drama. I have noticed when I use the term "drama eyes" rather than "pretend," off-task behaviour is minimized. (Jewel Bondar, special education teacher, 1994)

These rules can be reviewed with the class at the end of the lesson, and as Mr. Hughes pointed out, it is permissible — desirable even — to stop the drama when it does not appear to be going well. Again, language is important. "What can we do to fix it?" is better than "I don't like what's happening here."

## Time

Many of the drama strategies discussed here can be used as part of the regular curriculum as illustrated throughout this chapter. Drama does not need a special time or place. Nevertheless, finding time to implement drama was perceived as a difficulty by the teachers in the study. This concern is not specific to drama, but to all meaning-centred approaches. In classrooms where pupils are actively involved in learning, there will be lots of talk and writing, which are crucial for clarifying meaning.

## The Concert

During Edwards and Payne's two-year study, the teachers were perceived by their staff as the drama experts and were responsible for the annual school concert. The following guidelines facilitated this task:

- Use a presentational mode of drama. The forms presented in the section "Teaching Drama: Interpretation of Literature" would be appropriate.
- Where possible, allow the students to improvise dialogue and practise until they are fluent. This avoids scriptwriting and memorizing.
- Make the presentation as visual as possible, since most auditoriums have poor acoustics.
- Limit the amount of individual dialogue, since young students cannot project their voices sufficiently. Dialogue for a play can be recorded and the actions mimed. Choral work can be used.
- Allow students to choose how they will participate — for example, as performers, props makers, or scriptwriters.

## Evaluation

The teachers in the study discussed the importance of evaluating their lessons by reviewing the drama rules with the class. These teachers were using drama as a context for learning, so they judged the success of the drama in terms of the learning outcomes. When drama strategies were used as part of the writing process, the teachers noted a marked improvement in the quality of student writing. To evaluate each one of the dramatic forms listed under drama as interpretation of literature, one could devise a checklist specific to the particular form. The professional resources outlined at the end of the chapter would aid teachers in this task.

## Summary

The first part of this chapter describes several classroom scenarios that illustrate the range of activities labelled "drama." The way preservice and inservice teachers define drama determines their attitudes toward teaching drama and shapes their classroom practices. The next section of the chapter outlines four major conceptions of drama: drama as playing, drama as a context for learning, drama as interpretation of literature, and drama as theatre. These different types of drama make different demands on students and teachers. This chapter focusses mainly on two of these forms: drama as interpretation of literature and contextual drama. These forms can be readily integrated into the language arts program. Several lessons described make explicit the connections between drama and literacy. These connections underscore the importance of drama as a meaning-making process.

Throughout this chapter, numerous dramatic strategies are illustrated across a variety of dramatic forms. The similarities and differences between these less familiar drama strategies and those that are the more familiar, general teaching strategies are highlighted to encourage teachers to include drama in their language arts program. The last part of the chapter details the ways in which teachers can move their students into the dramatic context, and addresses some of the common concerns voiced by teachers beginning this drama journey.

## Selected Professional Resources

Barton, B. (1980). *Tell Me Another.* Markham, ON: Pembroke. This book is an excellent introduction to storytelling.

Booth, D. (1986). *Games for Everyone.* Markham, ON: Pembroke. This book outlines a variety of practical drama games to develop co-operation, problem solving, and movement. Each game is clearly described, with suggestions for follow-up activities.

Neelands, J. (1992). *Learning through Imagined Experience.* New York: Cambridge University Press. This book integrates the theory and practice of contextual drama very effectively. The relationship between drama and language is illustrated throughout, with many examples of drama strategies and units of study related to various curriculum areas.

O'Neill, C., Lambert, A., Linnell, R., and Warr-Wood, J. (1977). *Drama Guidelines.* London: Heinemann. This book is a classic, not only for its content, but also for its format. The lessons presented in this chapter are modelled on this text. Difficult ideas are made accessible through the use of clear language and sample lessons.

Schwartz, L. (1988). *Drama Themes: A Practical Guide for Teaching Drama.* Markham, ON: Pembroke. This is an excellent resource for teachers beginning work in drama. It contains many practical suggestions for using literature and drama in the language arts program.

Tarlington, C. and Verriour, P. (1983). *Offstage: Elementary Education through Drama.* Toronto: Oxford University Press. This is a comprehensive text containing games, drama exercises, examples of role dramas, and suggestions for drama as performance.

## Children's Books Noted in Chapter Twelve

Bahr, M. (1992). *The Memory Box.* Toronto: Albert Whitman.

Blos, J. (1987). *Old Henry.* New York: William Morrow.

Ciardi, J. (1983 [1962]). "Mummy Slept Late and Daddy Fixed Breakfast." Included in J. Prelutsky, *The Random House Book of Poetry* (p. 147). New York: Random House.

Galdone, P. (1981). *The Three Sillies.* New York: Houghton Mifflin.

Jacobs, J. (1973 [1854]). "King of the Cats." In *Starting Points in Reading*. Toronto: Ginn and Company.

Milne, A.A. (1983 [1928]). "The More It Snows." In *The House at Pooh Corner*. Illustrated by E.H. Shepard. Included in J. Prelutsky, *The Random House Book of Poetry* (p. 30). New York: Random House. Copyright 1928 by E.P. Dutton, renewed © 1956 by A.A. Milne. Used by permission of Dutton Children's Books, a division of Penguin Putnam Inc.

Slobodkina, E. (1947). *Caps for Sale*. New York: W.R. Scott.

## References

Barton, B. (1980). *Tell me another*. Markham, ON: Pembroke.

Bolton, G. (1979). *Towards a theory of drama in education*. London: Longman.

Booth, D. (1986). *Games for everyone*. Markham, ON: Pembroke.

Edwards, J. and Payne, P. (1994). A drama support group: Context for teacher change. *Youth Theatre*, *8* (3), 19–23.

Flynn, R.M. and Carr, G.A. (1994). Exploring classroom literature through drama: A specialist and a teacher collaborate. *Language Arts, 71*, 38–43.

Heathcote, D. (1972). *Three looms waiting: A BBC omnibus programme*. [Film]. Ipswich, UK: Concord Films.

Littledyke, M. and Baum, C. (1986). Structures for drama. *2D, 5* (2), 72–78.

McCaslin, N. (1996). *Creative drama in the classroom and beyond*. New York: Longman.

Moffett, J. (1983). *Student-centered language arts and reading*. Boston: Houghton Mifflin.

Neelands, J. (1992). *Learning through imagined experience*. New York: Cambridge University Press.

O'Neill, C., Lambert, A., Linnell, R., and Warr-Wood, J. (1977). *Drama guidelines*. London: Heinemann.

Schaffner, M. (1985). Drama and language. *2D, 4* (2), 35–44.

Schwartz, L. (1988). *Drama themes: A practical guide for teaching drama*. Markham, ON: Pembroke.

Sporre, D.J. (1993). *The art of theatre*. Englewood Cliffs, NJ: Prentice-Hall.

Stewig, J.W. (1983). *Informal drama in the elementary language arts program*. New York: Teachers College Press.

Tarlington, C. and Verriour, P. (1983). *Offstage: Elementary education through drama*. Toronto: Oxford University Press.

Vygotsky, L.S. (1978). *Mind in society: The development of higher psychological processes*. M. Cole, V. John-Steiner, S. Scribner, and E. Souberman (eds). Cambridge, MA: Harvard University Press.

# Chapter thirteen

# Technology in the Language Arts Classroom

**Computers in the Language Arts Classroom**
- Issues in Using Computer Technology
- The Role of Computers in Education

**The Internet**
- Basic Information
- The Promise of the Internet
- The Changing Face of Literacy Instruction and Learning
- Challenges and Issues
- Responding to the Challenges

**Learning with Computers**
- Operations (Learning How to Use the Computer)
- Productivity (Using the Computer as a Production Tool)
- Inquiry (Using the Computer for Problem Solving)

**Technology in the Language Arts Classroom**

**Evaluating Computer Software**
- General Guidelines
- A Checklist for Evaluating Software
- Research and Reviews

**Media Literacy**
- Goals of Instruction
- Media Literacy Instruction
- Issues and Challenges

During her undergraduate studies, Jennie Ng took an introductory course in computers that, according to the course description, was designed to help preservice teachers "become computer literate before your students do!" She now wonders what it means to be "computer literate" and if the course she experienced reflects what is occurring in today's elementary classrooms. Specifically, she is excited about some of the student learning programs she experienced and the way computer technology in general might support her teaching and her students' learning.

In addition to the introductory computer course, Jennie took a course that allowed her to learn on-line. The content for that course was organized into learning modules that were available on a Web site, and she had been able to access them from her home computer. She had chatted via the Internet with her fellow students and the course instructors on a regular basis. As well, she had completed and submitted her assign-

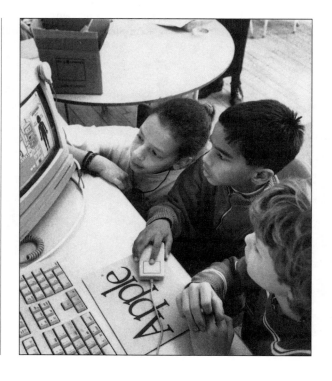

ments on-line and monitored her progress in the course. She completed a research paper on early literacy using on-line resources and, during her research, chatted with university students in Australia and Texas who had a similar interest. She accessed professional journals and communicated with practising teachers and university professors about her concerns and questions. She also created an electronic paper that investigated on-line resources for teaching children's literature. She is convinced that the Internet provides a teaching and learning resource of enormous potential, but she also has many questions. ∎

Jennie has a nagging concern that many programs are simply thinly guised, electronic worksheets, and she wonders if many of the computer "games" she has seen students playing are taking valuable time away from the development of critical computer and other literacy skills. She is also vaguely familiar with the Internet, but she often finds the new vocabulary of the World Wide Web almost overwhelming. In addition, she knows that children are exposed to far more technology than computers at school, at home, and in the community. Jennie has many questions that reflect these concerns:

- How are computers used in elementary classrooms, and does use of this technology increase children's learning?
- How can she choose the "best" software to meet the needs of her students?
- How can she use the Internet to effectively enhance elementary students' learning, language, and literacy development?
- What about television, films, photographs, videotapes, and recordings? How do these contribute to children's language and literacy learning?

This chapter is designed as an introduction to the current dimensions of electronic and media literacy. These are emerging fields, ones that are under constant expansion and transformation. Technology has profound implications for teaching and learning in classrooms, particularly from a constructivist perspective.

## Computers in the Language Arts Classroom

In this section, we begin by discussing some significant issues facing language arts teachers as they move into a technological era. From there, we move to a consideration of possible roles computers might play in children's language and literacy learning.

In the latter part of the twentieth century, our society developed a strong belief in technology. People envisioned and anticipated the "good life" with technology at its core: a computer on every desk, a diminishing need for writing abilities, everything they needed at the touch of a button. In spite of the fact that this vision has not materialized, computers are still viewed by many people as being "synonymous with human progress" (Postman, 1992, p. 12). Many people believe that computers have a far greater potential for revitalizing education than any other previous technological innovation. Some maintain that computers can revolutionize learning and teaching in classrooms, and that we need to either "get on board" with the computer revolution or be left behind.

But others, such as Olson and Sullivan (1993, p. 439), have urged caution: "It is plain that a new day is upon us. But where we are going is in question." It is clear that technology can help us achieve certain ends, but to what degree that happens depends on the abilities of the people who develop the technology, create software packages, load information onto computers, and make thoughtful choices about the uses of that information. Before looking at possible roles for computer technology in the language arts classroom, we first discuss some of the issues related to its use.

## Issues in Using Computer Technology

### The Impact of Computers on Language and Literacy Learning

The major issue surrounding the use of computers in literacy programs is whether they produce better learning than conventional approaches. Studies have explored the use of the computer in relation to quality and quantity of student writing, but the results have yielded somewhat contradictory findings (Sharp, 1999). Some studies offer favourable evidence supporting the use of word processing, while others (e.g., Daiute, 1985, as cited in Sharp, 1999) found that students did not write as much with word processors. These contradictory results appear to reflect the differences in implementation of not only word processing but other computer applications as well. A summary of several of these studies is presented in Table 13.1.

In addition to the impact of computer use on writing itself, researchers (e.g., Hatfield, 1996) have found that the positive attitudes of students toward the computer aids in motivating them and helping them to maintain a high level of interest.

**Table 13.1**  **Summary of Research on the Impact of Computer Technology on Language and Literacy Learning**

| Researcher | Level | Results |
| --- | --- | --- |
| Grégoire, Bracewell, and Laferrière (1996) | Grade 2 | • Children using computers showed greater improvement in their general writing skills and wrote longer compositions than control group.<br>• Use of word processors led to more focus on content and editing of text, and greater metacognitive awareness and incentive to think about language. |
| Jones (1994) | Grade 2 | • With use of word processors, there was overall improvement in the quality of each student's writing, and the stories tended to be longer. |
| Dybdahl, Shaw, and Blahous (1997) | Grade 5 | • There was no significant difference in the quantity of text produced by students who were or were not using computers. |
| Chang and Osguthorpe (1990, cited in Jones, 1994) | Kindergarten | • A computerized picture–word processor helped to improve children's writing and appeared to have positive effects on their attitude toward the subject. |
| Schrader (1990) | Ages 4 to 7 | • The word processor helped students to focus on content and meaning; by putting ideas and structures into print more quickly, children were less likely to forget them.<br>• Revising and editing were less costly in time and effort than with paper and pencil. |

Grégoire, Bracewell, and Laferrière (1996) concluded that students were not only drawn to the use of technology and were motivated by it, but that their motivation was sustained. The authors maintain that technology creates more interactive environments, presents more engaging content, and involves students more directly than textbooks and other traditional ways of teaching.

Students' literacy learning via computers is tied very strongly to the expertise of their teacher. Teachers who are considered "experts" in the use of computers in the classroom tend to guide their students in computer activities that support learning (Dillon and Gabbard, 1998). In a review of research findings related to computer implementation and use, Dillon and Gabbard (1998, p. 346) concluded that the pedagogical value of computer technology, particularly hypermedia, is limited at this time. However, they state, "We remain convinced that well-designed hypermedia offers the potential to enhance learning in a variety of ways." The lesson appears to be that current understanding of computer technology and its use requires refinement and development if teachers and students are to take full advantage of its potential.

## Issues Related to Power and Control

A fundamental issue in all aspects of language arts instruction, including computer technology, involves power and control. At the classroom level, computers appear on the surface to place more control into the hands of children, since computers are individually operated by children. However, the extent of the child's actual power with computers is, of course, determined by the ways in which computers are used in the classroom and the types of computer software made available to the learners. Some skill and drill programs do not empower children any more than workbooks and worksheets do. Whether computers will lead to individual autonomy or dependence in learners will vary according to how the teacher incorporates computers into classroom learning.

Olson and Sullivan (1993) note that questions about technology and the distribution of power go beyond the classroom door. Computers may appear to be classless and genderless, but even from the standpoint of availability, children in middle-class neighbourhoods have greater access to personal computers than do children in working-class neighbourhoods. This is true both at home and at school. Older schools frequently incur greater costs in acquiring computers because of the rewiring that must be completed for Internet access in the classrooms. The differences do not stop there. The type of training received with computers varies depending on whether it is being offered in the business stream or the academic stream. In the business stream, the emphasis is on "mechanical and routinized tasks"; in the academic stream, the emphasis is on "general and symbolic processes that lead to long-term control" (Olson and Sullivan, 1993, p. 429). Because of the uneven distribution of boys and girls in these two streams, many girls develop mechanical skills that do not lead to high-level careers. There is also a tendency for richer schools to teach programming skills, whereas schools in poorer districts use computer-assisted instruction. Olson and Sullivan argue that the use of computers in the schools appears to be doing little to equalize opportunities across class or gender, and that it indeed may lead to greater inequalities.

The National Association for the Education of Young Children (NAEYC, 1996) also cites evidence to show that

- boys use computers more than girls, both in and out of school,
- the presence of computers in schools does not ensure access,

- teachers believe that better-behaved students deserve more computer time, and
- teachers believe that the primary benefit of computers for low-achieving students is in the mastery of basic skills.

From this evidence, the organization concludes that computers often maintain and exaggerate inequalities related to gender, race, and social class. As teachers become more familiar with computer technology and its potential for all learners, a priority will be to take active steps to counter these trends.

### The Issue of Computer Acquisition vs. Professional Development

A further issue in the use of technology involves the degree of emphasis that is placed on acquiring computer hardware and software as compared with training teachers, planning curriculum, and integrating computers into the curriculum. Because nearly all of the focus has been on acquisition, even when computers are available in schools they are often underused (Rennie, 1990). Schools are also faced with the problems associated with provincially and locally mandated curriculums that are not supported with appropriate funding and technical support for teachers. Often these curriculum initiatives are "added" to an already full professional development agenda for teachers.

In addition to these concerns surrounding acquiring and applying computer technology are the particular issues related to using the Internet. These are discussed later in this chapter.

## The Role of Computers in Education

In 1980, Taylor proposed a framework for understanding the application of computers in education. He suggested that the computer can function in one of three modes: as tutor, as tool, and as tutee. As tutor, the computer is used to monitor student learning and provide practice, taking the role of instructor. As tool, the computer functions as an assistant, helping with handling and creating information. And as tutee, the computer takes the role of learner, where children are given opportunities to program and solve problems through their own directions to the computer.

More recently, these functions were reconceptualized by Jonassen (1996), who writes about the differences between learning *from* computers, learning *about* computers, and learning *with* computers. He maintains that, during the 1970s and 1980s, educators mainly saw "learning from" (computer-assisted instruction) and "learning about" (computer literacy) as possibilities for computer use in the classroom. Courses in computer-assisted instruction and computer literacy abounded. Yet, as Jonassen points out, we do not necessarily need to know about the computer in order to use one in our daily lives. Wilhelm, Friedemann, and Erickson (1998, p. 159) also reinforce this position by stating that "we don't need to know much about technology.... (W)hat is much more important and challenging is the need to know kids—how they think and learn—and how to teach them how to do and be more than they already are." In response, educators have moved beyond courses *about* the computer to learning *with* computers.

Jonassen and other educators (such as Reinking, 1997, and Leu, Karchmer, and Leu, 1999) are at the forefront of a move toward encouraging teachers to work with computers as cognitive tools—what Jonassen (1996) calls "mindtools"—in the classroom. Jonassen defines these as "computer-based tools and learning environments that have been adapted or developed to function as intellectual partners with the learner in order to engage and facilitate critical thinking and higher order learning" (p. 9). Mindtools include spreadsheets, databases, semantic networks, expert systems, computer conferencing, computer programming, microworld learning environments, and multimedia and hypermedia construction. These tools can

- provide a scaffold for meaningful thinking,
- assist children in recognizing and setting purposes for learning,
- aid children in asking questions,
- assist learners in finding information,
- help learners analyze and organize what they have learned, and
- assist learners in representing and revising their new and emerging understandings.

These computer tools "actively engage learners in the creation of knowledge that reflects their comprehension and conception of the information rather than focusing on the presentation of objective knowledge" (Jonassen, 1996, p. 10).

With the expansion of the meaning of literacy itself, which our technologically oriented world now requires, the use of computer mindtools becomes increasingly important. Mindtools can be symbolic systems serving as devices for expression and communication, or they can be strategies through which knowledge is transformed (Salomon, 1993).

> Before moving to the next section, spend a few minutes thinking about what roles computers have played in your own learning. How did your teachers use computers when you were in school, and was there any difference when you attended university courses on computers ? Although we recognize that learners are at different points in their knowledge and facility with computers, we believe that the major focus in language arts classrooms should be on learning *with*, rather than *about* and *from*, computers.

## Learning with Computers

> In this section, we organize our ideas for "learning with computers" using a framework devised by Alberta Education.

According to a scheme put forward by Alberta Education (1997), computer learning is placed into three categories—knowledge, skills, and attributes—each of which has a number of levels. The first level consists of foundational *operations* (including knowledge and concepts), the second level consists of processes for *productivity*, and the third involves processes for *inquiry*. The first level, foundational operations, includes basic computer, telecommunications, and multimedia technology operations, as well as ergonomic and safety issues. The second level, processes for productivity, focusses on text composition, data organization, media and process integration, electronic communication, and multimedia composition and manipulation. The third level, processes for inquiring, decision making, and problem solving, focusses on assessing information, researching, solving problems, and generally applying knowledge and skills in practical situations.

Alberta Education suggests that the three categories are interrelated and best learned when teachers integrate them into existing curricula and programs of study. These three categories provide a useful framework for discussing some of the specific skills that students need to develop electronic literacy.

## Operations (Learning How to Use the Computer)

Before students can use the computer productively, it appears that they must first understand and master certain processes and procedures. This "operations" category of learning outcomes includes

- using keyboarding skills,
- applying basic computer operations (such as saving to a disk, clicking on an icon, using and organizing files),
- applying safety procedures, and
- uploading and downloading text and graphics.

As students master such features as word wrapping, moving paragraphs, deleting words or sentences, and spell checking, they save time and reduce effort, which provides extra time for them to think about content (Sharp, 1999).

An important concern for teachers is when and how keyboarding skills should be taught. Many children who have not developed typing skills waste a great deal of time using a two-finger pick-and-peck method — time that could be better spent on the composing aspects of writing. Most educators agree that children do need to be taught keyboarding skills, using either computer programs designed for this purpose or more traditional teaching techniques (Strickland, Feeley, and Wepner, 1987; Rennie, 1990). We recommend that keyboarding be taught as soon as children are using word processors to compose on a more or less frequent basis.

## Productivity (Using the Computer as a Production Tool)

This category of learning outcomes is particularly relevant to many of the activities that constitute a language arts program. From reading, writing, spelling, charting ideas, using and creating databases, and working with spreadsheets, to importing clip art and audio recordings into a presentation and using the Internet to access information, technological production tools readily lend themselves to enhancing students' language learning.

### Word-Processing Programs

One of the most common ways computers serve as production tools in elementary language arts classrooms is in word processing. Children often use word-processing technology to compose, revise, edit, and print a wide variety of written compositions, including

- creative writing,
- reports across the curriculum,
- journal entries and letters to authors,
- class or school newspapers, and
- invitations and programs for school events.

It is difficult to recommend specific word-processing programs for use in elementary classrooms, because new computing technology and programs are constantly emerging. Even when a new program or technology appears on the market, most teachers are aware that it is highly likely that an "upgrade" with new and innovative features will follow in a relatively short time. With this in mind, we provide a sampling of currently available programs in Table 13.2 to indicate some of the potential that they have for supporting children's literacy growth in classrooms. Children are most commonly introduced to word processing around Grades 2 and 3, although some word-processing programs (such as KidWorks Deluxe) are available for younger children.

**Table 13.2**    **Word-Processing Programs**

| Title/Platform | Level | Features |
|---|---|---|
| ClarisWorks/AppleWorks (Windows/Macintosh) | Ages 9 and up | • Software contains four other modules in addition to word processing: spreadsheet, database, drawing, and communications.<br>• The word processor has file, edit, format, and spell-check features.<br>• The draw and paint program has standard tools such as fill, erase, draw, and spray can, and a large colour palette.<br>• The spreadsheet program allows children to create coloured graphs using various formats.<br>• The word processor allows the user to import text and graphics from other software programs into the text being created, and to export texts, graphs, database information, and graphics created with ClarisWorks into a presentation program such as Hyperstudio. |
| Student Writing Center (Windows/Macintosh) | Grades 4 and up | • Software emphasizes a writing process approach as well as writing across the curriculum.<br>• Critical thinking is related to the stages of writing through prewriting, drafting, revising, editing, and publishing.<br>• Templates allow students and teachers to create different types of documents easily.<br>• The program makes effective use of icons to select templates.<br>• Special borders, clip art, and letterhead choices add detail and interest to documents.<br>• The program cannot import graphics. |
| Storybook Weaver Deluxe (Windows/Macintosh) | Ages 6 to 14 | • Software allows children to create, write, and publish their own illustrated stories by placing, moving, and sizing pictures on the screen.<br>• Children choose borders and text colour, and select from hundreds of colourful graphics; they may also select from a range of sound effects and music.<br>• Once the scene is set, children write the story at the bottom of the screen in either English or Spanish.<br>• The story can be edited and printed.<br>• There is a modified spell-checker and a text-to-speech feature to allow children to hear their stories read aloud. |
| KidWorks Deluxe (Windows/Macintosh) | Ages 4 to 9 | • Software includes both a word processor and a paint program<br>• Optional features include sending and receiving stories on the Internet and accessing on-line help<br>• Children can change font, text, size, style, and colour, spread the story across multiple pages, and add stickers and sound effects. |

*(continued)*

**Table 13.2    Continued**

| Title/Platform | Level | Features |
|---|---|---|
|  |  | • The program is able to read the story the children have written. |
|  |  | • The paint feature includes drawing, filling in shapes, adding backgrounds, and adding words, stickers, animated stickers, and sound effects. |
|  |  | • Stories and multimedia presentations can be saved, printed, or sent over the Internet. |

## Database Programs

Students and teachers also use databases as production tools in the classroom. A database is a collection of data or information stored in a computer. Databases help manage large amounts of data, providing the data with a structure so that it can be manipulated and patterns or relationships noted.

A computer database can easily be understood by comparing it with an "old-fashioned" information system, such as the card catalogue in a school library. Databases organize information into files, records, and fields. A record is a set of data or information on a particular topic that is placed in a file. It is then treated as a unit. For example, each card in the library card catalogue can be considered a record, since it contains information about a single book. However, within a record there are fields. Each field contains a single, specific piece of information. The author, title, copyright date, and publishing company would be considered separate fields on the library card record. In a library catalogue system, data may be stored according to the various fields of author, title, intended age of readership, rating, abstract, and theme or topic of the book. A collection of information on a particular subject is called a file. For example, all records on authors would be considered a file. A group of related files is a database. Therefore, a library card catalogue system is considered a database. It consists of files on titles, authors, and subject matter.

To use database applications on the computer, children must be familiar with the concept of a database. This is most easily explained through examples children encounter in their own lives. The library catalogue is such an example. Computerized police records are another example that children see in movies and on television shows. Stolen vehicles, for example, are listed in a database that can be accessed immediately by the police if someone sees and reports an abandoned vehicle on the street.

Every database has a structure, a way in which it is organized to allow for the rapid retrieval of the information it contains. The structure includes file names, field headings, and data strings. Sorting information is an important function of a database. Information can be arranged alphabetically, numerically, or in chronological order. Fields can be sorted alphabetically from A to Z or from Z to A. If the fields are numeric, they can be arranged in the order of magnitude, from lowest to highest or highest to lowest. They can also be arranged according to date and time. Database programs also allow for changing and updating data as well as for adding and deleting information in the file.

In the past, only businesses and administrative offices used databases. Today, not only are teachers using databases in the classroom, but students are creating their own and using commercially developed ones. With the help of computer databases, students can sort, search, examine, and analyze information to discover relationships that exist in data that they have collected on a topic or concept. Students can conduct searches to discover answers to questions such as "What books has this specific author written?" or "What books on the topic of bears are appropriate for children aged 8 years?" Students can also make effective use of database programs in their research projects in science and social studies.

In some classrooms, children record information about the books they have read so that other children can use that information as a resource when making their own book choices or researching a topic. They are, in effect, creating their own database of book reviews and suggestions for reading. Edmonton Public Schools Resource Development Services (1998) has published 27 novel studies that involve computer-based work with databases. For example, *The Doll* by Cora Taylor (1987), a time-slip story set on the Canadian prairie, is one of the novels that has been incorporated into this database. Computer-based activities in this study include creating a database of prairie plants and animals, developing a family tree, and accessing Web sites to gain more information about pioneer settlers.

Teachers can also use databases for student record-keeping (e.g., test scores, books read, assignments completed, language strengths, and language needs), and for a number of instructional applications.

In making informed decisions about choice of database programs, Sharp (1999) reminds teachers to consider the possible search limitations of any particular program, the ease of adding to or changing data in its files, and its availability. For prepared databases, Sharp suggests that teachers determine the accuracy of the contents, the quality of the product, its ease of use, and its appropriateness for students.

A wide selection of database programs is available on the market, with varying prices and capabilities. Some are separate programs, while others are integrated with capabilities such as telecommunication, charting, word processing, and spreadsheet. Some examples of integrated software programs that are appropriate for elementary classroom use are ClarisWorks (included in the section on word processing above), ClarisWorks for Kids, and Microsoft Works.

Currently, the most widely used database program in elementary schools is ClarisWorks. Recently renamed AppleWorks (but still available for both Macintosh and Windows platforms), the database component of this integrated software package allows students to

- create their own databases,
- embed text, images, and movies in records,
- sort records and merge them with word-processing documents, and
- create labels and reports.

## Multimedia

In the 1970s and 1980s, the term *multimedia* was used to refer to technological combinations such as slide–tape presentations and interactive video. Today, the term refers to the integration of media such as sound, text, graphics, animation, and full-motion video into a single computer system. It is a computer-based method of presenting information in an interactive mode. The sophistication of current personal computers has made it possible for people to become publishers, artists, and video-producers themselves (Jonassen, 1996). Children in school today belong to a "video-generation" and are more apt to engage with multimedia presentations than with a single medium such as text. Multimedia programs are becoming an important part of many language arts programs.

Kevin Tok, a Grade 6 student at Sacred Heart School in Edmonton, created and presented a futuristic creation myth using PowerPoint presentation software. He downloaded background music from the Web (theme music from *Star Wars* and *2001: A Space Odyssey*), as well as animated cartoon characters, clip art, and graphics that he incorporated into his presentation. As he presented his story to the class, he "built" his story by having the text "fly in" from various sides of the screen, and the text was superimposed against a background of space scenes that he downloaded from the NASA Web site. His classmates were able to view Kevin's presentation on the large-screen monitor that is permanently mounted at the front of the classroom. Two pages from this presentation are presented in Exhibit 13.1.

According to Pan and Zbikowski (1997), multimedia applications and artificial speech technology make writing more appealing to students, enabling them to incorporate sound, drawing, video, and pictures in their compositions. In particular, synthetic speech can be a very stimulating way of adding dialogue between writer and audience and can serve to reduce inhibitions about beginning to write. As well, by composing with media other than text, students can learn to become more critical users of media in their everyday lives.

With multimedia resources and publication of students' work, young authors can now engage their readers through all the senses (Pan and Zbikowski, 1997). Because

**Exhibit 13.1    A Grade 6 Child's *PowerPoint* Presentation**

Aldaris returned to his creator giving him all the elements. "Well done Aldaris, " he said to Aldaris. Zel'naga absorbed the elements and created a black hole which brought comets, meteoroids and asteroids. He made them collide and create planets. He called the Fire God to merge his best stars to form the sun. He found a planet made from pure rock and made a comet to hit earth to create water and plants so that life could be there. All the planets were in the Sun's gravity which kept them balanced. Other planets and pieces went on beyond the stars. As the first animals and humans arrived on earth, new life began on Earth.

this allows for presenting information in a nonlinear, interactive way, students are able to develop a greater sense of the interconnectedness of different kinds of information. This helps them organize complex information in many media from different sources according to a particular theme. Galloway (1994) found that when students used the multimedia video tool QuickTime in writing compositions, their motivation and interest in the task increased.

Most of the electronic books and multimedia packages listed in this chapter use **hypertext**. This is nonsequential text (unlike conventional printed text, which is linear and read from beginning to end) developed by Ted Nelson in the mid-1960s. In hypertext, text, images, sound, and actions are linked in nonsequential associations that allow the reader to go through a topic in any order (Sharp, 1999). As Jonassen (1996, p. 188) says:

> [Hypertext is] a non-sequential, nonlinear method for organizing and displaying text that was designed to enable readers to access information from a text in ways that are most meaningful to them. Hypertext is super-text because the reader has much greater control of what is read and the sequence in which it is read. It is based on the assumption that the organization the reader imposes on a text is more personally meaningful than that imposed by the author.

The organization of hypertext is usually achieved through links, or "hot buttons," on which the reader clicks and is connected to yet another chunk of text. The use of computer word-processing systems and the Internet have made most learners familiar with the use of hypertext. Hypertext allows the reader to control the sequence in which information is accessed and the speed with which it is accessed (allowing browsing). However, many educators maintain that the success of hypertext depends entirely on how much prior knowledge the student can bring to the subject.

One of the problems for students in using hypertext is simply in navigating through it. However, a greater problem for teachers is in facilitating the learners' use of the information retrieved and the integration of it into their own knowledge structures. Jonassen (1996) suggests that the most effective way to use hypertext in the classroom is to have learners create their own hypertexts that reflect their personal understandings and perspectives (very much like writing for learning using a pen or a word-processing program).

**Hypermedia** is simply the combination of hypertext with multimedia systems. Hypermedia is computer software that is used to organize various types of multimedia information (such as sound, graphics, text, video, and animation) into a system so that the information can be accessed, retrieved, and modified easily (Wilhelm, Friedemann, and Erickson, 1998). Like hypertext, the different forms of information are linked together so that a user can move from one form to another in a nonlinear mode. Hypermedia components range from sound-enhanced documents that can be used on any computer to "stacks" (such as HyperCard or HyperStudio, described below) that carry sound, animation, and colour (Sharp, 1999). These are usually composed by multiple authors.

Hypermedia is a platform of the World Wide Web that is playing an increasing role in the presentation of composition and communication. It is relatively straightforward software for teachers and students to use. Wilhelm, Friedemann, and Erickson (1998) found that after having students engage in an extended journalism unit where they used hypermedia tools independently, motivation was sustained.

There are a number of powerful commercial software packages for producing multimedia programs. HyperCard and SuperCard (for the Macintosh) and ToolBook (for Windows machines) are the packages commonly used in schools. An example of an appropriate package for elementary school is HyperStudio.

HyperStudio (Macintosh), from Roger Wagner Publishing, is a production tool for students age 6 and up. It is a vehicle for presenting of their learning, especially research project work. The presentations the students create "stand alone"—that is, they are not made on the computer and then printed, but are viewed on the computer. The program works along the same principle as a stack of index cards, but in this case they are electronic cards and are connected through clicking on buttons. This moves the viewer from one card to another or initiates other actions. In each electronic stack of cards, information or a story is presented in a multimedia format. The hypercards might feature background layouts, scrolling text, clip art, animation, and sound created or selected by the student. As well, material from other software programs installed on the computer, such as ClarisWorks or Geograph, can be imported and placed on the cards. Graphs, maps, graphics, photos, data cards, video clips, sound bites, diagrams, and text from the Internet and from many CDs (including *Encarta*, for example) can be imported and placed on the hypercards. An example of a presentation prepared by an elementary student using HyperStudio is shown in Exhibit 13.2.

The manual *HyperStudio 3.0 in One Hour* (Sharp, 1995) is particularly helpful for teachers. It is well laid out and easy to follow, with sample projects and a tutorial to assist the user. The greatest challenge for learners in working with programs such as HyperStudio is in organizing and presenting information, and it is therefore in these areas that learners are called upon to stretch their abilities.

**Exhibit 13.2**    **An Elementary Student's *HyperStudio* Presentation on Saturn**

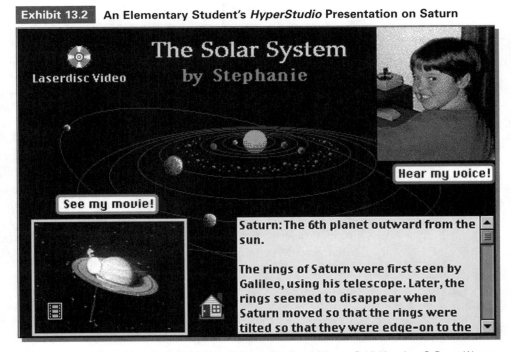

Source: Extracted from *HyperStudio 3.0* (1995). El Cajon, CA: Roger Wagner Publishing, Inc. © Roger Wagner Publishing Inc. All rights reserved. Reprinted with permission.

Elementary school children have created HyperStudio presentations on a myriad of topics, from ancient Greece to space travel and ecology. A research project (Ver Velde, Knight, and Shushok, 1997) conducted in a school in Arizona examined the learning of kindergarten/Grade 1 children (through a unit on weather) and Grade 6 children (through a unit on careers). The project was designed to determine whether this tool brought about children's learning, or alternatively, whether it was simply a means for children to show what they had already learned. While all the children completed writing assignments throughout the respective unit, it was the students who also created a multimedia presentation through HyperStudio who clearly showed a better grasp of the subject. Children deemed "at risk" seemed especially successful in enriching their HyperStudio stacks with detailed content and information. A follow-up study by the same research team, working with Grades 1, 2, and 6 children, indicated that learning was affected positively by the HyperStudio production. The researchers suggest that HyperStudio is a tool for learning as well as a medium for presentation. They also note, however, that multimedia productions are no substitute for effective classroom instruction. They highlight the importance of a teacher's knowledge of the children, subject matter, and art of teaching as well as how to use technology judiciously and skillfully (Ver Velde, Knight, and Shushok, 1997).

## Inquiry (Using the Computer for Problem Solving)

Although databases, hypertext, and hypermedia are referred to above as productivity tools, they also have the potential to be used for problem solving and higher-level thinking.

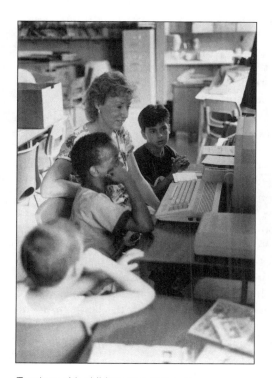

Teacher with children at a computer.

### Databases

According to Sharp (1999, p. 105), "a database is a perfect tool for teaching higher level critical thinking skills such as the ability to hypothesize, draw inferences, and use Boolean logic." Sharp goes on to explain that in addition to helping students develop higher-level thinking skills, databases support student learning of content material in any area of the curriculum. Once children have accessed information, they can reorganize it and make comparisons, developing new insights from this reorganization. The power of the database for inquiry lies in the ways it helps students to engage in creative thinking, predicting, and making generalizations and comparisons.

### Hypermedia

As with databases, a considerable amount of decision making is involved in developing hypermedia presentations. Student-created hypermedia, according to Wilhelm, Friedemann, and Erickson (1998, p. 15), "encourages students to name themselves as readers, writers, and learners and supports them in the achievement of better reading, idea development, sense of audience, classifying, organizing, collaborating, representing understandings, revising, and articulating and applying critical standards about the quality of work." And as with all software, it is how hypermedia is used in the classroom that will determine whether children go beyond productivity to inquiry in their learning.

## Electronic Books

The major focus in our description to this point has been on having children use computer software to create and represent ideas. However, materials produced by hypertext and hypermedia also have the potential to maximize the constructive and creative dimensions of reading. This is where electronic books come in.

An *electronic book* is a piece of software that has many features similar to those of a traditional book. The major difference is that the electronic book is accessed by a computer. Anderson-Inman and Horney (1999) provide the following general guidelines as to what may be considered an electronic book:

- It has an electronic text, and the text is visually presented to the reader.
- The software adopts the metaphor of a book in a significant way. For example, there may be a table of contents, and the information screens are referred to as "pages." Bookmarks may also be inserted, and in general, a reader will be familiar with the terms used.
- The software has a focus or an organizing theme. Large networks like the World Wide Web do not constitute a book even though they are "read."
- The visual text is primary, and any other media are used mainly to support the text.

Children can now access electronic books that incorporate a range of multimedia enhancements. Thus, in addition to reading the text, children interact with extensive illustrations, graphics, and animations. It is also becoming common for electronic books to have embedded speech, either pronunciations of individual words or spoken versions of the whole text. Overall, these enhancements can make the text more comprehensible and enriching for readers at all levels of expertise.

Some electronic books published on CD-ROMs (such as encyclopedias) are primarily for reference, while others have a strong pedagogical or instructional flavour. This latter group of books is designed to support the needs of a variety of readers. For example, books by key historical writers may contain links that describe the socio-cultural context in which the texts were written, while additional links may explicate literary devices or provide interpretations of difficult passages. Some are designed to support learning and studying by providing a large-scale network of graphics, related documents, video, and sound. Finally, some electronic books are intended simply for entertainment, and the feature links are designed to enhance the reader's enjoyment. As with any classroom reading, it is contingent upon the teacher to guide students toward reading experiences that will help them achieve the teacher's and the students' reading goals.

A major disadvantage of an electronic book is that it cannot be read without a computer, although lightweight, battery-operated, hand-held computerized readers called "e-books" are now becoming more common. (E-books enable a reader to set the reading speed so that the text scrolls continuously at a comfortable rate, and a technology is now available that adapts the e-book scrolling speed to the eye movement of the reader.) Another disadvantage is that to retrieve an electronic book from the Internet requires a modem, communication software, and a Web browser, while a CD-ROM text requires a CD-ROM drive and a relatively sophisticated operating system (Anderson-Inman and Horney, 1999).

These points aside, electronic books still have three important advantages over traditional formats. First, they are searchable, meaning that the user can easily track down information simply by entering key words or phrases into the computer's Find function. This is particularly helpful when students are searching for information in a large document, such as a CD-ROM encyclopedia. Students can also search the Web for resources related to particular topics, concepts, or themes, and all of the occurrences will be reported.

Second, electronic books are modifiable, meaning that a reader can change and adapt their font size and format as needed. This feature is particularly useful for students who have visual problems. Readers can also often choose a preferred language, as many electronic books come in more than one language. Other electronic books allow the reader to add personal notes and images and to annotate the text.

The third main advantage of electronic books is that they are enhanceable, which means that the student or teacher may add resources to them to enhance text processing and comprehension. Thus, the reader may also access embedded definitions, explanations, and pictures designed to enhance meaning construction or extend understanding. An electronic text downloaded from the Internet may also be linked to Web sites that contain information designed to expand the reader's background information. An example is the Frontier Girl Web site described later in this chapter.

Electronic book features such as the foregoing have the potential to improve comprehension and promote in-depth learning (Anderson-Inman and Horney, 1999). The critical element rests on the type of guidance that teachers provide, which in turn is often related to their comfort level with the technology.

One concern about computerized books is that the audiovisual effects and other options may distract children from the actual text. Another concern is that children will listen to the stories and engage in little, if any, reading themselves. It is helpful if teachers are aware of the strengths and drawbacks of electronic books and do not assume that children are acquiring literacy skills simply because they are engaging with a CD-ROM and a computer. A brief overview of selected electronic books is presented in Table 13.3.

**Table 13.3**  Overview of Selected Electronic Books

| Title | Level | Features |
|---|---|---|
| *Encarta Encyclopedia 98* (CD-ROM for Windows and Macintosh) | Ages 9 to 12 | • interactive, full-range encyclopedia<br>• allows students to access information through a list of contents, an index, information arranged by categories, and a Find feature<br>• an outline feature is available<br>• photographs, animation, Quick Time movies, sound maps, and diagrams can be used to elaborate the text<br>• graphics and text can be imported into word-processing and presentation programs<br>• text and graphics can be printed |
| *World Book Encyclopedia* (CD-ROM and Internet; Windows/Macintosh) http://www.worldbook.com | Ages 10 to adult | • a partial list of features includes videos, maps, simulations, animations, photos, and sound<br>• assistance is provided with texts, and "Homework Wizards" provide support and guidance<br>• Internet pages are devoted to both student learning and teacher resources |

*(continued)*

**Table 13.3**  Continued

| Title | Level | Features |
|---|---|---|
| | | • students can access the *World Book* archives, as well as linking to thousands of related Web sites |
| *Discis: Helping Children Read and Learn* (CD-ROM for Windows/Macintosh) | Ages 4 to 12 | • an older series with several titles, including *Paper Bag Princess* and *The Tale of Peter Rabbit*<br>• the text is read aloud, with phrases highlighted as they are read<br>• music accompanies the reading, and pages turn automatically or with the mouse<br>• students can click on pictures or words, which are then named |
| *Living Books* series (CD-ROM for Windows/Macintosh) | Ages 4 to 8 | • intended more for entertainment than education<br>• features animated stories and poetry<br>• students can choose between having the text read to them with accompanying animations and sound effects, or "playing" in the story, animating illustrations with a click of the mouse |
| *WiggleWorks: Scholastic Beginning Literacy System* (Floppy disks or CD-ROM for Windows/Macintosh) | Kindergarten to Grade 3 | • this is a multimedia literacy program<br>• there are three levels within each grade, and each grade has 24 books on disk or CD-ROM<br>• the series also includes children's books, teacher's guides, audio tapes, an assessment package, and other support materials<br>• for each electronic book, children can (1) have the book read to them, (2) read and request help with words, (3) modify the pictures and text and print their modified book, or (4) write their own story<br>• a magnetic board is available for word building, and children can develop a personal word list to serve as a writing resource<br>• the system includes a built-in management system for teachers |

Throughout this section, we have urged teachers to be critical consumers of computer software. How do you choose appropriate software to meet the learning needs of your students? This is the focus of the next section.

## Evaluating Computer Software

We provide both general guidelines and a detailed checklist to help teachers evaluate computer software.

### General Guidelines

In the early stages of the development of software intended to enhance reading and writing abilities, much of the material produced had the appearance of worksheets.

Hall and Martin (1999) point out that most educational software still focusses on drill and practice exercises, mainly because such software is relatively easy to implement and manage in the classroom. In addition, choices of software are often not made by teachers but by people outside the classroom, and such choices are most often dictated by cost and based on a limited knowledge of which software is appropriate for classroom use.

In our view, it is teachers who need to make choices about software, yet the steady stream of new educational programs constantly challenges them to make instructional decisions about which software best supports their literacy program. When teachers are asked to make decisions about software, they often have only very sketchy criteria for making the most productive decisions. The National Association for the Education of Young Children (1996) has developed a position statement on technology use and young children. Its guidelines include the following:

- Teachers should use professional judgement in deciding whether the technology is age appropriate, individually appropriate, and culturally appropriate. Used appropriately, technology can enhance children's cognitive and social abilities.
- Appropriate technology should be integrated into the regular learning environment and used as one of many options to support children's learning.
- All children should have equitable access to technology, and children with special needs should have increased access when this is helpful.
- Teachers must pay attention to eliminating stereotyping of any group and eliminating exposure to violence, especially as a problem-solving strategy.
- Teachers, in collaboration with parents, should advocate for more appropriate technology applications for all children.

These guidelines provide a useful framework to support teachers as they take a more active role in selecting the kinds of software that will support their students' literacy learning.

Hall and Martin (1999) also provide some general guidelines that busy teachers may use for appraising educational software. They suggest that teachers examine the software to determine whether

- it has clear objectives,
- the implied objectives are appropriate,
- it is age appropriate,
- it has supportive graphics and supportive text,
- it provides immediate feedback and encourages co-operative learning and critical thinking,
- it provides authentic scenarios and is easily integrated,
- the student maintains control, and
- it is accessible to special populations and represents the diversity of society.

## A Checklist for Evaluating Software

Shade (1996, p. 18) provides this general guideline for teachers who are trying to make appropriate software choices: "Avoid drill-and-practice software. Look for software that allows the child to make decisions about what she wants to do and which she can operate with little help." Shade suggests that a useful checklist of software can be grouped according to child, teacher, and technical features. These features have been adapted for the checklist presented in Table 13.4.

**Table 13.4**  Educational Software Review

| | | | |
|---|---|---|---|
| Title: | | | |
| Publisher: | | | |
| Intended ages: | | | |
| (A = acceptable        NA = not acceptable) | | | |

| Features | A | NA | Comments |
|---|---|---|---|
| **Student Learning Considerations** | | | |
| Child can independently operate | | | |
| Child controls pace and interaction | | | |
| Navigating directions are precise and clear | | | |
| Menu uses pictures or icons | | | |
| Speech supports operations | | | |
| Graphics and text are mutually supportive | | | |
| Intended curriculum outcomes are supported | | | |
| Objectives are clearly identifiable | | | |
| Engages student interest | | | |
| Encourages active learning | | | |
| • problem solving/decision making | | | |
| • critical thinking | | | |
| Provides appropriate feedback | | | |
| Encourages self-evaluation and monitoring | | | |
| | | | |
| **Technical Considerations** | | | |
| Easy to install and set up | | | |
| Minimal "wait" time for responses | | | |
| Can be customized | | | |
| Can be accessed by students with special needs | | | |
| Presents socially diverse populations | | | |
| Value (cost/educational benefits) | | | |
| Additional features: | | | |
| • | | | |
| • | | | |
| • | | | |
| Overall assessment | | | |

Source: Adapted from D.D. Shade (1996, September), "Software Evaluation." *Young Children*, pp. 17–21.

Overall, Shade suggests that teachers ask whether they have acquired "a powerful tool program that can be integrated across the curriculum (suitability), a program that will empower children to learn through self-directed exploration rather than through rote memorization and drill — *the educational value*" (p. 20). A consistent theme that is developed in most advice to teachers is echoed by Shade: "Avoid large, integrated learning systems. Look for software that allows the child to set the pace and stop anytime, experiment, operate from a picture menu, and control the interaction" (p. 19).

## Research and Reviews

As indicated at the beginning of this chapter, considerable research has been done on the impact of word processing on children's writing, but relatively little work on the effectiveness of specific software programs. There is also some research on electronic books. Results have shown that these types of books provide decoding practice (Miller,

Blackstock, and Miller, 1994), supply individual support for students with reading difficulties (Olson, Foltz, and Wise, 1986), and increase sight word knowledge (McKenna and Watkins, 1995). WiggleWorks, a multimedia-based literacy program, was the focus of a study by Schultz (1996) with Grade 1 students who used the software over a seven-month period. He found that these children made significantly greater gains on four subtests of the Iowa Test of Basic Skills (i.e., reading, language, vocabulary, and word analysis) than Grade 1 students who were not exposed to the WiggleWorks program. He also found that working with the WiggleWorks program positively affected advanced and weaker readers. Furthermore, there were highly significant differences in the writing samples between the WiggleWorks group and the comparison group on three writing scales that focussed on content, style, and mechanics. Schultz also noted that both teachers and students were enthusiastic about WiggleWorks.

There are a large number of software programs available and more being produced every day that are not reviewed except by the publishers. Careful evaluation and selection are required to ensure that computer technology is not used for its own sake, but rather to enhance children's learning. A useful reference for teachers is Reading Online (http://www.readingonline.org/home.html), which has a section devoted to reviews — often done by classroom teachers — of current software. Overall, the most important consideration when selecting computer software still remains the needs of learners.

> Computer software is only part of the picture. With the advent of the Internet, there has been an explosion in the amount of computer-based materials children are exposed to in both home and school contexts.

## The Internet

In this section, we provide some basic information about the Internet, examine some of the promise it holds, and offer examples of how this new learning environment is changing the way children learn and the way educators think about literacy and learning. Finally, we identify some of the growing pains associated with the Internet and its application to learning.

## Basic Information

The Internet is a vast network of computers that are connected to one another. The World Wide Web (often called simply "the Web") offers a means of linking texts, graphics, animation, and sound across any computer on the Internet. Internet users communicate using a special language that may prove daunting to the novice on first encounter. However, the central metaphor is one related to exploration and travel: users launch programs, visit Web sites, and navigate the Internet. Travellers on the information pathways visit sites that are linked to one another by guides called *servers*. In Table 13.5, we define some basic terms related to the Internet, and in Box 13.1 provide information on e-mail and Internet addresses.

## The Promise of the Internet

The Internet and the Web make it possible for learners to access thousands of archives all over the world. Library catalogues, text files, games, graphics, and organizational

**Table 13.5**   **A Quick Internet Primer**

| Term | Definition |
|---|---|
| World Wide Web (or WWW) | A facet of the Internet that consists of client and server computers handling multimedia documents. Internet users are sometimes called *Web crawlers*. |
| Browser software | Used by clients to view documents. Clicking on links brings documents located on a server to a browser, regardless of the server's geographic location. |
| Server | A program running on a computer that maintains Web documents that are accessible via a Web browser. Documents may contain text, images, sounds, and video, separately or in combination. |
| HTML (HyperText Markup Language) | A language used by authors to create Web documents. It offers short codes (also called *tags*) to designate graphical elements and links. |
| E-mail (electronic mail) | Part of the service provided by a server. To send and receive e-mail, a person must have an address listed on a server. |
| URL (uniform resource locator) | Addresses for documents. Clients and servers use a document's URL to find and distinguish among documents. |
| Search engine | A program that searches the World Wide Web to locate all of the documents that meet certain specifications given in search keys. Most search engines return a list of Web pages that are ordered by how well they match the specifications provided by the searcher. |
| Search key | A string of text entered by the user to guide a search engine. A key can include words, parts of words, or phrases. Users can specify keys that must be present, as well as those that must not be present. |
| Bookmarks | A means of electronically allowing users to store Web sites by name on the menu. Once a site is bookmarked, users do not have to enter the URL each time they want to visit a site, nor do they have to remember URLs. |
| Listserv | An on-line discussion group for e-mail subscribers. This is the most common program for this purpose, although other popular programs include Listproc and Majordomo. |

databases are available on almost any subject. Bulletin boards, computer conferencing, online journals, news networks, and discussion groups are totally changing the face of both information retrieval and learning. With these new developments, it is not

| **Box 13.1** | **E-mail and Internet Addresses** |

Sample e-mail address: aname@aserver.com
   **aname** identifies the user
Sample Internet address (URL): www.aserver.com
   **aserver.com** identifies the location of the server computer
   The **@** symbol (pronounced "at") separates the user name from the location of the server computer.
   Addresses use lowercase letters without any spaces. The name of a location contains at least a string and a suffix set apart by a dot. A three-letter suffix in the location name helps identify the kind of organization operating the server. Some locations use a two-letter geographical suffix.

Common suffixes for organizational affiliations include
.com (commercial)
.edu (educational)
.gov (government)
.mil (military)
.net (network)
.org (noncommercial)

Addresses from outside the United States often use a two-letter suffix designating a country. For example:
.ca (Canada)
.jp (Japan)
.uk (United Kingdom)
.nl (Netherlands)

surprising that some people are convinced that the Internet will revolutionize literacy education.

Educators are being forced to rethink traditional definitions of, and approaches to, literacy instruction. According to El-Hindi (1999), "Literacy now involves being able to make sense and navigate through several forms of information, including images, sounds, animation, and on-going discussion groups." She continues, "The idea of an isolated text no longer makes sense as children today are exposed to more fluid forms of information transfer." Student "talk" in these environments becomes the primary learning channel as they interact with one another and construct meaning in a universal classroom.

The Internet is an ideal environment for the social construction of meaning. As children navigate through a wide variety of information sources, they discriminate between important and unimportant information, respond to e-mail, and engage with other students in electronic chat sessions. In this process, what counts as knowledge is under constant construction, as the "knowledge base on the Internet becomes a function of social interaction among its users" (El-Hindi, 1999). The driving force in students' learning is not the teacher or a textbook, but their own natural curiosity. Once on-line, students can explore a wide variety of topics, engage in inquiry, and create unique and original responses using a range of multimedia technology. The teacher's primary task is to foster and support the establishment of learner-centred communities in which collaboration between teachers and students provides a means to develop and refine ideas.

Learning on and with the Internet promotes the active construction of meaning for several reasons:

- *Currency.* Learners have immediate access to current information. Nearly all major newspapers publish online versions, and research findings in most fields are now available. Most Web sites are constantly upgraded.
- *Relevancy.* Learners can choose lines of inquiry and pursue personal interests. Topics are linked and cross-referenced to enable Web crawlers to navigate their own inquiry pathways.
- *Immediacy.* Students can learn about events almost as they happen.

- *Multiple perspectives.* Learners using Web links can view and appraise the same information from a number of viewpoints.
- *Multiple dimensions.* The same event, concept, or topic is often available in multiple formats—text, chart, video, and sound. Regarding this aspect of learning with the Internet, Eagleton (1999) states, "Through transmediation, students have the opportunity to see how the same piece of information could be transformed in multiple ways through its participation in different systems of knowledge."

## The Changing Face of Literacy Instruction and Learning

Leu, Karchmer, and Leu (1999) describe the changing face of literacy instruction as "envisionments" that "take place when teachers and children imagine new possibilities for literacy and learning, transform existing technologies to construct this vision, and then share their work with others." They claim that it is through such envisionments that teachers and students are transcending traditional literacy materials by developing rich curriculum networks. They give an example of an envisionment where teachers and students in Tasmania, as part of a cultural study, developed and posted on the Internet a traditional Indonesian folk tale. This activity was picked up by a class in Indonesia, and through e-mail, the two classes learned about each other's culture. After reading about the experiences of the two classes, a school in the Netherlands integrated the original story into their own envisionment for literacy and learning. As other classrooms visit the original sites, numerous creation stories and myths from around the world are being made available on the Internet, and a rich curriculum resource developed by teachers and students is available for all to access and use.

The authors conclude that the Internet creates the possibility for new understandings of literacy. They suggest that "As new envisionments for literacy are regularly developed and exchanged, new definitions of literacy appear, requiring new forms of knowledge and new strategies for exploiting these information resources."

Thus, the Internet is transforming the way literacy is perceived and, in the process, is itself being transformed. The curriculum that evolves is therefore a response to the needs of the learners, who have the opportunity not only to acquire information, but to use it in new and constructive ways. Learning on the Internet is collaborative, as meanings are socially constructed and as new visions and altered states of knowing develop in a constant interactive flow. The critical idea that flows through all Internet exchanges is that they have purpose and personal significance (meaning) for the participants, regardless of age or location. They are not exercises to be marked, but projects that have meaning for the participants.

Leu, Karchmer, and Leu (1999) also report on an Internet exchange among students in Nagoya, Japan, and those in several countries around the world. The students in Nagoya were planning to visit Hiroshima and asked other classrooms to help them with developing interview and research questions. The focus that emerged from the exchanges was a worldwide project relating to world peace and international co-operation called "Passage to Hiroshima." Such projects are co-ordinated using an instructional framework called *Internet project*, "a collaborative instructional strategy in which learning experiences are developed and exchanged between two or more classrooms over the Internet."

It is apparent that the Internet is proving itself to be a valuable resource for both teachers and learners.

- It provides links and sites that can inform and encourage students' active partici-pation and inquiry.
- It can be a major source of literature as students read on-line.
- It can be used to develop and enhance background knowledge.
- It is a rich source of literacy activities that have been created by classroom teach-ers and their students.

Developing the conceptual knowledge that allows readers to fully appreciate the rich-ness of the text is made possible through hyperlinked sites. Hodgins (1999) shows how students reading the *Little House on the Prairie* series by Laura Ingalls Wilder can access the Frontier Girl Web site (http://webpages.marshall.edu/~irby1/laura/frames.html) to discover background information on the kind of prairie life that the author drew on for inspiration. Students can find diverse and intriguing information about prairie chickens, grasshopper plagues, sod houses and dugouts, muskrats, and winter bliz-zards, and all can be experienced through descriptions and photographs. In addition, students can gather information about the Ingalls family's personal life. A family tree provides personal glimpses, as do sound clips of the songs that Pa played on his fid-dle, such as "Pop Goes the Weasel" and the "Irish Washerwoman." These songs are ref-erenced to the book in which they are mentioned so that readers are able to hear the songs as they read the text. Hodgins concludes that the Laura Ingalls Wilder Web site can enrich the reader's background knowledge through both visual and auditory stim-uli. She maintains that "This multi-media approach benefits children with all type of learning styles" (1999, p. 8).

In addition, the Frontier Girl Web site has a listserv, which allows students to share their responses with other students, express opinions, ask questions, and generally share a wide range of opinions and responses to the literature being discussed. In essence, it becomes a global literature circle. Teachers also benefit by "listening in" on what other classes are doing and thinking and the kinds of activities that their col-leagues are engaging their students in. This kind of learning environment becomes a natural extension of a literature circle (see Chapter Eleven), as an Internet search read-ily lends itself to the roles of investigator, travel tracer, and connector. Internet activi-ties such as these have the potential to foster collaboration and interaction with oth-ers, allowing students to build a community of readers and writers on a global scale—classroom walls no longer define the boundaries of the literacy community.

In many ways, depending on how much opportunity students have to access the Internet, e-mail and chat rooms are replacing the telephone as the preferred medium of information exchange for today's students. According to Bruce (1999), "Using new communication and information technologies, teachers and students are discovering more ways to communicate with others to make things, to learn about the world, and to express themselves." That students engage in global chat-rooms, wherein they com-pose messages in an ongoing on-line conversation, has prompted Eagleton (1999) to conclude that the Internet may well serve to restore and reinforce the critical role that oral language plays in literacy learning.

In addition to sharing information and viewpoints via e-mail and chat-rooms, students are beginning to share themselves and their creativity through designing per-sonal Web pages using Web tools now available. As they do so, students communicate and share, inquire and question, and express and construct new meanings in an inte-grated manner. "Young people, and those not so young, are using the richly intertex-tual, multimedia canvas not just to learn, but to teach the world about themselves"

(Bruce, 1999). These Web pages often incorporate background music, personal photographs, video segments, graphics, the imaginative use of fonts, colour, backgrounds,
and clip art to create rich personal statements that are shared with others. All invite
response, and most conclude by letting readers know "I love to get e-mail!"

In the worldwide "chat" community, English-speaking students can post any of
their new language learning for response and support from native speakers of the language. And access to these Web sites is not restricted to English speakers only. New
translation technologies such as Systran (http://babelfish.altavista.com/cgi-bin/trans-
late), available on the AltaVista site (http://www.altavista.com), allow Web users to
translate their messages instantly from one language to another and post them on the
Web. Such translation technology allows students to talk with friends who speak different languages. Students can also "read" the news in a foreign language and then
translate it to check its meaning. Or they can write on a topic, translate it, post it, and
wait for responses. They can also choose a topic, translate it, search with the translated terms, and specify results in the target language. They can then translate the pages
that look interesting. The AltaVista "Translation Tips" page has more ideas that may
make second language learning interesting and enjoyable for students.

The Internet is creating global literacy communities that provide opportunities
for students to publish writing of all genres on the network. These opportunities not
only bring a sense of accomplishment, they also allow students to feel a sense of
belonging to a larger community of readers and writers (El-Hindi, 1998).

## Challenges and Issues

As we indicated in the introduction to this chapter, current research into the use of
computers in the classroom is somewhat equivocal. The research into the effects of
Internet use on literacy learning is very limited, both because of the network's relative
infancy and because of the fact that the technology is changing faster than our ability
to evaluate its utility using traditional approaches (Leu, Karchmer, and Leu, 1999).
Nevertheless, some of the basic questions that researchers face include (Reinking,
1997)

- What are the differences, if any, that networked literacy activities make for learners?
- Is the money and time required to get these systems up and running on-line a
  good investment in terms of student learning?
- What criteria could be used to measure successful learning?
- In a general sense, what is the best way to use this emerging technology and its
  resources?

Bruce (1999) suggests that responding to questions such as these might be difficult.
In the first place, the new information and communication technologies are no longer
discrete; rather, they exist as components of complex systems. Student learning cannot
be isolated as in the past, when all students read and responded to the same "basal" text.
An on-line student today may well be part of a discussion group that numbers in the
thousands and is geographically dispersed around the planet. In addition, because the
technology is constantly changing, it is likely that by the time research results are published, they may reflect the effect of an obsolete technology or procedure. This rapid
change becomes a critical factor in assessing how and what students learn.

Another difficulty in assessing the effect of the technology is the way the Internet
is continuously redefining the roles of both teachers and learners. Bruce (1999) gives
the example of how use of Internet technology in one setting may directly affect users

in other settings. Thus, to evaluate a "discussion group chat-room," one needs to look at the scale of the interaction. Often a single new contributor may make a critical difference in the learning of any student or all students who are part of a particular on-line project or discussion group.

## Responding to the Challenges

Research related to use of the Internet may rest almost entirely with classroom teachers. In the opinion of Leu, Karchmer, and Leu (1999), "Our understanding of effective literacy instruction may be informed more often by teachers who use continuously changing technologies on a daily basis and less often by traditional forms of research." Using the Internet, teachers can quickly spread the word about a useful teaching strategy. And multimedia resources, references, and unit and lesson plans can be downloaded instantly simply by accessing Web sites such as Canada's SchoolNet (http://www.schoolnet.ca) or ClassroomConnect (http://www.classroom. com). The home page of each of these sites is shown in Figures 13.1 and 13.2. These sites also provide a fund of professional references, and teachers may read online literacy articles by accessing sites such as Reading Online (http://www.readingonline. org/home.html), a site created and maintained by the International Reading Association.

**Figure 13.1**    **Canada's SchoolNet Home Page**

Source: Canada's SchoolNet (http://www.schoolnet.ca/home/e/index.html). Downloaded on November 18, 1999.

**Figure 13.2**   **Classroom Connect Home Page**

Source: ClassroomConnect (http://www.classroom.com/home.asp). Downloaded on November 18, 1999.

Other sites focus on a specific approach and provide teachers with a complete implementation guide and forum for discussing and sharing adaptations that they may incorporate into their instruction. One such site on "The Project Approach" (http://www.ualberta.ca/~schard/siteinfo/navigate.htm) has been developed and maintained by Dr. Sylvia Chard at the University of Alberta. This site provides explicit explanations of the theory, selection, planning, and structure of the "project approach" and is a favourite site for teachers who seek to promote active learning inquiry in their classrooms.

With this proliferation of material on the Internet, teachers and researchers alike are faced with the critical issues of how credible the on-line "shared" information is and how students can be prepared to evaluate the relative "truth" of the opinions and views that they access, including detecting distortion, bias, and outright prejudice. One way is to focus on assessing "the credibility of the advocates for different claims [rather] than on verifying the truth of their claims" (Leu, Karchmer, and Leu, 1999). Whatever the case, the Internet provides a compelling reason for students to learn how to recognize the propaganda devices by which writers seek to influence readers (discussed in Chapter Five). Ultimately, students will need to learn to actively question both the content of the writing that is being presented and the sources from which it originates.

While we recognize the great potential of the Internet to facilitate children's language and literacy learning, we also urge caution. It is not the technology itself that results in learning, but how that technology is used and integrated into the language arts program.

## Media Literacy

In this section, we describe the range of media that children experience in their daily lives, and then present goals for instruction in using of multimedia materials in language arts programs. We discuss some ways teachers use media as vehicles for instruction, and identify issues and challenges they face.

Children today are immersed in a multimedia world. From a very early age, the overwhelming majority of Canadian children have been subject to an unending stream of television images that shift approximately every seven seconds within a continuous background of musical and verbal messages (Flood, Heath, and Lapp, 1997). They are also surrounded with other media, including photography, recordings, radio, film, television, videotape, video games, computers, the performing arts, and virtual reality (Whipple, 1998).

Traditionally, nonprint media have been used in elementary classrooms as supplemental resources—that is, as follow-up activities, rewards, or "fillers" (Whipple, 1998). Seldom have they been regarded as suitable materials for literacy instruction. However, resistance to accepting media other than print as suitable learning vehicles is gradually being broken down, with many teachers beginning to use multimedia texts to enrich their students' meaning constructions. Increasingly, teachers in constructivist classrooms are helping students learn not only with and through media, but also about media (Hobbs, 1997).

Educators now realize that in the media world outside of school, children have opportunities to practise "essential skills such as self-presentation, role shifting, empathy building, sense of plot, and the ability to focus on several things simultaneously" (Flood, Heath, and Lapp, 1997, p. xvi). Building on this recognition, teachers in many constructivist classrooms now design learning activities that have students move among textbooks, trade books, films, and video in an attempt to help them develop in-depth conceptual understandings (Hobbs, 1997). As well, teachers are now encouraging students to think not only about the informational content of media, but also about the way information is presented. This is a key facet of media literacy instruction at all levels.

## Goals of Instruction

Media literacy instruction aims to provide students with skills and strategies for dealing critically with the media and the role they play in their lives. Specifically, the Media Literacy Resource Guide (Ontario Ministry of Education, 1989) suggests that students need to

- develop the skills, knowledge, and attitudes necessary for interpreting the way media present reality,
- become aware of the implications of these constructions and the values they present,

- develop an appreciation and aesthetic understanding of the media,
- be able to identify, interpret, and experience the techniques used to create media products,
- be able to decode media products in order to identify and examine the cultural practices, values, and ideas contained in them,
- recognize that media production is subject to political, cultural, and social constraints and factors, and
- recognize that the "meanings" in any media are socially constructed.

This facet of instruction tends to focus on the student as "consumer" of media, and the skills and attitudes to be developed are those that acknowledge the pervasive and often deleterious influence that media have in everyday living. A key concern is with the powerful influence that current and emerging media have on the listener/reader/viewer — that is, the consumer. In this framework, the media "text" needs to not only be decoded but examined and evaluated from a critical perspective before it is "consumed."

## Media Literacy Instruction

One of the most obvious media influences on elementary children's lives is that of advertising, and it is one aspect that most readily lends itself to helping children learn about media. Television advertising employs both explicit and implicit propaganda techniques (see Chapter Five) with one aim — to sell a product. Teacher and students viewing ads for breakfast cereals or toys and games might ask questions such as

- What do they want me to do?
- How are they trying to get me to do it?
- Is what they want me to do in my best interests or those of my community?
- What do I gain or lose if I do what they want me to do?

Questions such as these may lead to an examination of the various techniques (linguistic, auditory, and visual) that the media use to convey information. The Ontario Ministry of Education's *Media Literacy Resource Guide* (1989) provides useful suggestions for teachers who are helping students learn about media. It includes strategies for inquiring into and critically examining television, films, radio, popular music and rock videos, photography, and print. There is also a section that looks at advertising, sexuality, and violence in the media, as well as at how Canadian identity is represented.

A second aspect of media that is becoming more appealing for teachers is the way in which media can complement conventional literacy instruction (Flood, Heath, and Lapp, 1997). Hobbs (1997, p. 8) points out that "Many educators have discovered that the analysis of contemporary media can build skills that transfer to students' work with the written word." Whipple (1998) has demonstrated how rich intertextual connections can be when woven between literature and film. He argues that students are often much more familiar with the film/video genre because of its pervasiveness and are often more comfortable responding to it. In addition, says Whipple, by using both print and film, teachers can invite many students who are considered "at-risk" in predominantly print learning environments to participate in classroom discourse, to become part of the classroom learning community, and to be validated as learners and people. Students learn to read actors' body and language expressions and the details of setting and action, and they draw on background knowledge to anticipate and judge the events as they unfold.

Preliminary findings of research conducted by Mackey (1999b) indicate that students who move daily between print and other media worlds use similar strategies to read in both. She found that students applied the same "rules" or conventions for reading in print and other media. Students expected stories, whether they were presented in print, video, or CD-ROM games, to follow the same rules. One of the rules applied to "salience," meaning "what matters right now and what is likely to matter as the story progresses" (Mackey, 1999b, p. 8), while another applied to "configuration," meaning that which helps readers assemble the story as it proceeds. A final "rule" deals with "coherence," that which helps a reader make sense of the story as a whole and which usually comes into play after the reading is completed. Mackey found that students read all of the texts in pretty much the same fashion, and they made strategic "reading" decisions in much the same way in each medium.

Teachers who integrate nonprint media into their literacy curriculum have gained some valuable insights about student motivation. For example, experience has shown that once students become familiar with CD-ROM games and electronic books, they grow more demanding and readily reject those media that do not meet the level of sophistication that they demand (Mackey, 1999a). As a case in point, many children now regard the original Mario Brothers games as insultingly simple. As literacy teachers, we need to be aware that texts we think are appealing to students may, in many cases, not be so.

## Issues and Challenges

Whipple argues that we can either become resentful and reject the pervasive influence of children's home viewing habits and practices, or "we can look upon them as an opportunity to support literacy development and to make connections with more traditional media (i.e., written text)" (1998, p. 146). That said, a major challenge for teachers rests on how learning about and with media can be fitted into an already overcrowded curriculum.

There are no ready answers, but several possibilities provide support for the legitimacy of such integration:

- First, in a constructivist classroom where the concern is with building meaning, nonprint media provide opportunities for teachers and students to view ideas and events from several perspectives and thereby extend and enhance understanding.
- Second, media present more authentic learning experiences for some children. Video and film are frequently more relevant to students who come from impoverished print backgrounds, and they often provide the literacy links that teachers need.
- Third, from a social constructivist perspective, language and learning are social phenomena, and media experiences encourage collaborative interactions among students and teachers in ways that traditional print texts do not.
- Finally, students engage in active learning because they already have most of the necessary "reading" skills in place.

Another challenge for teachers who incorporate media into their instructional program rests on how their students' learning growth can be assessed. Although many provincial and local school authorities advocate integrating media literacy into the curriculum, few acknowledge students' achievement in viewing and representing. Large-scale provincial achievement tests still focus on measuring the traditional language arts skills of reading and writing. Even when students are asked to view and respond to a video, the "required responses" are evaluated according to fairly conventional criteria (Hobbs, 1997). Similarly, very few school districts provide space to report children's learning growth in media literacy.

One of the hallmarks of a balanced literacy program, as advocated in this text, is that it is built on the principles of integration and intertextual connections. Multimedia learning presents opportunities for children to build complementary skills and strategies. Integrative possibilities abound. Some involve viewing and listening to documentaries or docu-dramas, but even watching cartoons (one example might be *The Simpsons*) presents situations in which students can examine and critique social events in their immediate and distant worlds. Multimedia experiences provide opportunities for students to tie together many apparently disparate curriculum elements and create a more complete "meaning" of their lives and their culture.

> In the final analysis, children today are born into a media world, and most of the skills they need to operate in it are learned "on-line." Students benefit when constructivist teachers adapt their programs to this reality.

## Summary

Although many people strongly believe that computer technology is synonymous with human progress, teachers face several issues when planning to use technology in language arts programs. First, there is contradictory evidence about the impact of computer technology on aspects of language development such as writing. Children's learning is strongly tied to their teacher's expertise and ability to take full advantage of the potential of this technology. Another issue involves power and control. Computers appear to put more power into the hands of children, but this depends on the software selected and how computers are used. The issue of power and control goes beyond the school context, because the type of instruction children receive on a computer is dependent, at least to some extent, on their gender and socio-economic status. A third issue involves the degree of emphasis placed on acquiring hardware compared with that placed on training teachers and integrating computers into the curriculum.

Jonassen (1996) identifies three potential roles for computers in children's learning: learning *from* computers, learning *about* computers, and learning *with* computers. He recommends that teachers and children work *with* computers as cognitive tools or, as he calls them, mindtools. In programs designed for this purpose, instruction focusses on three levels: operations (including knowledge and concepts), productivity, and inquiry. The first level involves foundational operations such as basic computer, telecommunications, and multimedia operations. Productivity focusses on text composition (word processing), data organization (databases), electronic communications (e-mail and discussion groups), and multimedia composition (hypermedia). Inquiry involves using computer tools for decision making and problem solving.

There is a proliferation of software on the market, and more appears daily. Some of this material is reminiscent of worksheets and drill exercises, and it is important that teachers evaluate software to ensure that it will facilitate the learning of children in their classrooms. Shade (1996) recommends that teachers take into account child, teacher, and technical features when evaluating software. Child features include opportunities for active learning and child-controlled interaction, and the ability to set the pace and stop any time. Teacher features include curriculum congruence, suitability for children with different needs, and the ability of the software to be customized. Technical features include animation, realistic media effects, and clear speech effects.

The Internet provides learners with access to an enormous amount of information. It not only opens up new opportunities for literacy, but also for electronic communication. Learning on the Internet is current, relevant, immediate, and multidimensional, and it involves multiple perspectives. Some educators maintain that the Internet is changing the face of literacy education as children and teachers develop rich learning networks with their counterparts in other places in the world. The Internet is creating global literacy communities. However, research on the impact of the Internet is in its infancy, and there is a need for both teachers and children to critically examine material on the Web for both content and source.

Children live in a multimedia world. In addition to computer software and the Internet, they are exposed to films, television, photographs, and recordings in their daily lives. Although teachers have not always viewed these media as appropriate vehicles for instruction, increasingly they are becoming aware of the potential of these media to enrich children's constructions of meaning. One focus of instruction is to help students become critical consumers of media. Media are also being used to complement conventional literacy instruction, as when intertextual connections are woven between literature and film. Research is starting to show that children use similar strategies to "read" texts in both print and other media.

## Selected Professional Resources

Considine, D.M. and Haley, G.E. (1999). *Visual Messages: Integrating Imagery into Instruction* (2nd ed.). Englewood, CO: Teacher Ideas Press. This text provides teachers with a comprehensive and up-to-date overview of media literacy. The authors lead clearly and concisely from background information on a particular media to teaching suggestions and extensions identified with the grade level for which they are appropriate. The authors suggest a critical "student-centred approach" to media inquiry as they deal with how topics such as eating disorders, sex, violence, and alcohol are presented in the media. The authors also show how teachers can connect film and literature to effectively support (or scaffold) children's language learning.

Reading Online (http://www.readingonline.org/home.html). This is the online journal of the International Reading Association, and is an example of the many journals and professional resources that teachers can now access via the Internet. Reading Online contains articles that deal with all aspects of the literacy curriculum, including critical issues, electronic classrooms, international perspectives, research, and reviews. The key focus is on classroom applications of emerging technologies. Teachers can access archival material, as well as take part in on-line discussions with the authors of current articles and other classroom teachers.

## Software and Children's Materials Noted in Chapter Thirteen

Astound. (1998). Sunnyvale, CA: Astound.
ClarisWorks/AppleWorks. (1998). Cupertino, CA: Apple Computer.
ClarisWorks for Kids. (1997). Santa Clara, CA: Claris.
*Discis: Helping Children Read and Learn.* (1994). Buffalo, NY: Discis Knowledge Research.

*Encarta Encyclopedia 98*. (1997). Redmond, WA: Microsoft.

Holtz, M. (1995). ToolBox: The Multimedia Workshop. Belmont, CA: Wadsworth.

HyperCard. (1994). Cupertino, CA: Apple Computer.

HyperStudio. (1995). El Cajon, CA: Roger Wagner.

KidWorks Deluxe. (1996). Torrance, CA: Davidson & Associates.

Living Books. Novato, CA: Broderbund Software (Several titles with different dates of publication).

Microsoft Works. (1998). Redmond, WA: Microsoft.

Storybook Weaver Deluxe. (1996). Minneapolis, MN: MECC.

Student Writing Center. (1995). Minneapolis, MN: Learning Company.

SuperCard. (1997). San Diego, CA: Allegiant Technologies.

Taylor, C. (1987). *The Doll*. Toronto: Douglas & McIntyre.

Toliver, P.R. and Johnson, Y. (1997). *Microsoft PowerPoint*. Reading, MA: Addison-Wesley.

WiggleWorks: Scholastic Beginning Literacy System. (1994). New York: Scholastic.

Wilder, L.I. (1953). *Little House on the Prairie*. New York: Harper.

*World Book Encyclopedia*. (1995). Chicago: World Book.

## References

Alberta Education. (1997). *Learner outcomes in information and communication technology*. Edmonton: Alberta Education.

Anderson-Inman, L. and Horney, M. (1999). Electronic books: Reading and studying with supportive resources. Reading Online [an electronic journal of the International Reading Association]. Available at http://www.readingonline.org/home.html.

Bruce, B. (1991). Roles for computers in teaching the English language arts. In J. Flood, J.M. Jensen, D. Lapp, and J.R. Squire (eds.), *Handbook of research on teaching the English language arts* (pp. 536–541). New York: Macmillan.

Bruce, B. (1999). Learning through expression. Reading Online [an electronic journal of the International Reading Association]. Available at http://www.readingonline.org/home.html.

Chang, L. and Osguthorpe, R. (1990). The effects of computerized picture-word processing on kindergartners' language development. *Journal of Research in Childhood Education, 5*, 73–83.

Considine, D.M. and Haley, G.E. (1999). *Visual messages: Integrating imagery into instruction* (2nd ed.). Englewood, CO: Teacher Ideas Press.

Daiute, C. (1985). *Writing and computers*. Reading, MA: Addison Wesley.

Dillon, A. and Gabbard, R. (1998). Hypermedia as an educational technology: A review of the quantitative research literature on learner comprehension, control, and style. *Review of Educational Research, 68* (3), 322–349.

Dybdahl, C.S., Shaw, D.G., and Blahous, E. (1997). The impact of computers on writing: No simple answer. *Computers in the Schools, 13* (3/4), 41–53.

Eagleton, M. (1999). The benefits and challenges of a student-designed school website. Reading Online [an electronic journal of the International Reading Association]. Available at http://www.readingonline.org/home.html.

Edmonton Public Schools. (1998). *The Doll: A novel study*. Edmonton: EPSB Resource Development Services.

El-Hindi, A. (1998). Exploring literacy on the Internet. *The Reading Teacher, 51*, 694–700.

El-Hindi, A. (1999). Beyond classroom boundaries: Constructivist teaching with the Internet. Reading Online [an electronic journal of the International Reading Association]. Available at http://www.readingonline.org/home.html.

Flood, J., Heath, S.B., and Lapp, D. (eds). (1997). *Handbook of research on teaching literacy through the communicative and visual arts*. Old Tappan, NJ: Simon and Schuster.

Galloway, J.P. (1994). Effects of QuickTime multimedia tools on writing style and content. In J. Wills, B. Robin, and D.A. Wills (eds.), *Technology and teacher education annual* (pp. 94–97). Charlottesville, VA: Association for the Advancement of Computing in Education.

Grégoire, R., Bracewell, R., and Laferrière, T. (1996). *The contribution of new technologies to learning and teaching in elementary and secondary schools*. Available at http://www.tact.fse.ulaval.ca/fr/html/impactnt.html.

Hall, V.G. and Martin, L.E. (1999). Making decisions about software for classroom use. *Reading Research and Instruction, 38* (3), 187–196.

Hatfield, S. (1996). *Effective use of classroom computer stations across the curriculum.* ERIC D
Service No. ED 396 704.

Hobbs, R. (1997). Literacy for the information age. In J. Flood, S.B. Heath, and D. Lapp (ed
*Handbook of research on teaching literacy through the communicative and visual arts* (pp. 7–14
Old Tappan, NJ: Simon and Schuster.

Hodgins, K. (1999). Reading on the internet. Unpublished paper. University of Alberta, Edmonton, AB.

Jonassen, D. (1996). *Computers in the classroom: Mindtools for critical thinking.* Englewood Cliffs, NJ:
Prentice-Hall.

Jones, I. (1994). The effect of a word processor on the written composition of second grade pupils.
*Computers in the Schools, 11* (2), 43–53.

Leu, D.J., Jr., Karchmer, R.A., and Leu, D.D. (1999). The Miss Rumphius effect: Envisionments for literacy and learning that transform the Internet. Reading Online [an electronic journal of the
International Reading Association]. Available at http://www.readingonline.org/home.html.

Logan, R.K. (1995). *The fifth language: Learning a living in the computer age.* Toronto: Stoddart.

McKenna, M. and Watkins, J. (1995). Effects of computer-mediated books on the development of
beginning readers. Paper presented at the meeting of the National Reading Conference, New
Orleans, LA, November 1995.

Mackey, M. (1999a). Response to literature in media and multimedia. Unpublished paper, University
of Alberta, Edmonton, AB.

Mackey, M. (1999b). New literacies in action. Unpublished paper. University of Alberta, Edmonton, AB.

Miller, L., Blackstock, J., and Miller, R. (1994). An exploratory study into the use of CD-ROM storybooks. *Computers in Education, 22,* 187–204.

National Association for the Education of Young Children. (1996). NAEYC position statement:
Technology and young children ages three through eight. *Young Children, 51,* 11–15.

Olson, R., Foltz, G., and Wise, B. (1986). Reading instruction and remediation with the aid of computer speech. *Behavior Research Methods, Instruments and Computers, 18* (2), 93–99.

Olson, C.P. and Sullivan, E.V. (1993). Beyond the mania: Critical approaches to computers in education. In L.L. Stewin and S.J.H. McCann (eds.), *Contemporary educational issues: The Canadian
mosaic* (pp. 424–441). Toronto: Copp Clark Pitman.

Ontario Ministry of Education. (1989). *Media literacy resource guide.* Toronto: Queen's Printer for
Ontario.

Pan, A.C. and Zbikowski, J.M. (1997). Emerging technology for writing instruction: New directions
for teachers. *Computers in the Schools, 13* (3/4), 103–118.

Postman, N. (1992). The ideology of machines: Computer technology. In N. Postman (ed.),
*Technopoly: The surrender of culture to technology* (pp. 107–122). New York: Alfred A. Knopf.

Reinking, D. (1997). Me and my hypertext: A multiple digression analysis of technology and literacy. Reading Online [an electronic journal of the International Reading Association]. Available at
http://www.readingonline.org/home.html.

Rennie, J. (1990). Computers and literacy in schools. *Reflections on Canadian Literacy, 8* (1), 50–52.

Salomon, G. (1993). On the nature of pedagogic computer tools. The case of the writing partner. In
S.P. Lajoie and S.J. Derry (eds.), *Computers as cognitive tools* (pp. 179–196). Hillsdale, NJ:
Lawrence Erlbaum Associates.

Schrader, C.T. (1990). *The word processor as a tool for developing young writers.* ERIC Document
Reproduction Service No. ED 321 276.

Schultz, L. (1996). *A validation study of WiggleWorks, the Scholastic beginning literacy system.*
Cambridge, MA: Harvard University.

Shade, D.D. (1996). Software evaluation. *Young Children, 51,* 17–21.

Sharp, V. (1995). *HyperStudio 3.0 in one hour.* Eugene, OR: International Society for Technology in
Education.

Sharp, V. (1999). *Computer education for teachers* (3rd ed.). Boston: McGraw-Hill.

Strickland, D.S., Feeley, J.T., and Wepner, S.B. (1987). *Using computers in the teaching of reading.* New
York: Teachers College Press.

Taylor, R. (1980). *The computer in the school: Tutor, tool, tutee.* New York: Teachers College Press.

Ver Velde, P., Knight, M., and Shushok, K. (1997). *An assessment of the effects of student-produced multimedia productions upon the learning of academic content in elementary classrooms.* Flagstaff, AZ:
Report on applied research project sponsored by Northern Arizona University Office of Research
and Graduate Studies.

Whipple, M. (1998). Let's go to the movies: Rethinking the role of film in the elementary classroom.
*Language Arts, 76,* (2), 144–150.

Wilhelm, J.D., Friedemann, P.D., and Erickson, J. (1998). *Hyperlearning: Where projects, inquiry, and
technology meet.* York, ME: Stenhouse.

# chapter fourteen

# Planning and Organizing Language Arts Programs

**Program Planning**
- Balanced Revisited
- Components of Classroom Organization

**Selected Materials**
- Language Arts Series
- Trade Books
- Nonbook Resources
- Selecting a Range of Topics and Materials
- Thematic Organization

**Scheduling Time**
- Length of Time Blocks
- Whole Class, Small Group, and Individual Activities
- Time Guidelines

**Planning and Organizing Language Arts Programs**

**Organizing Space**
- Whole Class Activities
- Small Group Activities
- Individual Activities

**Organizing Children for Learning**
- Whole Class Instruction
- Grouping Children for Instruction
- Individual Reading and Writing

**Meeting the Needs of All Children**
- Non-Mainstream Backgrounds
- Limited English-Language Facility
- Learning Differences
- Mentally Challenged Students

**Reporting to Parents**
- Report Cards
- Student-Led Conferences
- Portfolios

Each day when the children enter David Paul's Grade 2 classroom, they are greeted with a letter to them on the chalkboard. In the letter, David tells about unusual class activities they will do that day or comments on class events from the day before. Today, the children read the letter and David helps them use strategies to identify unfamiliar words. The children use words on the classroom word wall as a resource to help them with words in the letter. On other days, David presents the letter as a minimal cues message.

David then draws the children together on the floor in a group and reads them a poem about a dragon to set the theme for the group composition they will write later. As he reads, he stops at the end of some lines to give the children an opportunity to predict meaningful words.

Next, David tells the children that they are going to write a composition together about an imaginary pet dragon. He planned this instructional activity

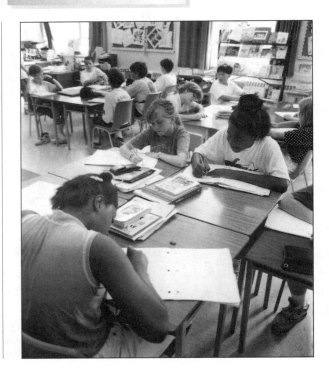

because he has noticed that many children in the class are having difficulty generating and organizing ideas in their compositions. As the children in the class brainstorm ideas, David writes them on the whiteboard. Then, with the assistance of his questions, the children organize the ideas into groups. As they do so, David uses coloured markers to circle ideas in each group — for example, how the pet dragon looks, what it does, and what it eats. The children discuss what they want to write and then dictate ideas while David records their ideas on chart paper. The completed composition is then read as a whole, and some suggestions are made for revisions. The revised composition, revision marks and all, is placed in the writing centre.

While the group is still intact, David and the children discuss how they will use their remaining time. He provides them with a sign-up chart to control the number of children who choose to work at each centre as well as to keep a record of what activities each child completes during the week. Some children indicate that they are going to continue writing a composition from their writing files. Others decide to read independently or write a response in their journal to a book they are reading. One group of children chooses to play a dragon game David has developed to reinforce a problematic spelling pattern (final *e*). Another group works on a puppet play based on a story they had read in class.

While the children are working independently or in small groups, David asks six children to join him at a small table in the corner of the room where he conducts a directed reading–thinking activity (see Chapter Five) with a level one text. He has noticed that these children are making limited use of their own knowledge when they read. Their responses to what they are reading tend to focus on story details rather than on linking story events or characters to their own lives. He will provide guided reading for another small group tomorrow, but will continue to work with this group in subsequent lessons until they are able to make more effective use of both print and knowledge-based information.

With five minutes left before recess, David asks the class to come back together to share what they learned that morning. One child talks about a book she is reading, and another shares a piece of writing. The group working on the puppet play say they have completed their puppets and are ready to share their play with the class the next day. ∎

The children in this classroom were involved in a variety of listening, talking, reading, and writing activities during the 90-minute period described as well as during other parts of the school day. They worked with the teacher, with other children, and by themselves. They completed some assigned activities and were able to select others based on their interests and skills. The children moved from one activity to another with very little waiting or off-task behaviour. This does not happen by accident, but rather reflects careful planning and organization of the program. Careful planning leads to meaningful learning for children, which in turn motivates them and reduces behaviour problems. Planning and organization are key to effective classroom management.

- How did David Paul plan the day described above?
- How can classrooms be organized to ensure that children are involved in balanced language arts programs?
- How can children be grouped to meet individual needs?
- How do teachers decide the amount of time to schedule for different aspects of language arts?
- How can the physical space in classrooms be organized to maximize children's learning?

- How can a language arts program be organized to meet the range of student learning needs found in any one classroom?

These are only a few of the questions you will ask yourself as you sit down to plan the language arts program in your classroom.

In the previous chapters in this text, we focussed heavily on instructional techniques for speaking, listening, reading, writing, viewing, and representing. But that is only part of the story. In this chapter, we discuss how to put these pieces together in a classroom context to meet the needs of all learners.

## Program Planning

We begin this chapter by revisiting the final section in Chapter One, where we discussed balance in language arts programs. We then identify the dimensions that teachers consider as they organize their classrooms to maximize learning.

### Balance Revisited

When language arts educators write about balance, they generally refer to the need for work on word identification and comprehension in reading and on meaning and mechanics (e.g., spelling, punctuation, and handwriting) in writing. However, as indicated in Chapter One, teachers who hold a social constructive perspective view "balance" from a broader perspective. They are interested in balancing not only *what* they teach but also *how* they teach and interact with children.

Even the *what* of language arts programs is itself not a simple matter of deciding how much emphasis to place on words and meaning as the "great debate" suggests. Important choices must be made about how much time to spend on each strand of language arts—reading, writing, speaking, listening, viewing, and representing. In relation to the *how* of language arts, all teachers—you included—are faced with even more difficult decisions. These include

- how much time to allocate for teaching and to practising and using strategies and skills,
- when to provide deductive instruction and when to provide inductive instruction,
- how to differentiate expectations, materials, and activities to meet the language needs of all learners,
- how to help children learn new strategies and develop automaticity in using the strategies they have learned,
- when to provide assistance to support children's learning and when to have them work independently,
- how to balance your control of children's learning with opportunities for them to control their own learning, and
- how to decide when children should work alone or with other children.

The answers to questions such as these begin with the words "It depends." Several factors affect the decisions you will make. Some of these include the needs of individual and groups of children, the stages children have reached in their learning, the resources available in your school, the program of studies mandated by government departments, your theoretical orientation to language arts and learning, and the philosophy of your school. As indicated at several points throughout this text, no one answer will be appropriate for all children at any one time or for any one child all the time. Organizational patterns change as children grow and change, but, increasingly, educators are recommending that balance is critical to effective language arts programs (Fountas and Pinnell, 1996; Cunningham and Allington, 1999).

The planning process always begins with children's learning needs. We described techniques earlier in this text for assessing children's oral language, emergent literacy, reading, and writing abilities. Another crucial piece of information that guides planning involves the provincial program of studies for language arts education. These programs of studies delineate objectives to be reached in each strand of language learning. One of your tasks in planning is to determine which objectives each child has already achieved and what he or she needs to learn next. Other tasks involve selecting appropriate materials, scheduling language arts time, organizing the physical space in the classroom to facilitate children's learning, and planning whole class, small group, and individual instruction and activities.

## Components of Classroom Organization

Different classrooms reflect different views of language learning. When desks are arranged in rows and children face the front, the focus is generally on teacher talk, with the teacher making most decisions about what children do and when they do it. When teachers arrange children's desks in groups with the children facing one another, they encourage student talk and co-operative learning. Other decisions you will make about the use of space include

- where to place the teacher's desk,
- whether to set up reading and writing centres,
- whether to have a classroom library in addition to the school library, and
- where to place computer and other equipment.

Space is just one of the variables teachers consider as they plan and organize their classrooms to facilitate children's learning.

Time is also a crucial variable. Most jurisdictions mandate the minimum amount of time schools must schedule for language arts instruction at each grade level. However, teachers have flexibility within this time allocation to decide whether to organize language arts instruction in one or two large time blocks or to devote small time blocks to specific skills or activities. They also make decisions about how to allocate time to ensure that children receive a balanced language arts program.

A third variable teachers take into account when planning a language arts program is materials and equipment. They make decisions such as the following:

- the extent to which language arts series are used as compared with **trade books**,
- the range of levels of reading materials included in classrooms,
- who selects materials or topics — children, teachers, or both, and
- whether materials are organized thematically or some other way.

Finally, the most critical variable teachers take into account when planning language arts programs is the children themselves. How can children be organized to maximize their learning? Teachers make daily decisions about when, why, and how to organize whole class, small group, and individual activities.

In the next four sections of this text, we describe ways teachers organize materials, time, space, and children to meet the need of learners in their classrooms.

## Selecting Materials

If you are 25 or older, you likely recall the characters Dick and Jane or Tom and Betty from your elementary school readers. Use of these materials was usually required by government departments, and your teacher had little choice about using them. In most school jurisdictions today, the practice of recommending language arts series is still in place, although teachers generally have the option of using them or other resources. We begin this section by describing different types of materials commonly used in language arts programs. We then discuss the need to select a range of topics and materials, and offer suggestions about how to organize thematic units.

## Language Arts Series

**Basal reading series** have dominated the teaching of reading in North America since the early part of this century. These series generally consist of teacher's guides, student anthologies, student workbooks, and other materials such as tests, worksheets, audiotapes, and computer software. Goodman, Shannon, Freeman, and Murphy (1988) indicate that basal readers were developed in the first two decades of the twentieth century to reflect the learning theories and research of that time and a concern about the quality of reading instruction. The explicit instructions in teacher's guides and structured skill development for students were presented as a solution to this concern. The promoters of basal series believed that all teachers needed to do was follow the instructions in the guides and children would learn to read.

Although this promise of basal readers has never been realized, these series dominated reading instruction throughout most of the twentieth century, and their format changed very little. Goodman, Shannon, Freeman, and Murphy (1988) reported that more than 90 percent of elementary school teachers in the United States were still using basal reading series in the 1980s. An examination of provincial department of education guidelines in the early 1990s in Canada revealed that all provinces included lists of language arts series, although the trend was toward recommending rather than mandating their use (Gordon, 1991).

Initially, basal reading series in Canada were essentially Canadianized versions of series from the United States (Murphy, 1991). However, over the past twenty years, Canadian series have begun to be developed in this country, and they are quite different from those produced in the United States. One major difference is the attempt by Canadian publishers to produce integrated language arts series rather than focussing primarily on reading.

Another major difference is an attempt to include more children's literature. Basal reading series in the United States have been criticized for including so much material written specifically to teach reading. Even when children's literature is included, it is often adapted to such an extent that it is almost unrecognizable (Goodman, Shannon, Freeman, and Murphy, 1988). In contrast, many Canadian series have made an effort to offer high-quality children's literature. Murphy (1991) analyzed five series that were authorized widely across the country in the early 1990s, to determine how much children's literature was actually incorporated. Beyond the Grade 1 level, she found that the Canadian series did contain a high proportion of reprinted children's literature, but at the Grade 1 level a considerable amount of material was written specifically for the series. While this material did not contain the controlled vocabulary of the basal series of the 1950s and 1960s, it did use predictable or repetitive patterns (note that these patterns did not occur in old series). Again, the result was that young children were exposed to limited, controlled material in the initial stages of learning to read.

Language arts series have continued to evolve in the 1990s. All still include teacher's guides, but rather than anthologies, many now provide children with many small books to read (e.g., Early Bird Collection, 1990; RefleXions, 1991). Few include workbooks or recommend use of worksheets. Some, such as MeadowBooks (1994), are packaged differently from the basal reading series of the past. In the MeadowBooks series, teacher's source books, theme library books, anthologies, cassettes, and activity cards are packaged into thematic kits. Supplementary materials include big books, an assessment guide, and a guide to help teachers develop children's word sense.

Regardless of whether language arts series are developed in Canada or the United States, they place considerable power and control in the hands of publishers rather than teachers and children (Shannon, 1989). Language arts series determine not only what children read, but also what teachers do with these materials. When these types of materials are used in language arts programs, the major challenge is for teachers and children to remain in charge of the programs, selecting from and adapting the materials provided rather than using them in a rigid, inflexible manner. This is not always easy to do.

The series are often intimidating, partly because they were developed by experts in language arts and cost a great deal to produce. Teacher's guides present many useful suggestions to help teachers promote active engagement and development of strategies. Indeed, they incorporate many of the instructional techniques recommended in this textbook. However, it is important to keep in mind that the experts who developed the materials are not familiar with the children in any one classroom. Teachers are the experts about the interests and needs of the children in their classrooms, and hence teachers are in the best position to critically examine the materials in language arts series to determine whether, when, and how they can be used to meet their students' needs.

## Trade Books

While language arts series are still widely recommended and used in Canada, most teachers who adopt these materials supplement them with trade books. This is what David Paul does in his classroom, exposing the children to a wide range of materials, not just a Canadian language arts series. Some teachers reject basal materials altogether and base their language arts program on children's literature.

The use of children's books either as the core of language arts programs or in addition to basal series has become so widespread that two chapters of this textbook were devoted to describing children's literature and how to use it in elementary classrooms. However, including children's literature in classrooms may not necessarily lead to a significant change in the nature of language arts instruction.

Jobe and Hart (1991, p. 147) have expressed concern about what they call "the basalization of children's literature." In other words, even when basal series are not being used, they may still influence what happens in classrooms. Jobe and Hart note that what many teachers are doing with children's books is very similar to what they did with stories in traditional basal reading materials. In novel studies, for example, many teachers still assign a chapter to be read and ten questions to be answered, develop fill-in-the-blank worksheet exercises about the stories, and ask children to define words on a list from the story and use them in a sentence. Jobe and Hart suggest that there is still a "dominant feeling that teachers have the answers and the kids must guess what they think" (1991, p. 147).

## Nonbook Resources

Sometimes we imply to children through what we do and say that books are the only legitimate source of reading materials. Yet, when we think about all the different items we read each day, books are only one of many reading sources. Some of the other items we read in a normal day include

- newspapers
- magazines
- TV guides
- brochures
- advertisements
- signs
- labels

If we want children to become literate and read widely for both information and pleasure, we need to ensure that they read a wide variety of materials in school.

Most young children are aware of print in their environment before they go to school. They know the sign for McDonald's, and they can identify their favourite cereal by looking at the box. When they begin school, they encounter print in their classrooms, including their names; the names of their classmates; the days of the week and months of the year on the calendar; words on tape recorders, computers, and other equipment; words on charts; and labels in work centres. By making this print the focus of instruction, teachers build on children's experiences with printed language and help children make use of it. In Chapter Three, we included suggestions to help teachers use **environmental print** to foster children's literacy learning.

For older children, the list of nonbook materials includes such items as

- pamphlets and brochures from a variety of sources (e.g., travel agencies, tourism bureaus, flyers, and advertisements)
- newspapers
- magazines
- material on the Internet and computer software

Because we are so inundated with advertisements trying to convince us to buy products, children benefit from learning to read these materials critically. For example, a Grade 6 class might discuss advertisements for jeans, discussing why the models are always young and attractive. A discussion of **critical literacy** was included in Chapter Five, with one section devoted to the detection of common propaganda devices used in advertisements and other materials.

Newspapers are a source of print that most of us read nearly every day. We read newspapers for both entertainment and information about current news and events in our area. We read them to decide where to shop for groceries and which movies to go to. Many local newspapers employ education specialists and provide newspapers and suggestions for their use to classroom teachers upon request.

There are also newspapers and magazines designed specifically for children. Materials are available at a range of reading levels and focus on a variety of areas, including outdoor life, science, and popular culture. Some of those available are listed in Box 14.1. These materials can be used for several instructional activities, particularly in relation to content area reading. They provide up-to-date information on a range of topics related both to curriculum and children's interests. Techniques for helping children construct meaning from informational material are presented in Chapter Five.

With the explosion of technology in classrooms, children are increasingly reading material on the Internet or in language arts software programs. Several of these programs are described in Chapter Thirteen, along with suggestions and cautions for their use. Like all other materials, those on the computer are only appropriate if they meet the needs of specific children in your classroom and are integrated into the curriculum.

---

**Box 14.1**  **Children's Periodicals**

**Let's Find Out and Storyworks**
- *Let's Find Out* (Kindergarten): Mini-books, news stories, classroom photo stories, activity pages.
- *Storyworks* (Grades 4 to 6): Fiction, nonfiction, poetry and classroom plays, interviews with authors, hands-on activities, student-written book reviews.
  Scholastic Canada Limited
  123 Newkirk Road
  Richmond Hill, ON  L4C 3G5
  http://www.scholastic.ca

**Ranger Rick**
Grades 4 to 6: Nonfiction, fiction, photo stories, activities, environmental tips about wildlife around the world.
  National Wildlife Federation
  PO Box 2049
  Harlan, IA  51593-0269

**National Geographic World**
Grades 4 to 6: Nonfiction, photo stories, activities for junior members of the National Geographic Society.
  National Geographic World
  PO Box 63001
  Tampa, FL  33663-3001

**Ladybug and Cricket**
- *Ladybug* (Kindergarten to Grade 3): Stories, poems, activities, songs, some nonfiction.
- *Cricket* (Grades 4 to 6): Stories, poems, activities, nonfiction.

Cricket Magazine Group
Box 300
Peru, IL  61354-9974
http://www.cricketmag.com

**Weekly Readers**
Several children's newspapers are available at a variety of age and grade levels.
  Xerox Educational Publications
  1250 Fairwood Ave.
  PO Box 444
  Columbus, OH  43216
  http://www.weeklyreader.com

**Chickadee and Owl**
- *Chickadee* (Ages 6 to 9) and *Chirp* (Ages 2 to 6): Stories, nonfiction, activities, posters.
- *Owl* (Ages 9 to 12): Nonfiction, activities, posters, comics.
  *Chirp, Chickadee,* and *Owl* Magazines
  PO Box 726 STN MAIN
  Markham, ON  L3P 0Z9

**Sesame Street and Kid City Magazines**
- *Sesame Street Magazine* (Ages 2 to 6): Stories, poems, activities, posters, children's drawing and writing.
- *Kid City Magazine* (Ages 6 to 9): Stories, puzzles, word games, projects.
  Children's Television Workshop
  PO Box 55518
  Boulder, CO  80328-5518
  http://www.ctw.org

# Selecting a Range of Topics and Materials

Whether or not teachers use a basal series as part of the language arts program, we recommend that a wide range of printed materials be available in classrooms. By including materials that cover a range of reading levels, all children have the opportunity to read both challenging and independent material every day. Having material on a range of topics and cultures provides at least some material related to each child's interests.

From the available materials, we recommend that children be allowed to choose at least some of the fiction and nonfiction books they read. When all materials are selected by someone else (the publisher or teacher), children do not gain a sense of ownership or control over their own reading. They often feel that they are reading for someone else rather than for themselves. David Paul gives children in his classroom control over what they read by allocating fifteen minutes every day to Drop Everything and Read (DEAR) right after lunch. This is a time when all the students read books of their own choice.

Similarly, children need opportunities to write on topics of their own choice. Not only does this take advantage of the unique knowledge and experience that each child brings to the classroom, but it also helps children feel like writers. If children learn to rely on story starters to serve as a beginning point for their writing, they may not develop a sense that their writing belongs to them. This does not mean that teachers will never assign specific books or topics, but that at least some of the time children can select what they read and write. On the day described at the beginning of this chapter, David Paul selected a writing topic to help children learn how to brainstorm and organize ideas before writing. When writing independently, the children wrote on topics of their own choice.

However, providing children with opportunities to make choices leads to many questions:

- What range of topics and materials is appropriate?
- Should children be allowed or encouraged to write about any topic they want in the classroom?
- Should children be allowed to read anything they want? For example, should comic books or Stephen King novels be considered acceptable classroom reading?

Mitchell and Cheverie (1989) discuss taste and sensibility in what children read and write. While provincial departments of education examine textbooks in relation to sexist, ageist, and racist guidelines, Mitchell and Cheverie suggest that teachers are on their own when it comes to issues of ethics, aesthetics, taste, and sensibility in the content of children's writing. What should teachers do, they ask, when children write "stories that contain excessive violence, a senseless slaughter of a kangaroo, the torture and torment of an alley cat, a play-by-play description of a violent television show or rock video" (p. 184)? What should teachers do when children write about problems at home such as divorce and abuse?

There are legal guidelines for teachers in handling knowledge or suspicion of abuse. Not so clear, however, is the role of teachers in managing a child's "right to write" and his or her socialization and moral development. Mitchell and Cheverie suggest that rather than censoring children's writing, teachers should use it as a basis for discussing issues of ethics, aesthetics, taste, and sensibility. With the rising spectre of school violence, it is becoming increasingly important for teachers to think through how such issues are to be handled. Some teachers set simple guidelines such as "No gore allowed."

# Thematic Organization

The most common way language arts materials are organized is according to themes. This organization is evident in most of the language arts series developed in Canada, with suggestions for teachers to provide children with opportunities to talk, read, and write about each theme. These themes often transcend the language arts period and are integrated into other subjects discussed during the day.

One advantage of **thematic organization** involves the transfer of knowledge and skills from one context to another. Another advantage is the opportunity for children to examine a topic more closely, going beyond the superficial to develop in-depth conceptual ways of thinking about information. In addition, by selecting books on a common topic at a variety of reading levels, the needs of learners at varying levels of reading proficiency can be met. Thematic organization also leads to opportunities for children to work co-operatively on a common topic or problem. However, themes are not the only way to organize language arts programs. In *Waves* (1992), for example, material is organized by genre. For each level, one book is devoted to science material, another to poetry, and others to folk tales and novels.

When considering whether to organize materials thematically, teachers also need to be aware of some potential disadvantages. One is that even when the teacher selects the theme in consultation with the children in the classroom, some children will be more interested in it and have a greater sense of ownership than others. Choosing broad themes rather than narrow topics is one way to get around this problem (e.g., not dinosaurs, but things larger than life). Another potential problem is that the theme might take precedence over curriculum concerns, with the result that goals in a specific subject area become secondary in importance. The most sensible approach is to make links when appropriate, but not to force links that distort curriculum goals or fail to serve children's learning needs.

Thus, while there are many advantages to thematic organization, several factors must be taken into account when planning thematic units. The most important of these is children's learning needs, but other factors include mandated outcomes, available resources, and district initiatives.

The vignette presented in Box 14.2 shows how one first-grade teacher organized most of her program thematically to provide her students with a continuous, integrated learning experience. She used a wide variety of materials and activities to meet the range of interests, learning styles, and learning needs she had identified through assessing the children. However, not all of her program was related to themes; she moved away from them at times to achieve specific learning goals and to meet the needs of individual children.

---

**Box 14.2**    **One Day in a Thematically Organized Grade 1 Classroom**

On the day of our visit to Theresa Pond's Grade 1 classroom, the children were working on the theme "myself and my friends," focussing on their body as part of the "Physical Me" aspect of the unit. Theresa planned activities related to this theme in all areas of the curriculum.

When the children arrived at school in the morning, they put their coats beside life-sized pictures of themselves that they had drawn and painted and that were hung next to their coat hooks. The children then worked in a circle group to discuss and group parts of the body. Theresa printed the names of the body parts on the chalk board, and the children read them. In mathematics, the children counted fingers and toes, and added and subtracted them. They then drew their friend's head and put a name on it.

*(continued)*

**Box 14.2**   **Continued**

Thematic work was discontinued at that point in the school day, and the children read individually from books in the classroom library. Everyone in the classroom read, including the teacher. Theresa then drew the children back together to reflect on what they had accomplished during the morning.

At that point, the school principal arrived. She lay down on a large piece of paper, and the children traced her outline. While they were doing this, the teacher asked them to think about body parts and what each part could do. When the outline was complete, the children discussed what each body part does. Hands, for example, are used for touching, patting, writing, dropping, and even doing handstands. Each body part was labelled, and each action was put on a card. These cards were then used in a learning game, where children put each part into action.

Following this, Theresa read the children a book called *Eyes Can*. As the final activity before lunch, each child drew an eye, and they discussed what the eye can do. This was followed by the children tidying up the classroom, made easier by the "mailboxes" hung on chair-backs and the trays set on each table for pencils and glue.

What we saw that day in Theresa's classroom was just the tip of the iceberg. What we did not see was the extensive and careful planning that went into each of the thematic units in her program. She began by selecting materials about the theme, choosing core books, and developing objectives related to the materials she had selected and the needs and interests of the children. She extracted main concepts and key vocabulary to develop tasks and activities across the curriculum.

At the time of our visit, Theresa was using semantic maps to organize the overall unit and daily lessons related to each aspect of the theme. On these semantic maps, she included the curriculum areas involved and the objectives she hoped to achieve in each area. When she completed graduate work on learning styles, she began to integrate this knowledge into the design of learning activities. Students were provided with opportunities to work on tasks consistent with their preferred learning style, and to try different ways of learning and thinking. Evaluation was based on an analysis of process and product using observation and questioning of the children. In this way, Theresa was able to assess the learning of each child while also planning the next thematic unit in her program.

Some teachers spend a great deal of time searching for the "perfect" book or other material to use with children in their classrooms. Although materials do vary in quality, it is *how* materials are used that determines whether children's language growth is maximized.

## Scheduling Time

Time is a very precious resource. There is never enough of it to do everything that needs to be done to meet children's needs. In this section, we begin by discussing the advantages and disadvantages of organizing language arts instruction in long versus short time blocks. We then present general guidelines for allocating time in classrooms for both younger and older students.

### Length of Time Blocks

In allocating time, teachers are faced with deciding whether to divide language arts into a series of separate time periods devoted to different aspects of language arts, or to designate large time blocks for language arts and organize a range of activities within these blocks.

#### Short Time Blocks

A major advantage of short time blocks is accountability: it is relatively easy to account for how much time has been spent on each aspect of the language arts curriculum. For example, if parents are concerned about spelling, you can assure them that a certain number of minutes are devoted exclusively to spelling instruction every week. This way of allocating time also provides a great deal of predictability for the children. They know what they will be doing at each point during the school day.

There are, however, also several disadvantages to organizing different aspects of language arts into separate time slots. First, it does little to foster links between talking, reading, and writing. For example, when phonics is taught in a separate ten-minute block each day, some children will not see its relevance for writing or reading. Second, separate time blocks make it difficult for the teacher to pursue children's needs and interests as they arise in the classroom. Instead of teaching children a strategy when they need it, the teaching is put on hold until the appropriate time in the school day. In addition, just when children get really interested in a topic they are discussing, it is often time to switch to another subject area. Third, short time blocks necessitate many changes in activity during the day, and a considerable amount of time is lost during transitions between activities. Children may spend up to 20 percent of the time allocated to language arts in transition between activities (Benterud, 1983).

## Long Time Blocks

An alternative to short time blocks is to organize one or two larger daily time blocks for language arts and to include language learning opportunities in other subject areas as well. The major disadvantage of this type of organization is the difficulty of balancing time spent on each area of the language arts. Careful planning and record-keeping are necessary to ensure that each child receives a balanced language arts program. However, the advantages far outweigh the disadvantages. There is more flexibility to pursue children's interests and learning needs. Activities are not cut off while children are still engaged in meaningful learning, nor are activities prolonged to fill a predetermined time slot when children are no longer interested or learning.

# Whole Class, Small Group, and Individual Activities

In the 1960s and 1970s, children spent most of the time allocated to reading instruction working in achievement groups or completing seat work. Today, many teachers devote at least some time to large group instruction.

Wiseman (1992) recommends two types of activities for use with the whole class: instructional or focus time, and sharing time. At the beginning of each day, many teachers bring children together to explain what they will do for the day. Some give children an opportunity to be involved in planning, and help them to set goals for their own learning.

Many teachers also teach a strategy or introduce a new genre to the whole class. In the example at the beginning of this chapter, David Paul used a minimal-cues message to teach strategies for identifying words to all the children in his class. He also read a poem to the class and had the children brainstorm ideas for a writing project. The amount of time spent on large group instruction varies with the day and needs of the children. Sharing time near the end of the language arts time block gives children an opportunity to talk about what they have accomplished and to evaluate their learning. They may discuss books they have read, read aloud what they have written, or talk about what they have learned. This provides the children and the teacher with an opportunity to evaluate the effectiveness of instruction and serves as the basis for planning the next day's objectives and activities.

While fewer teachers organize reading ability groups today than in the past, small groups are still an important feature of language arts classrooms. Fountas and Pinnell (1996) recommend dynamic rather than the fixed-ability groups of the past. In David Paul's classroom, children spend at least part of every language arts period in small groups, with support provided by the teacher when needed.

As indicated earlier in this chapter, children need to read and write independently every day, and during at least some of this time they need to be in control of what they read and write. In David Paul's classroom, time is set aside every day to drop everything and read. During this time, children select books of their own choice and read to themselves. Some sit at their desks, while others sit on pillows at the back of the room. David also reads, because he knows that he is a significant model for his students. He demonstrates his commitment to independent reading by allocating time for it and by reading himself during this time.

## Time Guidelines

Each teacher's actual daily timetable will depend on many factors, including the requirements of the school system or provincial department of education; the philosophy of the school; times allocated for recess, lunch break, gym, and library; the grade level involved; and children's learning needs. Some general guidelines for allocating time are provided in Tables 14.1 and 14.2.

**Table 14.1**  Guidelines for Allocating Time in Primary Language Arts

| Activities* | Kindergarten to Beginning Grade 1 | Grades 1 to 3 |
|---|---|---|
| Opening and closing routines | 10–15 minutes | 15–25 minutes |
| Reading to children | 10–15 minutes | 10–20 minutes |
| Shared reading and writing | 20–30 minutes | 10–15 minutes |
| Reading and writing instruction | 20–30 minutes | 40–60 minutes |
| Independent reading | 10–15 minutes | 15–30 minutes |
| Independent writing | 10–15 minutes | 15–30 minutes |

* These are scheduled daily. Other activities such as drama are scheduled less frequently.

**Table 14.2**  Guidelines for Allocating Time in Upper Elementary Language Arts

| Activities | Frequency | Time Allocation |
|---|---|---|
| Reading to children | Daily | 15–20 minutes |
| Independent reading | Daily | 20–30 minutes |
| Reading instruction | 2 or 3 times each week | 20–30 minutes |
| Writing instruction | 2 or 3 times each week | 30–40 minutes |
| Independent writing | 2 or 3 times each week | 20–30 minutes |
| Other activities* | Once each week | 15–20 minutes |

* Sharing a piece of reading or writing, reading with a buddy, and drama.

Cunningham and Allington (1999) suggest organizing instruction into four time blocks for language arts each day, in addition to including times for opening routines and summary activities. The four blocks they specify are for

- guided reading
- self-selected reading
- writing
- working with words

The guided reading component involves instruction to help children develop and use strategies as they read. The self-selected reading component involves the teacher reading aloud to children, shared reading, and children reading independently. The writing component involves shared writing, writer's workshop, and independent writing (Fountas and Pinnell, 1996).

Although most activities are completed every day in primary classrooms, some are completed less frequently with upper elementary students because older children often require longer time blocks for activities. The following guidelines are adapted from those presented by Cunningham and Allington (1999):

- *Every day*. Teacher reads aloud to students, and children read independently.
- *Two or three times a week*. Teacher leads guided reading, guided writing (writer's workshop), and working with words, and children write independently.
- *Once a week*. Children share something they have written or have read, read to or with a younger child, and do research related to their topic.
- *Once a month*. Children edit and publish something they have written.

It is important to keep in mind when using the guidelines in either Table 14.1 or 14.2 that the times recommended extend across subject boundaries, since language use is involved in all areas of the curriculum. This is particularly true at the upper elementary level, where a considerable amount of the reading and writing children do relates to social studies and science units.

As with everything else in language arts, there is no one best time schedule for all classrooms. We recommend that time schedules be used in a flexible way, extending the time for activities when children are obviously learning and discontinuing activities when they are not. The goal is to consistently provide the types of learning experiences described above without becoming a slave to your time schedule.

## Organizing Space

You will not have much control over the amount of space or type of equipment or furniture in your classroom, but you do have control over how that space and furniture are arranged. The physical arrangement of the classroom reflects the goals and philosophy of your language arts program.

In social constructivist classrooms, space is organized to facilitate

- children working together as a whole class,
- children working together in groups, and
- children working independently.

Reading and writing materials are also easily accessible.

## Whole Class Activities

The children's desks in David Paul's classroom are organized in rows. He uses this physical arrangement at the beginning of the day for large group instruction when children discuss the minimal cues message on the chalkboard. On the day described, he then asked the children to push aside the desks in the middle of the room to create a space for them to sit on the floor while he read them the poem. He preferred this arrangement so the children would be closer to the book and to one another.

In some classrooms, a rug in one corner provides a place for children to come together for whole class discussions, to listen to their teacher read, and to share what they have accomplished. Children can also be organized for whole class activities by having their desks placed together in groups, as shown in Figure 14.1, so that everyone can view the board and screen. Tables can easily replace groups of desks in this arrangement.

## Small Group Activities

In David Paul's classroom, children work together in groups in many different locations:

- They play learning games at a table placed at the perimeter of the room.
- They sit together in pairs on the floor or at adjacent desks to read books to one another.
- On the day recounted, a small group joined the teacher at a table for a lesson using the directed reading–thinking activity.

Group work encourages children to work co-operatively and provides opportunities for oral language development. The classroom organization depicted in Figure 14.1 places a high value on children working together. In addition to organizing desks in groups, a table on one side provides a place for children to come together to work with the teacher or to work with one another on projects.

**Figure 14.1**    **Physical Arrangement of the Classroom**

1. Chalkboard with pulldown overhead screen
2. Storage
3. Teacher's desk
4. Students' desks in groups
5. Storage
6. Centre
7. Small group meeting area
8. Writing centre
9. Display
10. Computer station
11. Listening centre
12. Reading centre

Learning centres are another way that teachers provide opportunities for children to work together in groups. Some centres, such as reading or writing centres, are permanent. Reading centres generally include a classroom library; comfortable rugs, chairs, or cushions; and often a listening centre with taped stories. Morrow (1989) recommends that

- materials selected for reading centres appeal to a variety of interests,
- materials be at a range of reading levels,
- materials include all the types of children's literature described in Chapter Ten, as well as newpapers and magazines,
- new books and materials be introduced to the centre regularly to ensure continued interest, and
- children be involved in planning and managing the reading centre, developing rules for its use, naming it, and keeping it neat.

Writing centres often include a display area for children's writing, materials for writing, and at least one computer and printer. Morrow (1989) also recommends including materials for making books, and placing books made by children in the reading centre to share with other children.

Other centres are less permanent, often being set up on a thematic basis related to topics in social studies, science, and other subject areas. While learning centres can be very useful in facilitating children's language development and co-operative learning, one caution is in order. Sometimes centres seem to be valued for their own sake rather than for how they contribute to learning and curricular goals. As with computers and other instructional tools, learning centres need to be integrated into the curriculum to maximize their usefulness.

## Individual Activities

In David Paul's classroom, most independent activities are completed by children at their desks. Having desks arranged in rows facilitates independent work, although children are still able to consult with their neighbour if they need help. The children in David's classroom also often find a quiet space on the floor when they are working independently.

While the classroom depicted in Figure 14.1 is more conducive to small group than individual work, children do have individual desks, and there are many spaces around the perimeter of the room where children can go to work alone. The reading centre, in particular, is appropriate for both group and individual reading.

## Organizing Children for Learning

When you were in the primary grades, it is likely that you were a member of one of three reading groups for reading instruction: the high group, the middle group, or the low group. Teachers set these groups up to reduce the extent of individual differences in reading ability and to adjust instruction to the needs of the group. When the teacher was not working with your group, you likely completed workbook pages or worksheets. Some people refer to this as a "three-ring circus."

In a review of literature on grouping practices, Barr and Dreeben (1991) note that, in the primary grades, most reading instruction is provided in ability groups, while in the intermediate grades, whole class instruction is dominant. When grouping children for instruction, Fountas and Pinnell (1996) recommend that teachers keep the following assumptions in mind:

- There is a wide range of experience, knowledge, and skills among any group of elementary children.
- Every child is different from every other child in some knowledge and skill.
- Children progress at different rates.

For these reasons, we recommend that children be organized in different ways throughout the school day.

## Whole Class Instruction

There are several advantages of whole class instruction. Talking and working together as a whole class helps to develop a community of learners — a community in which children help and respect one another. Children learn a great deal from one another. This learning is enhanced when children are provided with the opportunity to interact with others of differing abilities rather than only with those at a similar level of language achievement. Whole class instruction is also an efficient use of teacher time. When introducing children to a new theme or strategy, it is more efficient to work with all of them at the same time than to teach the same thing to each child individually. Because of individual differences in language development and needs, however, whole class instruction needs to be supplemented with other ways of organizing children.

## Grouping Children for Instruction

### Ability Grouping

The most common basis for organizing children into groups for reading instruction has been reading ability (Barr and Dreeben, 1991). Within schools, this involves assigning children to classes on the basis of their achievement scores or regrouping children from different classrooms together for language arts instruction. In the latter grouping pattern, children who achieve similar scores on achievement tests are brought together regardless of their age or number of years in school. Within classrooms, children are placed in ability groups for reading instruction, and sometimes these groups are maintained in other areas of language arts as well. Whether at the school or the classroom level, the major purpose of this type of grouping is to produce a more homogeneous group in terms of reading needs, making it easier for the teacher to plan and give appropriate instruction.

Despite the long history of ability grouping, recent reviews of research about it have produced few conclusive findings to either support or refute its impact on reading achievement. As a result, many educators are now questioning the value of this grouping practice (e.g., Barr and Dreeben, 1991; Indrisano and Paratore, 1991). Ability grouping may offer some advantage to academically gifted students, but results are far from clear even for this group and questionable for average- and low-ability groups. Even when teachers are very careful in the names they select for different groups, children know which group is high and which is low. This has negative implications for the self-esteem of children in the low group.

Researchers have also investigated whether children are taught reading differently in high-ability as compared with low-ability groups. Again the findings are inconsistent, although some studies indicate a stronger focus on decoding for low-ability students, more emphasis on critical thinking for high-ability students, and a lower rate of engaged time for low-ability students (Indrisano and Paratore, 1991). In light of these findings, ability grouping has come under considerable criticism. Some teachers have abandoned the practice, moving to whole class instruction instead.

While this solves the problems created by ability grouping, it does not meet the need of children to receive reading and writing instruction in their zone of proximal development. In order to meet this need, Fountas and Pinnell (1996) recommend combining grouping by similar reading abilities and text level with a wide range of other types of heterogeneous groups. They feel that grouping children on the basis of reading skill and experience is required for guided reading to be effective, but that in contrast to traditional ability grouping, these groups need to be dynamic. Any grouping is tentative and subject to change based on observations of the children's progress during instruction. These groups are more permanent than the skill needs groups described below, but far less fixed than the traditional so-called three-ring circus. And, perhaps most importantly, children are grouped in other ways for the remainder of their language arts instruction.

## Other Ways to Group Children

In the classroom described at the beginning of this chapter, David Paul organized children into interest groups, research groups, special needs groups, and pairs. All these groupings are far less permanent than ability groups. Interest groups in his classroom are sometimes set up for one day, for example, when children come together to play a game. Other groups, such as the one working on the puppet play, stay together for several days.

Interest groups are generally made up of children at different ability levels. They tend to exist for a relatively short time, disbanding when their purpose has been achieved.

Research groups are similar to interest groups in that they are temporary, although teachers are generally instrumental in a research group's formation. In addition, the focus of the research group is on a topic that the children research rather than on completing an activity or pursuing an interest. Often the teacher and students together set specific goals, and a written or oral presentation is produced at the end. Like interest groups, these groups are frequently composed of children of varying ability levels.

Special needs groups are set up for different reasons than interest or research groups. Through careful classroom observation, teachers identify an aspect of reading, writing, listening, or talking in which several children need help. David Paul identified several children who needed to make greater use of their own knowledge as they read. He brought these children together into a small group for a few lessons to help them understand the importance of their knowledge and develop strategies for using it as they read. Once the objectives for special needs instruction have been met, these groups are disbanded.

In collaborative pairs, children work together on a common activity, helping one another at points of difficulty. David organized the children in his classroom into collaborative pairs for part of the language arts time. Each pair found a space and shared books. While one child read, the other listened. This gave each child much more reading practice than is the case when children read orally in groups or the whole class. Because the children chose the books themselves, the books interested them and were

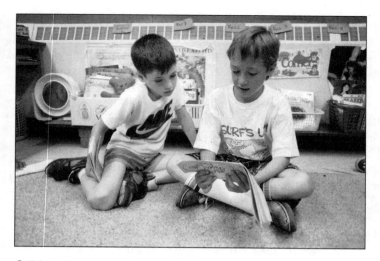

Collaborative pair: two Grade 3 children reading a book together.

also at an appropriate level. Collaborative pairs are also appropriate for other types of activities, such as problem solving and writing (Indrisano and Paratore, 1991).

A more common way of organizing children into pairs involves peer tutoring, either with same-age or cross-age dyads. Generally, a more proficient reader or writer is paired with one who is less proficient, and they complete a specific activity designed to facilitate skill development. This type of pairing can also be used when children need to access information from a common text in social studies or science. The child who has developed sufficient skills and strategies to construct meaning from the text reads it to the child who has not yet reached this level of reading proficiency. Another type of activity that is appropriate for peer tutoring is paired reading (see Chapter Six). As with most types of grouping, research has yielded conflicting results on peer tutoring, although it works best when programs are structured, short in duration, and focussed on specific skills (Indrisano and Paratore, 1991). According to Topping (1989), both the child being tutored and the one doing the tutoring benefit from the experience.

## Co-operative Learning

Many of the groupings described above lend themselves well to co-operative learning. Slavin (1980, p. 315) defines co-operative learning as a technique in which "students work on learning activities in small groups and receive rewards or recognition based on their group's performance." Golub (1994) provides several examples of co-operative groups in the language arts classroom. In one scenario, two students work together to complete a writing task, discussing what they will say and how they will say it. When they finish writing, they hand in one paper with both names on it. In another scenario, a group of students attempting to make sense of a poem first jots down questions about the poem and then discusses and shares different interpretations. The understanding the students come to as a group is different and often deeper than most children could have constructed individually. Still another example involves different students completing different parts of the same project and meeting regularly to discuss what they are doing. Again, one paper is handed in as a result of this work.

Co-operative learning changes the traditional authority structure of classrooms by placing more control in the hands of children. Another major difference is that, instead of each child being evaluated individually, children work together and are evaluated as a group. This encourages them to work co-operatively rather than competitively (which happens when teachers organize children into groups but still base rewards on individual achievement). Some of the additional benefits claimed for co-operative learning groups include (Mayfield, 1992)

- increased exchange of ideas,
- development of social skills,
- wider acceptance and respect for other children, and
- increased learning.

## Individual Reading and Writing

There is little doubt that children need classroom time to read and write in order to become good readers and writers. It is not enough to allow children to select a book for reading or to write something of their own choice after they complete their other work, or to suggest that they do these types of activities at home. Independent reading and writing must be scheduled into each school day.

> There is no one magic way to organize children so that all their needs are met all the time. The key to effective classroom organization is flexibility in organizing materials, time, space, and children. The challenge of organizing an effective language arts program becomes even greater when the learning needs of children considered by many to be at-risk are taken into account. The next section of this chapter focusses on the wide range of children in today's classrooms.

## Meeting the Needs of All Children

> We have recommended throughout this text that the goal of language arts teachers is to maximize the language learning of *all* children in their classrooms. Whether the children live in poverty, speak English as a second language, are members of a visible minority, or are labelled as having learning problems, the teacher's task is essentially the same — to figure out each child's learning needs and match instruction to these needs. Rather than focussing on what's "wrong" with children (a deficit view), we begin this section by suggesting that all labels are socially constructed.

The fact that labels change across time is one indication of their social nature. In the 1960s, for example, terms such as "emotional disturbance," "mental retardation," "cultural deprivation," and "neurological dysfunction" were widely used to label children who experienced difficulties learning in schools. Programs were funded to meet the needs of children given these labels. Included were compensatory programs for children living in poverty and labelled culturally deprived.

With the advent of the learning disabilities explanation for reading problems in the 1970s, compensatory programs for children from poor homes were replaced with remedial programs. Most definitions of learning disabilities had clauses that excluded children with sensory deficits, mental handicaps, or cultural deprivation from the learning disabilities category. These clauses effectively prevented most minority children from accessing remedial reading programs provided through learning disabilities funding.

The socio-political nature of learning differences is also reflected in changes in the way services have been provided for at-risk children. For many years, segregated classrooms and schools were the most prevalent and preferred system for educating these students. Children were labelled according to conditions (e.g., mental, physical, emotional, cultural, and learning deficits), and placement was based on this categorization. Some children with severe disabilities were denied education in publicly funded schools. However, in the mid-1970s, legislation was passed in the United States protecting the rights of individuals with disabilities. Since then there has been a sharp movement away from segregated classes and toward educating children in the "least restrictive environment" (Wilson and Cleland, 1985, p. 331).

The impact of this legislation has been felt in Canada, resulting in several provinces passing laws that require school boards to provide education for all students (Crealock and Bachor, 1995). There has also been a strong trend in Canadian classrooms away from segregation to **mainstreaming** for special needs children. Students are integrated for either all or part of the school day for instruction in regular classrooms.

Benefits of mainstreaming have been proposed for special needs children, other children in regular classes, and teachers. These potential advantages, as well as some disadvantages, are summarized in Box 14.3. As Crealock and Bachor (1995) indicate, the benefits of mainstreaming will not be attained if special needs children are simply dumped into regular classrooms with no support for either the teacher or the students. Support services and resources are needed to help teachers handle the increased workload involved in teaching a wider range of children.

The majority of at-risk students in schools are those with non-mainstream cultural backgrounds, a first language other than English, and mild disabilities. Children with visual impairments, hearing impairments, and severe mental disabilities make up a minority of special needs students. When they are placed in regular classrooms, we recommend that teachers collaborate with specialists to develop appropriate language learning programs for them. The remainder of this section focusses on

- children from non-mainstream backgrounds,
- those who are learning English as a second language, and
- those with mild disabilities.

## Non-Mainstream Backgrounds

As indicated in Chapter One, there is considerable evidence that literacy is related to socio-cultural variables. Literacy levels are lower among the poor than the rich, among rural than urban populations, and among minorities.

Jacobs and Jordan (1993) outline several explanations that have been given to account for the relative lack of success of children from non-mainstream homes in our schools. Most explanations place the responsibility for low school achievement on the cultural groups themselves. One explanation, now widely discredited, claimed that

---

**Box 14.3**   **Advantages and Disadvantages of Mainstreaming**

**Potential Advantages**

Children with Learning Differences
- greater independence
- more acceptance from others
- more positive self-concepts

Other Children
- expansion of awareness of individual differences
- positive attitudes toward handicapped students
- appreciation that all students can learn from one another

Teachers
- positive attitudes toward exceptional learners
- larger repertoire of instructional strategies

**Potential Disadvantages**
- decreased self-concept for children with learning differences unless instruction is adjusted to ensure success
- reduced instructional time for other children in the classroom if no additional support is provided to the teacher
- increased workload for the teacher

Source: Based on ideas presented by C. Crealock and D. Bachor (1995), *Instructional Strategies for Students with Special Needs*, pp. 6–7. Scarborough, ON: Allyn & Bacon Canada.

social class and IQ were largely the result of genetic differences. A more widely held view is that the child's home and community may be at fault by failing to provide the experiences, attitudes, and values the child needs to succeed in school. As a result, proponents of this explanation believe that children arrive at school with deficient language and cognitive development.

Both of these views have been reflected in a century of Aboriginal education in the United States and Canada (Deyhle and Swisher, 1997). Although there is considerable research to show that First Nations children are not inherently inferior, attitudes and beliefs of inferiority continue to contribute to a self-fulfilling prophesy for many of these children. The notion of cultural deprivation, a term that came into vogue in the 1960s, persists in the minds of many educators and has fuelled assimilationist solutions such as boarding schools and immersion of First Nations children in public schools. Nearly all research on Aboriginal education has focussed on students and their homes, with little attention being paid to schools or teachers.

This is also true for children living in poverty. A coalition of nineteen groups concerned about poverty in Canada states:

> Our kids are not deficient. They are simply different. By blaming the parents and children, these deficit theories divert attention from the education system and how it operates to produce certain outcomes, including failure. (End Legislated Poverty, 1993, p. 137)

Rather than blaming minority groups for the apparent shortcomings that children bring to school, social constructivists shift the focus to schools and society. Schools are seen as reproducing hierarchical social relationships and streaming groups into different economic slots. Those who hold this viewpoint claim that schools contribute to inequality by valuing the cultural capital (ways of talking, acting, and socializing) of mainstream children while devaluing that of others. According to Ogbu (1993), as non-mainstream children grow older and recognize inequalities within the school and restricted job opportunities in society, many demonstrate resistance to mainstream values and drop out of school. However, Deyhle and Swisher (1997) indicate that some First Nations students report feeling "pushed out" of schools.

One way the education system operates to produce unequal opportunities for learning is by ignoring discontinuities between ways language is used in the homes of non-mainstream children and at school. As Cazden (1988, p. 67) notes:

> In some of its aspects, the demands of classroom discourse are new to all children. In the classroom, the group is larger than even the largest family gathered at meals, and so getting a turn to talk is much harder. When one does get a turn, acceptable topics for talk are more restricted and more predetermined by someone else.... But beyond these commonalties, some children may be at a special disadvantage. For some children there will be greater cultural discontinuity, greater sociolinguistic interference, between home and school.

There are several ways that teachers can reduce the mismatch between the culture of the school and that of non-mainstream groups. A relatively easy way is to ensure that the literature in the classroom reflects the range of cultural backgrounds of the children. Inviting adults from the community into the classroom to share their knowledge and experiences also helps to reduce discontinuity. However, although a culturally sensitive curriculum is important, it is not the sole key to increasing school success. More important, yet more difficult, is the need to change the expectations of teachers and others in positions of authority toward children of different races, cultures, and social class.

In their study of low-income families in one American neighbourhood, Taylor and Dorsey-Gaines (1988) painted a picture of adaptation and survival rather than failure and deficiency. Despite inadequate housing, lack of essential services, limited access to higher education, and restricted job opportunities, the families they studied not only survived, but were active members in a literate society. Taylor and Dorsey-Gaines (p. 202) argue that "The myths and stereotypes that create images of specific groups … have no relevance when we stop counting and start observing and working with people." This is the perspective of teachers who work within a social constructive framework — they value rather than attempt to obliterate differences. They also expect children from diverse cultural backgrounds to be successful at school. By focussing on the special attributes and talents of each child, socio-cultural differences are seen in a positive rather than negative light.

## Limited English-Language Facility

Canada's current immigration policy is producing a steady flow of non–English-speaking immigrants into the country. It is likely that teachers at some point in their careers will have children with limited or no English language proficiency in their classrooms. For all children learning English as their second language (ESL), the goal of instruction is twofold: to help them learn English and to help them move ahead cognitively (Allen, 1991).

However, there is controversy regarding the role of first-language instruction in programs for these learners. Most language experts recommend that initial literacy instruction be provided in a learner's first language (e.g., Hudelson, 1987; Allen, 1991), and some earlier research supports this position (Rosier and Holm, 1980; Campos and Keatinge, 1984). To take advantage of language knowledge and abilities children bring to school, immersion and bilingual classrooms have been set up across the country to enable children whose first language is not English to learn to read and write in languages such as Spanish, German, Arabic, Cree, and Mandarin. However, not all beginning readers with limited English proficiency have access to these classrooms. The others are immersed in classrooms where English is the language of instruction, often without any special assistance to support them as they learn English.

Perhaps most crucial is that teachers immerse children in meaningful language experiences. This can be facilitated by

- selecting reading materials written with natural language patterns rather than contrived material with limited vocabulary,
- using visual aids such as pictures and films, as well as gestures and facial expressions, to clarify meaning,
- building in comprehension checks and responding to requests for clarification (Pica, Young, and Doughty, 1987),
- providing language instruction in a meaningful context (e.g., a learning centre set up as a store), and
- providing opportunities for children to work together in pairs and small groups with their English-speaking peers on meaningful tasks that involve purposeful talk.

It is unclear whether speaking more slowly or pausing between sentences, clauses, and phrases assists low-proficiency English speakers (Derwing, 1990).

Shared reading provides a rich context for the literacy learning of children with limited English proficiency. Big books are ideal to use with these children because of the support given by pictures. It is important to point to pictures during discussion of the story to help children link meaning to words being used in the story. Picture story books (listed in Chapter Ten) also provide a rich resource for helping children develop language and literacy knowledge. By watching the teacher run his or her finger under the printed words during reading, children who have been exposed to different writing systems (e.g., Mandarin or Hebrew) develop an understanding about the directional characteristics of the English language.

## Learning Differences

As noted above, all labels for learning differences are socially constructed, and the term *learning disabilities* is no exception. The notion of learning disabilities can be traced back to the work of James Hinshelwood who, in the late 1800s, began to study and write about what he called "congenital word-blindness." He hypothesized that the source of learning problems lay in children's brains, and this view persists to this day in spite of evidence to the contrary (Coles, 1987). In the 1920s, Orton replaced the term congenital word-blindness with "strephosymbolia" (mixed symbols), and this term was, in turn, replaced by *dyslexia*. In the 1960s, "learning disabilities" began to be used widely by educators, as it continues to be used today. The term "dyslexia" is used primarily by medical practitioners. Both terms, however, reflect the medical model: a problem needs to be labelled to indicate what's wrong with an individual before appropriate treatment can be prescribed. Indeed, in medicine, treatment follows logically from a diagnosis. If individuals have a bacterial infection, a doctor prescribes antibiotics and they get better. This is not the case for children who have difficulty learning to read. Being labelled with dyslexia does not lead directly to one's treatment, but it does have some other results.

For the child and the child's parents, the terms dyslexia and learning disability are both a help and a hindrance. On the one hand, the terms help parents feel that they did not do anything wrong in raising their children and give them a sense that they finally have an answer to the frustrating question of why their child is having difficulty learning to read. The terms also replace more derogatory labels such as "dumb," "lazy," or "bad."

On the other hand, because conditions such as dyslexia and a learning disability are viewed as relatively permanent, people view themselves as deficient learners for the rest of their lives. Hence, while the label might bring relief in the short term, it can be devastating for some individuals in the long term. Another problem involves the locus of responsibility for the problem. What the learning disabilities movement has done is remove the spotlight from society (homes, communities, and schools) and placed it squarely on the child. From this perspective, there is little need to consider the effectiveness of the school programs children are in or the social conditions they live in (Coles, 1987). According to Giroux (1987), the label also results in lowered expectations for at-risk learners that, in turn, result in further disempowerment as schools fail to give them the knowledge they need to deal with their everyday lives.

Instead of placing the responsibility for reading problems within children's heads, it appears that reading difficulties have multiple causes, including factors both within and outside of children. The combination of factors is somewhat different for each child who has difficulty learning to read. The effects of these factors also vary, from children who are word-callers (pronouncing words correctly but not constructing meaning) to children who have so much difficulty processing print that the meaning they construct reflects very little of the author's message. Other children have developed strategies for dealing with print but read so little that they have to direct most of their attention to word identification and therefore have little left for making meaning. The variations go on and on. Regardless of the nature of the child's problem, however, there is often a mismatch between the child's needs and the instructional program in the classroom. Most of these children are asked to read material that is far too difficult for them, either because they have inadequate strategies for processing cues in words, or they have insufficient background knowledge of the concepts involved.

Lipson and Wixson (1991) recommend that reading diagnosis focus on three areas:

1. analysis of the child's reading strategies and abilities,

2. analysis of teaching techniques and materials being used in the classroom, and

3. examination of the match between them and the needs of the child.

This approach is relatively unique in textbooks on reading difficulties. Most others focus almost exclusively on within-child variables and do not consider reading instruction as a possible source of the problem. This is not a finger-pointing or blaming exercise, but rather a recognition that both the source of and the solution to the child's difficulties lie in the interaction between the child and the instructional context. Our goal as teachers is to maximize the match between the child's needs and the instruction we provide.

## Mentally Challenged Children

Crealock and Bachor (1995) estimate that approximately 2 to 5 percent of the population have a mild mental handicap. As with learning disabilities, mental handicap (formerly called "mental retardation") is generally considered to reside in the individual. However, again, it is people who decide who is and is not mentally handicapped. For example, some say an IQ between 55 and 80 means a mental handicap, while others choose between 52 and 67. Other evidence of the social nature of mental handicaps is the fact that minority groups, children with behaviour problems, and males are overrepresented in this group (Gillespie-Silver, 1979). In addition, changing social values are reflected in different labels for children in this group over time. Learners we now label as mentally challenged were once referred to as morons and idiots.

The major distinguishing feature of these learners labelled as having mild mental handicaps is that they progress through the same stages of cognitive development as people of average intelligence, but at a slower rate (Bond, Tinker, Wasson, and Wasson, 1994). Similarly, language development in this group is slowed down but not qualitatively different. Hence, most of the teaching techniques suggested in this book are just as appropriate for children with mild mental handicaps as for other children. The major difference is the rate at which instruction proceeds, with numerous opportunities for repetition and practice. However, as with all children, the goal is to determine each child's individual needs and to match instruction as closely as possible to those needs.

Social constructivists view individual differences among children not as deficits, but as factors to take into account when planning instruction. We believe that appropriate instruction, not labelling, is the key to language learning.

## Reporting to Parents

Another challenge you face as a language arts teacher is how to report student progress most effectively to parents. How do you present an accurate picture of each child's learning without making some children feel like they are failures?

Parents have a right to know how their children are progressing in school, and they generally *want* to know. But what is the most effective way of conveying this information to them? Report cards have changed greatly in the past fifteen years, and an increased range of alternatives to the report card is now being used. These include parent–teacher–student conferences, portfolios to demonstrate student achievement, and student journals and anecdotal notes to show a record of student performance. Many of these strategies are used in conjunction with the more formal report card.

A number of issues arise to complicate the process of reporting to parents. For example, do parents want to know what their children can do, or do they want to know how their children stand in relation to the other students in the class? What is the role of effort and persistence with learning tasks, and what is the role of individual accomplishment and growth over a period of time? Do we regard reporting as equivalent to creating a "league table" (with all the repercussions that has for children who turn out to be at the bottom), or do we consider it a matter of focussing on the development and learning needs of the individual children?

In general, *how* we assess and report children's growth reflects what we value. What is tested, recorded, and reported becomes, in the end, the focus of teaching. When teachers know that persuasive writing will be tested on a provincial achievement test, then obviously they will teach persuasive writing. Not a bad thing. But what happens if the *emphasis* in testing is on grammar or spelling? Some people would think that, too, is not a bad thing, but we, along with many other educators, believe that it would not be helpful to the balanced nature of a language program or to the development of children's writing skills.

## Report Cards

Wiener and Cohen (1997) indicate that there are currently three basic types of report cards: letter grade reporting, narrative reporting, and combined reporting.

- Letter grades are more common in upper elementary and middle grades than at the primary level, where many school systems substitute descriptors such as E=excellent, S=satisfactory, U=unsatisfactory, and N=needs improvement.
- On narrative report cards, space is allocated next to each subject area for the teacher to indicate how the child is doing. Teachers usually focus on progress, strengths, and weaknesses in their descriptions.
- Combined report cards have space for both grades and teacher comments, and some also have a separate space for a mark for effort.

Teachers accumulate information about children's learning throughout the weeks of schooling. Many keep a file on each child with notes about her or his progress. Samples of writing, reading checklists, and other such instruments are kept in the file. At reporting time, the teacher converts this information into a grading system. Most teachers struggle with this task for a long time. How do we best represent the efforts of children in their schooling? There is no simple and straightforward answer to this question, and most teachers find their own way to amalgamate the data. The problem is that descriptive data have to be converted to a numerical grading system. What does a percentage mark mean? If a child gets 75 percent in reading, what does it mean? A parent will know that 75 percent is a better mark than 60 percent, but neither mark shows what a child can or cannot do, nor does it reflect individual student growth over time. Grades need to be accompanied by other, more descriptive reporting methods in order to have much value to parents.

Report cards are usually sent home three times each year in the elementary grades. Sometimes report cards are distributed to the children (especially the first one of the year) only when parents attend a parent–teacher–student conference at the school. This ensures that parents fully understand the report card, and that they also see evidence of what their child is doing in school. Parents find this more helpful than simply receiving the report card at home in an informational vacuum.

Even more helpful is ongoing communication between the school and home. Some teachers use regular interim progress updates through a dialogue journal of some type to keep parents and their child informed. This helps to ensure that the information in report cards is not a surprise. It may also help parents keep report cards in perspective and understand whose agendas they really serve.

## Student-Led Conferences

A recent development in reporting to parents is the student-led conference. Here, the students are in charge, each selecting the material to show his or her parents and explaining what these materials mean in terms of his or her progress. Obviously, the teacher plays a crucial role in preparing the children and materials for the conference. The teacher ensures that the children are well prepared, have selected appropriate materials to share, and can say why these materials reflect their growth and achievement.

## Portfolios

If portfolios are kept on an ongoing basis, then student-led conferences are much easier to facilitate. Student learning logs and journals can also be used to demonstrate a child's learning. Tests, special projects, and any other relevant materials can be put into the portfolio, and a selection of material from it can be used in the parent–child conference. Parents do not need to see everything their child has done. Students will have taken some work home on a daily or weekly basis before report time. Material in the portfolio is chosen for a particular reason, some of it by the child and some by the child and teacher together.

> We end this text on a familiar refrain: no one way of reporting is best for children or their parents. The combination of report card, teacher–parent–student conference, and portfolio will give parents and children a clearer picture than a report card alone of what the children are accomplishing in school, what they can successfully do, and what they need in order to learn most effectively.

# Summary

While no organizational structure is best for all classrooms, a major goal is to foster and support balanced language arts teaching and learning. Teachers take four major components into account as they plan and organize language arts programs: materials, time, space, and children.

Traditionally, basal reading series have provided the material for language arts programs throughout Canada and the United States. More recently, there has been a movement to increased use of children's literature and nonbook materials as well. Whether or not teachers choose to use a basal series, we believe that it is important that teachers make a wide range of materials available. These materials need to reflect the range of interests and the reading levels of the children. Many teachers select and organize materials according to themes, but the most important criterion to use when selecting any material, whether a book, magazine, videotape, or computer program, is the extent to which it is consistent with the philosophy of the language arts program and will contribute to children's language learning.

When making decisions about the organization of time, space, and children, teachers need to provide for whole class instruction, small group work, and independent practice. Whole class instruction is effective for helping the children set learning objectives, for teaching new strategies to all the children, for reading to the children, and for evaluating accomplishments. Allocating time for one or two large daily time blocks for language arts provides flexibility and facilitates integration.

Ability groups have traditionally dominated language arts classrooms, but more educators are now recommending a range of grouping practices to meet the diverse abilities and interests of children. These include interest, research, special needs, and paired groupings. Co-operative learning rather than individual competition is becoming increasingly common in elementary language arts classrooms. Learning centres are one way to encourage children to work in groups. It is also important that children have opportunities to read and write independently each day and that at least some of the time they choose what they read and write about.

One of the biggest challenges language arts teachers face is meeting the needs of all the children in their classrooms. Cultural, linguistic, social class, and learning differences among students need to be taken into account when planning and organizing language arts programs. We view the cultures of minority groups as different, not deficient. Increasing numbers of children are entering schools with English as their second language. It is important that these children understand what they see and hear, and that they be immersed in meaningful learning experiences. The labels "learning disabled" and "mentally handicapped" are both social constructions, and as for all children, the teacher's main goal is to maximize the match between each child's needs and the classroom teaching.

Another challenge to teachers is how to report effectively to parents on children's progress in language learning. Report cards have changed, and many alternative ways of reporting to parents are now being used in conjunction with the formal report card. Student-led conferences and sharing information in portfolios are two ways to help parents understand what their children can do and what they need to learn.

## Selected Professional Resources

Booth, D. (1994). *Classroom Voices: Language-Based Learning in the Elementary School.* Toronto: Harcourt Brace. The focus of this book is the language-based learning program in one Ontario school. The first two chapters are on planning and organizing programs. A special feature is the inclusion of numerous teachers' and children's stories throughout.

Fountas, I.C. and Pinnell, G.S. (1996). *Guided Reading: Good First Teaching for All Children.* Portsmouth, NH: Heinemann. The major question Fountas and Pinnell attempt to answer in this book is how a teacher can provide young readers with materials and instruction that fit their individual levels of development. The authors present a blueprint for a balanced literacy program, including how to provide guided reading instruction, what components to include in programs, and how to organize classrooms to implement these programs.

## Children's Materials Noted in Chapter Fourteen

Early Bird Collection. (1990). Scarborough, ON: Nelson Canada.
MeadowBooks. (1994). Toronto: Harcourt Brace.
RefleXions. (1991). Richmond Hill, ON: Scholastic Canada.
Waves. (1992). Toronto: Houghton Mifflin Canada.

## References

Allen, V.G. (1991). Teaching bilingual and ESL children. In J. Flood, J.M. Jensen, D. Lapp, and J.R. Squire (eds.), *Handbook of research on teaching the English language arts* (pp. 356–364). New York: Macmillan.

Barr, R. and Dreeben, R. (1991). Grouping students for reading instruction. In R. Barr, R.L. Kamil, P.B. Mosenthal, and P.D. Pearson (eds.), *Handbook of reading research, Volume II* (pp. 885–910). New York: Longman.

Benterud, J.G. (1983). Four first-graders' use of reading time during the language arts period in their natural classroom setting. MA thesis, University of Alberta, Edmonton, AB.

Bond, G.L., Tinker, M.A., Wasson, B.B., and Wasson, J.B. (1994). *Reading difficulties: Their diagnosis and correction.* Boston: Allyn & Bacon.

Booth, D. (1994). *Classroom voices: Language-based learning in the elementary school.* Toronto: Harcourt Brace.

Campos, J. and Keatinge, B. (1984). *The Carpinteria preschool program: Title VII second year evaluation report.* Washington, DC: Department of Education.

Cazden, C.B. (1988). *Classroom discourse.* Portsmouth, NH: Heinemann.

Coles, G.S. (1987). *The learning mystique.* New York: Pantheon Books.

Crealock, C. and Bachor, D. (1995). *Instructional strategies for students with special needs.* Scarborough, ON: Allyn & Bacon Canada.

Cunningham, P.M. and Allington, R.L. (1999). *Classrooms that work: They can all read and write* (2nd ed.). New York: Longman.

Derwing, T.M. (1990). Speech rate is no simple matter: Rate adjustment and NS-NNS interaction. *Studies in Second Language Acquisition, 12* (3), 303–313.

Deyhle, D. and Swisher, K. (1997). Research in American Indian and Alaska Native education: From assimilation to self-determination. In M. Apple (ed.), *Review of Research in Education* (pp. 113–194). Washington, DC: American Educational Research Association.

End Legislated Poverty. (1993). Poverty and school performance. In S. Baxter (ed.), *A child is not a toy* (pp. 133–143). Vancouver: New Star Books.

Fountas, I.C. and Pinnell, G.S. (1996). *Guided reading: Good first teaching for all children.* Portsmouth, NH: Heinemann.

Gillespie-Silver, P. (1979). *Teaching reading to children with special needs.* Columbus, OH: Charles E. Merrill.

Giroux, H.A. (1987). Critical literacy and student experience: Donald Graves' approach to literacy. *Language Arts, 64* (2), 175–181.

Golub, J.N. (1994). Cooperative learning. In A.C. Purves (ed.), *Encyclopedia of English studies and language arts* (pp. 298–299). New York: Scholastic.

Goodman, K., Shannon, P., Freeman, Y.S., and Murphy, S. (1988). *Report card on basal readers.* Katonah, NY: Richard C. Owen.

Gordon, C.J. (1991). English language arts instruction and assessment in Canada. *Reflections on Canadian Literacy, 9* (3 & 4), 153–158.

Hudelson, S. (1987). The role of native language literacy in the education of language minority children. *Language Arts, 64,* 827–841.

Indrisano, R. and Paratore, J.R. (1991). Classroom contexts for literacy learning. In J. Flood, J.M. Jensen, D. Lapp, and J.R. Squire (eds.), *Handbook of research on teaching the English language arts* (pp. 477–487). New York: Macmillan.

Jacobs, E. and Jordan, C. (1993). Understanding minority education: Framing the issues. In E. Jacob and C. Jordan (eds.), *Minority education: Anthropological perspectives* (pp. 3–13). Norwood, NJ: Ablex.

Jobe, R. and Hart, P. (1991). The basalization of children's literature. *Reflections on Canadian Literacy, 9* (3 & 4), 147–150.

Lipson, M.Y. and Wixson, K.K. (1991). *Assessment and instruction of reading disability: An interactive approach.* New York: HarperCollins.

Mayfield, M.I. (1992). Organizing for teaching and learning. In L.O. Ollila and M.I. Mayfield (eds.), *Emerging literacy: Preschool, kindergarten and primary grades* (pp. 166–195). Boston: Allyn & Bacon.

Mitchell, C.A. and Cheverie, A.E. (1989). "Now that we've got them writing ...": Addressing issues of ethics, aesthetics, taste, and sensibility within the content of student writing. *Reading-Canada-Lecture, 7* (3), 180–190.

Morrow, L.M. (1989). Designing the classroom to promote literacy development. In D.S. Strickland and L.M. Morrow (eds.), *Emerging literacy: Young children learn to read and write* (pp. 121–134). Newark, DE: International Reading Association.

Murphy, S. (1991). Authorship and discourse types in Canadian basal reading programs. *Reflections on Canadian Literacy, 9* (3 & 4), 133–138.

Ogbu, J.U. (1993). Frameworks — variability in minority school performance: A problem in search of an explanation. In E. Jacobs and C. Jordan (eds.), *Minority Education: Anthropological Perspectives* (pp. 83–111). Norwood, NJ: Ablex.

Pica, T., Young, R., and Doughty, C. (1987). The impact of interaction on comprehension. *TESOL Quarterly, 21,* 737–758.

Rosier, P. and Holm, W. (1980). *The Rock Point experience: A longitudinal study of a Navajo school.* Washington, DC: Center for Applied Linguistics.

Shannon, P. (1989). The struggle for control of literacy lessons. *Language Arts, 66* (6), 625–634.

Simner, M.L. (1993). A position paper on beginning reading instruction in Canadian schools. *Canadian Journal of School Psychology, 9* (1), 96–99.

Slavin, R.E. (1980). Cooperative learning. *Review of Educational Research, 50,* 315–342.

Taylor, D. and Dorsey-Gaines, L. (1988). *Growing up literate: Learning from inner-city families.* Portsmouth, NH: Heinemann.

Topping, K. (1989). Peer tutoring and paired reading: Combining two powerful techniques. *Reading Teacher, 42* (7), 488–494.

Wiener, R.B. and Cohen, J.H. (1997). *Literacy portfolios: Using assessment to guide instruction.* Columbus, OH: Merrill.

Wilson, R.M. and Cleland, C.J. (1985). *Diagnostic and remedial reading for classroom and clinic.* Columbus, OH: Charles E. Merrill.

Wiseman, D.L. (1992). *Learning to read with literature.* Boston: Allyn & Bacon.

# Glossary

**Aesthetic response** is a term coined by American educator Rosenblatt (1989) to describe the enjoyment or appreciation a reader feels while reading a text. An aesthetic response is not concerned with comprehension, word meanings, recall, or learning, but with the deep personal engagement of reader and text. Aesthetic responses are not necessarily pleasurable; some texts can be deeply moving and cause stress or discomfort rather than pleasure, but this is still considered to be an aesthetic response.

**Alphabetic principle** refers to the understanding that letters in written words stand for sounds in spoken words. Children demonstrate this understanding when they are able to map letters onto sounds to spell words, or sounds onto letters to identify words.

**Amelia Frances Howard-Gibbon Award** honours excellence in illustration in a children's book published in Canada. The award has been presented annually since 1971 by the Canadian Library Association. The award must go to a citizen or resident of Canada.

**Automaticity** is the ability to carry out a complex act rapidly and without conscious awareness or control. An important characteristic of automaticity is that an individual can perform a complex skill or act while at the same time performing another that may not be automatic. As readers become proficient and are able to identify most of the words in texts automatically, they are able to direct their mental resources to constructing meaning. Most experts feel that children need to engage in extensive reading to achieve automaticity.

**Basal reading series** are sets of materials for teaching reading and language arts. These series generally consist of teacher guides, student anthologies, workbooks, and supplemental materials such as assessment materials, big books, correlated trade books, audiovisual aids, and computer software. Initially, basal series focussed almost exclusively on reading, but in recent years they have included other areas of language arts as well. Basal series derive their name from the original intention that they form the basis of a program of instruction in reading.

**Basalization** occurs when a trade book (i.e., a published work of literature) is treated in a classroom in the same way as a basal reader. Trade books have different lessons to teach children than do basal readers. The objective of working with trade books is to teach children how to become readers. The ways in which texts work, and the enormous variety of text styles and formats, become apparent to readers of trade books. The essence of working with trade books is that children enjoy the reading experience and learn about the vast range of books available and the delight that reading can produce.

**Challenged books** are those that groups or individuals have attempted to censor by having them removed from the shelves of libraries, especially in schools. Not all challenges result in the removal of a book. Specific procedures are usually followed in dealing with a challenge to a book, and a committee of parents and teachers usually makes the final decision about whether a book should be removed from a school library.

**Chapter books** are beginning novels for children that are designed to facilitate a reader's transition from a reliance on illustrations for creating meaning (as is done with picture books), to a stronger reliance on text. Many chapter books are available for young readers, and a number of publishing companies are producing specific series of chapter books (e.g., Hodge Pog Publishing). Like picture books, chapter books include all of the major genres of literature. An example of a chapter book is *Harold and Harold* by Budge Wilson (1995).

**Children's Choice Awards** are usually presented at the regional level in Canada or at the state level in the United States. Voting for the awards is often conducted through the schools. Students must read a certain number of titles from a list created by teachers and librarians. The list consists of recent books, but not necessarily those published in the last year. The Silver Birch Award in Ontario, the Manitoba Young Reader's Choice Award, and the Red Cedar Award in British Columbia are examples of children's choice awards in Canada. The awards are highly regarded by authors and illustrators.

**Children's literature** is a term used in this book to refer to those print materials (fiction, nonfiction, magazines, and poetry) that possess an aesthetic quality, are written primarily with an audience of young readers in mind, are acknowledged by critics to meet high standards, are well-written and illustrated, and provide children with pleasurable and challenging reading experiences.

**Classification of dramatic forms** is based on the way drama is implemented: as part of dramatic play, as a way of interpreting text, as part of a performance for an audience, or as a way of creating a context for learning. Dramatic play, drama as interpretation of literature, contextual drama, and drama as theatre make different demands on students and teachers.

**Constructivism** is a theory of learning in which individuals use their knowledge to build or make meaning. Texts are viewed as providing cues to possible meanings rather than as containing meaning themselves. Readers are viewed as active meaning-makers rather than passive receivers of meaning, and because of variations in background knowledge, they construct variable meanings of the same text.

**Contemporary realistic fiction** is imaginative writing that accurately reflects life as it is lived today. Events and situations in such stories could conceivably happen to people living in the real world. Young readers consistently select contemporary realistic fiction as their preferred genre. Stories are often about characters growing up in the world and their manner of coping with the problems and dilemmas of the human condition. Examples of contemporary realistic fiction are *Pick-Up Sticks* by Sarah Ellis (1991) and *The Maestro* by Tim Wynne-Jones (1995).

**Context cues** are knowledge and linguistic cues that help a reader construct meaning when reading. Linguistic cues involve both syntactic (grammar or word order) and semantic (meaning) aspects of language. When children use context cues, they make predictions and monitor their reading in terms of what sounds right and makes sense.

**Contextual drama** is concerned with creating dramatic contexts within which teacher and students explore themes, issues, and relationships. As in dramatic play, the participants in a contextual drama construct the meaning of the dramatic situation as opposed to representing the ideas of an author or poet. Contextual drama has the spontaneous appearance of drama as play, but in fact it is carefully structured by the teacher to help students achieve new insights and understanding. Thus, contextual drama often requires the teacher to work in role and to facilitate the drama from within the context.

**Critical literacy** goes beyond providing students with conventional reading and writing skills to equipping them to critically examine how written language reflects power structures and inequalities. Temple (1993) refers to this as "reading against the grain." Critical literacy is seen as a necessary step in bringing about social change.

**Cuing systems** are the three systems of semantics, syntax, and grapho-phonics that are used by readers and writers to make meaning from printed symbols. Pictures, diagrams, and charts also act as cues for readers to construct meaning, but the term "cuing systems" usually refers to the text-based systems discussed in this book.

**Cursive writing** is handwriting where the letters are connected to one another with a continuous flow from one stroke to another. The most prevalent form of handwriting today is a combination of printing and cursive writing, with printed uppercase letters and cursive lowercase letters.

**Dialect** is a variety of a spoken language that is used in a geographic region or by members of a social class. Every dialect has distinctive patterns, rules, and features. Regional dialects are much less pronounced now than they were 50 years ago, but speech in the southeastern part of the United States, the north of England, the east coast of Australia, and maritime Canada are examples of dialects that remain distinct. The advent of radio, television, and movies has brought a more standard version of spoken language into our homes and schools.

**Dialogue** is conversation about a topic (either written or spoken) among any number of people. Unlike in a debate, no one tries to "win" or to make his or her particular view prevail. In a dialogue, the focus is on the stream of meaning flowing among and through the participants. A partnership is created with the other people based on compassion, acceptance, and a sincere interest in the others. In dialogue, when a mistake is discovered, everybody gains.

**Direct assessment** occurs when a sample of writing is used as a basis for writing assessment. Direct assessment takes longer to complete than indirect assessment (which consists of multiple-choice and short-answer questions that can be machine-scored), and is more open to subjective judgement, but it is generally agreed that it is the only way to assess a learner's writing ability authentically.

**Discourse** is a linguistics term used to describe a continuous stretch of spoken or written language longer than one sentence. Frequently, "discourse" is reserved for spoken language and the term "text" for written language. Discourse is also used to refer to specific topics or types of language (e.g., the discourse of high finance). As well, discourse can be perceived as process and text as product.

**Drama as a context for learning.** (See Classification of dramatic forms and Contextual drama.)

**Drama as interpretation of literature.** (See Classification of dramatic forms.)

**Drama as performance.** (See Classification of dramatic forms.)

**Drama as playing.** (See Classification of dramatic forms.)

**Drama as theatre.** (See Classification of dramatic forms.)

**Drama strategies** are the ways in which the drama form is created. Examples of strategies are narration, tableau, and voice-in-the-head. Such strategies can be used to create a variety of forms, though some are specific to a particular form (for example, teacher-in-role is used mainly in contextual drama).

**Dramatic forms** include storytelling, puppetry, choral speech, choric drama, readers' theatre, dramatization, and story theatre. All dramatic forms require students to create or interpret meaning within the "as if" world of drama. The forms described in this text require langugage to express this meaning. Scripts, props, and movement are also used. A particular combination of attributes defines a particular dramatic form.

**Efferent response** is a term coined by American educator Rosenblatt (1989) to describe a response to literature where the intent is to focus on what can be learned, observed, and taken away from the reading. Focussed on gaining information, an efferent response is at the opposite end of the continuum from an aesthetic response.

**Emergent literacy** is a term that was developed during the early 1980s to refer to the literacy development of young children. Sulzby (1985) defines emergent literacy as the reading and writing concepts, attitudes, and behaviours that precede and develop into conventional literacy. Emergent literacy begins early in children's lives at home, involves interactions with print, and is part of, rather than separate from, reading and writing development.

**Environmental print** is print in the home and community, such as on McDonald's signs and cereal boxes. The term is also used to refer to print in the classroom, such as labels, signs, calendars, charts, and lists used to organize the room.

**Expository writing** is a form of writing that provides information, detailed explanations, judgements, and supporting examples. It may be persuasive or argumentative writing.

**Expressive writing** is a term used by James Britton (Britton et al., 1975) to describe one of the three voices of writing (the others being poetic and transactional). Expressive writing is found in diaries, journals, and personal letters, where the writer's intent is to share personal points of view, ideas, thoughts, and questions. Expressive writing aims to communicate the personal identity of the writer.

**Fantasy** is a genre of literature that engages and stimulates the reader's imagination and gives free rein to endless possibilities. The reader is taken to worlds where animals and toys can speak, where people can travel across time and into completely fictional worlds. Modern fantasy is rooted in folk tales, myths, and dreams. Examples of modern fantasy literature include *Charlotte's Web* by E.B. White (1952) and *The Dark Is Rising* by Susan Cooper (1969).

**Genre** refers to the different literary and linguistic forms and functions of various texts. Narrative, for example, is different in form and function from expository text, which is different again from persuasive or descriptive text. Genre also refers to categories of literature such as myth, fable, poetry, fantasy, and contemporary realistic fiction. Each of these genres meets different functions and uses a variety of different forms to achieve the intentions of the text.

**Governor General's Award** for children's literature (established in 1975 as the Canada Council Children's Literature Prize) is awarded by the Canada Council. Up to four prizes are awarded annually in the following categories: text in an English-language book, text in a French-language book, illustrations in an English-language book, and illustrations in a French-language book. Recipients are selected by two separate juries, one for the English-language books and one for the French-language books. The award was originally given for best writing. Awards for illustration were added in 1977–78. The award honours Canadian citizens creating books for young people.

**Grammar** is an ambiguous term that has been largely replaced today by the term *syntax*. However, where "grammar" is used, it refers to three distinct perspectives on language: (1) systemic-functional grammar is a description of the choices made by language users based on context and intention in order to create meaning (e.g., see Halliday, 1969); (2) generative-transformational grammar is a description of how language actually works as a process and is based on language universals (e.g., see Chomsky, 1957); and (3) prescriptive grammar focusses on the rules of language and how language *should* work. Where most grammar taught in the first part of this century was prescriptive (frequently dealing with inappropriate usage as in *seed* and *saw*, most grammar taught today is descriptive and functional, and more like syntax.

**Graphophonics** refers to the print–sound relationship of text. Graphic cues generally include letters, letter clusters, words, and parts of words. Phonics (see below) refers to the relationships between graphic cues and sounds. Graphophonic cues are one of the cuing systems that help readers to identify words as they read. The reader identifies words by relating speech sounds to letters and letter clusters.

**Heuristics**— sometimes used to refer to educated guessing— is a process of discovery through exploration. Linguist Michael Halliday labelled one of the seven functions of language he identified as being heuristic. Some instructional methodology is based on heuristics in an attempt to have learners make discoveries for themselves and thus be more likely to have a meaningful learning experience than by simply being told.

**High fantasy** is a genre of literature usually involving a quest, elements of the mystical or magical, time travel, and time warps, and frequently takes place in a fictional setting and with a fictional language. Examples include *A Wizard of Earthsea* by Ursula LeGuin (1968) and *The Golden Compass* by Philip Pullman (1996). High fantasy is based on mythology (frequently Celtic). Elementary school children are aided in their reading of high fantasy when they have some familiarity with mythology.

**Historical fiction** is a genre of literature set in a specific place and time in the past. It requires a great deal of research, descriptive detail, and authentic language to be credible. Good historical fiction is both an aesthetic and an efferent reading experience. The reader will learn history from it, and will also appreciate and identify with the lives and concerns of the characters.

**Holistic scoring** is the assessment of writing according to a set of criteria that are either explicitly stated or implicitly required (as in general impression marking), and that provide an overall impression of the piece. The writing is read and responded to quickly, and many features of the writing are kept in mind at once. Holistic scoring is largely a matter of ranking and sorting. Holistic scoring does not focus on only one aspect of writing as do some other scoring procedures.

**Hypermedia** is computer software that is used to organize and manage various types of multimedia information (such as sound, graphics, text, video, and animation) into a system so that information can be accessed, retrieved, and modified easily. The different forms of information are linked together so that a user can move from one form to another in a nonlinear manner.

**Hypertext** is nonlinear writing. Text is linked together so that the reader is able to go through a topic in any order. Readers have greater control over what they read and the sequence in which they read it than with traditional texts.

**Instructional reading level** is the level of reading instruction that a child needs in order to make maximum progress learning to read. The material must be just difficult enough to help children develop reading strategies with the support of instruction. On an informal reading inventory, this is the highest level at which a child is able to accurately identify 90 percent of the words and answer 70 percent of the comprehension questions.

**Integration** is the organization of language arts into a unified curriculum so that reading, writing, speaking, and listening are taught together rather than separately. Another level of integration involves teaching and learning language arts in other subject areas. A third level involves integrating experiences inside and outside of school.

**Invented spelling** refers to a child's first attempts at transcribing spoken language into print symbols before learning the conventions of standard spelling. Children pay particular attention to the sounds of language, and invented spelling is a reflection of this focus.

**Literacy** is a term generally associated with reading and writing, but it has been defined in many different ways. Basic literacy is the ability to read and write. Functional literacy is frequently defined as those reading and writing skills needed by people to do everyday tasks such as write cheques and read instructions on a medicine bottle. Critical literacy goes beyond conventional reading and writing to an awareness of how written language reflects power and inequalities in society.

**Mainstreaming** is the practice of integrating students with special needs into regular classrooms. Children with mild disabilities are often integrated into regular classrooms for their entire day, while children with more severe disabilities are integrated for part of the day and receive specialized instruction for the remainder of the time.

**Manuscript printing**, sometimes called manuscript *writing*, is the first form of written language taught to children and consists of individual letters that are not connected. There are a number of styles of manuscript writing, but all of them are plain, easy to recognize, and easy for children to learn.

**Metacognition** is awareness and control of the thinking processes involved in developing an ability. In reading, metacognition includes knowledge of factors that affect reading, of reading tasks, and of reading strategies. The regulative or control dimension of metacognition in reading involves planning and monitoring.

**Metafiction** is a narrative mode used by authors to provide a constant and deliberate reminder that a book is something an author and reader create together, something that is not real but fictional and that is open to many interpretations. The device has been used by authors since the time of Chaucer. It is the opposite of literary realism. By drawing attention to how texts are structured, metafictions can show readers how texts "mean." Techniques used to this end include obtrusive narrators who directly address the reader, situations where characters and narrators change places, the insertion of parodies of other texts, typographic experimentation, and the mixing of genres and discourses. Works of metafiction usually employ any number of these techniques in combination. *Black and White* by David Macaulay (1990) and *Piggybook* by Anthony Browne (1986) are metafictions.

**Metalinguistic awareness** is the growing awareness and ability we have to think and talk about language as a formal code. With children, it refers to understanding terms such as *letter, word, sentence,* and *sound.*

**Miscues** is a term coined by Goodman (1969) for errors during oral reading. Goodman believes that analyzing oral miscues gives insights into the reading process, since miscues result from the same cues and processes as correct responses.

**Morphology** is the study of the structure of words, specifically the ways in which morphemes (the smallest units of meaning in a language) combine to create meanings. An example of a morpheme is *s*, which denotes plural in English. Hence *dog* means one creature, and *dogs* means more than one. Suffixes and prefixes are also morphemes. Morphology is one of the essential cuing systems readers use to make sense of the printed word. Morphology is distinct from syntax in that syntax deals with the meaning of language at the level of sentences and phrases.

**Narrative** consists of a story or a succession of related events. These events are frequently organized according to cause and effect or chronology. Narratives include descriptions of settings, events, and characters, as well as comments and observations. Narratives can have the structure of a story or a much looser structure without opening and closing sequences.

**Native speaker ability** is the ability to use language in many situations to accomplish a wide range of purposes. Idiomatic language, pragmatics, and dialect are all important in native speaker ability.

**Performance assessment** refers to assessment in which students demonstrate what they can do by actually doing it. Rather than using paper and pencil tests, teachers use their best judgement to evaluate performance along a continuum defined by increasingly demanding performance criteria. These criteria are written descriptions that capture quality performance at various levels of achievement. This form of assessment is frequently used for children's writing.

**Persuasive writing** is used to persuade others to do something, buy something, or believe something. Advertising, editorials, political campaign literature, religious tracts, and much of the unsolicited junk mail that arrives in mailboxes consists of persuasive writing. Children use persuasive writing when they create a poster presentation about a favourite book they have read or write a letter asking the school principal to consider changing a school rule.

**Phonemic awareness** is the ability to segment sounds (phonemes) in spoken words. For example, the spoken word *cat* consists of three separate phonemes, one related to each letter in the written word. Research shows that performance on phonological awareness tasks is related to the beginning of reading acquisition.

**Phonetics** refers to the way sounds are articulated and produced. The term *phonetics* is often used to describe the way children spell, sounding out a word so they can articulate individual sounds (phonemes) within a word and transcribe them into print symbols.

**Phonics** is the relationship between letters and their spoken sounds. Analytic or whole word phonics is the association

of sounds with larger clusters of letters such as phonograms or word families (e.g., *ight*). Synthetic phonics is the association of sounds with individual letters or letter clusters and the blending of these sounds to identify words.

**Phonology**, sometimes called phonemics, is the study of the patterns of sound that create meaning in language. In any one language, a number of sounds (phonemes) combine to produce words and meanings.

**Picture books** are books in which illustrations play an integral role in creating meaning. Picture books are not the same as illustrated books, where meaning does not depend on illustrations. In a picture book, text and pictures work together. Good examples of picture books are *Each Peach Pear Plum* by Janet and Allan Ahlberg (1976) and *The Tunnel* by Anthony Browne (1989).

**Poetic writing** is a term used by James Britton (Britton et al., 1975) to describe one of the three voices of writing (the others being expressive and transactional). Meant to have an aesthetic element to it, poetic writing consists of poetry and also fictional writing, including narrative and description. The purpose of poetic writing is purely pleasure or satisfaction on the part of the writer and audience. (Poetic writing is not necessarily pleasurable to read; it can, in fact, cause distress or discomfort for the reader.)

**Polysemic** is a semantics term that describes words with more than one meaning. A polysemic text allows the reader to draw inferences, make judgements, and interpret the text in several ways. Examples of polysemic texts are *Rosie's Walk* by Pat Hutchins (1969) and *The Golden Compass* by Philip Pullman (1996). A text that is not polysemic provides a narrower reading experience for accomplished readers.

**Portfolio assessment** uses a compilation of work done by a child over a period of time. Frequently, the portfolio items are selected by the learner or by the teacher and learner together.

Items included in a portfolio are chosen with deliberation in order to demonstrate what a learner can do. Teachers find portfolios useful in demonstrating a child's learning to parents and administrators, and in explaining to children what they need to focus on and what learning must be accomplished next. Portfolios also give teachers an opportunity to reflect on their teaching and the learning their students are engaged in. Portfolios provide children with an opportunity to see the range of work they have done over time and to assess what they are accomplishing.

**Pragmatics** is the study of how speakers create meaning. The emphasis in pragmatics is on the context of language use and on the intentions and presuppositions of the speakers. The focus is on what an individual speaker means and on how that meaning is communicated. Pragmatics examines relatively short stretches of language compared with discourse analysis, which studies linguistic patterns in longer stretches of language.

**Predictable books**, a term coined by Goodman (1969), are books that make reading easy for emergent readers. They have the following characteristics: the pictures support the text; large chunks of text are repeated; and the language has cadence, rhythm, or rhyme that supports the reading of the text. *Brown Bear, Brown Bear, What Do You See?* (Martin, 1972) and *Each Peach Pear Plum* (Ahlberg and Ahlberg, 1976) are examples of predictable books.

**Reading readiness** is the notion that children need to reach an appropriate stage of development in order to learn to read. Maturationists believe that reading instruction should be delayed until children reach this stage of development, whereas developmentalists believe that prereading experiences can hasten children's development.

**Reading series** (See Basal reading series.)

**Realistic fiction** (See Contemporary realistic fiction.)

**Schemata** (singular schema) are organized mental frameworks that develop through repeated exposure to ritualized experiences such as playing baseball, eating in restaurants, or singing on car trips. Schemata influence our expectations and impose structure on the information we receive.

**Semantic map** (or web) is a diagram that shows relationships among ideas. It consists of nodes containing key words, with connecting lines between the nodes. Teachers and students use semantic maps or webs to organize ideas about concepts, texts, or units of study.

**Semantics** is the meaning component of language. It does not simply refer to the denotational meanings of words but to the ways in which words are used, in both the actual choice of one word rather than another and the connotations created by those words. A semantic system includes idioms and compound words and the unique ways that words are used in different situations.

**Standardized tests** are norm-referenced tests comparing a student's performance with that of other students. These tests are developed by administering a test to a large number of students (the standardization group) to develop norms.

**Strategy** is an overall plan for performing a task. One strategy can be used in several learning situations. In contrast, skills are more specific and used in the service of a strategy. Examples of strategies include predicting words and meanings, summarizing, and monitoring.

**Syntax** (what used to be called grammar) is a linguistic term that refers to the structure of sentences. In the English language, syntax consists largely of word order. English is a non-inflected language. It does not depend on specific inflectional word endings to denote the role of a word in a sentence.

**Text structure** is the pattern or organization of ideas in a text. There are two major types of texts: narrative (story) and expository (informational). Knowledge of text structure helps us to construct meaning for texts when reading and writing.

**Thematic organization** is a way of organizing learning matter around a central concept (such as courage), the work of a particular author, or a topic (such as farms). The theory is that learning will be facilitated and deepened by connecting ideas to one another. Thematic units may be organized within language arts or extended across other areas of the curriculum as well.

**Time-slip fantasy** is a genre of literature that involves the main character or protagonist in two eras. An object often enables the character to slip from one era to the other. In *Who Is Francis Rain?* by Margaret Buffie (1987), the object is a pair of spectacles. In *Playing Beatie Bow* by Ruth Parks (1980), the object is a piece of fabric on a dress. In time-slip fantasy, the protagonist explores issues in the past that lead to an understanding of current issues.

**Trade books** are books published by publishing companies as works of literature and not as educational texts. Books published as part of an educational program and intended for use in schools are usually referred to as "textbooks."

**Transactional theory**, also called transactive theory, is based on the work of Louise Rosenblatt (1978) and posits that meaning comes from a transaction between a reader and a text in a specific context. Readers rely on the text itself and on their background knowledge, experiences, and world view to construct meaning while reading. The focus is on the reader's response to texts.

**Transactional writing** is a term used by James Britton (Britton et al., 1975) to describe one of the three voices of writing (the others being expressive and poetic). Like expository writing, with which it is often used interchangeably, transactional writing is meant to accomplish a specific practical goal. Business letters, reports, term papers, report cards, recipes, and shopping lists are all examples of transactional writing.

**Whole language** is a philosophy about learning, language, and the nature of relationships between children and adults. Meaning is seen as the essence of language learning, and children are viewed as learning language through using it. Language is also seen as indivisible and as personal, social, and cultural. Practices that have been associated with whole language include involving children in real reading and writing, immersing them in a print-rich environment that includes quality children's literature, and basing assessments on observations of children using language in the classroom.

**Zone of proximal development** is a term coined by Lev Vygotsky (1978) to refer to a level of difficulty just beyond that which a child can handle independently but at which he or she can manage with help from others. Providing children with the opportunity to work with others on problems or tasks at this level maximizes learning.

# Index

## Reader Reply Card

We are interested in your reaction to *Constructing Meaning: Balancing Elementary Language Arts,* Second Edition, by Joyce Bainbridge and Grace Malicky. You can help us to improve this book in future editions by completing this questionnaire.

1. What was your reason for using this book?

   ☐ university course    ☐ college course    ☐ continuing education course
   ☐ professional          ☐ personal         ☐ other _____
       development         interest            _____

2. If you are a student, please identify your school and the course in which you used this book.

3. Which chapters or parts of this book did you use? Which did you omit?

4. What did you like best about this book?

5. What did you like least?

6. Please identify any topics you think should be added to future editions.

7. Please add any comments or suggestions.

8. May we contact you for further information?

   Name: _____

   Address:_____

   Phone:_____

   E-mail: _____

(fold here and tape shut)

------------------------------------------------------------------------------------

MAIL ➤ POSTE

Canada Post Corporation / Société canadienne des postes

**Postage paid**
If mailed in Canada

**Port payé**
si posté au Canada

**Business
Reply**

**Réponse
d'affaires**

0116870399          01

0116870399-M8Z4X6-BR01

Director of Product Development
HARCOURT CANADA
55 HORNER AVENUE
TORONTO, ONTARIO
M8Z 9Z9